Crown, Church and Episcopate under Louis XIV

Crown, Church and Episcopate under Louis XIV

Joseph Bergin

Yale University Press
New Haven and London

For information about this and other Yale University Press publications, please contact:
U.S. Office: sales.press@yale.edu   yalebooks.com
Europe Office: sales@yaleup.co.uk www.yalebooks.co.uk

Set in Garamond 3 by SNP Best-set Typesetter Ltd., Hong Kong
Printed in Great Britain by St Edmundsbury Press Ltd., Bury St Edmunds

Library of Congress Cataloging-in-Publication Data

Bergin, Joseph, 1948–
    Crown, church, and episcopate under Louis XIV/Joseph Bergin – 1st ed.
       p.   cm.
Includes bibliographical references and index.
    ISBN 0-300-10356-5 (cloth: alk. paper)
    1. Catholic Church – France – Bishops – Appointment, call, and election – History   2. Patronage, Ecclesiastical – France – History.   3. Louis XIV, King of France, 1638–1715.   4. Church and state – France – History.   I. Title.
BX1529 .B456 2004   262′ .12244′09032 – dc22   2003026238

A catalogue record for this book is available from the British Library.

10 9 8 7 6 5 4 3 2 1

CONTENTS

PREFACE

THIS STUDY REPRESENTS the culmination of a number of lines of research which began life at different times and for different reasons during the past few decades. Of course, as any historian instinctively knows, the coherence of any body of work will seem much greater in retrospect than it did for many of the intervening years. It stems from a long-standing interest in the kinds of power that particular societies develop and sustain – in this case the power of an established church with deep roots in the history, culture and identity of early modern France. It examines some key features of the French church under Louis XIV, and does so by focusing on the governing elite of that church, its bishops. But since they were more than 'products' of that church, they are also examined here in connection with the society which 'formed' them in the first place. Of course, categories like 'church' and 'society' can be so broad as to be virtually meaningless. In the case of the French episcopate, the relation between the two categories was mediated by the French monarchy, which not only chose those individuals destined to become bishops, but also shaped the episcopate as a whole through its policies, religious and otherwise. Put at its simplest, these pages are the history of a triangular relationship in which one of France's governing elites is observed from several converging angles, in the hope that by the end it will be possible to grasp something of its distinctive make-up, its background, and its likely orientations, both pastoral and intellectual. More speculatively still, the objective is to reveal something of the kind of church that they were called upon to govern.

For all its apparent compactness, a study of Louis XIV's bishops is potentially a subject without in-built boundaries. Almost any aspect of it could justify years of sustained research, most obviously in the case of the search for the origins of bishops drawn from a wide spectrum of geographical and social backgrounds. The absence of a ready-made archive means that the necessary documentation has to be derived – some might say 'invented' – from a wide range of sources which in many cases may have little to do with the questions that are central to this book. Indeed the disproportion between the volume and the value of certain types of source becomes so acute in some cases, in particular the correspondence of the papal nuncios and French ambassadors in Rome, each of which runs to hundreds of volumes, that the only solution likely to produce results is to delve into those sources on an ad hoc basis. That these paper mountains so rarely mention episcopal patronage at all may be construed as evidence that the interested parties – the papacy, the crown, and church leaders in France itself – were broadly satisfied with the operation of the 'concordatory' system of episcopal patronage under Louis XIV.

Having made such decisions as the research for this book developed, it is difficult not to be conscious of the gaps in it and to regret the additional material that might have been mined by more prolonged work in French and Roman collections. But that, even had it been feasible, would probably only have slowed down the whole process indefinitely. For all its gaps and imperfections, I believe it is best to offer as full a treatment of the subject as the resources and time as my disposal allowed, in the hope that it will stimulate others to open up related fields of enquiry. If particular topics are not given the coverage they might be expected to receive in these pages, it is because other scholars have begun to open them up and I had no desire to trespass unduly on their terrain. I am thinking in particular of the work of Alison Forrestal, a former graduate student of mine, on the development of ideas about episcopacy during the seventeenth century, and of Jacques Grès-Gayer on the Paris theology faculty, which played such an important role in the history of the French episcopate.

I have been exceptionally fortunate in the support, material and academic, that I received while working on this book. Initially the British Academy's Small Grants fund enabled me to spend two periods in the Vatican Library and Archives, which must rate among the most agreeable places for anyone to engage in historical research. Thereafter, the almost unimaginable munificence of the Leverhulme Trust made possible the continuation and completion of the project, thanks to the award of one of its inaugural Major Research Fellowships in 2000, which allowed me to conduct sustained research in French libraries and archives, provincial as well as Parisian. The Trust's willingness not merely to consider unusual or unfashionable proposals, but to allow award-holders to develop or alter their ideas thereafter deserves applause and, more urgently, emulation at a time when it is increasingly difficult to secure support for research unless one advertises its conclusions in advance! I also thank my own department at the University of Manchester for making the necessary arrangements to enable me to undertake research and writing free from the usual distractions.

These are my principal debts, but there are others which I recognise just as willingly. Friends and scholars in several countries have followed and supported my research, and have in some cases allowed themselves to be called upon to provide references, confirm points of detail, and so on. I am not sure I can remember all of them, but I would like to mention Michael Hayden,

Louis Châtellier, Alain Tallon, Robert Descimon, Katia Béguin, Françoise Hildesheimer, Sharon Kettering, Mark Greengrass, Jacques Grès-Gayer, Patrick Ferté, James Collins, Giuliano Ferretti, Guy Rowlands, Yves-Marie Bercé, Michel Cassan, Bruno Neveu, Véronique Cassagnet, Fréderic Meyer, Julian Swann and Ignasi Fernandez Terricabras. To those I may have forgotten, I can only offer feeble but sincere apologies. Daniel Dessert has delved more deeply into Parisian archives than most historians of the period, and I am grateful to him for the readiness with which he passed on to me any reference that he felt I could put to good use. If there were a prize for all-round support and assistance, it would surely go to Olivier Poncet, *conservateur* at the Archives Nationales for much of the time while I was researching and writing this book, and who has uncomplainingly allowed himself to be bombarded with all kinds of requests for help throughout that time. As his escape from such importunity finally approaches, the publication of his own research on Franco-papal relations up to 1667 will shed invaluable light on many of the issues discussed in the following pages. Jérôme Ogerau greatly facilitated my work in the manuscripts department of the Bibliothèque Nationale at a crucial juncture. I also owe a special debt to Claire Berche, as obliging a librarian as anyone could hope to encounter. In a world where new technology does not always make historical research easier to pursue, it is the generosity of such friends and colleagues, as well as the goodwill of archivists and librarians, that continue to make scholarly research both possible and enjoyable. Long may that continue to be so!

MAPS

ABBREVIATIONS

AAE, France	Archives des Affaires Étrangères, Mémoires et Documents, France
AC	Archives Communales
AD	Archives Départementales
AN	Archives Nationales
Arch MEP	Archives des Missions Étrangères de Paris
ASS	Archives de Saint-Sulpice
ASV	Archivio Segreto Vaticano
AUP	Archives de l'Université de Paris
BAV	Bibliotheca Apostolica Vaticana
BIUT	Bibliothèque inter-universitaire, Toulouse
BM	Bibliothèque Municipale
BL	British Library
BN	Bibliothèque Nationale
Cab d'Hoz	Cabinet d'Hozier
Carrés d'Hoz	Carrés d'Hozier
Dangeau	Philippe de Courcillon, marquis de Dangeau, *Journal*, ed E Soulié et al, 19 vols, Paris 1854–60
DBF	*Dictionnaire de Biographie Française*
DGS	*Dictionnaire du Grand Siècle*
DHGE	*Dictionnaire d'Histoire et de Géographie Ecclésiastiques*
DLF	*Dictionnaire des Lettres Françaises, XVIIᵉ siècle.*
Doss bleus	Dossiers bleus
Gallia	*Gallia Christiana*
Gallia Chr Nov	*Gallia Christiana Novissima*
JRULM	John Rylands University Library Manchester
MC	Archives Nationales, Minutier Central
Misc Arm	Miscellanea Armarium
MS Fr	Manuscrit français
MS Lat	Manuscrit latin
MS Naf	Nouvelles acquisitions françaises
Nouv d'Hoz	Nouveau d'Hozier
Nunz Fr	Nunziatura di Francia
PC	Processus Consistoriales
PD	Processus Datariae
PO	Pièces Originales
Saint-Simon	Louis de Rouvroy, duc de Saint-Simon, *Mémoires*, ed A M de Boislisle et al, 43 vols, Paris 1879–1930
SHAT	Service Historique de l'Armée de Terre, château de Vincennes
Sourches	Louis-François du Bouchet, marquis de Sourches, *Mémoires*, ed G-J de Cosnac et al, 13 vols, Paris 1882–93

Legend:
— Ecclesiastical province
‡ Seat of Archbishop
▨ Avignon, its suffragans and Orange

St Omer
Boulogne
Arras
Cambrai
Amiens
Noyon
Laon
Rouen
Beauvais
Soissons
Reims
Coutances
Bayeux
Lisieux
Evreux
Senlis
Verdun
Metz
Avranches
Sées
Chartres
Paris
Meaux
Châlons-s-M
St Pol
Tréguier
Dol
St Malo
Rennes
Le Mans
Blois (1697)
Sens
Troyes
Toul
Quimper
St Brieuc
Vannes
Orléans
Langres
Nantes
Angers
Tours
Bourges
Auxerre
Nevers
Autun
Besançon
Luçon
Chalon-s-S
Poitiers
Mâcon
La Rochelle
Saintes
Angoulême
Limoges
Clermont
Lyon
Belley
Vienne
Périgueux
Tulle
St Flour
Le Puy
Grenoble
Bordeaux
Sarlat
Mende
Viviers
Valance
Die
Bazas
Agen
Cahors
Rodez
St Paul
Gap
Embrun
Condom
Montauban
Albi
Vabres
Alès (1694)
Uzès
Orange
Sisteron
Digne
Glandèves
Dax
Aire
Lectoure
Nîmes
Apt
Senez
Vence
Auch
Lavaur
Lodève
Riez
Lescar
Lombez
Toulouse
Castres
St Pons
Agde
Arles
Aix
Fréjus
Grasse
Bayonne
Oloron
Tarbes
Rieux
St Papoul
Montpellier
Béziers
Marseille
Toulon
Commminges
Mirepoix
Narbonne
Carcassonne
Couserans
Pamiers
Alet
Perpignan

0 — 50 miles
0 — 80 km

1   *French dioceses 1715*

INTRODUCTION

THE OLD PROBLEM of historical periodisation can present unexpected difficulties for anyone working in the field of early modern history. The phenomenon of the 'broken-back' century, whereby dates like 1555, 1648 or 1661 are viewed as major turning points, is so familiar as to pass virtually unnoticed. This might not matter had research and writing not been nudged into compartments inhibiting the search for a wider grasp of historical problems. Nowhere is this problem more evident than in France where the seventeenth century remains instantly recognisable as the 'grand siècle'. What it commonly means is something close to Voltaire's 'Century of Louis XIV' which, of course, leaves more than half of the century that preceded it badly adrift – not really part of the high 'civilisation' presided over by the *grand roi*. At best, those earlier decades are viewed as a perhaps necessary period of incubation and preparation for the 'greatness' of what was to follow; at worst, a spectacle of disorder and violence on which the age of Louis XIV would resolutely turn its back.

It may seem paradoxical, therefore, that historical research since World War II has *not* been concentrated on the *grand siècle* of Louis XIV, but on the more tumultuous, unruly and sometimes chaotic years from the end of the Wars of Religion to the Fronde. The ideological climate of the post-war decades largely accounts for this interest in the breakdown of royal authority, both centrally and locally. An impressive volume of research was devoted especially to the rebellions, mainly to those deemed 'popular' in character, which either provoked or followed that breakdown, and which culminated in the mid-century Fronde, so viscerally excoriated by state-focused historians of the Third Republic such as Lavisse.[1]

A different but in some ways complementary approach, much less connected to post-war sensibilities, was the study of 'state-building' during the

---

1 Ernest Lavisse, *Louis XIV*, 3 vols (*Histoire de la France illustrée jusqu'en 1789*) (Paris 1911, repr 1978), i, 46, 'rien n'est plus triste ni plus honteux dans notre histoire que ces quatre années de guerre sans honneur pour personne . . . il faut le conter pourtant, si vite que ce soit'.

same period, and the development of a powerful royal state personified by Louis XIV, the supreme absolute monarch.[2] But here, too, historical research focused far more on the 'heroic' state-building of ministers like Richelieu and Mazarin than on the monarch who enjoyed the fruit of their labours. Critics of this approach argue that the focus on institutions, political thought and state expansion too readily assumes intentions and a mindset which are too modern for the seventeenth century, however much the actual outcome may have strengthened the state in question. This challenge has come mainly from historians who stress the continuing dominance of dynastic thinking and interest at the highest level, beginning with the king himself; such ways of thinking were widely shared by the court-based governing elites whose ideals of service and duty were focused on the person of the king rather than on an abstract 'state'.[3]

An equally significant subject of research, also derived from recent concerns, has been the proliferation of corporate groups within French society over the *longue durée*, despite the destructiveness of the Revolution.[4] Given the expansion of such groups throughout the early modern period, even historians who may be sceptical of, or have little direct interest in state-building, have been drawn to study their genesis, composition, characteristics, and wider ramifications. So whether the subject is the magistrates of the sovereign courts, the oligarchies of cities and guilds, or the less obviously 'incorporated' groups of financiers who kept the monarchy in funds at crucial moments, the objective has been to understand how far they came to enjoy autonomous existence and power, and so became as much latent obstacles to full-blooded royal absolutism as its willing agents. The role played in this process by the venality and heredity of office, the scale of which was far greater in France than anywhere else in Europe, has attracted particular attention, since its side-effects, socially as well as politically, were enormous. As is well known, these corporate groups engaged in high levels of endogamy that enabled them largely to exclude newcomers. The fact that they were also vital

2 A Lloyd Moote, *The Revolt of the Judges. The Parlement of Paris and the Fronde 1643–1652* (Princeton 1971). Richard Bonney, *Political Change in France under Richelieu and Mazarin 1624–1661* (Oxford 1978). William F Church, *Richelieu and Reason of State* (Princeton 1972). Nannerl O Keohane, *Philosophy and the State in France. The Renaissance to the Enlightenment* (Princeton 1980). This listing is not intended to suggest that these authors shared any kind of common agenda or approach.

3 Herbert H Rowen, *The King's State. Proprietary Dynasticism in early modern France* (New Brunswick 1980); Sharon Kettering, *Patrons, Brokers and Clients in Seventeenth-Century France* (Oxford 1986); Roger Mettam, *Power and Faction in Louis XIV's France* (Oxford 1989); David Parrott, *Richelieu's Army* (Cambridge 2001); Guy Rowlands, *The Dynastic State and the Army under Louis XIV: Royal Service and Private Interest 1661–1701* (Cambridge 2002).

4 Michel Crozier, *La Société bloquée* (Paris 1970), for the most influential analysis of France as a 'stagnant society' because of privilege and corporate-group entrenchment. More recent concerns were triggered by Pierre Bourdieu, initially in his early book (with Jean-Claude Passeron), *Les Héritiers. Les Étudiants et leurs études* (Paris 1966) and later, *Noblesse d'état* (Paris 1989).

sources of credit to the crown meant that the latter had only limited means to determine their composition and behaviour.[5]

I

As studied by historians over the past half-century, most of these developments preceded the age of Louis XIV, whose long personal rule appears to have inherited and streamlined rather than genuinely innovated. The relatively few historians who have looked across the divide represented by Louis XIV's *de facto* accession to power in 1661 have invariably modified established interpretations, especially those concerning the crown's handling of dominant elites at the centre or in distant provinces. Compromise and the search for cooperation rather than 'domestication' of elites, social and corporate, emerged as the leitmotif of the crown's handling of this problem, and as the key to unprecedented political stability.[6]

Yet despite the obvious continuities at work across the seventeenth century as a whole, the personal rule of Louis XIV remains poorly charted territory. No historian familiar with the range and volume of research on French history from the 1580s to the 1650s, can fail to be surprised by the dearth of serious scholarship devoted to key aspects, with the exception of the artistic and cultural spheres, of the long reign which followed.[7] Apparently, entrenched myths about the reign have deterred historians from re-examining whole swathes of a familiar historical record, while the sheer length of Louis XIV's personal rule, its seemingly imperturbable stability, and the forbidding quantity of archival sources (mainly diplomatic and political) have discouraged all but the hardiest from tackling major research topics. Yet, paradoxically, the lack of research has not prevented over-interpretation of the reign, given the relative abundance of contemporary sources providing both detailed

5 William Doyle, *Venality. The Sale of Office in Eighteenth-Century France* (Oxford 1996); *idem, La Vénalité* (Paris 2000), both offer clear accounts and further references. The pioneering study by Roland Mousnier, *La Vénalité des offices sous Henri IV et Louis XIII* (Rouen 1945, 2nd edn, Paris 1971), as it title makes clear, does not concern itself with developments under Louis XIV. On the officeholders as corporate creditors, among David Bien's important essays see 'Offices, Corps and a System of State Credit: the Uses of Privilege under the ancien régime', in Keith M Baker, ed, *The French Revolution and the Creation of Modern Political Culture* (Oxford 1987), 89–114.

6 William Beik, *Absolutism and Society in Seventeenth-Century France* (Cambridge 1984), is the classic statement of this. Other examples include James B Collins, *Classes, Estates and Order in Early Modern Brittany* (Cambridge 1991). John J Hurt, *Louis XIV and the Parlements. The Assertion of Royal Power* (Manchester 2002) challenges this thesis as it refers to the crown's exploitation of the magistrates of the major courts of law.

7 This is evident from a perusal of the useful bibliography of monographic studies published between 1977 and 2000 compiled by Joël Cornette, 'L'Histoire au travail, le nouveau 'siècle de Louis XIV': un bilan historiographique depuis vingt ans (1980–2000)', *Histoire, Économie et Société*, 19 (2000), 561–620. Many of the monographs which figure in this list are primarily focused on the pre-1661 period.

information and ready-made comment on the most important events and personalities of the time, even though the bulk of them only cover the final decades of the reign. The most celebrated example is the *Mémoires* of Saint-Simon, which have left an indelible mark not merely on the years about which he writes (from 1693 onwards) but on the entire period after 1661.

From the vantage point of the present study of royal patronage in the French church, it is significant that the court of Versailles has always attracted attention, especially as it is inextricably linked to the inexhaustible but problematic output of biographies of Louis XIV himself. But analysis of the court as a political arena in the broadest sense has lagged well behind its artistic and architectural history.[8] The threadbare cliché of the sun king's court as a gilded prison for a domesticated aristocracy has, with a few exceptions, continued to serve as an obstacle to our understanding of either the court or the aristocracy.[9] Indeed, a major consequence of the prevailing stereotypes concerning the court was that they diverted attention away from the ministerial and sub-ministerial circles which gravitated within, and around, the council and the royal entourage, which itself became increasingly complex as the decades wore on. A major gap here is the lack of detailed studies of the forms and networks of patronage comparable to those that exist for the preceding period, whether they deal with the court of Henri III in the 1570s and 1580s, or the ministries of Richelieu and Mazarin.[10] André Corvisier had to admit to serious problems with reconstituting the Le Tellier clientele as soon as one moved beyond the obvious bounds of blood kinship, and nobody has tried to repeat for Colbert the minister what was so brilliantly done for his pre-ministerial history.[11] And if, despite the more recent work by Guy Rowlands on the Le Tellier dynasty, that can be said about the dominant planets of this particular universe, how much less sure is our understanding of the role of the smaller satellites.[12] Assumptions about political stability have not encouraged close scrutiny of the years of ministerial reshuffles (e.g. 1661, 1683, 1691, 1709) when the court-based political elites generally re-formed and

8   Gérard Sabatier, *Versailles, ou la figure du roi* (Paris 1999); William R Newton, *L'Espace du roi. La Cour de France au château de Versailles 1682–1789* (Paris 2000); Alexandre Maral, *La Chapelle royale de Versailles sous Louis XIV, cérémonial, liturgie et musique* (Paris 2002) are the most important recent contributions. See also Sabine du Crest, *Des Fêtes à Versailles. Les divertissements de Louis XIV* (Paris 1990).

9   Mettam, *Power and Faction in Louis XIV's France* was one of the first to argue for the continuing influence of the high court aristocracy, notably the faction gathered around the duc de Bourgogne, Louis XIV's grandson, in the final decades of the reign.

10 Nicolas Le Roux, *La Faveur du roi. Mignons et courtisans au temps des derniers Valois (vers 1547–vers 1589)* (Seyssel 2000); Xavier Le Person, *'Practiques' et 'practiqueurs'. La Vie politique à la fin du règne de Henri III (1584–1589)* (Geneva 2002); Kettering, *Patrons, Brokers and Clients*. The bibliography is obviously much larger than this, and each of these volumes refers extensively to it.

11 André Corvisier, *Louvois* (Paris 1983), 130ff. Jean-Louis Bourgeon, *Les Colbert avant Colbert* (Paris 1973).

12 Rowlands, *The Dynastic State*.

realigned. There are, of course, exceptions. Dessert's investigation of the financiers from the Fronde to the Regency, supplemented by Claude Michaud's study of the receivers-general of the French clergy, proposed a comprehensive analysis of the weaknesses of a state so consistently on the edge of bankruptcy.[13] His subsequent works on the royal navy follow related lines of enquiry which still need integration.[14] Recent research on military and diplomatic history, often regarded as the best known facets of the reign, has pointed up the many closely related but poorly understood issues that need serious attention.[15] Exactly how, for example, did the social elites, especially the provincial nobility, great and small, respond to the needs and opportunities of the expanding military machine?

Whatever the reasons for, and consequences of the scholarly neglect of this period in comparison with the preceding one, it should be noted that it *also* suffers from being lumped into a 'long eighteenth-century' or an 'ancien régime', both of which begin, depending on the subject of study, around 1660, more rarely around 1680, and focus essentially on the generations after 1715. This long-lens telescoping most affects the social, economic and cultural history of the period, but is evident in other areas, too.[16] It has direct relevance to the present study, for as we shall see shortly, certain features of the religious history of the reign have experienced just such a fate. The advantages of a longer perspective are undeniable, but it is usually the case that such studies treat the opening years or decades in a more perfunctory manner than those that follow, and are, therefore, more likely to perpetuate rather than question established views.

II

The French church may seems worlds apart from such considerations. Reinforcing this impression is the fact that its historiography has by and large run along different tracks for much of the past half-century. It has been much less

---

13 Daniel Dessert, *Argent pouvoir et société au grand siècle* (Paris 1984); Claude Michaud, *L'Église et l'argent sous l'ancien régime: les receveurs-généraux du clergé de France aux xvie–xviie siècles* (Paris 1991).
14 Daniel Dessert, *La Royale. Vaisseaux et marins du roi-soleil* (Paris 1996), esp chs 1–3; *idem, Tourville* (Paris 2002).
15 Paul Sonnino, *Louis XIV and the Origins of the Dutch War* (Cambridge 1988); Lucien Bély, *Espions et ambassadeurs au temps de Louis XIV* (Paris 1990). John Lynn, *Giant of the grand siècle, The French Army 1610–1715* (Cambridge 1996), Rowlands, *The Dynastic State*.
16 This trend is more visible in general surveys, the most recent of which is William Doyle, ed, *Old Regime France 1648–1789* (Oxford 2001), or Jeremy Black, *From Louis XIV to Napoleon: The Fate of a Great Power* (London 1999). But it is evident, too, in more detailed scholarship: for example, after a general introduction, William Doyle's study of eighteenth-century venality really begins in 1689: *Venality*, ch 2, 'Archomania: Venality at the Limit, 1689–1722'. Michael Kwass *Privilege and the Politics of Taxation in Eighteenth-Century France* (Cambridge 2000), incorporates material from the War of Spanish Succession and sometimes earlier.

inhibited by the problem of the 'broken-back' century discussed earlier, though the latter has created some problems. The only instantly recognisable point of contact with the recent studies of revolt was the attempt to see Jansenism as an ideology of opposition suitable for royal officeholders being sidelined by the state-building of the Richelieu-Mazarin ministry.[17] Few historians tried to imitate the example of Guy Lemarchand's attempt to demonstrate that the French church was the 'ideological apparatus' of the *ancien régime*.[18] Nevertheless, its historiography has had important underlying connections to the questions under discussion. The rather lifeless ecclesiastical historiography of the pre-World War II era, with its heavy emphasis on institutions and doctrinal questions, not to mention its own ideological *parti pris*, was unexpectedly rescued from what seemed like certain oblivion by the unforeseeable effects of the rise of the resolutely republican and *laïc* Annales school as mediated by established scholars like Gabriel Le Bras and Étienne Delaruelle. What followed, from the 1950s onwards, was a significant displacement of emphasis towards actual religion as lived and expressed by real communities, urban and rural, and which might be far removed from the prescriptions of 'official' religion and theological discourse. In successive decades, historians of the French church expanded their efforts from a historical sociology focused on the various types of clergy, ordination patterns, confraternities, to the history of mentalities and, more recently, to culture generally, of which religion was regarded as a manifestation. We should not perhaps over-emphasise the linearity or neatness of these shifts, given the lead-time involved in the preparation and diffusion of the most important works of research in this field. Extensive research remains to be done not merely because these successive trends have overlapped considerably, but also because they have not exhausted previous lines of research.[19]

Behind these methodological shifts, there have been some underlying constants. Probably the most important among them has been the focus on the penetration of reformist ideas and movements, especially in the half-century that followed the collapse of the Catholic League and its crusading vision of a catholic monarchy committed to the elimination of heresy and the purification of the church. The provenance of ideas on reform has been of enduring interest, since it raises the question of France's links to the wider church

---

17 Lucien Goldman, *The Hidden God. A Study of the Tragic Vision in the Pensées of Pascal and the Tragedies of Racine* (London 1964, original French edn, Paris 1955).

18 Guy Lemarchand, 'L'Église, appareil idéologique de l'ancien régime', *Annales Historiques de la Révolution Française* (1979), 250–79.

19 The shifts in historical writing within France are chronicled in considerable detail in the thirty-three articles in the *Revue d'Histoire de l'Église de France*, 86 (2000), 321–769, esp by Dominique Julia 'Sources nouvelles, sources revisitées' (409–36). A broader, more international as well as more thematic survey is contained in an 800-page number of the *Revue d'Histoire Ecclésiastique*, 95 (2000), in which Roger Aubert, 'Les nouvelles frontières de l'historiographie religieuse' (757–81), attempts a 'developmental' synthesis.

in the wake of the Council of Trent, and indeed of its dependence on the council itself for its programme of reform.[20] Yet piecing together a convincing chronological and geographical pattern of reforming activity within a Gallican church that was sensitive about its autonomy and indigenous traditions, remains a more elusive quest than the 'unity' of the French church under the wing of the monarchy would lead one to believe. Although the present work will not delve into that particular issue, it is worth pointing out that the calibre of the episcopate must form part of any explanation of the successes and failures of reform.[21]

In analysing the explosion of religious energies during the decades following the collapse of the Catholic League, there has been a growing recognition that the *dévots*, lay as well as clerical, female as well as male, played a decisive role as a 'leaven' capable of translating religious precepts into social practice. Nowhere is this more visible than in the urban associations and confraternities in which they came together in order to pursue those goals collectively rather than individually. The most celebrated of them, the Compagnie du Saint-Sacrement, may have had a relatively short life, at least in Paris, but it reached out into a large number of provincial cities and towns, and left its mark on key features of religious change – from anti-duelling campaigns to the creation of general hospitals and seminaries. Although it survived in many provincial centres after its suppressions in 1660 and 1666, its impact thereafter remains difficult to measure. The most satisfying study of the Compagnie to date combines a concise sociology of its membership with an extended analysis of the kind of religious culture it was trying to promote – action grounded in a specific interiorised spirituality.[22] A recent study of its sister organisation, the Congrégation de la Propagation de la Foi, shows how enterprising some local branches remained down to the end of the century in places like Lyon, Grenoble, Marseille and Montpellier, especially in the wake of the Revocation of the Edict of Nantes in 1685.[23] However, the decline of such associations that historians have chronicled did not signal the end of the *dévots*, merely that it has been harder to account for their activities and impact under Louis XIV. As we shall see later, *dévot* networks actively sought to transform the court of Louis XIV from the 1680s onwards, and had some success

20 Marie-Hélène and Michel Froeschlé-Chopard, *Atlas de la réforme pastorale en France de 1550 à 1790* (Paris 1986), which argues for the penetration of tridentine ideas into France via the south-east.

21 J Michael Hayden and Malcolm Greenshields, 'Les Réformations catholiques en France. Le témoignage des statuts synodaux', *Revue d'Histoire Moderne et Contemporaine*, 48 (2001), 5–29, which offers a foretaste of work in progress on synodal statutes and pastoral visitations between 1190 to 1789. It contests the standard interpretation and attempts to provide an alternative explanation.

22 Alain Tallon, *La Compagnie du Saint-Sacrement (1629–1667). Spiritualité et société* (Paris 1990).

23 Catherine Martin, *Les Compagnies de la Propagation de la foi (1632–1685). Étude d'un réseau d'associations fondé en France au temps de Louis XIII pour lutter contre l'hérésie des origines à la Révocation de l'édit de Nantes* (Geneva 200).

in doing so. It will come as no surprise that one of their major objectives was to influence the king in the choice of bishops.

It is, of course, problematic to speak of a unified and self-conscious *dévot* movement, because from the second quarter of the century onwards, there were also important internal differences on questions of theology which are usually identified under the heading of 'Jansenism'. But Jansen's presentation of the Augustinian theology of grace and free will was shared by relatively few of those who would subsequently be labelled 'Jansenists' in France: they were far more concerned with questions of 'applied' theology, that is their moral and pastoral implications, notably for the administration of the sacraments, the penitential discipline of the church, and so on. Here, too, post-war research has tried to revise a historiography in which anything that smacked of 'Jansenism' (and to a lesser extent the gallicanism that often accompanied it) had been demonised to the point where it became virtually a historical abstraction. The ensuing revision has revealed a far richer and more varied landscape, often fertilised by historical and patristic study, and a religious culture which moved much further towards a form of moral rigorism than any other part of Catholic Europe by Louis XIV's reign.[24] The scrutiny of episcopal patronage will show how far the initial choice of bishops and their subsequent behaviour were influenced by these shifts.

III

This study shares several features of the historiographies so far discussed. On the one hand, it examines a governing elite of a particular kind – territorially dispersed in a permanent rather than temporary way, unlike so many civilian and military officeholders, yet possessing a surprising and growing degree of unity despite genuine countervailing pressures. Functioning as it did under the tutelage of a gallican monarchy, the French episcopate bears strong resemblances to its secular elite counterparts. Bishops were drawn in considerable part from the same social groups. They may have held far fewer formal offices in royal service than their Spanish counterparts, but their informal roles as royal agents were as important as ever, despite the continuing expansion of venal officeholding throughout France.[25] Above all, the fact that episcopal office was clearly non-venal and non-hereditary in an age when the venality,

---

24   The bibliography is extensive, but landmark works include René Taveneaux, *Le Jansénisme en Lorraine (1648–1789)* (Paris 1960); Jean Orcibal, *Études d'histoire et de littérature religieuses* (collected essays) (Paris 1997); Bruno Neveu, *Érudition et religion aux xviie et xviiie siècles* (collected essays) (Paris 1994); Jean-Louis Quantin, *Le Catholicisme classique et les pères de l'église. Un retour aux sources (1669–1713)* (Paris 1999).

25   Mettam, *Power and Faction*, 247. Doyle, *Venality*, chs 1–2, is the most compact summary of research to date on venality.

legal and customary, and heredity of office both flourished – and when Louis XIV even abolished the venality of royal almonerships because it brought the episcopate a step closer to venality – should interest all historians. It raises the question of how the crown exercised the freedom to select individuals for what were important offices, unhampered by the kind of claims and outright property rights characterising so many secular offices. There were no *brevets de retenue* and no *survivances* to mortgage episcopal patronage, or to make the crown's freedom to choose more token than real. Yet the sheer weight of inherited custom and practice, inside and outside of the church, made it hard for the crown to change its spots when choosing the kind of bishop it wanted. What were the chances, at a time when *dévot* and reformist influences around the throne were by no means negligible, of an episcopate radically different in origin and background from the other elites? – a distinctive 'sacred militia', to use Louis XIV's own terminology, picked according to entirely different criteria? How capable was the crown of differentiating the different kinds of patronage at its disposal?

The French episcopate under Louis XIV suffers from being neither well known nor wholly unknown. Its diversity of origin and its geographical dispersion across the entire realm makes it quite unlike most of the corporate groups whose geographical stability and (commonly) origins provide both the incentive and the documentation for historians to study them.[26] This is certainly not the case with the episcopate, as emerged from studying its history for an earlier period.[27] Louis XIV's episcopate is not wholly unknown because of the relatively plentiful supply of published sources, mostly memoirs, journals and letters, in which bishops are frequently portrayed, and sometimes unforgettably so as by Mme de Sévigné or Saint-Simon. Yet it is obvious that the likes, dislikes, and religious sensitivities of a handful of authors are a slender, dubious basis, however well done their portraits of individuals may be, for a characterisation of the episcopate as a whole. Not even Saint-Simon, that inveterate purveyor of 'warts-and-all' sketches of French bishops, knew more than a handful of them, and no one else did either.

How Louis XIV's bishops have been presented by previous historians needs attention in order to explain the need for another study. It is here that the incorporation of the half century after 1661 into studies with a mainly eighteenth-century focus is most evident. Augustin Sicard's study of the episcopate 'before the Revolution' was the first of several volumes entitled the

---

26 The only roughly comparable civilian group would be the intendants, but even this comparison is weak, since virtually all of Louis XIV's intendants were Paris-based throughout most of their careers and, with some exceptions, an intendancy was not seen as a life-long career, but merely a stepping-stone to a better position within the officeholding hierarchy which produced intendants in the first place. See Annette Smedley-Weil, *Les Intendants de Louis XIV* (Paris 1995) and, for the preceding decades, the more substantial study by Bonney, *Political Change*.

27 Joseph Bergin, *The Making of the French Episcopate 1589–1661* (New Haven-London 1996).

'ancien clergé de France'. In his search for material for a study that covered a very wide range of subjects – court families and intrigues, political activities of bishops, gallicanism, Jansenism, and many others – Sicard frequently looked back as far as Richelieu whom he evidently regarded as a useful 'type'. On the one hand, Richelieu was representative of sixteenth-century practices which enabled under-aged clerics with court connections to obtain the mitre, but on the other he was responsible as chief minister for attempts to ensure the improved episcopate of subsequent generations. Sicard's use of evidence from Louis XIV's reign was, as we might expect, highly selective if increasingly extensive, and it largely dovetailed with his ultimate objective of defending the 'moral worth of the episcopate' of pre-Revolutionary France. Like several other Catholic historians of the later nineteenth- and early-twentieth century, Sicard evinces systematic hostility towards any bishop whom he regards as a Jansenist, and he even added a triumphant appendix 'on the defeat of Jansenism in the second half of the eighteenth century' to his book.[28] That same hostility was expressed in more biting terms by his contemporary, the Jesuit historian, Armand Jean, in his widely used and influential compilation on France's bishops between 1682 and the Concordat of 1801. It is worth noting that Jean's choice of starting date, the underlying motive for which was clearly ideological, had the effect of creating an episcopal 'long eighteenth century' *avant la lettre*.[29]

Although the two remaining studies of Louis XIV's bishops approach them from strikingly different perspectives, they, too, attempt to fit them into their own *longue durée*. Norman Ravitch's comparative study, *Sword and Mitre* is, as its subtitle indicates, a study of the relations of the crown and the episcopate in an age of aristocracy.[30] Apart from its discussion of gallicanism after 1682 and the financial relations of crown and clergy generally in the eighteenth century, it focuses primarily on the social origins of France's bishops and the routes to success at court in the competition for high office. Needless to say, the choice of starting date means that the analysis of Louis XIV's bishops is 'broken-backed' in yet another way, and can only provide limited guidance for an assessment of the episcopate as a whole after 1661. Nor do the subdivisions of the entire period (1682–1700, 1700–74, 1774–90), however justified for the author's purposes, facilitate comparison with the remainder of the personal rule, let alone with earlier periods of the seventeenth century.

28 Augustin Sicard, *L'Ancien Clergé de France. Les Évêques avant la Révolution* (1st edn, Paris 1893, 5th edn, 1912). The appendix is at pp 593–627 of the 1912 edition.
29 Armand Jean, *Les Évêques et les archevêques de France depuis 1682 jusqu'à 1801* (Paris 1891). For Jean, any notice favourable to a bishop in the *Gallia Christiana* was *prima facie* evidence of pro-Jansenist sentiments. The four Gallican Articles of 1682 were, for many nineteenth-century writers like Jean, a shameful blot on the reputation of the French episcopate.
30 *Sword and Mitre. Government and Episcopate in France and England in the Age of Aristocracy* (The Hague, 1966).

Despite appearing only a decade after Ravitch's book, Michel Péronnet's vast dissertation was both different in content and broader in scope.[31] His initial subject of enquiry, the episcopate of Louis XVI, became enveloped in his search for a comprehensive explanation of episcopal power, and that explanation required a *longue durée* of truly Braudelian proportions, beginning with the Concordat of Bologna of 1516. But Péronnet's work was notable less for its chronological sweep per se than for his realisation that the episcopate of Louis XVI was itself the product of a prolonged conjunction of ideas, aspirations and interests involving the crown, social groups and the French church, all of which were indispensable to understanding the episcopate of any generation from 1516 to 1789. His central theme was the 'regularisation of the episcopate', embracing such issues as the age of incoming bishops, their studies and degrees, as well as their pre-episcopal careers, to which might be added their social origins, their networks of family and patrons, and so on. The role of the crown was also central to this analysis, as Péronnet was anxious to show that when it was strong enough, it had an agenda of its own regarding bishops. The crown, in short, was itself another variable in the evolution of the episcopate, whose 'histoire totale' Péronnet attempted to delineate in a variant of the 'structure-conjoncture' paradigm. However, the extended chronological range of his work meant an inevitable telescoping of developments towards the mid-eighteenth century, as well as the elision of developments which had no place in his broader three-century panorama. The present author's study of the episcopate from the accession of Henri IV to the death of Mazarin, while applying many of Péronnet's methodological techniques, adopted a less teleological approach to its subject, and attempted to track the changes which occurred in the subsequent generations in a manner which allowed for the continuing interplay of interests – royal, social and ecclesiastical. Its shorter timescale clearly made it easier to allow for contingent developments and to provide nuanced explanations of particular changes, whether it was in the social composition of the episcopate or in the crown's approach to the patronage at its disposal. It also allowed for the possibility of further changes to the episcopate under Louis XIV, but without suggesting that they were merely side-effects of earlier developments.[32]

IV

It should be evident that there are compelling reasons for trying to exhume the 250 bishops who took office in the fifty-four years of Louis XIV's personal

---

31 *Les Évêques de l'ancienne France*, 2 vols (Lille 1977). This work, originally a dissertation for the Université of Paris-IV in 1976, was published without any evident changes, and was so poorly produced that it is virtually illegible in places. Many of its graphs and tables at the end of vol ii are impossible to decipher, so that some of his assertions and conclusions have to be taken on trust.

32 Bergin, *Making*.

rule. The following pages will add more, and leave no doubt that the changes which the episcopate underwent during the period were due to more than just impersonal long-term forces acting upon it. Contemporaries from the king and his entourage downwards were keenly aware of the importance of choosing bishops capable of fulfilling their obligations in a way that corresponded to ever-rising expectations. As will be argued later, given that episcopal power within the French church reached previously unparalleled heights under Louis XIV, our understanding of how that church worked is inaccurate and limited if we have only vague notions about the nature of its episcopate.

This book is, therefore, an attempt to remedy a major deficit in existing scholarship. It does not aspire to being an 'histoire totale' of a power elite at work throughout its life-cycle, and readers hoping for an account or an evaluation of the track-record of these bishops within their respective dioceses will be disappointed. A generation or more of high-quality research into the local and sub-provincial religious history of the seventeenth century, roughly from the end of the Wars of Religion to some usually undefined point in the second quarter of the eighteenth century, has enabled historians to escape from the stereotypes of earlier hagiography about the 'siècle des saints'. It would make little sense to return to the approach taken in previous generations and try to classify bishops as 'administrators' or 'pastors', 'resident' or 'non-resident', or 'rigorists' or 'laxists'. Furthermore, even a near-perfect knowledge of France's bishops at the outset of their episcopate would not always allow us to predict how they would behave once installed in their dioceses. Louis XIV's contemporaries themselves expressed surprise at the unpredictable shifts in the behaviour of some of them, notably those who moved towards a Jansenist posture. However 'programmed' they may have been before their nomination, it was not an infallible guide to their subsequent record. The bishops' own continuing development, whether it be intellectual or religious, and the multiple influences and constraints of the diocese that they found themselves governing, have to be taken into account if we are seeking to understand the kind of bishops they subsequently became.

Without assuming that the average bishop was any more absolute in his diocese than the king of France in his kingdom, it may be suggested that, as the decades passed, religious developments at local level were themselves bound to be affected by the type of bishop being put in place. As this book will show, France's bishops were increasingly geographic outsiders, and even those who were of 'local' extraction had frequently spent at least some of their pre-episcopal existence – from college and university onwards – elsewhere than their place of origin or their diocese of destination. This study accompanies them right up to the point where they embark on an episcopal career which took them far away from their diocese of origin and then, for a proportion of them, from their first diocese. This may suggest that the 124 dioceses which made up the French church by 1715 were like a giant chessboard on which the king and his confessor moved individuals around as they pleased.

But this was not the case, since for all kinds of reasons, French dioceses were highly unequal in their attractiveness, and the exercise of episcopal patronage had constantly to take account of that underlying constant.

Diocesan diversity, based on the size of revenues, location, status and so on, was not the only constant to influence the distribution of patronage. But it will not receive attention here, other than in the discussion of patterns of episcopal tenure and mobility in chapter nine. Because there was so little change to the actual mechanisms by which bishops were made, the material endowment of dioceses, and the royal practice of imposing pensions on episcopal revenues, there was little point in repeating the extensive analysis of them for the period from 1589 to 1661. Within individual chapters, however, comparisons will be made which will draw upon that earlier work, since it provides a basis for *moyenne durée* comparisons which seem particularly apt for a subject like the evolution of the episcopate under Louis XIV.

V

If the scope and the limitations of what follows are to be intelligible, a brief comment on its sources is essential. There is no conveniently constituted central archive with just the right kind of documentation for a study of the *ancien-régime* episcopate at a given juncture.[33] Neither the French crown nor the church itself generated or preserved records specifically related to the subject, and the disappearance of the papers which formed the basis of the *feuille des bénéfices* is particularly regrettable, since it means that historical analysis of the crown's ecclesiastical patronage is unavoidably one-dimensional.[34] This is partly offset by the volume of correspondance, journals, and memoirs for Louis XIV's reign, offering comment and speculation, but varying enormously in value and reliability in their explanations of royal decisions. In previous generations, correspondence exchanged between France and Rome by papal nuncios and French ambassadors offered sometimes invaluable information, especially about problematic individuals and decisions, but by the time of Mazarin's ministry Rome's long-standing anxieties about French episcopal patronage in general had largely disappeared, thus reducing the value of the correspondence.[35] No doubt some further nuggets could be mined from the several hundred volumes of surviving letters in both Rome and Paris, but several forays into them indicated that the results were likely

---

33 *Ibid*, 18–19.
34 The *feuille des bénéfices*, kept by the royal confessor under Louis XIV, was the list of names of candidates who were approved for church preferment. It generated a substantial volume of letters, petitions and consultation papers, none of which have survived.
35 The most complete study of this subject to date is Olivier Poncet's unpublished dissertation, 'La Papauté et la provision des abbayes et des évêchés français de 1595 à 1667' (Université de Paris IV-Sorbonne, 1998).

to be slight compared to the prolonged investment of time that a systematic trawl would require.[36] However, other Roman sources, such as the enquiries conducted into the background of newly nominated bishops, have been used systematically. For all their limitations, they proved to be the most convenient starting point for the next stage of the study, which focused upon the family history and social origins of the bishops. This research was based mainly, but not exclusively, on the resources of the *cabinet des titres* of the Bibliothèque Nationale.[37] After that, such 'homogeneity' of documentation as there was at the outset began to dissipate, and it became a question of tracking material, printed and manuscript, in whatever form it existed and wherever it could be found. Needless to say, for a subject which concerns the local history of virtually every corner of France, given the geographical origins and destinations of its bishops, the search for such material could be endless. In deciding when and where to stop the search, it was necessary to define the enquiry as an attempt to understand the making of the episcopate under Louis XIV. Readers will judge for themselves whether that has been the right decision.

The structure of the pages that follow reflects the issues, methodological and documentary, just discussed. The opening chapter presents a wide-angle view of the French church from the margins, as represented by the dioceses, in Roussillon, Artois-Hainaut and Franche-Comté, which it acquired between the 1640s and the 1670s. The challenge to the crown in its newly conquered provinces was not merely military or administrative, it was also religious and ecclesiastical, not least because these were regions whose own religious traditions were sometimes quite unlike those of gallican France. The ways in which the crown responded to these challenges seemed to offer an interesting test of its approach to church-crown relations in a context where the established reflexes needed to be rethought. It will also show how the crown compromised and negotiated by turn with Rome and local ecclesiastical elites, and how heavily it relied on hand-picked bishops to achieve its ambitions.

An obvious consequence of an overture of this kind is that it turns our attention to the 250 individuals who entered the episcopate under the *grand roi*. Between them, the three closely connected chapters which follow attempt to provide a collective portrait of the bishops at successive points beginning with their geographical, social and professional origins (ch 2), and progress-

36 The same impression can de derived from the two published sets of nuncios' correspondence for Louis XIV's reign, even though both nuncios were active at a time when episcopal patronage was a source of some difficulty between Rome and the French court. See *Correspondance du nonce en France Fabrizio Spada (1674–1675)*, ed Ségolène de Dainville-Barbiche (Rome 1982), and *Correspondance du nonce en France Angelo Ranuzzi (1683–1689)*, ed Bruno Neveu, 2 vols (Rome 1973).

37 For the problems of the *Cabinet des titres* as a historical source, see Robert Descimon's salutary, 'Élites parisiennes du xve au xviie siècle. Du bon usage du cabinet des titres', *Bibliothèque de l'École des Chartes*, 155 (1997), 607–44.

ing via their schooling and academic achievements (ch 3) to the careers and related activities which positioned them for entry to the episcopate (ch 4). Of course, we have no way of knowing how many others with identical trajectories either failed or perhaps never attempted to obtain royal approval for the mitre. This information, had it been available, would have been an invaluable 'control' for explaining the success of those who became bishops. Given the absence of any official explanation of the reasons for the vast majority of episcopal nominations, we can only judge the cursus of individual bishops against the record of the entire cohort, and paint as detailed a collective portrait as possible of the successful candidates themselves.

The second and longer part of the book deals with the exercise of episcopal patronage by Louis XIV. The obvious continuity provided here by the king's seemingly unchanging personal rule may seem to make the historian's task a relatively straightforward one. But it is equally evident that royal longevity is only one factor in explaining the ebb and flow of episcopal decision-making, so that combining the continuity and the shifts in the latter without unnecessary repetition or arbitrary periodisation raises real presentational difficulties – as it does for the history of other aspects of the reign. Consequently, this set of chapters is prefaced with one (ch 5) devoted to an analysis of the formal aspects of episcopal patronage, which offers an insight into the kind of 'system' that episcopal hopefuls themselves had to confront, and the means by which they could overcome the obstacles in their way. Thereafter, a broadly chronological analysis of the patterns of decision-making concerning episcopal patronage seems the best way to explain the short-term and newly emerging factors that affected patronage as the reign progressed, and to which no 'systemic' analysis can do justice. The 'early' (ch 6) and the 'late' (ch 8) phases of this story are separated by a chapter on the biggest crisis in bishop-making between the Wars of Religion and the French Revolution, that of the decade from 1682 to 1692. This solution may be open to objection for implying that the years of crisis were *also* a kind of watershed in the exercise of royal patronage, and therefore that the 'later' years were significantly different from those before 1682. The intention has certainly not been to contrive opposition where it does not exist, although it should not come as a surprise that changes did occur in the latter years when new influences and issues arose with a direct bearing on episcopal patronage. But whichever the approach one adopts in studying the crown's patronage, it is worth recalling a recent comment on Louis XIV's reign to the effect that the historian

can seldom listen in to the conversations of the king with individual ministers or other advisers, as few of them were summarized afterwards or reported in royal and ministerial letters to third parties. The decisions which resulted are known . . . yet the way in which a consensus was reached on an issue, the variety of different views which were discussed, the extent to which one minister or adviser had a decisive effect on the outcome, the role taken by Louis himself – all these matters remain concealed behind the closed doors of the council chamber or the royal apartments, and the historian has not been permitted to enter.[38]

That verdict might have been written with the history of episcopal patronage in mind.

The two final chapters attempt, from different but connected perspectives, to present an overall account of the kind of episcopate which emerged by the early eighteenth century. Chapter 9 steps back in order to examine the broad outlines of patterns of episcopal tenure and its determinants – age of entry, duration of careers, forms of mobility and promotion, and so on. It ends with an attempt to get beyond such external, objective patterns to an understanding of the mentality of a cross-section of the bishops as they drafted their wills and decided how to dispose of their bodies and their estates. Lastly, the conclusion attempts to look outwards beyond the episcopate in order to sketch its wider place within the French church at a time when its claims to greater authority and its search for unity were more ambitious than previously, yet were being counteracted from within by differences arising from issues such as gallicanism, Quietism and Jansenism, to mention only the most important. Can it be said that the French church was more 'episcopal' in character by 1715 that around 1660, and if so, what were the consequences of this? Of course, a systematic answer to such a question would involve exploring several aspects of eighteenth-century French history, but the value of raising it is that it affords an opportunity to assess the wider significance of the changes to the episcopate chronicled in the following pages.

---

38   Mettam, *Power and Faction*, 190. See also his comments at 98.

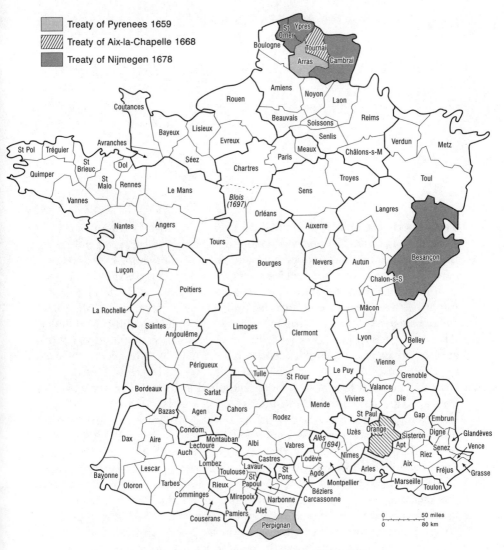

Treaty of Pyrenees 1659
Treaty of Aix-la-Chapelle 1668
Treaty of Nijmegen 1678

St Pol | Tréguier | Quimper | St Brieuc | St Malo | Rennes | Vannes | Nantes | Dol | Avranches | Coutances | Bayeux | Lisieux | Séez | Le Mans | Angers | Tours | Luçon | Poitiers | La Rochelle | Saintes | Angoulême | Bordeaux | Bazas | Agen | Dax | Aire | Condom | Lectoure | Auch | Montauban | Bayonne | Lescar | Oloron | Tarbes | Comminges | Rieux | Couserans | Pamiers | Mirepoix | Alet | Lombez | Toulouse | St Papoul | Lavaur | Castres | St Pons | Narbonne | Carcassonne | Perpignan | Albi | Cahors | Rodez | Vabres | Lodève | Béziers | Agde | Montpellier | Nîmes | Arles | Marseille | Toulon | Aix | Fréjus | Grasse | Senez | Vence | Glandèves | Riez | Apt | Digne | Sisteron | Embrun | Gap | Orange | Uzès | St Paul | Mende | Alès (1694) | Viviers | Die | Valance | Vienne | Grenoble | Belley | Lyon | Mâcon | Chalon-s-S | Besançon | Langres | Autun | Nevers | Bourges | Clermont | Limoges | Tulle | St Flour | Le Puy | Périgueux | Sarlat | Bordeaux | Rouen | Amiens | Noyon | Laon | Reims | Beauvais | Soissons | Senlis | Châlons-s-M | Verdun | Metz | Toul | Evreux | Paris | Meaux | Troyes | Chartres | Sens | Auxerre | Orléans | Blois (1697) | Boulogne | St Omer | Ypres | Tournai | Arras | Cambrai

0   50 miles
0   80 km

2   *New dioceses added to French church 1661–1715*

Note. Ypres and Tournai were lost in 1713.

CHAPTER 1

The French Church in the Age of the Pré Carré

THE MAP OF the church 'inherited' by Louis XV and his contemporaries in 1715 from Louis XIV is one which seems remarkably stable, apart from some limited additions along its northern and eastern frontiers. Like its counterparts elsewhere in Europe at the time, the French church was not much given to institutional or geographical reconfiguration. Even at the level where it might be thought that some such flexibility was desirable, that of the parish and *communauté d'habitants*, change was slow and genuinely difficult to undertake; new parishes were not as common as population shifts, especially in areas of urban growth, might seem to require, and were frequently blocked by a combination of institutional inertia and vested interests, both lay and clerical. The naval base of Rochefort catapulted in the space of a few decades from a village of six hundred inhabitants to a city of 10,000 by 1679, without any attempt to create a second parish or seriously improve the existing one.[1] Further up the ladder, the same phenomenon can be observed. The urge, or the need to alter the map of France's dioceses was if anything less acute, though a brief but interesting exception is provided by the problem of Protestantism in the 1680s and 1690s. When alterations to the diocesan map were proposed and taken seriously by church and crown, they became major events for contemporaries, but could take years to complete even when there was no great opposition to them. Being so unusual, they generated widespread comment, the gist of which may come as a surprise to later generations: for example, bishops who consented to the dismemberment of their dioceses, regardless of the circumstances, were routinely condemned for their weakness. Like Daniel de Cosnac, bishop of Valence-Die, most of them would prefer outright resignation of their office to the enduring shame such consent would entail.[2] Likewise, the first bishop of a newly established diocese was like a

---

1 Louis Pérouas, *Le Diocèse de la Rochelle de 1648 à 1724, sociologie et pastorale* (Paris 1964), 247–9.
2 Daniel de Cosnac, *Mémoires*, ed Gabriel-Jules de Cosnac, 2 vols (Paris 1852), ii 124, for his response to the planned breakup of his combined diocese of Valence-Die in 1687: 'je pris la résolution d'aller prendre congé de Sa Majesté, pour éviter un changement que, de bonne foi, je n'eusse jamais desiré'.

founding father, and at least one such bishop under Louis XIV, that of Alès in the Cévennes, always signed himself – and was commonly referred to by contemporaries – as 'the first bishop of Alès'.[3]

These remarks might suggest that there was virtually no difference in the episcopal map of France under Louis XIV and that of *his* predecessors. That change was limited is undeniable, yet when it is realised that the 113 dioceses of 1661 rose at one point during the reign to 126, before dropping back to 124 by 1715, it becomes apparent that change on a scale far beyond that experienced for several centuries did actually occur. A 10 per cent increase in the number of dioceses may not seem a particularly momentous matter for historians of seventeenth-century France, but the real significance of such a development does not lie in mere numbers or percentages. Rather it lies in the variety which characterises these changes and which reveals the range of problems with which the crown was faced either as a consequence of territorial expansion or of a desire to establish new dioceses. How and for what reasons were new dioceses added to the French church? How many of them were a response to what might be regarded as obvious religious needs rather than, say, an attempt to expand the fund of royal ecclesiastical patronage? Where were they located and what was the significance of the resulting geography?

As it happens, only two new dioceses were carved entirely out of existing ones, but the reasons, positive and well as negative, for this particular statistic deserve some attention. Elsewhere adjustments were made which may seem no more than 'cosmetic' rearrangements of the map – notably in the establishment of new ecclesiastical provinces. And as in previous periods, the question of the relations between 'ordinary' bishops and their metropolitan superiors, the archbishops, especially across political frontiers, proved to be as thorny as ever. Since they involved monarchies as sensitive as the French and Spanish about their sovereign rights, these were not regarded as trivial by either political or ecclesiastical decision-makers at a time when claiming and implementing such rights could generate a climate which, especially in the 1680s, made war ever more likely.

It may seem perverse to begin a study of the French episcopate at the margins, both institutional and geographical, but it has the advantage of contrasting the novel with the taken-for-granted elements of a particular historical problem – the relations between the monarchy and the church, but also involving leading figures from the episcopate of the day. The issues just mentioned can be looked at from a number of angles, grouped together under several headings, and thus revealing much more than one might suspect about the temper of relations between the crown and the church under Louis XIV. In particular, where the 'new' dioceses in question were in fact 'old' dioceses located in recently conquered territories, they can help us to understand not

3   The bishop in question was François Chevalier de Saulx, who governed Alès from 1694 to his
    death in 1712. See below, p 43.

just the way in which the French monarchy dealt with newly acquired lands generally, but also to identify the distinctiveness of the 'gallican' traditions, royal and ecclesiastical. It is worth remembering that not all of the problems encountered under Louis XIV were unprecedented, and the analysis that follows overlaps on several points with the present author's earlier study of the French church before Louis XIV.[4]

I

It does not require much familiarity with Louis XIV's reign to guess that one important source of new dioceses lay in France's territorial expansion. That in turn ensured that the main problems to be faced were those of absorbing and integrating existing foreign dioceses rather than creating entirely new ones. And while most of the expansion occurred along the north-eastern borders, in Artois and Flanders, it was not confined to them by any means. Moreover, most of the gains, as far as new dioceses was concerned, occurred relatively early during the king's personal rule; some of them, however, involved acquisitions which went back to the end of Louis XIII's reign, and which constituted 'unfinished business' until the late 1660s. To understand the approach adopted by the new regime after Mazarin's death towards these bishoprics, we need to review the 'pre-history' of the most important of these cases.

The first of them involved not the Spanish Netherlands, but France's Roussillon-Catalan frontier. The Spanish diocese of Elne, whose bishop actually resided in Perpignan since 1601, was one of several to be affected by the Catalan revolt of 1640 and the subsequent French occupation of the region. Most of the six local Catalan bishops, only two of whom were native Catalans, either fled or were expelled from French-occupied Catalonia between 1641 and 1646 rather than cooperate with the rebels and their French patrons. Staying on and cooperating would have entailed them taking the same oath of fidelity to Louis XIII as that taken by the lay supporters of Catalan independence from Castille and incorporation into France. In some cases, these bishops subsequently either died or were transferred, as was the bishop of Elne himself, to sees elsewhere in the Spanish monarchy, leaving their previous sees vacant *de jure* as well as *de facto*. Those unable to obtain such a transfer refused formally to resign their sees, thereby complicating the situation from a French point of view, since the French crown was inevitably drawn into dealing with the ensuing problems. Ironically, by sending men such as Pierre de Marca, bishop of Couserans, Michele Mazarin, the cardinal-minister's brother who was also archbishop of Aix, Hyacinthe Serroni, bishop of Orange and protégé of Michele Mazarin, and Bernard Duval, the Carmelite bishop of 'Babylon' *in partibus infidelium*, to Catalonia in the mid-1640s, the French crown ensured

4   Bergin, *Making*, ch 1, esp 27–43.

that the region was certainly not without consecrated bishops who could perform episcopal functions *in spiritualibus*, even though they could not legitimately exercise episcopal jurisdiction in the dioceses concerned.

The collapse of the French cause in 1652 and Catalonia's return to allegiance to Philip IV was not quite the end of this episode, since the question of filling vacant bishoprics had by then produced contradictory French and Spanish nominations which would take many years to resolve. A key reason for the stalemate was the papacy's refusal to confirm any nomination to a vacant Catalan see so long as France and Spain were at war – as it also did with nominations to Portuguese dioceses during the Portuguese revolt against Philip IV after 1640. At various dates from 1641 onwards, first Louis XIII and then Mazarin attempted to impose 'French' candidates – none was actually French by birth – on vacant sees such as Urgell, Tarragona, Girona, Lerida and Elne when they fell vacant, but not one of them obtained their provisions from Rome. When France and Spain did finally make peace in 1659, only one Spanish diocese, that of Elne-Perpignan in Roussillon, was transferred to French sovereignty. Twelve years earlier, in 1647, Mazarin had already nominated Vicenç Margarit, brother of the leading pro-French Catalan noble during the revolt, to Elne, and he could finally look forward to claiming his reward for supporting France at such heavy cost to himself and his family.

The situation in Artois during these years was not wholly dissimilar. The last Walloon bishop of Arras had died in 1635, five years before the French conquered the city. Although Madrid nominated a successor in 1637, his confirmation failed to materialise since Rome and the Spanish crown were by then involved in an acrimonious dispute of a kind not unfamiliar to the French monarchy, concerning the wider patronage claims of the Spanish crown over the province's major benefices. Rome claimed that the monarchy's title was based purely on an indult granted by the pope to each successive ruler and that no such indult covered Artois in the late 1630s. By the time this particular dispute was resolved and a new indult was granted to Philip IV in October 1640, it was too late: the city of Arras had been in French hands for just two months by then. Even if they were not sure of how to proceed thereafter, neither Richelieu nor Mazarin was prepared to allow a candidate of proven loyalty to Spain to occupy the see of Arras. This was why it was not until April 1656 that Mazarin nominated a candidate for the bishopric – Étienne Moreau, abbot of St Josse, better known for having been secretary and diary-keeper of the 1635 Assembly of Clergy. Two years later, shortly before the Treaty of the Pyrenees was signed, Philip IV finally abandoned any hope of nominating to Arras, a concession which should have opened the way for a quick French succession there.[5]

---

5   See the excellent account, which brings out the complexities of French policy and the need for prudence in its dealings with Rome, by Olivier Poncet, 'Un aspect de la conquête française de l'Artois: les nominations aux bénéfices majeurs de 1640 à 1668', *Revue d'Histoire de l'Eglise de France*, 82 (1996), 263–99.

But the Treaty of the Pyrenees did not resolve the problem of episcopal nominations, either in Roussillon or in Flanders, even though the king of Spain had formally transferred to his French counterpart his 'rights of sovereignty, property, régale, patronage, advoswson, jurisdiction, nomination, prerogatives and pre-eminences over the bishoprics, cathedral churches and other abbeys, priories, dignities, parishes and all other benefices situated in the said countries, towns and *bailliages* in question'. This seemingly comprehensive clause notwithstanding, a nine-year impasse ensued in both cases, the reasons for which far transcend local history, revealing as they do some key assumptions of France's ecclesiastical policy at the time.[6] In both cases, it was relations with a third party, Rome, that were the decisive factor, something which no amount of bluster by an impatient and imperious young Louis XIV could disguise.

For much of the war with Spain, a good deal of calculation and restraint prevailed over nominations to major benefices, abbeys as well as bishoprics, in disputed areas like Artois and Roussillon, for fear of insoluble complications at a later date. Rome, as we have seen, refused to take sides in the conflict or to approve the nominations of either party while the outcome of war was uncertain, even though the price to be paid was exceptionally prolonged vacancies and the usurpations of temporalities and other benefices that often accompanied them.[7] It was really only after the 1659 peace treaty that the practical implications of conquest could, and had finally to be faced. Initially, the official French line was that the king was entitled to nominate to vacant bishoprics in Artois and Roussillon by virtue of the Concordat of Bologna of 1516, which was interpreted as automatically applicable to territories that came under French sovereignty; the case seemed all the more clear-cut since the territories involved had been French before François I ceded them to Charles V in 1529. The concordat was judged by ministers (though not by Mazarin himself) and gallican lawyers alike to be co-extensive with that sovereignty; any other stance, such as petitioning the pope for an indult, was, in this view, beneath the dignity of the king of France. The papacy, however, viewed the concordat very differently, and strongly resisted the notion that it was designed to cover anything beyond the lands actually subject to the French crown not merely in 1516 but in 1439, the date of the Pragmatic Sanction which the Concordat was designed to supersede. Having concluded

6 This account is based mainly on Joan Busquets, 'Bisbes espanyols i francesos a Catalunya durant la guerra dels segadors', in Albert Rossich and August Rafanell, eds, *El barroc català* (Barcelona 1989), 61–87. I wish to thank Ignacio Fernandez Terricábras for bringing this essay to my attention, and for generously providing me with additional information on the career of Margarit. A more general account of the Catalan situation is in J H Elliott's classic study, *The Revolt of the Catalans* (Cambridge 1963).

7 See Olivier Poncet, 'Les Contradictions d'une diplomatie. Le Saint-Siège face aux demandes indultaires des souverains catholiques (Espagne, France, Portugal) de 1640 à 1668', in Lucien Bély, ed, *L'Europe des traités de Westphalie. Esprit de la diplomatie et diplomatie de l'esprit* (Paris 2000), 254–65 for the dilemmas faced by the papacy in relation to France and its neighbours or allies.

that Leo X had conceded altogether too much to François I in 1516, successive popes were reluctant to heap more favours on his successors, even though Henri III was the last king of France who needed to ask for a special papal indult in order to nominate bishops in Brittany or Provence, provinces not covered by the concordat. Under Henri IV, the newly acquired see of Belley was subject to a similar tug-of-war before Paul V granted the necessary indult to him to nominate its bishop. By the 1650s and 1660s, the arguments had already been well rehearsed by both sides, but neither was prepared to give ground readily, leaving the unfortunate Margarit and Moreau to wait even longer for an eventual outcome. Interestingly, one of the principal architects of the shift which did occur in French policy after 1659 was the Béarnais Pierre de Marca, by now archbishop of Toulouse, and who had played a major role as France's visitor-general in Catalonia in the 1640s. Marca, who had had to trim his own gallican principles in order to secure papal confirmation as bishop of Couserans in the 1640s, found himself taking the lead after 1659 in moderating the hard-line position previously adopted concerning French episcopal nominations in these new provinces. The upshot was that after unsuccessful discussions in Rome in the years 1660 to 1662, the French crown was forced to abandon its arguments and change tack; there was nothing to be gained from sticking to one's gallican guns, and it seemed better to seek negotiations for indults with Rome than to bury one's head in the sand of putative sovereignty rights under the concordat.[8]

This new-found realism was also a by-product of the poor relations between France and Rome under the pontificates of Innocent X and particularly of Alexander VII (1655–67), whose dislike of Mazarin and, beyond that, of French policies in general, was no secret.[9] It was a dislike which, as we shall see later, would affect other episcopal nominations of Louis XIV's early years. Alexander's humiliation by Louis XIV over the Corsican guard affair in the early 1660s did nothing to repair the damage; on the contrary, it left the French to complain about his 'bad humour' and 'mauvaise affection' towards the king's requests. Consequently, even after the king and his ministers had sacrificed their insistence on the Concordat for negotiated indults by October 1661, they could still obtain hardly any concessions from Rome – with the exception of an indult in 1664 for the *trois-évêchés* of Metz, Toul and Verdun, which will be discussed later in this chapter.[10] As so often, it required a change of pope for this to happen, so Louis XIV and his ministers had to wait until

8   The most succinct and clear account of these problems is by R Darricau, 'Louis XIV et le Saint-Siège. Les Indults de nomination aux bénéfices consistoriaux (1643–1670)', *Bulletin de Littérature Ecclésiastique*, 66 (1965), 16–34, 107–31.

9   See *Enciclopedia dei Papi*, ed Istituto della Enciclopedia Italiana, vol iii (Rome 2000), 321–35 and 336–48 for extensive notices on Innocent X and Alexander VII. The latter's experience as papal nuncio at the Peace of Westphalia negotiations had much to do with his attitude.

10 See Paul Sonnino, *Louis XIV's View of the Papacy* (Berkeley-Los Angleles 1966). Sonnino notes repeatedly how at this stage Louis and his ministers regarded the papacy as corrupted by nepotism and in serious need of reform.

Clement IX Rospigliosi's election in 1667. Of course, episcopal nominations were not the only items on the new pope's agenda, as the 'Clementine Peace' of 1669 (also known as the Peace of the Church), which temporarily ended the disputes over the anti-Jansenist Formulary, clearly attests.[11] Clement IX, who had been France's candidate in the recent conclave, generously granted a perpetual rather than the conventional *ad vitam* indult in 1668 to Louis XIV to nominate to both Arras and Elne-Perpignan. This finally enabled the long-suffering but now elderly Moreau de Saint-Josse and Margarit to obtain their provisions as full bishops, but that could not make up for the years they had lost in waiting: Moreau 'reigned' for just two years, Margarit for four. But what is striking about the papal concessions of 1668 is how clearly the papacy displayed its vigilance in dealing with local differences: the indult for Elne, for example, demanded confirmation of the local Inquisition, annual publication of the famous bull *In Coena Domini* condemning the *appel comme d'abus* to secular tribunals and threatening to excommunicate any lay person usurping ecclesiastical jurisdiction, implementation of the decrees of Trent, exemption from the *régale*, and permission for the apostolic chamber to collect the revenues of the see during a vacancy, as well as part of the estate of a deceased bishop (the *ius spolii*).[12] These conditions were all highly foreign to gallican traditions. But in Artois, the papacy proceeded very differently, granting two distinct indults, one for the see of Arras, another for the remaining major benefices, but without the restrictive conditions laid down for Perpignan. The indult for the see of Arras was perpetual, while the second was valid only during Louis XIV's lifetime.[13] Such an outcome, and the differences accompanying it have been well summarised: 'the long road leading to the indult of 1668 reflects as much the determination of Rome not to make the least additional concession to Louis XIV as it does the king's desire to obtain the canonical regularisation of his nominations to benefices'.[14]

By 1668, coincidentally, Louis XIV had begun making the first of his own contributions to the further expansion of France. The Treaty of Aix-la-Chapelle ending the so-called War of Devolution over the Spanish Netherlands netted him the substantial see of Tournai. In this instance, the timing could not have been better and it was here that the French change of approach towards episcopal nominations paid rapid dividends, since within three months of the treaty, the benevolent Clement IX had granted Louis XIV an indult to nominate to Tournai in addition to Arras. Eleven years later, in 1679, under the terms of the Treaty of Nijmegen which concluded the Dutch War,

---

11   R Darricau, 'Une heure mémorable dans les rapports entre la France et le Saint-Siège: le pontificat de Clément IX (1667–1669)', *Bolletino Storico Pistoiese*, 61 (1869), 78–98.

12   Raymond Sala, *Dieu, le roi et les hommes. Perpignan et le Roussillon (1580–1830)* (Perpignan 1996), 336.

13   Darricau, 'Louis XIV et le Saint-Siège. Les Indults de nomination', 124–5. There is a copy of the papal brief to Louis XIV in ASV, PC 66, fo 2 (Moreau dossier *de vita et moribus*).

14   Poncet, 'Un aspect de la conquête française de l'Artois', 294–6 (quotation from p 296).

the king added no fewer than four further dioceses to his tally – Saint-Omer, Ypres and Cambrai in the Spanish Netherlands, and Besançon in the Franche-Comté.

These were the last of the previously foreign dioceses acquired by Louis XIV and incorporated into the French church. Papal indults enabling the king to nominate their bishops duly followed, albeit with delays of varying lengths, so that the last of them only materialised in 1698.[15] Here, too, there were some differences worth noting. Cambrai and Besançon were archiepiscopal sees and both, strictly speaking, belonged to the *Reichskirche*. In both of them, the cathedral chapter retained the formal right to elect their archbishop, however much the Spanish monarchy may have been able to determine the outcome in practice. Of the two, Besançon was probably the more genuinely 'autonomous', something which was undergirded by the fact that the Franche-Comté was both highly localist and pro-Roman in sentiment, with little sympathy for gallican ideas on church-polity relations.[16] As it happened, when the two sees became French in the 1670s, they were governed by prelates in mid-career who, unlike the Catalan bishops a generation earlier, quickly transferred their allegiance to Louis XIV, thus avoiding a potentially dangerous conflict which would have certainly involved Rome at a time when the pope, Innocent XI, was increasingly at odds with France over the *régale* and other issues. The question of a French succession would only arise later.

But if Besançon and Cambrai were not identical cases to those of a Tournai or a Saint-Omer, neither were they in the same category as Strasbourg, the most celebrated of all Louis XIV's territorial acquisitions. The fact that it was a fully German-speaking and hugely wealthy prince-bishopric that genuinely and actively belonged to the Empire more than offset its lower status as a 'mere' bishopric.[17] And with a highly aristocratic chapter enjoying the right to elect its bishop, there was little prospect of a papal indult, even were it to be granted, being sufficient to establish direct royal episcopal patronage there. So at no time after its acquisition by France in 1681 was there any question of undermining the formal right of election at Strasbourg: such a course of action would have been regarded as a highly provocative political gesture into the bargain. In the years immediately after the acquisition, there was no urgent need for action, since Strasbourg was held by the strongly pro-French Cardinal Fürstenberg. But during the last few years of his tenure, the crown's efforts focused sharply on securing the election of a French successor whose nobility, if not his autonomy, could rival that of the Empire: Armand-Gaston de Rohan-Soubise was finally elected coadjutor with succession rights in

---

15 The indult for the Flanders dioceses was perpetual (BN, MS Fr 23498, fo 131, *Nouvelles Ecclésiastiques*, 12 Oct 1686), but that for Besançon was 'ad vitam regis'. See also François de Dainville, *Cartes anciennes de l'église de France* (Paris 1956), 278–9.

16 B Grosperrin, *L'Influence française et le sentiment national français en Franche-Comté de la conquête à la Révolution* (1674–1789) (Paris 1967), 14–16.

17 Franklin L Ford, *Strasbourg in Transition* (Cambridge, Mass. 1958), ch 2.

1701.[18] Rohan was not the only French house to hanker after a prize as valuable as Strasbourg – that of Bouillon and possibly others did so, too.[19] Its attractiveness lay mainly in the possibilities it offered them of acting as virtually independent 'princes étrangers' in relation to the French monarchy. In fact all parties, the crown included, adjusted well enough to the singularity of Strasbourg. Each of the successive Rohan bishops of eighteenth-century Strasbourg had to be elected in a manner which the French church and crown had both long forgotten, while the monarchy soon found there were numerous ways in which it could effectively oversee and control the affairs of the diocese.[20]

This comparison does not account for all of the quirks of geography, political and ecclesiastical, along France's eastern marches. Ever since the early 1630s, France had also had to deal with the hostility of the duke of Lorraine, whose lands it occupied after 1633. But the French presence in this region was actually much older than that. Since their occupation by Henri II in 1551, the *trois-évêchés* of Metz, Toul and Verdun had been regarded as vital to the defence of the realm; but only in 1648 was actual possession legally acknowledged and they finally become *de jure* part of France. Significant temporal lordships in their own right, they also broke up the territorial unity of the duchy of Lorraine. But as their name suggests, they also possessed a prominent ecclesiastical dimension resembling that of the German prince-bishoprics across the Rhine, even though the French monarchy would always be unwilling to allow their bishops to play the autonomous politico-military role of their imperial counterparts. But apart from that, the French monarchy was extraordinarily slow to integrate these bishoprics into its political and ecclesiastical structures, and relatively little was done until well into the seventeenth century. Politically, it took the establishment of a parlement at Metz in 1633 and the despatch of a regular intendant, as well as the introduction of venality of office, for the administrative and political structures there to begin to change.[21] Until the 1620s, the three bishoprics were dominated ecclesiastically by the house of Lorraine and their clients, facilitated by the survival there of the election of bishops by cathedral chapters. Henri IV had realised that Metz, as the most important of the three in strategic terms, needed to be held by a reliable French client, and before his death in 1610 he made arrangements for it to pass to one of his bastard sons, Henri de Bourbon-Verneuil, who was an unconsecrated bishop there from 1612 until 1652, when

18   René Metz, *La Monarchie française et la provision des bénéfices ecclésiastiques en Alsace de la paix de Westphalie à la fin de l'ancien régime 1648–1789* (Strasbourg-Paris 1947), pt 2, ch 3, pp 295–331, 'l'artifice des élections épiscopales'.
19   AN, L 745, pièce no 1, Strasbourg. Cardinal Bouillon was incensed that his nephew, the abbé d'Auvergne, was passed over in favour of the younger Rohan-Soubise.
20   See Louis Châtellier, *Tradition chrétienne et renouveau catholique dans le cadre de l'ancien diocèse de Strasbourg 1650–1770* (Paris 1981), esp ch vi.
21   Taveneaux, *Le Jansénisme en Lorraine*, 54–5.

Louis XIV unceremoniously obliged him to abandon it in order to marry! His successor for a time was no less a figure than Mazarin, whom Rome firmly refused to confirm. Effectively administered by suffragans for over half a century and vacant *de jure* after 1652, Metz only finally swung into the French ecclesiastical orbit with the transfer there of the archbishop of Embrun, Aubusson de la Feuillade, in 1669.[22] Its cathedral chapter had twice attempted to elect a new bishop during the 1660s, but it failed in the face of opposition from *both* Rome and Paris, a relatively uncommon occurrence in such matters and at that juncture.[23] At neighbouring Toul, by far the biggest of the three sees and having Nancy within its jurisdiction, Louis XIII and Richelieu had failed to engineer the succession of a French candidate, Henri Arnauld, in the 1630s and 1640s.[24] Although a former vicar-general of Paris, André du Saussay, became bishop there in 1655, the papacy formally declined to recognise him as the nominee of Louis XIV.[25] It was not until the mid-1670s that a royal nominee for Toul was accepted as such by the curia. By contrast, Verdun, another former *chasse gardée* of the house of Lorraine and vacant only since 1661, had a French nominee, approved as such by Rome, by as early as 1665.[26] It is ironic that it should have been Alexander VII, so unresponsive in other respects towards French interests, who made the concessions which accelerated the process of integrating the *trois-évêchés* at this crucial moment. In 1664, the year he had to apologise to Louis XIV for the Corsican guard incident in Rome, he granted an indult to the king enabling him to nominate to the three bishoprics, while excluding all other benefices within their boundaries. This deliberately limited concession, designed explicitly to obtain French assistance in ending an anti-papal revolt in Avignon, actually angered the king and his ministers, but it proved a short-lived slight, since the more generous Clement IX removed that exclusion by a new indult in 1668.[27] Needless to say, the fact that the three bishoprics had been in French hands for over a century by that point facilitated their subsequent integration into the French church. It was in the nature of Franco-papal relations that *de facto* powers tended to be slowly translated, by the medium of indults, into *de jure*

22 After Mazarin abandoned his efforts to become titular bishop of Metz, he ensured that the French claim to it passed to the pro-French prince, Guillaume Egon von Fürstenberg, who held it for an unspecified number of years before 1669. ASV, PC 66, fo 189, Louis XIV to Clement IX, 25 June 1668, nominating Aubusson 'en conséquence de la cession et renonciation faite entre nos mains par nostre très cher et bien amé cousin, Messire Guillaume Egon langrave de Furstenberg prince du Saint Empire nommé et postulé aud Evesché'.

23 See Taveneaux, *Jansénisme en Lorraine*, 217–19.

24 Bergin, *Making*, 482–3.

25 Taveneaux, *Jansénisme en Lorraine*, 110–12.

26 This is most evident in the career of the last episcopal member of the house of Lorraine to hold Verdun, François de Lorraine, who died in July 1661, and had been neither a priest nor a consecrated bishop during his thirty-eight-year tenure. See Taveneaux, *Jansénisme en Lorraine*, 169.

27 Sonnino, *Louis XIV's View of the Papacy*, 67. Taveneaux, *Jansénisme en Lorraine*, 58, n 15.

rights in which the papacy often found itself surrendering the substance while keeping the semblance of power. If the *trois-évêchés* remained outside the 'Clergé de France' and did not send deputies to the general assemblies of the French clergy, their integration into the French church is nevertheless vouched for by the readiness with which the king transferred bishops both to and from them in subsequent decades.

A final case-study for our present purposes is provided by the southern see of Orange which, like the smaller principality of Orange itself, was a virtual enclave within the papal *Comtat Venaissin*. With a largely Protestant population, it was occupied on several occasions by Louis XIV during his wars against the Dutch and the house of Nassau-Orange. But it was always restored on the conclusion of peace until, finally, the Treaty of Utrecht (1713) confirmed its latest seizure by France in 1703 and its submission to French sovereignty. However, since Louis XIII's time, its bishops were increasingly French clients, even though the kings of France had no formal right whatever to nominate them. From 1572 to 1646, it was held by three successive members of the Tulles family, the last of whom was transferred to Lavaur in recompense for his services to Mazarin. This pattern was repeated with two successors, both Mazarin clients, the Italian Dominican Hyacinthe Serroni, who was transferred to Mende in early 1661, and his successor, Alessandro Fabri.[28] One of Mazarin's last acts of episcopal patronage was to secure the Orange 'nomination' for Fabri, but he was then made to wait six years for his provisions while Rome disputed the validity of the 'presentation' and tried, unsuccessfully, to impose its own candidate.[29] By contrast, Fabri's successor Jean-Jacques d'Obeilh was a French subject, born in Autun diocese and a doctor of the Paris theology faculty.[30] Although neither he nor Fabri later moved to another diocese, it is clear that there was no aversion to such a transfer, as when it was rumoured in 1687 that Obeilh was earmarked to take the see of Nîmes.[31] It is possible that Obeilh's forty-three year tenure temporarily obscured the see of Orange's connection to France, since it was not until his death in 1720 that the Regent, Philippe d'Orléans, formally nominated a bishop of Orange.[32] In fact, the crown had not waited until 1720 before acting. It was Louis XIV himself who, having occupied Orange again in 1703, requested the indult and, surprisingly given that his possession of Orange was not yet validated by a peace treaty, obtained it from the highly pro-French

---

28 Bergin, *Making*, 38–9, 709.
29 SHAT, Archives de la Guerre, A¹ 171, no 63, minute of Louis XIV's letter of nomination of Fabri to Alexander VII, 28 Feb 1661. Pierre Blet, *Les Nonces du pape à la cour de Louis XIV* (Paris 2002), 37–8, for an account based on the nuncio's correspondence. Serroni, Fabri's predecessor, resigned Orange to him in Feb 1661 on the eve of his own nomination to Mende. Fabri had been given a French abbey *in commendam*, and was consecrated by French prelates in Paris 1668.
30 *Hierarchia Catholica*, v, 106, 'Aurasciensis'. *Correspondance du nonce Spada*, no 571, Spada to Cardinal Altieri, 9 Nov 1674.
31 BN, MS Fr 23498, fo 168v, *Nouvelles Ecclésiastiques*, 15 Feb 1687.
32 *Hierarchia Catholica*, v, 106, 'Aurasciensis', n 4.

Clement XI in 1706.[33] Down to this point the nomination rights to Orange theoretically belonged to the Protestant prince of Orange, and in 1661 and probably later, the French crown did at least seek the prince's formal cooperation in obtaining the confirmation of new bishops.[34] But behind this façade an instructively different reality prevailed: thanks initially to Mazarin's unique capacity to pull French and Roman levers simultaneously, only someone approved by the king of France could become bishop of Orange, but as with other dioceses in a similarly ambiguous position, Rome delayed for as long as possible before publicly acknowledging such a state of affairs.

The impression of a haphazard, slow-moving acquisition and integration of existing bishoprics into the French church is confirmed by another test of the pattern of integration, namely whether newly acquired dioceses were included in the 'Clergé de France', in other words whether they participated in the assemblies of clergy. One of the main incentives in this direction, at least from the crown's point of view, was to ensure that the new dioceses would contribute to the *décimes* and *dons gratuits* which the clergy voted to it at regular intervals, sums which were to grow substantially in the latter de-cades of Louis XIV's reign. But in this area the king's ability to get what he wanted was far more limited. Since it was ecclesiastical provinces rather than individual dioceses which were represented at the assemblies, everything depended on whether the dioceses in question were part of a 'French' ecclesi-astical province. In the case of Elne-Perpignan, whose contemporary affilia-tion was to the Spanish province of Tarragona, the problem was 'resolved' unilaterally during the 1670s by Louis XIV himself: tiring of waiting for a papal response to his requests, he reunited it to the French province of Nar-bonne, to which it had once belonged. But that did not make Perpignan a French diocese 'comme les autres' and it did not participate in elections to general assemblies by the Narbonne province.[35] Elsewhere clear-cut solutions were just as elusive. The crown was hightly fortunate that the Artois-Flanders sees of Arras, Tournai and Saint-Omer were all part of the province of Cambrai acquired at virtually the same time as them, so problems arising from subordination to a foreign metropolitan were neatly avoided. The one

33   *Recueil des instructions données aux ambassadeurs et ministres de France depuis les traités de Westphalie jusqu'à la Révolution française, Rome*, 2 vols (Paris 1884–1911), ii, ed Jean Hanoteau, 586–603, instruction from Cardinal Dubois to abbé de Tencin, 6 Aug 1722, p 590, which mentions the Orange indult in the context of a discussion of the indults that needed to be renewed after Louis XIV's death.

34   SHAT, Archives de la Guerre, A^1 171, no 63, minute of letter of Louis XIV to prince of Orange, 28 Feb 1661 announcing that Bishop Serroni was moving from Orange to Mende, and asking the prince to deliver the necessary papers so that Alessandro Fabri, a Mazarin servant, could succeed him.

35   Sala, *Dieu, le roi et les hommes*, 337. Rome had been formally approached and some work done in preparation for a decision in mid-1676, which seems to have been shelved: ASV, Archivio congregationis consistorialis, 1676, fos 527–33.

exception here was Ypres, which belonged to the province of Malines, but its removal, along with that of Tournai, from French control by the Treaty of Utrecht in 1713 effectively 'solved' the problem of how to incorporate it into the 'Clergé de France'. On the other hand, Metz, Toul and Verdun as well as the more recently acquired Besançon fully retained their singularity. The *trois-évêchés* remained part of the German province of Trier, and did not send deputies to the assemblies since their archbishop could hardly be required to convene his suffragans to send deputies to a French assembly! Likewise, the archiepiscopal see of Besançon, whose province included the non-French sees of Lausanne and Basle, also stood outside of the 'Clergé'. Orange, which historically belonged to the province of Arles, could be more readily incorporated once the crown formally acquired nomination rights, but this did not happen until after 1720.[36]

II

To limit the analysis of the effectiveness or otherwise of the absorption of new dioceses into the French church to the institutional domain would be one-sided. Contemporaries themselves would have paid just as much attention to the manner in which the crown employed the patronage rights which it acquired in order to achieve its objectives. As we have just seen in the case of Orange, a diocese could strictly speaking remain entirely 'outside' of the French church, yet the crown's ability to impose its own choice of bishop ensured it would be the real master there. It would also be perverse to imagine that, at a time when the filling of all vacant bishoprics required careful consideration, decisions affecting sees as diverse as those examined here did not attract at least as much deliberation. How the crown approached these decisions for the dioceses we are examining should offer valuable additional insight into its tactics and priorities.

In every respect, the bishopric of Elne-Perpignan was the most 'foreign' of the new additions. Not only were its language and culture Catalan, but it was also wedded to Spanish ecclesiastical traditions which were quite foreign to those of France. Mazarin's initial nomination of a Catalan, Margarit, to the vacant see was a typically pragmatic move which was upheld by Louis XIV because by the 1650s Margarit and his family had lost their lands and offices in Spain on account of their support for the French. As we saw, the papal indults of 1668 insisted that the ecclesiological status quo remain unchanged after Elne's transfer to France. Margarit's death in 1672 led to the rapid nomination, in early February 1673, of Jean-Louis de Bruelh, son of the

---

36 The archbishop of Arles tried to organise the election of the bishop of Orange to the 1705 Assembly of Clergy but this was successfully opposed by others present, for whom Orange was 'comme ceux de Flandres qui ne sont point du corps du clergé de France': BN, MS Fr 19212, fo 147r, 18 April 1705, Père Léonard's 'mémoires ecclésiastiques'.

French governor of Perpignan. Nephew of an earlier bishop of Mende, he had himself been made Inquisitor of Roussillon in 1662, so he might be regarded as a semi-native of the province, even though his mission as Inquisitor was to reduce the powers of the Inquisition! However, his nomination to Perpignan coincided with a dispute between France and Rome over the powers of the Inquisition in Roussillon and when he died early in 1675 he had not been confirmed by Rome. His 'successor', also the scion of a family with an episcopal track record, Jean-Baptiste d'Etampes de Valençay, was a native of Orléans diocese. However, having also also waited several years in vain for his bulls, he abandoned Perpignan for Marseille in 1679. As far as Perpignan was concerned, the problem was that the French crown was now increasingly unwilling to accept the 'liberties of the church' in Roussillon which Rome had written into the 1668 indult. The discontinuity of episcopal tenure in the decade after Margarit's brief reign opened the way for royal intervention in pursuit of what has been called a policy of 'gallicanisation' of Roussillon. The temporal *régale* was imposed when the see fell vacant in both 1672 and 1675, though early attempts at imposing the spiritual *régale* (i.e. appointing to vacant benefices in the bishop's gift) were less successful since Rome and the local clergy were both hostile to it. After the 1673 decree, which extended the *régale* throughout France generally, even Orange was targeted by the crown, but Perpignan was unable to mount the same successful defence of its autonomy as Orange had done.[37] The new French *conseil supérieur* of Roussillon vigorously applied gallican jurisdictional maxims there, especially the *appel comme d'abus*, in order to curb ecclesiastical courts and exemptions from secular jurisdiction. The Inquisition also gradually found itself squeezed out of the picture, and a more recognisably French diocesan administrative structure began to fall into place. But it was not until 1682 that the long vacancy of Perpignan itself finally ended, and from then until 1721, it was host to just two bishops, as episcopal stability became the order of the day. Significantly, both were northerners – firstly, Louis Habert de Montmort, son of a Parisian financial and judicial family with several distinguished members of the Académie Française, and then Jean-Hervé de Bazan, a product of Saint-Sulpice and a protégé of Madame de Maintenon's director, Godet, bishop of Chartres.[38] Both, it should be said, frequently found themselves at loggerheads with the *conseil supérieur* on questions of jurisdiction. Even the war minister Louvois, who was the real instigator of the gallicanisation policy, once admitted that 'ces usages de France' had been 'used and abused' in

---

37   BM Avignon, MS 2648, fos 340–50, for a dossier of *avis*, decrees of the royal council etc 1676–8 on the question of whether Orange was subject to the *régale*. For the context of these moves, see Pierre Blet, *Les Assemblées du clergé et Louis XIV de 1670 à 1693* (Rome 1972), 149–50.

38   Joseph Capeilles, *Dictionnaire des biographies roussillonnaises* (Paris 1914), 211–12 (Bazan). Bergin, *Making*, 637–8, for a notice on the Habert family and Pierre Habert bishop of Cahors under Louis XIII.

Roussillon.[39] On the other hand, it would seem that gallican principles on questions such as episcopal control of religious orders and so on must have been highly welcome to these bishops.[40]

There is no question of building an interpretation of French political ecclesiology under Louis XIV on the evidence of how it went about pruning Roussillon of its un-gallican traditions. A more balanced perspective can be achieved by comparing Roussillon with the northern dioceses acquired during the same period. When the first French bishop of Arras, Étienne Moreau whose abbey of Saint-Josse (the name by which he was commonly known) was situated in the neighbouring diocese of Boulogne, died in January 1670, within little more than a week the crown nominated a successor who was in many ways typical of the newer kind of bishop of the period. Guy de Sève was not yet thirty-years old, but was exceptionally well linked to Parisian high-robe families, and was a cousin of Colbert, whose hand is not hard to detect in his promotion; at the same time, he was a priest and doctor of theology of Paris since 1666 and had been formed at Saint-Sulpice by its celebrated superior, Louis Tronson, who was also a cousin of his.[41] A rigorist on questions of morality and an energetic legislator, he spent the next fifty-four years governing a diocese which, as in the past, lay in the path of the armies of France and its enemies.

By contrast, Louis XIV was to have more than one opportunity to appoint bishops to the neighbouring see of Tournai, which happened to fall vacant shortly before it was confirmed as a French possession in 1667. Almost inevitably, this led to rival Spanish and French nominations, and few incidents better illustrate the differences between the two crowns than their approach to finding a successor of their choice.[42] The previous bishop had died only the year before, in 1666, having failed to obtain the coadjutorship and succession for his nephew in the face of his cathedral chapter's opposition. The chapter then initiated the search for a successor and the governor-general despatched a circular to the bishops and abbots of the Spanish Netherlands to elicit suitable names. The council of state in Brussels examined the names suggested and prepared two lists for the governor-general, one containing those distinguished by birth, the other those of intellectual or ecclesiastical distinction, and adding only that the governor should *not* consider a regular

---

39   Sala, *Dieu, le roi et les hommes*, 338. BN, MS Fr 23502, fos 179v; MS Fr 23503, fos 3v–4, *Nouvelles Ecclésiastiques*, for reports on bishop's attempts in 1692–3 to curb the powers of the *conseil supérieur* by appealing to king and ministers in Paris.

40   Sala, *Dieu, le roi et les hommes*, 347–50.

41   His extensive correspondence with Tronson concerning his diocese, and in particular over synodal statutes and other decrees, was published in part in *Correspondance de Louis Tronson: lettres choisies*, ed A L Bertrand, 3 vols (Paris 1904), iii, esp 49–54, 58–61, 73–6, 85–6, but most of it survives unpublished in the Saint-Sulpice archives.

42   This account is based primarily on F Desmons, *Etudes historiques, économiques et religieuses sur Tournai durant le règne de Louis XIV. L'épiscopat de Gilbert de Choiseul 1671–1689* (Tournai 1907), 1–41.

for the position. He ignored the second list and went for a man of birth, Alphonse de Berghes, a former grand almoner to Philip IV of Spain, who duly obtained the approval of the Regent of Spain in October 1667. But exactly as with Arras in 1640, Tournai had fallen into French hands only a few months earlier, and Berghes was not an acceptable candidate to them, especially as he seemed unwilling to take the oath of fidelity to Louis XIV. Although Louis XIV had no title whatever to nominate to Tournai at this point, he ensured Berghes's confirmation was effectively blocked in Rome. He further raised the stakes in August 1668 by nominating a highly placed French curial official, Louis de Bourlemont, to Tournai, but Bourlemont was either not ready for such a move or wanted something better, for he returned the *brevet de nomination*. Some months later, Louis XIV was duly given his indult to nominate to Tournai by Clement IX, while Berghes's nomination as archbishop of Malines in 1669 conveniently opened the way to an uncontested succession. In contrast to the Spanish mode of consultation and selection just observed, virtually nothing is known about how Louis XIV decided to nominate first Bourlemont and then Gilbert de Choiseul, who accepted the nomination and who would govern Tournai until his death in 1689. Choiseul, scion of a high-ranking military family, was not an unknown quantity by then. Bishop of Comminges since 1646, he had fallen out of favour under Mazarin for refusing to sign the censure of Antoine Arnauld during the Jansenist affair in 1655–6, but he regained it by his strongly gallican stance during the Paris theology faculty disputes of the early 1660s and the negotiations leading to the Peace of the Church of 1669. The precise reasons for the king's choice remain a matter of speculation, as Choiseul's apparent rejection of an earlier offer of a promotion to Narbonne suggests he had no great desire to change diocese; it is conceivable that the court felt that it would be easier to keep an eye on an independently minded and Jansenist-leaning figure like him in Tournai than in Comminges. What may also be suggested is that as bishop of the southern frontier diocese of Comminges he had as much experience of Spanish ecclesiastical traditions as it was possible for a French bishop to acquire; moving him to another frontier diocese which had hitherto been Spanish would seem to have played some part in the king's decision. The unknown factor was how a gallican bishop with known pro-Jansenist sentiments like him would fare in Flanders.[43]

Less than a decade later it was the turn of the neighbouring sees of Saint-Omer, Ypres and Cambrai to pass into French sovereignty. The biggest problem might have arisen with the metropolitan see of Cambrai itself, but it turned out to be the least complicated of the three. Trouble was averted because the archbishop, the Liégeois Jacques de Bryas, proved willing, unlike other

43   For his record as a hard-line reformer in Comminges, see Serge Brunet, *Les Prêtres des montagnes. La Vie, la mort, la foi dans les Pyrénées centrales sous l'ancien régime* (Aspet 2001), 157–9, 'l'implacable apogée de la réfome'. There is a hint that the move to Tournai was involuntary on Choiseul's part, and may have been decided with a view to better surveillance of his activities.

subjects of the king of Spain before him, to recognise Louis XIV and take the oath of fidelity.[44] He and Choiseul even represented the Cambrai province at the celebrated Assembly of Clergy of 1682 which approved the four Gallican Articles. It was around this time that preliminary steps were taken towards ensuring a successor to Bryas who would be French in every sense. There was no point in seeking a papal indult for Cambrai as for the other dioceses, since Cambrai's chapter still enjoyed the right of election, and Rome would not unilaterally abolish it. The French crown opted instead for direct negotiation with the chapter, and a bargain was agreed whereby the chapter surrendered its electoral rights and the crown undertook *not* to introduce the *régale* into Cambrai. Matters rested there until Bryas's death in 1694: it was only then that the crown applied to Rome for the indult, since the 1682 'treaty' with the Cambrai chapter needed the approval of the pope, the 'lord of the benefices' in canon law. The delay in nominating Bryas's successor was partly due to the time it took to obtain papal approval, but when it is realised that the delay in question was less than three months, it is clear that times had changed radically since the 1660s. The first French archbishop of Cambrai, Fénelon, encountered no significant obstacles to his tenure there – in fact, that came from his French neighbour and confrère, Le Tellier of Reims![45]

In the mid-1670s, when Jacques de Bryas had moved to Cambrai from Saint-Omer, not only did Louis XIV follow the precedent he had set at Tournai in 1669 by nominating a reigning French bishop to Saint-Omer, but he nominated one who also held a Pyreneean frontier diocese, Tarbes. However, in his desire to react quickly to an episcopal vacancy, he did so before obtaining the required indult from Rome, and by the later 1670s, Innocent XI was, as we noted above, increasingly unwilling to heap favours on Louis XIV by expediting his episcopal nominations. But having waited in vain for several years for his bulls, the bishop of Tarbes finally lost patience and accepted the offer of the great southern see of Auch instead. At that point, in May 1684, the king showed how consistent he could be by awarding Saint-Omer to yet another bishop of a Pyreneean see, Louis Alphonse de Valbelle, successor of the famous Pavillon at Alet. It was only in 1686 that Innocent XI finally granted the king the indults he sought for Saint-Omer and Ypres, while still refusing them for Cambrai and Besançon, neither of which was vacant.[46] However, well before 1686, the Saint-Omer succession had, like many others as we shall see

---

44   Fénelon, *Correspondance*, ed Jean Orcibal et al, 17 vols (Paris 1972–99), xiv, no 1443, to Tellier, royal confessor, 5 Feb 1711. Fénelon, successor to Bryas, recounts that he was told about Bryas's decision by Cardinal Bouillon and Archbishop Le Tellier of Reims, who persuaded Bryas to take the *serment* two years before the treaty of Aix-la-Chapelle was actually signed.

45   Philippe Guignet, 'Évangélisation et apaisement d'un conflit séculaire avec l'archevêché de Reims', in Gilles Deregnaucourt and Philippe Guignet, eds, *Fénelon évêque et pasteur en son temps* (Lille 1996), 44–55. Since Cambrai's elevation to the rank of archbishopric in 1559 by Philip II of Spain, archbishops of Reims had refused to recognise its new status, and Le Tellier was reiterating that opposition nearly 150 years later.

46   *Correspondance du nonce Ranuzzi*, i, 90 (editor's introduction).

later, become entangled in the crisis of Franco-papal relations from 1682 to 1692, so that Valbelle did not obtain his provisions until November 1693. Saint-Omer had been vacant for eighteen years by then.

The experience of Ypres resembled that of Saint-Omer. Its Flemish bishop died in August 1678, and the king of Spain nominated a candidate whom Rome would not confirm, but as on previous occasions, the papacy would not allow a French candidate to be confirmed so long as his Spanish rival lived or had not been given another diocese. Everyone had to wait until his death in December 1693 before a successor could be approved. As was to be expected, the French crown had not stood idly by until that date, though it is not known who was Louis XIV's first nominee. In 1689, however, he made an interesting choice – this time, his candidate was not a reigning bishop from a Pyreneean diocese, but someone who came close enough to being one and who also had experience on 'foreign' soil – Martin Ratabon, the first French vicar-general of Strasbourg since 1684.[47] He, too, had to await the resolution of the Franco-papal impasse before obtaining his provisions in late 1693. As we shall see, he came very close to being the last as well as the first French bishop of Ypres.

The experience of Besançon paralleled that of Cambrai in some respects, but with noteworthy differences, too. When the province finally became subject to French sovereignty in 1679, the see of Besançon was not vacant but was occupied by Antoine-Pierre de Grammont, the second of a line of four archbishops from a powerful franc-comtois family, and who was still only in mid-career. Within a few years he took advantage of his and his family's pro-French stance by obtaining the installation of his nephew as his auxiliary (suffragan) bishop. This was less of a success than obtaining him as his coadjutor would have been, since the latter carried rights of automatic succession. Whether he attempted to secure a coadjutorship or not at this juncture, we do not know. Certainly, the refusal of Innocent XI to grant Louis XIV an indult for Besançon and Cambrai in 1686 strongly suggests that Grammont may have settled for an auxiliary-bishop solution as a possible stepping-stone to family succession at a later date. When the archbishop died in early May 1698, nothing had been settled and there was a sudden flurry of activity: the crown quickly stepped in to strike an identical deal with the Besançon chapter as it had done with Cambrai in 1682 – the chapter forfeited its election rights, the crown would not introduce the *régale* into the province.[48] On this basis the king sought a papal indult to nominate the new archbishop and Innocent XII granted it almost immediately.[49] The impression given by such rapidity

47   See the entry on him in *Biographie Nationale* (Belge), xvii, cols 763–70.
48   Sourches, vi, 37, 30 May 1698.
49   ASV, Nunz Fr 195, fo 814, nuncio to Cardinal Spada, secretary of state, 30 June 1698; Nunz Fr 196, fo 62, same to same, 14 July; *ibid*, fos 119–20, 18 July; Nunz Fr 384, fos 146, 153v–54r, Spada to nuncio, 8 July, 9 July and 5 Aug respectively. Grosperrin, *L'Influence française et le sentiment national français en Franche-Comté*, 37–9.

— it all took no more than three months at the most — is that of a well-oiled machine which by now knew precisely how to negotiate and resolve such issues without fear of disruption or unpleasant surprises. What was less clear at that juncture was whether the Grammont hold on Besançon would be extended to another generation. The diarist, the marquis de Sourches, reported that the comte de Grammont came to court immediately after his uncle's death to ask for Besançon for his brother, the auxiliary bishop, but it is possible that he did not receive any firm assurances.[50] Once news of the papal indult was known, Sourches wrote that 'great cabales were formed to prevent it from being given to the bishop of Philadelphia (i.e. Grammont)' in the weeks before the king's decision was due.[51] In the event, the suffragan-bishop was duly nominated to succeed his uncle at Assumption 1698.[52] Even if a Grammont uncle-to-nephew succession was always the most likely outcome, the steps taken in 1698 evinced a clear determination to eliminate any ambiguity about the crown's grip on Besançon. Once that was assured, it could even allow yet another Grammont to become suffragan of Besançon in 1707.[53]

III

The successive papal indults which enabled Louis XIV to nominate to dioceses like those of Perpignan and Artois-Flanders all specified that they were only valid so long as he remained master of the lands in question. The twists and turns of war could also undo such exposed gains, and it is worth observing how the French monarchy went about defending them when the tide of fortune turned against it. In the event, it was the Flanders dioceses, and not the likes of Perpignan or Besançon, which proved the most vulnerable. By the latter years of the War of Spanish Succession, Ypres and Tournai were both occupied by the allied powers, and Saint-Omer was not safe for much of the time. Their bishops became increasingly concerned about their future, but the crown's dilemma was similar to that of the Castilian monarchy in Catalonia in the 1640s — if the bishops were to leave or be transferred to other sees, would that not play into the hands of France's enemies, allowing them to declare the dioceses vacant or *en régale* and, as a result, begin

---

50   Sourches, vi, 31, 8 May 1698.
51   Sourches, vi, 48, 23 July 1698; 52, 4 Aug; 55, 15 Aug. Philadelphia was the title of the suffragan's diocese *in partibus infidelium*.
52   ASV, PC 93, fos 64–76, Grammont's *de vita et moribus* dossier; the letter of nomination is dated 17 Aug 1698; *Hierarchia Catholica*, v, 120, 'Bisuntin'.
53   Sourches, ix, 438, 14 Dec 1705, reporting that the archbishop had obtained royal permission to take his cousin as his suffragan to assist him in governing what was a vast diocese. Rome did not confirm this until 1707: *Hierarchia Catholica*, v, 97, 'Arethusin', n 2, Antoine-François de Grammont. He did not succed his cousin on the latter's death in 1717, but *his* nephew, Antoine-Pierre II, did regain Besançon for the Grammont family in 1735.

to fill empty benefices there? Martin Ratabon, whose residence in Ypres had been somewhat erratic, cast around for another see, and Louis XIV finally consented to his resignation of Ypres in January 1713 before nominating him to Viviers a few months later.[54] Crucially, the changeover was kept secret for long enough to nominate a French successor *and* to obtain Rome's approval of the nomination before the inevitable handover of Ypres to the allies by peace treaty.[55] The choice of incoming bishop for Ypres is also worth noting: Charles de Laval-Montmorency, priest, doctor of theology and vicar-general of Cambrai, was, as his name alone suggests, as blue-blooded a candidate as one could find, belonging to a family with historic ties to the Flanders high nobility. However, Louis XIV's success proved unexpectedly short-lived: when Montmorency died suddenly in late August 1713, only a few months after taking up office, it was too late to repeat the 'coup' of a few months earlier.[56] Peace had finally been made in April 1713, after which Ypres came under Austrian sovereignty.[57]

Neighbouring Tournai, which had had three French bishops since Choiseul's death – one of them also a former Strasbourg vicar-general like Ratabon, the other two reigning bishops who were translated from French sees – was to follow the same path as Ypres, but its fate reveals much more about French tactics and motivation in adversity. Its last French bishop, René-François de Beauvau, had been transferred from Bayonne – yet another frontier diocese with Spain! – to Tournai as recently as 1707, and was soon in serious difficulties. With the allied occupation of Tournai in July 1709, he was forced out since he would not take the oath of fidelity to a foreign prince; the diocese was in the hands of the Dutch who treated the see as vacant (and therefore *en régale*) since, they claimed, its bishop had effectively abandoned it. By late 1710, Louis XIV was under several contradictory pressures. The papal nuncio was pressing strongly for Beauvau to be sent back if not to Tournai itself, then to neighbouring Cambrai where he would be in a position to protect his diocese. Fénelon, the metropolitan of Tournai, claimed that the Dutch were favouring Jansenists in the diocese; the bishop himself protested that his return to Tournai would achieve nothing. Unwilling to give Beauvau permission to return to Tournai itself on account of the oath of

54   ASV, Nunz Fr 226, fo 72, nuncio to Cardinal Paulucci, secretary of state, 23 Jan 1713.

55   *Ibid*, fo 192, same to same, 6 March 1713, noting that the 'preconisation' of Laval-Montmorency was the only item on the special consistory in question. See Philippe de Courcillon, marquis de Dangeau, *Journal*, ed Feuillet de Conches, 19 vols (Paris 1853–60), xiv, 368, 20 March 1713 (cited hereafter as Dangeau): 'le roi y nomma l' abbé de Laval, grand vicaire de Cambray, et envoya à Rome pour avoir des bulles, et jusqu' à ce qu' elles aient été expédiées on a tenu l' affaire secrète. Comme le roi doit rendre Ypres par la paix, il a été bien aise d' avoir là un nouvel évêque avant la conclusion de la paix.'

56   Fénelon, *Correspondance*, xvi, no 1737a, Père Tellier to Fénelon, 7 Oct 1713. In this letter the confessor discusses possible ways of persuading the emperor in Vienna to nominate an anti-Jansenist successor to Laval-Montmorency.

57   *Hierarchia Catholica*, v, 420, 'Yprensis'.

fidelity, Louis was ready to nominate him to another diocese provided he could be sure that the pope would *not* confirm as his replacement at Tournai anyone nominated by an enemy power.[58] The shoe was now firmly on the other foot! The king tried to insist that since he had been given the indult to nominate to Tournai, he alone had the right to decide who should be Tournai's next incumbent – precisely the reverse of the French stance decades earlier, when the indult belonged to the king of Spain.[59] An attempt to promote Beauvau to Toulouse while retaining Tournai until a peace settlement was completed had to be abandoned in the face of a papal *non placet*.[60] In February 1711, after discussions with his confessor, the foreign secretary Colbert de Torcy, and others, Louis XIV announced he was prepared to agree on a successor who would also be acceptable to the allies, and to drop his insistence on the explicit use of his indult in the nomination procedures. But here, too, the real problem lay in finding acceptable candidates who would be willing to accept the not inconsiderable risks involved. The first French candidate for Tournai, Thomas-Philippe Hennin de Bossut, was a Brussels-born cleric who would become archbishop of Malines in 1714 and be known later as the Cardinal of Alsace. But since he was in Rome in 1711 and apparently working on behalf of the disgraced French Cardinal Bouillon, doubts soon arose about his suitability, leading to discussions which are highly revealing as to the expectations, admittedly in peculiar circumstances, of the elderly monarch and his circle about candidates for the mitre.[61] As Torcy put it, they began by 'remarking favourably on his morals and his personal qualities, which is what one normally does when considering someone for promotion'. Bossut's brother's attachment to Louis XIV's grandson, Philip V of Spain, was also held to be an advantage, but his own service to Bouillon became the sticking point; as Torcy put it, 'this employment being extremely unworthy of a man of his birth, it did not reveal good intentions towards the king'. When Torcy himself suggested they could test Hennin de Bossut's attitude by seeing whether the offer of Tournai would induce him to leave Bouillon's service, it was Louis XIV who seemed reluctant to proceed, 'fearing that his conscience would be somewhat afflicted by letting him (Bossut) glimpse the prospect of a

58   ASV, Nunz Fr 219, fo 522, nuncio to secretary of state, 17 Nov 1710; Nunz Fr 222, fos 714, 734, same to same, 10 and 17 Nov 1710.

59   *Journal inédit de Jean-Baptiste Colbert marquis de Torcy, ministre et secrétaire d'état aux affaires étrangères pendant les années 1709, 1710 et 1711*, ed Frédéric Masson (Paris 1884), 277, 279, 300–1, Sept–Nov 1710 for these discussions. Fénelon, *Oeuvres*, ed J Gosselin, 10 vols (Paris 1851–2), viii, 419–21, for his *mémoire* to Père Tellier, the confessor. See also Fénelon, *Correspondance*, xiv, no 1434, to duc de Chevreuse, 5 Jan 1711; no 1443, to Tellier, 5 Feb 1711; no 1444, to bishop of Tournai, same date; no 1459, to same, 30 March 1711.

60   ASV, Nunz Fr 223, fo 36, nuncio to secretary of state, 29 Jan 1711; Dangeau, xiii, 344.

61   See Lucien Ceyssens, 'Le Cardinal d'Alsace (1679–1759)', in his, *Le Sort de la bulle Unigenitus* (Louvain 1992), 567–603. Ceyssens was unaware that Hennin was a potential French candidate for the mitre. The Hennin-Liétard family, to which the cardinal belonged, had several branches settled in France, one of which produced a bishop of Alès in 1713, Jean-François de Hennin-Liétard. The situation in early 1711 was further complicated by Bouillon's flight to Tournai itself where he enjoyed Dutch protection.

substantial diocese in return for renouncing the commission given him by Bouillon'. Such a proposition – 'you can have Tournai if you abandon Bouillon' – evidently struck the king as not far removed from simony. But when he asked Torcy whether his confessor, the Jesuit père Tellier, was of a similar mind on the question, the reply was in the negative: Tellier could see no issue of conscience here, and believed there was nothing wrong in ensuring they were not making a mistake in promoting someone currently serving a rebel who had behaved as badly towards his sovereign as Cardinal Bouillon had.[62] The idea was only dropped when Hennin himself, who probably had more patrons in Vienna and Rome than in Versailles, understandably would not take the French bait.[63] By then, April 1711, Beauvau had made, with royal approval and in response mainly to papal pressure, the first of his fruitless attempts to return to Tournai.[64] But in early 1713, as peace finally approached, Louis XIV partly achieved his objective for Tournai. The curriculum vitae of its new bishop, Johan-Ernst von Löwenstein-Wertheim from Würzburg diocese, was far closer to that of Germany's prince-bishops than that of their French counterparts: although aged forty-five, he was neither a priest nor a university graduate. But he was dean of Strasbourg cathedral and abbot *in commendam* of Saint-Vincent of Laon and Saint-Jean-des-Prés of Saint-Malo, two benefices in the gift of the king of France and, above all, he was a nephew of the famously pro-French bishop of Strasbourg, whom we have already encountered, Cardinal Fürstenberg. These 'qualities' would no longer have enabled him to become a bishop in France 'according to the standards of the present time', as Saint-Simon said of others like him, but they made him a more valuable compromise candidate for Tournai in 1713 than other contenders.[65] At last, having dropped a plan to move the see of Tournai to Lille, Louis XIV now had full papal support on the Tournai succession: by prior agreement the papal consistory that confirmed him in May 1713 made no mention of a royal nomination, thus affirming papal assertions to act independently, on paper at least, but there is no doubt that Clement XI's willingness to accept Löwenstein pleased Louis XIV far more than it did Emperor Charles VI.[66] It was the last time the king would manage such a feat,

---

62 Torcy, *Journal*, 383–7, 19–20 Feb 1711, for an extensive account of these discussions. Torcy reports here that 'Sa Majesté craignit que la conscience ne fût un peu blessée dans la proposition de faire entrevoir au comte de Bossu un évêché considérable s'il renonçait à la commission que le cardinal de Bouillon lui avait donnée.'

63 Torcy, *Journal*, 422–3, 12 April 1711.

64 ASV, Nunz Fr 223, fos 8, 21, 36, 126–7, 152, 181, 193, 207, 236, 266, 293, 307, 331, 409, 462–3, 546, 585, 683, for a series of despatches from the nuncio in Paris, often once weekly, reporting to Rome on Beauvau's movements and intentions, from Jan to Nov 1711.

65 Abbé François Gaultier, a French agent in London, approached the pope directly with a view to obtaining Tournai, claiming to enjoy the support of Queen Anne. But given that he also felt he deserved a cardinal's hat for his services, it may be asked how serious a candidate he was: Lucien Bély, *Espions et ambassadeurs au temps de Louis XIV* (Paris 1990), 186–7, quoting from his letter to Clement XI, 10 Nov 1712.

66 ASV, Nunz Fr 225, fos 95, 97, 107, 123, 127, 141, nuncio to secretary of state, 6 and 13 Feb, 3, 10, 17 and 19 April, 5 June 1713 respectively. Dangeau, xiv, 414, 4 June 1713,

and the right to nominate to Tournai reverted after 1713 to the Emperor in his capacity as count of Flanders.[67]

It is clear from this exposition that the French crown did rather better in defending its ecclesiastical patronage than conditions might lead us to believe. In its own way, it confirms what historians have long known about the capacity of French diplomacy under Louis XIV to limit the anticipated consequences of military setbacks. Up to the eve of the Treaty of Utrecht, the papacy was willing to endorse his choice of new bishops for sees no longer actually in French hands, in singular contrast to the situation early in Louis's reign when papal 'neutrality' towards French nominations could be tinged with hostility. Times had indeed changed in other ways and for other reasons, too: 1713 was also the year of the anti-Jansenist bull *Unigenitus*, which Clement XI allegedly said he could not deny to Louis XIV given how much good he had done to the church.[68] In most of the cases we have seen here, episcopal nominations to newly occupied dioceses were made as soon as they fell vacant, regardless of whether the king had any actual title to do so; that problem could be faced later once the time for diplomacy had come, but in the meantime it was essential to stake one's claim rather than allowing it to lapse by default. After all, if Louis XIV was prepared formally to press the pope to confirm *his* preferred candidate for the Sicilian archbishopric of Messina during that city's revolt against Spain in 1676 – a brother, like Margarit in Catalonia, of the leader of the anti-Spanish revolt there – we should hardly expect him to be any slower to do the same for dioceses much closer to home.[69]

It would take an enquiry which is beyond the scope of this study to establish how successfully or otherwise the prelates despatched to Roussillon, Flanders or elsewhere dealt with local religious traditions, or whether French traditions of episcopal authority had to be partly set aside in order successfully to govern such dioceses. But we should not assume that the crown operated a 'one-size-fits-all' policy in dealing with its newly acquired dioceses. The willingness, which we noted earlier, to allow the Grammont, uncle and nephew, to continue governing Besançon was probably as much a concession to the peculiarity of the Franche-Comté as to the family's own

     commenting on papal generosity towards Löwenstein in allowing him to keep all of his other benefices in both the Empire and France 'et lui a accordé toutes ces graces quoiqu'il ne fût point prêtre . . . il était venu à la cour député du chapitre de Strasbourg, et n'ayant aucune vue de se faire évêque'. See Fénelon, *Correspondance*, xvi, no 1720, Fénelon to Tellier, 10 Aug 1713.

67   *Hierarchia Catholica*, v, 383, 'Tornacen', n 6.

68   See Lucien Ceyssens, *Autour de la bulle Unigenitus* (Louvain 1988), 737–88, for a study of Clement XI. The pope's remark may well have been a later invention – see Pierre Blet, *Le Clergé de France, Louis XIV et le Saint-Siège de 1695 à 1715* (Vatican City 1989), 386, n 29.

69   ASV, Nunz Fr 155, fo 627, Louis XIV to French ambassador, 19 July 1677. Although the language of the letter makes it clear that Louis XIV was not claiming the right formally to nominate a candidate for the pope's approval as he would for a French see, his insistence makes plain his will to pressurise the pope into satisfying him. BN, MS Fr 23504, fo 167v, *Nouvelles Ecclésiastiques*, for a reference to Caffaro's presence in Paris in 1695.

ambitions.[70] The bishops of Perpignan of northern French origin certainly found themselves dealing with recalcitrant local clergy, secular and regular, but they were also often at loggerheads with French officials in Roussillon and their gallican maxims. More paradoxical still is the experience of Toul after the restoration of the independent duchy of Lorraine in 1698, an event which did not alter the crown's rights to nominate to the 'three bishoprics'. The restored duke of Lorraine was determined to apply his own version of the gallican maxims, as embodied in the new *Code Léopold*, within his lands, only to find himself being vigorously opposed by Bishop Bissy of Toul, who was in the happy position of having his defence of ecclesiastical prerogatives there receive the support of the French monarchy! The problem was solved not by a change of maxims by either side, since what the duke was attempting to do in Lorraine was scarcely different from the practices of the French monarchy at home. Typically, the conflict was defused by a change of personnel: the Lorraine 'interest' at Versailles badgered Louis XIV so effectively in 1704 that Bissy was transferred to Meaux and a more 'understanding' successor was sent to Toul.[71] On the other hand, Fénelon's twenty years at Cambrai passed off with few serious problems, for which outcome his social status, diplomacy and intelligence may hold the key, though when it came to 'difficult matters of canon law' – probably short-hand for problems concerning benefices – he admitted that he could not rely on natives of Cambrai diocese.[72] In sum, the varying admixture of 'good birth' and prior experience as a bishop or a vicar-general among those appointed to sees like Tournai, Saint-Omer and Ypres certainly suggests that considerable care was taken in selecting them, and that this was not confined to moments of most acute difficulty after 1709. Of these three particular sees, only Saint-Omer remained French after Utrecht, and that was clearly underlined by the unbroken tenure of the see by three members of the Marseille-based Valbelle family from the 1680s down to 1754.[73]

IV

By comparison with these unexpected additions to, or subtractions from the French church, the creation of new dioceses within France must seem rather limited in scale and historical interest. Enormous discrepancies in size

70   The Regent actually nominated yet another Grammont in 1717, but he died before being confirmed by Rome.

71   AN, L 737, no 29, Meaux, 1704. Abbé Ledieu, *Mémoires et journal sur la vie et les ouvrages de Bossuet*, ed Abbé Guettée, 4 vols (Paris 1856–7), *Journal*, ii, 110, 9 May 1704; 180, 31 Oct 1704. Sourches, viii, 352–3, 10 May 1704. Taveneaux, *Jansénisme en Lorraine*, 268–70.

72   Fénelon, *Correspondance*, xiv, no 1373, p 238, to Madame Guyon [May 1710]. See Gilles Deregnaucourt, 'Fénelon à Cambrai: remarques sur un épiscopat et perspectives de recherches', *XVII Siècle*, 52 (2000), 97–110.

73   See the brief study of H Laplane, *Messieurs de Valbelle évêques de Saint-Omer* (Saint-Omer 1872).

between contiguous dioceses were as common in France as elsewhere in Europe, but even when there was a willingness to deal with this problem in a particular instance – no sign of any *general* perception of the problem has so far come to light – the obstacles to change were as daunting as ever. Historically, any new creation inevitably meant the division of existing dioceses, and the protracted canonical process defined in previous centuries by the papacy had opened the door for entrenched interests to oppose change and even to muster support in Rome, without whose approval nothing could be achieved. The royal administration was by no means anxious to tear up the map of French dioceses and start again; in the *pays d'états* like Languedoc, Brittany and elsewhere it had made the dioceses the basis of its tax-collection system. When ideas for new dioceses did take shape, it is not certain if it was ecclesiastics or laymen who generated them in the first place. Likewise, it is hard to know how seriously some of them were taken, even by their initiators. For example, there was a proposal around 1670 to subdivide the huge diocese of Rouen, the biggest in France measured by the number of its parishes, into about seven or eight dioceses. The starting point for the proposal may have been the status of the archdeaconry of Pontoise, which was itself virtually a diocese, in close proximity to the court at Versailles and administered by an archdeacon with little control from Rouen. But if Pontoise could be converted into a real diocese, so, it was argued, could Fécamp, Le Havre and other towns, while the archbishop of Rouen would himself gain by becoming the metropolitan of the most numerous ecclesiastical province in all of France.[74] It is not known whether the idea was taken up in governing circles, and it did not resurface later. Twenty-five years later, the creation of the new diocese of Blois did lead to a discussion of the need to subdivide some other large dioceses, and Mme de Maintenon herself claimed she supported the idea.[75] But once again, the more ambitious the scheme, the less likely it was to be adopted for actual implementation.

In the century before 1660 no new dioceses had been created in France, so that the emergence of even as few as two entirely new dioceses under Louis XIV should not be underestimated. Both were triggered by arguably the most notorious decision of the reign – to revoke the Edict of Nantes in 1685, one of the alleged grounds for which was the superfluity of the edict in the light of the recent and massive conversions of France's Huguenot population to Catholicism. A half a century earlier, in the 1620s, when the final phase of the religious wars had opened, Louis XIII and his advisers hardly gave any thought to reorganising France's unevenly sized dioceses to cope with the Protestant problem where it was most acute – in the great arc from La Rochelle to the Dauphiné. Their only gesture was to move the seat of the

---

74   Jean Lesaulnier, ed, *Port-Royal insolite: Receueil critique des choses diverses* (Paris 1992), 578.
75   *Lettres de Madame de Maintenon*, ed Marcel Langlois, 5 vols (Paris 1934–9), v, no 1064, 33–5, letter to Archbishop Noailles of Paris, 9 March 1696.

diocese of Maillezais into the newly conquered La Rochelle and to rename the diocese accordingly, but even that took nearly twenty years to complete. Few suggestions about other changes to the map were made then or in subsequent decades. But it was soon obvious after 'the Revocation' of 1685 that the problem of the Huguenots had not been solved, and that under the label of Nouveaux Catholiques, they had become an even thornier one. Their heart-lands might have contracted, but the weight of numbers was inescapable in the Cévennes and elsewhere, as the experience of the crown-sponsored missions there in 1685 and later demonstrated – missions on which, incidentally, a number of future bishops served. How the crown approached the question of diocesan subdivision remains hard to grasp, though there is a strong impression of *ad hoc*, circumstantial reactions. The easiest decision was one which did not entail the creation of a new diocese at all, but rather the restora-tion of a historical status quo: namely the separation of the Dauphinois see of Die from its long-standing 'twin', Valence. Both dioceses had substantial 'New Catholic' populations, and the decision to separate them was made easier by the simultaneous promotion of their incumbent bishop, Daniel de Cosnac, to Aix-en-Provence.[76] The idea had been tried at least once before, in 1654, but it had been blocked in the curia and dropped for a time.[77] In the case of Nîmes, a major Protestant bastion where, as Robert Sauzet has so convinc-ingly shown, the failure of re-Catholicisation campaigns throughout the century in the face of Huguenot tenacity made some reorganisation desirable, the age and opinions of the incumbent bishop may have played a part.[78] Jacques Séguier, cousin of the former chancellor, was nearly eighty years old and clearly unable to cope with the post-1685 problems when he agreed, reluctantly it seems, to resign in 1687. He was replaced by the celebrated preacher, Fléchier, on the understanding that he consent to the subdivision of Nîmes, with a new diocese to be established at Alès in the heart of the Cévennes. The oblong shape of Nîmes diocese – strangely similar to La Rochelle which was *not* subdivided in 1648 – also justified the decision. But the new diocese did not materialise until 1694, delayed by the continuing dispute between France and Rome which suspended all episcopal confirma-tions in the curia until 1692–3. Meanwhile, the crown had not been inactive, preparing the ground for the new diocese, eliciting the necessary and vital agreement of the Nîmes cathedral chapter and other interested parties, as well as working out how to endow the new see. The new bishop, François Cheva-lier, was nominated as early as August 1687 and was active as vicar-general

76   Jules Chevalier, *Essai historique sur l'église et la ville de Die*, 3 vols (Montelimar-Valence 1888–1909), iii, 523–5.

77   ASV, Acta congregationis consistorialis, 1654, fos 169–75, 238, 24 Sept 1654. I owe this ref-erence to Olivier Poncet.

78   Robert Sauzet, *Contre-Réforme et Réforme catholique en Bas-Languedoc. Le Diocèse de Nîmes au xviiᵉ siècle* (Paris-Louvain 1979).

of the parts of the diocese of Nîmes earmarked to constitute the future diocese by at least 1688, but he had to wait until May 1694 for his provisions.[79]

Apart from Alès, the only other new diocese to be created after 1685 was that of Blois, extracted from the huge diocese of Chartres because of the substantial Huguenot presence in the southern parts of the diocese around Blois and Vendôme. Unlike Nîmes, no attempt was made to pension off into retirement the elderly bishop of Chartres, Ferdinand de Neufville, doubtless because as the uncle of marshal Villeroy and a patron of the La Chaize family, he could not be as easily disposed of as a Séguier. It was only when he finally died in January 1690 that the process could begin. His eventual successor, Godet de Marais, who was already director of conscience to Mme de Maintenon, explicitly gave his consent for the creation of Blois diocese.[80] Possibly because of the slow progress at Alès, there was no rapid formal episcopal nomination to Blois, even though it was no secret that a candidate had been selected and was being sent as a vicar-general to work in precisely the area designated for the new diocese – David-Nicolas de Bertier, son of a great Toulouse *parlementaire* and episcopal family![81] For all the support this project enjoyed at the highest level at Versailles, the canonical procedures proved as slow as elsewhere, and Bertier was not confirmed as bishop until 1697.[82]

---

79 *Ibid*, 405–17, 489–90, for valuable brief studies of Séguier, Fléchier and Chevalier.

80 Godet des Marais was Madame de Maintenon's confessor, and the new *maison royale de Saint-Cyr* which she was sponsoring was located in Chartres diocese. Louis XIV and his confessor, La Chaize, were fully persuaded of the scheme to establish an *évêché* in Blois. In Nîmes, Chevalier de Saulx was made vicar-general in 1687 of the area to be covered by the future diocese of Alès of which he was the first bishop. The records show that both Bertier and Chevalier were resident, active vicars-general. This issue will be discussed more generally in chapter seven, in the context of the suspension of episcopal provisions during the decade 1682–92.

81 Bertier's nomination to Blois was not formalised until March 1693: ASV, PC 91, fo 40, Louis XIV to Innocent XII, 21 March 1693, letter of nomination. In fact, the nomination to Blois was initially offered to Michel Le Peletier, son of the *contrôleur-général des finances* and bishop of Angers in 1692, but it was turned down by father and son even before it was formalised. See *Correspondance de Louis Tronson*, iii, 305–6, Tronson to Michel le Peletier, abbé de Jouy, 5 Jan 1690, 'si Monsieur votre père ne croit pas que Blois vous convienne, je ne vous conseillerois pas d'y penser. Mais si sa réponse au P de La Chaise n'a été fondée que sur ce qu'il ne savoit pas que vous l'accepteriez volontiers, vous pouvez en seureté lui témoigner que vous suivrez sur cela ses sentiments; et que, comme il peut mieux connoitre que vous-même ce qui vous peut convenir, vous n'avez point d'autre mesure à prendre que de faire ce qu'il croira de meilleur pour vous, soit pour Blois, soit pour un autre évêché; l'un et l'autre vous étant d'ailleurs indifférent et assez égal. Vous pouvez meme lui proposer sans scrupules les avantages que vous auriez à Blois. Renoncez seulement, avant que de lui parler, à tout ce que la nature pourroit mêler d'impur dans vos intentions.'

82 J Gallerand, 'L'Erection de l'évêché de Blois', *Revue d'Histoire de l'Eglise de France*, 42 (1956), 175–228, esp 179, 181ff. See also Robert Sauzet, 'La Création du diocèse d'Alès (1694), prototype de l'érection de celui de Blois' and Olivier Poncet, 'La Cour de Rome et les créations de diocèses au xviiᵉ siècle: L'exemple du diocese de Blois (1693–1697)', both in Gerald Chaix, ed, *Le Diocèse: espaces, représentations, pouvoirs. France xvᵉ–xxᵉ siècles* (Paris 2002), 33–46, 47–66 respectively.

Despite the seriousness with which the Huguenot problem was viewed in these years, the crown's already limited appetite for making new dioceses quickly evaporated. No doubt more pressing issues, especially war, claimed its attention from 1688 onwards. But there is every reason to believe it continued to share the widespread aversion to such changes to be found not merely among sections of the clergy but among the population at large. When the notary-cum-chronicler of Nîmes, Étienne Borelly, first heard of the creation of Alès, he wrote quite uncomprehendingly that 'since the beginning of the world, never has there been such a change'.[83] The success of the Blois creation seems to owe a great deal to the tenacity of the *dévots* close to Mme de Maintenon. If Alès and Blois have a common distinguishing feature of broader significance, one to which we shall return later, it is the despatch of their first bishop after his initial nomination and with the full consent of the incumbent bishop of the existing diocese, to his new, albeit still 'virtual' diocese, with the title and function of vicar-general. Rather than waiting as idle observers for many years while the crown and the papacy went through the normal but protracted bureaucratic procedures which such creations entailed, this tactic enabled them to accelerate the establishment of the new dioceses on the ground. It is hard to imagine such a solution either being tried let alone working in previous generations, as it entailed a considerable unity of views at the highest level of ecclesiastical politics, as well as the confidence that local opposition could be successfully dealt with during the interim. But, as we shall see, even this novel tactic was not invented for dioceses in the process of creation; it was widely used in 'normal' dioceses during the crisis of the 1680s, from which it was adapted for use in Blois and Alès.

V

Since the development of the regular assemblies of clergy after 1560, the role and shape of France's ecclesiastical 'provinces' had taken on greater significance. A highly unusual but revealing example of sensitivity on the subject is provided by the establishment of the see of Quebec in 1674. Archbishop Harlay of Paris had previously refused when he was archbishop of Rouen to accept the need for a diocese at all, claiming that Quebec was no more than an extension of Rouen diocese![84] Later, vigorous objections were elicited by the prospect that the new diocese might stand on its own rather than be subject to an archbishop. In accordance with French maxims on church

83 Quoted in Robert Sauzet, *Le Notaire et son roi. Étienne Borelly (1633–1718). Un Nîmois sous Louis XIV* (Paris 1998), 181, 'depuis que le monde est monde on n'avoit pas veu tel changement'.
84 BN, MS Fr 23508, fos 250–5, *Nouvelles Ecclésiastiques* (ca 1678), for a long contemporary account of the disputes over Quebec. See also *Histoire du christianisme*, ed Jean-Marie Mayeur et al, 14 vols (Paris 1990–2000), ix, 675.

government (*police ecclésiastique*), it was argued that either the archbishop of
Rouen or, perhaps, of Paris, should act as his ecclesiastical superior in case of
appeals, since the idea of his being directly subject to Rome was just as unacceptable to French bishops as would be its total autonomy.[85] The most recent
creation of an ecclesiastical province in seventeenth-century France had been
that of Paris in 1622, but it was not until the 1660s that Louis XIV and his
ministers finally buried the regular protests against that decision by the archbishop of Sens, the previous metropolitan of Paris, by offering him financial
compensation.[86] But since it took the form of an abbey in distant and often
war-torn Flanders, it is hard to know how pleased the archbishop was with
the king's largesse. Disputes continued between the Paris and Sens over the
election of deputies and officers for the assemblies of clergy, and in 1670 the
crown intervened to oblige the two provinces to vote jointly for an incoming
agent-général du clergé.[87] But behind it all lay the emergence of Paris as the most
important see, politically and ecclesiastically, in the realm. That process was
seriously slowed down by the tenure of the last two Gondi archbishops from
1622 to 1661 when the Cardinal de Retz, from his exile in Rome, finally consented to resign Paris outright. Louis XIV soon made his intentions towards
Paris plain by nominating his own former preceptor, Bishop Péréfixe of Rodez
and, when he died in 1671, by replacing him with the undisputed master
politician within the French church of his generation, François de Harlay of
Rouen. It was under Harlay, in 1674, that the king also created the peerage
of Saint Cloud, the first of its kind since the thirteenth century, for the archbishops of Paris. Even though this peerage remained separate from the six
other ecclesiastical peerages, there was no doubting the royal determination
to boost the standing of Paris. The only prize to elude Harlay during his
twenty-four-year tenure in Paris was the cardinal's hat but, although this
failure was the source of constant comment during and after his life, he was
in better company than he or contemporaries could have known. Only one
archbishop of Paris before the Revolution, Harlay's immediate successor,
Noailles, managed to do that, but when he found himself in the eye of a very
different political storm, the post-*Unigenitus* crisis of 1713–14, his adversaries,
as we shall see presently, cast around for other, more surprising forms of episcopal status to bring him to heel.

The long drawn-out sequel to the creation of the archbishopric of Paris
would itself have cautioned Louis XIV and his ministers against hasty
rearrangements of France's ecclesiastical provinces. Some of them, such as
Arles, were tiny both geographically and in the number of their suffragan-
bishops. Sens was left with only three suffragans after the creation of its rival,
Paris, which ended up with four after Blois became a diocese in 1697. The

85   BN, Morel de Thoisy 2, fos 42–3, undated 'mémoire sur l'érection de l'évêché de Quebeq dans
     la Nouvelle France'.
86   Bergin, *Making*, 40–1.
87   Blet, *Les Assemblées du clergé et Louis XIV*, 8.

largest province by far of the existing provinces was Bourges, with Tours, the metropolitan of the nine Breton sees despite its own non-Breton location, coming a close second.[88] But it was Bourges, and not Tours which was to be dismembered with the creation of the province of Albi in the late 1670s. Yet even after the dismemberment Bourges was still the largest province in purely territorial terms. Bourges diocese itself stretched southwards as far as Castres and Vabres to the northeast of Toulouse. Not only did sheer distance seem to make it difficult to exercise metropolitan jurisdiction, but Bourges was as poorly endowed as any low-ranking 'ordinary' French diocese. The same was true of Tours but, unlike Tours, Bourges at least had one suffragan, Albi, which was immensely rich – a useful factor when it came to compensating Bourges for its prospective loss of suffragans and jurisdiction. It was also argued that creating a new province of Albi would help to deal more effectively with the Huguenots who were far more numerous in the southern dioceses such as Castres, Vabres and Mende. As with Paris in 1622, care was taken not to alienate the incumbent whose province was to be dismembered, and the first moves were only made after Archbishop Montpezat of Bourges was nominated to Sens in October 1674. The most difficult part of the ensuing negotiations was not just determining the extent of the new province of Albi or the exact amount of the indemnity payable to Bourges, but how and from which sources the latter should be taken, since the crown also realised there was a genuine need to raise its endowment substantially. In the end it was agreed that Bourges would be entitled to collect the revenues of specific areas within the distant diocese of Albi itself, revenues fixed at 15,000 *livres* per annum – which was actually more than Bourges's current value – and consisting mostly of church tithes.[89] Such an arrangement, which brought further complications later, would not have encouraged the crown to repeat the move elsewhere, even though, by raising the total number of archbishoprics, it increased its fund of 'promotional' episcopal patronage.

VI

One unmistakable feature of the records of the period under examination is the apparently extravagant titles, both secular and ecclesiastical, by which

---

88 Tours was also metropolitan of Angers and Le Mans. Bourges had the same number of suffragans – eleven.

89 *Correspondance du nonce Spada*, no 142, Spada to Cardinal Altieri, 20 April 1674, for the financial conditions proposed from the outset. But by the 1690s, the archbishop of Bourges was claiming that the crown's decision, taken in the mid-1680s, to raise the monetary value of the *portion congrue*, the proportion of the tithe to be paid directly to serving parish priests there, had decimated the value of the archbishop of Bourges's indemnity! He consequently sought and obtained redress from the parlement of Paris: AN, L 729, pièce 1, Bourges, no 10, mémoire-factum for Archbishop Potier de Gesvres of Bourges against Archbishop Le Goux de la Berchère of Albi; no 15, Père Léonard's comments.

French bishops described themselves. Several archbishops, for example, laid claim to primatial or patriarchal rank, which usually referred to provinces of the Roman Empire. Whereas Bourges claimed to be primate and patriarch of Aquitaine, and Sens primate of the Gauls and Germanie, Lyon proclaimed itself, simply, primate of the Gauls.[90] Despite its recent upgrading, Paris was at a disadvantage here, being unable to compete with these more ancient sees. Needless to say, as in other spheres of seventeenth-century life, such claims give rise to quarrels over precedence on public occasions, especially when those involved were outside of their own dioceses. But did they matter any more than that? At a relatively mundane level they could, since the primates in question enjoyed 'primatial' as well as 'ordinary' or even 'metropolitan' jurisdiction, and had officials and lawcourts specially designated to hear appeals and exercise the relevant jurisdiction.[91] But beyond that, historians have usually assumed that the significance of the primatial claims for the workings of the French church was non-existent. Yet it may be suggested, until further research into the subject has been done, that they should not be dismissed out of hand. Particular archbishops certainly appear to have taken them seriously enough to wish to impose them, by appealing to the crown if necessary. The archbishop of Lyon actually fought a highly publicised lawsuit against his counterpart of Rouen in the late 1690s in order to establish his primacy over Rouen, but lost the case which was judged before the king himself – hardly an indication of its inconsequential nature. He explained afterwards to the archbishop of Rouen, Jacques-Nicolas Colbert, that there was nothing personal about the case, and that he had merely sought a legal determination of the situation.[92] The whole episode may strike us as typical of a status-obsessed *ancien-régime* society, in which any increment in one's existing status was highly desirable. In this case, the fact that all of those claiming primatial rank were also archbishops at the head of ecclesiastical provinces naturally makes it extremely difficult to disentangle their two roles. Under Louis XIV, archbishops generally seem, if anything, to have taken on greater importance, and this despite the strong sense of equal worth professed by all bishops within the gallican tradition. As we shall see later, this was also signalled by the king's habit – to which there were a few but widely remarked exceptions – of only nominating to archdiocesan sees bishops who had already served in 'ordinary' dioceses. One reason for this shift was the greater frequency of assemblies, especially in the latter part of the reign, which meant the archbishops were more actively involved in convening provincial assemblies to elect deputies and draft cahiers for presentation to the general assemblies. But the latter decades of the reign also witnessed provincial assemblies convened

90   Dainville, *Cartes anciennes de l'église de France*, 275.
91   Some of the ecclesiastical archives held in the G series of French departmental archives contain indications of the activities of primatial and metropolitan courts and officials from the seventeenth century and earlier.
92   AN, L 736, Lyon, for large dossier relating to this case. Sources, v, 360, 20 Nov 1697.

specifically to 'receive' and accept papal pronouncements such as the condemnation of Fénelon's *Maximes des Saints* in 1699, and of Jansenist ideas in 1705 and later.[93] The crown may have decided against supporting 'primatial' powers within the French church in the Lyon versus Rouen case in 1698, but circumstances could change its mind in unexpected ways. Thus, in the last days of the reign and at the height of the *Unigenitus* crisis in 1714–15, when Cardinal Noailles, the archbishop of Paris, whose see had no claim to primatial status, was still defying the king over the bull, one of the tactics considered in order to bring about his submission was, in addition to a national council of the gallican church, recourse to the primatial authority of the archbishop of Lyon.[94] The death of Louis XIV soon put paid to such extraordinary plans, and one can only speculate on their outcome had they been tried. That either instrument, especially the second, was considered at all says much about the remaining potential for service in exceptional situations of institutions and titles which historians often ignore too readily.

The complexity as well as the size of the French episcopate will be readily apparent from the issues discussed in this chapter, even though the great majority of the bishops and their dioceses did not fall under the headings we have been examining so far. One final observation will serve as a preface to the following chapters. In an age when the French church was, following in the footsteps of the monarchy, also expanding territorially, and when Vauban's idea of France as a precisely defined 'pré carré' was taking shape, the speed and degree to which new dioceses were absorbed into the inherited structures of both the church and the monarchy were well below what might have been expected. Ecclesiastical structures were even less amenable to reformatting than secular ones, so that from Saint-Omer to Orange via the *trois-évêchés* and Besançon, there was still an impressive number of loose ends for the eighteenth-century monarchy to deal with. Above all, there is good reason to believe that under Louis XIV the crown paid more attention to the individuals whom it designated to serve as bishops in these far-flung dioceses: it was they rather than changes to laws, customs or institutions who would make the difference in the new provinces, and draw them gradually into the embrace of the French church. Sometimes, as we saw in this chapter, the crown chose men who were already experienced as bishops elsewhere in France; sometimes it sent younger, less experienced but well-connected figures, some of whom might later be transferred to dioceses within France itself. This variation in its choices is an invitation to turn the spotlight on the wider French episcopate, beginning with an exploration of the identity and backgrounds of the 250 individuals who entered its ranks under Louis XIV.

93   Blet, *Le Clergé de France, Louis XIV et le Saint-Siège*, ch 3, 'l'heure des métropoles'.
94   *Ibid*, book iii, 'la bataille de l'Unigenitus'; Ceyssens, *Autour de la bulle Unigenitus*, no 13, 'Le Cardinal de Noailles', 649–733.

CHAPTER 2

Points of Departure

To BEGIN A study of the bishops seated between early 1661 and mid-1715 with an enquiry into their origins would seem, on the face of it, a straightforward step, unlikely to invite needless controversy. But even now, despite the researches of several historians, the long shadow of the 'petit duc' hovers implacably over any attempt to understand the social history of the power elites – military, ministerial, ecclesiastical – of the period we are dealing with. Ever since the indefatigable Saint-Simon lambasted his least favourite monarch for his many faults, and in particular for his willingness to promote parvenus to positions that should have been out of bounds to them, historians of Louis XIV have been unable to avoid confronting the enduring stereotype of a 'long règne de vile bourgeoisie'. Coming from a writer whose pen was uniquely equal to the challenge set by his prejudices, Saint-Simon's trenchant verdict has tended to elicit equally one-dimensional responses from later commentators and historians.[1] Apart from judging an entire reign by one yardstick, this approach, as François Bluche observed, assumes that a king like Louis XIV should have chosen his most important servitors according to one criterion, their social status, in order to ensure that political power was in the hands of the great nobility, its only rightful holders in Saint-Simon's view.[2] Moreover, his critique also tends to colour interpretations of the reign in areas that have little to do with the original source of Saint-Simon's ire, so that it is likely that his prejudices still weigh most heavily on those areas, such as the church and the upper clergy, which have *not* been the subject of much serious research. A more careful and systematic reading of the duke's own verdicts on Louis XIV's bishops soon makes it clear that his ideal bishop

---

1 The edition of his *Mémoires* used throughout this study is that of the *Grands écrivains de France* collection, on account of its editorial principles and its extensive annotation and numerous appendices, which make it an unrivalled feat of historical scholarship in its own right: Louis de Rouvroy, duc de Saint-Simon, *Mémoires*, ed A M de Boislisle, L Lecestre, J de Boislisle, 43 vols (Paris 1879–1930).

2 François Bluche, 'The Social Origins of the Secretaries of State under Louis XIV, 1661–1715', in Ranghild M Hatton, ed, *Louis XIV and Absolutism* (London 1976), 85–7.

had a rich panoply of qualities, one of which was undoubtedly *naissance*; it is also evident that those qualities *could* be acquired without *naissance*, though Saint-Simon did not advertise this too loudly. Furthermore, he was convinced that Louis XIV had rather too often, especially in his latter years, nominated men who, lacking such qualities, were simply too obscure to bring credit to the episcopate.[3] Most of those who found a place in the duke's portrait gallery have been enduringly marked by his judgements, especially those unfortunate enough not to correspond to his expectations. By extension, the historical image of the episcopate as a whole has been heavily coloured by Saint-Simon's preferences.

Identifying and categorising the king's bishops under the headings that will be proposed in this and subsequent chapters is, therefore, a task which proves to be more contentious than it initially appears, and some of its findings will have implications for our broader understanding of the reign. The study of origins, whether they be geographical, social, professional or other, may have its limitations, but it is still capable of bringing significant benefits to historical analysis. To confine it, however, to a study of blood-lines and pedigree would be imprison both the historian and the subject itself in a Saint-Simonian straightjacket, and would limit unnecessarily the range of the enquiry. The following pages will offer a preliminary exploration of a series of interconnected questions which, as will soon become apparent, it would take a full-length study to deal with exhaustively.

I

One feature of Saint-Simon's pen portraits of his contemporaries, ecclesiastical as well as lay, is his concern with the degree to which they conformed to the stereotypical image of the provinces from which they originated. Natives of Normandy and Maine were particularly likely to receive such treatment.[4] There is no need to share the duke's enthusiasms or aversions in order to ask how geographically inclusive a group like the episcopate, one of the few genuinely 'national' groups of the day, was under Louis XIV. Historians have devoted much ingenuity to mapping the clerical geography of modern France, beginning mostly with the eighteenth century, and have found that some regions were even then, for reasons not always easy to discover, either under- or over-producers of clergy.[5] Although these studies are essentially focused on the lower clergy, they suggest posing the question as to whether there were

3 Many of Saint-Simon's verdicts on bishops are to be found in the end-of-year entries in his *Mémoires* where he recorded the deaths of individuals in any given year. They are too numerous to cite in detail here.

4 See comments on Froullay de Tessé from Maine in Saint-Simon, iii, 129 and n 2.

5 These enquiries are summarised and explained in Timothy Tackett and Claude Langlois, 'Ecclesiastical structures and clerical geography on the eve of the French Revolution', *French*

parts of France which produced few or no bishops, or others which enjoyed undue 'success' in this field. And if significant imbalances are discovered, how are they to be explained?

Bearing in mind how little is still known – and knowable – about a surprising number of Louis XIV's bishops, it is essential to realise the kinds of problems which these questions raise.[6] The first is that all official documents concerning clerics during the ancien regime referred to their diocese of birth, however fleeting their association with it might be thereafter. This was not the inconsequential product of pure inertia, since individuals wishing to take clerical orders at a later date were obliged to present themselves before the bishop of their diocese of birth, or obtain his permission if they wanted to be ordained elsewhere. Thus, Marc Malier du Houssay, a Parisian who became bishop of Tarbes, would be routinely described as a cleric or priest of Venice because he was born while his father was ambassador there. Likewise, François Hébert, bishop of Agen, was officially a 'priest of Tours', since he was born there during the Fronde when his parents had probably left Paris for a brief time.[7] Many other examples like these abound, not least for sons of peripatetic provincial intendants, as contemporaries themselves were aware: in certain cases, witnesses giving evidence to the papal nuncio would affirm that although a royal nominee had been born in a given diocese, he had spent virtually all of his career elsewhere.[8] In all but one or two instances, it has been possible to establish precisely the actual place of origin and of residence of the bishops in question and, consequently, to assign a family 'seat' to them. But this too can be more problematic than it seems: what does one make of those well-born bishops whose families were habitually resident in 'Paris' – often meaning the court – but who possessed lands in one or more parts of France? Even when it is relatively easy to find their province or diocese of origin, that is not necessarily the best guide to fixing their subsequent geographical base. The highly influential Noailles family originated in the Limousin, where they still had significant landed holdings and although they were largely court-based in our period, they should be reckoned as Limousins rather than as Parisians. Yet to think of them as 'merely' Limousins or Parisians is also inadequate, since like many other aristocratic families, their importance was

Historical Studies, 11 (1980), 715–45; Timothy Tackett, 'L'Histoire sociale du clergé diocésain dans la France du xviiie siècle', *Revue d'Histoire Moderne et Contemporaine*, 26 (1979), 198–234; Timothy Tackett, *Religion, Revolution and Regional Culture in Eighteenth-Century France. The Ecclesiastical Oath of 1791* (Princeton 1986). See also John McManners, *Church and Society in Eighteenth-Century France*, 2 vols (Oxford 1998), i, ch 11.

6 See the fuller discussion of these questions for the pre-Louis XIV period in Bergin, *Making*, 167–73.

7 ASV, PC 67, fos 728–52. *Hierarchia Catholica*, v, 368, 'Tarbien', n 2 (Malier). AD Lot-et-Garonne, G/E 70, Hébert papers, 'extrait des registres des baptesmes de l'église St Pierre du Boille [sic]', Tours, 13–9-1651.

8 One example among many: Pierre de la Broue, bishop of Mirepoix in 1679, was born in Moissac, where his father was governor, but he lived in Toulouse: ASV, PC 78, fos 352v–3r.

more 'national' than provincial. Historians have discussed geographical mobility much less than its social counterpart, and have done so mainly in terms of 'lower-class' movement in search of land, employment and relief from distress.[9] But higher-status families could and did move, for reasons that we do not always fully understand. Intermarriage involving heiresses with more attractive lands elsewhere; military, urban or provincial governorships, as well as other opportunities would seem to be the most prominent motives among the dominant social groups. For families intent on acquiring nobility via office-holding, the 'sovereign courts' acted as magnets comparable to the royal court and Paris for the established nobility. Lastly, some families, though probably not more than a few, even moved to a new location on account of a family member entering the episcopate.[10] Whatever the reasons, the outcome is one which makes the allocation of bishops' families to particular provinces or dioceses problematic and, therefore, makes the geography of episcopal origins more interesting and elusive than we might imagine at first.

We can see the implications of this most clearly in the case of the single largest geographical contingent among Louis XIV's bishops – Parisians. If we were to take normal residence as the main criterion, then eighty-three out of 250 bishops, virtually one-third of the total, could be described as Parisians. This is exactly the same number as for the period from 1589 to 1661, but it represents a 10 per cent increase overall. Even when we remove at least fifteen bishops from distinguished noble families whose Parisian attachments were fundamentally court-centred rather than urban, the resulting overall total, sixty-eight, would still show an increase of nearly 5 per cent on the preceding period. Given the common assumption of a greater proportion of provincial nobles among the episcopate after 1661, this increase may come as a surprise worth investigating. In the case of the Noailles family just mentioned, not even the future cardinal's promotion to the see of Paris in 1695 could really make them 'Parisian'. Contrariwise, the label of Parisian rather than Languedocian seems far more appropriate for a bishop like Martin Ratabon, whose father had moved from the Cévennes to make his fortune in Paris under Richelieu and Mazarin, where he had married into the powerful Sanguin family. Numerous other cases like his exist, thanks largely to the attraction of office in the sovereign courts of the capital, or in the royal finances. Ideally, the best test of how 'Parisian' these bishops actually were would be the number of generations of family residence there. The results

9   James B Collins, 'Geographic and Social Mobility in Early Modern France', *Journal of Social History*, 24 (1991), 563–77, summarises research and opens up new avenues in this area.

10 The family of Bishop Lescure de Valderiès of Luçon (1699–1723) had for centuries lived in the Albi region, but the main branch followed him to Poitou and was still there until the Revolution, participating in the Vendée rebellion of 1793. See the brief sketch by Jean-Louis Biget in *Les Tarnais, dictionnaire biographique* (Albi 1996), 202–3. In his will, the bishop refers to several family members and also to the lands he had purchased in Poitou: AD Vendée, 1 G 5, 5 March 1723.

involve a good deal of approximation as to the place of birth of earlier generations, but it seems as if about fifteen of the sixty-eighty bishops were first-generation Parisians, sons of fathers who had themselves originated elsewhere. Between them, the Colbert and Desmarets families alone account for six of the fifteen; the others were mainly sons of either financiers, like Ratabon above, or of royal physicians or surgeons such as the Aquin, Vallot or Fagon. At the other end of the spectrum, bishops who were at least fifth-generation Parisians were more numerous – about eighteen at a conservative estimate – and included names such as the Séguier, Neufville, Phélypeaux, Potier, Le Tellier and others which had once figured among the city's bourgeoisie but which had subsequently scaled the 'hauteurs de l'état', their urban-merchant origins long forgotten as, in some cases, they joined the titled higher nobility.[11]

At any rate, the presence of so many Parisians, new or old, among Louis XIV's bishops was the bedrock for the presence of 'northerners' in the episcopate as a whole. The pattern that has been observed for the eighteenth century, in which the majority of bishops were drawn from (noble) families from south of the Loire, seems to be on the point of emerging in our period.[12] But it is reasonable to ask what exactly that proves, since two-thirds of seventeenth-century France was south of the Loire, as was about the same proportion of its dioceses. Measured in these terms, and taking into account the problem of placing lop-sized dioceses either south or north of as meandering a river as the Loire (see map), about 140 bishops in all, well over half of the total, were 'northerners' (on a line running from Nantes to Basle), in our period. This is in fact a 10 per cent increase on the total of 159 out of 351 bishops for the period from Henri IV to 1661. Leaving Paris and its sixty-eight bishops to one side, the remaining seventy-two northerners were relatively well scattered across the northern provinces, with few significant clusters visible on the map. Areas in the close vicinity of Paris did not fare well, since the pull of the capital was evidently such as to engineer a 'desert effect' in its hinterland. The big dioceses of Rouen and Amiens, which dominated upper Normandy and Picardy, only produced three bishops apiece, while their immediate neighbours, big and small, were reduced at best to either one or two. It is only towards the westward side of Paris that things begin to look differently, but not exceptionally so, since even substantial dioceses like Chartres, Le Mans, Coutances and Rennes, covering much of the Beauce, Perche, Mayenne, lower Normandy and eastern Brittany, only provided between four and six bishops each. Of the Loire valley dioceses, Tours stands out as a major contributor with eight bishops to its credit, though few

---

11   Denis Richet, *De la Réforme à la Révolution* (Paris 1991), part ii, 143–306, provides the most interesting account of this process in his extended analysis of the Séguier and other high-robe families.

12   Péronnet, *Évêques de l'ancienne France*, 536ff.

3 *French bishops by diocese of origin*

of them were from the city itself. Considering the historical and linguistic distinctiveness of Brittany, it may also seem surprising that it did not provide more than thirteen bishops under Louis XIV. Apart from Rennes (five), only the dioceses of Quimper (two), Nantes and Vannes (three each) did so at all. In fact the overall total is identical to that of the period 1589 to 1661, which means the proportion is actually higher; the main difference lies in the more limited geographical origins of the post-1661 bishops born in the province. But there is a second difference which is arguably more significant, and that is that well under half of them (only five in all) were chosen to serve in Breton dioceses.

The geographical 'spread' of episcopal origins south of the Nantes-Basle line is, not surprisingly, distinguished by the absence of any competitor for the role that Paris played in northern France. Major urban centres like Toulouse (nine), Aix (five) and Marseille (six) do stand out against their immediate hinterlands, but other provincial capitals like Lyon, Bordeaux and Grenoble figure less prominently, especially the latter two, despite both of them being seats of 'sovereign' courts. With the exception of the Aix-Marseilles cluster, to which we shall return, it was the big, inland and mainly rural dioceses like Poitiers, Limoges, Clermont, and Lyon which were the more fertile soil for future bishops, as they had been under Louis XIV's father and grandfather, but their huge size should also be taken into account when comparing their 'scores' with those of their often much smaller neighbours. While their overall contributions remain roughly the same by comparison with the period 1589 to 1661, it was Clermont which supplanted Limoges (and Toulouse) in providing the largest cohort of any single diocese after Paris, with ten future bishops. Most of these Auvergnat bishops were sons of old noble families, but like the episcopate as a whole, they also contained a minority that was of commoner and newly ennobled stock still based in towns like Clermont and Riom. Beyond this, it was Provence which out-distanced the other southern provinces in providing new bishops. Its overall total of eighteen bishops contrasts with one of thirteen from 1589 to 1661, while the contribution of its neighbours Dauphiné and Languedoc dropped from sixteen to nine and from twenty-five to fifteen respectively. It was the area covered by the contiguous dioceses of Aix and Marseille which accounted for most of Provence's contribution. That in turn was due largely to the vitality, connections and ambition of families like the Vintimille, Forbin, Simiane, whose origins and continuing residence lay for the most part in the two cities. But over time they had also accumulated land and titles throughout Provence, thanks in no small part to their extraordinarily dense marriage alliances, which in turn enabled less prominent families to secure episcopal office for their sons. By comparison, the falling off in Languedoc's contribution to the episcopate under Louis XIV is noteworthy, especially given the high number of dioceses in the province (twenty-three with Alès after 1694); were it not for the continuing capacity of Toulouse parlementaire families to promote their *cadets d'église*, bishops born in Languedoc would have indeed been few and far between. Finally, the cultural and linguistic traditions of the dioceses of Béarn had, rather like those of Brittany, ensured that a good number of its bishops since at least Henri IV's reign would be native sons. But it is evident that this pattern was waning here, too, with the two Béarnais dioceses of Lescar and Oloron only providing five bishops, compared to twelve in the preceding period.[13]

But perhaps the most significant difference between Louis XIV's episcopate and that of previous generations is that it scarcely contains any foreigners at all. In fact, only one bishop could be genuinely described as foreign – the Catalan Margarit, the first 'French' bishop of Perpignan. By comparison, the two Lorrainers, four Franc-comtois and six natives of Avignon and the Comtat Venaissin were French-speakers whose status as 'regnicoles' was not problematic in that none of them required royal 'lettres de naturalité' to hold office or benefices in France. Only one of them, as far as we know, ever revealed any sense of conflicting loyalties, and that was due to peculiar circumstances: Pierre Sabatier, a native of Vaison and resident of Saint-Sulpice seminary in the early 1680s, was reluctant to support the four Gallican Articles of 1682 in his Sorbonne examinations lest he alienate the pope, whose subject he also was, and upon whom his subsequent career, as then undetermined, might well depend.[14] The key point is that virtually all of these men, as Sabatier's own example shows, had either studied in France, belonged to families in royal service, or had themselves spent their pre-episcopal careers almost wholly in France. The Catalan, Margarit, whom we have already encountered, lost all his goods and prospects on account of his pro-French stance during the Catalan revolt, so French patronage was only to be expected. For all Mazarin's own efforts to advance his many Italian clients, the days when emigré foreign clerics – usually the sons of important Italian families with French affiliations – could hope to enter the French church at the highest levels were well over by Louis's reign. And with the French monarchy pushing back its northeastern and eastern frontiers, previously separate regions like the *trois-évêchés* and the Franche-Comté were themselves becoming fully French. The effects of such change could not but be felt by the episcopate which was by now more wholly 'franco-français' in its composition than at any time since the Renaissance.

---

13 See Bergin, *Making*, 169–78, for the pattern obtaining during the period from 1589 to 1661.
14 ASV, Nunz Fr 174, fo 115, Pierre Sabatier to Cardinal Cibo, 11 June 1685, defending his actions in the Sorbonne which had been criticised by Rome on the grounds that there was no obligation on him to take his doctorate from a French university if he disagreed with the Gallican Articles. He had earlier sought but failed to get permission to exclude the four articles from his 'defences', but went ahead despite Rome's unhappiness. The nuncio had investigated the case, and Sabatier had prepared a paper defending his 'theses': *ibid*, fos 105–6, 111–13. See the other references and documents about the case in *Correspondance du nonce Ranuzzi*, i, nos 231, 288, 356, 1136, 1188.

The conclusion to which this analysis points is that the episcopate under Louis XIV was one characterised by wide geographical recruitment, and in which there were fewer dominant clusters than might be expected – Paris and, perhaps, Provence excepted. But in other respects, Paris and Provence stand at opposite ends of the spectrum. Paris is, of course, *sui generis* and the long process of 'social centralisation' that its growth represents was evidently still bearing fruit under Louis XIV. The geographical spread of episcopal origins was, hardly surprisingly, uneven in other respects. Virtually the same number of dioceses, thirty-eight in all, as in the period from 1589 to 1661 produced no bishops at all, but since many of them were small southern dioceses, the significance of this figure should not be inflated. By contrast, it should be noted that much of the greater south-west (Gascony and Aquitaine), much of the Loire valley, Champagne-Burgundy, as well as eastern Languedoc and the Dauphiné, contributed few bishops relative to their size. One decisive reason for the scattered geographical origins of these bishops is that fewer and fewer dioceses were being given to men who were natives of the diocese or even of the province in which they were situated. If Provence and, to a lesser extent, Béarn produced as many bishops as they did, it was because they remained the only provinces where native-born bishops still managed to make a strong showing, but that should not be exaggerated. Over two-thirds of the Provençaux promoted to the episcopate by Louis XIV occupied seats in their own province or in close proximity to it (e.g. Digne or Saint-Paul-Trois-Châteaux). It was only later in their episcopal careers that, via transfers, some of them managed to govern a diocese elsewhere in the kingdom. It would be excessive to think of this kind of phenomenon in terms of 'ghettos', but the lack of attractiveness of particular dioceses or provinces to outsiders cannot be ignored when considering the connections between family origins and ecclesiastical geography. The significance of geographical factors to an understanding of the French church's governing elite is, needless to say, also inseparable from trends, both long- and short-term, in the crown's exercise of its episcopal patronage.

II

In the preceding discussion, questions of geography have more than once pointed in the direction of the social status of Louis XIV's bishops. Indeed, in his attempts to explain the geographical origins of eighteenth-century bishops Michel Péronnet asked whether the significant presence of southerners among them might not be due to the density and durability of the noble families of provinces such as Dauphiné, Provence and Languedoc – a durability which, he argued, might also explain why they were perfectly at home in the network of relations without which there was no chance of success in the search for a mitre.[15] The analysis so far in this chapter would seem to cast some doubt on whether such a connection was quite as operative in the second half of the preceding century. But even without such a link, the question of the social background of those who became bishops under Louis XIV loses none of its importance. Dealing with it, however, is not as simple as it seems. It requires rather more than establishing the social status of 250 individuals by determining the numbers and proportions drawn from the ranks of the nobility or the commoners, as these 'hold-all' categories are too 'inert' as well as too loose to explain a great deal by themselves. Some attempt has also to be made to connect social status – itself usually the result of a sequence of activities or careers over several generations – to 'professional' occupations, for want of a less anachronistic term, in order to convey some idea of how the latter may have contributed toward the elevation of individuals to the episcopate.

Given the intensity of Saint-Simon's jeremiad against the social climbers of the reign, it is not surprising that previous historians should have attempted to see how far the duke's judgements were borne out in the ecclesiastical world. In an influential synthesis, which drew heavily on the abbé Sicard's study of the pre-Revolutionary episcopate of 1893, René Taveneaux wrote 'that of all the early modern period the reign of Louis XIV was the one in which birth counted least in opening the way to the episcopate', something which Taveneaux attributed to the king's understanding that a good episcopate was also of value to the monarchy.[16] Both Sicard and Taveneaux seem to rely on virtually identical items of evidence to reach a conclusion which, while turning Saint-Simon's views on their head, can easily give the misleading impression of a monarchy and a church which were unexpectedly 'open' to those with talent and ability. In recent decades two historians have attempted empirically to test the basis of such an enduring generalisation – though both of them were really more concerned with the eighteenth century than with the preceding half-century. In his study comparing the Anglican and French episcopates 'in an age of aristocracy', Norman Ravitch estimated that of the 124 French bishops already in office in 1682, the *terminus a quo* of his research, 114 (92 per cent) were noble of all stripes, with only a handful of genuine commoners to make up the numbers. In the years from 1682 to 1715, he argued that the picture only changed marginally, with the proportion of nobles – 135 out of 144 – rising slightly overall, though Ravitch did discern a dip in their presence during the final six years of the reign, which

---

15 Péronnet, *Évêques de l'ancienne France*, 523.

16 René Taveneaux, *Le Catholicisme dans la France classique*, 2 vols (2nd edn, Paris 1994), i, 103. Augustin Sicard, *L'Ancien clergé de France. Les évêques avant la Révolution* (Paris 1893, 5th edn, 1912), 4–5. Sicard quotes Ferdinand Brunetière to the effect that 'under the ancien regime, with the exception of embassies and the major military commands, every post from that of a *commis* in the tax farms to that of first minister, was accessible to everyone'. Sicard himself adds, 'that was so under Louis XIV'.

corresponded to the confessorship of Michel Tellier (1709–15).[17] The other
substantial contribution to the discussion came from Michel Péronnet in his
longue durée analysis of the entire early modern French episcopate. His figures
for the period 1660 to 1715 do not diverge wildly from those of Ravitch. The
nobility as a whole claimed seven-eighths (87.75 per cent) of all episcopal
appointments, with bishops of commoner origin doing particularly badly
(a mere 4.2 per cent) and the residual category of 'uncertains' (8 per cent)
probably containing as many nobles as commoners.[18] Péronnet commented
that 'Louis XIV had no intention of altering the social recruitment of the
episcopate', being more concerned with ensuring that bishops would possess
the necessary learning, piety and devotion to duty'. The real hallmark of the
reign, according to Péronnet, was the 'regularisation' of the episcopate on
several fronts – education, age, previous experience, and so on. But he did
detect a long-term trend at work in the episcopate after 1685, and that was
the falling-off of sons of nobles in crown service (court, army, office): their
places were increasingly taken by sons of provincial nobles whose service
records were far less impressive.[19] Both Péronnet's figures and his interpretation of them support the earlier findings of Ravitch, whose work he seems
not to have known. Between them, they would cast serious doubt on the 'traditional' view, as expressed by Sicard and Taveneaux, that this was a period
when the dominance of the nobility was *not* so extensive as to leave virtually
no room for social 'outsiders'. Insofar as one can judge from the figures provided by these historians, it may be that they paid insufficient attention to
the actual social status of bishops' families at their birth, and may well have
judged them to be noble in relation to their *later* history. A family clearly
ennobled by 1700 or 1750 might have been in a very different position around
1620, especially for those whose ennoblement was 'gradual'. And in the case
of families gaining 'immediate' nobility by one method of another, a few years
could obviously make a difference as to whether a son entering the episcopate
was noble or not by birth. Trivial as they may seem, such considerations have
a direct bearing on the statistics which underpin a social interpretation of the
French episcopate.

Before attempting to measure as accurately as the surviving evidence allows
the social origins of the Ludovican episcopate, it is essential to understand the
problems presented to the historian by the fragility of the social categories to
which families and individuals are usually assigned. Those of 'nobles' and
'commoners' are simply too basic to serve as more than an initial guide, while
elaborate social typologies can easily lead to uncertainty and confusion. The
evolution and differentiation of French society itself during the period defies
efforts to simplify questions of personal status. The gradual codification of the

17   Ravitch, *Sword and Mitre*, 72, table iv.
18   Péronnet, *Évêques de l'ancienne France*, ii, 1440–1, table 59 (i).
19   *Ibid*, i, 520–7.

privileges of nobility inevitably generated a strong desire to share them on the part of families and individuals with money and ambition. The proliferation of officeholding and the piecemeal extension of the privileges of nobility to a growing constellation of royal officials were the best-known response to such a situation, one which ensured that the monarchy would play a pivotal role in facilitating or denying entry to the nobility. These avenues to nobility, beginning in time with the ennoblement of holders of municipal office in certain towns, broadened in due course, not least in times of war when urgent royal financial needs could mean instant social alchemy for those with ready cash. Letters of ennoblement or purporting to restore earlier noble status allegedly lost through mercantile or similar 'derogating' activities, as well as offices of *secrétaire du roi* – all purchased for ready cash – were among the most common mechanisms which enabled the crown and the moneyed elites to obtain what they wanted. The vast majority of the constantly expanding mass of royal offices either conferred no claim to nobility at all or only did so by degrees, so that hereditary nobility via officeholding was only acquired after three successive generations in office. From the sixteenth century onwards, the monarchy was increasingly anxious to channel and, if possible, exert some sort of control over the forms of social mobility, not least because uncontrolled entry into the ranks of the nobility would end up sapping its tax base. This concern was already manifest under Henri III and Henri IV, when royal legislation tried to prevent the usurpation of noble privileges. But it was only from the mid-seventeenth century onwards, and especially in the first years of Louis XIV's personal rule that systematic, if often flawed, attempts were made to stabilise the social structure of the provinces by the institution of *recherches de noblesse* conducted by the provincial intendants. Even such a step could be viewed as yet another fiscal expedient, since fines were levied on convicted 'usurpers' of nobility. But it was no secret, either then or in later enquiries that 'understanding' investigators could accept dubious claims, for all kinds of reasons. The older nobility might welcome these efforts at stemming the inflow of newcomers to their ranks, but the king's subsequent wars re-opened the gates as widely as at any time in the past. However, tacit ennoblement of the kind that was widespread in the previous century had disappeared – or at least it was no longer recognised as valid. The 'juridification' of nobility was complete by the 1660s at the latest, with the important consequence that only service to the crown could now bring about a change in one's social status.[20]

---

20 The bibliography of this subject is extensive, and is represented at opposite ends of the scale by the recent, general account in Laurent Bourquin, *La Noblesse dans la France moderne* (Paris 2002), esp ch 2, 'le Roi, alchimiste social', and the more monographic study of Jean Meyer, *La Noblesse bretonne au xviiᵉ siècle*, 2 vols (Paris 1966), i, ch 2, 'La Réformation de la noblesse de 1668 à 1672'. The latter provides a revealing evocation of the problems of noble status in a single province with its own distinct customs on the matter.

Table 2.1   Social origins of French bishops 1661–1715

	Nominations	Nobility	Commoners	Unknown/ uncertain
1660s	35	27	6	2
1670s	55	39	11	5
1680s	44	32	10	2
1690s	42	35	5	2
1700s	45	39	6	0
1710s	29	24	5	0
Total	250	196 (78.4%)	43 (17.2)	11 (4.4%)

This account of the mechanisms of social change might seem otiose were it not for the fact that in analysing the social background of Louis XIV's bishops virtually every outcome that contemporary practice made possible is to be encountered – which is itself an initial indication of the social complexity of the episcopate. With so many bishops born between the 1620s and 1650s, a time when the mechanisms just described were working at full throttle, it is hardly surprising that resolving problems relating to their social origins can prove genuinely tricky. Put differently, it means that the results obtained by the analysis involve a large measure of subjective judgement and should, therefore, not be over-interpreted. But as they stand, how far do they bear out the conventional assumptions about the episcopate of the reign? Or can they be used to demonstrate patterns that would not otherwise come to our attention?

The most succinct presentation of the results is to be found in table 2.1. Its value is mainly indicative, since the three categories involved are themselves so broad in scope, though it no longer needs a column entitled 'foreigners' as it would have for earlier periods.[21] It will be evident straightaway that with over 78 per cent of all bishops, the nobility took the lion's share of church patronage under Louis XIV – since similar if not greater proportions could probably be registered for the abbeys and priories also in the king's gift. At the same time, it is no less clear that the dominance of the nobility was not as all conquering as it would be in the next century – or as it had been prior to the wars of religion. Commoners and 'unknowns' still retained a significant foothold in the episcopate. Moreover, the eleven individuals in the category of 'unknown' and 'uncertain' were almost certainly of commoner origins, sons of families on the road towards nobility but not yet in full sight of it. It can be suggested, therefore, that the figures for the nobility in table 2.1 would be unlikely to rise much in the light of further research. Taken

21   The one foreign-born bishop, Margarit of Perpignan, has been entered here as a noble.

together, the combined total for commoners and 'uncertains' amounts to just over one-fifth (21.6 per cent) of the episcopate.

These figures bear out the more impressionistic judgements of historians from Sicard to Taveneaux about the social diversity of the episcopate of this period, without however demonstrating that access to the episcopate was quite as 'open' as they claimed. Furthermore, when the figures are viewed on a decade-by-decade basis, as in table 2.1, they can be equally revealing. It would seem as if the early decades, from the 1660s to the 1680s were as good a period for commoners seeking the mitre as the 1640s and 1650s, though much less so than the 1620s and 1630s. The proportion of commoners (and 'uncertains') among incoming bishops, having hovered below or just around 20 per cent from the 1640s to the 1680s, looked set to collapse in the 1690s and 1700s, before making a perhaps unexpected recovery in the last few years of the reign after 1710. This would, on the face of it, support the contention of Saint-Simon, echoed by Norman Ravitch's figures, that the last confessor, Tellier, had somehow obtained preferment for more commoners than had previously been the case. Similarly, the dip in known and possible commoners obtaining the mitre in the 1690s and 1700s may well give credence to a comment made privately by Fénelon early in the Nine Years' War in 1690. Replying to a vicar-general of his own native diocese, Cahors, who was contemplating moving to court and seeking a royal almonership, Fénelon wrote to discourage him, claiming that in wartime the king would give the benefices his correspondent had his eye on to the sons or brothers of the military officers fighting his wars.[22] Fénelon probably meant non-episcopal benefices in this particular context, but the figures in table 2.1 could be read to mean that the king was either unable or unwilling to make such a strict distinction between them and bishoprics.

For nearly one in five bishops under Louis XIV to have been born commoners may seem unremarkable. But their significance should not be minimised either. This was an age in which social change had already begun to slow considerably compared with the previous century, and in which relatively fewer 'new' families appeared; the successful 'new' families of recent generations had been taking advantage of the generous scope for entry into the nobility which the French monarchy provided for those with the financial means and ambition. Only a preference for offices providing gradual ennoblement would keep them in a commoner or transitional status for a number of generations. For that reason also, the commoners among Louis XIV's bishops must count among the most 'self-made' of the reign. The term 'self-made' would seem out of place in any discussion of the seventeenth century, not least after the brilliant destruction of the legend of Colbert as a self-made bourgeois from Reims. It is no paradox, however, that some of them bore some of the most famous names associated with the reign – no

22   Fénelon, *Correspondance*, ii, no 142, p. 194, letter to canon de Fouillac, 8 Sept 1690.

fewer than four Colberts; Fleury, Louis XV's *premier ministre*; Mascaron, Fléchier and Soanen, three of the greatest preachers of the day, were born commoners. In this limited sense, the French church even under Louis XIV still offered more scope than most other domains for those with particular talents – provided, no doubt, they were able to capitalise on them by attaching themselves to the networks of relationships which could lead to ecclesiastical preferment.

Because the proportion of nobles entering the episcopate in our period falls well short of what we know for the early sixteenth century and the pre-Revolution period, it would be tempting, but anachronistic, to regard their record under Louis XIV as some kind of aberration. As early as the wars of religion, their numbers among the episcopate had dropped significantly, and they were not especially quick to recover lost ground under Henri IV and Louis XIII. The first clear signs of such a recovery are visible in the 1640s and 1650s, but even then the evidence does not point to anything like a clean sweep of episcopal appointments. Furthermore, the proportions they achieved in the 1640s and 1650s are not seriously out of line with those of the early decades of the king's personal rule after 1661. As with their commoner counterparts, the period from the 1640s to the 1680s represents a kind of plateau, after which their relative share of episcopal patronage began to shift upwards again – though only further research could determine how quickly or otherwise the pattern of noble monopoly observed for Louis XVI's reign took shape.

The French nobility, as already noted, was a house of many mansions. It is crucial, but infinitely more difficult, to form some idea of the kind of nobility from which bishops emerged in this period. Were they drawn, as their eighteenth-century successors increasingly were, from the older 'noblesse de race', the effect of which was to more or less shut out, not just commoners, but even most of the 'noblesse de robe'? Likewise, assuming that the latter type of nobility continued to attract royal attention under Louis XIV, we need to know how they had attained their nobility and, if possible, for how long they had possessed it. Clearly, if many families of bishops were only recently ennobled – or, better still, 'instantly' ennobled – then the distance between commoners and a given proportion of the formally noble bishops was minimal, and would reinforce the argument just advanced about the social profile of Louis XIV's episcopate.

Table 2.2 is an attempt at an internal classification of the nobility represented in the ranks of the episcopate, but it requires some preliminary explanation if it is to make sense. In theory there was only one nobility in France, whose privileges were enjoyed equally by all its members. But for the historian, this legalist argument cannot be the last word. Distinguishing between different types of noble families involves tracing their 'principe de noblesse', a rather grandiose term which signifies the manner in which they acceded to their privileged status and, wherever possible, putting a date on it. Of course,

Table 2.2 – Origins-typology of nobility of Louis XIV's
bishops

Pre 1400	79
1400–1560	36
Officeholding	37
Cloche	12
SR	15
Letters-patent	17
Total	196

ancient noble roots, so lost in the mists of time that a prior state of impurity could not be imputed to the lineage in question, were the most highly prized of all in the extremely competitive seventeenth-century, as evidenced by the huge volume of 'incredible genealogies' it witnessed.[23] It was the very absence of a precise moment of accession to nobility that was the hallmark of the true 'noblesse de race'. In principle, this latter category was reserved for families who could trace their nobility back to 1400 and who were untainted either by commoner blemishes or even by an act of ennoblement. It was to this ancient nobility that the eighteenth century monarchy reserved the 'honneurs de la cour' and other favours. As a consequence of the mid-seventeenth-century investigations of noble titles, the monarchy also fixed a more recent date, that of 1560, for those individuals or families wishing to prove their status as 'nobles de race': failure to produce the necessary proof meant being refused a patent upholding one's noble status and the prospect of being obliged to pay the *taille* again. Here too, there was no question of dating precisely the beginnings of their nobility: it was merely 'recognised' as having existed before a fixed date. By contrast, immediate access to noble status could be obtained in several ways. Surprisingly perhaps, the oldest was through tenure of the position of mayor or councillor in a relatively small number of cities, beginning with Poitiers in 1372 and ending, no less surprisingly, with Paris under Louis XIV in 1706.[24] Ennoblement by letters from the crown was itself a long-standing custom, going back in the case of some of the episcopal families to the fourteenth century, when it was obviously less discredited from overuse than it would become later, especially during the wars of religion. For the historian, these forms of 'fast-track' ennoblement do not seem a world apart from the acquisition of instant noble status by purchasing an office of *secrétaire du roi*, a practice usually indulged in by financial

23 Roberto Bizocchi, *Genealogie incredibili: scritti di storia nell'Europa moderna* (Bologna 1995), on the nature of the genealogical 'culture' fostered by the search for nobility.
24 François Bluche and Pierre Durye, *L'Anoblissement par charges avant 1789*, 2 vols (*Les Cahiers nobles*, np 1962), i, 23–4.

officials from the sixteenth century onwards – and one which proved to be the source of the nobility of even some royal ministers under Louis XIV. More familiar, however, to most historians is the gradual process of ennoblement, spread out over three generations, achieved by the continuous tenure of certain categories of royal office, categories which themselves shifted over time, usually in response to the crown's financial needs.[25]

The most obvious point to make about the figures in table 2.2 is how significantly bigger than any other category were the bishops drawn from the older *noblesse de race*. In some instances, it is difficult to know for certain whether particular families had successfully 'proved' noble origins pre-dating 1400. The family of Claude de Saint-Georges, archbishop of Lyon in 1693, could prove their filiation back to 1404, which means they came very close, but not close enough, to making it into the pre-1400 category. Of course, identical problems arise with families proving their nobility back to 1560, since they probably found it easier to present the proofs needed to pass scrutiny and to secure letters of 'maintenue de noblesse' – leaving it to the crown's own genealogists to pick holes in the evidence at some later date. These uncertainties are less problematic if we pool together the pre-1400 and the pre-1560 nobility. After all, both were characterised by the fact that they had always been reputed as nobles, or had entered the nobility 'par agréga-tion' – not excluding what would later be classed as simple 'usurpation'. The combined total for the two categories of 'old' nobility, 115, means that between them they counted for 46 per cent of the entire episcopate, and 58.7 per cent of the 196 nobles becoming bishops under Louis XIV.[26] But however substantial, this is significantly short of the figures reported for the following century, when the proportion of noble bishops was much higher anyway, and it clearly left substantial room for men with quite different noble origins, often of recent vintage.

With two out of every five noble bishops descended from families which had been formally ennobled at some moment in their history, it is worth considering the routes they followed towards nobility. The most socially acceptable form of ennoblement, spread across two or more generations of officeholding was, as table 2.2 also shows, well represented among the fami-lies of Louis XIV's bishops. The lion's share, amounting to virtually two-thirds of the families of the thirty-seven bishops concerned, belonged to Parisian officeholders, most of whom were by Louis XIV's time ensconced in the par-lement. Some of them, like the Séguier, Le Tellier, Phélypeaux, Potier, had already held ministerial office or were moving in that direction after 1661. The scions of the Parisian robe to be found among the episcopate were not drawn from the families of obscure *conseillers*, but from those of its presidents,

25 *Ibid*, vol i, which provides a breakdown and chronology of the offices in question, including those of *secrétaire du roi* which are considered under the heading of *noblesse de chancellerie*.
26 Péronnet, *Évêques de l'ancienne France*, ii, 1440–1, appendix 59 (i) combines the 'noblesse de race' and 'noblesse étrangère' with the 'anoblis anciens' and obtains a figure of 67.8 per cent.

procureurs-généraux and the like. As hinted at earlier in this chapter, bishops from provincial capitals like Toulouse, Bordeaux, Grenoble and elsewhere, were drawn mainly from the same parlementaire milieux. Bishops whose families' nobility derived from officeholding in lesser 'sovereign' courts like the *grand conseil*, *cour des monnaies*, or *chambre des comptes* were also far fewer in number.

Although gradual ennoblement through tenure of certain offices was the biggest single category in table 2.2 after that of the 'old' nobility, its total is lower than that of the various 'fast-track' alternatives available to those seeking to shed commoner status. The oldest of these was ennoblement via municipal office. Despite its admittedly modest total of twelve, it should not be dismissed as an aberration or the 'poor man's' route to superior social status. Such ennoblement was only in the gift of fifteen cities for the period with which we are concerned – Paris was *not* one of them – and some famous families began life in the second estate thanks to it. In most cases, the offices in question had been part of a family's cursus during the sixteenth century or earlier, so that the nobility of the families in question was itself often venerable. The oldest case of this kind of ennoblement of a bishop's family was that of the Bertier family of Toulouse in the late fifteenth century, the most recent that of the father of Gabriel de Roquette, bishop of Autun, who was a Toulouse city councillor – a *capitoul* – as late as 1620. And since, with a few exceptions, the cities in question were not exactly among the most prominent in France, the beneficiaries of their ennobling privileges often sought later either to join the ranks of the local gentry or, in the absence of attractive local royal offices, to move to more important cities in search of better opportunities. The Nesmond family, ennobled by municipal office in sixteenth-century Angoulême, then moved to the Bordeaux and Paris parlements in search of professional and social advancement. Residents of Toulouse, by contrast, did not have to look so far afield, given that the *capitoulat* could be a natural prelude to office in the local parlement, as the history of families like the Bertier, Catelan, Dreuillet and others shows. If the Milon family's ennoblement via municipal office in Tours was open to objection, then their tenure of ennobling financial office in subsequent generations resolved that particular question.[27] As often as not, 'municipal' nobility was a stage, though not a necessary one, along the road to much longer careers in the ranks of the 'robe'.

As already noted, straightforward ennoblement, usually by letters patent, had become increasingly discredited by 1600 and the crown's cynical practice of revoking them at some later date did nothing to redeem their reputation. Yet this was the road to nobility taken by families as prominent in the

---

27 Bluche and Durye, *Anoblissement par charges*, i, 36. The parlement of Paris placed heavy restrictions on the ennoblement of Tours civic officeholders such that only those in office between 1589 and 1667 could be sure of their status.

seventeenth century as the Le Camus, Maupeou, and Fortin de la Hoguette. An alternative, which neatly avoided the imputation of commoner status, was the grant of letters purporting to restore an older noble status of which a family's more recent (usually mercantile) activities had deprived them. This was the method used under Henri IV by the Argouges family from Tours, for whom it had the added advantage of allowing them to claim a distant common origin with a better-known Norman family of the same name; numerous other families followed exactly the same pattern. Louis XIV also imitated his predecessors by ennobling a number of favoured 'domestics', particularly physicians, in his and the royal family's service. Among the beneficiaries of this practice to provide bishops in our period were the Ancelin, Vallot and Aquin families, though only one of the bishops in question, Louis d'Aquin, bishop of Sées, was born *after* the ennoblement in question and thus qualifies to figure among the nobility.[28] The father of Pierre de Langle, bishop of Boulogne, was one of many middling royal officials ennobled in 1661 as part of the celebrations for the Treaty of the Pyrenees, but his son had been born several years earlier and cannot therefore be considered of noble extraction. As with other forms of 'instant' ennoblement, establishing the social status of children of ennobled parents often does come down to precise dates. But it would be misleading to think that families ennobled in this way were mostly parvenus of recent vintage buying their way into the second estate. Instances of such ennoblement among the families of bishops go back to the fifteenth and even fourteenth century, and were, like some of the cases just seen, rewards for genuine service to the crown. Avignon-based families like the Brancas or Berton de Crillon, whose descendants would enter the French peerage in later centuries, were ennobled in this way, the Brancas as commensals of René d'Anjou, count of Provence, in the fifteenth century, the Crillon for military services to Henri II in the mid-sixteenth century.[29] And the famous Turgot family attracted a similar reward as far back as 1472, long before they began providing *maîtres des requêtes* in generation after generation.[30]

The bishops owing their status as nobles to the no less criticised offices of *secrétaire du roi* (SR) also deserve attention, and not merely because of the numbers, fifteen in all, involved. Firstly, judged in relation to the careers of the bishops concerned, not all of the offices had been recently bought by ambitious fathers or grandfathers anxious to avoid the tedium of gradual ennoblement. The oldest instance involves the ancestor of the two Brûlart bishops who had been a *secrétaire du roi* under Louis XI and Charles VIII. The Villeroy, Le Jay and Loménie families followed their example in the next two generations – and in each case, their descendants rose to the summits of ministerial

28   Saint-Simon, xxviii, 524–31, appendix 7, 'la nourrice de Louis XIV et sa descendance', a carefully documented study by the principal editor of the *Mémoires*, A M de Boislisle.
29   L-H Labande, *Avignon au xve siecle* (Paris 1920), 22–3, 550–60.
30   Pierre Foncin, 'Remarques sur la généalogie des Turgot', *Revue Historique*, 115 (1914), 64–84.

or parlementaire office. The remaining families in this list were ennobled between the 1550s and the 1630s, in a chronology which in most cases is mirrored by the subsequent chronology of their descendants' accession to the episcopate. The last two among them – Le Peletier and Fleuriau, ennobled in 1634 and 1637 respectively – were families which were to match the achievements of those just mentioned, since they, too, would hold ministerial office under Louis XIV and his successor. Moreover, despite the opprobrium heaped by contemporaries on the nobility of the *secrétaires du roi*, it should be noted that within a few years of acquiring the office in question, several ancestors of bishops in our period went on to become *maîtres des requêtes*, magistrates in sovereign courts, or even serving councillors of state, and thus moved well beyond their point of entry to the nobility: their upward advancement was driven essentially by service and favour. As some of these names suggest, different combinations of luck, connections and ability could lead individuals to high political office which, if ministerial in character, brought corresponding social status in its wake. Strictly speaking, it was the acquisition of an office of *secrétaire du roi* which brought nobility to some of them. However, for the historian of bishops descended from such families the problem is to determine the status of these families at particular moments of their history – such as the date when a future bishop was born! – since the crown, from Louis XIII to Louis XIV, frequently extended, altered, or abrogated the entitlement to nobility attached to certain offices. Nor are we dealing with a homogeneous body of families with titles to nobility. Men like Claude Bouthillier and Jean-Baptiste Colbert were both commoners when they became royal ministers, but their exalted functions as ministers close to the king were such as to bring them nobility 'in the first degree', that is to say, full and immediate ennoblement. Consequently, by the time the two Bouthillier bishops of Louis's reign were born, their nobility was beyond any doubt, since both their father and grandfather respectively had served as royal ministers. But Jean-Baptiste Colbert's elevation came well after the birth of his son Jacques-Nicolas, who must therefore be listed among the commoner bishops of the reign. Likewise, his cousin and namesake, Jean-Baptiste Colbert de Saint-Pouange, only acquired his office in the *chambre des comptes* in the 1620s, not early enough for his two episcopal sons to qualify as nobles. On the other hand, Colbert's brother and future foreign minister, Croissy, was, by virtue of becoming a *maître des requêtes* in 1663, ennobled just soon enough for his son, the Jansenist bishop of Montpellier, to be born noble in 1667.

With the 'nobility' of Louis XIV's bishops ranging from that of the likes of a Colbert de Croissy to a Béthune or an Adhémar de Grignan, it is worth asking how, or indeed if, their fortunes rose or fell in relation to each other across the fifty-four years of the king's rule. Did Fénelon's remark about the king favouring a certain kind of cleric during wartime have any basis in fact and, if it did, was it part of a broader pattern not necessarily confined to the impact of war? Is there evidence that older noble families claimed a greater

Table 2.3   Variations in noble presence among episcopate

Decade	pre-1400	1400–1560	Charges	Cloche	SR	Ennobled
1661–69	11	6	5	2	3	0
1670–9	14	9	8	2	3	3
1680–9	14	7	6	1	5	4
1690–9	16	6	6	3	2	2
1700–9	15	10	9	3	0	2
1710–15	9	3	3	1	2	6
Totals	79	36	37	12	15	17

proportion of the ecclesiastical spoils as the reign progressed, and thus in some way prefigure the pattern already revealed for the following century? Table 2.3 shows that as far as the episcopate was concerned, there are few obvious signs of any such development. Across the six decades of the king's rule the combined *noblesse de race*, with noble origins going back to 1560 or earlier, accounted for a relatively stable proportion of all nobles entering the episcopate, moving within a fairly narrow band which varies from slightly under two-thirds to a half. Nor is there any noticeable upward trend, more of a pendulum swing, since their contribution during the 1660s was already as high as it would be in any subsequent decade, the 1700s being the exception; but even then the difference was quite small. It seems, on reflection, that whenever incoming bishops of commoner origin were more numerous, the crown was also likely to promote bishops whose nobility was more recent than that of the *noblesse de race*. On the other hand, someone in Fénelon's position and writing around 1690, after a decade in which the older nobility's contribution had dropped to 50 per cent of all nobles, might have been justified in believing that this situation would change in wartime. The old nobility *did* actually fare rather better in the 1690s and 1700s, when it reached its highest figure for the whole reign. But as already observed, it merely regained the share in episcopal patronage that it had already enjoyed in the 1660s, while the five years from 1710 to 1715 showed that even that gain could be reversed.

III

One of the limitations of discussing the social origins of France's bishops along these lines is that it unwittingly treats them as largely nameless individuals to be brought together only under aggregates of one type or another, with the consequence that their own ways of seeing themselves can easily be ignored. Yet the previous pages have referred more than once to families either producing bishops over several generations or several bishops within a single generation. As we shall see, neither the Colbert nor the Béthune, to take instantly recognisable examples, were alone in doing so. In general, it is fair to claim that opportunities for entry into the episcopate, as to other bodies secular as well as ecclesiastical, were nearly always more likely to come the way of those with a family history, past or ongoing, of holding such office; and families with such a track record were also more than likely to actively seek to retain – or regain – the advantages such office had once brought them. The implications of such traditions, and the pressure that resulted from them, for the crown's use of church patronage can easily be imagined. For the historian, it raises a different question, though one which is related to the subjects discussed so far in this chapter – namely, the extent to which the episcopate was 'colonised', not merely by particular social groups, but also by clerics who were brothers, nephews, cousins or more distant relatives of bishops, present and past. At its simplest, the question is – to what degree did kin-groups, mostly but not exclusively drawn from the nobility, populate Louis XIV's episcopate?

All that can be attempted here is a series of sketchy observations, since it would require a virtually unattainable mastery of the genealogies of the families of the bishops in order to properly understand their kinship networks and how they actually worked. Shared patronymics are only a crude pointer here: although social rank and title were transmitted 'patrilineally' in *ancien régime* France, it is clear that kinship derived from the marriages of female family members counted for just as much as those of males in the minds of contemporaries. But it is precisely this kind of information which the sources, largely genealogical in form, used by social and family historians often simply omit or ignore. Consequently, once we move beyond the obvious commonalities provided by family names, our understanding of the meanings of 'family' in its extended sense of kinship for seventeenth-century society is strikingly deficient, which puts us at disadvantage in deciphering their behaviour as they sought for favour and preferment for themselves and those they regarded as relatives. Memoirs, journals and letters abound with references to their authors' relatives ('parents'), but it is often extremely difficult to uncover the nature or origins of these ties; they occasionally allude to the efforts of certain families to 'court' better-known families bearing the same name as themselves in order to achieve the kind of 'recognition' that would increase their social capital, especially in the marriage market of the day.[31] One example will illustrate this general point for our present purposes. According to Saint-Simon, Fénelon had 'brought up' Guy de Laval-Montmorency, bishop of Ypres in 1713, being 'un peu son parent': it turns out that the husband of Fénelon's sister was Laval's cousin to the sixth or seventh degree – i.e. that their kinship

---

31 Saint-Simon, *Mémoires*, i, 381, recounts how Bishop Clermont-Tonnerre of Noyon, to whom he was himself related, rebuffed the claims of Bishop Clermont-Chaste of Laon to be from the same family as himself. The Isoré d'Hervault claimed to be first cousins with the Beauvillier de Saint-Aignan, but although this was not true, the family connection did go back three generations on the female side.

was indirect, and went back to end of the fifteenth century. This may seem far-fetched – and one might suspect that Saint-Simon's legendary genealogical knowledge went too far here – except that Fénelon did indeed behave as he was reported to have done, taking Laval under his wing in 1704 and 'making' his career over the following decade. It is possible that among aristocratic families like these, awareness of such seemingly remote family ties was more acute than it was further down the social scale. Yet it seems that officeholding families in Paris and elsewhere behaved no differently, no doubt because of the kind of endogamy that they practised so assiduously. A further example will make the same point: the families of at least three of Louis XIV's bishops – Argouges, Amelot and Maupeou – were related to each other owing to their sons marrying the daughters of just one Parisian magistrate, Jean de Creil, whose own family name appears on no episcopal list.[32]

With these caveats in mind, a simple trawl of an admittedly limited range of sources indicates that at least two-thirds of all French bishops under Louis XIV were related to previous or contemporary bishops. No doubt this figure would rise further if ties to sixteenth-century bishops could be determined. The remaining one-third cannot readily be fitted under a single label, but it will not come as a surprise that many of them were commoners by birth, lacking the social capital represented by having episcopal predecessors in their families. Yet it would be mistaken to think that all of them fitted into this particular category: bishops who were sons of *secrétaires du roi* or from recently ennobled families could, for obvious reasons, be in a similar position. However, the lack of relatives, be they predecessors or contemporaries, in the episcopate should not lead to the conclusion that these bishops were necessarily isolated individuals; some more than made up for this defect, if that is what it is, by having powerful supporters – fathers, brothers, relatives – whose current political favour was of decisive importance for their careers. Although a commoner by birth, Jean-François Chamillart, bishop of Dol in 1692, did not really need 'episcopal' relatives when he could count upon the influence of his brother, Michel, who was by then within a few years of becoming *contrôleur-général des finances*. The first of the Colbert bishops, Nicolas, owed his promotion to Mazarin, Jean-Baptiste's employer, but after 1661 it was the latter himself who could place his cousins and son in high church office – and he had few equals in that particular skill.

At a conservative estimate, at least 106 bishops (42.4 per cent) were related somehow to bishops of the pre-Louis XIV era (i.e. pre-1661), and in some cases not to just one, but to several predecessors. Three of the 106 bishops under discussion here had an elder brother in the episcopate since Mazarin's day (La Mothe-Houdancourt, Carbon de Montpezat and Anglure de

---

32   BN, MS Fr 32138, 'généalogies des maîtres des requêtes', p 435. Actually two Creil sisters married two Maupeou brothers. Another married René de Marillac, *maître des requêtes* and son of Michel de Marillac, Richelieu's disgraced rival.

Bourlemont), while one had the even more unusual distinction of succeeding his father (Marc Malier du Houssay, bishop of Tarbes in 1668). It seems that about one-third of the 106 bishops were nephews, paternal or maternal, of bishops promoted under Louis XIII and Mazarin; the rest were great-nephews, cousins or more distant relatives. More to the point, a considerable number of bishops, sixty-three in all, were related to pre-Louis XIV bishops who were *still* in office in or after 1661. Even when there was no direct overlap between the generations, the surviving sources indicate a keen awareness of the kinship ties in question, ties that were undoubtedly a powerful incentive to the following generation to repeat their earlier attainments. When an Alleman or a Brisay de Denonville was nominated a bishop by Louis XIV, witnesses were able to testify on their behalf (no doubt because they had been 'primed' to do so) that the family had produced bishops as long ago as 1500 or earlier still.[33] In certain instances, it is via a particular bishop that the historian perceives the ramification of such kinship ties. It is no surprise, therefore, that clusters of related families like the Colbert, the Béthune, the Forbin, the Séguier, the Beauvau and the La Baume de la Suze were disproportionately influential sources of kinship among Louis XIV's bishops.

Among the 250 bishops promoted by Louis XIV after 1661, a slightly higher but still conservative figure of 120 were related among themselves by blood. Within the familiar networks of *cousinage*, a number of concentrations stand out. In addition to the three pairs of brothers already in office, the king added seven more, men whose names are closely associated with his rule – Colbert (albeit from the Saint-Pouange branch), their two Desmarets cousins, Béthune, Grignan, Matignon, Noailles and Mailly; the last two sets testifying to the influence in the 1690s of Mme de Maintenon, to whose family they were recently related by marriage. Uncle and nephew combinations were more common, with about twenty instances recorded, though one or two may actually involve great-uncles and grand nephews. It would be tempting to imagine that such couplings, which did not preclude those involved also being cousins to yet other bishops, represented a rather greater staying power on the part of the (mostly) noble families involved than that of more short-lived ministerial families. But such a sharp contrast cannot be sustained. Ministerial families and longevity were not as uncommon under Louis XIV as in other periods, which enabled some of them to match the record of ostensibly more entrenched noble families like the Matignon, Forbin, Grignan or Noailles. The record of the Colbert clan speaks for itself – six bishops in all if we included Nicolas, brother of the minister, nominated in the last days of the Mazarin regime; and it grows further still when we include their close relatives the Desmarets (two), Le Camus, Sève, Beauvillier (one each). With three bishops, the Phélypeaux family were some way behind, but they could

---

33   ASV, PC 87, fos 227–31, Brisay enquiry *de vita et moribus*, 3 July 1693; PC 101, fos 136–43, Alleman enquiry, 1 Dec 1707.

also point to their Bouthillier, Habert and Maupeou cousins in the episcopate. The Le Tellier only managed to secure one promotion for themselves,
though it was to Reims, but they, too, could point to their Cassagnet and Le
Peletier relatives at Mâcon and Angers. What the Colbert clan and others have
in common with the aristocratic Grignan and the Beauvau, but also the much
less visible Poncet de la Rivière dynasty of *maîtres des requêtes*-cum-intendants,
was a capacity to secure episcopal preferment across three generations.

If this analysis were extended to embrace the post-1715 episcopate, it
would no doubt produce equally considerable evidence of kinship between
Louis XIV's bishops and their successors. The names of the best connected
bishops might change somewhat, and a few surprises might emerge,[34] but it
would probably not add a new dimension to what we have seen in the previous pages. If the evidence of a social closure of the episcopate in our period
is not as convincing as is sometimes imagined, the impression generated by
even the relatively limited analysis attempted here shows that a substantial
proportion of the bishops' bench was made up of individuals with numerous
ties of kinship to each other. These ties were inter-generational, and given
the marriage practices of the period, they could involve bishops whose social
backgrounds were far from identical. Episcopal cousins could be commoners
by birth, but their families could already be 'allied' to, or in the process
of becoming allied to recently ennobled families, especially if they were
in robe and administrative circles, while the latter, depending on their
activities, could find themselves marrying their daughters into the ranks of
the nobility, great as well as small. Vertical kinship ties were not as common
as horizontal ones, but were not out of place either. The mechanisms whereby
the episcopate was becoming more like the *chasse gardée* of the following
century were clearly at work, even if they were not exactly a creation of Louis
XIV's reign.

IV

One obvious effect of the criss-crossing of kinship ties within the episcopate
is to draw attention to the way in which bishops and their families positioned
themselves in order to obtain a share of the *bienfaits du roi*. It also displaces
social status per se as the principal or sole avenue to ecclesiastical preferment
by emphasising the role of other, complementary factors. With royal choices
of bishops representing the final stage of a process of proposing and filtering
the names of potential candidates, it is worth asking how far the professional
activities of their families constituted an additional element in their success.
In discussing this point for an earlier period, attention was drawn to the

34 The Dauphiné family of Revol had produced a bishop of Dol in Brittany down to 1629, but
    then disappeared from view until 1705, when Joseph de Revol was made bishop of Oloron, a
    see that would pass from uncle to nephew thereafter until 1783.

Table 2.4   Professions of fathers of Louis XIV's bishops

Court 5	Royal minister/secret state 8	Medical practitioners 8
Diplomacy 3	*Conseiller d'etat* 5	Barristers 5
Marshals of France 7	*Maître des requêtes* 14	*Marchand-bourgeois* 3
Military commands 26	President in parlement 12	*Procureur* 1
Military (unspecified) 25	*Avocat/proc-général* 5	Peasant 1
Navy 1	*Cons* parlement 16	Others 2
Prov gov/lieut-gen 8	Pres/*cons* in other sovereign	*Sub-total 20*
Urban governor 6	courts 11	
Baillis/sénéchaux 8	Financiers/financial	*Unknown 41*
Sub-total 89	official 17	Total 250
	Lesser royal officials 9	
	Urban magistrates 3	
	Sub-total 100	

limitations of the documentation and to the danger of anachronism posed by modern assumptions about 'profession' and 'career' when transposed to the seventeenth century.[35] At more than one rung of the social scale, careers could be made up of successive activities, while among the higher nobility, the *simultaneous* tenure of more than one *charge* was the most convincing sign of power and favour. Ideally, the analysis should include the careers not just of the fathers' of bishops, but also of their grandfathers, maternal as well as paternal; and it could also be extended to uncles on both sides of the family, especially to their ecclesiastical members. But as with the study of kinship among bishops, it will hardly be surprising to learn that the information needed to conduct such an analysis is extremely patchy and becomes more elusive the further one moves away from the bishops themselves.[36] For these reasons, it seems best to focus on the careers of the fathers of the bishops, as that promises to provide the most useful snapshot of the professional background of the episcopate. It should be added, however, that incoming bishops were often known to contemporaries as much by the activities of their brothers as by those of their fathers; that was particularly true of bishops from noble families following military careers, which in turn is testimony both to the toll taken by Louis XIV's wars on noble families and to their continuing commitment to military activity.

Table 2.4 attempts to group together the available data under three main

35 Bergin, *Making*, 202.
36 One major problem here arises from the proliferation of noble titles in seventeenth-century France when the crown was busy raising the status of numerous families and their lands. Families themselves were subdividing into often numerous branches, which might be distinguishable only by titles of 'comte', 'marquis' or 'seigneur'. That, along with what seem like purely 'courtesy' titles within families, can render the precise identification of the individuals referred to in contemporary documents, often merely as 'Monsieur', extremely hazardous. It is also frequently impossible to know whether they are referring to fathers, sons or uncles.

headings. With sons of *noblesse de race* families so prominent in Louis XIV's episcopate, it is to be expected that the major professional activity of their fathers should have been military. However, the overall figures for this in table 2.4 should be regarded as minima, since almost certainly a proportion of the 'unknowns' were nobles who may *not* have stayed at home during the wars. The reason why so many military careers are labelled 'unspecified' in the table is that large numbers of provincial nobles often served in minor positions and possibly for short periods in the royal armies. The father of Fénelon is probably representative of many such nobles: detailed research on him has only enabled his historian to say that 'Pons de Fénelon *appears to have had* a relatively honourable military career'.[37] The same could be said of many others about whom we know far less. Beyond that, it is highly likely that those holding provincial or town governorships had probably seen military service of some kind, but which is not otherwise documented. A similar point might be made about some or all of those involved in diplomatic or court-based careers. The small number of 'courtiers' entered here should not be misinterpreted: it refers only to those for whom no *other* substantial activity apart from their court position can be found. All but one of them were noble – and that was Malezieu, born a commoner, but whose career was primarily that of preceptor to the sons of Louis XIV's son, the duc du Maine, at whose court he subsequently became a highly prominent figure. By the same token, it will be obvious that a number of those designated as following military careers were also nominally attached to the court by office, whether it was a sinecure or not. On balance, however, it seems truer to the historical record to place them in the 'professional' category which best accounts for their career. Certainly the nobility had ample opportunity to demonstrate their military commitment ever since the Huguenot wars of the 1620s, when some of the earliest bishops of the post 1661 period were born. And of course as the century progressed, French armies grew in size and number, a more elaborate hierarchy of posts emerged, and a more militarily experienced nobility than that of previous generations took shape. As is well known, such military activity led to the extinction of families, and a number of Louis XIV's bishops were the last surviving male members of their lineage. Compared to the period from 1589 to 1661, fewer bishops were sons of the top-flight military commanders, the marshals of France, despite the rise in the number of marshals in service. But there is no mistaking the presence of those immediately below them – sons of lieutenants-general, brigadiers, colonels of regiments and so on listed under the heading 'military commands' in table 2.4. The total for those with otherwise unspecified military careers would probably also rise if the careers of the 'unknowns' in the table were discovered. As in the preceding period, sons of naval officers hardly figure at all in the episcopate: the only one to do so under Louis XIV was a Valbelle from Marseille, where

37   Fénelon, *Correspondance*, i, 25–6 (editor's introduction). The italics are mine.

for several generations fathers and sons were key figures in the admiralty. This virtual absence of the navy was partly historical accident and should not be exaggerated: the rebuilding of the French navy and its campaigns under Louis XIV explains why a number of bishops were brothers or relatives of major naval commanders like Coëtlogon, Estrées, La Luzerne and Nesmond. This, of course, serves to remind us that bishops' brothers, both older and younger, usually sustained their family's military traditions, and in many cases improved on the record of their fathers, at least in terms of their position in the military hierarchy. Their success in doing so probably played a part, admittedly one that it is difficult to determine, in securing ecclesiastical preferment for their siblings, especially as the latter normally entered the epis-copate between the ages of thirty and fifty-five. Finally, as we shall see again later, a handful of future bishops had been military and naval officers them-selves in their early careers.

It might seem surprising that bishops who were sons of fathers serving at court, in the army or in provincial or town governorships, should be fewer than those with fathers in royal 'civilian' office. One obvious explanation is that this second group is broadly cast, running all the way from a local tax official, the *élu*, upwards to the minister or secretary of state. All of them, apart from a few ministers and elected urban magistrates, have in common the ownership and exercise of an office. At the very top, the happy few who were sons of ministers were genuinely rare, and three of the eight were sons of men from the Richelieu and Mazarin era (Loménie, Bouthillier, Phélypeaux de La Vrillière). Only five of Louis's ministers (Le Tellier, Colbert, Croissy, Le Peletier and Beauvillier) managed to place sons in the episcopate, although some of those who 'failed' only did so because they had no sons at all or too few sons to place them in the church (Ponthcartrain, Boucherat), while a min-ister like Arnauld de Pomponne was too compromised by his Jansenist-leaning family to secure such preferment for his son, the abbé Pomponne (1669–1756), although the young man accumulated virtually everything short of a bishopric.[38] At fourteen, the number of sons of *maîtres des requêtes* may also seem on the low side, considering the expansion of this pivotal corps of high-ranking *officiers* since the Richelieu ministry. But it should be noted that several of those listed in table 2.4 as sons of either *conseillers d'état* or as presidents in the parlements or other sovereign courts had previously been *maîtres des requêtes*, which itself accurately reflects the reality of their place within the royal administration – in principle located within the parlement, but actually serving in the various royal councils. But what is most note-worthy about the second column of table 2.4 is that nearly half (44) of those in this group were officeholders in a sovereign court, Parisian or provincial, and that two-thirds (28) of them were in turn seated in a parlement. It is

---

38 See Alexander Sedgwick, *The Travails of Conscience. The Arnauld Family and the Ancien Régime* (Cambridge, Mass 1998), 246–51, for an excellent account of the abbé's career and affiliations.

obvious that a presidency in a parlement was itself no mean advantage, especially if it was in Toulouse, where half of the eight bishops who were natives of the city were sons of presidents in the parlement. In the light of the discussion of bishops' geographical origins earlier in this chapter, it should be added that in this broad 'middle' tier of royal officials, Parisians are less prominent than might be anticipated. Accounting for only twenty-five out of seventy officials in this middle band, Parisians were concentrated mostly among the financial officials and the non-parlementaire sovereign courts. Only three bishops were sons of 'mere' *conseillers* in the parlement, whereas double that number were sons of presidents or of *avocats-généraux* or *procureurs-généraux* based in Paris. Likewise only four of the twenty-one lesser royal officials and urban magistrates were based in Paris, the bulk of whom were widely scattered through the provinces.

The presence of seventeen sons of financiers or financial officials among the episcopate also warrants comment. Once again, all were holders of royal offices, but that common denominator disguises the often considerable internal differences in this group, which ranges from officials like *élus* and *trésoriers de France*, who were essentially magistrates, to full-time financiers. Within this group, eight can be clearly identified as active financiers for most of their careers, which were spread in time between the reign of Henri IV and the ministry of Mazarin. Virtually all of them were either dead or had ceased their activity by the 1660s when the *chambre de justice* sat, and the bishops' generation of family members turned to more socially respectable careers.[39] None of the great financiers who were active in underwriting Louis XIV's many wars managed to secure a mitre for a son while the king lived.[40]

As for the last and smallest grouping in table 2.4, which refers to the fathers of just twenty bishops, it provides some interesting contrasts with what we have seen. The common denominator of what is a heterogeneous list is that all of the professions involved would have been regarded as incompatible with nobility, even though as we shall see in some cases, they were not an insuperable barrier to ennoblement. The father of Claude Joly, bishop of Agen, cannot really be classed as anything other than a peasant, but the sources indicate that he was a *coq de village*, a rural or village notable who was probably moving beyond the horizons of the peasant world. Probably the closest to him in this list were Michel Fléchier, a candlemaker from near Carpentras, and Étienne Ancelin, father of the bishop of Tulle, who was a coachman from Poissy. But there the similarities between them end. Ancelin's wife was Louis XIV's wetnurse, and that sufficed to transform the family fortunes within a generation, leading to ennoblement and household office at court, whereas the

---

39   The exceptions were Pierre Maurel, *trésorier* of the Estates of Provence, and Alexandre Milon, a major tax farmer of the 1660s. See Daniel Dessert, *Argent, pouvoir et société au grand siècle* (Paris 1984), 644, 649.

40   See the dictionary of the major financiers of the reign in *ibid*, 519–703.

Joly and Fléchier families, especially the former, seem to have remained largely confined to their local horizons.[41] The three *marchands-bourgeois* were wealthy, so that within a generation their offspring were also moving into officehold-ing and, to a lesser degree, financial affairs. The barristers and *procureur* were, with one exception, all from provincial towns, and so probably further adrift from officeholding than they might have been in major cities with parlements or sovereign courts. The biggest surprise, however, comes with the group of eight medical practicioners. Only one of them did not practise in Paris, and it remains to be proven for certain that Pierre Le Neboux, bishop of Saint-Pol-de-Léon in Brittany, was actually the son of a 'surgeon' from Angoulême. The others, however, are of a wholly different calibre. All were physicians or surgeons in royal service, two of whom had served Henri IV or Louis XIII.[42] The remainder included *all* of the adult Louis XIV's own *premiers médecins*, as well as Félix de Tassy, his best-known *premier chirurgien*, whose skills saved the king's life in the famous fistula operation of 1686. All of Louis's principal physicians managed to enrich themselves quite considerably; some succeeded in adding ennoblement to riches and, above all, they placed their children in attractive positions, usually as far removed from medicine as possible. In doing so, none of them felt that the episcopate was beyond their reach, and the king and his confessor evidently did not dissent from that ambition.

At the end of this survey, whose tentative character will be evident, it seems clear enough that the vast majority of Louis XIV's bishops were born into families that were engaged in activities which, in one way or another, had something to do with the service of the monarchy. The numbers of those without such a common feature was miniscule. From a marshal of France to a physician might seem a huge leap, but they at least could frequent each other in the anti-chambers of Versailles – and contemporary commentators knew perfectly well that the real favour of a 'mere' physician might some-times be far greater than that of a marshal. However, most of those individ-uals under consideration here probably never set foot at court, but in numerous ways they and their families would have had, via intermediaries, at least some contact with the military and politico-administrative hierarchies of capital and province. This analysis of the professions of bishops' fathers should extend our understanding of who France's bishops were beyond the rather one-dimensional and frozen world of social status. But precisely because bishops were celibate individuals whose offices were not venal or hereditary in any of the senses understood by contemporaries, their careers do not map automatically onto those of secular elites, one important consequence of which

---

41   A brother and cousin of Joly followed him to Paris, but little is known about their later history. See references to them in the bishop's testament, a copy of which is in BN, MS Fr 23508, fos 46v–8r, *Nouvelles Ecclésiastiques*, 10 Oct 1678.

42   The latter include André du Laurens (father of Pierre, bishop of Belley), *premier médecin* of Henri IV, and Simon Le Tellier (father of François, bishop of Digne), *médecin ordinaire* in Louis XIII's household.

was, as this chapter has suggested, that other family members, especially paternal and maternal uncles, inside as well as outside of the church, could and did contribute to their careers. The difference between success and failure in the church obviously depended on their ability to tap into the combined capital represented by their origins, kinship networks or professional backgrounds. But the combination of celibacy and non-venality also made it easier to ensure that they would have to contribute something of their own to that success, and it is these particular ingredients that the following chapters will attempt to uncover.

CHAPTER 3

College, University and Seminary

COLLEGE, SEMINARY, UNIVERSITY – this trinity summarises a virtually canonical sequence in the careers of countless churchmen, great and small, since the Counter-Reformation. However, it is easy to forget that such a sequence was still in gestation in the seventeenth century, when the connection between the three was by no means evident. This was particularly so in the case of the last two of them: seminaries were still far from fully developed and even where they did exist, attendance at university could still dispense clerics from spending time in seminaries whose value for university graduates was still seriously debated. Down to the end of Louis XIV's reign, the relationship between the three types of institution did not cease to evolve in the wake of changes to one or the other of them.

By the middle decades of the seventeenth-century it had become clear that future bishops, whatever their social background might be, needed to have received a solid education, ideally rounded off by a university degree in either law or theology. But this prescription, first articulated in the Concordat of Bologna and later adopted by the Council of Trent, had taken an inordinately long time to make its mark. Even though the crown frequently ignored it when it came to selecting bishops for much of the century or so after Bologna, efforts to confine many of the most attractive second-rank positions in the church – those of canons in cathedrals, parish priests in the major towns and cities, episcopal officials, and others – to university graduates, helped to increase both the demand for, and value of university degrees among the clerical elite in general. Of course, it would be naive to believe that the crown's legislation produced major changes on its own, and in legislating as it did, it may have been doing little more than mirroring and formalising changes that were occurring anyway within the middle ranks of the French clergy. But in a world where competition for attractive benefices was, if anything, more intense than ever before, the act of reserving offices for certain categories of ecclesiastic was bound to have an effect on all of those concerned. It might seem, on a literal reading of the clauses of the Concordat and of Trent, that the episcopate was similarly 'reserved' to graduates, but crown and papacy were often prepared to overlook the absence of a university degree in candidates for the episcopate. The first pope overtly to show his disapproval of this was, it seems, Urban VIII, during whose reign a number of French bishops were singled out as needing a special dispensation for having no university degree. The message, as it happened, registered fairly quickly, as is evident in the spectacle of newly nominated bishops rushing to take their degrees so that the dossier to be sent to Rome by the nuncio could truthfully state that they did indeed have a degree.[1] As we shall see, a number of Louis XIV's bishops were to do exactly the same. Moreover, the French church itself was developing in such a way that the role of bishops as guardians and teachers of the true faith rose markedly during the century, especially under Louis XIV, as the Jansenist, Quietist and other controversies make clear. No doubt the spectrum of intellectual achievement within the episcopate was a rather broad one, to say the least. Not everyone had the education or the ability of a Bossuet or a Fénelon, but one only needs to read some of the correspondence of these two men alongside that of far less well-known figures to realise how heavily involved all of them could become in pastoral and theological disputes.[2] Fénelon's frequently caustic comments on the intellectual limitations of some of his confrères, many of whom were doctors of the Paris theology faculty, only make sense in such a context.[3]

It may seem perverse to preface a discussion of the education of France's bishops with considerations of this order, but the following pages will show how far an awareness of the appropriate educational requirements, informal as much as formal, became widely disseminated throughout the French church before and during Louis XIV's reign. The educational profile of the French episcopate represents a series of adjustments to those requirements. For example, one of the questions put to those testifying on behalf of new bishops by the papal nuncio or others conducting the *de vita et moribus* enquiry was whether nominees held a degree from 'a famous university'. In the sixteenth and early seventeenth-centuries, it was common for witnesses – themselves bishops, well-placed clergy, and sometimes laymen – to express contemporary attitudes by defending the nomination of non-graduates with reference to noble birth, the possession of other forms of learning, or membership of certain mendicant orders; by Louis XIV's time, none of these excuses apart from the last one was acceptable anymore. And when witnesses were not

---

1 See Bergin, *Making*, ch 6, esp 224ff.
2 See *Correspondance de Tronson*, iii, 49–54, 58–61, 73–6, 85–6, and also ASS, Correspondance des supérieurs-généraux, iii, for numerous exchanges between Tronson and Guy de Sève de Rochechouart, bishop of Arras, concerning the bishop's pastoral instructions and other disciplinary decrees. Sève's own letters are not preserved in this collection. Similar exchanges between Fleuriau d'Armenonville, bishop of Aire, and Tronson's successor, Leschassier, can also be found here.
3 See, for example, his frank evaluation of the bishops of Tournai, Meaux, Saint-Omer and Rouen in 1709: Fénelon *Correspondance*, xiv, no 1340, 177–80, Fénelon to duc de Chevreuse, 19 Dec 1709.

absolutely sure if a nominee was a graduate, they could always point to the evidence of the benefices or offices he had held, on the grounds that they were reserved for those with degrees.[4] When non-graduates were nominated, swift remedial action was possible, as we shall see later in this chapter, but such nominations tended to attract adverse comment and encouraged speculation, usually unflattering, about the new bishop's intellectual limitations. In the later years of the reign, at least one important nomination had to be delayed because the king's choice had not taken his theology degree and needed the time to do so.[5] But only a candidate with exceptionally influential patrons could contemplate taking that kind of risk, and the overwhelming majority of those seeking bishoprics made sure their chances were not jeopardised by such embarrassing gaps in their curriculum vitae. The most convincing proof, to which we shall return later, that this message was being taken seriously lies in the growing willingness from the 1630s onwards of the most natural candidates for episcopal office, the French nobility, great as well as small, to send its church-bound sons to college and then to university to take degrees. Cardinal de Retz typically boasted that he was the first of his (elevated) social rank to take a theology doctorate in Paris, but however exaggerated his claim, he was putting his finger on a change that would gather pace in the decades to follow, precisely when the bulk of Louis XIV's future bishops were pursuing their own studies.[6]

I

Any attempt to reconstruct the educational history of a group like the French episcopate must begin by accepting that there will be large gaps in both its evidence and conclusions. Given their widely scattered geographical origins, which stand in strong contrast with most of the groups that have attracted historians of ancien-regime corps, discovering anything significant about the early education of Louis's bishops is particularly difficult. This caveat covers not merely their earliest schooling but also their subsequent attendance at college, enrolment records for which have rarely or, at best, only haphazardly survived. Nor does what we know in general about family practices in this

---

4   ASV, PC 86, fo 647v–8v, evidence given in the *de vita et moribus* enquiry for François-Louis Polastron, nominated to Lectoure, 1692. One of the witnesses was the vicar-general of Auch who expressly stated that only graduates were admitted to positions in the cathedral chapter there.

5   Godet des Marais's successor and nephew, Des Montiers de Mérinville. Special arrangements were made in the Paris theology faculty to enable him to complete the licence and doctorate more quickly than was normally allowed: BN, MS Fr 19212, 225r, n d, for Père Léonard's comments on his nomination: 'il auroit esté plustost nommé s'il avoit soustenu ses actes de licence'.

6   Cardinal de Retz, *Mémoires*, in *Oeuvres* (ed La Pléiade) (Paris 1984), 136.

sphere always make the historian's task any easier. Younger sons destined for
clerical careers were rarely without uncles or older relatives already in the
church, whether bishops, canons, or mere curates. Family 'understandings',
sometimes arising from the initial provision of financial support for clerics
(the *titre clérical*, without which they could not take orders), usually placed
some responsibility on those clerical shoulders for educating younger
members in due course. Subsequently, the peculiarities of the clerical *cursus
honorum* – especially for those who were university graduates and thus in a
position to compete for 'reserved' benefices – could often take them far away
from their places of origin. As a direct consequence, their younger kin might
be sent away from home from an early age to join them and acquire an education under their supervision, which might in due course involve attendance
at a college and or a university which 'family geography' would not lead one
to suspect. Bearing in mind what we saw in the last chapter about the number
of future bishops related by blood to serving bishops in seventeenth-century
France, there is good reason to think that many of them were entrusted to
their episcopal relatives from an early age.[7]

In such an environment, early education and upbringing in the broad sense
were inextricably linked. The older generation of clerics might actually begin
the formal education of their younger kin, but if they did not, there were
usually other clerics available for the task, especially when younger sons were
destined for a church career. Wealthy families, ranging from the nobility to
officeholders and merchants, could not only afford tutors for their children,
but in many cases they would continue to serve in that capacity even when
their young charges began attending college or even university. Ultimately,
their contribution to the education of their charges may have been more decisive than that of the institutions they attended, but it is rare to find this ade-
quately documented. A very substantial number of Louis XIV's bishops were
probably the beneficiaries of such practices, while a far smaller number of
them filled the role of tutor, Fléchier of Nîmes being the most celebrated
example, which proved to be the starting point for careers to which they could
not otherwise have aspired.[8] Some of these points can be illustrated by the
experience of René Le Sauvage, bishop of Lavaur in Languedoc (1673–7). Born
around 1630 in Granville, in lower Normandy, where his father and brother
were successively *lieutenants* in the local admiralty court, his parents' early
deaths left the eldest son to raise his siblings. An uncle, Pierre, was a priest
who had himself moved to Paris and joined the resident but probably
unbeneficed clergy of the parish of Saint-Séverin. René was duly sent to Paris
to live with him, probably in the early- to mid-1640s, and completed his
humanities in one of the colleges of the university, where he became an MA

---

7   See above, p 70ff.
8   Fléchier began his career in Paris as tutor to the children of président Lefèbvre de Caumartin,
    whom he accompanied during the *grands jours* in Auvergne 1666.

in 1650. Supported by an annuity (the *titre clérical* mentioned above) and occasional ex gratia payments from his elder brother, he was a doctor of theology and member of the Compagnie du Saint-Sacrement by 1657, having also taught philosophy in one of the university colleges.[9] Short of some disaster, he was sure to surpass his uncle's modest attainments and to end up perhaps as a teaching doctor in the theology faculty, a canon of a cathedral, or an official to a bishop.[10] That none of these honourable but relatively anonymous destinies claimed him was due to the fact that two years later he was chosen to be preceptor to the young duc d'Albret, then beginning his studies in the University of Paris. After fifteen years of devoted service as tutor, factotum and companion, Albret and his celebrated uncle, marshal Turenne, obtained the see of Lavaur in Languedoc for Le Sauvage. But this kind of outcome did not quite turn the ecclesiastical establishment on its head: in the meantime, Le Sauvage's patron, Albret, had become the Cardinal de Bouillon, and we can only speculate on what more he might have accomplished for his old tutor had Le Sauvage's health not collapsed after a few years in Languedoc.[11]

At any rate, it was during the decades between about 1630 to 1680, when the vast majority of Louis XIV's bishops were students, that France's educational institutions finally took the shape they retained until the Revolution. It was then that France became dotted with colleges of various types and, to a lesser degree, with seminaries.[12] The Jesuits, readmitted to France in 1603 and having recovered the colleges they had lost during their expulsion, went on to found new or take over existing ones in provincial towns at an impressive rate. Of course, some towns avoided the Jesuits altogether, either because they already had a college of their own, or preferred to have an Oratorian or 'Doctrinaire' college instead. The rivalry of the religious orders over the running of colleges remained as sharp as ever, and it increased again from the mid-1680s, when the Jesuits finally abandoned their policy of refusing to run seminaries in France. With large numbers of offers to run new or established diocesan seminaries, the Jesuits often devised ways of closely coordinating the running of colleges and seminaries, ensuring that the conventional distinction between the two types of institution was largely blurred for those who passed through the seminary. The later affiliations – theological, pastoral and

9 His passage through the theology faculty, from his supplication for admission to the *primum cursus* in August 1653 to his taking of the *serment* required of new doctors in Sept 1658, can be traced in AN, MM 252, fos 180v, 184v, 187r, 219r, 227r, 238v.

10 His uncle is probably the Jacques Le Sauvage from Coutances diocese who took the baccalaureate in theology in 1636 – AN, MM, 252, fos 25v, 30v, 31r, 38r.

11 For Le Sauvage's career as a whole, see René du Coudray, 'René Le Sauvage, évêque de Lavaur 1630–1677', *Le Pays de Grandville*, 5 (1909), 1–36.

12 Dominique Julia, 'La Constitution du réseau des collèges en France du xviᵉ au xviiiᵉ siècle', in *Objet et Méthodes de l'histoire de la culture* (Budapest-Paris 1982), 73–94. The study by Marie-Madeleine Compère and Domique Julia, *Les Collèges français xviᵉ–xviiiᵉ siècles*, 2 vols (Paris 1984–8) offers an abundance of material on individual colleges and seminaries, but it does not cover northern and eastern France.

institutional – of French bishops were enduringly affected by these developments, though it should not be automatically assumed that the alumni of the Jesuit, Oratorian, Doctrinaire or other colleges were bound to them for life thereafter: some of the Jesuits strongest episcopal opponents, such as Colbert de Croissy of Montpellier, were former students, while alumni of the Oratorians or Doctrinaires were not necessarily Augustinian, let alone pro-Jansenist in theological or pastoral outlook.

With colleges growing so steadily in size and numbers, it is paradoxical that it should be so difficult to discover the patterns of attendance in them by France's future bishops. It seems that in previous generations, when university graduates among the episcopate were distinctly fewer and private tuition was probably more extensive, contemporaries were markedly more curious about the colleges they had frequented. But once university graduates came to dominate its ranks, that curiosity seems to have been displaced in the direction of their university background. It is striking that, under Louis XIV, even bishops testifying about newly nominated colleagues whom they had known since their early years, virtually never bother to mention the colleges they attended – and perhaps attended along with them! – while never failing to mention it if they were contemporaries at university. Such a reflex says a great deal about the shifts in their educational priorities.

Despite this drawback, it is possible to make some comments, on the basis of the very limited information we do possess, much of it second-hand, on the college attendance of Louis XIV's bishops. That a substantial number, perhaps even the majority, attended Jesuit colleges at some point will come as no great surprise, since their colleges increasingly outnumbered those of, say, the Oratory or the Doctrinaires (the latter being largely confined to southern France). However, in cities like Aix, Lyon, Toulouse, Bordeaux, which had universities and where there was a greater choice of college, it may *not* be safe to assume that adolescent clerics were sent as a matter of course to the Jesuit colleges in preference to others. Families often had long-standing connections with particular institutions and would not easily break with them. Many Parisian families maintained such ties to particular colleges of the University. Moreover, some had their own reasons for liking or disliking the Jesuits, and those preferences were probably transmitted in some measure to their sons who would later become bishops.[13] Out of fifty-seven bishops for whom information survives, twenty-eight had been to a Jesuit college, compared with eight for the Oratory – a proportion which may hold for the episcopate as a whole. But bishops educated between the 1620s and the 1650s may not conform to such expectations, since the college network was far from complete by then. The odd bishop frequented schools run by the Benedictines, the Doctrinaires, or the Barnabites. The famous Pierre-Daniel Huet, bishop

13 In 1663 when the Jesuits finally obtained a foothold within Clermont, there was a riot. It was widely known who their main supporters and opponents among the most prominent city families were: one of the strongest opponents was Joseph Girard de la Bournat, father of Antoine, bishop of Poitiers 1698–1702. See Régine Pouzet, *Chronique des Pascal* (Paris 2000), 225–7.

of Avranches, went first to that of the Crosiers in Caen before moving to the local Jesuit school. Above all, for reasons that will soon become apparent, it would be mistaken to ignore the continuing attraction of the colleges that formed part of the University of Paris or, to a lesser extent, Toulouse or Aix, not least because some of those colleges had strong historic connections with particular dioceses.[14]

Only occasionally, as in the case of Huet above, do we have information about individuals who frequented more than one college. But it was probably more and more common as the century progressed, being greatly facilitated by the network of colleges run by the major teaching orders. One of the features of these networks of colleges was the possibility that individual students could be singled out, sometimes at an early age, for their ability or future prospects, and then 'forwarded' to better-placed or better-known institutions. Needless to say, families with strategies tailored to their ambitions were disposed to take advantage of such possibilities. Of course, movement between colleges might have had more mundane reasons, namely that the classes in some colleges did not go far enough for those wishing to continue at university, especially in theology. But the active 'sponsorship' of their brightest pupils (in the broadest sense) by the Jesuits, Oratorians and other orders should not be underestimated. Working out quite how many future bishops may have been treated in this way is, unfortunately, impossible, but the experience of someone like René Le Sauvage shows that the *peregrinatio academica* could begin at a surprisingly early age.

There was another quite important reason for frequenting more than one college. More future bishops than ever before were taking theology degrees in the University of Paris; but to qualify for admission to the Paris theology course, they had to be MAs of the university – and that meant they had to take their classes, and defend their theses in philosophy in the university itself. Enrolments, especially in the humanities, may have shrunk over time in the Paris university colleges because of the competition from the Jesuits of the college of Clermont – renamed Louis le Grand during Louis XIV's own reign – but a combination of family traditions and academic requirements ensured that the university colleges would continue to attract young adolescents with designs on a theology degree. Even pupils of the college of Clermont across the street from the University of Paris had to follow these rules if they wanted Paris theology degrees. Only one of Louis XIV's bishops got away with *not* taking a degree on the grounds that he had studied philosophy and theology with the Jesuits of Paris – but Gilles de la Baume le Blanc, nominated bishop of Nantes in 1668, had the singular advantage of being an uncle of Louis XIV's current mistress, Louise de la Vallière.[15] With approximately 157 MAs from Paris among the 250 bishops nominated by Louis XIV, it is apparent how

---

14 The best guide to these colleges and their educational programmes is the incomplete work of Compère and Julia, *Les Collèges français*.

15 ASV, PC 67, fos 378–84, evidence given to papal nuncio on La Baume de la Vallière's behalf on his nomination to Nantes in 1666.

substantial a proportion of the episcopate obtained at least part of their 'arts' (i.e. philosophy) education there.[16] But the real figure is undoubtedly higher still, since the one just given does not include those, many of them Parisians by birth or residence, who having completed their college studies, went on to take law degrees – or no degree at all.[17]

II

Compared with the problems of tracking the secondary education of Louis XIV's bishops, accounting for their university record appears to pose fewer problems. It should be realised from the outset that even here there are pitfalls awaiting the unwary. For one thing, the information we do possess is often highly laconic, and refers far more to examinations sat, and degrees taken, than to studies actually undertaken. University faculties, beginning with the Paris theology faculty, to which we shall return later, were primarily examining rather than teaching bodies, so their records naturally mirror what they actually did.[18] But for all its limitations, this type of information is the obvious starting point for analysis. Which universities did the bishops frequent? What kinds of university degree did they take? How far did established trends continue? And what was the significance of the changes that may have occurred for the overall profile of the episcopate?

Establishing exactly which universities were frequented by Louis XIV's subjects as distinct from those at which they took their degrees is probably an impossible task, given the absence of matriculation or registration records for most French universities of the day.[19] Glimpses of a particular individual's movements can, of course, be obtained from more purely 'biographical' sources, but the problem of how far one can make general statements based upon them is ultimately insuperable. However, as far as the bishops are concerned, there are good grounds for believing that those who moved from university to university were not especially numerous, and that such movement was also unusual enough to attract comment from their contemporaries. Our sources indicate that only about twenty-five bishops, just 10 per cent of

---

16 This figure is derived from BN, MS Lat 9153–6, which lists MAs from the 1610s to 1706.

17 They would not have taken an MA at the university, so their presence there is not attested by the surviving records.

18 This is the most striking feature of the surviving records of the Paris theology faculty: other questions, sometimes of far greater importance in a general historical sense, appear only infrequently among them – AN, MM 252–5, for the period from 1630 to 1717.

19 The most useful and systematic survey to date has been published as a book-length contribution to Dominique Julia and Jacques Revel, eds, *Les Universités européennes du xviᵉ au xviiiᵉ siècle*, 2 vols (Paris 1984–9), vol ii: *Histoire sociale des populations étudiantes* (Paris 1989), 25–486, 'Les Étudiants et leurs études dans la France moderne'. This vast 'chapter', written by Julia and Revel, is based on a detailed survey of surviving university records and a statistical processing of the figures for enrolment and graduation, where they are available.

the total, frequented more than one university, and that includes cases where it may be suspected that the second university was only frequented for as long as it took to sit the examinations in question! Furthermore, most of the equally few bishops who took more than one degree, tended to take them at the same university rather than moving elsewhere. This picture of 'sedentariness' is reinforced by other changes which were to make the map of university attendance by the episcopate more uniform than previously. Firstly, the fact that Louis XIV only nominated one clear foreigner whom we have already encountered – the Catalan Dominican Vicenç Margarit – to a French diocese, the newly conquered Perpignan, contrasts with the previous experience of the French church down to Mazarin's ministry, when foreign-born clerics, especially Italians who had mostly studied in their own countries, were a regular presence in the episcopate. Three other nominations involved natives of French-speaking frontier regions. Claude Joly and Louis de Bourlemont were both born in Lorraine and, although their careers were almost wholly French, both took their degrees at Pont à Mousson. The franc-comtois François-Joseph Grammont was born a subject of the king of Spain and, although he spent some months at Saint-Sulpice in the 1660s, he followed family tradition by studying and taking his degree at the University of Dole. The second point to note is that scarcely any of Louis's French-born bishops was attracted to a foreign university. Only the Avignon-born François Berton de Crillon was, not unnaturally, tempted by Rome, where he took a doctorate in theology, though he also took the precaution of getting a law degree in his native university.[20] His nephew, Jean-Louis, one of Louis XIV's last episcopal appointments, settled for an Avignon degree. It may well be, of course, that the elder Crillon's Roman university experience was little more than an academic formality arranged while he was sojourning there for unrelated reasons. In their different ways, though, these isolated cases underline just how massively 'French' Louis XIV's bishops were in their education.[21] And that leads naturally to the question – which universities appealed to them most?

The evidence compiled in table 3.1 is based on every surviving mention of universities attended by Louis XIV's bishops, and includes instances where bishops attended two or even three universities. Not that there were many of the latter category – only twenty-five in all, as noted above. However, there is reason to believe that these entries are conservative, given the haphazardness of our sources of information, and they should only be read as orders of magnitude. In any case, what is not in doubt is the attractiveness of Paris as a place of study. Although hardly new, this trend continued to rise sharply: whereas it accounted for about 35 per cent of attendance among bishops nominated from Henri IV to Mazarin, that percentage more than doubled for Louis XIV's episcopate (74.5 per cent). Universities like Bordeaux, Toulouse,

20 ASV, PC 91, fos 530–4, evidence before papal nuncio, 17 Aug 1697.
21 Bergin, *Making*, 231, for the pattern of the preceding period.

Table 3.1   Universities attended by Louis XIV's bishops

Aix	4	Cahors	4	Poitiers	1
Angers	1	Dole	1	Reims	1
Avignon	5	Orléans	5	Toulouse	10
Bordeaux	6	Paris	189	Valence	5
Bourges	17	Pont-à-	2	Unknown	6
Caen	2	Mousson		None	6

Note. This table includes all universities attended, and not just one per individual.

Aix, Avignon and Valence seem to have mainly attracted students from neighbouring provinces, though with such comparatively small returns, trying to account for their record is problematic. Moreover, the presence – however temporary and whatever the reason – of an ecclesiastic in a university city might prompt him to obtain a degree there, since it might be necessary to enable him to take up a post reserved for graduates. This certainly seems to be the only reason why Angers and Poitiers, with just one graduate each, figure in the list of universities attended; one of Caen's two graduates was a Provençal who was briefly in the service of the bishop of Bayeux.[22] Similar cases could doubtless be found elsewhere, and a group of 250 individuals, especially of the kind being considered here, probably does not reflect the general patterns of university attendance.[23] Among the provincial universities which made any show of resisting Paris, only Toulouse and Bourges reached double figures. Orléans declined further, not merely because it was possible to take the degree in civil as well as canon law in Paris after 1679, but also because, as we shall see presently, law studies themselves attracted fewer and fewer future bishops. The figures given in the table for Bourges, Cahors and Valence, none of which had attracted more than a few students each in the preceding period, also reflect the increased demand for theology degrees.

The dominance of Paris is so overwhelming that it seems to need little additional commentary. In fact, that dominance is probably under-represented by the figures, since it is almost certain that some of those bishops who are recorded only as having taken law degrees at Orléans before 1679 or

22 Jean Gaillard, bishop of Apt (1671–75), was archdeacon in Bayeux during the 1660s, and Caen was within the diocese: ASV, PC 70, fos 67–8, a certificate showing that he obtained his baccalaureate in theology at Caen, 30 Jan 1666. The other Caen graduate was Huet, bishop of Avranches, who was a native of the town.

23 Julia and Revel, 'Les Étudiants et leurs études dans la France moderne' is a helpful attempt to weigh the wider factors which determined university attendance in France as a whole and across the 'higher faculties' of law, medicine and theology. See also Laurence Brockliss, *French Higher Education in the Seventeenth and Eighteenth Centuries* (Oxford 1987), ch 1, with comment on both attendance and provision of teaching within universities and, later, the university-affiliated seminaries. Patrick Ferté has published the first of several volumes arising from his research into the southern universities for the early modern period – *Répértoire géographique des étudiants du Midi de la France (1561–1793)*, vol i (Toulouse 2002).

theology degrees at Bourges, Cahors and Valence, had studied mainly in Paris and had hardly set foot in the universities of which they were officially graduates. Already evident for the preceding period, the trend for provincial families, especially of the nobility, to send their sons to college and university in Paris in preference to their local ones, continued strongly since, as we saw in the previous chapter, native Parisians were not more markedly numerous among France's bishops than in the past. The advantages of mixing with the sons of the kingdom's political and social elites were not lost on the families involved, while the question of how significant the networking engaged in by future bishops during their university years will be addressed later in this study. And further reasons for the attractiveness of Paris will emerge in the discussion of the degrees taken by bishops.

III

Measured by the degrees they held, the academic achievement of the bishops of our period can be viewed as a broad spectrum – at one end, the bishop with no degree at all; at the other, the bishop with two (one in law, one in theology) degrees, and which in turned ranged from the baccalaureate to the doctorate. It may seem peculiar to begin with those without any degree at all, but it does shed light on some wider issues. To begin with, the number of bishops without a degree was extremely low – only six in all. It is *likely* that there was one other, the Benedictine Pierre Marion, bishop of Gap, for whom we have no information at all.[24] We have already encountered one of the six being considered here, La Baume le Blanc of Nantes. Of the others, three were members of religious orders whose rules did not permit members to take degrees, and the remaining two were Oratorians, both of them renowned as preachers, Soanen and Mascaron.[25] Oratorians were not regulars who shunned university degrees but, as we shall see later, their own programmes of study were so highly developed that members could be called upon to *teach* theology in their colleges even if they held no degree in the subject. Of the six non-graduates, only one, La Baume, could be regarded as a 'natural' candidate for the mitre: he was the nephew of his predecessor at Nantes and had Bourbon blood in his veins as well as being a relative of Louise de la Vallière. None of the others remotely enjoyed the advantages of birth that he did.

With 243 known graduates out of 250 bishops, there is little doubt that the terms of the Concordat and of the Council of Trent about bishops needing

24 One eighteenth-century source claims that during his years as a Benedictine, he attended the University of Angers *incognito* and took a law degree there: AD Hautes-Alpes, G 1533, 'Histoire des évêques de Gap'. But there is no mention of a degree in any of the seventeenth-century sources relating to his episcopate. One problem is that the *de vita et moribus* enquiry on Marion no longer exists in the Vatican archives.

25 The others were Bacoué of Glandèves, Allart of Vence, Roger of Lombez.

to have university degrees were being fully respected under Louis XIV. This is highlighted in an unexpected manner by a category of bishop not unrelated to those we have just seen – namely, those who had not taken a degree during their normal time of study, however one defines it, but who hastened to do so just *after* their episcopal nomination. There were eleven of them in all, although there is reason to believe that a few degrees taken only weeks *before* a nomination were probably the result of some kind of prior knowledge of an impending royal decision.[26] In strict logic, of course, the eleven individuals under consideration should be recorded alongside those without a degree, since the decision to nominate them was evidently taken without regard to the lack of a university qualification. But strict logic may not help the historian much here and it is more instructive to turn the question on its head: why did eleven of the seventeen royal nominees without degrees decide to take one, so that by the time they were proposed for confirmation in the papal consistory, they would conform to the same rules as everyone else? The simplest answer may be that they had been 'advised' to do so, probably by the king's confessor, and that was advice which it would have been perilous to ignore. But it is equally likely that they themselves realised that they should imitate what others before them had done in their situation, and seek to take the necessary examinations. To do so even when it no longer seemed to have much point was itself a clear acknowledgement of the force of the requirements for a bishop, even if it could not entirely suppress unflattering comment by their contemporaries about bishops 'who had not studied' – a far stronger insult than we might imagine in an age which French bishops were intent on claiming full powers to define and defend sound doctrine. Indeed, it is also probable that similar considerations convinced a small number of incoming bishops to 'upgrade' their existing degrees – whether from baccalaureate to licence or licence to doctorate – at the time of their nomination.[27]

Equally revealing are the bishops on the very opposite end of the spectrum, those with more than one degree, which invariably meant some combination of law and theology. Their numbers were also relatively limited, no more than nineteen according to the available sources. Spread relatively thinly across the period as a whole, it is difficult to connect them to a particular development or to gauge the motives of those taking two degrees, sometimes at considerable intervals. They may well have included a few compulsive degree-collectors, of course, although only three of them are recorded as holding

26   François Hébert, curé of Versailles, was one of those taking his degree during the weeks after their nomination: given the *brevet* for Agen at Christmas 1703, he took his theology degree in Bourges in Jan 1704.

27   Aube de Roquemartine of Saint-Paul-Trois-Châteaux took his baccalaureate in canon law at Avignon in 1644, and returned there in 1675 to take his licence, a few months after his nomination as bishop: ASV, PC 75, fos 253–5, for copies of his degree diplomas. One of Louis XIV's later nominations, Villeroy of Lyon, took first place in the Paris theology licence of 1702, but only took his doctorate after his nomination to Lyon in 1714.

double doctorates. One of the latter, Mathieu d'Hervault, seems to have taken his law doctorate in 1681 purely so that he could take up the post of Auditor of the Roman Rota *already* offered him by Louis XIV.[28] But the most frequent combination of degrees that we find among this group is the baccalaureate in theology, mostly from Paris, and a higher-ranking degree in law, either from Paris or another university. Such a combination is not as accidental as it might seem. The Paris theology licence in particular could be an intimidating prospect, and large numbers of those who began theology there would break off after the baccalaureate examinations before commencing the highly intensive two-year licence cycle. But since the baccalaureate itself was not a full-blown degree, despite its holders being considered 'graduates' for the purpose of obtaining benefices reserved for graduates, there *was* a genuine incentive to round it out with a licence or doctorate in law, often canon law. Moreover, the evidence suggests that this decision was more likely to be taken by clerics from robe families, who might either be tempted by certain offices in the parlements and sovereign courts reserved for clerics, or be pressed by their families to take up 'lay' offices before they took 'major' clerical orders.[29] So it is hardly surprising to find familiar names on this list – Thomassin, Colbert, Maupeou, Foresta, Desmarets, Turgot, though it should be added that it also includes a Béthune, a Montpezat and two Matignon brothers, all of more aristocratic stripe.

However, the vast majority of the Ludovican episcopate settled for a *single* degree in either law or theology. It is unnecessary at this point to rehearse the long-standing debates about which of these degrees was more suitable for a bishop. Neither the Concordat of Bologna nor the Council of Trent attempted to settle the issue once and for all, thus leaving it to individual clerics to make their own choices. It was, consequently, influences or pressures at work within the contemporary French church itself which would determine the preferences of each generation as they made their way through university. In previous centuries, to the extent that bishops had taken degrees at all, they were more likely to be in law than in theology. But by the middle decades of the seventeenth century, the historic dominance of the lawyers seemed to be under serious threat; theology graduates became increasingly numerous from the 1630s onwards, reaching parity with the lawyers among the bishops nominated in the decade immediately before Louis XIV assumed the reins of government.[30] Would the trend be sustained or reversed under the new regime?

28 AN, O¹ 25, fo 67, 6 March 1681, 'dispense d'estude en faveur du sr abbé d'Hervault pour estre licencié en droit'. AN, MM 1120, Catalogue of Paris law graduates, 1679–90, pp 5–6, 9/10 March 1681, for degrees taken by 'noble' Mathieu Isoré, abbé d'Hervault, doctor of theology of Paris, 'recently designated' as Auditor of Rota by Louis XIV.
29 For example, Maupeou of Castres and Maurel of Saint-Paul-Trois-Châteaux, were both sons of robe families, and in Maupeou's case taking a law degree enabled him to succeed an elder brother who died suddenly while holding the office of *avocat-général* of the *grand conseil*.
30 See Bergin, *Making*, 235–40.

Table 3.2   Episcopal graduates by decade of nomination

Decade	All noms	All degrees taken	No of graduates	All law graduates	Law-only graduates	Law as % all noms	Law as % all degrees	Theology degrees	% all noms	% all degrees
1660s	35	36	33	10	7	28.57	27.78	26	74.20	72.22
1670s	55	56	52	21	17	38.18	37.50	35	63.60	62.50
1680s	44	47	43	12	9	27.27	25.53	35	77.70	74.47
1690s	42	42	41	7	4	16.67	16.67	36	90.20	85.71
1700s	45	47	45	5	3	11.11	10.64	42	91.30	89.36
1710s	29	32	29	4	1	13.79	12.50	28	96.50	87.50
Total	250	260	243	59	41	23.60	22.69	202	80.80	77.69

Table 3.3   Episcopal graduates by decade of birth

Decade	Noms	All grads	Law grads	Law only graduates	% of noms	% of grads	Theology graduates	Theology % of noms	% of graduates
1590s	1	1	0	0	0	0	1	100.00	100.00
1600s	6	5	1	1	16.67	20.00	4	66.67	80.00
1610s	11	7	2	2	18.18	28.57	5	45.45	71.43
1620s	17	17	9	6	52.94	52.94	11	64.71	64.71
1630s	44	43	19	17	43.18	44.19	26	59.09	60.47
1640s	56	55	16	8	28.57	29.09	47	83.93	85.45
1650s	58	58	8	3	13.79	13.79	54	93.10	93.10
1660s	39	39	4	4	10.26	10.26	36	92.31	92.31
1670s	14	14	0	0	0	0	14	100.00	100.00
1680s	4	4	0	0	0	0	4	100.00	100.00
Total	250	243	59	41	23.60	22.69	202	80.80	77.69

The figures in tables 3.2 and 3.3, which compare the 'scores' of law and theology among the episcopate from different perspectives, make it abundantly clear that the trend just noted not merely continued under Louis XIV, but that by the later decades of the reign, the rout of the lawyers was virtually complete. During this entire period, forty-one 'law-only' graduates became bishops; the total number of law graduates rises to fifty-nine when we include those who had a law and well as a theology degree – which gives a minimum of 16.4 per cent, a maximum of 23.6 per cent of the total. Either way, the overall picture is clear enough, though for our present purposes it is the law-only graduates who are of primary interest. The decline of the lawyers is visible as early as the 1660s when their share of nominations suddenly slipped far more sharply than in previous decades. During the 1670s, which boasted the highest numbers of appointments for any decade of Louis's reign, law graduates seemed to manage something of a rally, but this did not remotely reach previous percentages and in any case it proved to be a prelude to a more dramatic collapse. After the 1690s, incoming bishops with only a law degree in their curriculum vitae were becoming as rare as hen's teeth. The last law-only graduate to join their ranks under Louis XIV stands out incongruously in a sea of theologians: Joseph de Mesgrigny, son of a *premier président* of the parlements of Aix and Rouen, was nominated to Grasse in 1711, but he was an elderly friar who had taken his canon law degree in Paris as long ago as 1672, almost as a precaution, on the eve of his entry to the Capuchins![31] Indeed, on detailed inspection, it could be said that most of the relatively few law-only graduates nominated since the mid-1680s were in some way exceptional. Some, as already noted, took their law degrees in a hurry after their nomination; others took them in mid-career, like the Sulpician Bazan de Flamanville, who took his law degree while temporarily in the service of the bishop of Angers, and for purely utilitarian purposes.[32]

No less suggestive are the results of observing these figures in terms not of the chronology of royal nominations, but of the age-cohorts of the bishops themselves (table 3.3). The oldest of Louis XIV's bishops was born in 1594, the youngest in 1685. In between, the big battalions belong to the 1640s and 1650s, with the 1630s and 1660s in strong supporting roles. Bishops born in these particular decades would, therefore, dominate the educational profile of the episcopate from thirty to fifty years later. It is clear from the table that the last 'generation' of bishops with a substantial number of law degrees was the one born in the 1630s. Now, if law graduates were to retain a signifi-cant presence in the episcopate of Louis XIV's middle years, they had to be numerous among those born in the 1640s and 1650s, yet it is precisely at this point that their numbers start to really collapse: if represented on a graph, the two sets of figures would be moving in radically different directions. Those bishops born in the 1650s and 1660s only comprised a handful of lawyers, those of the 1670s and 1680s not a single one.

Finally, the law graduates in question were, as table 3.4 shows, very unequally distributed among France's law faculties, largely reflecting the pat-terns of attendance we have already discussed. Orléans, the one law faculty that in the past would have challenged the dominance of Paris, comes a very poor second after the capital, followed by Avignon and Toulouse. Whether we look at law-only graduates separately or along with law-and-theology graduates, the pattern is the same: Paris provides more of them than all the other universities combined. That dominance is also reflected in the fact that bishops taking a canon law degree easily outnumbered those taking the one

---

31 ASV, PC 101a, fos 123v–24v, *de vita et moribus* enquiry, at which Archbishop Montmorin of Vienne testified that Mesgrigny became a Capucin in May 1672. AN, MM 1116, fos 33r, 34r, law degrees, 4 and 6 Aug 1672.

32 ASV, PC 89, fo 226, *de vita et moribus* enquiry, testimony of Gaston de Noailles, future bishop of Châlons, 22 Oct 1695.

Table 3.4   Universities where bishops took law degrees

PARIS	31
Orléans	5
Avignon	4
Toulouse	3
Aix	2
Others	7
Unknown	7
Total	59

in civil and canon law (*in utroque jure*). Given that most of these degrees were taken before the teaching of civil law and the awarding of degrees *in utroque jure* by the Paris law faculty had really got going, the figures underscore another important trend which we shall observe in the next chapter – the continuing clericalisation of the world from which bishops were chosen. Fewer and fewer of them took the law degree (*in utroque jure*) that would have been required to hold a royal secular office. By choosing canon law for their degree, even those who were steering clear of theology were nevertheless committing themselves to a career in the church.

IV

On the flipside of the rout of the lawyers stands the triumph of the theologians, and its consequences would be far-reaching. If there was a time when theology finally became the 'queen of the sciences' as far as entry to the episcopate was concerned, this was it. Whereas in the 1620s Richelieu had been hard put to find a doctor of theology among the bishops who could engage in the stormy debates of the theology faculty, Louis XIV was faced with an embarrassment of riches.[33] Indeed, by the time of the king's death in September 1715, all but six of France's 121 sitting bishops were theologians by training, even if some of them had also stopped to take a law degree en route.[34] The wider significance of this shift can be highlighted by comparing developments in France with those in Castile and León, where for the entire early modern period from 1556 to 1834, the theologians were only marginally more numerous in the episcopate than the lawyers – 53 to 45 per cent respectively. But even this aggregate cloaks as much as it reveals, since the highest proportion of theologians in the Castilian episcopate (60 per cent) was registered

33 Laurence Brockliss, 'Richelieu, Education and the State', in Joseph Bergin and Laurence Brockliss, eds, *Richelieu and his Age* (Oxford 1992), 252–4.
34 Three dioceses fell vacant in early-mid 1715 and nominations were *not* made to them by Louis XIV.

under Philip II, falling back to about 45 per cent under Louis XIV's counter-part, Charles II, before finally returning under the French Bourbon monarchy in the eighteenth century to something close to the favour they enjoyed under Philip II.[35]

The outline of the quite different experience of the French episcopate will be evident from the contents of tables 3.2 and 3.3. It should be noted that the overall numbers and percentages for theology graduates among the epis-copate include those 'double-degree' graduates whom we have already counted as taking a law degree. But counting them again among the theologians does not really misrepresent the proportions between law and theology, whereas *not* to count them would constitute a genuine distortion: all the evidence to hand indicates that those with two degrees spent far more time engaged in theology than in law studies, even if the theology degree in question was just the baccalaureate, especially from Paris.

The entries in tables 3.2 and 3.3 show how the dominance of the theolo-gians over the lawyers took shape. As suggested earlier, these figures reflect a growing demand among the French clergy for theology degrees. Even before seminaries affiliated to university theology faculties began to inflate the numbers of those holding theology degrees generally, it seems that most of France's theology faculties witnessed an expansion in numbers during the seventeenth century, although that expansion can usually only be measured indirectly, via the number of those who graduated.[36] The Paris theology faculty clearly did so (even though the other faculties there did not, it seems), and the numbers of bachelors of theology rose inexorably from the 1640s onwards.[37] Those taking the licence examinations easily tripled between 1630 and 1714, rising from thirty-six to 131, while a high proportion of the licentiates went on to take the doctorate.[38] As the figures in table 3.5 show, the dominant position of Paris stands out, with all of the other universities between them only managing to account for just 25.8 per cent of the theol-ogy graduates. At first sight, Paris may seem less all-conquering in theology than in law. Missing from these graduation figures are those future bishops who took their MA in Paris, perhaps embarked on the study of theology there, and either completed the *tentativa* examination (which entitled them to the baccalaureate) or, before they got that far, moved sideways in search of a law (usually canon law) degree. An alternative solution for some was to resort to the theology faculties of Bourges, Cahors or Valence after completing the bac-calaureate in Paris, and to obtain the licence or doctorate there. The Bourges

35   Maximiliano Barrio, *Les Obispos de Castilla y León durante en antiguo régimen (1556–1834). Estudio socio-económico* (Madrid 2000), 65–7, esp tables 8–10.

36   See the analysis and data in Julia and Revel, 'Les Étudiants et leurs études dans la France moderne', ch 3, 191–241.

37   Jacques M Grès-Gayer, 'Tradition et modernité. La réforme des études en Sorbonne 1673–1715', *Revue d'Histoire de l'Église de France*, 88 (2002), 343.

38   These figures are taken from the lists compiled in BN, MS Lat 15440. See also Julia and Revel, 'Les Étudiants et leurs études', 375–6, 450–3.

Table 3.5   Theology graduates among the episcopate

Decade	Noms	Theology graduates	Paris theology graduates	Other universities	Theology % of all noms	Paris as % of theology graduates	Paris as % of all noms
1660s	35	26	15	11	74.29	57.69	42.86
1670s	55	35	32	3	63.64	91.43	58.18
1680s	44	35	27	8	79.55	77.14	61.36
1690s	42	36	30	6	85.71	83.33	71.43
1700s	45	42	25	17	93.33	59.52	55.56
1710s	29	28	19	9	96.55	67.86	65.52
Total	250	202	148	54	80.80	73.27	59.20

theology faculty seems to have been as lax as its law counterpart at Orléans, since at one time it even allowed candidates to present themselves before a Paris-based Jesuit who was a doctor 'agrégé' of Bourges in order to obtain the baccalaureate or the degree of 'external' doctor.[39] It seems likely that some of our bishops took this latter option – particularly mid-career clerics without degrees, but whose nomination to the episcopate made quick remedial action necessary. The fact that Bourges contributed nearly one in ten of the theology graduates to become bishops under Louis XIV, and that it was still attracting them in the latter decades of the reign, seems due mainly to its function as a 'refuge' for many of those unable or unwilling to take their degrees in Paris. Valence may have served a similar function, especially towards the end of the reign. Yet, overall, only a small percentage of future bishops who had commenced their studies in Paris availed themselves of this relatively painless option – mindful, perhaps, that it might not enhance their reputation, and that it was in any case outweighed by the advantage of graduating as a licentiate or doctor from Paris itself. These impressions are borne out by the evidence of the accompanying table which deserves brief comment. As early as the mid-1670s, Paris theology graduates came close to monopolising episcopal nominations of *theology* graduates, but their grip relaxed somewhat in the next two decades, while remaining relatively stable as a proportion of the overall number of all bishops being nominated in those decades. It is from the mid-1690s onwards that a second gap opens up: for about a decade, Parisian theology graduates slipped again, at a time when episcopal nominations were still rising and theologians were virtually monopolising them. The gap in question was filled mainly by theology graduates of Bourges and Valence before Parisian theologians regained some of their earlier dominance in the last few years of the reign.

39   Julia and Revel, 'Les Étudiants et leurs études', 441.

Aggregates like these, however, do not tell the full story. Even more inter-esting is the way in which clusters of Paris theology licentiates became bishops. From the mid-1630s to the mid-1650s, no more than one or two graduates per licence cycle did so, even though the number of licentiates graduating was steadily rising into the fifties. But from 1658, when four future bishops graduated, things began to change markedly, and until the early 1690s as many as eight to eleven graduates per cycle went on to become bishops. Between 1658 and 1692 inclusive, 104 future bishops took the Paris theology licentiate, a period when the total number of graduates per cycle oscillated between seventy-five and 120. The most productive of all licences of the period was that of 1666 when eleven out of the eighty-two graduates became bishops, followed by 1674 (ten out of eighty-eight) and 1684 (nine out of 107). Naturally, these proportions fall off from the mid-1690s onwards, given the lead-time between taking degrees and being nominated a bishop, but there is every reason to believe that the cohorts of Paris theology gradu-ates from the last twenty years of Louis XIV's reign were no less prominent among new bishops under his successor.

Less easy to establish is how well these future bishops performed academ-ically. The only indicator we possess is the official rank-order for each licence in Paris over the period as a whole. The bulk of the 134 future bishops con-cerned were well scattered through each list, so the top and bottom places of each list may repay closer scrutiny. Thirty-two of the 134 were ranked in the first five places, and among them sixteen actually came first. However, there is more than a suggestion that when a first-ranked licentiate was called Le Tellier (twice), Colbert (twice), Noailles (twice), Estrées or Beauvillier, the faculty was continuing a well established practice of acknowledging social and political distinction and, therefore, that real intellectual distinction belonged to the second- or third-placed graduates. But this cannot always be clearly demonstrated, since on other occasions the top-ranked graduates were of no such eminence, and were listed well ahead of infinitely better-connected fellow graduates. This impression is borne out by a look at those placed among the *last* five of each licence. The overall total is virtually identical – thirty-one – and the tail-enders seem to cluster together most clearly during the licences of the 1660s and 1670s, when for several cycles, the lowest-ranked regularly contained one or more future bishops. Indeed, the single largest group – eleven in all – among this cohort consists of those ranked last, and there is no reason to presume that questions of status counted for as much at this end of the scale. For example, the 1664 licence contained five future bishops out of seventy-eight graduates: the highest ranked of them came in seventy-third, while the others filled the last four places. Elsewhere those ranked last include men with names like Bouthillier de Chavigny, Clermont-Tonnerre, Potier de Gesvres, du Cambout de Coislin, Saint-Georges, Étampes de Valançay, whose social distinction might have earned them a better ranking. Statistics like this may suggest that some, especially well-born bishops, were neither bright enough nor, more likely, assiduous enough to do more than scrape through their licence. The faculty's frequent complaints about absence and negligence may well refer to students like them with other objectives to pursue along-side their studies. Certainly, some contemporaries questioned their mastery of theological questions, few more acidly than Fénelon, a doctor of Cahors who may well have been settling a score with some of his Paris-educated colleagues. But any verdict based on such sources, negative as well as positive, should be treated with care. The great intellectuals of the upper clergy under Louis XIV, such as Huet of Avranches and Fénelon himself, were not products of the Paris theology faculty at all, and the same is true of its great episcopal 'orateurs sacrés', Bossuet and one or two others excepted. It is also sobering to discover that Antoine Arnauld, probably the most prolific theologian of his day, only took fiftieth place out of fifty-five in the 1640 licence.[40]

With Paris dwarfing its rivals, it is worth attempting an internal analysis of its theology graduates among Louis XIV's bishops. Only fourteen 'mere' bachelors of theology are to be found among them. No fewer than six of the fourteen also took either a licence or doctorate in law which, as suggested earlier, may denote an unwillingness on their part to face the challenge of the Paris theology licence. This switch may also have been motivated by a desire to avoid being caught up in the gallican or Jansenist issues hotly debated there, especially in the early decades of the reign.[41] Four out of every five Paris theology graduates among the bishops pursued the theology course to the doctorate itself, and the tendency to do so increased significantly as the reign progressed: most of the 'mere' bachelors or licentiates are to be found among the bishops of the early decades. The reasons for this trend were not purely academic, since the *épreuves* for the doctorate were largely a formality com-pared to those of the licence. One traditional reason for not taking it was that it was expensive, beyond the reach of graduates with limited means. There is, obviously, no way to fathom the intentions of those who had just completed their licence or exactly how they viewed taking the doctorate, but it would be naive to rule out the growth of peer pressure among such a self-consciously elite 'society'. Of course, not all took the doctorate in the months following the licence as they were entitled, and some even waited for several years before doing so. Yet the figures seem to speak for themselves: for the vast majority, the doctorate was desirable, it would open doors of many kinds to its holders, and they seized the chance. There are few signs that the failure, or refusal, on the part of future bishops to take it was based on lack of financial resources. As the case of René Le Sauvage mentioned earlier suggests, even families of relatively modest means could muster the resources to finance their younger sons' studies, and the prospect of having a doctor of the Paris theology faculty

40   These figures and rankings are all taken from BN, MS Lat 15440.
41   Jacques M Grès-Gayer, *Le Jansénisme en Sorbonne 1643–1656* (Paris 1996), 282.

among their number was incentive enough to find additional funds for taking the doctorate itself. It also seems clear that the prestige of the Paris theology doctorate had been rising since Louis XIII's time, not least because sons of major noble families proved willing to take it. We have already encountered the Cardinal de Bouillon studying in Paris for his theology degree while still known as the duc d'Albret. Within a generation, he would be succeeded by clerics with august names like La Trémoïlle, Lorraine, Estrées, Polignac, Grimaldi, Beauvillier, Rohan-Soubise to name but a few; their presence, along with that of sons of royal ministers, contributed enormously to transforming the faculty's image and attractiveness. This in turn may be one of several reasons why, entitled to call themselves doctors of theology 'of the faculty of Paris' where everyone else was simply a 'doctor of theology', they gradually began to resemble an ecclesiastical aristocracy.

There are many signs that the Paris faculty itself was not entirely at ease with this change in its student body. It could hardly deal with blue-blooded abbés, whose ambitions might even include the cardinal's hat, in the same way as it traditionally dealt with its more socially modest bourgeois students. The more socially elevated students were apt to ask for dispensations from the normal regime of study or sequence of examinations as laid down by the faculty's statutes – ill health, particular disabilities, urgent affairs elsewhere being the most common grounds. Refusing them was difficult, especially when there was ministerial or royal intervention on their behalf.[42] But then leading churchmen, especially the archbishop of Paris, could behave in identical manner where their own nephews, relatives or protegés were involved.[43] Overt external intervention seems to have occurred much less than in the law faculty, and the theology faculty, traditionally very touchy about its internal autonomy and making its decisions by debate and ballot, did not welcome it. Some rule-bending did obviously follow, but the faculty would then make it clear that this had only happened because of intervention from on high (implying that favours would not have been given on the merits of the case alone), or would ask that future interventions be confined to genuine cases.[44]

---

42 AN, MM 253, fo 45v, 1 Dec 1663, petition from Bouillon to be allowed to skip one year of study so he could enter the *primum cursus* leading to the baccalaureate, with reference to his glorious name and titles; fos 176v, 5 June 1675, petition to faculty by Colbert's son, Jacques-Nicolas, to be allowed to join licence without having to take outstanding examinations (and references to his birth and status); fos 177v–8r, 1 Aug 1675, J-N Colbert's thanks the faculty for its decision. It had also agreed that his *tentativa* would be presided over by Archbishop Harlay of Paris! Other examples are cited in Grès-Gayer, 'Tradition et modernité', 383, n 372.

43 AN, MM 253, 31v, 5 Feb 1663, Archbishop Péréfixe intervened to enable Charles-Maurice Le Tellier to skip examinations so he could enter the licence beginning in Jan 1664. On the same day, a similar petition was made (not by Péréfixe) on behalf of André de Marillac, with reference being made to his illustrious name and previous family actions.

44 AN, MM 254, fo 337, text of 'supplique' to be submitted to king, early 1693, complaining about the deleterious effects of dispensations on studies and orders.

The growing attractiveness of the Paris faculty had other effects, too, which are important for a broader understanding of the episcopate. As the numbers of licentiates per licence cycle who went on to become bishops suggests, the Paris faculty was becoming a distant precursor of the *grandes écoles*. In 1681, Le Tellier of Reims described it simply as 'l'école du royaume'.[45] Those emerging from the same licence would remind others of the common bond between them decades later.[46] The opportunities for networking and developing life-long friendships there must have been considerable, though subsequent divisions on issues like Jansenism should caution us against making easy assumptions about their solidarity in all circumstances. Even closer contacts could derive from membership of particular colleges of the University, especially as only a few colleges presented students for theology degrees. The strongest bonds seem to have been generated by the college of Navarre: smaller than the Sorbonne, which was a theology-only college, Navarre housed students from their early teens through to the theology licence, which may be the real reason for the strength of the ties between former Navarristes; the fact that it was known for favouring 'Augustinian' theology was also important in an age of renewed religious controversy. Admission to the fellowship (*société*) of the college of the Sorbonne seems to have had a similar bonding effect among other Paris theology graduates. But it would be wrong to imagine that these bonds were confined to one's student contemporaries: significant inter-generational ties also developed, involving distinguished former members of the colleges who retained close connections with it. It may be misleading to cite someone like Bossuet as typical of anything, but he remained heavily involved with his college of Navarre after completing his doctorate there in the mid-1650s. For almost fifty years thereafter, he returned regularly to preside over examinations and theses defences.[47] His willingness to do so was an honour for the students in question: it was patronage asked for and granted, and he was sometimes able to secure positions in royal service for some of them.

Furthermore, young students with attractive career prospects ahead of them could readily draw either existing graduates or fellow-students into their circle – as we saw in the case of Bouillon and Le Sauvage. When Colbert, in typical fashion, wanted to ensure that his son, Jacques-Nicolas, would come through his licence without difficulty, he recruited the brightest graduates he could to act as a collective mentor to his son.[48] And when men like Colbert

---

45   Quoted by Grès-Gayer, 'Tradition et modernité', 341.
46   As appears frequently in evidence they gave to the papal nuncio on behalf of newly nominated bishops and scattered through ASV, PC, vols 63 to 105.
47   See Bosuet, *Correspondance*, ed Charles Urbain and Eugène Levesque, 15 vols (Paris 1909–25), xv, 431–516, 'Chronologie de la vie de Bossuet', for the evidence. He was due to preside over a *tentativa* (baccalaureate) defence by abbé Colbert de Maulevrier in Jan 1704, only months before his death (516).
48   Eugène Levesque, 'Liste des élèves de l'ancien séminaire de Saint-Sulpice', *Bulletin trimestriel des*

fils became bishops, they frequently called upon these contemporaries to serve them in key administrative posts such as grand-vicar, *théologal* and *official*, or simply as private theologians.[49] Nobody, as far as we know, went quite as far as the bishop of Limoges who, on hearing of the future Cardinal de Noailles's performance in the licence, wrote to Louis XIV asking him to nominate Noailles as his successor![50] In an age when bishops found themselves publishing more pastoral instructions and the like than ever before, their need for theologians more professional than themselves grew apace, and individual bishops were sometimes accused, particularly during the Jansenist crisis of the end of the reign, of being excessively dependent on these backroom mentors.[51]

Contacts with reigning bishops also became easier to establish when more and more of the bishops were themselves doctors of the faculty. It is notable how often, when sons of ministers, courtiers, or great nobles generally took their theology examinations, bishops who were doctors of the faculty either themselves sought, or were asked to preside on the day.[52] In some cases, it may well have been a tactic to ensure that neither the distinguished candidate nor the president would be embarrassed by the outcome of the disputations. Similarly, bishops on business in Paris would also attend particular examinations and even if they were not necessarily involved in promoting the candidates in question, they could spread news of their achievements. Cardinal de Retz agreed to preside at the baccalaureate examination (the *tentativa*) of the future Cardinal Le Camus in November 1652, at a point during the Fronde when it might be imagined he had other things to preoccupy him.[53] Such things cut both ways, as students of illustrious birth could bestow honour on those who presided at their examinations. An early example was that of the prince of Conti, enrolled in the theology faculty in the mid-1640s when he was being groomed for a church career. Four bishops were on hand to take charge of his preliminary examination enabling him formally to *begin* the study of theology; had he persevered, even as far as the baccalaureate, one can imagine the competition to participate in examining

anciens élèves de Saint-Sulpice (1905–7), nos 1350–1. I used a separately paginated copy from the Saint-Sulpice library, but as entries are actually numbered in the list, references to particular individuals by numbers rather than by pages are easier to check. Even at Saint-Sulpice, Jacques-Nicolas Colbert was accompanied by his doctor of theology, abbé Feu.

49 The *théologal* was the canon-theologian of the cathedral, with responsibilities for educating the clergy, preaching and so on, while the *official* was entrusted with exercising the bishop's jurisdiction in the episcopal court. Pierre Clément, later bishop of Périgueux, was a member of the Compagnie de Saint-Sulpice who accompanied Colbert to Rouen and eventually became his vicar-general in 1691. See the notice on him below.

50 BN, MS Fr 23506, fo 32v, *Nouvelles ecclésiastiques*, n d, but late 1675 to early 1676.

51 For the dependence of Le Tellier of Reims, at least in his early years, on his doctor, Antoine Faure, see Lesaulnier, *Port-Royal insolite*, 524.

52 Evidence for this is scattered across the 'conclusions' of the meetings of the theology faculty in AN, MM 252–5.

53 AN, MM 252, fo 174r.

him.[54] Lastly, the practice of students dedicating their theses to 'the great and the good' of church and state, already visible under Richelieu and Mazarin, continued to grow, and offered a more numerous openings for those seeking future patrons.[55]

V

The final member of the trinity to be discussed in this chapter, seminaries, resembles the first (colleges) more than the second (universities) in its elusiveness. By Louis XIV's time, the slow-moving Catholic Reformation in France had spawned an impressive number of seminaries of various types, yet it was nowhere stated that frequenting one was a prerequisite for entry to the episcopate: the French church was still far more concerned to improve seminary provision for the mass of the lower clergy, and there were still enormous discrepancies in the obligations of attendance imposed on them from one diocese to another. Those involved in founding seminaries never consciously intended to create one specially designed for bishops and other high-ranking clergy, though a handful of such elite institutions did come to exist over time.[56] But as we saw in relation to university degrees, wider trends could envelop, however unintentionally, those who in one way or another belonged to the clerical milieux from which bishops were selected. For one thing, as Louis XIV's reign progressed, more bishops were refusing to ordain clerics from their dioceses as priests, deacons or subdeacons unless they had spent a stipulated amount of time in their diocesan seminary, and they were prepared to deny them the *lettres dimissoires* which would enable them to be ordained elsewhere. What is more surprising, however, is that students of the theology faculty of Paris, and no doubt elsewhere, also found themselves being subjected to such conditions for the first time. Action of this particular kind – or the threat of it – may only have been taken by a minority of rigorist bishops, but by the 1680s they included highly reputable figures like Cardinal Grimaldi of Aix and Bishop Coislin of Orléans, a royal favourite.[57] How fully

54   AN, MM 252, fo 140r, 2 July 1646.
55   V Meyer, 'Les Thèses, leur soutenance et leurs illustrations dans les universités françaises de l'ancien régime', *Mélanges de la Bibliothèque de la Sorbonne*, 12 (1993), 87–109. This subject deserves further study, not least because an engraved thesis dedicated to the king himself or his ministers was extremely expensive to produce.
56   See Dominique Julia, 'L'Éducation des ecclésiastiques en France aux xviiᵉ et xviiiᵉ siècles', in *Problèmes d'Histoire de l'Éducation* (Collection de l'École Française de Rome, 104) (Rome 1988), 141–205.
57   AN, MM 253, fo 214, 2 Jan 1681 (Orléans); fo 215r, 1 March 1681 (Aix). Candidates caught unprepared by such demands would petition the faculty to dispense them from *its* demands on the understanding that they would take the orders as soon as they could after finishing their studies. One such candidate in 1681 was Jean Le Normand, native of Orléans, bishop of Evreux in 1711.

they enforced their policies in respect of students in theology faculties it is impossible to say, but as far as Paris was concerned, they were theoretically in a strong position to do so: those entering the theology licence had to be at least subdeacons; they would normally wish to take the doctorate very shortly after the licence, but for that they needed to have been ordained priests. If made obligatory, residence in seminaries before each rite of ordination could seriously upset their academic calculations or require them to adjust them. None of this enables us to say with confidence what proportion of Louis XIV's bishops set foot in a seminary, but at the very least it seems that if Paris theology students could be made to do so before taking orders, an increasing number of French bishops were likely to have personal experience of some such institution.

With demands like those just noted gradually taking shape, it may be asked whether an institution like the Paris theology faculty itself attempted to do more than examine the intellectual capacity of its students. Was it perhaps also a seminary of some kind? As early as 1665, the future *procureur-général* of the parlement, Achille de Harlay, declared the faculty to be 'séminaire des évêques', but he probably used the word in its more generic sense of a seedbed. The evidence points, it seems, in more directions than one. First of all, as just noted, the faculty did consciously link the passage through the final cycle of theology study, the licence, to the taking of specific 'major' orders. Indeed, the respective cycles of studies and clerical orders became more dovetailed as the seventeenth-century wore on, and the rules were applied with increasing strictness, as requests for exemptions or special treatment themselves suggest. In addition, there is some evidence of attempts being made after 1700, probably with the approval of Cardinal Noailles, to develop a more seminary-like regime, at least for the arts students at the well-attended College of Navarre, but whether it affected the fee-paying boarders (*pensionnaires*) rather than the poorer scholarship-holders (*boursiers*) may be doubted.[58] Success there would have been significant, as Navarre was the only college to house both arts and theology students. Finally, in 1724, Jean Bonnet, the superior-general of the Lazarists, who by then were directing a large number of seminaries throughout France, tantalisingly referred to 'a substantial instruction provided by the Sorbonne to the young bachelors in order to assist them in preparing for their licence and in learning the discipline of the church'.[59] Whatever its actual contents, the need for such guidance probably stemmed

---

58 Liam Chambers, 'The Life and Writings of Michael Moore (ca 1639–1726)' (Ph D thesis, National University of Ireland, 2001), ch 6, pp 194ff, using material from the University records in AN, MM 243. Moore, principal of the Arts students of Navarre after 1703, held strong views on the need for learning to be accompanied by piety and discipline, and practised them within the College himself. His record as a former director of the seminary of Montefiascone in Italy may have been the reason Noailles appointed him to Navarre in 1703.

59 Raymond Darricau, *La Formation des professeurs de séminaire au début du xviii siècle d'après le directoire de M Jean Bonnet (1664–1735) supérieur général de la congrégation de la Mission* (Piacenza 1966), 15, 'une instruction bien ample qui se donne en Sorbonne aux jeunes bacheliers pour

from longer-standing disciplinary concerns about theology students as they approached the critical moment of their studies. The faculty minutes record frequent calls for a proper implementation of its rules and requirements, both intellectual and moral. The faculty regularly nominated members to supervise licence students and report on their behaviour. Its concerns were not limited to absenteeism or granting dispensations to the well connected. The instruction mentioned by Bonnet probably had its roots in efforts like this.[60]

Yet the increasing size and social diversity of the student body (especially its growing contingent of blue-blooded 'abbés de qualité', as contemporaries called them) of the Paris theology faculty probably made efforts to turn it into anything resembling a seminary unrealistic. It is in this particular context that we may view a familiar but genuinely significant development associated with Louis XIV's reign – the emergence of a small group of elite seminaries based in Paris, one of which would triumph over its competitors by the mid-eighteenth century. The oldest of them was the seminary of Saint-Magloire which began in the early 1620s. The official seminary of the Paris diocese, it was entrusted by Archbishop Gondi to Bérulle's Oratory, and it was here that Paris ordinands were sent for examination and instruction before taking orders. Subsequently, the former college of the Bons-Enfants and Vincent de Paul's foundation at Saint-Lazare also served a similar function in preparing some Paris ordinands, but attendance at de Paul's conferences by Retz and his contemporaries shows that he attracted some of the future ecclesiastical elite from the late 1630s onwards. Neither seminary was capable of coping with all of the Paris clergy, needless to say, and Saint-Lazare under de Paul had no aspirations to form an intellectual elite. The gradual emergence of the Saint-Nicolas-du-Chardonnet and Saint-Sulpice seminaries out of parish-based communities of clergy offered the diocese and capital badly-needed additional resources for clerical formation.[61] Finally, the Missions Étrangères de Paris, founded by members of the defunct Compagnie du Saint-Sacrement, established their own seminary in Paris during the 1660s. Although its emphasis was on providing clergy for missions in Quebec, Asia and elsewhere, its genealogy ensured that it was not cut off from the French church, especially during the decades from the 1670s to the 1690s when missions at home (to the Huguenots) attracted numerous younger ecclesiastics.

Unfortunately, none of these seminaries bar one, Saint-Sulpice, has left serviceable records of its own, and even these are highly laconic. Consequently, gauging the relative attractiveness of the seminaries, and establishing either when, or for how long, individuals resided there during the decades from the

les disposer à bien fournir leur licence et à bien apprendre la discipline de l'église'. Bonnet's text may seem to suggest the Sorbonne guidance was primarily academic in content, but it also hints at rather more than that.

60   See Grès-Gayer, 'Tradition et modernité', 344–5.
61   See Antoine Degert, *Histoire des séminaires français jusqu'à la Révolution*, 2 vols (Paris 1912), i, 173–91.

1640s to the 1700s is frequently impossible, which in turn means that measuring the possible influence of the seminary experience on them is also hazardous. Despite these difficulties, a comparison of the numbers frequenting the different Paris seminaries, based on a collation of all the available sources, will shed surprising as well as useful light on the preferences of many of France's future bishops.

We may begin with the most marginal of them, Bons-Enfants and Missions Étrangères. The first of them seems to have been host to only three future bishops, two of whom moved on quickly to Saint-Sulpice, but the real total may be somewhat higher. Missions Étrangères fared better, no doubt because of its Compagnie du Saint-Sacrement roots. It seems that at least ten future bishops had some connection with it, though it is not clear from the surviving records how many of them were 'patrons' rather than 'products' of it – or even a combination of the two. In the early 1680s, Bouthillier de Chavigny, the future bishop of Troyes, was cited as one of 'nos abbés' when Archbishop Harlay came to lay the foundation stone of the Missions Étrangères chapel, but no complete list of the others in that cohort seems to have survived.[62] Louis Milon, a protégé of Fénelon and future bishop of Condom, was made a director of the seminary in 1688, while Antoine Girard and Henri Le Pileur, future bishops of Poitiers and Saintes respectively, were among those identified as 'attachés au séminaire'.[63] Other abbés bearing 'episcopal' names like Grignan and Phélypeaux were also associated with the Missions Étrangères, but the exact nature of the connection is not known.[64] The overall number would have been fractionally higher than the total of ten proposed here if the abbé Saint-Valier had preferred the French diocese offered him by Louis XIV over Quebec[65] or if two of its superiors had not flatly rejected the nomination as bishop of Chartres proposed to them in the 1690s.[66] By that point the seminary was also in the good graces of *dévots* like Mme de Maintenon and her circle, and one future bishop, Berger of Gap, was said to have resided successively in Saint-Magloire and Missions Étrangères, according as one replaced the other as Maintenon's favourite![67]

It may come as a surprise that Saint-Magloire, run by the Oratory since the 1620s and housing some very distinguished scholars of its own, did not attract many more future bishops than the Missions Étrangères. A major reason for this limited success was that for long periods of Louis's reign, Saint-Magloire

---

62 Arch MEP, MS 9, p 156, 24 April 1683.
63 *Ibid*, MS 94, p 7.
64 *Ibid*, MS 9, p 159.
65 Sourches, i, 174, Jan 1685. Sourches, who makes no mention of the double offer to Saint-Valier, records the consternation of other family members over his decision to accept Quebec.
66 AN, L 729, pièce 1, Chartres, no 81, Père Léonard papers. Godet des Marais, Maintenon's director, wished to resign Chartres in late 1694, and successively proposed Louis Tiberge and Claude Brisacier, whom Louis XIV accepted, but both argued their vocation was of a different order.
67 AN, L 730, pièce 1, Gap, no 30, Père Léonard papers. The same assertion about Missions Étrangères is made in AN, L 744, pièce 1, no 24, La Bourdonnaye bishop of Saint-Pol-de-Léon.

– and the Oratory in general – were under suspicion of harbouring Jansenist ideas, and that would have made it a risky choice for many ambitious clerics. The aversion of Archbishop Harlay to it was well known, in strong contrast to the goodwill shown to it by his successor Noailles, so it is hardly surprising that several bishops who owed their promotion in part to Noailles during the king's final years had spent some time there. The nine bishops who had done so included Berger of Gap and Barillon of Luçon, both of whom had also resided in the Missions Étrangères at some point.[68] To this group we should add the six members of the Oratory who themselves entered the episcopate under Louis XIV, and who had probably spent some time at Saint-Magloire or another Oratory-run seminary. Not all of these 'alumni', the Oratorians themselves included, turned out to be Jansenists, but for the many 'Augustinians' (only some deserving the label of 'Jansenists') of the later seventeenth century generally the reputation of Saint-Magloire as the flagship of proper ecclesiastical standards, piety and scholarship eclipsed that of all of its rivals. Under Louis XIV its professors and residents did include, after all, figures as eminent as Louis Thomassin, Richard Simon and Pasquier Quesnel.[69]

The most prominent of Saint-Magloire's rivals was, of course, Saint-Sulpice. Saint-Nicholas-du-Chardonnet, the other seminary to evolve from a parish-based community, would boast a number of bishops among its alumni, but not under Louis XIV.[70] Saint-Sulpice's eighteenth- and nineteenth-century ascendancy over the French episcopate, itself exaggerated, has tended to be projected backwards into the reign of Louis XIV. The endlessly rehearsed comments of an author like Saint-Simon have reinforced that impression, precisely because he regarded the influence of Saint-Sulpice on the episcopate as deeply harmful. This particular issue will resurface in a later chapter, but meanwhile it is essential to try accurately to evaluate Saint-Sulpice's part in providing France with bishops under Louis XIV.

It is common to think of Saint-Sulpice in the singular, but as it grew during Louis XIV's reign it was actually a cluster of establishments. The seminary proper evolved in the direction of providing spiritual and moral formation for future clergy while they were studying theology at the University of Paris, though it did gradually add some complementary intellectual provision of its

---

68 The others were Abbadie of Dax, Desmarets of Saint-Malo, Fromentières of Aire, Montmorin de Saint-Herem of Aire, Moret de Bourchenu of Vence, Revol of Oloron, Rousseau of Nîmes. The Oratorians were Baglion du Saillant of Tréguier, Mascaron of Agen, Quiqueran of Castres, Soanen of Senez, Verjus of Grasse, Verthamon of Couserans.

69 The lack of substantial critical studies of the Oratory, especially in Paris, in the age of Louis XIV remains a serious lacuna in the religious historiography of the period. The suspicion of Jansenism, which would increase during the eighteenth century, has also been a deterrent to research, and leaves historians heavily dependent on works like those of Louis Batterel, written in the eighteenth century but not published until much later – *Mémoires domestiques pour servir à l'histoire de l'Oratoire*, ed A-M-P Ingold, 5 vols (Paris 1902–11).

70 P Schoenher, *Histoire du séminaire de Saint-Nicolas-du-Chardonnet*, 2 vols (Paris 1909), i, 354ff.

own – in moral theology, canon law, liturgy and preaching. In 1705, its superior, Leschassier, wrote that it only admitted clerics about to commence their theology studies at the university, though in some instances it would accept those who needed to revise their philosophy in order to take the MA – but the revision had to take place 'privately' within the seminary itself while the students were formally studying theology.[71] By 1706, the *grand séminaire* had eighty-four residents, the *petit séminaire* fifty-five.[72] Most of the future bishops chosen by Louis XIV who frequented Saint-Sulpice only resided in the 'main' seminary (*grand* or *petit*, depending purely on whether they paid the full or the half pension) for relatively short periods of time. Once they had obtained their degrees and been ordained, some of the *élèves* joined the parish's very large community of priests, itself the origin of the seminary, in order to complete their pastoral formation: as Paris's largest parish, with possibly 150,000 inhabitants, there was no shortage of work for them to do there. Additionally, an early *petite communauté* operated from 1672 to 1690, and it attracted a smaller number of members whose health did not permit them to observe the rule of the seminary: among its earliest members were both Fénelon and Godet des Marais of Chartres, two of the most eminent 'Sulpicians' among Louis XIV's episcopate. A second *petite communauté* took shape in a Paris university college in 1693 and was integrated into the main seminary in 1708. Finally, Saint-Sulpice also developed a much smaller community, the 'solitude' of Issy, which had thirteen residents in 1706 and became famous for hosting the conferences involving Bossuet and Fénelon and designed to settle the dispute over Quietism in the 1690s.[73] The absence of records, especially of entry, for most of these 'institutions' complicates the historian's task, but by the same token it underlines how varied affiliation to, or residence at Saint-Sulpice could be. The ultimate commitment, of course, lay in joining the new congregation itself – that of the 'prêtres de Saint-Sulpice', who for the most part were engaged in directing or teaching in the many seminaries that Saint-Sulpice managed throughout France.

These distinctions are important if we are not to be misled by some of what has been written about the seminary under Louis XIV. It will be obvious that the chances of being enduringly 'marked' by Saint-Sulpice varied significantly from one individual to the next. For Saint-Simon the world had really been turned upside down when a Sulpician like François Madot could be elevated to the episcopate, even though the see itself was Belley, which in the past had attracted mainly regulars. What made this intolerable for the duke was that Madot, like his successor at Belley, Jean du Doucet, had spent his entire career

---

71   ASS, Correspondance des supérieurs-généraux, iii, no 1107, Leschassier to marquis de Denonville, 17 Aug 1705.

72   *Ibid*, iii, no 1126, Leschassier to M de Montigny, n d (Feb 1706). At this point, the *grand* and *petit séminaires* were distinguished only by the difference in the pension paid by those admitted, and not, as later, by the age of their inmates.

73   See Degert, *Histoire des séminaires français*, i, 186–91.

Table 3.6   *'Élèves' of Saint-Sulpice entering the episcopate*

Decades	At St-Sulpice	Nominated Bishop
1640s	2	0
1650s	5	0
1660s	9	4
1670s	5	9
1680s	9	3
1690s	6	7
1700s	2	10
1710s	0	5
Total	38	38

serving in Saint-Sulpice parish under the orders of its curé. His social obscurity was rivalled by that of his subsequent career, which Saint-Simon could only view as an affront to the dignity of the episcopate.[74] But to regard Madot as a 'typical' product of Saint-Sulpice is a serious distortion of the real picture, as it begs the rather large question of what it meant to be a 'Sulpician' at this point in its history.

According to the 'liste des anciens élèves du séminaire', based on Saint-Sulpice's own archives of entry and exit, it appears that thirty-eight of Louis XIV's bishops attended the seminary between the early 1640s and the early 1700s.[75] Only one of them, Languet de Gergy of Soissons, seems to have begun in the half-fee *petit séminaire*, but he graduated quickly to the full-fee *grand séminaire*.[76] Episcopal office had already beckoned for three of its earliest members during Mazarin's ministry. Among the thirty-eight who followed after 1661, the first was Claude Joly, bishop of Agen, another early member of Olier's community; the last was François de Beauvillier, half-brother of the royal minister, bishop of Beauvais in 1713, who entered the vastly-enlarged institution as late as July 1700. Their ranks also included, as we noted earlier, a few men who had spent some time in Bons-Enfants, Saint-Magloire, or Missions Étrangères, so it would be wise not to exaggerate the distinctiveness of these institutions at this point in their history. Saint-Sulpice's total accounts for just 15 per cent of the episcopate, which may seem a rather modest achievement. But allowance should be made for at least two things – firstly, the fact that it was still in its infancy in the years after 1643, just when most of the future royal nominees of the 1660s and 1670s were university students; secondly, the fact that for equally obvious reasons few of those

74   Saint-Simon, iv, 299–300; xi, 114.
75   Figures based on Levesque, 'Liste des élèves'.
76   *Ibid*, part ii, no 25. The annual fee in the *grand séminaire* at the time was 400 *livres*, in the *petit séminaire* 200. See *Correspondance de Tronson*, iii, 437–9, Tronson to Mme Languet, 30 Nov 1691.

attending Saint-Sulpice around or after 1700 stood much chance of becoming bishops *before* the king's death in 1715. Most of those classed as 'élèves' and obtaining the mitre under Louis XIV form a cluster from the late 1650s to the 1690s, as a decade-by-decade breakdown of their presence in Saint-Sulpice compared to the numbers of Sulpicians entering the episcopate makes clear (table 3.6).

But this table is clearly limited in what it can reveal, apart altogether from the fact that it deals only with those classed as 'élèves' of the seminary. One obvious way to measure the impact of Saint-Sulpice, as of any other institution, would to calculate the time that future bishops resided there. But this, too, is by no means straightforward, since exit dates for these early decades are not always available, especially for those who, their studies completed, joined one of its communities or even the nascent congregation itself. Consequently, the data on which to build a statistic are rather thin, aggravated by the fact that any set of averages can be hugely distorted if it contains even one individual who resided for several years in the seminary. At a glance, it does seem that for the more conventional *élèves*, the period of their stay did lengthen as the decades passed, a feature of seminary development generally at this time, but there is nothing inexorable about this pattern. Beauvillier, one of the last of Louis XIV's appointments to have entered Saint-Sulpice, stayed for nine years, but his contemporary there, La Tour du Pin Montauban of Toulon, stayed for only sixteen months in 1700–1.[77] Likewise, the later champion of *Unigenitus*, Languet de Gergy, bishop of Soissons, stayed for ten years from 1692 to 1702 until his cousin, Bossuet, finally 'placed' him at court. But it is clear that the vast majority never came remotely near such figures: even in the later years of Louis's reign, periods of six to eighteen months were more common. It is hardly surprising, therefore, that the average stay would be shorter still in the early decades of the king's personal rule. A bishop like Beaumanoir de Lavardin of Rennes qualifies as an *élève* even though he is recorded as only staying two and a half weeks there in June–July 1661; ten years later, Jean-Jacques de Gourgues, future bishop of Bazas, stayed for just five weeks, while Colbert's son, Jacques-Nicolas, the future archbishop of Rouen, moved in with his preceptor in December 1678 and left the following April, only days after taking his theology doctorate.[78] Short stays like this were closer to extended retreats for ordinands, another distinctive aspect of French seminary development, and in Colbert's case, it was designed mainly to enable him to take his university degrees. Colbert should not, however, be regarded as typical, and a comparison of the timescales of sojourns at Saint-Sulpice (and others seminaries, no doubt) and of the taking of university degrees by future bishops fails to demonstrate that the two dovetailed during Louis XIV's reign.

77 Levesque 'Liste des élèves', part i, nos 2121, 2113 respectively.
78 *Ibid*, nos 667, 1134, 1350, respectively.

It seems clear, therefore, that precisely because of its diversity and its still unfinished institutional development, the impact of Saint-Sulpice, and no doubt that of its rivals, cannot be fully understood in terms of a more modern notion of *élèves*. In addition to the thirty-eight future bishops already mentioned, we know that at least another nine of Louis XIV's bishops frequented Saint-Sulpice in other ways. It would be hard to imagine bishops more Sulpician in their background and formation than du Doucet, just mentioned, and François Madot, his predecessor at Belley: yet neither man figures among its *élèves*, even though both served for many years in the parish community and were regarded by contemporaries as pure products of Saint-Sulpice.[79] Nor should we imagine that such affiliation was, as a reading of Saint-Simon might suggest, confined to low-born clerics prepared to take on modest roles within the Sulpician enterprise, since most of these ten bishops were of an altogether different stripe, and were sons of aristocratic or ministerial families. As already mentioned, Fénelon and Godet des Marais resided for a time in the first *petite communauté*, under the direction of the influential superior, Louis Tronson.[80] Among their contemporaries there was the first bishop of Blois, Bertier. Others again, such as Bishops Vény d'Arbouze of Clermont or Loménie de Brienne of Coutances, may have lived briefly in the parish community (Vény) or performed some pastoral functions connected to it (Brienne), indicating that their links were with the parish community itself.[81] Both of them, especially Brienne, remained life-long *dirigés* of Tronson, and that was assuredly more decisive than a stay within the seminary or parish.[82] Other associations with Saint-Sulpice, the precise nature of which we cannot establish because they went unrecorded, continued into the latter years of the reign.[83] In some instances, the sojourn at Saint-Sulpice came *after* the individuals had completed their studies, or it was part of a search for a place of retreat or pastoral experience. These elusive, often brief, encounters contrast sharply with the commitment of the six future bishops who joined the *petite communauté* between the 1660s and its suppression in the early 1690s, since all of them were previously *élèves* of the seminary.[84] And, of course, the most committed

---

79 For du Doucet, see AN, MC, LXXXII, 115, 27 July 1712, for enquiry *de vita et moribus*, evidence from Bishop Saint-Valier of Quebec. For Madot, see ASS, *fiches* Bertrand, 'Madot'.

80 Fénelon, *Correspondance*, i, 143ff, where the duration of Fénelon's stay at Saint-Sulpice is shown to have been shorter than usually thought, but not his connection to Louis Tronson or the parish of Saint-Sulpice itself. Fénelon was not formally enrolled at the Paris theology faculty, and eventually took his theology doctorate at Cahors in 1677.

81 The references to their activities are usually to be found in the enquiries *de vita et moribus*, which are listed in the sources for the individual entries in the accompanying biographical dictionary.

82 *Correspondance de Tronson*, iii, 66–7, 69–71 for letters of direction to Brienne, 1678–9.

83 AN, MC, LXXXII, 111, 16 Sept 1711, enquiry *de vita et moribus* for Christophe Turpin de Sanzay, nominated to Rennes. In his evidence Bishop Rousseau of Nîmes claimed to know Turpin from their time in Saint-Sulpice together, yet Turpin does not figure in the lists published by Levesque.

84 Godet of Chartres, Bazan de Flamanville of Perpignan, Le Peletier of Angers, Gaston de Noailles, Fleuriau of Aire, Languet of Soissons.

of all were the five individuals who went a step further and joined the nascent Sulpician Compagnie itself.[85]

Thus, despite the limitations of our sources, it is clear that we should not view the influence of seminaries like Saint-Sulpice, Saint-Magloire or Missions Étrangères in terms of the length of a precisely dateable initial stay sufficient to generate an enduring mindset among their *alumni*. Their influence was more subtle than that because, as we noted above, they remained embedded in the wider world of religious reform from which they had emerged. There is abundant evidence that many bishops returned to them in later years, residing there during visits to the capital, especially during the assemblies of clergy. Some would retire to follow a retreat there, notably during the days or weeks before their consecration as bishops; a few bishops retired there after they had given up their dioceses altogether. The correspondence of Tronson and his successor at Saint-Sulpice, Leschassier, also frequently shows them engaging in delicate rounds of diplomacy when 'gens de qualité', bishops or others, were seeking temporary lodging in an establishment that was already heavily overcrowded.[86] By these means, existing affiliations were progressively consolidated over a period of years. Many of them remained under the spiritual direction of seminary superiors like La Tour (Oratory) or Tronson for many years after entering the episcopate.

VI

The contribution of France's still developing seminaries towards shaping the episcopate under Louis XIV may well seem fairly limited if viewed in tightly defined terms. As far as we can tell, between one-fifth and one-quarter of the bishops (when allowance is made for attendance by some bishops at more than one seminary) attended the major Parisian seminaries; perhaps as many again may have attended diocesan seminaries for a time possibly because, as we noted earlier in this chapter, they could no longer take major orders without doing so. It will also be abundantly obvious from the foregoing discussion of both the Paris theology faculty and of seminaries like Saint-Sulpice that the borderline between education and early career for France's bishops is extremely difficult to draw, and is to some extent an anachronistic modern distinction. In one sense, it could be argued that potentially the least 'Sulpician' bishops

---

85 Bazan de Flamanville of Perpignan, Lescure of Luçon, Champflour of La Rochelle, Clément of Périgueux, Sabatier of Amiens.

86 *Correspondance de Tronson*, esp vol. iii, contains several letters from Tronson to bishops requesting lodgings at Saint-Sulpice. See also ASS, Correspondance des supérieurs-généraux, iii, no 465, Leschassier to bishop of Alet, Taffoureau, 31 March 1700, replying to his request to be allowed to reside in the *petite communauté* when in Paris, and pointing out to him that the *petite communauté* no longer existed! The bishop of Alet was *not* a former associate or inmate of Saint-Sulpice as far as is known.

of Louis XIV's day were the 'mere' *élèves*, who for the most part spent anything from a month to a year or so within its walls. At the other end of the
spectrum we might place those future bishops who were seminary teachers or
directors, and for whom seminaries represented far more than just a brief
period of personal initiation. By the time they were completing their degrees,
residing in seminaries, or taking orders, many future bishops had already
embarked on careers which could take them down unexpected avenues leading
years later to dioceses they might know little or nothing about. It is to this
question of their pre-episcopal careers that the next chapter will be devoted.

CHAPTER 4

Paths to Preferment

DESPITE THE ALLUSION in the previous chapter to the Paris theology faculty emerging under Louis XIV as a kind of *grande école* for high-flying churchmen who, once their studies had been completed, were launched on careers that would prepare them to govern the French church, it would be misguided to take that analogy with more recent career patterns too literally. The discussion of studies and degrees also noted how many future bishops either did *not* take their degrees in Paris, or preferred to abridge their studies by taking law degrees. Moreover, it seems that many of those who did study theology in Paris were not exclusively engaged in academic pursuits during their years there. Many were already, in one way or another, embarked on what may be called their careers by then, and the traditions of both the church and the university allowed them to pursue them simultaneously with their studies. Even during the two years of the theology licence, when they should have been assiduously attending faculty disputations and examinations, considerable numbers of them asked for permission to be absent for periods of time because of other obligations elsewhere.[1] And of course, it should not be forgotten that large numbers of them took their degrees when they were in their late twenties, thirties, and even older. To that extent, we cannot fold 'studies' and 'careers' into two neatly separated sequences; they overlap in ways that have become unfamiliar since the end of the *ancien-régime* church. And there is a further element that needs to be taken into consideration before we can understand the pre-episcopal careers of Louis XIV's bishops – their clerical status.

I

The previous chapter noted that the university degrees taken by future bishops reflected a clericalisation of the future ecclesiastical elite; it also showed how

1 The requests for such permission are scattered throughout the minutes of the faculty in AN, MM 252–5, covering the period 1634 to 1717. Grès-Gayer, 'Tradition et modernité', 344, considers such absences as one of the major problems of the Paris theology faculty.

the determination of French bishops to regulate and control the taking of 'major' orders culminating in the priesthood itself could affect those study-ing at universities like Paris.[2] By insisting that the highest degrees were only available to those in major orders, the Paris theology faculty was fully in step with this wider movement. If efforts like these were successful and the younger generations of clergy were obliged to comply with them, then there would seem to be little for historians to say on the subject of the clerical status of newly nominated bishops. But legislation and reality could diverge widely, as contemporaries themselves fully appreciated, and in any case those who took no degree or who held one in law were not subject to the constraints just mentioned. Moreover, the age-profile of incoming bishops was far from stable, and the range of ages – anywhere from thirty to sixty – was consider-able enough for one to suspect at least some variations in the clerical status of these men. In this connection, it should not be forgotten that large numbers of *ancien-régime* clerics, especially among those from elite backgrounds, stopped well short of the priesthood itself; the pressures on them to take full orders were not especially strong in an age when being a priest was *not* a sine qua non for a wide range of ecclesiastical offices and when large numbers of attractive benefices were without cure of souls. It was a prerequisite for the episcopate, of course, ever since the Concordat had included a stipulation to that effect, but that clause had been breached on numerous occasions under Louis XIV's predecessors. Moreover, this was also a society in which it was not unusual for laymen to become bishops within virtually no time at all of 'entering the church', or for clerics who were still in minor orders to accede to similar positions. How far did these habits, well documented for the sixteenth and early seventeenth century, persist thereafter? Could a small minority of well-placed laymen still hope to be treated as they had been for centuries? Or was the collective leadership of the French church which took shape under Louis XIV one which, after a long period of gestation, was now cast in an exclusively clerical mould which left little or no room for 'out-siders'? Questions like these clearly involve placing pre-episcopal careers in a wider perspective.

It can be said without qualification that Louis XIV was never called upon to nominate a layman to the episcopate. This does not mean that some of the bishops he did choose had not *been* laymen for part or even most of their pre-vious careers, merely that all traces of that part of their existence had been comprehensively erased by the time of their selection. The 'halcyon' days of his grandfather, Henri IV, when laymen, present or very recent, had often been among the king's choices, were well and truly over. Indeed, they had scarcely figured at all among Louis XIII's or Mazarin's bishops.[3] That Louis should

2   See, pp 104–5.
3   See the discussion of this subject for the period 1589 to 1661 in my *Making of the French Episcopate*, ch 8.

Table 4.1   New bishops by number of years in priestly orders

Decade	None	Under 1	1 to 2	2 to 5	5 to 9	10 to 15	15 to 20	20 to 25	25+	Unknown	Total noms
1661–9	1	2	6	4	5	3	2	3	5	4	35
1670–9	1	7	3	10	14	7	4	6	1	2	55
1680–9	0	2	0	6	20	5	4	0	2	5	44
1690–9	0	0	1	3	10	7	8	4	1	8	42
1700–9	0	0	0	4	9	11	10	5	0	6	45
1710–15	0	0	0	2	7	5	5	4	2	4	29
Total	2	11	10	29	65	38	33	22	11	28	250

follow them rather than resurrect older practices is thus no surprise. Even those of his bishops known to have followed a lay career only became bishops several years – sometimes a decade or more – after they had abandoned it to take orders. And, as we shall see later, all of them had subsequently embarked on activities that did nothing to distinguish them from bishops who had never been anything else but clerics.

This means that in a formal sense we are dealing with a highly homogeneous group, all of them clerics in some degree or other. But given the protean shape of the clerical world to which they belonged, it is essential to determine if there was any significant internal differentiation among them, and whether there were trends emerging during the period after 1661 which can be connected to earlier or later patterns. In doing so, it should be remembered that the minimum age for priestly orders was twenty-four, while that for entry to the episcopate was twenty-six, so that anyone at the time wishing to break records without needing some kind of dispensation had to be especially fortunate or well connected. We can begin by asking for how long those who were made bishops had been in priestly orders before their promotion. With the age of new bishops varying considerably, it makes little sense to calculate an average across the period as a whole, as it might prove to be a purely arithmetical fiction. It seems best, therefore, to think in terms of a series of thresholds varying from one year to twenty years and beyond. The discussion which follows is based on information of differing degrees of precision: actual dates of priestly ordination have been found for sixty-nine bishops, the year of ordination for 142 others, leaving just twenty-nine individuals scattered fairly randomly across the period as a whole for whom no reliable guess can be attempted. The data in the accompanying table (4.1) may also be compared to that covering the main decades of the Richelieu and Mazarin ministries (1629–1661) in order to obtain a broader perspective.[4]

4   *Ibid*, 256.

The first point to underline is that Louis XIV only nominated two bishops not already in full priestly orders at the date of their nomination, and that was relatively early during the reign, in 1666 and 1671 respectively. Nor were the lucky individuals in question among those, just mentioned, who had previously followed a lay career, as one might expect for an earlier age. The first of these exceptions was made for Pierre du Cambout, the future Cardinal de Coislin, grandson of Chancellor Séguier, brother of a duke and peer, and offspring of a Richelieu-related family.[5] Despite holding high ecclesiastical office at court, where he enjoyed the king's favour from an early age, Coislin's reputation for rectitude and piety was, and would remain impeccable until his death forty years later, so that his early failure to take priestly orders ought not to be ascribed to any lack of commitment on his part.[6] Indeed, like many other Port-Royal or philo-Jansenist figures of this period, his slowness to become a priest – he was aged thirty in 1666 – probably had more to do with self-doubt and scruples than with negligence on his part. For reasons that remain unclear, Coislin shared his exceptional favour with Michel Amelot, son of a Parisian robe family still on a steep upward trajectory. Nominated to Lavaur in Languedoc in early 1671 and ordained priest a month later, he had been a *conseiller* in the Paris parlement since 1648, the year he had also received his first major benefice. Here, too, there is no evidence of insouciance that might explain his slowness to take full orders.[7]

No more than eleven bishops were ordained priests within less than a year before their nomination by the king. There is good reason, based on the identity of those involved, to think that in these cases there was either a strong hint of impending royal favour or a simple desire to be *en règle* so that royal favour might not be jeopardised by the lack of priestly status. In the first category belong undoubtedly the three bishops promoted in the mid-1670s whose dates of ordination and nomination as bishops were only a few *days* apart; in the second, those whose ordination dates varied between a few weeks and a full year before their nominations.[8] Once again, all of these nominations took place in the early decades of the reign, and it is not irrelevant to note that the last two of them, involving a Colbert and an Estrées, date from

5　ASV, PC 64, fos 56–7, certificate from archbishop of Paris that he ordained du Cambout on 16 Aug 1666 *extra tempora* by virtue of a papal dispensation. The royal letter of nomination of 24 May 1666 describes du Cambout as a deacon: fo 54.

6　He had been the king's *premier aumônier* since 1657 and would become *grand aumônier de France* in 1700, when the disgraced Cardinal Bouillon forfeited the office: BN, MS Fr 7854, fo 353r, royal household offices in 1653.

7　ASV, PC 70, fos 1130–58, enquiry *de vita et moribus* for Amelot, 19 Feb 1671. One of the witnesses, Claude Auvry, former bishop of Coutances, had ordained him a priest a few days earlier. He had also sponsored the reformed observance of the Maurists in his abbey.

8　Michel Phélypeaux de la Vrillière (Uzès), Jacques Potier de Novion (Sisteron) and Michel Cassagnet (Mâcon). The second group includes Monchy d'Hocquincourt (Verdun), Vallot (Nevers), La Garde de Chambonas (Lodève), Thomassin (Vence), Beauvau du Rivau (Nantes), as well as Colbert (Rouen) and Estrées (Laon).

1680 and 1681 respectively. A roughly similar number of bishops had been priests for between one and two years before being promoted. Once again, all but one of them was an early appointment. Between 1677 and 1715 the *only* bishop in this category was a Noailles, the cardinal's younger brother, Gaston, who was nominated to succeed him at Châlons in 1695. It is, therefore, primarily among those who had recently taken full orders that we are most likely to find the most 'natural' (based on status, connections and previous favours from the crown) candidates for high church office. The crown's approach to this question as the reign progressed resembles its behaviour towards young candidates for the mitre, and it is highlighted by a fascinating case which helps to show just how reluctant the king could be to 'parachute' seemingly uncommitted clerics into the episcopate. Although the case only concerns a single individual, its derives added weight from the dramatis personae. Cardinal d'Estrées, frequently absent on missions in Rome, decided to follow the traditions of both his family and cardinals in general by ensuring that his diocese of Laon passed directly and without fuss to his young nephew, Jean, in 1681. The transfer was eased by the nephew's being in full orders and taking first place in the Paris theology licence, followed immediately by the doctorate, in 1680. These triumphs would have been fresh in everyone's mind, the king's and the confessor's included, when less than a year later the cardinal made his move to obtain Laon for him. His timing suggests that the move was delayed so that any objections, based on the nephew's relative youth, would have fallen away.[9] The Laon succession encountered no obstacles, but Jean d'Estrées died in his early forties in 1694, and the long Estrées presence in the highest ranks of the French church seemed in jeopardy.[10] In an earlier age, the cardinal, who was still alive, would have reclaimed his former diocese for himself and started making new succession plans. However, the first of these options had also ceased to obtain as the seventeenth century progressed, but the second could still be tried. He had another clerical nephew, also named Jean, who was by then French envoy to Portugal, and the cardinal duly asked that he be named as successor to Laon. But Louis XIV objected that the abbé d'Estrées was not in full orders and even for him to take orders at short notice and then to be nominated to a prestigious see was more than the royal conscience would allow.[11] Estrées's own services and those of his ancestors and

9 Jean d'Estrées was just under thirty years old in 1681.
10 Laon, one of France's most poorly endowed dioceses, attracted aristocratic families because it carried the title of *duc et pair*.
11 JRULM, MS French 90, fos 297, Mme d'Huxelles to marquis de la Garde, 3 Dec 1694. The bishop of Laon died on 1 Dec and Huxelles reports on speculation that the abbé d'Estrées, who was only a deacon, could be ordained a priest in order to ensure the succession 'si c'est la volonté de Sa Majesté'. *Ibid*, fos 159–60, same to same, 25 Dec 1694, reporting on the distribution of benefices published on Christmas Day: 'M le Cardinal d'Estrée avoit demandé aussy l'Evesché de Laon pour cet Ambassadeur, mais Sa Majesté respondit qu'Elle en auroit trop de scrupule, *à cause qu'il ne seroit prestre que pour cela*' (italics mine). Dangeau, v, 125, 25 Dec 1694, and Sourches, iv, 413, 24 Dec 1694, both record that Estrées received the abbey of Préaux worth

living relatives – diplomatic, military and courtly – were unrivalled, and on such grounds alone the king would normally have been as ready to reward the abbé as his predecessors Henri IV and Louis XIII before him. Indeed, he showed his goodwill to abbé d'Estrées on the same day as he awarded Laon to a different candidate by giving him an abbey *in commendam* that was twice as well endowed as Laon itself! But on the main issue of episcopal preferment, he held firm, prompted perhaps by his confessor, and Jean d'Estrées was never to become a bishop under Louis XIV.[12] It is also likely that the king was wary of making a decision which would have quickly been seen as opening the door to other *abbés de qualité* like Estrées to press for episcopal office.[13]

This decision – and perhaps others we know nothing about – would have made it amply clear to even well-born contemporaries that the mitre would be available only to those who had been ordained priests as a normal part of a clerical *cursus*. It did not preclude the nomination of relatively young and inexperienced individuals who were virtually always sons of families close to the levers of power. It would be easy to deduce from this that opportunism and ambition drove them to take orders relatively young, but as we saw in the previous chapter, more and more of them were taking the Paris theology doctorate, for which priestly orders were an absolute prerequisite.

Closing this parenthesis and returning to the figures in table 4.1, it is clear that the great majority of Louis's bishops had to wait far longer after ordination than those discussed above, with three out of every four for whom information survives being a priest for over five years before their turn came. By comparison with the pattern observed for the years from 1629 to 1661,[14] the table shows that after 1661 the number of bishops who were ordained priests less than a year before their promotion fell by well over half, while those in orders for between five and twenty years increased by 10 per cent. Perhaps the most important point of all is that from about 1680, for reasons which we will return to elsewhere, virtually nobody in priestly orders for less than two years became a bishop, while the numbers of those in orders for less than five years were also falling. These changes, which doubtless relate in part to the rising average age of incoming bishops, may not seem particularly startling, but judged across a period of close to a century, they have genuine significance. In addition, these figures can be viewed in more ways than one.

twice the value of Laon in income, but say nothing about the king's preference for another candidate to Laon.

12 He seems to have been rejected for Béziers, along with other *abbés de qualité*, in 1702: JRULM, MS French 94, fo 101, Huxelles to La Garde, 12 May 1702: 'le roi estoit las de disputer contre les abbés de qualité, le Père de la Chaise de soutenir la dispute, qui les favorisait, n'estant question que des Messieurs d'Estrées, de Pomponne et de Castres'. In late 1715, after Louis XIV's death, the Regent nominated him as Fénelon's successor at Cambrai, but he died before he could obtain his papal provisions.

13 See AN, L 401, for Père Léonard's portraits of 'ces abbés qui épiscopalisent', most of them from the same generation as the abbé d'Estrées himself.

14 Bergin, *Making*, 256, table 7.4

The one which is most revealing, because it can be connected to the evolution of episcopal patronage, is that which gives a breakdown of these figures decade by decade. Without rehearsing points already made, it emerges that in the 1660s and 1670s, those who had been priests for less than five years before their nomination as bishops came close to 40 per cent of the total, with even a marginal increase during the bountiful 1670s. However, this proportion halved during the 1680s and then it halved again in the 1690s, falling to around 10 per cent by the end of the 1690s; it levelled off in subsequent years and then dropped further to around 8 per cent in the last decade of the reign. As this particular cohort was falling in size, the numbers of those in full orders for between five and ten years rose sharply in the 1670s and especially the 1680s, the transitional decade, only to halve even more suddenly in the 1690s and to remain steady thereafter. The corollary of this particular trend is that bishops in orders for over ten years came into their own as a proportion of incoming bishops. This movement becomes especially evident in the 1690s and was fully sustained thereafter, accounting for nearly two out of three newcomers in the final decades of the reign. For the present, we can only speculate as to why a trend of this kind took shape. Was it due to pressures that contemporaries were scarcely aware of? Or did an ageing monarch – in the process of becoming something of a *dévot* under the influence of Mme de Maintenon – and his even more elderly confessor increasingly prefer those who had been in orders for a respectable number of years, compared with the 'younger' ones of the 1660s and 1670s? However we answer this question, it is surely clear that the clerical milieux from which French bishops were drawn did not wholly escape the pressures within the Counter-Reformation church on clerics to proceed to take full orders. Clearly, some delayed doing so far longer than others, for reasons which we can do no more than surmise. Some of those reasons may well have been related to the pre-episcopal careers which they adopted.

II

Historians of the eighteenth-century French church are accustomed to seeing France's bishops emerge mainly from the ranks of the grand-vicars of existing bishops. This development was regarded as bringing significant advantages to the French church, since it guaranteed that its governance would be in the hands of men of experience for whom episcopal office held few or no secrets when they finally assumed it in their own name. Put in these terms, such a widely chosen career-track suggests that an important element of 'meritocracy', or at the least some proto-professionalism, had emerged within a world not instantly recognisable in such modern terms. At the same time, it puts paid to one of the most tenacious clichés regarding the French episcopate of the *ancien régime* – that not only were bishops appointed at an unseemly young age, but they had done little more than accumulate church benefices and wait impatiently for the king and his advisers to promote them. It also challenges other intimately connected stereotypes about those obtaining episcopal office, particularly the one that they were mostly *abbés de cour*, holders of sinecures whose only preoccupation was to stay at court in order to keep an eye on 'the main chance'. Paradoxically, however, this form of meritocracy did not undermine, intentionally or otherwise, the increasing dominance of the nobility, especially the older nobility, among the eighteenth-century episcopate. Just as the sons of the nobility proved themselves willing to attend university and take degrees, especially in theology, so they accepted that a stint, sometimes a long one, as a vicar-general was an indispensable element of the curriculum vitae of future bishops. However tedious or onerous this obligation might be, without it no ambitious cleric could be sure of being placed on the *feuille des bénéfices*, which was the decisive moment in any attempt to position oneself in the competition for royal attention and favour.

The well-oiled workings of this ecclesiastical world seem highly remote from that of the sixteenth and early-seventeenth centuries, when there was no such 'royal road' to the episcopate, but rather an impressively eclectic series of avenues converging somewhat haphazardly at the same point. This immediately raises the question of whether the personal government of Louis XIV, with all the elements of continuity that royal longevity provided, somehow laid the foundations for the dominant pattern of the following century. And if it did so, what were the intentions and influences that contributed towards it? Of course, the search for the early development of a pattern that was later to dominate the episcopate may easily give the impression that, as with other searches for origins, it is the subsequent outcome that should be the central focus of the analysis. That would be to predetermine the findings of the analysis that follows here: even if the reign did lay the foundations for the future, it is also essential to measure them in relation to traditions which did *not* conform to the emerging pattern. Having formed some idea of the length of time future bishops had been in full orders, we can now attempt to situate their pre-episcopal careers in their proper historical context. A preliminary view of their multifarious activities and careers is outlined in table 4.2, though as we shall see, some of its entries require careful interpretation.

We have already seen that Louis XIV did not nominate a single layman to the episcopate. The last such case had occurred in 1621 when Louis XIII had chosen the young Thomas Bonsi to preserve that family's tenure of Béziers. But, as already noted, this is not to say that subsequent decades did not witness incoming bishops whose careers had been either partly or mainly lay careers. A total of forty-six (13 per cent) bishops seated from 1589 to 1661 had pursued a lay career of greater or lesser duration, and there was no noticeable falling off of such nominations under Richelieu and Mazarin, quite the contrary. Some were probably tonsured clerics who, like François Bosquet,

Table 4.2   *Pre-episcopal activities of Louis XIV's bishops*

Activities		Activities	
regulars	10	chapter dignitaries	39
		archdeacons/priests	30
royal almoner, etc	42	*official*	18
royal tutor etc	9	*théologal*	6
agent-général du clergé	18	grand-vicar	86
sovereign courts	10	seminary direction	8
service to grands	2	convent superiors etc	11
conseillers d'état	2	missions	19
papal service	3	preaching	18
		parish priest	12
cathedral canons	72		
other chapters	13		

Note. Because it includes the known activities of future bishops, the total in this table exceeds the total number of bishops.

bishop of Lodève and Montpellier, had pursued lay careers for several years, only to abandon them and take orders in mid-life. Better known for obvious reasons were those who, like Pierre de Marca, had married, raised families and then, usually in widowhood, had taken orders with a view to seeking church office. The most unusual case of all occurred only a few years before Louis XIV's personal rule began, when the former provincial intendant, François de Villemontée, was nominated to Saint-Malo while his wife was still alive, albeit legally separated from him.[15] With the exception of the first and the last of these examples, similar patterns would recur in the decades after 1661.

There is little doubt that the proportion of former laymen becoming bishops under Louis XIV was considerably smaller than during the two previous reigns. Reaching a reliable total figure is, curiously, more difficult than might be imagined. Although contemporaries were apt to comment when former laymen moved into the ecclesiastical hierarchy, sources such as the papal enquiries into new bishops are often discreet, if not wholly silent, on this aspect of their biography, highlighting their ecclesiastical activities instead. When bishops were tonsured at a relatively 'advanced' age – in their twenties or later – we may suspect that a lay career had been their first choice (or that of their families for them), but corroborative evidence is often lacking. In the end, it seems that no more than thirteen of Louis XIV's 250 bishops, a mere 5 per cent, had followed a lay career at some point in their lives – a substantial reduction compared to the period after 1589. A further three cases

15   Bergin, *Making*, 261.

illustrate the continuing ambiguities of clerical status: the great scholar, Pierre-Daniel Huet, was not tonsured until he was twenty six, and it took him twenty years more before he was ordained a priest in 1676. His learned pursuits were scarcely interrupted by such digressions, but there is no compelling reason to see such a career as a secular one: Huet the scholar was a *clericus* in every sense of the term. The two other cases involved men who were initially Knights of Malta, a career which, though military in fact, was, in principle at least, clerical, since the knights were celibates bound by the three religious vows.[16]

Although statistically close to insignificant, these lay careers can tell us more than we might expect about who became bishops under Louis XIV. The first surprise is that no fewer than seven of the thirteen had been military officers, while another had been in military administration as a modest *commissaire des guerres*.[17] None had risen to any eminence within the military hierarchy; only one of them was aged over thirty when he quit the sword for the church, whereas most of the others were at best in their mid-twenties, the youngest only nineteen. Consequently, their taste of military life was relatively short, and leaving it behind was doubtless facilitated by the fact that none of them bar one had married.[18] Of the remaining five with lay careers behind them, two had been *conseillers* in a parlement, one was a minor financial official, and one had taken over his father's business in Paris.[19] Here, too, there was no record of high-level service to the crown, and there was only one marriage to delay a decision to change career. In all thirteen cases, therefore, those involved had abandoned their secular careers many years before they became bishops, even though the speed with which they subsequently proceeded to take orders varied hugely. For several of them, it seems that it was the attraction of *retraite*, in the sense that the term was understood at the time, which prompted their withdrawal from secular careers rather than a rapid change of course designed to secure high church office. Some entered the Oratory or religious orders, while others associated themselves with Saint-Sulpice or other *bonnes oeuvres*. Yet despite their seeming uncertainty, all but one had been in priestly orders for over three years before their nomination as bishops; the exception was made not for the younger brother of the future *contrôleur-général*, Desmarets, but for a boyhood companion of Louis XIV,

16   Henri de Barillon (Luçon) and Charles-François Desmontiers de Mérinville (Chartres).
17   Lacaris (Limoges), Baglion du Saillant (Tréguier), Frézeau (La Rochelle), Desmarets (Saint-Malo), Frétat (Saint-Brieuc) and Montmorin (Die). The *commissaire* was Pierre Marion (Gap).
18   Joseph-Gaspard de Montmorin de Saint-Hérem, bishop of Aire in 1710, only embraced an ecclesiastical career when his wife died in 1700. He was succeeded as bishop of Aire in 1723 by one of his own sons!
19   Desclaux (Lescar) and Francheville (Périgueux) were *conseillers* in the Pau and Rennes parlements. Aubert (Senez) was a financial official at the court of the young Louis XIV (as *maître* in the *chambre des deniers*). Mathurin Savary (Sées) inherited his father's profession as an iron merchant in Paris. There is no evidence that Ignace de Foresta-Coulongue (Apt) embarked on a career after taking his law degree in 1672.

Lascaris d'Urfé, bishop of Limoges in 1676.[20] Aged forty, Lascaris was the second youngest of these men to accede to the episcopate; the eleven others were all in their mid-forties and over.[21] This brief collective profile demonstrates beyond reasonable doubt that the bridge linking secular careers and entry to the episcopate was by then an extremely narrow one; above all, it was in no sense the 'fast-track' option for the ambitious. It is striking that, among the group being considered here, not one of them was a senior ministerial or political figure of the kind who in previous generations would have seen the episcopate as a natural and immediate exit from a secular career. In this respect, the age of Louis XIV knew neither a Duprat nor a du Vair.

Before moving to consider what the great mass of France's bishops had done before obtaining the mitre, there is another marginal group which deserves consideration, since its place within the episcopate at any moment can illuminate general features of the latter in a way that its limited numbers might not suggest. Genuine regulars among Louis XIV's new bishops amounted to no more than ten, though a number of others, to whom we shall return later, might well be classified under the same heading. It also appears that two or three bishops may have been regulars at one stage during their early careers, but this was, like the seculars we have just discussed, a distant memory by the time of their promotion.[22] Apart from that, connections between the two groups were virtually non-existent, since only two of the thirteen former 'seculars', Pierre Marion and Joseph-Ignace de Mesgrigny, had entered a religious order on abandoning their previous career in royal service. The other eight regulars seem to have spent all their post-adolescent years in the religious life, and not to have exercised any responsibilities outside of their orders. But perhaps the biggest surprise of all is that six of the ten regulars belonged to the old monastic orders,[23] leaving the older mendicants (Dominicans and various Franciscans) with just one bishop each.[24] Compared to the period 1589 to 1661, the numbers of regulars entering the episcopate dropped four-fold; and that fall was virtually complete by the early 1680s, since only two regulars were appointed after 1682. What *all* of the regulars have in common, however, is that they were sent to dioceses that were geographically peripheral, some of which were also on vulnerable frontiers (Gap, Glandèves, Belley,

20 Lascaris, known as the comte de Sommerive in his early career, was ordained a priest in 1675, a year before his nomination, but he had abandoned his courtly-military career as long ago as 1660 for a life of retreat, and spent some time at Saint-Sulpice, although he was not in any orders.

21 Aubert de Villeserin (Senez) was the youngest at thirty-six, possibly because he was a godson of Louis XIV and successively an almoner to his mother and wife.

22 Vény d'Arbouze (Clermont) had been a highly rebellious Benedictine, the great preacher Fléchier (Nîmes) a Doctrinaire, and Armand de Montmorin (Die) allegedly a Feuillant.

23 Marion (Gap), Belin (Belley), Roger (Lombez), du Laurens (Belley), Baudry (Mende), and Mailly (Lavaur).

24 Margarit, a Dominican (Perpignan), Bacoué, a Franciscan (Glandèves), Allart, a Récollet (Vence), Mesgrigny, a Capuchin (Grasse).

Perpignan), or which were otherwise regarded as distinctly unattractive (Grasse, Vence, Lombez, Lavaur). Moreover, none of them succeeded in moving to another, more desirable see.[25] They were, clearly, marginal figures in more than one sense of the term.

The tiny number of bishops drawn from the more pastorally active mendicant orders, old and new, does raise wider questions about the composition of the French episcopate, especially when the latter is compared to the episcopates of the Italian and Iberian worlds of the day.[26] Their limited presence should, perhaps, be considered alongside that of another relatively small group which straddles the divide between the secular and regular clergy. Six Oratorians and one Lazarist also became bishops under Louis XIV. Of course, neither the Oratory nor the Lazarists (*recte*, Congrégation of the Mission) can be regarded as religious orders: both were quite consciously different from the existing orders and their members were secular clergy. But they shared their congregational organisation, constitutions and hierarchy with the conventional regulars, making it legitimate to discuss them alongside the latter. The six Oratorians who followed in the footsteps of the three nominated under Richelieu and Mazarin were promoted between the early 1670s and 1708, mostly to dioceses similar to those given to regulars, although some of the Oratorians did succeed in moving to better sees later. That there should have been that many Oratorians at all may come as a surprise, given how suspect the Oratory was on doctrinal grounds under Louis XIV, and it raises the question of how many more of its members might have joined them had it not been so tainted. Vincent de Paul's Lazarists, on the other hand, had a reputation for unwavering orthodoxy, so it is yet another surprise that the one Lazarist to enter the episcopate, François Hébert, bishop of Agen, was Augustinian in his views and a combative supporter of Cardinal Noailles during the battles leading up to *Unigenitus*.

In seventeenth-century terms, being a regular represented as much a condition (*état*) as an activity. The great majority of those regulars elevated to the episcopate, the Oratorians included, had held office within their orders, but they did not need to have been heads of their orders before attracting the notice of the king and his advisors. Being prior of Saint-Martin-des-Champs or Saint-Victor, both in Paris, could be just as useful, because these houses enjoyed connections to wider court and ecclesiastical circles. The only Récollet bishop of this period, Théodore Allart, had held several high offices in his order (a reformed branch of the Franciscans) but seems to have attracted royal attention mainly for bringing the Récollet houses of Flanders under

25   When Fénelon wrote to his friends to advertise the merits of his distant relative and protegé, Laval-Montmorency, the nearest he could bring himself to recommend him for the episcopate was to say that he might be considered for the see of Lombez! – Fénelon, *Correspondance*, xiv, no 1434, 308, letter to duc de Chevreuse, 5 Jan 1711, 'je ne demande rien pour M l'abbé de Laval . . . il me semble que Lombez conviendrait pour faire une experience à cet abbé'.

26   See Bergin, *Making*, 269, 547–8.

French authority after France's territorial gains in the Spanish Netherlands. Some regulars combined a relatively uneventful existence – as far as we can tell – with that of writer who could, in some instances, offer his services to the crown.[27] But the most common source of their wider reputation, and thus of their success in attracting royal patronage, lay in their activity as preachers. This was perhaps the main reason why the Oratory did so well in supplanting the older mendicant orders in the episcopate. Mascaron and Soanen were among the most celebrated preachers of their day, and other Oratorians, trained by, or following the example of their influential superior-general and preacher, Jean-François Sénault, enjoyed a solid if less spectacular reputation in their day. And because they often began their preaching career in the provincial colleges where they had been sent as teachers, their reputation was frequently more than merely Parisian. Even if the style of individual preachers could differ considerably, as contemporaries observed with extreme acuity, it does seem that the substance of Oratorian preaching had a greater appeal to France's elites than that of the older orders. But as some contemporaries observed with regret, far too few of the ablest preachers of the day were rewarded with a mitre.

III

More than any other, Louis XIV's reign has long been seen as the epitome of the 'court society' phenomenon. Anecdotes abound about royal suspicion of individuals the king did not know or had not seen at court for long periods. Yet there is good reason to be wary of such commonplaces, and we should be ready to allow that, in principle at least, the familiarity generated by 'the king's gaze' was not always a prerequisite for ecclesiastical preferment. At the same time, such familiarity was always *likely* to be an advantage, especially when the king and his advisers were becoming elderly. Probably the most obvious way to acquire the kind of familiarity with the royal entourage which contemporaries judged essential to advancement was to hold some kind of post in the various royal households at court. In an age when clerics in full orders monopolised access to the episcopate, that meant, above all, the royal almonerships. But, for reasons that will become clear, the list should also include preceptors, tutors, and 'royal' preachers whose route to the court was probably somewhat different involving, as it did, some element of intellectual distinction. There are a few unusual cases, as we ought to expect, in such matters. A handful of the former 'seculars' discussed earlier had been based at court *before* entering the church, and it was always possible, depending on their connections, for them to return there later in new clothes. Louis Aubert de Villeserin succeeded his father as a financial official (*maître* in the *chambre*

27 Belin of Belley, Bacoué of Glandèves.

aux deniers) at court in the late 1650s, and returned there as a royal almoner a few years after entering the church: the fact that he was a godson of Louis and his mother Anne of Austria may have smoothed the way for him. On the other hand, the king's boyhood *enfant d'honneur*, Lascaris d'Urfé, eschewed such an easy option during the sixteen years between his first encounters with Saint-Sulpice in 1660 and his nomination to Limoges in 1676.

This is not the place to examine the evolution of the court under Louis XIV, but a few points of direct relevance to the present discussion need to be made in order to understand the figures in tables 4.2 and 4.3. Perhaps the most unexpected of them is that while the overall size of the court may have been expanding, Louis XIV gradually curtailed the huge proliferation of honorary but purchasable almonerships characteristic of the court since the mid-sixteenth century; nor did he stop there, since he also gradually abolished the venality of the almonerships themselves.[28] Compared with the 1640s and 1650s, when non-serving almoners proliferated, the size of royal ecclesiastical households fell considerably, if progressively – a development which ought to have been to the benefit of the (fewer) almoners who actually served there. As far as the scrappy and laconic extant sources enable us to generalise at all, it appears that there were significant reductions rather than a complete elimination during the 1660s in the number of almoners without quarter or salary ('sans quartier ni gages'): the norm for the king's chapel remained fixed at eight almoners, two of whom would serve per quarter, with one of them subsequently serving the Dauphin.[29] That reduction was, it seems, partially offset by the rising number of royal establishments within the court owing to the proliferation of royal offspring, legitimate and illegitimate, as well as the simultaneous presence there of several generations of the royal family in the latter decades of the reign. It will be obvious that all of these offered more promising openings not just to prospective almoners but also to tutors and preceptors to younger family members.

Fifty-one of Louis XIV's bishops, just over one-fifth of the total, are known to have been attached to the various ecclesiastical households at court.[30] As an overall proportion, this is marginally *lower* than that for the period 1589

28 Abbé Oroux, *Histoire ecclésiastique de la Cour*, 2 vols (Paris 1777), ii, 532, who compares the number of ecclesiastical sinecures with those of the court generally, especially under Mazarin, 'qui aimoit à faire argent de tout'. Saint-Simon, iv, 94–5 also discusses this decision.

29 In the successive volumes of the *État de la France*, which itemise the personnel of the royal chapel for the period, only the eight serving almoners are identified by name. All of the others are covered by the unvarying remark – 'je ne parle point de tant de prédicateurs et aumosniers ad honorem, qui n'ont ici aucun rang' (e.g. N Besongne, *État de la France*, 1698, i, 29). Who or how numerous they were and whether they actually frequented the court remains virtually impossible to establish.

30 This figure is compiled from several sources, which range from the enquiries *de vita et moribus* of individual bishops to the partial *états* of the royal households in BN, MS Fr 7854, fos 331–60; BN, MS Clairambault 814, fos 177–267, *état* of king's household for 1673; BN, MS 32757, *tableau de la France*, pp 883–7 (1680 and later); and individual volumes of Besongne, *État de la France*, for 1663, 1665, 1692, 1698, 1712.

to 1661, and to that extent it dispels the idea that the episcopate was increasingly reserved, literally, for *abbés de cour*. By far the biggest subgroup among them consisted of the forty-two who were almoners of one rank or another, but also 'masters' in the royal chapel (*maîtres de chapelle*). Only five of these men held the more prestigious positions of *premier aumônier*, which usually signalled a much closer relationship with particular members of the royal family. Among them, of course, the best placed were those who started out rather than finished as either a *premier aumônier* or a *maître de chapelle*. It is thus no surprise that these men bore names like Cambout de Coislin (uncle and nephew), Le Tellier, Lavergne de Tressan, Simiane de Gordes or, at the end of the reign, Turgot. Moreover, these high-status posts were compatible with episcopal office, which meant that, unlike the 'ordinary' almonerships, they did not have to be given up on promotion to the episcopate – a privilege which of course gave their holders continuing access to royal favour once they had been promoted bishops. By the same token, such an arrangement explains why there might be so little upward movement within royal ecclesiastical households for the 'ordinary' almoners. During the years when almonerships were still venal – the usual price in the 1660s and 1670s was 75,000 *livres* – they were not necessarily socially 'exclusive', so it is not surprising to find sons of financiers with names like Le Camus, Forcoal and Milon, or of court-service families of commoner background like Ancelin, Aubert or Vallot, among their ranks. One consequence of the suppression of the venality of almonerships after 1685 may indeed have been to make them more socially exclusive than hitherto – a possibly unintended consequence of royal intentions, since Louis XIV's scruples about such venality were based on the confession by an almoner, Henri Feydeau, nominated bishop of Amiens in 1685, that he had purchased his office explicitly with a view to episcopal preferment.[31] The fact that the almoners becoming bishops in the last two or three decades of the reign were increasingly from noble families of some antiquity would suggest that what we are seeing are the effects of the gradual disappearance of venality.

The reduction in the numbers of honorific almonerships probably resulted in the 'ordinary' almoners serving in a more continuous and exclusive fashion at an increasingly regulated court. That in turn may have strengthened the ties of clientship between the almoners and the Bourbon ruling family and, therefore, their chances of entry to the episcopate. This was all the more likely in that the king's almoners did not always literally serve the king himself, but also other members of the expanding royal family, who were often willing to press their case for episcopal promotion in later years. Still, for some of our bishops the almonership may have been a useful *état* rather than a genuine activity. Exactly half of them held no other post concurrently with it, nor engaged in any other sustained activity that has so far come to light. This, of

31 Oroux, *Histoire ecclésiastique*, 532–3. Saint-Simon, xx, 219.

course, did not preclude a certain amount of occasional preaching or involve-ment in missions to the Huguenot areas of France on the part of some almoners. Most of them, needless to say, held benefices *in commendam* or other posts which did not involve either residence or cure of souls. Thus, to be simultaneously either a canon of Saint-Jean of Lyon, Montpellier or Notre Dame of Paris was an agreeable benefit to those enjoying good connections, not a headache, since they were largely sinecures for which dispensations for non-residence were readily given. Whatever the means whereby almonerships and 'masterships' (*maîtrises*) in the royal chapel were obtained, they tended to be remarkably 'self-sufficient' for their holders until the latter decades of the reign. The most important exceptions to this pattern are represented by those of their number who, as we shall see later, went on to be vicars-general of dioceses or *agents-généraux* of the French clergy.

The handful of future bishops who served as preceptors, tutors, or *lecteurs* to members of the royal family were almost certainly busier than the almoners. By contrast, the duration of their service was necessarily limited, even if it was never precisely spelled out in a contract. Louis XIV's longevity as well as the progeny produced by his successive liaisons ensured that this form of employment would not be lacking from the 1670s onwards. It was not a cler-ical monopoly, on the contrary, but clerical intellectuals were bound to be serious candidates for some of the posts on offer. As far as we know, only one candidate *failing* to obtain such a position, in the education of the Dauphin, was actually given – unexpectedly, no doubt, since he was a Franciscan – a bishopric instead![32] The normal route was service first, with reward, not nec-essarily in the form of a mitre, following later. The total number of future bishops employed in this way was no more than nine, but they included some of the most distinguished bishops of the age – Bossuet, Huet, Fénelon. The last of the nine, Nicolas Malezieu, who became a bishop in 1713, was the only example of a father-son team of tutors. His father had begun by teach-ing Louis XIV's sons the ducs du Maine and de Bourgogne and, having sub-sequently established himself as Maine's chancellor and confidant, he ensured that his son would tutor the duc's son, the prince de Dombes. Malezieu *père* had, in fact, owed his initial advancement to Bossuet when the latter was in royal service during the 1670s, but Bossuet's patronage did not end there, since he also managed to place future bishops like Jean Catelan and Antoine Girard, neither of whom would have had much of a claim on high office in the church, in the service of the duc de Bourgogne and comte de Toulouse respectively. With the exception of the well-born Fénelon, who was also the

---

32 Léon Bacoué, the Franciscan, who got the modest Provençal see of Glandèves in 1673. BN, Mélanges Colbert 176bis, fos 877–8, undated letter to Colbert: 'ce pays estant le pays de l'elo-quence et de la politesse où les valets de chambre de la Cour parlent plus purement que les Avocats Généraux de nos parlements de province, et en comparaison duquel le reste de la France est Barbare, il seroit fort necessaire pour l'heureux succes de la composition de mon ouvrage que j'y (the court) demeurasse' (fo 878r).

most admired and successful of royal preceptors, few of these men were offered attractive dioceses: most were a very considerable distance from the court. The debates over how Fénelon could continue to act as the duc de Bourgogne's preceptor while archbishop of Cambrai notwithstanding, it seems that these episcopal promotions were intended finally to draw a line under the activity in question and to separate the tutors or *lecteurs* from their royal charges in a very public way.[33]

It is, unfortunately, far more difficult to gauge the contribution of preaching activity to episcopal preferment. Like its counterparts elsewhere in Europe, the French royal court had its complement of pensioned preachers, the *prédicateurs du roi*. But under Louis XIV the formal connection between preachers who obtained the mitre and those who held posts of *prédicateur du roi* seems loose to an extent that defies expectations, given how many bishops were among the best-known preachers of the day. The surviving lists of *prédicateurs du roi* show that, like the almoners 'sans quartier', their numbers rose and then fell during the 1640s and 1650s, settling at around ten by the early 1660s but dropping, it seems, to as low as four in later decades.[34] Nobody on those early lists ever became a bishop. Yet between twenty and twenty-five bishops were active and well-known preachers before the episcopate, and in some cases that was their primary claim to royal attention. This may not seem a significant number, and it could probably be increased if we knew more about particular individual biographies. Obviously, not all of them were the equals of Bossuet, Fléchier or Mascaron. Only one or two bishops, such as Fromentières of Aire and the celebrated Mascaron, are recorded as having been a *prédicateur du roi*. For his part, Bossuet only obtained his court position as tutor to Louis XIV's eldest son *after* he had become bishop, so his preaching had not been acknowledged in any formal way before his nomination to Condom in 1669. Fléchier, for his part, was made a royal almoner, and so would probably not have needed any additional title to advertise his oratorical gifts. No doubt the same could be said of the six other known preachers who were almoners or tutors in royal service. Several of them had preached in major Parisian churches, delivered funeral orations for members of the royal family or major military or political figures, or done the Advent or Lenten 'stations' at court. Others again may have waited until they became bishops before displaying their oratorical talents on a wider stage. What few seem to have actively sought was a position of *prédicateur du roi*, which at one level makes it more difficult to estimate the contribution of their oratorical talents to the promotion of several bishops. In any case, rarely were the triumphs and setbacks, the strengths and weaknesses of preachers scrutinised

33 Not all of these nominations fit the same pattern. Nicolas Malezieu was given the distant see of Lavaur in Languedoc, but the duc du Maine was governor of the province and Malezieu's father was his *secrétaire des commandements* for Languedoc!

34 BN, MS Fr 19212, fo 23v, Père Léonard papers, 21 Jan 1704, referring to Père Séraphim as 'un des quatre prédicateurs de Sa Majesté *couché sur l'estat*' (italics mine).

with such seriousness by France's elites, particularly those of the capital, as during the personal rule. Even ambitious clerics, like Archbishop Harlay's future secretary, the abbé Le Gendre, was awestruck by the abundance of such talent on display when he first arrived in Paris and began preaching there himself.[35] It took more than one good sermon to win a mitre, of course, and many able preachers were overlooked, but contemporaries readily agreed on the appropriateness of such promotions. Even Saint-Simon was prepared to ignore the frequently undistinguished origins of these men and applaud their qualities, especially if their preaching was in a morally rigorist vein.

If contemporaries of Louis XIV had been asked to point to a 'high road' to the episcopate, they would almost certainly have singled out not the court positions we have just examined, but the elective and short-term post of *agent-général* of the clergy. However, this perception would only have become widespread during the latter decades of Louis's reign. Since the emergence of the regular assemblies of clergy after 1560, the *agents*, of whom there were normally two at any one time – one elected by a northern province, one by a southern one, each one serving a five-year term – had become important intermediaries between the crown and the clergy. This alone sufficed to ensure that their election was a matter of some importance, with royal ministers from Richelieu onwards doing everything possible to ensure that reliable men would be elected by whichever province enjoyed the rotating right of election. As we shall see, it was equally normal for ambitious members of the clergy to canvass election to such pivotal positions capable of opening up far greater prospects for them. Once elected, those prospects depended heavily on how they managed to satisfy both of their official masters, the French clergy in assembly, and the crown in the form of its ministers, especially the *contrôleur-général* of the finances. Contemporary views of these men are borne out by the statistics which, for once, enable us to determine actual success rates.[36] The oldest *agent-général* to become a bishop under Louis XIV (Moreau de Saint-Josse) had been elected an agent as long ago as 1630, the last one (a Turgot) as late as 1708. Between those dates a total of thirty-eight individuals were elected as *agents-généraux*, a higher figure than might be expected, given the normal five-year term of tenure. Of the thirty-eight, no fewer than twenty-seven (71 per cent) became bishops, and eighteen of them served as agents under, and were made bishops by, Louis XIV – an impressive tally. The record for the *agents* of Henri III, Henri IV and Louis XIII was in no way comparable, with no more than two of them becoming bishops during the first fifty years of the 'agency'! It was the three *agents* elected by the 1635 Assembly of Clergy, thanks largely to their connections with Richelieu, who started a trend that would be regarded as wholly normal a generation or so

---

35   Louis Le Gendre, *Mémoires*, ed M Roux (Paris 1863), 8–22, for his verdicts on several preachers.

36   There is a convenient list of them, from 1579 to 1789, provided by Pierre Blet in Lucien Bély, ed, *Dictionnaire de l'ancien régime* (Paris 1996), 41–2.

later. Mazarin imitated the 'grand cardinal' in this regard, but up to the late 1660s only one out of every two *agents* joined the episcopal corps.[37] However, beginning with the Assembly of 1670, virtually every *agent-général* for the next forty years became a bishop – though the last few obviously had to wait until the next reign to do so. For a few years in the late 1690s, the agency seemed to be on the verge of becoming a revolving door through which agents briefly entered only to leave as bishops well before serving their full term. Whatever lay behind this unusual episode, it was not repeated thereafter, though it was not unknown for individual agents to become bishops half-way through their term as *agent*. There were, as we should expect, a handful of exceptions – a few early deaths and, more surprisingly, actual refusals of episcopal promotion, one of them by the only *agent-général* to serve for two terms: Charles Andrault de Maulevrier turned down Autun in 1710 after months of reflection, possibly on the same grounds that he had given on a previous occasion, namely that the 'agency' was altogether a more attractive and well-remunerated position, and with fewer headaches![38] Insofar as we can detect a pattern developing during the early decades of the reign, it was that the *agents-généraux* would serve out their full term, concluding with the five-year assembly where they acted as secretaries or *promoteurs*, and during which vacant dioceses would be earmarked for them. With just one exception, this remained the case until the 1690s, when there was a spate of nominations to the episcopate of recently installed *agents-généraux*. This in turn continued to occur, though less frequently, down to 1710, when the last of the *agents-généraux*, Dominique Turgot, was made bishop after just two years in post. But just as there was early promotion for some agents, it could be substantially delayed for others. Louis d'Aquin, an *agent-général* elected in 1690, suffered from the disgrace of his powerful brother, the king's *premier médecin*, in 1693, since he was not promoted on ending his *agence* in 1695; he had to engineer his uncle's resignation in his favour in 1697 before his fortunes changed. Less easy to understand is why Balthasar Phélypeaux, who ended his *agence* in 1705, had to wait until 1713 and even then to be given a remote Provençal diocese, Riez, given the ministerial eminence of his powerful cousin, Chancellor Pontchartrain.

Because of its strategic importance, it might be thought that the *agence générale du clergé* would be reserved to men who already possessed substantial experience in other spheres. But this was precisely why it was no less certain to attract the ambitious and well-connected younger clerics.[39] Down to the mid-1690s roughly, the incoming *agents-généraux* had had relatively little previous experience, with the exception of two royal almoners. Many of them

---

37 See Bergin, *Making*, 291.

38 BN, MS Fr 19211, fo 77, Père Léonard's *mémoires ecclésiastiques*, 27 Dec 1703, 'estant à son ayse et sans embarras et avec train, disant que son agence pour le revenu lui vaut un evesché'.

39 See Albert Cans, *L'Organisation financière du clergé de France au temps de Louis XIV* (Paris 1910), ch 7, 'les agents généraux'.

had only completed their theology degrees as recently as the year of their election, all of them in Paris, which no doubt brought them to the attention of
senior figures in the French church and among the royal entourage. An
extreme example is provided by Armand Bazin de Bezons, future archbishop
of Bordeaux, who was no more than a twenty-five-year-old bachelor in
theology when elected *agent* in 1680 by the province of Narbonne, an election
probably engineered by one of his patrons, Cardinal Bonsi, archbishop of Narbonne.[40] He duly continued his studies, taking his licence and doctorate
during his first two years as *agent-général*! Ten years previously, Archbishop
Péréfixe of Paris had engineered the election as *agent* of his nephew, Fortin
de la Hoguette, by the province of Paris. Other names among these early
agents-généraux with high-ranking connections and relatively little prior experience include Colbert de Saint-Pouange, Grignan, Desmarets, Aquin and
Phélypeaux. Something of a record would be set in 1696 when *both* the new
agents-généraux were Colberts (Croissy and a Villacerf), the first of whom
was bishop of Montpellier within a year; Villacerf's personal behaviour
subsequently debarred him from preferment.[41] In the last decade or so of the
reign, the Phélypeaux and Desmarets families succeeded in having a second
family member elected *agent-général* and then nominated bishop. But there is
one noticeable difference by this point – the *agents-généraux* of the mid-1690s
and later were slightly older and had previously been active as vicars-general
or in other church posts. Limited though it may be, this shift is symptomatic
of changes which we shall shortly revisit.

IV

What we have seen so far only accounts for the early careers of approximately
a quarter of all Louis XIV's bishops. With fewer regulars than ever before
entering the episcopate, court-based posts of royal almoner, preacher and royal
tutor, not to mention those of *agents-généraux*, could never provide more
than a fraction of incoming bishops in a church the size of that of France. By
comparison, the complex superstructure of offices, benefices, 'dignities' and
functions provided by the church was almost boundless, and it was in fact
growing rather than contracting in ways that would be important for the
recruitment of new bishops in our period. It was here that the great mass of
France's bishops would have had to exercise their talents, if not exactly prove
their fitness for the episcopate.

We may begin looking at the historical launch-pads of future bishops –
chapters, cathedral and collegiate and, for want of a more historically exact

40 Bazin's father had served for twenty years as intendant in Languedoc until 1673 where he had
    worked closely with Bonsi, then its dominant political figure. Moreover, the cardinal's sister,
    the marquise de Castries, was also godmother to the future bishop.
41 Saint-Simon, vi, 580.

term, diocesan administration. There is no need to rehearse here the reasons why a place in a chapter attracted clerics from established families ranging from the leading provincial aristocracy to the urban bourgeoisie and office-holders. As far as the episcopate itself is concerned, the figures would seem to speak for themselves, since at least 107 of Louis XIV's 250 bishops had belonged at some point to a chapter. This figure should be taken as an absolute minimum, since it is not known how many of the vicars-general and other officials whom we shall encounter presently were simultaneously canons of a chapter. Of the 107 canons on our list, only thirteen had belonged to a collegiate rather that to a cathedral chapter. A few of them did migrate from a *collégiale* to a cathedral, while yet others went on to hold offices which were not chapter-based at all. Such movement should not be regarded as essential pre-requisites for their subsequent careers, since 'mere' collegiate chapters like Saint-Martin-de-Tours or Saint-Thomas-du-Louvre were far more distinguished than most cathedral chapters. When the figures are looked at more closely, it transpires that only four of Louis XIV's bishops had never been anything other than a cathedral canon before their promotion. But before jumping to the conclusion that their elevation must have been something of a miracle, we should briefly note who they were. One of them was a Béthune, nephew of the archbishop of Bordeaux, Henri de Béthune; another the brother of the king's physician, Aquin; the two others were a Colbert and a Lezay de Lusignan respectively. None of them would, we can safely wager, have made it to the episcopate without the name and favour that their names alone suggest. And both of the collegiate-church canons who remained in their chapters of origin, Gourgues and Lalanne, were from prominent Bordeaux *parlementaire* families who went on to govern dioceses in their native region (Bazas and Bayonne). These figures amply bear out the verdict of Philippe Loupès for the chapters of Guyenne, namely that 'mere' cathedral or collegiate canons stood very little chance of entering the episcopate unless they were sufficiently well connected not to need other church positions along the way.[42]

This should not be taken to mean that the remaining canons in our list lacked for such advantages, merely that we are unlikely to uncover the reasons for, or the circumstances in which they went on to hold higher positions in their chapters – or beyond. Frequently, of course, they combined the two. Of the seventy-two bishops known to have begun their careers as canons in a chapter, sixty-eight later moved upwards or outwards. Moreover, because of long-standing family connections and the canon law governing benefices, which facilitated the passing on of offices by 'resignatio in favorem', many of the future bishops who passed through cathedral or collegiate chapters did

---

42 P Loupès, *Chapitres et chanoines de Guyenne aux xvii*ᵉ *et xviii*ᵉ *siècles* (Paris 1985), 260, reporting that only five canons from the region's chapters became bishops over three centuries, a success rate of just 1–2 per cent.

not have to begin their careers as 'mere' canons and in the hope that something better would come their way in due course. Approximately thirty-three
of the 107 canons under discussion actually began further up the ladder,
securing posts of 'dignity', as they were called, at an often early age. For that
reason,providing reliable figures about the exact numbers of bishops occupying
these different positions raises real difficulties. In many cases, the dignities in
question were in cathedrals where future bishops had uncles or other relatives
in whose gift they were. Thus, Armand de Béthune, whose uncle had made
him a canon of Bordeaux, made his own younger brother, a future bishop of
Verdun, dean of Le Puy sometime after he became bishop there in 1665. The
two Matignon brothers were successively deans of Lisieux in the 1660s and
1670s, thanks to their uncle, the local bishop. Many other examples of the
recycling of such offices within families could be cited, especially in the
chapters of Provence, whose closely interrelated noble families were past
masters of the conservation of family heirlooms. What these examples show is
that these dignitaries were sometimes from entrenched 'provincial' families,
sometimes from ones with far more extensive 'national' connections. It should
also be noted that at least some of these canons and dignitaries owed their
initial positions – and not just their ultimate episcopal one – to the crown
itself, thanks to the *régale* which enabled the king to nominate to vacant
positions such as those of cathedral and collegiate chapters, since they did not
involve cure of souls.[43]

The 'dignities' mentioned above – provost, archdeacon, dean, archpriest,
cantor, sacristan and others – placed their holders among the most prominent
clergy of the dioceses in question, even when they were not related to
reigning bishops. They enabled them to seek election to general assemblies
of the clergy, provincial councils, diocesan assemblies, local estates (where
they existed) and various other bodies. As members of a chapter with its
own corporate interests to defend, especially against bishops often deemed
to be 'authoritarian', the dignitaries might not be on the best of terms
with their bishop, who in turn might therefore not sing their praises in high
places. But such 'structural' rivalries did not always have such negative effects,
nor prevent individual dignitaries from becoming heavily involved in
administering the diocese. What the historian cannot do, unfortunately, is
to deduce from the dignities in question the extent to which their holders
were either assiduous or absentees. We may well ask what, if anything,
the twenty-one year-old Henri Félix, son of Louis XIV's *premier chirurgien*
and a future bishop of Digne, made of his position as archdeacon of Auch
in distant Gascony: the chances are he may never have set foot in Auch

---

43 Examples of this are to be found scattered throughout BN, MS Fr 20969, a compilation known,
     quite mistakenly, as the 'feuille des bénéfices' 1672–1702. For the nomination of Charles-
     Gaspard de Vintimille as canon and sacristan of Toulon 'vacant en régale', Nov 1675 (fo 15r);
     René-François de Beauvau to a canonicate in Sarlat, April 1689 (fo 76v); of Bernard de Poudenx
     as canon and archdeacon in Tarbes, Dec 1689 (fo 119r).

before his father's favour secured him a more attractive benefice closer to Paris.[44]

One of the most common dignities encountered in the curricula vitae of Louis XIV's bishops is that of archdeacon which, in principle, entailed a measure of 'geographical' responsibility within a diocese. At least thirty future bishops had held that position.[45] We know that for some future bishops, that responsibility was genuine and involved them in pastoral visitations, oversight of the clergy of the area, the organisation of ecclesiastical conferences and so on – in short, the kind of experience that would be invaluable in their subsequent careers. Nicolas Taffoureau, bishop of Alet in 1698, is a good example of this: he began as a chaplain in Sens cathedral, became a canon and then dean of the chapter, before being made archdeacon of the Gâtinais by his archbishop. This involved, among other things, oversight of the female religious communities of the area, but for all his labours, Taffoureau might well have remained one of a legion of anonymous, unnoticed archdeacons were it not for his encounter with the Beauvillier family, whose daughters were nuns at Montargis. The potential for expanded activity among archdeacons seems to have increased as the reign progressed. Of the thirty future bishops who had held the position, nineteen were either simultaneously or successively grand-vicars to their bishops; by the latter decades of the reign, virtually *every* one of these former archdeacons in question had also served as a grand-vicar. If it is possible to talk of French bishops as at least partially coopting their collective successors, then the line of investigation has to start further down the line than is usual, with the groups which produced cathedral chapter canons and their dignitaries.

This conclusion could be taken to mean that nothing had changed within the French church since the later middle ages when cathedral chapters elected bishops from their own members. Such a view would be untenable. There is no doubt that most French bishops in the seventeenth century felt that they needed their own *hommes de confiance* in positions of authority under their direct control. As in the past, some of these men would be family members, clients of one kind or another, sometimes even contemporaries or mentors from their years at university. Moreover, some of the posts that bishops could usually offer these men were still evolving in our period, and from a bishop's point of view, their value lay in that they were not part of, or subject to, the supervision of the chapter. Consequently, holders of posts of *official*, *théologal* and vicar-general (or grand-vicar) came to serve as the core of diocesan administration, answerable to the bishop himself.[46] The presence of future bishops in

---

44 Félix became archdeacon in Auch cathedral in 1662, possibly thanks to the privileges attached to university graduate status. By 1664, he was treasurer of the Sainte Chapelle of Vincennes, an attractive and well remunerated benefice; he also became a royal almoner during the 1660s.
45 In some southern dioceses, the equivalent of the archdeacon was the archpriest.
46 See p 103, n 49.

such posts is, therefore, an excellent indicator of their closeness to the generation of bishops that preceded them. It was the post of *théologal*, or canon
theologian, which attracted the smallest number of future bishops – only
five in all. There is no obvious explanation for this except perhaps to say
that with seminaries beginning to take shape as formal institutions, the
function and value of the *théologal* was perhaps more problematic than in
the past. Secondly, French bishops seem to have begun employing theologians
in a more purely private capacity than previously and, in an age when
episcopal pronouncements on religious questions were more common
than ever before, these theological confidants were not short of work. The
number of future bishops who had been an *official* was higher, but not remarkably so, at fourteen in all. Intriguingly, none of the bishops nominated
before the 1680s had held this post, which involved the exercise of episcopal
penal authority. It is only post-1700 that the number of *officiaux* begins
to rise, if we can really use the word in relation to very limited figures.
But the most interesting feature of its development by that point is how often
it was confided to someone who was *simultaneously* a vicar-general. At first
sight, there is no apparent reason for this amalgamation of duties beyond the
reigning bishop's own convenience or personal approach to governing his
diocese. But because of its increasing frequency, the connection deserves a
closer look.

V

The post of vicar-general was perhaps the least 'autonomous' within the upper
levels of the diocesan administration and its clergy. Appointed by the bishop
to act as his right-hand man and exercise his jurisdiction, the vicar-general
was not necessarily a member, let alone a dignitary, of the cathedral chapter,
though episcopal patronage might of course secure such a position for him.
His position was thus radically different from that of an archdeacon well
ensconced in the chapter. An episcopal succession might suddenly leave him
without employment, obliged to look elsewhere or return to his previous
occupations. But his value to a reigning bishop lay in that ultimate depend-
ency, even if there is little evidence of vicars-general being disgraced in large
numbers by their capricious masters. On the contrary, there is more evidence
of continuity of service by these men across several episcopal reigns. Their
value is also underlined by the fact that bishops, especially in large dioceses,
began to appoint several of them to assist them, which explains why the terms
vicar-general and grand-vicar tend to be used interchangeably to describe
them. The early chronology of this development remains obscure, but it
probably took off in earnest under Louis XIV as a French adaptation of Carlo
Borromeo's *vicaires forains*. A good example of this is the reorganisation of the
diocese of Albi in 1695 which saw its four archdiaconates transformed into

Table 4.3   *Pre-episcopal activities by decade*

Activity	1660s	1670s	1680s	1690s	1700s	1710s	Total
almoner, chapel	8	12	7	7	3	5	42
royal tutors etc	1	2	1	3	1	1	9
agent-général	2	4	3	4	5	0	18
papal/Roman service	0	1	0	2	0	0	3
sovereign courts	1	3	3	1	2	0	10
conseiller d'état	0	1	1	0	0	0	2
service to grands	1	1	0	0	0	0	2
cathedral canons only	1	2	1	0	0	0	4
cathedral canons 'plus'	10	12	8	12	19	7	68
other chapters	3	1	1	3	3	2	13
chapter dignitaries	6	7	7	5	13	1	39
archdeacon/priest	3	9	2	7	7	2	30
official	0	0	3	2	11	2	18
théologal	2	2	0	1	1	0	6
grand-vicar	4	5	3	19	41	14	86
seminary direction	1	0	1	1	4	1	8
convent superiorships	1	4	0	5	0	1	11
missions	0	2	6	7	4	0	19
preaching	3	7	2	4	3	0	19
parish priests	3	2	1	1	4	1	12

twenty-one districts, each subject to a *vicaire forain*.[47] To what extent did Louis XIV's bishops bear the imprint of these changes?

An initial glance at the king's nominees suggests that that impact was rather limited and slow to materialise (see table 4.3). About ninety bishops – slightly more than a third of the total – had been grand-vicars before their promotion. However, when we break down this aggregate on a decade-by-decade basis, the figures begin to take on a different construction. From the 1660s to the 1680s included, grand-vicars are scattered around fairly evenly, but are easily outnumbered by royal almoners and members of cathedral chapters. Four or five representatives per decade, and totalling only fourteen over three decades, hardly amounts to a significant presence. Such a pattern differs very little from that of the half century before 1661. It is in the 1690s that the situation changes quite dramatically – the numbers simply soar onto a different plane altogether, *and* the change proves to be a sustained one, even

47   *Répertoire des visites pastorales de la France. Première série: anciens dioceses (jusqu'en 1790)*, 4 vols (Paris 1977–85), i, 55. The archbishop of Albi, Le Goux de la Berchère, was a capable and respected figure. It might be added that a neighbouring diocese, Saint-Pons, with just forty parishes, was divided a few years after Albi into six similar districts known as 'conférences' (p 225).

though the numbers drop back temporarily during the last few years of the reign. There is no doubt that the origins of the eighteenth-century pattern of pre-episcopal careers lies here. But why did it happen then, and why was it so rapid, unheralded by any obvious longer-term prior trends?

If there is an answer to this question, it probably lies in the experiences of the ten-year freeze from 1682 to 1692 in the provision of new bishops to vacant dioceses, which was a consequence of the gallican crisis of 1682. This problem will be discussed in greater detail later, but for the present it should suffice to say that the crown tried to get round the obstacles that the embargo caused by ensuring that the king's nominees could already participate in the governing of their dioceses through having the cathedral chapters coopt them as vicars-capitular *sede vacante*, with neighbouring bishops performing the religious functions reserved for consecrated bishops.[48] By the time the crisis was finally resolved in 1692–3, a large number of bishops had been active for several years as vicars-general in effect. This did not provoke an immediate revolution in the way in which episcopal nominations were made, but by the end of the 1690s something like a clear pattern was undoubtedly emerging. Forty-five per cent of all bishops of that decade had been grand-vicars, compared to no more than 5 per cent hitherto, and that proportion would nearly double again (to 82 per cent!) during the 1700s. The drop to a still substantial 65 per cent during the last five years of the reign may, in turn, have something to do with the politics of those years, dominated as they were by the battles that preceded and followed the bull *Unigenitus*. But it does not affect the overall shift of emphasis in royal patronage during the last twenty-five years of the reign.

As already noted, the development of the functions of grand-vicars within individual French dioceses remains obscure. One diocese which seems to have played an important role in this regard was Lyon under its long-serving and masterful archbishop, Camille de Neufville-Villeroy (1653–93) and especially under his successor, Claude de Saint-Georges (1693–1714), although relatively little is known about this aspect of its history.[49] At any rate, the Lyon model, as refined and perfected by Saint-Georges, was subsequently exported to other dioceses by those who had served there or attempted to copy it. An impressive instance of such export was Poitiers under Jean-Claude de la Poype

---

48 While a diocese was vacant, it was governed on behalf of the cathedral chapter by two or more vicars-capitular elected by the chapter (hence their title) for that purpose. When Bishop Le Goux of Lavaur was promoted to Albi in 1687, and his successor at Lavaur, Victor de Mailly, was sent there as vicar-capitular, it was understood that Le Goux would continue to perform the bishop's exclusive religious functions. Indeed it seems that both men were active in Lavaur for the next year or more: 'Annales de l'église de Lavaur' by G-M Audran, who served as confidant and adviser of successive bishops of Lavaur, cited by Jean-Claude Ferret, 'L'Action des évêques de Lavaur dans la réforme pastorale de leur diocèse aux xviie et xviiie siècles' (Mémoire de maîtrise, Université de Toulouse-II, 2000).

49 Philip T Hoffman, *Church and Community in the Diocese of Lyon 1500–1789* (New Haven-London 1984), does not deal with this question in an otherwise valuable study.

de Vertrieu, a Lyonnais who had been the principal grand-vicar under Saint-Georges and who became bishop of Poitiers in 1702. His short lived predecessor, Antoine Girard, had worked himself into an early grave as he tried to tackle a poorly run diocese, but the experienced and better organised La Poype governed it 'souverainement' for thirty years. From the outset, he employed six grand-vicars to help him govern what was also a vast diocese of 750 parishes with a large ex-Huguenot population and numerous religious orders, male and female. As one of his best informed and shrewdest contemporaries noted, La Poype delegated most of the ordinary business to the grand-vicars, each of whom had his own territorial area of competence; together they reported on petitions, grievances and other issues requiring decisions at weekly meetings at which La Poype presided and where decisions were apparently made by a vote of those present. This left La Poype free to take a broad view of the needs of his diocese, and also the time and energy to bombard anyone, especially at court, who could provide help, financial or otherwise, for his diocese.[50] Three points are relevant for our purposes here. Firstly, virtually all of La Poype's early grand-vicars were fellow Lyonnais, who may also have been in Saint-Georges's service like himself. Secondly, these posts were clearly *ad laborem*, and not *ad honorem*, as the contemporary distinction had it – that is, they were *not* sinecures. Finally and crucially, three of his six earliest grand-vicars were made bishops by Louis XIV, with no fewer than six more under Louis XV – which may be a record for the century to follow and help explain why Poitiers under La Poype was regarded as a school for bishops. And his grand-vicars were not 'purs produits' of Saint-Sulpice of the kind that Saint-Simon tirelessly ridiculed. All were well-born nobles, and two of them, *grands seigneurs* bearing the names of Villeroy and Châteauneuf de Rochebonne, went on to become archbishops of Lyon itself in due course.[51]

It is not necessary to assume that the Lyon-Poitiers model was the only one taking shape under Louis XIV. La Poype's neighbour at La Rochelle, Champflour, refused to have any grand-vicars, at least during his early years there.[52] Some future bishops are known to have served as grand-vicars in two or three dioceses, which may indicate either a change of bishop or a search for a better position elsewhere. Taken together, however, developments like these show that the growth of grand-vicarships and, above all, the demand for them on the part of well-born clergy in search of high office was having something

50 AN, L 740, pièce 1, Poitiers, no 53,'mémoire concernant Mr l'Evesque de Poictiers, le 7 nov 1705'. Mme de Maintenon, Ponthchartrain, Desmarets and doubtless others received endless missives announcing plans and pleading for assistance. His letters to Maintenon are scattered through her unpublished correspondence in BM Versailles, MS G 331; his correspondence with Desmarets, the *contrôleur-général*, is in AN, G⁷, 542b, nos 262–99.

51 Paulze-d'Ivoy de la Poype, *Un Évêque de Poitiers au xviiiᵉ siecle. Mgr Jean-Claude de la Poype de Vertrieu* (Poitiers 1889), a well documented if one-sided study.

52 Étienne de Champflour was also completely out of sympathy with the proclivities of his rigorst, anti-Jesuit predecessor, Laval-Boisdauphin. See Louis Pérouas, *Le Diocèse de La Rochelle de 1648 à 1724. Sociologie et Pastorale* (Paris 1964), 358–9.

akin to a capillary-action effect. That the message was being heard and acted upon is apparent when, in addition to the names just cited, Paris theology graduates calling themselves Beauvillier, Forbin-Janson, Caylus or Laval-Montmorency went off in search of grand-vicarships when, in an earlier age, they would probably have regarded their pedigree, benefices, and a court position as more than sufficient. It is remarkable, and an early sign of subsequent developments, that a growing number of the king's last episcopal appointees had only *one* item on their curriculum vitae – a grand-vicarship! The 'discovery of the vicar-general' by the crown may have been largely accidental to begin with, but once it had been made its effects were considerable, with even the most unlikely types of cleric queuing up to gain the experience that it provided and which now seemed an indispensable element of a future bishop's career pattern. In this regard, it comes as no small surprise that eight out of the nineteen royal almoners and tutors for the same period had also been grand-vicars before the episcopate; and if one plots these figures chronologically, there is no doubt that the curve is a rising one. This is all the more striking, given how few of these men would have felt any need whatsoever to bother themselves with other church posts in previous generations.

VI

One of the questions put to witnesses testifying on behalf of the king's nominees for bishoprics was whether they had experience of cure of souls. This question was intended to be understood in the restricted sense of holding an office or position to which cure of souls was formally attached. Put in such terms, it was a question that could not often be answered with an unqualified affirmative during Louis XIV's reign; witnesses would frequently cast around for activities that could be associated with the cure of souls pointing, for example, to a candidate's commendable record as a preacher, a missionary, a superior of nuns or of a seminary, and the like. In the generations before Louis XIV few of these latter activities would have received any mention. Even if we may remain skeptical as to how active some candidates had really been in these roles, there is no doubt that the development of the roles themselves was a prominent feature of the seventeenth-century French church, and that, consequently, some at least of the major figures involved with them could, and did, attract the attention of the crown. The example of seminaries will give us some idea of what is meant here, despite the limited numbers involved. A total of eight bishops had actually directed a seminary at some point in their career. The first was Louis Abelly, one of Vincent de Paul's major disciples and his first biographer, nominated to Rodez as early as 1662; fifty years later, in 1712, it was the turn of Pierre Rogier, bishop of Le Mans, who had been superior of the Rennes seminary. The six other seminary directors nominated bishops between those terminal dates were mostly promoted after

1690, beginning with the highly influential figure of Godet des Marais, bishop of Chartres and closely associated with the Parisian Trente-Trois and Saint-Sulpice seminaries, whose growing influence is also visible in some of these pre-episcopal careers. At this stage, even within Saint-Sulpice, being a seminary director was not necessarily a life-long career, and it might be either interrupted or succeeded by other related activities. Moreover, in some dioceses, bishops were already looking to the directors of their seminaries for more than what their nominal functions entailed. Some were concurrently grand-vicars *de facto* if not always *de jure*, as in Limoges in the 1680s where Étienne Champflour was seminary director and grand-vicar to all intents and purposes. La Poype of Poitiers may not have gone quite so far, but the Poitiers seminary director always attended the weekly meetings of his grand-vicars and other *bras droits*.[53] It also seems that Rogier du Crévy was superior of Rennes seminary in his capacity of grand-vicar.[54] But however admirable individuals may have been as seminary directors, that alone was unlikely to bring them to the attention of Louis XIV and his successors: it was most likely to happen if they belonged to, or were closely connected to Paris-based institutions like Saint-Sulpice, the Lazarists or the Oratory.

Not wholly unrelated were the activities of another small group of bishops who had been involved in acting as superiors of religious establishments, particularly convents of nuns. For four of these ten men, the superiorships are their only known pre-episcopal activity, but it should not be concluded from this that these were not serious obligations. Bishops like Michel Poncet of Sisteron and Henri Le Pileur of Saintes seem to have made something of a speciality of such superiorships; both did so in Paris whose multiplicity of religious establishments, new and old, provided unlimited scope for action as well as invaluable connections to elite families. Another four more or less succeeded each other from the late 1670s onwards as superior of the Paris house of the Nouvelles Catholiques, a more controversial position to hold since it was a boarding school for girls forced to abjure Protestantism during the crucial decades either side of the Revocation of the Edict of Nantes. It was a role for a grand *dévot*, as their names alone suggest – Noailles, Fénelon, Milon and Girard.[55] Of the final two religious superiors, Bishop Taffoureau of Alet, is already familiar as the director of the convents of the Montargis area. Yet it is worth reiterating the point that whereas the superiorship derived from his being dean and archdeacon of Sens, his episcopal promotion came about because of the Beauvillier family connection which arose from his superiorship.[56] Likewise, one of grand-vicars of Poitiers before 1705, Joseph Revol, was given the superiorship of all the diocese's

53 AN, L 740, pièce 1, Poitiers, no 53, Père Léonard papers, notes on the Bishop of Poitiers, 1705.
54 ASS, Correspondance des supérieurs-généraux, iii, no 509, Leschassier to Rogier, superior of Rennes seminary, mid-1700.
55 Fénelon, *Correspondance*, i, 155–60.
56 See above, p 137.

many convents alongside his grand-vicarship.[57] It seems likely that many of these superiorships were increasingly being brought under episcopal oversight and, consequently, given to grand-vicars or others in the employ of French bishops whose ambitions to control the religious orders in their dioceses were no secret.

Mention of the houses of the Nouvelles Catholiques raises the related question of whether Louis XIV's future bishops played any part in the Huguenot conversion campaigns *before* the episcopate. Although there is abundant evidence that some of them did so, putting a precise figure on such activity is extremely difficult, given that our sources often refer indifferently to their taking part in preaching, catechising and missionary campaigns. They range from Bossuet's early disputations with Huguenot ministers during his years in Metz to those of Fénelon, Milon and others in western France or the Cévennes in the late 1680s and beyond.[58] By a conservative estimate, at least twenty bishops had participated in these campaigns. The first of them was promoted bishop in 1670, the last in 1711, but most of the appointments came in the 1680s and 1690s. For about one-third of them, missionary involvement is the only known element of their pre-episcopal curriculum, while for the others it was only one of several activities. For reasons that will emerge in a later chapter, however, it seems that for a short time missionary work in Huguenot dominated areas came close to becoming the 'royal road' to the episcopate, but as the missions themselves dropped off in the 1690s, so too did their impact on episcopal patronage, which moved back into more conventional grooves.[59] Not many bishops could rival François Chevalier de Saulx, who had briefly been a seminary director before engaging in missionary work in the Cévennes. The latter was the only thing contemporaries could associate with him, making his nomination as the first bishop of Alès seem wholly appropriate to everyone who commented on it.[60]

It would be absurd to conclude that the promotion of a Bossuet, a Fénelon or a Milon depended mainly on their missionary campaigns. In Fénelon's case, it is quite clear that it did not, since two attempts to obtain western dioceses for him in the mid-1680s while he was actively preaching there were promptly vetoed.[61] What the discussion here has revealed, however, is the sheer fluidity and range of the activities engaged in by a substantial number of bishops of their generation, activities which fitted beside each other almost seamlessly, and which combined established responsibilities within the church alongside newer, more pastorally oriented ones which cannot be pinned down

---

57   AN, L 740, pièce 1, Poitiers, no 53, Père Léonard, notes on Bishop of Poitiers, 1705.
58   Fénelon, *Correspondance*, i, 171–89, with abundant references to the preaching activities of Fénelon and his contemporaries, especially in western France.
59   See below, p 248.
60   AN, L 727, Alès dossier, fo 24, Père Léonard papers.
61   Fénelon, *Correspondance*, i, 165–6.

either in space or time with the same precision. This plasticity of some pre-episcopal careers is most evident in the fact that few of the bishops involved in these related activities confined themselves to just one of them. Some of them also belonged to the compagnies du Saint-Sacrement that survived in one form or another in provincial cities like Marseille, Toulouse or Lyon, and the label of *dévots* fits them perfectly.[62]

In providing significant new opportunities for future bishops to exercise their talents, the seventeenth-century church had not abolished the ones that already existed, including those of a conventionally pastoral kind. A small minority of bishops had indeed exercised the kind of parish ministry covered by the term 'cure of souls' as then understood. Of the eleven men in question, two were just curates – though it should be added that the parish in question was Saint-Sulpice. As in the previous period, a few of these curés seem to have held the parish 'title' rather than actually served in it, but proof either way has not come to light. About half of them had subsequently moved onwards towards more promising occupations, but the other six still held their parishes at the moment of their nomination as bishops, which was unusual in any age. Five of the six parishes in the latter group were Parisian, if we include François Hébert, who had held a Paris parish before occupying possibly the most high-profile parish in Louis XIV's kingdom, that of Versailles itself. But he and the other Parisian curés and curates elevated to the episcopate were, in their different ways, much more than just what their labels suggest. One of them, François Le Tellier, was even a royal almoner. Claude Joly and Louis Abelly were widely known through their many other activities, especially for being close associates of Olier and Vincent de Paul respectively. Broadly similar comments could be made about the few provincial curés who became bishops, but they would not change the overall picture. The path to the episcopate was such a narrow one as to be non-existent for those without activities to their credit capable of generating other sources of reputation and patronage.

The implications of this discussion so far are that, to a considerable degree, Louis XIV's reign witnessed the arrival of a kind of bishop whose early career differed in significant ways from those of previous generations of bishops. But it is worth asking if such a conclusion tells the full story. Did the new really replace the old to that extent? Before concluding in favour of one or the other, we need to look more closely at the familiar and the unchanged in the careers of new bishops.

Some of the familiar and the unchanged have already been discussed – the regulars, the royal almoners, and other court-based clerics. We can also point to a scattering of magistrates in parlements, parisian and provincial,

---

62 For the activities of La Poype of Poitiers while at Lyon, see Catherine Martin, *Les Compagnies de la propagation de la foi (1632–1685)* (Geneva 2000), 320. For Foresta-Coulongue, future bishop of Apt, at Marseille, see Raoul Allier, *Une Société secrete au xvii siècle. La Compagnie du très saint-sacrement de l'autel à Marseille* (Paris 1909), 8, 98, 375ff.

numbering just eleven in total. Two bishops even obtained *brevets* as *conseillers d'état*, but one was a Bouthillier, the other a Desmarets, son and a brother respectively of royal ministers, past and future. Only two seem to have owed their careers virtually entirely to the *grands* – Condé and Bouillon – whom they served in the fullest sense of the term, a considerable contrast with previous periods, but which should not be taken to mean that the *grands* in general did not intervene to secure a mitre for other clients. And just as there were fewer graduates from foreign universities, so too there were fewer bishops with any career experience outside of France. Only two had spent their early careers in Rome in the high-ranking post of Auditor of the Rota, which in the past had just as often led to a diplomatic career crowned by a red hat. Neither of these men – Louis de Bourlemont and Mathieu d'Hervault – managed to achieve such heights, although both finished their careers as arch-bishops in France. A third 'Roman', Léon Potier de Gesvres, seemed destined for a red hat while in the pope's service in Rome during the 1680s, but his prospects were unexpectedly blighted by the crisis in relations with France in the late 1680s. Fortunately, his family connections were good enough for him to return home and restart his career in France as archbishop of Bourges in the mid-1690s: he did get his red hat in the end, although the wait was far longer than it would otherwise have been.[63]

Together, the individuals just discussed number no more than seventeen. But as in the previous generations, they were outnumbered by another enduring category of *ancien-régime* cleric, the twenty-five individuals without any known position or activity prior to the episcopate. The proportion is much lower than for the period from Henri IV to 1661, though the difference may be due in part to nothing more than better sources of information. It is tempting to see them as the ultimate privileged elite who did not even feel they needed to become royal almoners in order to enter the episcopate. There is no doubt that many of them were well connected – sons of great nobles like La Mothe-Houdancourt, Monchy d'Hocquincourt, Étampes, Beauvau or Estrées; sons or close relatives of ministers like Colbert, Sève, Cassagnet, Le Peletier or Loménie; and finally, like Antoine Fagon, the son of an esteemed royal *premier médecin*. But a substantial proportion of them did not enjoy such obvious pedigrees, even though they could in no sense be regarded as outsiders. In the case of some of these names, it was not the supposed certainty of the mitre which explains their blank curriculum vitae, but the fact that they became bishops at a relatively young age – if we can define 'youth' for the present purposes as the age at which they completed their studies rather than their score of years per se. In trying to understand this it is the chronology of their nominations which is of greatest interest, since it clearly confirms some of the tendencies we noted earlier in this chapter.

---

63 Saint-Simon, vi, 411–12. He only received the red hat in 1719 when he took the title of Car-
    dinal de Gesvres.

No fewer than twenty-two of the twenty-five bishops with no recorded pre-episcopal activities received the royal *brevet* between the 1660s and the 1680s, when nominations of this kind were fairly evenly distributed. By comparison, the remaining three beneficiaries, nominated in 1692, 1694 and 1711, seem like throwbacks to a forgotten age, especially the last and most isolated of them.

No doubt further research would lead to a drop in the number of future bishops without any recorded pre-episcopal office or activity. But their presence should not be regarded as evidence that the king and his advisers were somehow occasionally 'irresponsible' in their choices of bishop. A number of the bishops in question were clearly 'heirs' in the sense of being well-placed – nephews of ruling bishops, sons of highly prominent families, relatives of ministers, and so on. Some, but certainly not all of them, secured early promotions, but that was by no means guaranteed in every case. Fagon *fils* was, after all, forty-five when he was nominated to the minor and distant see of Lombez in 1711. It also seems that some among them led lives of quasi-withdrawal, which was far from unusual under Louis XIV, only to be plucked out of it and projected into high office by a king who sometimes liked to confound his advisers by reaching for the forgotten or the 'outsiders', as we shall see in later chapters.

VII

There is one additional feature of the curriculum vitae of the 'average' French bishop from the Concordat to the Revolution which, if not classifiable as an activity, helps to explain why some ecclesiastics rather than others became bishops. Obtaining benefices *in commendam* before elevation to the episcopate indicates a capacity to attract royal attention and patronage, though in many cases such benefices would have been in family hands for one or more generations. Families and individual ecclesiastics were not averse to 'trading-in' their existing benefices to obtain better ones: all depended on how well positioned they were to benefit from royal goodwill towards them. As we saw above, some future bishops took advantage of the *régale* in order to obtain benefices only in the king's gift during episcopal *interregna*. Insofar as the extant sources permit, we can give some idea of how successful future bishops were in availing of the royal bounty during their early careers. At least 150 out of them (60 per cent) held one or more benefices in the gift of the crown before their nomination. Only twenty-four were definitely 'empty-handed' under this heading at the same date, and three-quarters of them were regulars, Oratorians and the like, whose status precluded such good fortune. That leaves us with a relatively large figure of seventy-six (30.4 per cent) for whom we have no information, so the likelihood is that the real proportion of those with benefices before the episcopate was around two-thirds or higher. Only a handful (eight in all) of the 150 with benefices held three or more and, as one might expect, they were from court-based or ministerial families. Cases like these apart, it seems that Louis XIV distributed such benefices in a fairly even-handed way: even the well-beneficed Cardinal Bouillon could not rival predecessors like Cardinals Guise, Joyeuse or La Valette. The vast majority of the new bishops had, therefore, to settle for one or two benefices, but mere numbers can be misleading here: one wealthy abbey – a Fécamp, La Chaise-Dieu or Bonnecombe – might be worth more than a half-dozen lesser abbeys or priories. For reasons that remain mysterious because spread randomly across the years, a small number of individuals were required to give up such benefices on being nominated bishops.

For an unquantifiable cross section of benefice-holders, of course, obtaining benefices was not an end in itself, but a means of ensuring the possibility of being elected as a deputy to an assembly of clergy, since only those holding benefices in an ecclesiastical province could be candidates for election by that province. The benefices in question did not have to be in the king's gift, and even minor 'chapellenies' in cathedral churches would suffice for the purpose.[64] This was a genuine incentive for ambitious clerics to diversify, at least geographically, their portfolio of benefices, and the evidence from the provincial assemblies held to elect deputies shows a number of them switching their attention between provinces that were often far apart.[65] Crucial to success in these endeavours, however, was the ability to persuade the metropolitan and/or the most influential bishops of a province to support one's candidacy, and fragments of correspondence suggest how intensive the ensuing lobbying could be. As one bishop wrote without illusions on the subject to a colleague: 'the rules prescribe that these deputations only be discussed when it is time for the elections, but the rules are so ignored that anyone wishing to follow them would be ignored'.[66] Here too, some candidates

---

64 Dominique Turgot, bishop of Sées in 1710, was a prebendary in Bayonne cathedral at the time of his nomination, which led the historian of Bayonne to speculate on his reasons and to wonder if he was not perhaps a vicar-general to the bishop of Bayonne: J B Daranatz, 'Dominique Turgot de Saint-Clair, évêque de Sées en 1710', *Bulletin de la Société des Sciences, Lettres, Arts et Études Régionales de Bayonne*, new series, 1 (1928), 171–5.

65 This passage is based mainly on the *procurations* for deputies to general assemblies from the provincial assemblies that elected them, and which give the names of those attending the latter assemblies. The procurations for the years 1645–50, 1675–85, 1695–1711 are in AN, G⁸ 88–9. For the assemblies for which there are no surviving *procurations* (1655–70, 1690–3) the names and 'qualités' of the elected deputies are provided by the *Collection des procès-verbaux des assemblées générales du clergé de France depuis l'année 1560 jusqu'à présent*, ed Antoine Duranthon, 9 vols (Paris 1767–78), iv, 10–21, 460–6, 815–26; v, 4–6, 640–1; vi, 8–10

66 AN, 109 AP 14, no 204, Bishop Montmorin of Aire to Bishop Gourgues of Bazas, 28 Aug 1713, 'les règles voudroint qu'on ne parlast de ces deputations que lors qu'il faut nommer, mais ces règles sont tellement negligées que qui voudroit les suivre seroit apparemment oublié'. Montmorin was asking for Gourgues's vote for one of his sons who was seeking election by the Auch province, and added that he had written to the archbishop and the other bishops of the province. Other letters in this volume show candidates and patrons seeking the Bishop of Bazas's vote in elections to other assemblies.

evidently started with serious advantages over their competitors, and the best connected of court clerics could obtain interventions on their behalf by ministers or even members of the royal family.[67] It is not hard to understand why four out of the five Colbert bishops had been deputies to an assembly of clergy before the episcopate. It would require a detailed study in order to determine how much freedom of action such assemblies really enjoyed when electing deputies, though it may have been greater in the case of second-order deputies than in that of their episcopal counterparts. At any rate, seventy-five future bishops – almost one-third of the total – were elected as second-order deputies, some of them more than once, to the assemblies held between the 1640s and the early 1710s. We should place alongside them the eighteen *agents-généraux du clergé*, who were not elected as deputies to the assemblies per se, but whose involvement with the assemblies was *ex officio*, and whose chances of episcopal promotion were, as we also saw, better – and getting more so – than those of the ordinary deputies.[68] There is clear evidence that as the reign progressed virtually all of the deputies – though not the *agents-généraux* – were already vicars-general and thus extremely well positioned within the church establishment to seek election to an assembly. But there is no obvious pattern to the success rate of assembly deputies (excluding the *agents-généraux*) becoming bishops after 1661. From the 1660s to the 1680s, the proportions were within the one-third to one-quarter band, but they dropped in the 1690s to slightly over one-fifth, only to jump again in the 1700s and 1710s to their highest levels for the reign, at just over 35 per cent. If we add the figures for *agents-généraux* becoming bishops to each of the above cohorts, we find that the proportion of bishops jumped from 20 per cent in the 1660s to just under 45 per cent by the 1710s.

These figures suggest something important about the evolution of the crown's episcopal patronage and the French clergy's response to it, a subject for analysis in later chapters. The increased frequency of assemblies in Louis XIV's final years, especially after 1700, and the return of the Jansenist problem during the same period, probably explain why the proportion of former deputies becoming bishops reached such figures. Mazarin's tactic of keeping dioceses vacant while assemblies were in session and then rewarding loyal deputies once they had finished was used far more sparingly under Louis XIV – the most notorious instance of it was that of the Assembly of 1710,

67 See AD Haute-Vienne, G 216, letters from Anne of Austria and Philippe d'Orléans to bishop of Limoges, Jan 1665, requesting his support for abbé Lavergne de Tressan. Evidence for such intervention is easier to find with regard to episcopal elections to the assemblies. See Jean-Baptiste Colbert, *Lettres, instructions et mémoires*, ed Pierre Clément, 8 vols (Paris 1861–82), vi, 128, Colbert to Bishop Vialart of Châlons-sur-Marne, 28 March 1680, thanking him for supporting his nephew, Desmarets's election as *agent-général*; *ibid*, 156–8, letters from Colbert to archbishop of Rouen and bishop of Avranches, 21 and 29 July 1681 respectively, informing them of king's wishes for election of episcopal deputies by Rouen province for 1681 Assembly.
68 At least one *agent-général*, Louis-Alphonse de Valbelle, bishop of Alet and Saint-Omer, had been a deputy to an assembly before his election as *agent*.

as we shall see in a later chapter. Of the thirty-six second-order deputies who attended the most famous of all the assemblies, that of 1682, thirteen (36 per cent) went on to become bishops – which was probably a record for any assembly of the period. But only two of them were nominated at the end of the assembly itself. The rest had to wait rather longer: nine in all had been rewarded before the decade was out, but the last of them had to wait until 1702 – long enough, it may be suggested, for his contribution to the 1682 Assembly not to be the obvious reason for his promotion.[69] Elsewhere, while it is clear that some nominations followed particular assemblies fairly closely, in just as many cases several years might elapse before a former deputy was singled out for the mitre.[70] Needless to say, the 'great' assemblies (meeting in mid-decade) were an ideal opportunity for the crown and its advisers, especially the king's confessor, to study and observe the deputies in attendance, but also for their patrons (who might also be their bishop and a first-order deputy to the same assembly) to draw them to the attention of the court. With their longer sessions and their special commissions, they were always likely to offer more opportunities to ambitious deputies than the 'small' assemblies, but the latter may also have made observation of individual deputies by the confessor and others easier than the larger assemblies, if we can judge by the 'success rates' of deputies to both kinds of assembly. Above all, as we shall see later, these assemblies did not usually interfere with the routine established by Louis XIV of only nominating bishops at certain times of the year. That in turn suggests that by then the crown felt sufficiently in control of the conduct of the assemblies not to need to resort to the blandishments that Mazarin devised in order to obtain what he wanted from them.[71]

It is far from easy to conclude this analysis of the 'personnel files' of incoming bishops in a way which does full justice to the enormous diversity of their recorded activity, or which does not take an anachronistic view of 'activity' and 'inactivity' in securing high church office. But some important features do emerge from that diversity. It is clear that Louis XIV's bishops had not remained aloof from the changes occurring within the French church itself, changes which they would have to deal with themselves once they had become bishops. The virtual disappearance after the 1680s of men without any recorded pre-episcopal position or activity to their credit is one obvious element of this pattern. Converging indices show beyond reasonable doubt that by the 1690s some of the longest-standing past practises were also dis-

---

69   See Blet, *Assemblées du clergé et Louis XIV*, 603–10, list of deputies to the 1682 Assembly. The last of the deputies to become a bishop was Bertrand de Sénaux, nominated to Autun on the resignation of his uncle, Gabriel de Roquette.

70   For example, Moret de Bourchenu, nominated to Vence in May 1714, had attended the Assembly of Clergy in 1700.

71   Assemblies of clergy were usually intended to begin their sessions on 25 May of the year when they met, but they often failed to keep to that timetable. Under the management of Archbishop Harlay they often concluded their business within a month or so, but episcopal nominations were usually held over until the feast of the Assumption on 15 August.

appearing. As we saw, laymen and clerics not in full orders no longer figured among incoming bishops, while those in orders for over five, ten or twenty years were on the increase, and on a remarkably similar timescale. It is particularly noticeable that the curricula vitae of bishops thereafter are far fuller than for the preceding decades, and that this is not just the consequence of better sources of information. Many of those whom we observed acting as archdeacons, preachers or even parish priests had in fact either combined such activities or moved from one to another over time. When even royal almoners and the sons of leading nobles and ministers felt the need to seek service under a ruling bishop as an *official* or grand-vicar, it is evident that a clear message was not merely being transmitted, but was being acted upon by them. We cannot be sure that these men were actually made to work as hard as their less well-placed colleagues for whom a grand-vicarship was the absolute limit of their ambition and attainments. As time passed and teams of grand-vicars grew in size, it is virtually certain that some of these posts were more honorific than others, but that point may not have been reached during the *grand roi*'s reign.[72] Yet we should be wary of concluding that the cumulative effect of these shifts was a revolution in the make-up of the French episcopate, personified by the emergence of a dramatically new type of bishop during the second half of the reign. Neither the *ancien-régime* church nor monarchy was revolutionary, and it is in many respects highly symbolic that one of Louis XIV's very last bishops, nominated in January 1715, was a royal almoner whom Saint-Simon depicts as an inveterate *homme d'antichambre*, and whose main claim to remembrance is that his father's diary provides the most detailed account we have of that court from the 1680s to the 1710s.[73]

---

72 McManners, *Church and Society*, i, 232–3.
73 Jean-Louis du Bouchet de Sourches, bishop of Dol 1715–48 was son of the marquis de Sourches, *grand prévôt de l'hôtel du roi*, whose diaries begin in 1682 and end in 1712.

CHAPTER 5

The Context of Episcopal Patronage

IN FEW PARTS of Catholic Europe in the early modern period were the arrangements for the selection of bishops as clearly defined as in France. This was due in part to the detail and precision of the Concordat of Bologna, a bilateral treaty between François I and Leo X, negotiated as early as 1516. During the following century and a half it was sustained, clarified and, in some respects, extended by the vigilance that was characteristic of a gallican mindset that was capable of seeing the advance of papal jurisdiction in action even in the collection of information by the papal nuncio on the qualities of the king's choices of bishop.[1] This singularity becomes particularly apparent when France is compared to other countries in Catholic Europe that had to live with much less clear-cut conventions, with some of them only securing a concordat with the papacy as late as the mid-eighteenth century.[2] The so-called Germanic Concordat of 1449 – which governed the provision of benefices in some of the lands from Franche-Comté and Alsace to the Spanish Netherlands which France would acquire under Louis XIV – preserved papal rights over benefices to an extent that was by then unacceptable in gallican France, and which explains in part the disputes chronicled in chapter one over the indults requested not merely for episcopal nominations, but for other major benefices in the territories concerned. The resort to diplomacy in order to resolve these particular issues was a pragmatic move which did not mean that the gallican understanding of Bologna was being jettisoned, as Cardinal Dubois was still reminding French diplomats in Rome in the 1720s.[3] The status of the

---

1 For the issues and arguments this raised, see Pierre Blet, 'Le Concordat de Bologne et la réforme tridentine', *Gregorianum*, 45 (1964), 241–79.

2 Olivier Poncet, 'La Papauté et la provision des abbayes et des évêchés français de 1595 à 1667' (unpublished thesis, Université de Paris IV-Sorbonne, 1998), 42–9, for a concise and accurate survey. The Treaty of Barcelona of 1529 allowed Charles V, as king of Naples, to nominate to twenty-four of the 131 bishoprics within the kingdom. See Mario Spedicato, *Il Mercato della mitra. Episcopato regio e privilegio dell'alternativa nel regno di Napoli in età spagnola (1529–1714)* (Bari 1996), esp ch 1.

3 *Recueil des instructions données aux ambassadeurs et ministres de France, Rome* ii, 586–603, instruction from Cardinal Dubois to abbé de Tencin, 6 Aug 1722.

Bologna Concordat was sometimes questioned in Louis XIV's France, but only on particular points, such as the need for indults, or in periods of acute crisis, such as the 1680s.

I

By vesting the right to select bishops and many other benefice-holders in the king and by reducing to a minimum the rights of the papacy to overturn his selections, Bologna laid – or, more accurately, consolidated – the foundations of an ecclesiastical superstructure already closely entwined with the monarchy. But the clarity that Bologna brought to the question of episcopal provision in France is less evident when we turn to sphere of actual practice. The terms of the Concordat make it easy enough to enumerate the crown's patronage rights, but they provide few signposts as to how those rights were actually exercised. For that reason, this chapter will attempt to sketch the central features of French episcopal patronage in order to provide a context for an understanding of the options facing, and taken up by, the crown under Louis XIV. In order to do this some comparisons with the preceding generations are essential.

During the century and a half after Bologna, the crown's handling of its episcopal patronage – the only feature of its huge fund of patronage to attract extensive research – experienced relatively few major changes. Much depended, needless to say, on the crown's own political strength, which would determine whether episcopal patronage would be used to serve the interests of particular social groups, factions or families rather than the crown's own purposes, though we should not push that distinction into anachronism. For example, a combination of royal weakness and dynastic custom ensured that for long periods, parts of that patronage were even 'alienated' to third parties such as apanage-holders, widowed queen mothers, or royal favourites, who could formally 'present' their candidates for benefices for royal approval.[4] In addition, the French tradition of royal 'liberality' remained enormously resilient, with the result that for a long time even major church positions were granted as 'gratifications' of one kind or another. Above all, by leaving so much room for considerations based on ties of patronage and clientage, service and reward – often in respect of families and factions rather than of the individuals who received major church benefices – liberality as practised by the French monarchy was extremely slow to make room for formal procedures for ensuring what might be regarded as the 'proper' distribution of such positions. Indeed, as Olivier Poncet has clearly shown, once the king had

---

4   See the accounts in Frederic J Baumgartner, *Change and Continuity in the French Episcopate: The Bishops and the Wars of Religion 1547–1610* (Durham, North Carolina 1986); Bergin, *Making*; Poncet, 'La Papauté'.

demonstrated his liberality by, say, nominating someone to a vacant diocese, he then withdrew from the picture: thereafter it was the responsibility of the nominee to do whatever was necessary to obtain confirmation in Rome; only if the crown's assistance was requested or its rights seemed likely to suffer, would it re-enter the picture.[5] The contrast between the well-oiled administrative machinery of the papal curia, which made a large part of its livelihood out of provision to benefices, and the highly informal and elusive character of the French monarchy's approach to managing its ecclesiastical patronage is a striking one.

This conclusion is clearly borne out by another feature which might seem rather unimportant to anyone but a historian – the record-keeping practices of the crown and the survival of the documentation that church patronage generated. The crown never developed an equivalent of either the Spanish *Patronato Real* or the Roman Datary, so that no systematic record of the exercise of church patronage was kept, let alone survived. Strange as it may seem, systematic, if not necessarily wholly up-to-date, lists of French benefices were more likely to be found in Rome than at the French court.[6] This did begin to change in one respect at least under Louis XIV, notably for bishoprics, when the *économats* were reorganised from the 1670s onwards in response to the widening of the *régale* and the earmarking of a proportion of the revenues of vacant dioceses for the 'new converts' from Protestantism. Gradually the *économats* began to generate their own administrative 'system' and records, but their focus was essentially financial in scope, and it was not until the following century that their wider value to the crown became fully apparent.[7] It is thus no small paradox that even under the so-called *monarchie administrative* of Louis XIV, the most extensive records of royal nominations to major benefices are to be found in the diaries of two lay courtiers, Sourches and Dangeau. Both of them literally copied the names and details, virtually without any comment, from the lists circulated at court when decisions over benefices were announced, but they only cover the period from the early 1680s onwards. A substantial but unpublished compilation covering the years 1673 to 1702 is sometimes referred to as the *feuille des bénéfices*. Although it was based on the original of the *feuille* kept by the royal confessor – to which we shall return later – it, too, is seriously incomplete. One need but point out

5   Poncet, 'La Papauté', 188. Of course, letters of nomination were addressed to the pope via the French ambassador in Rome, but this did not mean the ambassador was seriously involved in seeking papal provisions. It was the *banquiers expéditionnaires* and their agents in the curia who did virtually all the work.

6   *Ibid*, 69–84.

7   Jean Orcibal, *Louis XIV et les Protestants* (Paris 1951), ch 2, 'la caisse des conversions'. The *économes* were responsible for administering the temporalities of dioceses during vacancies, which of course provided often detailed data on leases and revenues. This could be useful in deciding whether to award pensions to third parties when nominating new bishops, or whether dioceses were poor enough to require additional endowments in the form of benefices 'incorporated' into the episcopal *mense*.

that it was put together at the behest of a private collector and antiquarian with good connections to imagine its limitations. So, as with the pre-Louis XIV period, the only 'systematic' information on new French bishops is to be found in Roman archives, but even here the 'gallican' vigilance alluded to earlier in this chapter played a characteristic part in limiting its scope and, consequently, its value to historians.[8] Finally, the reconstitution of the workings of episcopal patronage in France is seriously restricted by the virtual secrecy in which candidates were discussed and decisions made – all in sharp contrast with the Spanish practice that we noted in an earlier chapter.[9]

II

To contemporaries concerned about the exercise of royal church patronage, most of these issues were of secondary importance. From at least the Council of Trent onwards, French ecclesiastical figures had protested against the unacceptable consequences for the French church of royal 'liberality' regarding bishoprics, initially demanding the return of episcopal elections and, when that proved an impractical objective, the establishment of a special section of the royal council to deal with these issues. The term 'conseil de conscience', used initially as a loose description of the duty to discharge the crown's obligations under the Concordat properly, began to acquire currency during the later 1610s and 1620s, but it was only after Louis XIII's death in 1643 that it actually took the form of a body of advisers whose task it was to scrutinise candidates for major benefices, especially bishoprics, and to make recommendations to the king for formal nomination. But the status of the *conseil de conscience* as a clearing-house for church patronage was fragile from the outset. It never became a fully-fledged branch of the royal council, and its ad hoc character was evident in its also being referred to as a 'congregation'; by 1661, when Louis XIV assumed responsibility for government, it was being labelled the 'conseil establi pour les bénéfices'.[10] It thus lacked the clear institutional and juridical foundations that would have made it the full French equivalent of the Spanish *Patronato Real*, which was firmly entrenched within the

8   When witnesses give the age, orders or degrees of incoming bishops, they usually make their assertions 'ex fide baptismi', or refer to the 'litteras quas vidi' – 'the letters (*scil* certificates) which I have seen'. Gallican sensitivity to anything smacking of the exercise of papal jurisdiction on French soil by the nuncios could embrace the collection of information of this kind. Spanish, Flemish and other dossiers in the Vatican archives normally include these documents. Unlike their Spanish and perhaps other counterparts, papal nuncios in France could not require the king's nominees to furnish, as part of their dossier for the papal consistory, certificates of baptism, ordination or university graduation, even though it is perfectly clear that these documents were usually presented to, and inspected by those testifying before the nuncio on their behalf.

9   See above, pp 32–3.

10   *Mémoriaux du conseil de 1661*, ed J de Boislisle, 3 vols (Paris 1905), ii, 330–42.

conciliar structures of the Madrid monarchy. This may well be partly because the real force behind the *conseil de conscience* were the *dévots* who had flourished during Richelieu's ministry, and who were more concerned with improving the calibre of the episcopate than with bureaucratic arrangements per se. Its early history during Mazarin's ministry, hardly a period of political or ministerial stability, soon revealed its limitations.

Yet the very fact that the *conseil de conscience* returned to the agenda immediately after *both* Mazarin's death in 1661 and Louis XIV's in 1715 is indicative of the continuing problem of how best to deal with royal church patronage in France. Clearly, neither adult monarchs, committed to governing in their own name, nor chief ministers like Richelieu and Mazarin or, later, Dubois and Fleury, would willingly accept the restraints on their freedom of decision personified by even a purely consultative rather than a deliberative *conseil de conscience*.[11] But since the *conseil* was not necessarily seen as a formally constituted body in its early days, someone like Richelieu could claim that, as a chief minister who was also a senior ecclesiastical figure, he personally exercised its functions thanks to his proximity to the king, Louis XIII, himself an adult king. After Louis's death in 1643, only one element in this equation was present – a cardinal who was chief minister, Mazarin, but he was a foreigner with little experience of France where, unlike his mentor Richelieu, he had never served as a bishop. He thus found himself having to accept a formally constituted *conseil* which was intended to met regularly and handle 'affaires ecclésiastiques'. Relations between the *conseil* and Mazarin, who was himself a member of it and who signed its recommendations, were not smooth at the best of times, and they degenerated further during the Fronde. His political comeback after his two exiles enabled him to confine its effective membership to himself and the young king's confessor.[12] To all intents and purposes, by his last years he held a similar grip on episcopal patronage as Richelieu had over two decades previously. It ought to be added that Mazarin's own political style was as openly clientelist as that of any minister over the previous century, so the prospects of an *entente cordiale* between him and something as novel as the *conseil* were never good. None of this amounts to suggesting that either the power of chief ministers or the fate of the *conseil* determined how well or badly, if we can use such terms, the French crown handled its responsibilities over episcopal patronage. Its value lies rather in suggesting the nature of the options and constraints which could affect the latter at the point when Louis XIV was about to assume the plenitude of kingship.

Historians are so familiar with the absence of a chief minister after Mazarin that there seems little left to say about it. The king's willingness to shoulder the burdens of kingship, as advised by Mazarin himself, was widely welcomed.

11   See McManners, *Church and Society*, i, 49.
12   Bergin, *Making*, 529.

But even when accepting that the transition was relatively trouble-free – the Fouquet affair and the *chambre de justice* excepted – this decision did not of itself provide a solution to every problem. Few at the time really knew what it meant, and some, beginning with Anne of Austria, did not expect it to last long[13]. Too often, however, Louis XIV in 1661 is seen as effecting, or at least intending, a kind of *tabula rasa* of recent ways of governing. His desire to rule as well as to reign undoubtedly enhanced royal legitimacy. But no dynastic, divine-right prince could put himself in the shoes of the kind of ministerial figure who emerged from within the political rough-and-tumble of the court and the council, whose hold on power might be short and unpredictable, and who had his own family, clients and supporters to rely on and to support if he was himself to survive. Yet France had, to all intents and purposes, been managed politically in such a way by chief ministers for nearly forty years before 1661. From our point of view, of course, the fact that Richelieu and Mazarin were cardinals is of crucial importance. While their earlier careers and 'statut dans l'église' were far from identical, both operated from 'inside' the French church, as would their eighteenth-century successors, Dubois and Fleury. This means that they were perfectly placed to expand and promote their ecclesiastical clientèles directly and without having to defer to, or work through a ministerial hierarchy placed above them. The power and ambition deriving from this is one obvious explanation of their unease in having to defer to a *conseil de conscience*, however constituted. Thus the decision taken in 1661 to end government by chief ministers, which in France had only taken the 'cardinalitial' form, was bound to have major implications for the workings of ecclesiastical patronage: the lines of communication and the strategies adopted by those seeking advancement had now to adjust to an unfamiliar political landscape. From this perspective, too, yet another of Louis XIV's life-long resolutions takes on its full significance – his refusal, as expressed in response to Anne of Austria's pressure, to have a cardinal as a member of his inner council, no doubt because he might aspire to hold the position of a Richelieu or a Mazarin.[14] It was possibly also in this connection that a further, albeit less well-established promise was made – not to seek the red hat for any future archbishop of Paris.[15] Senior church figures were therefore to be kept at two removes, rather than just one, from the council chamber.

In 1661, however, the immediate solution arising from the king's preferences was a revamp of the *conseil de conscience*, with Pierre de Marca no doubt intended to be its major figure. Since the *conseil* had never been formally scrapped, this decision went largely unremarked. In the late 1650s, Mazarin

13   Abbé de Choisy, *Mémoires*, ed Georges Mongrédien (Paris 1966), 80. Anne may well have remembered Louis XIII's identical promise of 1621 after Luynes's death.
14   Michel Antoine, *Le Conseil du roi sous Louis XV* (Geneva-Paris 1970), 44ff. John B Woolf, *Louis XIV* (New York 1968), ch 12, which remains a shrewd analysis of Louis XIV's political choices in 1661.
15   BN, MS Fr 23506, fo 165r, *Nouvelles ecclésiastiques* (n d, c 1676).

and François Annat, the king's confessor, effectively constituted the *conseil de conscience* and, separately or jointly, they signed the 'résultats' of its deliberations, though what form the latter actually took remains a complete mystery.[16] But if practice did not quite match theory, the *idea* of such a council was past burying by then. Within a week of Mazarin's death, it had been resurrected and its membership reconstituted, with its first meeting taking place on 18 March 1661. Annat was now joined by Pierre de Marca and his eventual successor in Paris, Péréfixe, as well as Anne of Austria's *premier aumônier*, La Mothe-Houdancourt, the former bishop of Rennes.[17] Marca may have been its single most important member, given his services and reputation, but Louis XIV was probably just as inclined to listen to his confessor or his former preceptor, Péréfixe. In any case, Marca's membership was too short-lived for us to draw any valid conclusions on this point, and he was not replaced when he died in June 1662. The precise nature of La Mothe-Houdancourt's participation, which underscores the queen mother's continuing influence, also seems open to question: he was nominated to the distant metropolitan see of Auch in Gascony only days after Marca's death, although his bulls were not granted until early 1664. In any case, even without such a transfer, he would probably have lost any remaining influence after Anne's death in 1666. This time, significantly, there was no equivalent of Vincent de Paul or his less known fellow-member of the original *conseil*, Jacques Charton. Apart from the confessor, the revived *conseil* consisted wholly of bishops.

There is no sign, however, that the king or his ministers were worried that this would make the *conseil* a more difficult body to manage, or that it would have a distinctive agenda of its own. In his ghost-written memoirs for the instruction of the Dauphin, Louis XIV expatiated on his prerogatives and responsibilities towards religion and the church in the early 1660s. Without exaggerating the degree to which such pedagogic rather than autobiographical sentiments reveal his actual convictions, they do offer a clue to some of the young king's own preferences and prejudices – and, no doubt, to those of the circles from which he recruited his ministers, advisers, and confidants. Asking rhetorically if there was anything more important for the 'tranquillity of our subjects' than the conscientious distribution of benefices to the best candidates available, he declared that it was the 'piety, knowledge and behaviour' of the latter that one should examine most closely before making decisions. Knowledge, he confessed, was probably the most difficult of the three for kings to fathom, but he claimed to have resolved that problem to his own satisfaction by preferring doctors of the Sorbonne above all others – an aspiration which, as we saw, was far less true at the time of writing than it would become later in the reign. On the other hand, piety, morals and behaviour were less difficult to discern, and kings only needed to listen and observe carefully before

---

16   *Mémoriaux du conseil de 1661*, i, 145 n 5.
17   Antoine, *Le Conseil du roi sous Louis XV*, 61. *Mémoriaux du conseil de 1661*, i, 202, n 1.

making up their minds about individuals, without having to delve more deeply into individual cases. Having added the familiar *topos* of the saintliest men not necessarily proving to be the best suited for the mitre, Louis allowed himself a fleeting utopian moment in which he imagined that bishops and the like would be chosen from preachers, missionaries to the Huguenots, or even simple parish priests or curates. Bishops, he continued, were the commanding officers of a 'sacred militia', but they would have previously moved through the ranks – just like the sons of great nobles who, before they commanded France's armies, would have started out as simple musketeers in the royal guards. Sensing no doubt the improbability of this scenario, he immediately injected a note of realism by admitting that kings could only secure slow, progressive change, since any attempt at legislation based on such premises would either discredit the laws or lead to their being ignored.[18] The abbé de Choisy, who frequented the court and ministerial circles of the early 1660s, recalled in his *Mémoires* how contemporaries viewed the theory behind the newly reformed *conseil de conscience*: 'the merits of individual candidates were severely discussed by three or four men who did not always agree among themselves, and by such means the prince could see where the truth lay'.[19]

Yet with so little direct information about its activities, it is difficult to make a judgement about the revived *conseil* of the early 1660s. It is not clear, as we shall see later, that it really managed to control episcopal patronage, or that its individual members wielded enough influence to promote men close to them. For example, Marca confided to his long-time friend, François Bosquet, bishop of Montpellier, that he wanted him for his successor in Toulouse if he himself were promoted to Paris, but nothing came of it. Marca's equally strenuous efforts to promote his own nephew, abbé Faget, for whom he obtained the strategically placed post of *agent-général*, were also curtailed by his early death.[20] Nor is there any evidence that his colleague, and successor in Paris, Péréfixe was in any way responsible for choosing *his* successor in Rodez, Louis Abelly. At any rate, by the mid- to late 1660s the non-renewal of its membership, which Mazarin had apparently recommended to the king on his deathbed, had once again reduced the *conseil* to a rump, and a pattern that would be familiar for the rest of the reign was emerging.[21] During the

18 Louis XIV, *Mémoires pour l'instruction du dauphin*, ed Pierre Goubert (Paris 1992), 139–41. There is a scholarly English translation of this text by Paul Sonnino, *Mémoires for the Instruction of the Dauphin* (New York 1970), 106–7.

19 Choisy, *Mémoires*, 82. The *conseil* is also referred to as the *conseil des bénéfices* in the Le Tellier papers in the war archives at Vincennes.

20 BN, MS Baluze, 121, fo 52, 31 Jan 1662. It is probable that since Marca's resignation of Toulouse did not take effect before his death, his personal wishes could be more easily ignored there. Faget was made *agent-général* of the clergy, normally a sound bet for episcopal promotion, but he failed to translate it into reality.

21 Raymond Darricau, 'La Feuille des bénéfices', *Dictionnaire du grand siècle*, ed François Bluche (Paris 1990), 185, based on the account of Mazarin's death by the Italian Theatine, Angelo Bisarro.

Jansenist dispute in 1668, the new papal nuncio, Bargellini, reported that the king had actually disbanded it altogether during his dispute with Alexander VII just before the Treaty of Pisa (1664), and that the impetus for the decision had come largely from the Jansenists, anxious to avoid sanctions if they refused to sign the Formulary[22]. The nuncio's explanation for the decision may be partisan and his chronology doubtful, but when he asked the king to reconvene the *conseil* in 1668 in order to deal with Jansenist issues, Louis replied that he had indeed disbanded it, but would take advice from well-intentioned people.[23] By royal admission the *conseil de conscience* in the form it had taken since 1643 no longer really functioned, but this did not necessarily mean that it had been completely obliterated, let alone formally abolished. Stray references to it during the rest of the reign should make it easier to understand why it was resurrected in 1715 and 1720, only to encounter similar problems.[24]

III

The king's admission of 1668 meant that church patronage (and ecclesiastical affairs more generally) were by then effectively the subject of deliberations involving himself, his confessor and the archbishop of Paris. That the king's confessor should be closely involved with episcopal patronage was not new in itself.[25] All of Annat's predecessors had certainly been, but the power of Richelieu and Mazarin had seriously reduced their scope for providing independent, authoritative advice, let alone dictating the direction of episcopal nominations. Moreover, those earlier confessors who reputedly harboured such ambitions had elicited hostility among the episcopate itself, whose members were reluctant to accept that any confessor, especially a regular, should enjoy such enormous influence: Richelieu had capitalised on that hostility in order to rein in some of the royal confessors before his own position reached full strength.[26]

The mothballing of the *conseil de conscience* in the 1660s meant that Louis XIV was about to raise his confessor to a position of influence that few of his

---

22 Pierre Blet, 'Louis XIV et les papes aux prises avec le jansénisme', part ii, *Archivum Historiae Pontificiae*, 32 (1994), 94.

23 ASV, Nunz Fr 135, fos 55–6, Bargellini to Rome, 8 June 1668. The word Bargellini used here was 'licentiato', corresponding to the French 'licencié'.

24 Antoine, *Le Conseil du roi sous Louis XV*, 82, 83 n 138, 109–13, 128–31. See also the account in Peter R Campbell, *Power and Politics in Old Régime France* (London 1996), 47–8, who says 'the conseil *seems* to have ceased to exist at some time after 1733, although it is mentioned in the *Etat de la France* for 1736' – a good indication that the uncertainties of its earlier history remained into the eighteenth century.

25 The only general study of the royal confessors is that of Georges Minois, *Le Confesseur du roi* (Paris 1988), but it is superficial and based on what seem to be second-hand sources.

26 Bergin, 'Richelieu and his bishops?', in *Richelieu and Age*, 185–6.

predecessors had enjoyed. For the king himself, this may have been an early manifestation of his preference for familiar faces and, above all, his well-documented preference for dealing with ministers and advisers singly rather than as a group. A *roi-bureaucrate* as much as a *roi de guerre*, Louis settled into the habit of working with his confessor on a regular basis, usually on Fridays but also on the eve of the major feast-days of the Christian calendar. A contrast in style was only to be expected from one confessor to the next. As far as church patronage was concerned, Annat was regarded by contemporaries – possibly because of his earlier experience of the *conseil* in the 1650s and of having to play minor fiddle to Mazarin – as being far more 'collegial' in his approach than his successors, especially Ferrier. Increasingly elderly, this probably also meant that he was not especially forceful in pushing forward particular candidates. If true, one implication of this is that Péréfixe, who died only six months after Annat, on New Year's Day 1671, may well have played a more important role in these matters than some of *his* successors. Péréfixe no doubt enjoyed the king's confidence as his former preceptor, but he was not installed as archbishop of Paris until 1664 while the absence of a place in the king's council may also have limited his influence. By the time Annat died, aged eighty, in 1670, Jean Ferrier (1614–74) had already been virtually installed as his right-hand man, so there was little discussion or surprise at his succession. His anti-Jansenist activities, which had begun while he was still rector at Toulouse, had already earned him a reputation for combativeness. Less of a courtier than his predecessor or successor, as confessor he preferred a more exclusive king-and-confessor arrangement which, logically, involved either shutting out the archbishop of Paris altogether or relegating him to seeing the king separately. But this was easier said – or intended – than done, for within months of his becoming confessor, Ferrier was confronted by a new archbishop of Paris, François de Harlay, previously archbishop of Rouen. By far the ablest ecclesiastical politician of his day, his many skills were appreciated by Louis XIV. But because of persistent rumours about his private life, his reputation ebbed and flowed for the next twenty-five years, so that however valuable he proved to be, a place in council continued to escape him, and it was only in his last years that Louis finally resolved to nominate him as his candidate for the cardinal's hat.

Within four years of Harlay's installation in Paris, Ferrier himself died and was succeeded by the longest-serving of all royal confessors, François de La Chaize (1624–1709), from a noble family of the Forez area west of Lyon. Previously Jesuit rector and then provincial superior in Lyon, he was also a grand-nephew of Henri IV's most famous confessor, Pierre Coton. Despite possessing such unique credentials for the post, there was an uncharacteristically long delay of four months before he was finally chosen in February 1675, and it appears that the intervention of La Chaize's local patron, the archbishop of Lyon, Camille de Villeroy, was decisive in bringing him to the king's attention at a time when the Parisian Jesuits were anxious to see one of their own chosen for the role. La Chaize was to spend thirty-four years in post, and his successive attempts to retire in the final ten years or so were always rebuffed by Louis XIV, another instance of the king's attachment to familiar figures which became more pronounced with old age.[27] La Chaize did not lend his own pen to the anti-Jansenist campaigns as Louis's other confessors did – indeed, he was an admirer of Quesnel's *Réflexions morales* – and if anything his intellectual interests were more antiquarian than theological. That judgements on him varied considerably is only to be expected: his lengthy tenure inevitably made it seem that he exercised an unseemly hold on the king. On the one hand, even someone as poorly disposed to the Jesuits as Saint-Simon found him to be a 'perfect gentleman', cultivated, urbane and respectful, who rose above the mediocrity that the duke increasingly saw in the French clergy generally.[28] Fénelon, no enemy of the Jesuits, famously but anonymously denounced him to the king in 1693 as 'the dupe of all those who flatter him'. But Fénelon's real target here was not La Chaize but the king who elevated his confessors 'beyond all the proper limits. Previous royal confessors had never been the only ones to make bishops or to make decisions on matters of conscience.' For Fénelon, as for so many others before him, the real scandal was that the king 'had made a minister out of a regular'.[29] Mme de Maintenon, a more dangerous opponent also writing during the 1690s, considered La Chaize to be a disaster, a man whose principles had been sapped by too much contact with the court, and who could not be counted on to defend the *dévot* cause.[30] Long years of service and old age were unlikely to change the habits of a lifetime, but even in his early years she criticised him for evading his confessorial responsibilities towards his royal penitent, preferring to absent himself from Versailles at the major feast-days rather than confront the monarch over his adulteries.[31] As we shall see later, his long confessorship meant that his influence on episcopal patronage went through different phases, and that at particular junctures it seemed in danger of being eclipsed entirely. Thus generalising judgements of him attempting to fit his thirty-four years in office under one heading can miss much of what the historian would wish to know. Clearly no zealot, he was less of a polar opposite to Archbishop Harlay than either his predecessor or his successor.

27   See Georges Guitton, *Le Père de la Chaize, confesseur de Louis XIV*, 2 vols (Paris 1959). Saint-Simon, xvii, 49–50.
28   In addition to his depiction of La Chaize in his *Mémoires*, Saint-Simon compares him to Louis XIV's other confessors in a text which resembles his famous 'parallel' of the first three Bourbon monarchs: *Écrits inédits de Saint-Simon*, ed A-P Faugère, 8 vols (Paris 1880–93), ii, 'Mélanges', 463–80, esp 464–70.
29   Fénelon, *Correspondance*, ii, no 249, pp 278–9. This text is also in Fénelon, *Oeuvres* (Pléiade) ed Le Brun (Paris 1983–92), i, 549–50.
30   See *Lettres de Maintenon* (ed Langlois), vols iv–v, especially her letters to the future Cardinal Noailles in the 1690s, which endlessly lament La Chaize's aversion to virtue and devotion.
31   *Ibid*, ii, 176, Maintenon to Mme de Saint-Géran, 26 July 1676, 'Le P de la Chaise est un honneste homme mais l'air de la cour gaste la vertu la plus dure et adoucit la plus sévère'.

The tenure of La Chaize's successor, Michel Tellier (1643–1719), was correspondingly short, terminated by the king's death.[32] Tellier's anti-Jansenist writings before the confessorship, his tactics in dealing with the problem during his term, and the kind of ecclesiastics he promoted to the episcopate alienated so many, inside and outside the episcopate, that his disgrace in 1715 was a foregone conclusion. Some of Saint-Simon's most devastating comments are reserved for him, but others probably shared them at least in part.[33] Louis XIV's successors would retain their Jesuit confessors, but Tellier was the last of his kind, since the confessor's responsibility for advising the king on church patronage lapsed in 1715 and was formally removed in 1725, only two years after Louis XV's majority.[34] This task was now entrusted to a bishop or cardinal, a decision which made it easier and more natural to call them the *ministres de la feuille*, and which was more acceptable to the higher clergy generally.

Perhaps the most intriguing trait the four confessors have in common is *not* to have been disgraced by Louis XIV – which compares very favourably to the lot of royal confessors in previous generations. Only Tellier came close to disgrace, in 1711, although that was for his own intrigues against Cardinal Noailles in the Jansenist affair, and not for his activities in distributing benefices. Coinciding in large part with Harlay's tenure of Paris, La Chaize's own long 'reign' as confessor established a clearer sense of the role of the confessor. For a time, Louis XIV worked with both men during their weekly sessions at court, but by some point in the 1680s, he decided to meet them separately. This is probably why some contemporaries remarked then that the *conseil de conscience* no longer existed.[35] However mistaken that may be, it seems that a crude division of labour had emerged, in which Harlay's value lay mainly in his handling of the affairs of the French clergy generally, especially its assemblies, the Paris theology faculty and the religious orders, while the confessor's brief mainly concerned church patronage, missions to the Protestant population, and so on. This did not mean that they were not consulted by the king on matters relating to the other's sphere of competence – after all, the king's lifelong strategy for political survival was to do just that, so as not to be without alternative sources of advice and information. Nor did it mean that Harlay was unable to promote protégés of his to the episcopate. But it was precisely the king's *méfiance* which enabled opponents of La Chaize to hope to supplant him in the king's favour. As we shall see in more detail later, Mme de Maintenon probably aimed to do just that from relatively soon

32 The family name was Tellier, and he seems himself to have added the 'le' to it. Because of possible confusion with the ministerial family of that name, and the long-serving archbishop of Reims, Charles-Maurice Le Tellier, I use the 'Tellier' form here.

33 *Écrits inédits de Saint-Simon*, ii, 470–80, for Saint-Simon's most extensive portrait of him. The only recent scholarly study is also drawn in negative and sombre colours: Lucien Ceyssens, 'Le P Michel Le Tellier 1643–1719', in *Autour de l'Unigenitus*, 333–400.

34 Sicard, *Ancien clergé de France*, 496. McManners, *Church and Society*, i, 51–3.

35 Guitton, *Le Père de la Chaize*, i, 179.

after her marriage, but in the event she had to wait for the installation of *dévot* bishops like Godet of Chartres and Noailles of Paris before potential counter-weights to the confessor were available. Noailles's succession to Paris in 1695 gave her hope of sidelining La Chaize, but although the king did consult Noailles, as he had Harlay before him, the experienced confessor and the habit-dominated king weathered the siege, partly because Noailles was compromised by his pro-Jansenist leanings, thus leaving Maintenon to sputter with rage at La Chaize's indolence, timidity, and frank dislike of the *dévots*. Maintenon felt much more content with La Chaize's successor, Tellier, whose approach to episcopal promotion as well as his anti-Jansenism accorded largely with her views.

IV

The fact that a monarch like Louis XIV was ready to lock himself away with his confessor (with or without the archbishop of Paris being present) at regular intervals to discuss ecclesiastical promotions for hours on end should not lead us to misread what was happening. Both the confessor and the archbishop were advisers who at no time enjoyed a monopoly on advice and information to the king, let alone, as we shall see, a veto on actual decisions. To describe the confessor as a 'minister' of ecclesiastical, or more narrowly 'religious' affairs, is to impose an anachronistic format on a rather more undefined, 'archaic' state of affairs, one in which a 'domestic' servant of the king, to employ contemporary categories, was permitted to wield considerable influence without acquiring any public title which would confirm a move out of the 'domestic' sphere where it suited the monarch to keep his confessor. One consequence of this, namely the absence of anything resembling an archive of the confessor's activities, compounds the problem of the historian while helping to perceive its origin more clearly. Yet in performing his role, there is no doubt that the confessor engaged in an extensive correspondence with many people, including actual and future bishops. 'Having burned an infinity of papers' before his death, only a few desultory items of La Chaize's correspondence have survived here and there; they are mostly letters written by, rather than to him, frequently congratulating or even informing new bishops of their elevation, and sometimes conveying to them the rationale for their nomination and, consequently, explaining what was expected of them.[36]

36　Some letters have been published here and there – as in Régis de Chantelauze, *Le Père de la Chaize confesseur de Louis XIV* (Lyon 1859), appendix. For an example of an unpublished letter, see AN, 109 AP (Gourgues papers), 14, no 125, La Chaize to Jacques-Joseph de Gourgues, 31 May 1684, 'enfin, Monseigneur, le Roy convaincu de vostre mérite, vous a nommé à l'évesché de Bazas, vous scavés quil y a beaucoup à travailler. C'est pour cela quil y falloit un ouvrier de vostre force, et quil faut que Sa Mté aye pour vous personnellement la consideration que vous merités pour vous avoir placé si fort à vostre bienséance et conformément à vostre zèle. Je ne

But the real volume of correspondence, incoming and outgoing, was apparently enough to require the confessor to have a full-time secretary, who was a fellow Jesuit rather than a royal official, for just that purpose.[37] The incoming correspondence, some of it certainly petitions or *placets*, must have been substantial, and when La Chaize died in 1709, the Jesuits presented Louis XIV with the keys to a large consignment of his surviving papers and correspondence that he kept in their house in Paris.[38] With the constantly expanding web of Jesuit houses and colleges throughout France, one ready-made source of information on clerics seeking church preferment was easily available to the confessors. It is also apparent that particular bishops were themselves close to the confessor, who doubtless turned to them for advice, and who in turn could bring the names of individuals they approved of to the confessor's attention. This was all the more likely at a time when more and more incoming bishops were serving as vicars-general in dioceses, and recommendations, solicited or unsolicited, concerning their merits and behaviour could be directed to the confessor. Le Goux de la Berchère, successively bishop of Lavaur (1677–93) and archbishop of Albi (1693–1703) and Narbonne (1703–19) was even known by contemporaries as a 'mignon' of La Chaize, whose early efforts to promote him to Aix in 1685 backfired.[39] A key figure in Languedoc politics – he was, not surprisingly, Bonsi's successor at Narbonne – Le Goux was almost certainly not alone in acting as a conduit to and from the confessor, whose confidence in him would not have escaped observers and who could consequently have acted as a kind of 'broker' for those in search of advancement. In his last years at Cambrai, Fénelon regularly supplied the confessor, Tellier, with *his* views on candidates for episcopal patronage, some of them existing bishops with ambitions for promotion to a better see. How many other correspondents did likewise we can merely

---

sçauroys vous expliquer la joy que jay de vous voir dans cet employ.' Gourgues had been nominated the same day, 31 May. The phrase alluding to Gourgues's *bienséance* refers to the fact that the Gourgues family were a parlementaire family from neighbouring Bordeaux. For congratulations on an episcopal nomination, AD Saône-et-Loire, F 604, letters from Claude Thyard de Bissy to La Chaize on his son's nomination to Toul, 4 and 10 April 1687. JRULM, MS French 92, fo 154, Huxelles to La Garde, Nov 1699, 'Le R Père de la Chaise a mandé à Mr l'abbé de Fleury que l'évesché de Fréius est affermé 32 mille livres de rente, sur quoy il y a une pension de 4 mille à M le chevalier de Tilladet et une de 3,000 à l'ancien évesque relegué en Bretagne'. Fleury, the future cardinal, had just been nominated to Fréjus, and evidently wanted to know of its financial situation before accepting it. Cardinal Noailles complained bitterly to Mme de Maintenon that he had been left in the dark about the name of the new bishop of Orléans, a Paris suffragan diocese, in 1706, while La Chaize openly announced it during one of his audiences: *Lettres de Mme de Maintenon*, 8 vols (Amsterdam 1766), iv, 280–4, n d (but early April 1706).

37 For many years his secretary was Antoine Verjus, brother of François, bishop of Grasse, 1692–1710.

38 Dangeau, xii, 312; Sourches, xi, 253, 20 Jan 1709.

39 *Lettres de Germain Vuillart ami de Port-Royal à M Louis de Préfontaine (1694–1700)*, ed Ruth Clark (Geneva-Lille 1951), no 96, 11 June 1699, referring to the nomination to Luçon of Jean-François de Lescure, a vicar-general of the archbishop of Albi, 'mignon du P de la Chaize'.

guess. A number of bishops nominated by Louis XIV were wholly unknown to the king and the court, so that their promotions, often to dioceses that were not particularly desirable, cannot be explained by the normal workings of court-centred patronage and clientage. The confessor's many sources of information and recommendation were probably crucial in many, if not all of these decisions, and to that extent they can be viewed as an alternative or parallel network of patron-client politics, not its antithesis.

Contemporaries also spoke of the throng of petitioners, especially ecclesiastics, who filled the antichamber of La Chaize's apartment when he gave audiences in the Jesuit house in Paris where he resided. More specific evidence exists for prelates like the ageing Bossuet, a lifelong opponent of the Jesuits' theology, desperately courting La Chaize at the end of his life in order to obtain the Meaux succession for his unworthy nephew.[40] No doubt ambitious young ecclesiastics, with or without family members in the episcopate, also did the same.[41] Some of the most acid contemporary comment was directed towards those ecclesiastics who had been known to be anti-Jesuit but who in order to pursue their personal ambitions decided to court the 'bons pères', often by attending public events like *soutenances de thèses* at their colleges or preaching on major feast-days like that of Ignatius of Loyola. In addition, individual Jesuits resident in Paris and reputed to be on good terms with the confessor could also be approached by petitioners; men as well known as Bourdaloue, Bouhours or Rapin, all experienced this pressure at various times. But as often as not they had to confess that their intercession was, or would be fruitless, since Ferrier and La Chaize in particular were wary of such approaches, and knew how to stonewall them, as the exiled writer Bussy-Rabutin among many others was to discover.[42]

V

Attention to the confessor and his network of informants and agents who were involved, directly or indirectly, in the channelling of high church patronage should not make us lose sight of the many other players in the field. As with the royal finances, we should be wary of treating the 'système apparent' as if it was the 'système réel'.[43] The following chapters will provide more circumstantial evidence of the involvement of courtiers, ministers and others, so only

---

40   Abbé Ledieu, *Journal*, ii, 420–1, 427–9, 443, 444, 464–6.
41   Pasquier Quesnel, *Correspondance*, ed Mme Albert Le Roy, 2 vols (Paris 1900), ii, 136, letter to Vuillart, 9 March 1701, referring to Cardinal Janson taking with him to Rome a nephew of père La Chaize 'chargé de bénéfices que des évêques de la cour lui ont donné pour faire la cour à son oncle' – benefices which, Quesnel adds, his uncle had refused to help him obtain in the first place.
42   See below, pp 177–8.
43   Dessert, *Argent pouvoir et société au grand siècle*.

general indications need be provided here. It should be noted at the outset that the confessors themselves relied to varying degrees on laymen as sources of information and recommendation. La Chaize probably paid as much attention to the opinions of the long-serving Languedoc intendant, Lamoignon de Basville, who was as pro-Jesuit as Archbishop Le Goux or any other bishop.[44] Another intendant, Foucault, boasted in his memoirs that he had been instrumental in setting at least two episcopal nominations in train, and did so by recommending them *directly* to La Chaize and Archbishop Harlay rather than to royal ministers.[45] There is no reason to imagine that these are isolated cases, but the disappearance of the correspondence in question makes it impossible to do anything more than hint at the usefulness of intendants or other leading officials to a confessor known to welcome recommendations or who was seeking information on individuals.[46] The fact that the French monarchy had little time for the formal intervention of local interests in episcopal patronage also makes it difficult to trace the source of at least some episcopal nominations. Since the abolition of elections, lobbying sometimes took the form of petitions from provincial estates for particular individuals, as exemplified by the Breton estates under Mazarin.[47] It probably continued after 1661, but there is no direct evidence for it at present. Yet intervention of a less 'institutional' kind by local interests was not out of the question, as is evident from the rare recorded instances of a kind of *vox populi* petition designed to influence the royal decision. The first, an appeal to Louis XIV in 1679 to ensure that Cahors be given a successor in the same vein as Alain de Solminihac and the recently deceased Nicolas Sévin, claimed that the 'suffrages and prayers' of the diocese 'designated' the future Cardinal de Noailles as the man best fitted for the task. According to the *Nouvelles Ecclésiastiques*, 'this extraordinary *placet* created a great stir in town and at court, and everyone reacted to it according to their opinions or their passions'. When the author of the *placet*, a priest of Cahors, was asked to produce the procuration which would prove that it was based on the *suffragia cleri* and the *vota populi*, he had to admit there was no such thing. The final comment on this incident – 'on a fait passer cette action pour ce que l'on a voulu' – perfectly captures the incomprehension and perhaps embarrassment that it elicited.[48] Over

---

44   It was Basville, for example, who brought the resignation of Méliand of Alet to court in 1698: JRULM, MS Fr 92, fo 103, Huxelles to La Garde, 18 Aug 1698. For a memorable if overdrawn portrait of Basville, see Saint-Simon, iii, 325–7; xi, 80–1, 134–41.

45   Nicolas-Joseph Foucault, *Mémoires*, ed F Baudry (Paris 1862), 28 (Montauban, 1674), 116–17 (Dax, 1685).

46   Quesnel wrote that Foresta-Coulongue, vicar-general of Marseille, was thought to owe his nomination to Apt in 1695 to his cooperation with the intendant of Provence, Le Bret, but did not specify what form it took – *Correspondance*, i, 378–9, to du Vaucel, 16 Sept 1695.

47   See Bergin, *Making*, 288.

48   BN, MS Fr 23508, fo 99, *Nouvelles Ecclésiastiques,* n d, but early 1679. The French text is practically untranslatable, but it suggests that the initiative was regarded as the work of a madman or a fool.

twenty years later, in 1700, some kind of petition was also put together in the diocese of Bayonne, asking that the next bishop *not* be a native of the area![49] Yet however out of season such gestures may have been in a monarchy like that of Louis XIV, both actually bore fruit: Noailles did get Cahors in 1679 and, whatever the form it actually took, the message from Bayonne was heard in 1700 in that the new bishop was a northerner, René-François de Beauvau. It is not inconceivable that further research might unearth further instances of such intervention on behalf of particular dioceses or candidates.

In any case, whatever their source, requests for ecclesiastical advancement did not have to be addressed exclusively to the confessor, although it is not possible to say how much practices altered as the reign progressed or as confessors changed. Contemporary accounts leave little doubt that requests for vacant dioceses or abbeys were made by a wide range of individuals – family members, *grands*, members of the royal family, courtiers, ministers, senior churchmen, to name only a few obvious ones – and that such interventions, made sometimes to the king in person, were not concealed as if somehow shameful.[50] Only in some cases do we know who the petitioners in question were; for the majority we can only make enlightened guesses, but with little certainty of accuracy, especially when kinship relations were not involved. Thus we discover, for example, that the Récollet friar Théodore Allart probably owed his promotion to Vence in 1681 to the king's long-serving and trusted *premier valet*, Bontemps, who then paid most of the new bishop's expenses.[51] No kinship relation seems to have existed between them, so the connection may well have been one arising from Allart's activities as a regular, possibly as a family confessor or confidant. The use of third parties to present candidates to the king and his entourage did not prevent well-placed candidates themselves from directly approaching them from the outset.[52] The evidence for this may be thin and scattered, but it does suggest that those

---

49　AN, L 728, pièce 1, Bayonne, no 47, Père Léonard papers. The recently deceased bishop of Bayonne, Léon de Lalanne, was from a family with Bordeaux and local connections, but Père Léonard neither alludes to the reasons for the Bayonne petition nor the actual form that it took.

50　One example of this matter-of-fact reporting in JRULM, MS French 90, fo 46, Huxelles to La Garde, 17 May 1694, 'M de Lannion demande Tréguier pour son frère l'abbé'.

51　BN, MS Fr 23510, fo 48v, *Nouvelles Ecclésiastiques,* 4 July 1682.

52　By way of example, see BN, Mélanges Colbert 176bis, fos 612–13, Joseph de Montpezat, bishop of Saint-Papoul to [Colbert], 24 Jan 1672, reminding him that the king, aware of his poverty, had expressed a desire to 'me faire du bien' when he took leave of him at court. The opportunity to do so had just arisen with a 'grande vacance', and he asks Colbert's help in securing his advancement 'auprès du roi'. Louis de Bourlemont, then based in Rome as France's Auditor of the Rota, asked for the see of Toulouse directly in 1674. See Desmons, *Études historiques, économiques et religieuses sur Tournai,* 9, note, quoting his letter of 24 Oct 1674 to Colbert: 'j'ose supplier très humblement le Roy que si, après un travail de 17 ans continuels que j'ai employez à la charge d'Auditeur de Rote à Rome, S M jugeoit que je puisse à present mériter ses graces pour la servir à l'archevesché de Toulouse, qui est vacant, je me remets à tout ce qu'il plaira à sa royale bonté d'en ordonner'. The *Correspondance du nonce Spada,* no 99, n 10, refers to a similar letter to Pomponne, foreign minister, of the same date.

who were known to the king and confessor were emboldened to take the most direct route towards advancement.

Bishops who achieved their ambitions by means like these fit naturally into the categories proposed for the eighteenth-century episcopate by Michel Péronnet – of which the most important was the 'network of relations' (*réseau relationnel*) which converged on the court and the decision-makers. This in turn assumes that future bishops were known in royal circles and were 'active' candidates for preferment in some sense. There is enough evidence from Louis XIV's reign to suggest that we should not take either of these assumptions for granted. The more intriguing category of the two consists of those who, as far as contemporaries could discern, were *not* candidates at all. Hagiographers concerned to highlight the virtues of their heroes invariably insisted that episcopal office came their way without warning, and especially without any effort on their part; it was a *topos* which, decrying the benefice-hunter in all his forms, the Catholic Reformation in France had re-vivified in the writings of its most distinguished champions. Under Louis XIV, attacks on courtier-bishops and abbots were as scathing and widespread as at any time in the past. Court-based observers were perfectly placed to record the nomination of 'non-candidates' to particular dioceses; and they evinced even greater surprise when those individuals were not known to the king, though it is hard to measure what they meant by the term 'known' in this case.[53] We shall see later that at various times either side of 1700 Louis himself seemed anxious to nominate bishops who did *not* belong to the established *réseaux relationnels*. Dangeau recounts how at All Saints 1698, the king proposed to nominate to Alet one such unknown, Nicolas Taffoureau, whom he knew only by repute and who had not been explicitly recommended to him by anyone. He asked La Chaize to approach his archbishop to confirm whether the reports he had about Taffoureau were correct. The Archbishop of Sens responded as requested, but used the opportunity of recommending someone else for promotion. However, he was rebuffed and Taffoureau, 'who had no thought of becoming a bishop', was duly nominated a day after the other bishops of that promotion.[54] In this case, we happen to know from other sources that the king had been informed about Taffoureau by no less a figure than the duc de Beauvillier, who had encountered Taffoureau because his daughters, nuns at Montargis, were under his overall superiorship in Sens diocese. Whether

---

53 A relatively early example of this is Henri de Barillon, bishop of Luçon in 1671, who was presented to the king by his uncle, Barrillon de Morangis, later ambassador to England, after his nomination. Barrillon was hardly an 'outsider', but the king's confessor himself declared that he had not been a candidate for the episcopate, 'il en est d'autant plus digne qu'il n'a point sollicité ni fait solliciter personne pour l'obtenir': *Documents pour l'histoire de Luçon*, no 1104, Jean Ferrier to Barillon de Morangis, 16 Oct 1671.

54 Dangeau, vi, 453, 2 Nov 1698. AN, L 727, Alet, no 36. Père Léonard adds the name of Fortin's own candidate, who was also a grand-vicar at Sens, Pas de Feuquières, the son of a great military family, who had been passed over for the Angers succession in 1692, but who would become bishop of Agde in 1702.

Beauvillier had merely praised Taffoureau for his ability as a vicar-general or formally recommended him in the accepted sense for promotion, we cannot be sure, but there was nothing to prevent the king from taking praise for recommendation. As Sourches noted in his diary, also in 1698, one of the reasons for the scandal caused by the annulment of an episcopal nomination made earlier that year to Poitiers that was already public knowledge was that the king's nominee had *not* asked for it.[55] We must, therefore, allow for at least a modest percentage of Louis XIV's bishops not having consciously sought their good fortune, and indeed that this may itself have been a consequence of the 'système réel' of recommendation and presentation which saw the numbers of candidates listed in the *feuille des bénéfices* inflate. It seems that both the king and his confessor were tempted, though not necessarily in the same instances or for the same reasons, to escape from the ensuing pressure and to look to individuals from 'outside of the loop'. On one or two occasions, an irate monarch is recorded as warning the *abbés de cour* that they should not take promotion for granted.[56] He was also capable of springing surprises in order to remind La Chaize of the confessor's subordinate place within the ecclesiastical patronage system.[57]

The nomination of bishops who were in no sense active candidates for the mitre raises a related question to which contemporaries were also sensitive, namely the degree to which the king actually 'knew' those he was promoting. 'Non-candidates', after all, stood a strong chance of also being 'unknowns'. When Mme de Maintenon wrote that Louis had nominated just two bishops 'whom he does not know at all', she could not help adding, as if in some trepidation, 'please God that he has done the right thing'.[58] To do this was evidently felt to be a serious risk by the king himself, but what did being 'known' amount to? Clearly royal almoners, tutors, court preachers, sons of major courtiers and ministers would be known, sometimes personally, to the king himself, but beyond these relatively limited numbers, the meaning of the term becomes far more uncertain. Moreover, the disquiet arising from nominating 'unknown' bishops probably grew in the latter decades of the

55   Sourches, vi, 24, 19 April 1698.
56   JRULM, MS French 94, fo 101, Huxelles to La Garde, 12 May 1702, with reference to recent nomination to Béziers of a vicar-general from Carcassonne, des Alrics, when all of La Chaize's suggestions were *abbés de cour*, she says 'enfin le Roy demandant un grand vicaire, celuy-cy fut nommé et pris au bond de la balle'. *Ibid*, fo 233, to same, 27 Nov 1702, she says the *abbés de cour* 'ont eu sur les oreilles particulièrement pour les évêchés', and some of them had departed to take up other occupations and wait for times to change.
57   This seems to be what happened in the succession to Dax in 1692, as reported by Quesnel, who quoted the king as saying to La Chaize during their discussions, ' "Il y a un curé de ce pays-là dont on m'a dit beaucoup de bien. Quel inconvenient y aurait-il de lui donner l'évêché?" Le Père n'ayant rien à dire contre, cela fut fait': Quesnel, *Correspondance*, i, 237, to du Vaucel, 14 Nov 1692.
58   Maintenon, *Correspondance* (ed Lavallée), v, no ccxcv, 227, to Noailles, 2 Nov 1703, 'le roi . . . a disposé des évêchés vacants en faveur de deux hommes qu'il ne connait pas. Dieu veuille qu'il ait bien choisi!

reign. A strong clue as to what defined an 'unknown' in this context is provided in early 1690 by the superior-general of Saint-Sulpice, Tronson, a man
perfectly placed to know what he was talking about when commenting on
the choice of Godet des Marais to the see of Chartres: 'what is truly singular
about this nomination, is that the king chose him without knowing him
except by reputation, and without his being on the Père de la Chaize's list'.[59]
Godet, who within a few years would himself play an important role in determining episcopal patronage, was already spiritual director to Louis's wife,
Maintenon and involved with the running of Saint-Cyr before 1690, which
would certainly have been enough for the king to know him 'by reputation
only'. Tronson's further comment that Godet was not on La Chaize's list – the
feuille des bénéfices – is probably the key point here: before an individual figured
on that list, his merits would have had to be discussed by the king, confessor and others like the archbishop of Paris (and Godet himself in later
years), sometimes more than once and involving discreet enquiries about them
among reigning bishops, provincial intendants, rectors of Jesuit colleges and
others. To be 'known' was to be approved in principle for preferment, even
though one might be passed over many times before one's turn arrived; to
become a bishop without previously figuring on the list was to be an
'unknown'.

VI

Ever since Saint-Simon's bitter critique of Louis XIV's government, which
argued that ministers were permitted to wield disproportionate power, there
has been a natural tendency to assume that they also played a key role in the
nomination of bishops. It was, after all, one of the most influential of them,
Michel Le Tellier, who informed a petitioner for a vacant abbey in May 1661
that those seeking ecclesiastical preferment should henceforth approach the
king himself directly, and not via ministers or courtiers.[60] But this injunction,
which was not intended to be confined to the ecclesiastical sphere, was as
utopian as it was short-lived. Even if we discount some of Saint-Simon's claims,
it is clear that ministers, because of their virtually daily contact with the king,
could be invaluable conduits for petitioning and lobbying precisely, although
petitioners would not have felt obliged to approach them exclusively. This is
not the place for an extended analysis of the ministerial history of the reign,
nor of their relative success in securing bishoprics for kinsmen and clients. But
a number of general points need to be made. Firstly, being a minister or
secretary of state did not necessarily indicate an equal capacity to influence

59 *Correspondance de Tronson* i, 148, letter to Rigoley, superior of Autun seminary, 12 Feb 1690.
   Tronson had himself been involved in discussions about who should be given the new see of
   Blois to be carved out of Chartres.
60 SHAT, Archives de la Guerre, A¹ 168, 13 May 1661.

royal decisions. Throughout the reign, certain secretaries of state – Loménie de Brienne and Phélypeaux de Châteauneuf among others – were known to have very little influence in the royal entourage, while some of their colleagues enjoyed correspondingly disproportionate favour. Given the longevity of ministerial careers under Louis XIV, this means that genuine ministerial influence in episcopal affairs was confined to a relatively short list of names – essentially the Le Tellier clan (Le Tellier, Louvois, Barbézieux, and their relative Le Peletier), the Colbert clan (Colbert himself, Seignelay, Croissy, Torcy, Desmarets, as well as their in-laws the ducs de Beauvillier and Chevreuse), the Phélypeaux (La Vrillière, Châteauneuf, Pontchartrain father and son), as well as Chamillart. At the outset of the king's personal rule, Le Tellier influence was by far the strongest, and it was sustained and expanded by the long partnership between the future chancellor and his son and successor as war minister, Louvois. When the latter died in 1691, his son Barbézieux was simply unable to repeat this feat, especially when faced by the competition that had emerged in the intervening decades. By then, the Colbert influence had gradually separated from its initial roots under the Le Tellier tree, and was still growing at the time of its creator, Jean-Baptiste's death in 1683. His sons, nephews (Desmarets, Torcy) and son-in-law (Beauvillier) remained formidably entrenched in various ministerial offices down to 1715. Yet it would be mistaken to take the Le Tellier-Colbert clash too literally, especially in those early decades: it had more to do with rivalry over policy and resources, and did not prevent them from cooperating to advance the careers of their relatives and dependents. The Phélypeaux were actually the oldest of all Louis XIV's ministerial clans, but it was not until the 1690s and later that they really came to resemble the Le Tellier or Colbert in the scale of their presence, with Chancellor Pontchartrain and his son, Jérôme, the navy minister, enjoying true ministerial influence for the first time during the last decades of the reign. The longevity of these ministerial dynasties ensured that they could act as patrons and supporters of episcopal candidates over prolonged periods of time. By comparison with these groups, individual ministers like Boucherat or Chamillart were more isolated and short-lived. However, as far as we are concerned, they all had one thing in common, namely the capacity to obtain significant church benefices, bishoprics included, for their own family members. Ministerial influence, like charity, began at home. This had always been accepted as a 'natural' consequence of the personal service they rendered to the crown, which was honour-bound to show its liberality to its own ministers. Here too, some were more successful, doubtless because more ambitious and insistent, than others. Even insignificant political figures like Brienne and Châteauneuf were beneficiaries of that tradition. Royal generosity towards the Colbert clan was no less spectacular for being assiduously solicited, with five members following Colbert's own brother, Nicolas, into the episcopate after 1661, a total that can be increased if we include relatives like the Desmarets (two bishops), Sève and Beauvillier (one each). The Le Tellier, for all their early dominance, only managed to place one son – admittedly at Reims – and two cousins (a Cassagnet and a Le Peletier), though it ought to be noted that the two Colbert de Saint-Pouange bishops (and their family generally) were closer to their Le Tellier than their Colbert cousins. The Phélypeaux, with three bishops, were only slightly less successful, though all but one of them was placed before Pontchartrain reached the height of his influence as chancellor after 1699. In a previous generation, they would have themselves been clients of a former ministerial family to which they had since become related by marriage, the Bouthillier, but by the 1690s, when a Bouthillier uncle-nephew succession was negotiated for Troyes, those roles were probably reversed. Chamillart placed his brother in the episcopate, while Boucherat, who had no sons, extended his patronage to a nephew of his wife.

Ministerial influence did not end 'at home', however. Yet as soon as we move away from the hard 'objective' evidence in the shape of bishops with demonstrable family ties to ministers, it becomes much more difficult to gauge their precise activity and influence on church patronage since, as André Corvisier pointed out in connection with the Le Tellier, reconstituting their non-kin clientèle networks is still problematic. For the Le Tellier family, with its uninterrupted tenure of the war ministry from 1643 to 1701, it would be natural to expect a clientèle consisting in large part of military nobles and officials, and Corvisier identified the Bazin de Bezons and Bochart de Saron families, each of which produced a bishop under Louis XIV, as belonging to it, yet these were robe rather than military families. A similar analysis has yet to be done for other ministerial clientèles, especially that of Colbert, who seems for much of the 1660s at least to have been a relatively inactive intermediary for church posts not involving family members: his incoming correspondence, even during years such as 1668 or 1671 when episcopal nominations were especially numerous, certainly bears out this impression. That and the lack of anything like continuous or uniform information on epis-copal decision-making means it is much easier to surmise than to determine the role of successive ministers – as indeed of royal favourites and well-placed courtiers. In any case, the likelihood is that a large number of petitions for episcopal preferment were made verbally rather than in written form, and for that reason what we can know about the background to them is inevitably uneven and haphazard. In July 1687 alone, for example, Louvois forwarded to La Chaize three petitions for the grant of major benefices (none of them bishoprics, however), so that he could bring them to the king's attention when they met to discuss church patronage.[61] In the late 1680s and after the death

---

61 SHAT, Vincennes A[1] vol 784, nos 113, 126, 448, Louvois to La Chaize, 7 (two) and 22 July 1687. The first of the letters reads: 'Je vous adresse Mon Reverend Père un placet du sr Rouillé auquel je vous supplie d'estre favorable lorsque vous rendés compte au Roy de ceux qui deman-dent le prieuré de St Frémont qui est vaccant en Normandie'. Unfortunately, the *placets* them-selves have not survived, but this example gives some idea of the volume of written supplications reaching the confessor.

of Colbert, Louvois was also the dominant and longest-serving minister, so there was every reason for 'prétendants' to have recourse to him.[62] Other ministers handled similar petitions, but to forward them to La Chaize – as Louvois did with a covering letter in each of the cases just mentioned – ought not to be read as leaving the matter purely in the confessor's hands from there onwards. It was, at the very least, a way of reminding the confessor that he needed to take account of the minister's own possible interest in the case. If all such petitions had to end up on the confessor's desk, that did not make him the master of what might ensue. Petitioners wrote to ministers rather than to the confessor in the strong expectation and, sometimes, the knowledge that they would press their claims on the king himself. If the king then insisted on adding further names to the existing list of candidates for benefices, it was probably a response to such approaches.[63]

It is rare to catch a glimpse of what soliciting ministerial intervention might mean from the point of view of those in search of a mitre. In April 1710, Gabriel Boisot, the influential *premier président* of the parlement of Besançon, wrote to Desmarets, the *contrôleur-général*, on behalf of his son, a doctor of the Sorbonne and a preacher. He had been encouraged to do so, he confided to Desmarets, by no less a figure than Bishop Bissy of Meaux, whom his son had been serving as vicar-general for the past four years. Bissy, whose star was rising at just that moment and whose anti-Jansenist efforts would win him a red hat a few years later, had assured him that his son had 'the good morals, sound doctrine and the other qualities needed for the good government of a church'. Consequently, Bissy had decided to present him to père Tellier, the confessor, as a candidate for a bishopric, possibly Nîmes, which was then vacant. But Boisot senior realised that other competitors would have their eyes on the same prize and that it was vital to convince the king himself if the desired outcome was to be obtained when few dioceses were available. Since Bissy would vouch for his son to La Chaize, all that Boisot could do was to itemise his own services – and those of his numerous and well-placed family – to Louis XIV in the generation since the conquest of Franche-Comté. He presented the promotion of his son to Desmarets as his own indemnity and reward by reminding him how poorly he had been paid for his services over the years. Doubtless like many others in a similar situation, Boisot did not overrate the chances of persuasion by letter, so he also informed Desmarets that the Cardinal d'Estrées and his nephew, the abbé-ambassador d'Estrées, would both approach him in order to persuade him to intervene with the king. Desmarets did indeed discuss the case with Louis XIV, but his subsequent note to the effect that 'His Majesty seemed to me

62 Only more detailed research in the voluminous Louvois correspondence in the war ministry archives could establish the full extent of his role in church patronage distribution. Preliminary *sondages* indicate that his correspondence with La Chaize may not have been voluminous, nor concerned exclusively about patronage issues.

63 See below, pp 177–8.

well disposed to grant him marks of his satisfaction as occasions arise' may be seen as an instance of Louis XIV's trademark response ('on y verra') or a plain lack of enthusiasm for abbé Boisot.[64] In the event, Boisot's careful briefing and lobbying achieved nothing, and despite Bissy's growing influence in the coming years, Boisot did not make it into the episcopate, either under Louis XIV or Louis XV. We can only guess as to why this was so, since Boisot's approach seems well tailored to the outcome he sought. On this occasion at least, it seems that other candidates had more impressive credentials or more persuasive advocates, ministerial or otherwise, on their side.

VII

Regardless of who they approached or how they did so, what all of these petitioners wanted, either for themselves or their clients, was to have their names entered on the celebrated but elusive *feuille des bénéfices*. The *feuille* seems to have made its appearance with the first *conseil de conscience*, and it is not too far-fetched to see it as a prototype of the *listes d'aptitude* which designate those regarded as deserving promotion to particular positions – in this case, benefices in the gift of the crown. To be entered on the *feuille* was an indispensable, if only a first step towards preferment.[65] Discussions for this purpose could take place between king, confessor and archbishop at any time, even if there were no, or only insignificant, benefices to distribute, as contemporaries like Sourches clearly indicate. It also seems that the *feuille* was always kept by the confessor, since there is no evidence that either a secretary of state or a royal *secrétaire de cabinet* were in any way involved in these matters until after decisions had been taken and formal documents needed despatching to Rome.[66] Most of the time, it seems that the names and details of those entered on the working *feuille* could be quite sketchy, enough merely to discuss the merits of individual cases.[67] But once decisions to promote individuals were

64 *Correspondance des contrôleurs-généraux des finances avec les intendants de province*, ed A-M de Bois-lisle, 3 vols (Paris 1874–97), iii, no 740, 282–3, Boisot to Desmarets, 4 April 1710, which also includes Desmarets's own 'apostille' recounting the royal response. The Boisot were an influential parlementaire family, with some well known ecclesiastics among their ranks. The abbé Boisot may not have become a bishop, but the *premier président*'s eldest son succeeded him in his office in 1714 and held it until 1750. For the service record of successive generations of the Boisot family, see Maurice Gresset, 'Un fidèle de Louis XIV en Franche-Comté: Claude Boisot', in Yves Durand, ed, *Hommage à Roland Mousnier. Clientèles et fidélités en Europe à l'époque moderne* (Paris 1981), 169–82.

65 The first *conseil de conscience* had, it seems, done more than merely discuss who should be promoted to actual vacant posts; it had attempted, at least in its early days, to designate individuals as suitable for promotion.

66 The secretary of state 'en quartier' would of course be responsible for drafting and counter-signing the formal letters of nomination, so he would take cognisance of the *feuille*, but at a later stage and for purely 'bureaucratic' purposes.

67 See the *feuilles* in *Memoriaux du conseil pour 1661*, ii, 332–40, where the gaps are very

actually made, this sort of approximation would no longer do. Only when the missing details were supplied would the *feuille* be signed by the king; but until that formality was completed, the decisions taken were regarded as provisional and revocable, as some aspirants found out to their cost.[68] There are a few scattered references to the confessor having to write to obtain the necessary personal details about the successful candidates, so that the letters of nomination at least (which were addressed in person to the pope) would be complete and accurate.[69] It is not inconceivable that mistakes could occur because of such vagueness, especially where individuals with similar names were concerned. Archbishop Harlay's secretary, abbé Le Gendre, claimed that La Chaize gave an abbey destined for him to another cleric of the same name: the mixup was never openly admitted, as Louis XIV stood by La Chaize, but Le Gendre claimed that this was not the first such mistake made by the confessor.[70] Even with such a 'relaxed' approach, it seems unlikely that any French bishop owed his promotion to a case of mistaken identity. But at least one such case was reported in 1687, when Louis XIV decided to nominate the abbé Bochart to Valence on the request of his brother, the governor of Péronne. It turned out that there were two abbés bearing that name – a Bochart de Champigny and a Bochart de Saron – and that the 'wrong' one, Champigny, obtained the nomination. It was only when he was subsequently presented to the king that the mistake was realised. La Chaize subsequently claimed that he had acted in good faith, in the absence of a more precise identification by the king. *Noblesse oblige*, the king declined to revoke a nomination which had already been made public and letters sent to Rome for its confirmation. The king's intended choice, Champigny's cousin, Bochart de Saron, was not forgotten and a few years later he was chosen as bishop of Clermont.[71] When Louis felt obliged to actually withdraw an

considerable, and give some idea of the work needing to be done before formal letters of nomination could be drafted and signed.

68   At Easter 1698, nominations were made on 29 March, but Mme d'Huxelles reports that the *feuille* was not signed by the king until 19 April, which, she adds, 'a esté fatal à Mr l'abbé de Coadelets, car il n'est plus evesque, et on déclara que S M avoit change la première disposition': JRULM, MS French 92, fo 42, letter to M de la Garde, 2 April 1698; also fo 49, 20 April. For the incident in question, see below, pp 178–9.

69   BN, MS Fr 20969, fo 93, extract from letter (from La Chaize?) to the *premier commis* of Croissy, minister for foreign affairs, (n d, Nov 1694): 'je me suis esclaircy que l'abbaye de Bonnevaux que le Roy a donné à Mr l'abbé de la Salle est dans le diocèse de Poitiers et non pas dans celuy de Limoges. Je vous prie de le faire mettre ainsy dans les expéditions, et quand j'iray à Versailles je le corrigeray de ma main sur la feuille'.

70   Le Gendre, *Mémoires*, 204–5.

71   AN, L 746, Valence, no 1, Père Léonard papers: 'Quand il fut pour remercier le Roy, Sa Majesté fut surprise et dit à son confesseur que ce n'estoit pas luy qu'il avoit entendu etc. Ce Jésuite luy dit que ne s'estant pas expliqué il l'avoit cru ainsy, qu'il estoit fasché de s'estre trompé mais que le bruit s'estant respandu et le brevet expédié pour Rome, ce seroit luy faire un affront insigne etc, que Sa Ma auroit l'occasion de placer l'autre etc, ainsy l'abbé de Champigny resta evesque de Valence'.

episcopal nomination, albeit on different grounds, as with the abbé Coëteletz in 1698,[72] he was furious with La Chaize for allowing himself to be duped and, consequently, for duping the king himself.[73]

Exchanges like these also highlight the nature of the relationship between the king and his closest advisers on church patronage. It was, after all, possible to trust someone like Harlay – or not trust his successor Noailles – on wider questions of church politics, but where matters of patronage were concerned, personalities, families, services rendered, favours due and so on, could be viewed very differently by the king than by his confessor or the archbishop. It is fair to assume that Louis behaved in the same way towards the latter as he did with his ministers generally – keeping them guessing, even refusing particular requests for no obvious reason other than to keep them on their guard. But with so little surviving direct evidence of how he, his confessors, the archbishops of Paris, and others actually dealt with church patronage, it is risky to build an interpretation on hearsay or hindsight provided by non-participants in the actual decision-making. But some recorded incidents do give what seems like an authentic flavour of how things may have worked. Virtually all the evidence derives from the La Chaize era, and it may not, therefore, be valid for the preceding or succeeding periods.

There is absolutely no doubt that the king retained the prerogative of making actual decisions, however often he would take the advice he received on individual promotions. In the normal run of things, he was probably not determined to push candidates whom he had not previously discussed with the confessor and/or the archbishop, or whom they could not recommend to him as worthy of promotion. An unquantifiable proportion of their encounters with him involved discussing individuals who had already been proposed for promotion and who might already figure on the *feuille* kept by the confessor. But such a routine could be interrupted at any point. In June 1677, relatively early during the La Chaize confessorship, the Jesuit Rapin reported Louis XIV as personally taking the *feuille* from La Chaize and adding the names of about twenty people to whom he wanted to give benefices. Rapin also claimed there were no fewer than 200 names on the list by then – which, if true, meant that satisfying all of them might take several years.[74] Rapin's correspondent on this matter was no less a figure than Bussy-Rabutin, then in exile in Burgundy. Bussy replied to this news hoping that he was one of the twenty new names but, after so many years of exile and false hopes, he

72 BN, MS Fr 6919, fo 178, Louis XIV to Noailles, 8 April 1698. The incident was widely commented on. See Sourches, vi, 24, 19 April 1698, 'jamais affaire n'a fait tant de bruit dans le monde que celle-là, et l'abbé de Coadeletz fut plaint également de ses amis et de ceux qui ne le connoissoient pas, parce qu'il n'avoit pas demandé cet évêché, et qu'on le lui otoit d'une manière si nouvelle'. AN, L 740, pièce 1, Poitiers, no 36.

73 *Lettres de Germain Vuillart*, no 54, 10 May 1698.

74 Roger de Bussy-Rabutin, *Correspondance avec le père René Rapin*, ed C Rouben (Paris 1983), no 58, 142, Rapin to Bussy, 24 June 1677, 'le Roy a pris luy mesme la feuille du P de la Chaise

also knew that he needed to be patient: 'my turn will come, and God will grant Père La Chaise a greater share in future distributions of benefices than in this one'.[75] Rapin wrote to say he was unable to discover from La Chaize if Bussy's name had been added or not by the king, and went on to say: 'Père de la Chaise offers no explanation for this. The king has forbidden him to say [anything] when benefices become vacant; when he goes to Versailles, the King is tired of the number of candidates which grows bigger each day. You must not get disheartened.'[76] What makes this exchange, which is neither gossip nor a matter of later recall, worthy of attention is that it conveys some sense of how the 'system' practised by Louis XIV worked, even for those such as Bussy-Rabutin who were in search of relatively minor benefices. At the same time, it highlights the duty of confidentiality imposed on the confessor, one which, for obvious reasons, suited the latter when confronted by enquiries or complaints from the disappointed. How long it lasted like this is unclear, as the incident may well be a case of royal uncertainty about a recently installed confessor. Over twenty years later, in 1698, when informed by a third party that a man just nominated to a bishopric was alleged to have been gambling during Holy Week, the king felt he could only resolve the problem by asking for a further opinion. Without inflating the importance of a single case, his vulnerability as well as his dilemma are acutely presented by the language of his candid, even pathetic appeal to Archbishop Noailles of Paris:

> I thought I did the right thing in nominating the abbé de Coadelets to the see of Poitiers. His name is on the list of those who do their duty correctly . . . for my part, I shall not sign the *feuille* until I have seen you. Continue to 'me divertir de tout', and pray God to enlighten me, as I have great need of this, given the great variation in the things that I hear. You must believe that I shall always pay special regard to advice which comes to me via you. Let me know who are those most suited for this diocese'.[77]

pour y metre les noms d'environ vint personnes à qui il veut donner des bénéfices. Il y en avoit près de 200.'

75 *Ibid*, no 59, 143–4, Bussy to Rapin, 2 July 1677, 'mon tour viendra, et Dieu donnera une autre fois au P de la Chaise plus de part dans la distribution des bénéfices qu'il n'en a en celle cy.'

76 *Ibid*, no 60, 145, Rapin to Bussy, 12 July 1677, 'Je n'ay peu savoir si le Roy mit votre nom sur la feuille. Le P de la Chaise ne s'explique pas de cela. Il a défence du Roy de dire quand il vaque des bénéfices; et quand il va à Versailles, le Roy est fatigué du nombre de prétendans qui croit tous les jours. Il ne faut pas, s'il vous plaist, vous rebutter.'

77 BN, MS Fr 6919, fo 178, Louis XIV to Louis-Antoine de Noailles, 8 April 1698. 'J'ay creu bien faire en nommant l'abbé de Coadelets à l'evesché de Poictiers. Il est sur le mémoire que jay de ceux qui font bien leur devoir, en trouvés vous encore de sa conduite . . . de mon costé je ne signeray point la feuille que je ne vous aie veu. Continués à me divertir de tout et priés Dieu qu'il mesclaire, jen ay grand besoin dans la diversité des choses quon me dit. Vous devés croire que je distingueray toujours celles qui me viendront par vous. Mandés moy ceux que vous croiés les plus propres pour cet evesché.' This is the only letter of its kind in a collection of letters from the king to Noailles stretching over many years.

It will be clear from this discussion that becoming a bishop under Louis XIV could be a long and extremely uncertain process; particular names might remain on the confessor's list of *episcopabili* for years on end, and some might never obtain their reward. The quasi-confidentiality of the decision-making means we know little or nothing about why particular individuals were nominated or promoted. As we have also seen, even getting onto the confessor's list of those who were in principle deemed worthy of reward was fraught with danger. Once individual names were known to be subject to such discussions, they were exposed to rumour and disinformation, which could be disseminated in the royal entourage – as clearly happened in the case of the unfortunate Coëteletz above. In such cases, the confessor and perhaps others were likely to be asked to make their own enquiries to see if there was any substance to the allegations. This was the meat and drink of court politics, and no doubt much of it could be, and was, ignored. But if we recall Mme de Maintenon's characterisation of Louis XIV as being 'implacable when it came to other people's failings', then well-chosen accusations stood a chance of evoking a response. La Chaize himself was accused of labelling some candidates as Jansenists in order to ensure that the king would not insist on promoting them.[78]

VIII

One of the most original aspects of episcopal nominations – and benefice distributions in general – under Louis XIV was their 'seasonality'. To the diarists and commentators of the final decades of the reign, they had become part of an unvarying annual cycle defined by the major feastdays of the religious calendar. But to project this pattern back to the earlier decades without further ado would be mistaken. Neither Louis XIII nor Mazarin 'tied' their religious decision-making in this way, and the young Louis XIV did little to alter those earlier, more haphazard procedures. This is not contradicted by the presence of repeated examples from these early years of several nominations – some interconnected, some not – being made on the same date, or so close as to be virtually so. The most famous instance of this came in 1671, when twenty-two bishops in all (some of them, admittedly, promotions or transfers) were involved. Thirteen of them were bishops being nominated for the first time. Of the twenty-two, thirteen were nominated or promoted during January 1671 alone, with no fewer than seven of them on the same day, 5 January, with the remainder following on the 16th and 28th. One could point to similar groupings of nominations in January 1673 (four in one day), Sept 1675 (nine during the third week of September), February 1679 (five on 24 February) or 1681 or 1683 (eight during May in both years). But there is much less evidence of coordinated nominations during the 1660s. Nominations, which

---

78 *Lettres de Maintenon* (ed Langlois), v, no 1461, to Noailles, 2 Nov 1701.

were in any case fewer during that decade, were fairly randomly scattered through the calendar year, largely ad hoc responses to deaths and retirements. It seems that a significant shift away from isolated, single nominations – a shift that was never absolute for reasons we need not discuss here – only began during the 1670s, and that the practice which we have just observed of making several nominations en bloc on the same date or a few dates was a *sine qua non* for the subsequent decision to reserve such activity to the major feast-days – Christmas, Easter, Whit, Assumption and All Souls and, sometimes, the Purification in early February. This latter development is in turn probably connected to the king's own private life, and specifically the long string of affairs which kept him away from the sacraments for many years, despite the efforts of Ferrier (blunt but ineffective) and La Chaize (initially ineffective and 'diplomatic'). It was, it would appear, from the mid-1680s onwards, after he had abandoned Mme de Montespan and married Mme de Maintenon, that the coordinated nominations of the previous decade or so were increasingly confined to the feast-days when the king henceforth performed his 'grandes dévotions', a connection which no doubt served to underline, if it needed to be, the 'seriousness' of episcopal patronage.[79] On the eve of the feasts in question, the confessor would come from Paris to court, be closeted with the king for several hours, and decisions would be made; on some occasions, it seems that a second session would follow on the feast day itself before the decisions were finally announced. Once king and confessor had settled into this routine, it was unlikely to change unexpectedly. Diarists like Sourches or Dangeau chronicle this year-in, year-out routine in virtually unchanging language. Of course, there could be unforeseen problems or accidents, as contemporary observers noted. If the king was unwell, taking unusual medicine, or was otherwise unable to perform his 'grandes dévotions', then a postponement, usually brief, was announced.[80] Likewise, if an elderly confessor like La Chaize, in his mid-eighties when he died in 1709, was indisposed, there would be postponements. In mid-August 1695, the usual round of nominations was postponed purely because the task of finding Harlay's successor for Paris was in full swing, and normal business did not resume until early September.[81] Mme d'Huxelles reported the diocese of Pamiers as being given 'extraordinairement' in mid-January 1708, meaning simply that it was given

---

79 Maintenon's comment in 1692 confirms that this was a well-established practice by then: 'Je ne crois pas Monsieur que le Roy dispose des abaies qui sont vacquantes qu'à la première feste qu'il fera ses devotions, au moins c'est sa coustume': *Lettres de Maintenon* (ed Langlois), iv, 58, to comte de Caylus, 24 June 1692.

80 Sourches, vii, 434, 23 Dec 1702, the king announced a one-week postponement of the distribution of benefices because La Chaize was unwell. In Feb 1709, the new confessor, Tellier, missed his very first working session with the king because he was unwell (xi, 281, 22 Feb 1709).

81 Four nominations were made on 8 Sept, when the king performed his 'grandes dévotions', but as Dangeau noted, not even the scrofulous turned up for the king's touch on that date, as no one had been informed of the king's intentions (Dangeau, v, 275, 8 Sept 1695).

outside of the normal timetable.[82] Saint-Simon accused La Chaize's successor, père Tellier, of bringing some of these occasions forward without any fore-warning in order, evidently, to catch candidates and their supporters off-guard, and to push through his own preferences with less difficulty. But as we shall see later, apart from a batch of eight nominations in mid-July rather than mid-August 1710, there seems to be little evidence of that.[83] This 'bunching' of nominations at certain times of the year should not be blown out of its proper proportions – frequently the number of bishops appointed on any given date might be as few as one, two or three; the large numbers we have seen above were not the norm from the 1670s onwards, merely examples of what could happen in particular circumstances. But even when that is allowed for, it is evident that the grouping of nominations like this both reduced the singularity of individual nominations as acts of princely liberality and emphasised what they had in common, obliging actors and observers alike to regard them as more strategic acts based on something resembling 'horses-for-courses' considerations. Furthermore, by confining nominations to particular occasions when the king (and the royal family as a whole) engaged in a full round of religious practices and made his confession, the importance of the confessor to the business of making bishops was doubly underlined. Making bishops had itself become a ritual within a ritual.

It is not difficult to imagine the knock-on effects of this bunching of epis-copal patronage. Vacancies, whatever their cause, could be left to accumulate over several weeks or months – something which only happened while assem-blies of clergy were in session during Mazarin's ministry. In fact, one of the more interesting and significant features of the post-Mazarin era was, as noted in the previous chapter, that the assemblies of clergy had less and less of an impact on episcopal appointments. From relatively early in the reign, thanks largely to Archbishop Harlay's efforts, the assemblies granted the subsidies asked of them, thereby reducing the need felt previously by the crown to use vacant dioceses to induce them to conform to royal wishes.[84] Candidates for bishoprics and their supporters were now denied the opportunity to extract a 'snap' decision from the king based on inside knowledge or on being in the right place at the right time, though the *conseil de conscience* had probably put paid to such practices anyway. During those intervals, the *feuille des bénéfices* would no doubt have new names added to it, and individual cases would be discussed between king, confessor and perhaps others. Deaths of bishops occurring within days or a few weeks of the next major feast would obviously

---

82   JRULM, MS French 95, fo 16v, to La Garde, 19 Jan 1708.
83   The nominations, which included one promotion, were made on 11 and 12 July, when 15 Aug, the feast of the Assumption, was the normal mid-summer date for such decisions.
84   Ravitch, *Sword and Mitre*, 159, quoting a document from 1722 which confirms the view that the crown no longer needed to defer nominations while the assemblies were in session. Mazarin's practice was linked to limited control and the need to play every available card to get what he wanted.

complicate the tentative decisions that might already have been taken; but as often as not, these 'last-minute' deaths were simply ignored, and the selection of a successor would be postponed until the next feastday.[85] It was in such instances that royal tolerance of changes of mind by, or requests from candidates for nomination to a better but more recently vacated diocese could lead to delays and uncertainties – and therefore to the backlogs which can explain in part the variations in the numbers of bishops nominated across individual years. Contemporaries commenting on these issues did not know all the reasons why a particular diocese might be left vacant for an unusual period of time. For example, Toulouse, not an insignificant see, was kept vacant from July 1710 until July 1713. Feastdays, *grandes dévotions* and other nominations came and went, but court observers like Sourches were evidently baffled by its continuing vacancy.[86] The fact is that the king had decided to reserve it for the bishop of Tournai, René de Beauvau, whom we encountered in chapter one, but did not wish to see him vacate Tournai until the last possible moment, when all hope to retaining it had vanished.[87] By contrast, the bishop of Ypres, who was as desperate as Beauvau to find another diocese, was given a diocese that had been vacant for only two months. Special cases like this were not numerous but must have added to the sense of uncertainty and anticipation surrounding nominations. As the feastdays themselves approached, many of the ecclesiastics in the running for benefices and their supporters converged on the court itself to await the outcome. The parents of Bossuet's nephew came to Paris and the court at the Assumption in 1703 in the firm expectation of obtaining the Meaux succession after months of assiduous efforts by Bossuet and his nephew to court the confessor, Noailles, Maintenon and others. The 'eagle of Meaux's' own *états de service* across a long and distinguished career were surely deserving of such reward; Bossuet himself joined them after the king's devotions as they waited agitatedly for the nominations to be announced; even the letters of congratulation to their son, who had remained at Meaux, had been prepared in case of success. But their hopes were soon dashed: there was no mention of Meaux, and they departed hurriedly without waiting for the remaining announcements. But the younger Bossuet was ultimately more fortunate than the abbé Boisot whom we encountered earlier: after a thirteen-year wait he obtained the see of Troyes during the regency.[88]

85   This becomes evident when the dates for the deaths of reigning bishops are compared with those of episcopal nominations generally.

86   Sourches, xii, 272, 14 July 1710; 322, 15 Aug 1710; 391, 31 Oct 1710; xiii, 79, 5 April 1711; 477, 15 Aug 1712; 521, 1 Nov 1712; 552, 24 Dec 1712.

87   See above, p 38.

88   Ledieu, *Journal*, ii, 465–6, 15 Aug 1703. Ledieu, Bossuet's secretary, provides a uniquely detailed account of the activities, spread out over the previous four months, to prepare the ground for a successful transfer of Meaux from uncle to nephew. His dislike of the nephew is patent, but does not reduce the value of his account. Bossuet himself died the following year, which must have seemed the end of the road for his nephew.

IX

That a bishop of Bossuet's stature could be kept in the dark as much as everyone else says a great deal about the way in which such decisions were kept secret until the last possible moment. No doubt, losers were unlikely to have bad news broken to them in any other way, and Bossuet's disappointment was due largely to his nephew's failings and his own blindness towards them. But if considerable secrecy enveloped the decision-making process, it was heavily compensated for by the publicity given to its outcome. The announcement, presumably made *viva voce* to the waiting throng at court on the feast-days in question, was soon available to those not present, initially as simply 'the list' – 'la feuille'. Diarists like Sourches and Dangeau made a point of procuring a copy of it and consigned the details to their journals, making them the most accessible source of information on the filling of bishoprics. But it was not just those with their eyes on posterity who acted like this. In her letters to her daughter – who was sister-in-law to more than one Grignan bishop – Mme de Sévigné made a point of keeping her informed of episcopal nominations that she knew would interest her.[89] Noting, for example, the odds being offered in Paris for Archbishop Harlay's successor in August 1695, when many seemed to think it would go to Fénelon, only recently installed at Cambrai, she cut the guessing short by saying the suspense would be ended on the following Monday.[90] Mme d'Huxelles used the lists circulating at court to convey news to her correspondents in the provinces, knowing that they would want to be kept informed of at least some of the details.[91] Even the secretary of state, Jérôme de Pontchartrain, was in the habit of enclosing them with his letters to his wife for her perusal.[92] Finally, in his Brussels exile, Quesnel eagerly read the lists and willingly commented to his correspondents

---

89 Marie de Rabutin-Chantal Sévigné, *Lettres*, ed Louis Monmerqué and Paul Mesnard, 14 vols, Paris (1862–6), vi, no 774, 207, 24 Jan 1680, 'je regarde toujours ce qui se passe pour les évêchés à cause de notre bel abbé'. The 'bel abbé' in question was Louis-Joseph de Grignan who would become bishop of Carcassonne in 1681.

90 *Ibid*, xi, no 1426, pp 304–5, 12 Aug 1695.

91 JRULM, MS French 93, fos 291, 411, 442, 'distribution des bénéfices' at Easter, All Saints and Christmas 1701 respectively. Other instances of this are scattered throughout this correspondence which begins in 1689 and continues, with interruptions, until 1708.

92 AN, 257 AP 3 (Pontchartrain papers), nos 62 and 187, two letters without indication of year or date. In the second he says he has no news worth relating, except what is in the list of benefices distributed, which he asks her to show to his parents. Although it does not concern bishoprics, what he adds is not without interest: 'mon père s'est doublement trompé sur l'abaye des Cleretz: premièrement, elle a esté donnée a Mme de Bouthillier, ce qu'il desiroit sans le croire; deuxièmement cette Mme Bouthillier est soeur de l'évêque de Troyes le jeune, par consequence de nos parentes et Chavigny et non Rancé. L'abaye du Pré est donnée à Mme de Beringhen fille ainée de M le premier sur la démission faite de Me d'Aumont tante de Me de Beringhen . . .' A few punctuation marks not in the original have been added in order to make the text comprehensible. I would like to thank Sara Chapman for bringing this collection of letters to my attention.

upon the royal choices.[93] But these lists were more than a kind of tolerated *samizdat*. Since the beginning of the reign, the highly official *Gazette* carried details of nominations to benefices. Mme d'Huxelles, Vuillart and papal nuncios would frequently skip the details of nominations in their letters, referring their correspondents to the *Gazette* if they wished to know more about them.[94] This was not the only service rendered by the *Gazette* to France's bishops: it regularly included accounts of their consecrations and sometimes lengthy obituaries in later years, which probably remain the principal source of most subsequent accounts of their careers.

If there was a final act in the rituals of selecting bishops under Louis XIV, it was their formal presentation to the king shortly after the announcement. No doubt presentations of some kind had always existed, if only because bishops had to take the oath of fidelity to the king in person at court between receiving their provisions from Rome and taking formal possession of their see. However, as a special ritual normally conducted within days of the nomination, the 'presentation' seems to date from Louis's reign only. One of the first instances of it may have occurred only days before Mazarin's death, when Le Tellier requested that Nesmond, president in the parlement, take his son, whom Mazarin had just nominated to Bayeux, to court and present him to the king – 'it is another manoeuvre, but the Cardinal wishes it, and he is dying', Le Tellier is supposed to have commented. The king used the occasion to say to Nesmond *père* the kind of thing he would repeat to many others, bishops included, over the next fifty years: 'I believe you son will do his duty, I have had good reports of him'.[95] Later, the king would sometimes be less laconic than that and, of course, address his recommendations directly to the nominees themselves. For example, when at Christmas 1695, he told the new bishop of Langres that he had given him a diocese in which there was much to be done and which required 'regular residence' – counsels which may strike us as anodine enough – it was as a consequence of a sharp exchange over the record of his predecessor who had a weakness for gambling.[96] It is not hard

---

93 Quesnel, *Correspondance*, i, 225–6, to Louis du Vaucel, 29 Aug 1692; 378–9, to same, 16 Sept 1695; ii, 28, to same, 8 Nov 1698 for a few examples of his reactions.

94 *Lettres de Germain Vuillart*, no 76, 6 Nov 1696, surmising that his correspondent will have seen in the *Gazette* that the abbé Colbert de Croissy had been nominated to Montpellier. BN, MS Fr 23498 fo 58, *Nouvelles Ecclésiastiques*, 25 Jan 1686, 'je ne vous parle pas de la nomination aux évêchés, La Gazette l'expliquant'.

95 Choisy, *Mémoires*, 79–80. What exactly the term 'manoeuvre' was intended to convey is another matter; it may have been Mazarin's idea of giving the king an opportunity to impress on those who had received his graces to act accordingly.

96 Sourches, v, 83, 25 Dec 1695, 'ce qui faisoit assez connoitre qu'on avoit rendu auprès du roi de très mauvais offices à l'évêque qui venoit de mourir, quoiqu'on pût dire avec vérité que son diocèse n'étoit pas de ceux du royaume qui étoient les plus mal réglés.' The previous bishop, Louis de Simiane de Gordes had been bishop since 1671. When Cardinal Bouillon defended his record to Louis XIV he argued that although he gambled, he only did so *outside* of his diocese, which he did manage well. Obviously, the king did not fully accept this version of the facts: JRULM, MS French 91, fo 142, Huxelles to La Garde, 24 Nov 1696. The king had

to imagine similarly well-chosen remarks been made to bishops appointed to dioceses previously held by bishops suspected of Jansenist leanings, but there were limits to how far the king could go in a public presentation of a new bishop. No doubt in particular cases, the confessor also took a more discreet hand in briefing new bishops as to what was expected of them, although we can only guess as to the nature of such exchanges. These formal court presentations could be ordeals as much as triumphs, especially for ecclesiastics who had not previously been there, but they usually involved the presence of family members or patrons – some of whom were perhaps instrumental in securing the nomination in the first place.[97] As we have seen, at least one such presentation enabled the king to realise that he had named the wrong person to a diocese![98] As for the steady trickle of those refusing the king's graces – whether to a first diocese or a transfer to another – we can assume that the audience, if there was one at all, was more private: this was hardly the sort of rebuff that could be made, let alone witnessed, in public.[99]

X

French bishops were 'made' in France rather than Rome, but the latter's role in their making was far from unimportant, as the following chapters will make amply clear. All that needs to be noted here are the persistent structural features of that Roman connection. It is clear that even before Louis XIV assumed his full powers in 1661 a combination of efforts in both Rome and France had ensured the elimination of virtually all of the irregularities which had affected episcopal patronage in the century or so following the

previously questioned Bishop Simiane about his gambling, but without taking any action, *ibid*, MS French 90, fo 292, Huxelles to La Garde, 27 Dec 1695.

97 In 1671, Henri de Barillon, newly nominated to Luçon, was presented to Louis XIV by his uncle, who would continue in subsequent years to promote his interests, including a transfer from Luçon, with its unhealthy climate and marshlands, to a better diocese: see *Documents pour l'histoire de Luçon*, no 1111, Ferrier, king's confessor, to Barillon de Morangis, 23 Oct 1671. At Christmas 1695, the new bishop of Langres, Clermont-Tonnerre, was presented by his uncle, the bishop of Noyon, while the duc de Noailles and his brother, the archbishop of Paris, presented their brother, Gaston, who had just been nominated to Châlons-sur-Marne. The latter apparently had the rare privilege of an audience in the king's cabinet behind closed doors: Sourches, v, 83, 25 and 26 Dec 1695.

98 AN, L 746, pièce 1, Valence, no 1, Père Léonard papers.

99 JRULM, MS French 92, fo 16v–17r, Huxelles to La Garde, 3 Feb 1698, in which she says that Bissy, bishop of Toul 'balance d'accepter Bordeaux, disant n'estre pas assés riche et M son père ne le voulant point aider, il eut hier là dessus, *à ce que l'on présume*, une longue conférence avec le Roy'. Bissy did refuse Bordeaux (*ibid*, fo 18, letter of 5 Feb, to same), as the bishop of Saint-Pol-de-Léon in Brittany had done in 1680 when summoned all the way to court to accept Alet in the Pyrenees: *Correspondance de Rancé*, ii, 471–2, Le Neboux de la Brousse to Rancé, 18 Dec 1680. ASV, Nunz Fr 166, fo 20, Lauri, auditor of Paris nunciature, to Cardinal Cibo, 10 Jan 1681, on Le Neboux's voyage to Paris and king's acceptance of his unwillingness to change diocese.

Concordat. As Olivier Poncet has shown, one of the ways that Rome dealt with instances of episcopal resignation, requests for pensions or coadjutors, or the increasingly rare nominations of underage bishops, was to entrust consideration of them to the vigilant consistorial congregation, whose work then enabled the papacy to take a tougher stance than previously. And the relative rarity of French dossiers, compared to those of other parts of Europe and Spanish overseas territories, among the congregation's surviving papers shows how effective an agency of reform it was. Louis XIV's reign would witness serious disputes with Rome which directly affected French bishops, as the following chapters will show, but the calibre or appropriateness (*idoneitas*) of the individual royal nominations were rarely at issue, and when they were it was nearly always because of ideological (Jansenist or gallican) issues.[100] Indeed, if only a handful of them, in comparison with earlier generations of French bishops, went to Rome under Louis XIV to seek their provisions or have themselves consecrated, it was partly because so few of them needed to seek dispensations or other favours. As nominations increasingly corresponded to post-tridentine norms, they attracted less and less attention in instructions to papal nuncios and in the reports the latter sent back to the curia. Most the time, nuncios only mentioned new bishops when they conducted the enquiry *de vita et moribus* and received their profession of faith, but those reports were overwhelmingly short and formulaic, unless of course the new bishops were requesting special favours (usually the reduction in the costs of bulls) or were relatives of ministers and major figures at court. Arguably the high point of such confidence in the patronage system came in 1712 when a new nuncio wrote apologetically to Cardinal Paulucci, the secretary of state, to say that in future he would not bother the cardinal with news of episcopal nominations, since the court lists would give him all the information he needed.[101] But the date of this utterance should not lead us to conclude that it had been a long, uphill struggle before such perfection was reached: in fact, Bentivoglio's offer might well been made by virtually any of his predecessors under Louis XIV, who consistently relied heavily upon the lists and the *Gazette* to keep Rome informed of nominations. One issue, however, represents an exception to this trend, because it alone led nuncios to increase the mentions accorded to new bishops in their despatches from the early 1690s onwards. After the resolution of the decade-long crisis to which the extension of the *régale* to France's southern dioceses gave rise after 1682, the papacy insisted that incoming bishops receive from the nuncio a papal brief admonishing them not to actively consent to the extension and to sign

---

100 The last of these cases dates from 1713, when the duc de Beauvillier's half-brother, nominated to Beauvais, was being denied his provisions by Clement XI on account of his defence of the four articles of 1682 in his theses for the doctorate of theology at the Sorbonne – theses, it should be noted, he was obliged to defend on the king's own orders.

101 ASV, Nunz Fr 224, fo 620, letter from Nuncio Bentivoglio, 29 Aug 1712, 'mi riportaró in avvenire ad essi (the lists) per non aggravare maggiormente Vestra Eminenza.'

Table 5.1   From nomination to confirmation (in years)

1661–9	0.75	1690	0.6
1670–9	1.1	1700–9	0.5
1680–9	4.4	1710–15	0.4

a declaration to that effect. Nuncios often reported difficulty tracking down some of the bishops, occasionally hinting that they were playing cat-and-mouse with them, unwilling to sign such a declaration.[102] But none of this actually delayed the despatch to those concerned of their papal provisions, and nothing demonstrates better the fluency of the entire system than the speed with which royal nominations were turned into papal confirmations during the half-century after 1661. A breakdown of the time elapsed between nomination and confirmation per decade makes this clear (table 5.1).

Crude as it is, this table reflects developments to which we shall return in due course, notably the delays which arose out of worsening relations with Rome under Clement X and Innocent XI from the mid-1670s onwards, and then the suspension of provisions altogether between 1682 and 1692. But if we put them to one side, bearing in mind that it was political disputes between crown and papacy rather than problems with individual nominees to the episcopate that were the issue, it is quite clear that Rome found fewer and fewer reasons to delay provisions for French bishops. The falling averages for the last two and a half decades of the reign are the clearest sign of that, indicating both that new bishops were anxious to complete the formalities in France with genuine rapidity, and that Rome responded in kind for its part. By the standards of any age, turn-around times of four to six months are impressive. Apart from diplomatic crises, delays could arise for a wide variety of reasons, which we need not itemise here, while the curial bureaucracy was unforgiving if incomplete or inaccurately compiled dossiers were sent from France. Suffice it to say that the lowest average for any decade, that of the 1710s, would have been lower still had some royal nominees not had to wait several months in 1712 for the arrival of a new nuncio, since during the interim the crown firmly refused to allow anyone else at the nunciature to conduct the enquiry *de vita et moribus* or receive the profession of faith from new bishops.[103]

---

102   For an instance of this, see ASV, Nunz Fr 224, fo 988, nuncio to secretary of state, 19 Nov 1712, claiming that despite all of his efforts he had so far failed to present the brief to the new bishop of Toulon, whom he suspected of evasiveness, even though La Tour du Pin, the bishop in question, was no gallican. See also the account in Blet, *Les Assemblées du clergé et Louis XIV*, 542ff.

103   ASV, Nunz Fr 224, fo 321, Carlo Borio, auditor of the nunciature, to secretary of state, 23 May 1712; fo 337, same to same, 30 May. The nuncio arrived in late July and promptly conducted the enquiry for the incoming bishop of Belley: fo 542, Bentivoglio to secretary of state, 1 Aug 1712.

There is little doubt that the exercise of episcopal patronage during the half-century after 1661 is considerably easier to follow than that of any preceding period since the Concordat of Bologna. This is partly because the regularisation and ritualisation sketched out in this chapter went hand in hand, and generated far more comment than in the past. Reading the accounts, sometimes quite circumstantial, of diarists and correspondents, it is all too easy to infer that the system held so few secrets for participants and observers alike that surprises were virtually eliminated, and that there was little room for change over five and a half decades. Yet if one resists the temptation to assume that contemporaries really did know the 'inside story' of episcopal nominations, it becomes clear that surprises did occur, involving both the selection of 'outsiders' and the passing over of 'natural' candidates for high office. There is, therefore, every reason to subject the crown's handling of its patronage to closer scrutiny, in order to judge how far short-term considerations inflected the main features of royal policy. The three chapters that follow will attempt to follow the pattern of episcopal patronage in chronological perspective and in sufficient detail to uncover its continuities and variations.

CHAPTER 6

A New Dispensation?

CARDINAL MAZARIN REMAINED a busy, anxious man in the last few weeks of his life, despite his visibly failing health. There was, of course, a great deal still to be done – ensuring that the young Louis XIV would accept his political legacy and retain the ministers he had promoted, marrying off the last of his nieces, arranging the terms and destination of his gigantic fortune, to name only a few. Ecclesiastical affairs were also among those requiring His Eminence's attention. For one thing, his own unrivalled collection of great abbeys had to be split up and earmarked for successors of his own choosing.[1] A considerable backlog of episcopal nominations had also built up since October 1659, the date of the last round. This arose in large part from Mazarin's own habitual tactic of not making such decisions while an assembly of clergy was in immediate prospect or in session, in the hope of bending deputies to his will with expectations of advancement. But the 'little' Assembly of 1660, which had begun in August 1660 and which would not normally have involved extended deliberations, was still in session when the cardinal died in early March 1661.[2] This no doubt explains why in the last few weeks of his life, sensing that the Assembly might outlast him, Mazarin made no fewer than eight episcopal appointments, most of them a mere ten days before his death.[3] In this he was doing precisely what his royal pupil and godson, repeatedly pressed by *his* confessor, would steadfastly refuse to do half a century later.[4] Consequently, not a single French diocese was without a nominee when Mazarin died, so Louis XIV would have to await further deaths or resignations before he could exercise the patronage which the cardinal had so jealously guarded for himself until the end. During the following months Mazarin's last nominees, with a few exceptions as we shall see later, would receive their bulls and be consecrated, mostly in Parisian churches, taking

---

1 Choisy, *Mémoires*, 78–9. See also *Mémoriaux du conseil de 1661*, i, 101.
2 Pierre Blet, *Le Clergé de France et la monarchie*, 2 vols (Rome-Paris 1959), ii, 255ff.
3 *Mémoriaux du conseil de 1661*, i, 145, n 5. One of the eight nominations was to Orange, technically not part of the French church.
4 Saint-Simon, xxvii, 253; xxix, 331.

their place alongside the other 105 or so bishops already in place. But in order to understand how the young Louis XIV went about dispensing episcopal patronage when it did become available, it is essential to have some idea of the kind of episcopate which he inherited at Mazarin's death. The brief overview that follows will cover only a limited number of features; and it assumes, moreover, that the discussion in previous chapters of their social and geographical background as well as their intellectual attainments can be taken as familiar.

I

The point of departure is the realisation that between them, the size of the French church – as expressed in the number of dioceses – and the age-profile of its bishops were enough to ensure that the turnover of bishops would be relatively slow. With the average age of incoming bishops hovering around – and mostly above – forty years, careers spanning around twenty-four years were the norm by mid-century. Given Mazarin's eighteen years in power, it follows that the majority of France's bishops in 1661 had come into office during his ministry – seventy-seven out of 108 to be precise (71 per cent). This is not to assert that they all owed him some kind of deep personal debt for their elevation, as his control over episcopal patronage was never absolute and was at times, especially before and during the Fronde, distinctly limited. His skill lay rather in understanding the interests and ambitions of those directly concerned with high church office in such a way that they could also serve his multifarious purposes, political and personal. This is most evident in his management of church patronage during the post-Fronde years. He did, of course, place a number of his own clients in the episcopate, and some of them would play important roles in church politics long after his death. Of the remaining thirty-one bishops in office in 1661 and who did not owe their advancement to him, twenty-seven had been seated during Richelieu's ministry. There were just four hardy survivors from the world as it was before the cardinal-ministers. Even an elite like the bishops were not unaffected by the mortality rates of seventeenth-century France, so we should not expect these men to have died off or retired in a conveniently pre-ordained sequence. Indeed, the two oldest bishops among them, both seated in the 1610s, lived until 1671 and 1690 respectively – a good deal longer than many of Mazarin's men from the 1650s.[5] The rate at which the pre-1661 bishops died or retired is conveyed most succinctly by the following table (6.1).

This breakdown gives some idea of the durability of the bishops of the Richelieu and Mazarin era and, consequently, of the scope left to Louis XIV

5   Louis Duchaine, nominated coadjutor of Senez in 1617, and Louis de la Baume de Suze, nominated to Viviers in 1613.

Table 6.1   Death/retirement of pre-Louis XIV bishops

1661–9	31
1670–9	38
1680–9	24
1690–9	12
1700–9	4
1710–15	2

for renewing the episcopate in the short term. It does not, of course, tell the full story: after all, bishops promoted after 1661 were themselves also dying, retiring, or moving to other dioceses during these same decades. Even so, the figures given above for the 1660s and especially the 1670s suggest something of the speed at which a new generation of bishops *could* emerge. Equally, the longevity of those who survived until the 1690s and beyond is remarkable, and it would be rivalled by several of the king's own nominees, some of whom reigned, as we shall see later, for over fifty years. The career of one of the very last of Mazarin's nominees from late February 1661, François de Nesmond, bishop of Bayeux, maps almost perfectly onto that of Louis XIV himself, since he died only a few months before the king, in May 1715. In terms of sheer longevity, he was actually outdone by two of the best known diplomats of Louis's reign, both cardinals, Toussaint de Forbin-Janson (died March 1713) and César d'Estrées (died December 1714) who had become bishops in 1653 and 1655 respectively.

Moreover, nineteen of the 105 bishops in office at Mazarin's death had already moved from their first diocese. If there is a category of bishop that is worth singling out from among those in office before 1661, it would be the archbishops, whose role as titular heads of ecclesiastical provinces in an age of frequent assemblies of clergy, was still growing in importance; and for some of them that was enhanced by their leadership role in the *pays d'états*. Four of the nineteen bishops to have moved to a second diocese by 1661 had already become archbishops. Louis XIV would himself promote several 'mere' bishops to archiepiscopal sees in the decade or so after 1661 and some of these 'happy few' survived nearly as long as he did himself.[6] A few of those who were already archbishops – Pierre de Marca of Toulouse or François de Harlay of Rouen being prime examples – were promoted by Louis to yet more attractive dioceses. As we shall see later, the king's approach to such nominations was characterised by careful deliberation of a kind not always exhibited by his predecessors. But here, too, his freedom of action was for long limited by the fact that a significant number of those already ensconced in their archiepiscopal sees before 1661 survived for several more decades – the archbishops of

6   The longest living of these men was Daniel de Cosnac, bishop of Valence in 1654 and archbishop of Aix-en-Provence after Grimaldi. He died in 1708.

Lyon and Vienne (died 1693), Arles (1689), Aix (1685), Bordeaux (1680), Sens (1674) led the field and included some of the most independently-minded prelates of their time.[7]

II

For all his last-minute activity in early 1661, there were major items of unfinished business which not even a master politician like Mazarin could successfully resolve. A close look at them will reveal the kinds of issue – some enduring, some purely short-term – which episcopal patronage raised, then and later, during Louis's reign. Others, already familiar from an earlier chapter, need not be discussed further: the problem of Elne-Perpignan and Arras went far beyond the normal routines of episcopal patronage, and could not be resolved without active papal cooperation. The first two cases to be examined here are far more conventional, but they highlight the problems generated, even when the crown was compliant, by the ambitions of families to retain a diocese over several generations. Strictly speaking, the Rieux succession belongs to the last years of the Mazarin regime, but because it was still stalled in early 1661, its beneficiary can be regarded as belonging among Louis XIV's first bishops. The Languedoc see of Rieux had been held by two members of the powerful Toulouse parlementaire family of Bertier since 1602. In 1657, Jean-Louis de Bertier, wishing to transmit it to his nephew, André-François, obtained royal permission to resign it in his favour, while reserving half of its revenues for himself as a pension. But Rome objected in principle to the size of the pension, and considered the fact that the younger Bertier was far from indigent as wholly irrelevant. The matter proceeded slowly, it seems, possibly because the elder Bertier bishop was still alive and in post, so nothing had happened by the time of Mazarin's death over three years later. Louis XIV duly allowed the nomination to proceed, Rome continued to resist but, having examined the case again, it finally relented.[8] While allowing the succession to take its course, it tried to put restrictions on its terms, and especially on the pension.[9] André-François de Bertier duly obtained his provisions

7   In the case of Arles, the archbishop's death in 1689 did not create a vacancy, since he had installed a nephew as his coadjutor as early as 1666. Grimaldi, a former papal nuncio to France under Mazarin, had emerged as a reforming and rigorist archbishop at Aix, whose politics did not endear him to the court. Gondrin of Sens, a relative of the king's mistress Mme de Montespan, was feared even by the king himself, who also allowed enormous latitude in the Lyonnais to the archbishop, uncle of the marshal Villeroy.

8   ASV, Acta congregationis consistorialis 1660–3, fo 60, 27 Sept 1661. It imposed several restrictions on the retiring bishop's pension and privileges: *Hierarchia Catholica*, iv, 296, 'Riven', n 4.

9   *Hierarchia Catholica*, iv, 296, 'Riven', n 4: the pension amounted to half of the revenues, but Rome stipulated that it should only be paid provided 1,000 *livres* remained for the new bishop. In the event, the latter did not have to pay the pension, since his uncle died in early June 1662.

at last in April 1662. When he died, forty-three years later in 1705, with a reputation for Jansenist proclivities, there was little chance of yet another Bertier succession in Rieux.

In 1661, a second Languedoc see had also been vacant since 1657, but this time through death rather than retirement. Like Rieux, Lombez had been held by successive members of another famous Toulouse *parlementaire* dynasty, the Daffis, and that also seemed set to continue when Mazarin agreed to nominate Charles de Roquépine, a maternal nephew of the last Daffis bishop and *agent-général* of the clergy since 1655. But he died in December 1660 while still awaiting his bulls, a delay which it remains hard to explain.[10] A successor, Nicolas Le Maistre was chosen in February 1661, one of Mazarin's last episcopal nominees.[11] But he too died, in October 1661, having received his bulls but before being consecrated or 'taking possession' of his see.[12] Finally, a cousin of Chancellor Séguier, Jacques Séguier de la Verrière, was chosen to succeed these two 'local' predecessors, though the fact that his relatively modest diocese was burdened with pensions for a Colbert and a Cassagnet (a nephew of Le Tellier) casts its own light upon the power shifts within the royal entourage.[13]

Cases like Rieux and Lombez serve as reminders of the kinds of problem or event – the premature death of a royal nominee being just one – which could inordinately prolong an episcopal vacancy. They also show, as was suggested in the previous chapter, how much more intractable Rome had now become on questions such as the size of pensions, and how it would block appointments at a time when it was usually capable of processing unproblematic royal nominations within a few months. The days when Rome complained about excessively long vacancies in the French church might be over, but Louis XIV's reign experienced its share of them from the outset, while the crisis of the decade 1682–92 would outstrip even the previous record for such vacancies during the latter phase of the Wars of Religion. Both Rieux and Lombez belonged among the lesser French dioceses, and the problem of filling them probably did not cause the king and his advisers too many headaches. But there were other dioceses that were capable of doing just that. Louis XIV inherited from Mazarin two cases that went far beyond the conventional stakes of episcopal promotion and patronage, since they involved two archbishoprics of prime importance.

Since 1654, the archbishop of Paris was the ex-Frondeur, the Cardinal de Retz and, like the Bertier and the Daffis we have just seen, he too was the scion of a family that had filled the see of Paris for generations, since 1569 in fact. But his role in the Fronde, which brought him a red hat and made him

10   *Mémoriaux du conseil de 1661*, i, 261–3, for reference to his activity as *agent-général* and *promoteur* of the Assembly of 1660–1.
11   SHAT, Archives de la Guerre, A¹ 171, no 68, minute of *brevet de nomination*, 28 Feb 1661.
12   G Couarraze, *Au Pays de Savès. Lombez évêché rural* (Lombez 1973), 130–1.
13   *Hierarchia Catholica*, iv, 223, 'Lomberiensis', n 5.

Mazarin's main rival for the position of chief minister, had led to his arrest in 1652. Having escaped two years later to Rome, where Mazarin's enemy, Alexander VII, protected him, he refused thereafter to cooperate with the Mazarin government, let alone resign his see. A stalemate ensued during which Mazarin and Retz engaged in a kind of guerrilla war – labelled the 'third Fronde' by one historian – for the control of the diocese of Paris.[14] It was only after Mazarin's death that, still in exile, Retz finally agreed to resign Paris outright. Officially, he did so on the same day as the pope confirmed his successor in consistory, on 5 June 1662, but the final negotiations were not as simple or clinical as this suggests: by insisting on the simultaneous resignation and succession in Paris Alexander VII was trying to demonstrate that, at least where cardinals were concerned, the essential decisions were his. Needless to say, this display of papal authority was more formal than real, as the real decisions had already been made elsewhere. From the crown's point of view, the Paris succession was of vital importance, and Louis XIV was persuaded, by Michel Le Tellier it seems, to choose the same man as Mazarin would certainly have done.[15] Pierre de Marca, whom we have already encountered, owed his episcopal career almost entirely to Mazarin's patronage, as his translation from Couserans to Toulouse in 1652 at the end of the Fronde suggests; it was confirmed by his major role thereafter in both diplomacy and church-state politics – in which, incidentally, he emerged as an implacable enemy of Retz. Promoted to the *conseil de conscience* in 1661, he was by then mainly resident at court, so his translation to Paris, to which he was formally nominated on 26 February 1662, the same day as Retz's resignation papers reached the court, surprised nobody.[16] A bureaucratic hitch delayed his confirmation by Rome until 5 June, but by the time his bulls arrived in Paris on 26 June, he had only three days to live; he was, technically, only archbishop of Paris for twenty-four days. By then the king and his advisers already knew that death was close and had earmarked a successor. On 1 July, only two days after Marca's death, the identity of his successor became known – Hardouin de Péréfixe, bishop of Rodez since 1649, but most of all the king's former preceptor. He had also been Louis's personal preference as successor to Retz earlier that year, but he had deferred then to Le Tellier's arguments that the Jansenist and related problems in the post-Retz capital

---

14   Richard M Golden, *The Godly Rebellion. Parisian curés and the Religious Fronde 1652–62* (Chapel Hill 1981), esp ch 4.

15   René Rapin, *Mémoires sur l'église et la société, la cour, la ville et le jansénisme*, ed Léon Aubineau, 3 vols (Paris 1865), ii, 166. Marca himself reported that two other bishops, both clients of Mazarin, had been proposed for Paris – Charles de Bourlemont, bishop of Castres, and Hyacinthe Serroni, recently transferred from Orange to Mende: BN, MS Baluze 121, fo 52, letter to Bishop Bosquet of Montpellier, 31 Jan 1662.

16   F Gaquère, *Pierre de Marca (1594–1662), sa vie, ses oeuvres, son gallicanisme* (Paris 1932), 293–304. Gaquère explains that while Marca was not aware of the king's decision before it was made public, he had engaged in discreet lobbying behind the scenes in the preceding weeks.

needed a man of Marca's proven capacity and experience.[17] The choice of Péréfixe, which Le Tellier could hardly oppose for a second time, was an early example of the king's enduring preference for men he knew. It was also alleged later by a writer with unusually good sources of information, Louis Fouquet, that the Retz succession had made the king resolve never to seek the red hat for an archbishop of Paris, since he would then either want to become a minister or Rome would protect him from royal reprisals in case of conflict.[18]

The Paris succession involved a cardinal from a distinguished ducal family with powerful ties to the clergy and elites of the capital. That of Reims, long held by members of the Guise family and whose archbishop was the first peer of France, enjoying considerable prestige within both church and state, was an even more convoluted piece of unfinished business left by Mazarin. The last papally approved archbishop of Reims, Léonor d'Etampes de Valençay, had died in April 1651. Mazarin's first choice of successor, Henri de Savoie-Nemours, was clearly prompted by Fronde politics, but in 1655 Nemours, still unconfirmed and unconsecrated, became head of his house and decided to marry. Mazarin's second choice of archbishop for Reims was even more problematic, though for entirely different reasons. Cardinal Antonio Barberini had fled to France in the mid-1640s due to Innocent X's attack on Urban VIII's family, and had remained there under Mazarin's protection whereas his elder brother and family rival, Cardinal Francesco Barberini, made his peace with Innocent and returned to Rome. Mazarin had originally nominated Antonio to Poitiers in 1652 but Innocent X refused to confirm the nomination, and his successor, Alexander VII, another *bête noire* of Mazarin, did likewise. Not surprisingly, Antonio's nomination to Reims in 1657, which followed his installation as *grand aumônier de France* in 1653, again thanks to Mazarin's patronage, was no more acceptable to Rome than his previous one to Poitiers. Barberini was trapped in the animosity and sniping which characterised Franco-papal relations for the final years of Mazarin's ministry and Alexander VII's papacy. The pope initially argued that Barberini could not have Reims since the duty of residence it imposed clashed with an identical duty for his office of chamberlain (*camerlengo*) of the Roman church. Fearing that this was a ploy to ease him out of a high-ranking dignity which could then be given to a papal client, Louis XIV bluntly refused to allow Barberini

---

17 See Golden, *The Godly Rebellion*, for the best account of the post-Fronde problems of Paris and its clergy.

18 BN, MS Fr 23506 fo 168, *Nouvelles Ecclésiastiques* (n d, but ca 1676), 'c'est je croy ici l'endroit de vous faire souvenir de la résolution qui fut prise à la cour du tems que Mr le Cardinal de Rets donna sa démission de l'archevesché de Paris de ne plus jamais nommer au Cardinalat aucun archevesque de Paris tant de peur qu'il ne prist des liaisons trop estroites avec le pape que de peur que les Cardinaux ne rentrassent dans le ministère.' Fouquet's own anti-court animus is evident from his comment on such royal decisions: 'il n'y a point de maxime en France et rien n'y est stable, aucune chose ne s'y décide par le veritable interest ou de l'église ou de l'estat mais tout par l'intrigue et par la faveur.' He was, of course, writing many years before Louis XIV would seek to obtain a red hat for Archbishop Harlay of Paris.

to resign Reims in order to satisfy the pope.[19] The deadlock remained even when Antonio returned to Italy after Mazarin's death, and Alexander found various reasons to refuse him the bulls for Reims.

As so often, it took a new pope, Clement IX, elected in June 1667, to break the logjam, and within weeks of his election Reims finally had a titular archbishop.[20] But it was also clear by then that Barberini, even though he was only sixty years old, was unlikely to return to govern Reims in person. Despite the king's objections to coadjutorships, this was the prospect soon being canvassed for Reims, not least because after so many years of neglect and vacancy, it genuinely needed a resident archbishop.[21] The problem, naturally, was that, as the premier peerage of the kingdom, it was bound to attract powerful and intense competition. The most delicate claim to deal with was presented by marshal Turenne, then on the verge of converting to Catholicism and acting on behalf of his young nephew, the abbé d'Albret, who had recently taken his doctorate at the Sorbonne and was being openly groomed for high ecclesiastical honours.[22] Turenne, who knew how to look after his own, was determined that his nephew would benefit handsomely from his planned conversion, but Louis XIV and his advisers cannot have viewed with equanimity the prospect of a son of the duc de Bouillon installed at Reims, given its proximity to lands like Sedan which had until recently belonged to the La Marck-Bouillon family and where, under Richelieu and Mazarin, Albret's own father had engaged in rebellion against the crown. It was probably to block the Turenne-Bouillon claim that a 'ministerial' candidate, the young Charles-Maurice Le Tellier, son of the war minister, Michel Le Tellier, was put forward. His – or rather his family's – episcopal aspirations for him were no secret since *his* theology doctorate a few years earlier. Initially their efforts focused on securing the succession to another diocese with a peerage – that of Langres, held since 1655 by yet another former rival to Mazarin, Barbier de la Rivière. In their negotiations with Barbier, the latter was, it seems, ruthlessly outmanoeuvred by Le Tellier *père*, who secured the coadjutorship of Langres for his son on 30 May 1668.[23] Yet within less than two weeks, on 12 June, Le Tellier was offered, with Barberini's full consent, the Reims coadjutorship and he promptly accepted it. Within less than a month, his bulls were granted in Rome – compelling evidence of the perceived need to resolve this question quickly rather than allow it to

19 The French case is stated in BN, Morel de Thoisy 2, fos 45–7. See *Mémoriaux du conseil de 1661*, i, 251, 254–5, nn 22–3; ii, 38–40, for a summary of the negotiations down to 1661.

20 His bulls were dated 18 July 1667, a month after Clement IX's election: *Hierarchia Catholica*, iv, 295, 'Rhemen'.

21 Long neglected by its Guise incumbents since the Cardinal of Lorraine's death in 1574, Reims was administered for long stretches either by suffragan-bishops or vicars-general.

22 Albret was son of Turenne's brother, the duc de Bouillon, who had converted to Catholicism on his marriage to Elisabeth de Bergh in 1634 and who died in 1652, leaving his son under Turenne's care.

23 *Lettres du cardinal Le Camus, évêque et prince de Grenoble (1632–1707)*, ed A P M Ingold (Paris 1892), 13–18, letter to Sébastien du Cambout de Pontchâteau, 16 Feb 1670.

rumble on and leave the door open to further intrigue. By comparison with some of the cases we have just examined, the Reims succession was wrapped up with almost unseemly haste – so much so that a particularly well-informed source, Lefèvre d'Ormesson, claimed that Louis XIV realised only later that Le Tellier senior had pulled the wool over his eyes by giving him the impression that there was virtually no difference between Langres and Reims.[24] Ormesson also alleged that the Langres coadjutorship was deliberately contrived, and that their real objective from the outset was the succession to Reims, but whether the king or his confessor were aware of this remains unclear.[25] Turenne and his supporters were certainly taken aback by these developments, and attempted to discredit the nomination of Le Tellier in the most obvious manner they could, by alleging that his low social status made him clearly unworthy of such an elevated rank in the French church.[26] Turenne himself, not the most tactful figure in the king's circle, embarrassed Le Tellier senior by claiming that his famous 'modesty' was a mere cover for unwarranted ambitions, while marshal Bellefonds and others unnamed appear to have openly disapproved of the nomination in council.[27] In the event, Le Tellier's coadjutorship at Reims was to be both relatively short and unhampered by his absentee superior Barberini, who died in August 1671. Le Tellier would remain at Reims as full archbishop until his death nearly forty years later and, as a hardline gallican and anti-Jesuit figure, play a major part in French ecclesiastical affairs for much of that time.

Louis XIV may well have regretted making a hasty decision about the Reims coadjutorship, but that was quickly forgotten as another challenge connected to it had to be faced. Just as Le Tellier used the Langres coadjutorship in order to secure the real prize, Reims, so Turenne and his nephew, the future Cardinal de Bouillon, were themselves angling to use the Reims case to obtain an even more desirable one – that of Paris. While still abbé d'Albret, Bouillon began to ingratiate himself with Archbishop Péréfixe, especially after taking his doctorate in 1668, to the extent that the latter was ready to do for him what Barberini did for the young Le Tellier. According to the abbé de Choisy, it was Bouillon who persuaded the irate Turenne to moderate his

24 Olivier Lefèvre d'Ormesson, *Journal et extraits des mémoires d'André Lefèvre d'Ormesson*, ed Adolphe Chéruel, 2 vols (Paris 1860–1), ii, 545–6, 550.

25 *Ibid*, 545, 'Il y avoit longtemps qu'il ménageoit cette coadjutorerie avec M le cardinal Antoine, et l'on croit que celle de Langres n'avoit esté recherchée et obtenue que pour faciliter l'obtention de la première. Quoy qu'il en soit, la coadjutorerie de Langres a fait réussir la seconde . . .'

26 *Ibid*, 546–7, for Turenne repudiating the pretence of Le Tellier being too modest to dare dream of Reims for his son. As Ormesson put it, 'tout le monde considère cette grace comme trop considérable'. Turenne may have been the one whom Ormesson claims pointed out to Louis XIV that if the king had a son he wished to place in the church, he could not do better than Reims (p 550). If true, this story raises questions about the king's relative lack of understanding of the kind of church patronage at his disposal and of the absence of advice from Annat, Péréfixe or others on this occasion.

27 *Correspondance du nonce Spada*, no 199, Spada to Cardinal Altieri, 18 May 1674. This report, written several years later, need not be taken as fully accurate.

anti-Le Tellier sentiments over Reims: better for that particular coadjutorship to go through, he suggested, since it would make it extremely difficult for the king, on the defensive for promoting a young ecclesiastic of inappropriate rank, to deny even greater advancement to Bouillon, who had already lined up two more desirable targets. But when Turenne, less tactically astute on the ecclesiastical than the military battlefield, asked for the first of them, the Paris coadjutorship, Louis XIV refused point-blank recalling, according to Choisy, the role of Retz, then coadjutor of Paris, as a leading rebel during the Fronde. However, quickly realising that snubbing the Bouillon-Turenne interest like this was potentially troublesome, Louis readily agreed to nominate Turenne's nephew for the red hat – which was probably what they wanted most of all – though it did not eliminate, either then or later, his ambition to hold a major French bishopric.[28]

The interest of successions like those of Reims and Paris, although their outcomes have taken us far from the immediate aftermath of Mazarin's death, lies in what they reveal about the young Louis XIV's handling of major items of episcopal patronage. More crucially, they lay bare not just the undiminished competitiveness of the ministerial and aristocratic groups aiming at high church office, but also their willingness and ability to hoodwink the monarch on occasion. They are also a reminder that, especially at the highest levels, the outcome of individual successions, far from closing off such competition, only ensured that the parties would carry over, as Turenne did, a kind of 'profit and loss' account for use on subsequent occasions. Finally, it should be remembered that the Reims succession, drawn out over seventeen years, had become entangled with yet other items of unfinished business which were surveyed in the opening chapter, notably that of the indults to nominate bishops in recently acquired dioceses like Elne or Arras.[29] Instructions to French envoys in Rome in 1661 and later raised these issues alongside each other, and in language that did not conceal irritation at the papacy's stubborn refusal to bring them to a conclusion. The worse diplomatic relations generally between France and Rome were, the more these 'secondary' questions were unlikely to be dealt with expeditiously or in their own terms – and down to Alexander VII's death in mid 1667 a series of incidents, misunderstandings and slights, alleged or real, all ensured that they remained troubled.[30]

There is perhaps one additional element of the Mazarin inheritance that ought to be noted here, although it constituted 'fall-out' rather than unfin-

---

28 Choisy, _Mémoires_, 230–5, for the most substantial account of these two affairs. Choisy was close to Bouillon and wished to show that he had a far better grasp of ecclesiastical politics than his uncle. Bouillon was the sole cardinal promoted in the consistory of 5 Aug 1669. See Bouillon's letters to his agent in Rome during 1669 in _Lettres de Turenne_, ed Suzanne d'Huart (Paris 1971), 603–13.

29 _Recueil des instructions aux ambassadeurs: Rome_, i, 92–4, for instructions to envoy to Rome, d'Aubeville, 1661.

30 See Sonnino, _Louis XIV's View of the Papacy_, 20.

ished business, since it emerged only as a consequence of the most notable political change to follow the cardinal's death – the disgrace of Fouquet. The latter's wide connections to the *dévots* and to the most influential social and literary circles of his day made him a formidable problem for those around the king who plotted his downfall and elimination. Moreover, he had two brothers, as well as more distant relatives and clients, who were bishops. In the event, it was his brothers who paid the heaviest penalties after the *surintendant* himself. His elder brother, François, had been coadjutor and then full archbishop of Narbonne (since 1659), while his younger brother, Louis, became bishop of Agde, vacated for him by François, in 1656. Mazarin's protection had enabled them to move untroubled and simultaneously into two highly desirable southern dioceses.[31] Narbonne was not Paris, but along with Aix it was probably the most politically important see of southern France, whose incumbent presided over the Estates of Languedoc and enjoyed potentially enormous power in the province. The Fouquet brothers understood this, too, as did Louis XIV, Colbert and others who dominated the post-Fouquet ministry. Consequently, François Fouquet was quickly sent into internal exile in 1661 by *lettre de cachet*, dying in 1673 in Alençon in remotest Normandy. He had apparently tried to resign Narbonne at some point during the 1660s to Gilbert de Choiseul, bishop of Comminges, but there was little chance of such a decision winning royal acceptance, since Choiseul himself was not the kind of biddable character the crown would wish to see in such an important position.[32] This enabled Pierre de Marca's immediate successor in Toulouse, Charles de Bourlemont, to become the major player in the provincial Estates after 1661, but after his death in 1669 it was a different kind of episcopal dynast with good Mazarinist credentials, Pierre de Bonsi, previously bishop of Béziers, who stepped into that role, while waiting his turn to secure the Narbonne succession after François Fouquet's death in 1673. As for the younger of the Fouquet brothers, Louis, bishop of Agde until his death in 1702, he had to suffer nearly thirty years (until 1690) of outright exile from Agde, followed by twelve years of confinement within his diocese, the kind of retribution which his combative Jansenist proclivities did nothing to relieve.[33] It was he who founded the original, unpublished *Nouvelles Ecclésiastiques* which became a *locus classicus* of a rigorist, anti-court view of contemporary religious affairs and, in particular, of the proper conduct of bishops.[34]

31 See Bergin, *Making*, 626–7, for notices on them. François, a bishop since the 1630s, had become coadjutor of Narbonne in 1656, with a view to governing this vital see in the years to come. Louis moved into his old diocese of Agde shortly afterwards.
32 Brunet, *Les Prêtres des montagnes*, 157–9, and 190, n 64.
33 Xavier Azéma, *Un Prélat janséniste. Louis Foucquet évêque et comte d'Agde 1656–1702* (Paris 1963).
34 *Ibid*, ch 8, 'Une entreprise épiscopale d'information janséniste: les *Nouvelles Ecclésiastiques*'. They have survived in various manuscript collections, the most complete of which is BN, MS Fr 23498-24510.

III

Louis XIV's reign would witness several other cases of bishops who were disgraced or exiled, but it would be misleading to imagine that either the Retz or the Fouquet cases somehow set a tone that would be typical of the decades to follow. The different *cas de figure* we have just seen highlight the variety of problems with which a new regime could be confronted, and the ease and speed – or lack of them – with which they were resolved. Inevitably, the most intractable of them have also taken the analysis well past the beginnings of the king's personal rule. It is, therefore, time to focus attention on the mainstream of episcopal patronage and its distribution in the aftermath of Mazarin's death. However politically inexperienced Louis XIV may have been at that point, he did begin exercising power in a much more favourable situation than either Henri IV in 1589 or the young Louis XIII in 1617. There was little sign of regime-threatening problems with religious connotations in 1661. As we saw, one of Louis's first decisions, to revamp the *conseil de conscience*, was not intended as part of a 'revolution of 1661', as the king's subsequent defence of the virtue of prudence in episcopal affairs specifically confirms. As a preliminary to looking in closer detail at how the new regime handled episcopal nominations it will be useful to have some grasp of the overall scope of what was available to it.

The broad outlines of the 'volume' of episcopal patronage between March 1661 and early 1682, when relations with Rome nose-dived so badly that episcopal confirmations were suspended for a decade, are presented in the accompanying year-by-year table (6.2). During this period a total of 105 new bishops were nominated and received their provisions from Rome; one or two more nominations, already held up by unresolved disputes with Rome concerning recently acquired dioceses like Saint-Omer, were stalled further by the 1682 break.[35] Seen in purely numerical terms, Louis XIV virtually renewed the entire French episcopate during these first two decades. The table also confirms (column two) something already noted in this chapter: the many acts of patronage involving reigning bishops – transfers and promotions – which were just as important to the evolution of the episcopate and which totalled forty-three in all between 1661 and early 1682. Less than half of these transfers, seventeen in all, involved promotions to higher-status archbishoprics, but in most cases they created vacancies that were more premeditated, and less random than those arising from the death of bishops.[36] In order to grasp the extent and even the unpredictability of royal decisions, it is also worth noting that there were at least thirty-two nominations – or at

35   For example, La Baume de Suze, bishop of Tarbes, was nominated to Saint-Omer in 1677, but as the indult was delayed by Innocent XI until 1686, his bulls were not forthcoming.

36   This figure includes Bossuet, who had resigned as bishop of Condom in 1671, and who rejoined the episcopate as bishop of Meaux in 1681. He was not a 'new' face in 1681, having been usually called 'Monsieur de Condom' during the previous decade.

Table 6.2   Patterns of episcopal nomination per year 1661–82

Year	1	2	3	Total
1661	4	2(0)	5	11
1662	1	5(4)	0	6
1663	0	0	0	0
1664	7	2(1)	0	9
1665	3	0	1	4
1666	6	1(0)	2	9
1667	4	0	1	5
1668	6	2(0)	3	11
1669	4	2(1)	1	7
1670	3	1(0)	2	6
1671	13	9(3)	1	23
1672	1	0	0	1
1673	3	2(2)	3	8
1674	4	3(3)	0	7
1675	11	1(0)	1	13
1676	5	1(1)	3	9
1677	7	2(1)	2	11
1678	2	0	1	3
1679	6	2(0)	1	9
1680	7	5(1)	4	16
1681	7	2(0)	4	16
1682	1	0	0	1
Total	105	42	32	179

Col 1 = new nominations; col 2 = transfers (promotions in brackets); col 3 = nominations without effect.

The year 1682 has only one entry, since all of the other nominations that year were blocked by the dispute over papal provisions for new bishops.

least offers of dioceses to individuals – which did *not* take effect (column three).

As a perusal of table 6.2 shows, there is no obvious correlation between its three main categories. However, as they stand, the figures from column three ('no effect') offer some interesting points for analysis. Firstly, only three of the thirty-two cases involved a refusal of episcopal office by someone who would not subsequently become a bishop. Whether anyone at the time would have sensed the finality of returning the royal *brevet* obviously cannot be known, but some of the refusals which may have seemed 'absolute' at the moment they were made – that is, rejections of episcopal office itself rather than of a particular diocese – proved not to be so in subsequent years, as the experience of Étienne Le Camus of Grenoble, Louis de Bourlemont of Bordeaux, and others shows.[37] Of the three absolute refusals mentioned above, the first was by a former Mazarin *fidèle* and bishop of Coutances, Claude Auvry, who rejected the invitation to come out of retirement and return there in 1666, while the neighbouring see of Avranches was turned down by François d'Aligre, son of the future chancellor, in 1668.[38] The remaining refusal was made by Charles Bourlon, a canon-regular and nephew of the bishop of Soissons, who in 1677 rejected the offer of Digne, a see that had uncommon difficulty not just in finding takers but also in keeping them.[39] As for the other royal choices which did not take effect, in two cases death supervened, while a third nominee tired of waiting for Rome's confirmation and sought nomination to another diocese altogether.[40]

In fact, most of the 'no effect' cases resemble this last one in important respects. Throughout Louis XIV's reign, it was not uncommon for *episcopabili* nominated to one diocese to switch their attention to a more attractive diocese if one became available soon after their original nomination, and to lobby for a change of *brevet* by the king. As we shall see later in this chapter, some of these switches occurred so rapidly that they attracted virtually no comment at the time; that they took place at all only becomes apparent after a detailed analysis of the chronology of all nominations. They commonly occurred as part of a series of interconnected nominations involving transfers, promotions and new nominations, the accumulation of which faintly resembles house-buying 'chains'. Some of them could take place over a few days, others over several weeks or months. One individual's decision to accept or reject a particular diocese or, more usually, to sit on a nomination in the hope that something better would come his way in the following weeks or months, was bound to affect the others in the chain; they in turn would feel entitled to suitable compensation when new dioceses became available later, a sentiment which was shared in part at least by the king and his advisers. An obvious effect of such refusals, whether outright or merely tactical, was to slow down, sometimes quite significantly, the speed with which individual dioceses were filled. It is more difficult to fathom the reasons why some of those rejecting a nomination were subsequently rewarded more quickly than others with another diocese – though family connections and patronage probably played a major part. For example, in early 1673, Louis

---

37   For Le Camus, see below, p 225. Bourlemont, then Auditor of the Roman Rota, would be offered Tournai in 1668–9, Lavaur in 1671, but would fruitlessly ask for Toulouse in 1673, only to be offered Fréjus, Carcassonne and Bordeaux in quick succession in 1679–80.

38   Lefèvre d'Ormesson, *Journal*, ii, 534, Jan 1668, 'M d'Aligre estoit là pour remercier le roy de l'évêché d'Avranches, vacant par la mort de Boisleve, et que le roy avoit donné à son fils le religieux'. See David Sturdy, *The d'Aligres de la Rivière. Servants of the Bourbon State in the Seventeenth Century* (Woodbridge 1986), 209–12.

39   BN, MS Fr 7652, no 38 (*bienfaits du roi*).

40   Jean d'Étampes, nominated to Perpignan in 1675, waited for his bulls until 1679, and then opted for Marseille when it was vacated by the future Cardinal Forbin-Janson, who moved to Beauvais.

made three attempts in quick succession to fill the see of Lavaur, but the first two nominees, a Bénard de Rezay and a Colbert de Saint-Pouange turned it down in quick succession, doubtless in the hope of something better in the near future. Not surprisingly, Colbert fared better than Bénard: he obtained Montauban only a year later, while Bénard's turn did not come round again.[41]

Returning to the overall figures for *new* bishops, table 6.2 (column one) clearly shows the impact of the episcopal 'monde plein' bequeathed by Mazarin to Louis XIV. New faces are relatively few in number for the 1660s – thirty-eight down to 1670 compared to sixty-seven for the long 'decade' from 1671 to January 1682. Year on year, the totals vary dramatically, and we can only speculate on how far these swings affected the relative chances of success for bishops-in-waiting and, as suggested above, how individuals might react to their nomination to a given diocese. The annual average of 4.6 new bishops per annum for the entire personal rule was only bettered during eleven of the first twenty-one years, and over half of these clustered in the years after 1674. The 1670s, however, were not without their 'meagre' years, among which 1672 and 1678 stand out, both coming immediately after relatively bountiful ones. The year 1671 was, in some respects, a turning point – no fewer than thirteen new bishops, as well as nine transfers and promotions, and only a single nomination that did not take effect. The unusual numbers involved and the fact that most of the nominations occurred in January and February of that year struck contemporaries forcibly.[42] No other year would ever match it, even if 1675 and 1702, with eleven new bishops each, came closer than most. It would be tempting to imagine that rates of mortality among the episcopate must have fluctuated equally wildly during these same years, which by comparison with the last decades of the reign are not known to have been particularly afflicted by epidemics and high population loss. But in fact, the numerical disparity in nominations, especially in record years like 1671 and 1675, derives less from the impact of the grim reaper than from the slowness of the crown to make decisions about vacant sees: in some cases, up to two years elapsed before a definitive nomination was made, and the vacancy was inevitably prolonged if there were diplomatic problems with Rome or if the latter became suspicious of the king's choices. The bunching of nominations in particular years and the absence of nominations in others can be partly explained in this way.

These general aspects of episcopal patronage as a whole before 1682 need to be borne in mind as we turn to discuss particular aspects of the question. As we have seen, Mazarin's last bout of bishop-making ensured there would not be much episcopal business for the revamped *conseil de conscience* to

---

41　The abbé de Rezay nominated to Lavaur should not be confused with his nephew, whose full name was identical to his, and who became bishop of Angoulême in 1692.

42　Lesaulnier, *Port-Royal insolite*, 579–85, 'evesques faits le 5-1-1671'.

transact. From the outset it convened each week on Fridays, though we do not know how long this habit endured. Its surviving *feuilles* from 1661 clearly show that it was involved in distributing all kinds of benefices (abbeys, priories, chapels) and pensions, with nomination to posts or benefices vacant during a period of *régale* also being a normal feature of its work.[43] But even a relatively 'quiet' year like 1661 shows something of the unpredictability of episcopal patronage. Three bishops (Evreux, La Rochelle and Auch) died by the end of the year, while Hugues de Lionne's elderly father finally decided to retire from Gap. Between them the first two vacancies, at Evreux and La Rochelle, generated no fewer than ten nominations, some of which were more in the nature of promises than outright nominations, and five of them remained a dead letter. Part of the reason for this apparent drift was a desire to reward certain Mazarin clients who had been overlooked before his death – unfinished business of yet another kind! – and Anne of Austria's continuing ability to promote clerics in her service, even to the extent of persuading Louis XIV to change his decisions in order to satisfy her.[44] With Evreux and La Rochelle finally being given to reigning bishops, further vacancies and nominations were inevitable, which in turn explains why the number of promises and nominations was so high. And when one of those 'second-phase' vacancies, that of Saint-Pol-de-Léon in Brittany, arose, the nomination was offered to Claude Joly, who hesitated for six months before finally turning it down: he would have to wait three more years before being offered, and accepting, a second nomination, that of Agen.[45] And, as we might expect, Louis XIV seems to have allowed Lionne a completely free hand in finding a successor to his father at Gap.[46] For a relatively 'meagre' year, this volume of activity may seem disproportionate. But it was partly the result of transferring existing bishops to newly vacant sees and having to find successors for their previous one. By contrast, the following year, 1662, witnessed only one nomination of a new bishop – Louis Abelly to Rodez – while the five others were the result of the need to fill senior positions like the archbishoprics of Paris and Toulouse, but also of Bourges and Auch which had become vacant by death. Unlike the pattern observed for the previous year, none of those singled out for reward in 1662 turned it down. The year 1663 is unique for

43 Some of them survive among Le Tellier's correspondence in the secretary of state for war's archives in Vincennes, SHAT, A1 171 (1659–61), and are reproduced in the *Mémoriaux du conseil de 1661*, ii, 332–42.

44 *Mémoriaux du conseil de 1661*, i, 154, n 1.

45 Philippe de Coulanges, *Mémoires*, ed Louis de Monmerqué (Paris, 1820), 380. Lesaulnier, *Port-Royal insolite*, 602.

46 See Bergin, *Making*, 659–60. There is frequent reference to the Gap succession in 'Lettres inédites de Hugues de Lionne', ed Ulysse Chevallier, in *Bulletin de la Société d'Archéologie et de Statistique de la Drôme*, 11 (1877), 272–306, 382–402; 12 (1878), 5–30, 105–38, 254–87, 313–44, but the trail goes cold after 31 Dec 1660, when Lionne informed his uncle that he had received several offers for the Gap succession and that all he had to do was to come to an agreement with one of the candidates.

the entire personal rule, since it alone witnessed no act of episcopal patronage of *any* kind.

Limited as these early years may be as a vantage point, they do offer a glimpse of some important features of episcopal patronage after Mazarin. It seems likely that the step-by-step policy towards the choice of archbishops, to which we shall return presently, owed something to the reinstatement of the *conseil de conscience*. Yet, from what we have observed so far, there were from the outset limits to the functional capacity of the *conseil*, limits which were always likely to open the door to an even more clientelist exercise of patronage. Le Tellier's decisive intervention in favour of Marca for the Paris succession in 1662 may well have had such clientelist undertones, but it also indicates that some decisions were too important to be left to 'specialists'. In the early 1660s, as we have seen, Anne of Austria, Lionne, and perhaps others were able to advance their own interests in the face of a king whose own preferences may have been less firmly defined than his *Mémoires* suggest, and whose confessor may not have had either the will or the personality to oppose those interests. When Saint-Flour and Clermont, which were part of Anne's jointure lands, both fell vacant in within a month of each other in early 1664, she exercised her 'presentation' rights to both sees, and Louis XIV acquiesced without demur in her choices; the absence of third parties is evident enough from the speed with which these successions were finally settled.[47] Anne's death heralded the end of a distinctive historical tradition, in which bishoprics were included alongside other benefices in the presentation rights of apanage- and dower-holders. Like his uncle, Gaston d'Orléans before him, Philippe d'Orléans, the king's brother, enjoyed no formal right to make episcopal presentations. Nor was any such concession provided for in Louis's own marriage contract with Marie-Thérèse in 1659. After Anne's death in 1666, Louis was the first monarch in a long time to enjoy theoretically unfettered rights to select each and every one of France's bishops in the first instance. It may not have revolutionised the actual exercise of episcopal patronage, but it was a milestone in the minor mode.

Yet it would be wrong to think that episcopal patronage in the two decades after 1661 was subject only to the interplay of interest and ambition. The king's dislike of quasi-hereditary arrangements surfaced as early as April 1661, when Le Tellier informed the elderly bishop of La Rochelle that he could not have a coadjutor.[48] With a few notable exceptions, he did not change his views thereafter. While never explicitly stated, reserving archbishoprics for incumbent bishops was another *de facto* rule from the outset, one of which contemporaries were aware – indeed to such an extent that when Louis XIV did break

---

47 The bishop of Clermont, Louis d'Estaing, died on 15 March 1664, and his successor, Vény d'Arbouze, from a family with close connections to Anne of Austria, was nominated on 12 April. Bishop Montrouge of Saint-Flour died 20 April 1664 and was quickly succeeded by Jérôme de la Mothe-Houdancourt, nominated on 1 May, a younger brother of Anne's *premier aumônier*.

48 SHAT, Archives de la Guerre, A¹ 168, no 273, letter of 15 April 1661.

it in subsequent years, it caused surprised comment, so contrary did it seem to his longstanding custom.[49] None of his predecessors had felt compelled to adopt such an approach, and Mazarin was no innovator in this respect. Of the seventeen archiepiscopal nominations made between 1661 and 1682, only one involved a newcomer to the episcopate: in 1668, Brûlart de Genlis was given Embrun, whose geographical position may have made it seem less important to the king and his advisers. This clear exception apart, it seems fair to say that in one limited but nevertheless important respect, the king did implement at least one feature of his dream of a 'sacred militia' moving upward, as he put it, 'from post to post' (*de charge en charge*). We have already seen instances of it in the Paris double succession of 1662 and that of Reims with Barberini, and it is also demonstrated by the other archiepiscopal nominations of the first twenty years of the personal rule. No doubt the Le Tellier coadjutorship at Reims was a double infringement of these maxims, but a coadjutorship like this one was probably seen as an apprenticeship that would in due course provide him with all the experience needed by a full archbishop. As Embrun and other cases already seen suggest, even within the upper ranks of the episcopate, some decisions were regarded as more crucial than others. This was not purely because the crown decided to make them so: that depended at least as much on the attractiveness of particular sees and, therefore, the competition to secure them. Auch in Gascony was no more distant from the court than Narbonne was, and was much better endowed financially, but it was regarded as the less attractive of the two. Giving Auch to Anne of Austria's *premier aumônier* and former bishop of Rennes, La Mothe-Houdancourt in 1662, was seen as a way of removing from court and the *conseil de conscience* a well-known pro-Roman ecclesiastic at a time when gallican disputes were again causing problems.[50] Not for the last time, apparently prestigious episcopal nominations or promotions could in reality be marks of disfavour for their recipients or a means of removing them from places where they were henceforth undesirable.

There is little doubt that, in terms of their importance for the French church for the key decades of Louis XIV's rule, the most decisive acts of episcopal patronage came in the early 1670s rather than a decade earlier, yet they are intimately connected to the issues already discussed in this chapter. An unexpected third Paris succession arose less than ten years after Mazarin's death, when Archbishop Péréfixe died on New Year's Day 1671. Unlike the Barberini-Le Tellier arrangement for the Reims succession, in the absence of a coadjutor the identity of Péréfixe's successor was not yet known. Given the

49 BN, MS Fr 23505, fo 12, *Nouvelles Ecclésiastiques*, Feb 1695, referring to the nomination of Fénelon to Cambrai as well as the new archbishops of Vienne and Bourges, the author concludes 'il est bon de remarquer . . . que les maximes ont entièrement changé sur les grandes places' – the 'grandes places' being archbishoprics in general.
50 See Jacques M Grès-Gayer, *Le Gallicanisme de Sorbonne* (Paris 2002), esp chs 2–3; A-G Martimort, *Le Gallicanisme de Bossuet* (Paris 1953), chs 5–9.

rapidity with which his successor was nominated – on 4 January 1671 – it might seem unlikely that there was much time for potential candidates to show their face. Cardinal Bouillon, who had failed to secure the coadjutor-ship in 1669, admitted to Olivier Lefèvre d'Ormesson on 3 January 'that he would take care not to ask for it (Paris), having already been raised to a quite extraordinary rank (*dignité*) by the king for someone of his age'.[51] Not for the last time, Bouillon's denials were couched in terms which make his true ambi-tion clear, and it is doubtful if anyone took them seriously, since he was fre-quently quoted as being interested in subsequent archiepiscopal successions. On this occasion, he was probably also diverted from chasing the Paris suc-cession by the prospect, which duly materialised, of succeeding Antonio Bar-berini as *grand aumônier de France*, since Louis XIV declared that he absolutely wanted the post to go to a cardinal, of whom there were very few in France in 1671.[52] As in 1668–9 with the red hat, the grand almonership was used to placate and satisfy Bouillon, while ensuring Paris was in a safer pair of hands. Moreover the question of age and experience was vital for Paris, and even Bouillon, then only twenty-seven years old, could see that the king would want an archbishop with the required curriculum vitae. Indeed, it seems wholly likely that the king's mind was already made up, and in Arch-bishop Harlay of Rouen, he found someone far better suited than Péréfixe had proved to be for the task ahead of him. Experienced, well connected (espe-cially to Colbert), learned, and an excellent orator, he had already clearly emerged as the man to manage the assemblies of clergy – and therefore eccle-siastical affairs generally. Even some of those close to Port-Royal were pleased with the news of his promotion.[53] For the next twenty years, this master chameleon would be the king's man *par excellence* in the French church – respected by many, detested by some, but retaining a firm grip on affairs despite setbacks and personal failings which might have sunk someone less naturally or less wholly 'political'.[54] Of course, Harlay's translation to Paris meant the archiepiscopal see of Rouen was up for grabs, and whoever obtained it might aspire to move further upwards to Paris in due course. There was perhaps less urgency about filling Rouen but the decision followed within less than two weeks, long enough to give potential candidates time to show their hand. The names of at least three candidates, all of them actual or future car-dinals, are known – and all of them are recorded as refusing Rouen for one reason or another. It is hard to know whether Bouillon, clearly willing to entertain governing a prominent see, rejected an actual royal offer or simply

51 Lefèvre d'Ormesson, *Journal*, ii, 607, recording a conversation with Bouillon on 3 Jan 1671.
52 ASV, Nunz Fr 145, fo 206, Michele Vibo, *chargé d'affaires* at Paris nunciature to Cardinal Altieri, 18 June 1671.
53 Lesaulnier, *Port-Royal insolite*, 579.
54 There is no full study of Harlay, for whom few personal papers have survived. The best appre-ciations of his political skills are to be found in the works of Pierre Blet on the assemblies of clergy from the 1650s to the 1690s.

the idea that he might put his name forward. Another ecclesiastical grandee, César d'Estrées, the bishop of Laon whom Bouillon had pipped for the red hat in 1669, was also reported as turning it down on the grounds of 'not wanting to take Harlay's leftovers'. Finally, another future cardinal, Coislin, bishop of Orléans since 1666, rejected Rouen on the grounds that 'he was already married to a bride' whom he would not leave for another.[55] In fact, he really wanted the grand almonership, which Louis XIV had virtually promised to him, only to be left empty-handed and furious once the king decided that satisfying the Turenne-Bouillon interest was more important.[56] The outcome was that Rouen went to another aristocratic bishop, François Rouxel de Médavy, bishop of Sées in Normandy since 1651 and already nominated to the now vacant see of Langres since September 1670. With powerful family connections in both Burgundy and Normandy, it would have been difficult to second-guess what he might do when presented with the luxury of choosing between such desirable offerings. In the event he preferred Rouen, an archbishopric with primatial status and of which he had hitherto been a suffragan, to the peerage of Langres, and governed it for the next twenty years.

The Narbonne succession finally arose in October 1673 with the death of François Fouquet. Its attraction lay essentially in the fact that its incumbent was *ex officio* president of the Estates of Languedoc. Although holding a more attractive see in most respects, archbishops of Toulouse normally aspired to move to Narbonne, making this particular translation the clearest instance of a hierarchy of mobility within the upper clergy. Fouquet's long disgrace from 1661 to 1673 constituted an unscripted interruption of the normal course of events, so that successive archbishops of Toulouse – Marca (before his transfer to Paris), Charles de Bourlemont, and Pierre de Bonsi – already found themselves taking his place in Languedoc politics. As the youngest of the three, it was Bonsi who reaped the harvest to the fullest extent. His diplomatic missions to Venice, Tuscany and Poland, which led to him being tipped as a possible successor to Lionne as foreign minister in 1671, as well as the cardinal's hat which he secured in 1672, greatly fortified to his claims on Narbonne.[57] It does not seem that there were any serious competitors to oppose him when Archbishop Fouquet died in October 1673.[58] Not only that, but Bonsi made sure to be at court immediately after Fouquet's death, and his elevation was duly announced only days later. There was, however, a highly

55   Lesaulnier, *Port-Royal insolite*, 584–5, 'Monsieur d'Orléans a refusé le Roy de l'archevesché de Rouen, disant qu'il vouloit s'attacher à son espouse'. As the king's *premier aumônier*, du Cambout was close to Louis XIV, who had a high regard for him.
56   Choisy, *Mémoires*, 248–56.
57   Sonnino, *Louis XIV and the Origins of the Dutch War*, 164, 'the betting in the city was on the wily Bonsi, Archbishop of Toulouse – ignoring, for some reason, Louis' aversion to another eventual cardinal-minister'.
58   *Lettres du cardinal Le Camus*, 107–9, letter to Pontchâteau, nd (1673). He had spent the previous months following the court during the military campaign in the Netherlands: Blet, *Les Nonces à la cour de Louis XIV*, 92–6.

interesting twist to this appointment. Bonsi's see of Toulouse was, according to contemporary observers, initially given to the archbishop of Bourges, Montpezat de Carbon, in order to counteract Bonsi's influence in the province, which was already judged excessive. Despite his southern origins and earlier career at Saint-Papoul, Montpezat evidently hesitated about such a prospect and he opted instead for Sens when it became vacant in 1674, leaving his younger brother and successor at Saint-Papoul to move into Toulouse. How seriously the crown wanted to see Bonsi curbed at this point in his career is a moot point, but his ambition to place relatives and dependents in key posts in Languedoc was no secret and was not always successful.[59] He was to hold Narbonne for the next thirty years. When he finally lost his political ascendancy in Languedoc after his patron Colbert's death in the mid-1680s, it was not to a rival prelate but to the provincial intendant and Le Tellier protégé, Lamoignon de Basville.[60] Meanwhile, the Montpezat brothers had achieved the very uncommon feat of scooping up two major archbishoprics in a short space of time. The younger of them, Joseph, would play such a prominent role in the *régale* and related disputes, especially in the affairs of Pamiers, one of his suffragan dioceses, that Innocent XI would later publicly condemn him for his actions.[61]

This sequence of 'major' nominations, virtually all involving the transfer of existing bishops, set a pattern for the reign as a whole. But their importance also lay in the fact that they installed a group of men who in their different ways, with the possible except of Rouxel of Rouen and Brûlart of Embrun, would remain dominant figures in the affairs of the French church for a long time.[62] All but two of them had become bishops at different times during the Mazarin ministry. If Louis XIV was content to continue employing his godfather's ministers, the same might be said of those he chose to be the leading figures in the French church for a generation or more. It would not be until the 1680s and beyond that bishops installed early during his personal rule would find themselves moving into the dominant positions. As already noted, Louis XIV would have to wait a very long time to place his choice of archbishop in other senior sees like Lyon, Vienne, Aix, Arles or Bordeaux, whose archbishops – men with names like Villeroy, Villars, Grimaldi, Grignan and Béthune respectively – enjoyed exceptionally long tenure and were figures of considerable independence despite being, especially

---

59 *Correspondance du nonce Spada*, no 400, Spada to Cardinal Altieri, 31 Aug 1674, relating Bonsi's efforts to keep the post of *lieutenant du roi* in Languedoc in family hands, and the reasons this might not be accepted at court.

60 William Beik, *Absolutism and Society in Seventeenth-Century France* (Cambridge 1984), 241–3, for an account of Bonsi's 'reign' and his replacement after Colbert's death.

61 Sourches, i, 95, April 1682. See Blet, *Les Assemblées du clergé et Louis XIV*, 197–203, 384–5.

62 Brûlart seems to have been especially reluctant to be elected a deputy to the assemblies of clergy by his province, which he frequently did not even attend. See AN, G⁸ 88, *procurations* to general assemblies of 1680 and 1685 from Embrun province.

in the case of Grimaldi, often out of favour.[63] In the case of Lyon and Vienne, archiepiscopal longevity stretched to as far away as 1693! Of the remaining metropolitans, Sens, Bourges and Tours were filled at various times during the 1660s and 1670s, while Albi was elevated to archiepiscopal rank in the mid-1670s. In the case of Sens, the most important consideration seems to have been to ensure that the pro-Jansenist Gondrin de Pardailhan, the truculent uncle of the king's mistress Montespan, was replaced by someone who would eradicate alleged Jansenist influences in a very large diocese, but in the event the king's choice of the elder of the Montpezat brothers proved to be a poor one.[64] Tours was the only one of the sees just mentioned which might be thought of as having a big political role to play, given it was the metropolitan of the 'province' of Brittany. Yet it was decidedly *not* the northern equivalent of Narbonne, since it played no real part in the Estates of Brittany where the local bishops, even those holding minor sees like Dol or Vannes, were far more prominent. Victor Bouthillier, uncle of the former royal minister, Chavigny, had long wanted his famous nephew Rancé, the reformer of La Trappe abbey and the oracle of those who regarded episcopal office with trepidation, to succeed him at Tours, but that prospect had already evaporated well before Bouthillier's death in 1670.[65] Four months later, the king offered Tours instead to Charles de Rosmadec, bishop of Vannes, who did not particularly want it either, given its combination of mediocre revenues and substantial expenses, but according to one account, the king himself successfully urged him to accept it by reassuring him on that point.[66] When he died only two years later, in 1673, his successor, the former *conseiller* in the Paris parlement who was by now bishop of Lavaur, Michel Amelot, does not seem to have required similar royal cajoling: Tours, it may be suggested, was more than attractive to someone with greater personal means but far lower social status than a Rosmadec.[67] Similarly, it seems that in nominating the former

63 For Grimaldi, see René Pillorget, *Les Mouvements insurrectionnels de Provence entre 1596 et 1715* (Paris 1978), 743–4, 835, 867. *Mémoriaux du conseil de 1661*, i, 112, 276. In 1662 an attempt was made to persuade him that a move from Aix to Toulouse 'feroit plaisir au Roi . . . pour le tirer de la Provence, où l'on ne veut point qu'il retourne; on parle mesme de lui ordonner de retourner à Rome': BN, Baluze 121, fo 53, Pierre de Marca to Bosquet of Montpellier, 31 Jan 1662. Later, he was exiled from his diocese to his abbey of Saint-Florent de Saumur.

64 BM Sens, MS 77, Charles-Henri Fenel, 'Mémoires pour l'histoire des archevêques de Sens', ii, pp 1113–15. Fenel, dean of Sens and contemporary historian of the archbishops of Sens, claims that the elderly Montpezat lacked the energy to do more than restore the Jesuits to their pastoral activities, from which Gondrin had banned them, and to confide the seminary to the Lazarists.

65 Armand-Jean Bouthillier de Rancé, *Correspondance*, ed A J Krailsheimer, 4 vols (Paris 1993), i, 80–1, 168, 354, letters to Louise Rogier, '1658', 2 Feb 1661, 1 Dec 1670 respectively, all referring obliquely to his uncle's designs for him.

66 Lesaulnier, *Port-Royal insolite*, 582, 'il a refusé Tours parce qu'il l'engageoit à trop de despence. Le Roy l'a porté à le prendre et qu'il ne se mist pas en peine.'

67 Cardinal de Retz, *Oeuvres*, ed A Feillet *et al*, 10 vols (Paris 1870–1920), xi, 134–5, Retz to Francesco Barberini, 9 April 1673, interceding for Amelot, 'mio singularissimo amico', and asking for reduction in cost of bulls, since he had only recently paid for provisions to Lavaur. Rome obliged him and Amelot thanked Cardinal Altieri in due course.

Dominican friar, Serroni, to be the first archbishop of Albi in 1676, the crown felt that such an unexpected promotion would dampen potential opposition to the planned diversion of a slice of its very substantial revenues to its much poorer former metropolitan, Bourges.[68]

IV

Whatever the logic of particular choices of archbishop, they virtually always led to vacancies in ordinary dioceses. In considering how nominations to 'ordinary' dioceses were handled after 1661, it will be useful to look first at those located in the most prominent and politically important of the *pays d'états*, in which bishops played key political roles. Among them, Brittany stands out because of its historical traditions of linguistic and political autonomy, with the added ingredient under Louis XIV of also witnessing the last major anti-government revolt of the age. As we have seen, its nine dioceses belonged to one ecclesiastical province whose metropolitan, Tours, was not located in Brittany at all. The brief tenure of Tours (1671–2) by a Breton, Charles de Rosmadec, previously bishop of Vannes, was unique for the century since Henri IV and would not be repeated. Leaving Tours to one side, it appears that the province as a whole experienced eleven episcopal nominations between 1661 and 1682, of which only two were transfers (Saint-Pol-de-Léon and Vannes) and one a coadjutor (Quimper). Within Brittany itself, only one diocese, Dol, did not welcome a new bishop between 1661 and 1682, but that was because its bishop refused the nomination to Rennes in 1676. The biggest of its dioceses, Nantes, had been held by Gabriel de Beauvau, a Richelieu relative and client since 1635, and it would remain firmly in family hands until the post-Louis XIV Regency. The Beauvau had some serious advantages: in addition to old Bourbon blood in their veins they were, as already noted, close relatives of Louis XIV's mistress, Louise de la Vallière, whose influence was doubtless instrumental in transferring the diocese to her uncle in 1667, after whom it reverted to a Beauvau. Apart from them, all of the nominations to Breton dioceses until the mid-1670s were of Breton – or 'virtually' Breton – ecclesiastics, some of whose families (e.g. Visdelou, Coëtlogon, Guémadeuc) were prominent in Breton governorships or the Estates, or both. In the case of the first of the two Coëtlogon to enter the Breton episcopate under Louis, the intervention of the Estates on his behalf shows that the old traditions of petitioning for natives as bishops were not dead in the 1660s.[69] The first non-Breton among the new bishops, Le Neboux

---

68 See Sévigné, *Correspondance*, v, 30–1, Sévigné to Mme de Grignan, 21 Aug 1676, says that, notwithstanding rumours to contrary, Serroni would accept Albi, despite pensions payable to third parties from its revenues. Serroni, a friend of Mazarin's brother, the Dominican and cardinal, Michele, had previously been bishop of Orange and Mende.

69 *La Bretagne en 1665 d'après le rapport de Colbert de Croissy*, ed Jean Kerhervé, François Roudaut and Jean Tanguy (Brest 1978), 194, n 18.

de la Brousse, nominated to Saint-Pol-de-Léon in 1671, may not have had such overt support, but he could hardly have been better integrated in the province: although born near Angoulême, he had spent his entire career in the service of the bishop of Saint-Brieuc, La Barde, also a non-native, and he was singled out by the governor of Brittany, the duc de Chaulnes, for the political skills he had shown in the Breton Estates. If there was a break in this sequence, it came in September 1675, in the immediate aftermath of the revolt in lower Brittany, with the nomination to neighbouring Saint-Brieuc of Fortin de la Hoguette, outgoing *agent-général* of the clergy, who had no known Breton connections and who, in any case, moved on to Poitiers in 1680. Arguably, a far more unconventional appointment was that of an Oratorian of Lyonnais extraction, Baglion, to Breton-speaking Tréguier, in 1679, but he confounded everyone by learning to speak and preach in Breton in subsequent years. However, the most difficult of all, it seems, was the search for a bishop of Rennes, epicentre of the urban revolt of 1675, when it fell vacant in January 1676. Never the preserve of Bretons or Breton-speakers, Rennes was promptly offered to François Bouthillier de Chavigny, perhaps in the hope that his connections to what remained of Richelieu's clientele in Brittany might be useful. But having sought and even obtained provisions from Rome, he got cold feet by mid-1676 and resigned his rights to it.[70] It was then offered to the sitting bishop of Dol, an old Mazarin client of some political ability, but he, too, turned it down, leaving the way open for his intended successor at Dol, Beaumanoir de Lavardin, to be nominated to Rennes instead.[71] Here, too, Beaumanoir family connections must have been an important consideration – one of the most powerful families in the neighbouring province of Maine, they were Breton by origin and the new bishop's cousin, the marquis de Lavardin, was *lieutenant-général* in Brittany at that moment.[72] Thereafter, episcopal nominations in Brittany dropped off markedly and did not pick up again until the 1690s and beyond. Perhaps the most interesting development of the latter part of the reign was that, sees like Dol and Saint-Malo apart, more and more of Brittany's bishops were Bretons or from families with strong ties to the province. Even the Breton-speaking dioceses of the western part had more Breton-speaking bishops during these latter years than they had since prior to the Richelieu ministry when French-speaking outsiders had become more common. The Breton-speaking Oratorian, Baglion, may have left Tréguier for Poitiers in the mid-1680s, but

---

70   ASV, PC 75, fo 550, Louis XIV to pope, 3 Feb 1676, nominating Bouthillier to Rennes. ASV, Acta congregationis consistorialis 1678–9, fo 432, 2 Feb 1679, recapitulating Bouthillier's nomination and subsequent rejection of Rennes.

71   BN, MS Fr 7652 (*bienfaits du roi*), fo 58, for the sequence of nominations to Rennes and Dol in 1676. ASV, PC 76, fo 781, Louis XIV to pope 26 Nov 1676, nominating Lavardin to Rennes.

72   The see of Le Mans was held by two members of the Beaumanoir family from 1610–37 and 1649–71: Bergin, *Making*, 570–1. Governors of Maine and holders of high military posts, they included more than one *maréchal de France* during the seventeenth century.

his two successors were both Bretons. It is possible that this trend towards a native or quasi-native episcopate is itself evidence of the diminished attractiveness of the province's dioceses to outsiders at a time when post-revolt Brittany as a whole was facing decline and social closure.[73]

Still a frontier province until the conquest of Franche-Comté in the 1670s, the territory covered by the Estates of Burgundy contained just four bishoprics – Auxerre, Autun, Chalon-sur-Saône, and Mâcon, the last of which had long had its own 'états particuliers'. Nothing like the particularism of Brittany survived here, and with the princes of Condé restored as governors by Louis XIV, the episcopal stakes were bound to be of great interest. The Condé reputation for tight control of patronage in their governorships was made evident in the first, and most crucial, episcopal nomination in post-Mazarin Burgundy – that of Gabriel de Roquette to Autun in 1666. Roquette had served many masters in previous years, in particular Condé's brother, Conti, but also Brienne and Le Tellier, so he enjoyed a wide range of patrons. And Autun was also the key Burgundian diocese, since its bishop presided *ex officio* over the sessions of the Estates. His long tenure (to 1702) left little room for competitors for that particular role.[74] The fate of the two dioceses of Auxerre and Mâcon are no less interesting, because they, too, clearly involved ministerial patronage. First Mâcon (1666) and then Auxerre (1671) was granted to members of the Colbert family, though it was only in Auxerre that this feat was subsequently repeated (1676). In reality, the picture is more complex than that. Michel Colbert, bishop of Mâcon in 1666, was a Saint-Pouange whose ties to their Le Tellier relatives were closer than to the other Colbert, which in turn helps explain the choice of a successor for him at Mâcon in 1676: Michel Cassagnet de Tilladet was a first cousin of Louvois. As for Auxerre, the Colbert interest in the see was not just a matter of ministerial patronage or local political influence. It was the acquisition of the marquisate of Seignelay and other properties there by Jean-Baptiste in the late 1660s which led him to press his reluctant brother, Nicolas, to leave Luçon for Auxerre when it fell vacant in 1671 and, when he died in 1676, to secure it for his more obscure Reims nephew, André Colbert. But whereas Autun, Auxerre and Mâcon experienced relatively little mobility after the 1670s, Chalon-sur-Saône, held by a Maupeou since 1659, only fell vacant in 1677. It attracted a different type of bishop with his own close ties to the king and court: Henri Félix de Tassy, the son of a royal physician, already bishop of the perennially unattractive see of Digne, moved to Chalon and held it until his death in 1711.

Beyond these two ends of the spectrum, Brittany and Burgundy, we find the vast space stretching from eastern Provence to Gascony, Béarn and Navarre

---

73 See Alain Croix, *L'Âge d'or de la Bretagne 1532–1675* (Rennes 1993), ch 14, 'le paradis perdu'; James B Collins, *Classes, Estates and Order in Early Modern Brittany* (Cambridge 1994), 274ff.

74 AN, L 728, Autun, nos 28–30. Roquette fought a successful defence of his presidency against Colbert of Auxerre in subsequent years.

in the extreme south-west, a space with provincial and local estates as well as a disproportionately high number of dioceses, many of them tiny and varying considerably in degrees of desirability. Only those of Lescar and Oloron in Béarn resembled the lower Breton dioceses in their linguistic particularism and, therefore, their tradition of having indigenous bishops. Louis XIV, whose first opportunity to appoint to either see only came in early 1682, maintained that tradition intact until 1705, when the first outsider bishop was nominated to Oloron. The bishops of some of the neighbouring Pyreneean dioceses, such as Pamiers in the county of Foix, were also involved in presiding over local estates, but possibly for that very reason 'native' bishops were not a distinctive part of their recent history. Across the twenty-two dioceses of Languedoc, the biggest of all the *pays d'états*, the existing admixture of families from within the province and from elsewhere continued after 1661. There were thirty-one nominations in all there between 1661 and early 1682, a figure which is inflated by unusually short tenures in a number of dioceses (Rodez, Lavaur, Vabres, Uzès). Nine of the thirty-one nominations were transfers, all of them of bishops *already* seated in Languedoc, of which four were to archbishoprics. Only one of the eight bishops involved in these transfers was a native of the province, though as the fifth (and last) of the Bonsi dynasty to hold Béziers since 1576, Pierre de Bonsi was hardly an outsider 'comme les autres'. Of the twenty-two remaining nominations, fourteen were of outsiders, as against eight native Languedocians. Northerners of every stripe, Parisians included, were numerous among the incoming bishops, but we also find natives of neighbouring provinces (Provence, Gascony and Dauphiné). When it came to promotions, either before 1682 or later, nine of the twenty-two newcomers were singled out, a much higher proportion than for the episcopate generally. Five of the nine moved within the province itself, three of them to archbishoprics. Of the four others, two secured archbishoprics outside of Languedoc. If we combine these perspectives in order to see how natives fared against outsiders where transfers were concerned, it is clear that the outsiders did twice as well, above all when it came to transfers to dioceses *outside* of Languedoc – something which their wider origins and connections no doubt facilitated. The pattern of episcopal tenure in the province is perhaps best illustrated by the fact that not a single newcomer became an archbishop there at first nomination, even though the existence of such an ambition among some of them would not have surprised anyone. Unlike Brittany or Burgundy, whose dioceses experienced much lower levels of episcopal mobility, the relatively high levels of the latter in Languedoc in the early decades of Louis's rule was partly the result of its two archbishoprics falling vacant four times by the early 1670s, followed by the creation of the archbishopric of Albi in 1676. Three metropolitan sees offered much more scope for upward movement than was the case in other provinces of France, and it was thanks to this mechanism that Albi, Toulouse and Narbonne each witnessed a succession of archbishops who were carefully chosen for their own – and, as often, their family's – service record to the crown. A Le Goux de la Berchère might begin at Lavaur but then move to Toulouse and finally Narbonne; a Colbert de Saint-Pouange or a Nesmond might begin in Montauban and then step up to Toulouse or Albi respectively at a later date. And in doing this, they only needed to follow in the steps of Pierre de Marca or Pierre de Bonsi from a previous generation.

The position of the nineteen dioceses located to the east of Languedoc in the four ecclesiastical provinces of the Provence-Dauphiné area was different again.[75] They had their own history of faction and turbulence, especially Provence, but their Estates, cities and sovereign courts were by now less troublesome than under the cardinal-ministers. Moreover, many of their dioceses, which included some of France's smallest, were among the least attractive to outsiders in the entire French church – which did not prevent outsiders from being sent there, on the contrary. The entrenched power of the Provençal nobility was both cause and consequence of this situation, and the crown had to acknowledge the importance of satisfying their ambitions. The fact that one of the earliest of the few coadjutorships agreed by Louis XIV, that for the archbishopric of Arles, was awarded to a Grignan is eloquent enough in this regard – and Louis, *bon prince*, immediately renewed the concession when the beneficiary died almost immediately in 1666.[76] The possibilities of mobility similar to that of Languedoc were singularly reduced in the early decades of the personal rule through the fact that of the region's four archbishoprics, only one – Embrun – became vacant, and it did so only the once (1668). Those in search of better dioceses in the area had, therefore, to look to 'ordinary' sees like Marseille, Fréjus or Toulon. It is in this context that the problems of a see like Digne – problems of which the king himself was apparently aware – find their explanation: all three of its earliest bishops after 1661 moved elsewhere, and the Parisian, François Le Tellier, nominated in 1678, was notoriously reluctant to reside there.

A general view of the entire Provence-Dauphiné region can be gleaned from a few simple statistics. Of the twenty-three individuals nominated to sixteen dioceses there between 1661 and 1682, fifteen were outsiders, but the eight natives accounted for three out of four instances of movement between local dioceses, which involved Provençal rather than other dioceses. By contrast, as we have already noted for Languedoc, it was the outsiders who virtually scooped the pool when it came to moving onwards to dioceses *outside* of the region. The only exception here was Forbin-Janson's move from Marseille to Beauvais in 1679, but this scion of the great Marseille family was by then more than a local church magnate. The Forbin family's Vintimille cousins would repeat this feat over a generation later when Charles de Vintimille

75 The provinces were Vienne, Embrun, Arles and Aix. The total given here does not include Viviers, a suffragan of Vienne, because it was part of Languedoc.
76 Jean, *Évêques et archevêques de France*, 34.

succeeded Cardinal Noailles in Paris in 1729. It will not be immediately evident why, with so many small or relatively unattractive dioceses, Provence attracted so many outsider bishops. The majority of these outsiders occupying such sees were, it is fair to say, of relatively low social or ecclesiastical status: they included, for example, three members of religious orders and one Parisian parish priest, while another Parisian was semi-native by virtue of having spent much of his existence in the service of his uncle, who was bishop of Riez.[77] It was when higher-status or better connected outsiders were sent to some of these dioceses that problems could arise. Louis Aubert, bishop of Senez, was convinced he was on his way to Toul as coadjutor in 1674, only to fall foul of Colbert over an entirely unrelated issue, so he remained where he was for the next twenty years.[78] Michel Poncet and Jacques Potier de Novion were both sons of prominent Paris robe families, and both engaged in obscure and complex manoeuvres to extricate themselves, successfully as it happens, from Sisteron in eastern Provence during the late 1670s; both of them also turned down a transfer to Fréjus, and their subsequent problems may have arisen because they were aiming at more attractive northern dioceses (Bourges and Evreux) respectively.[79] Indeed, Fréjus was declined by three sitting or future bishops between 1674 and 1679, as each of them looked to capitalise on their credit with the royal entourage by seeking a more suitable diocese. The last of them, Louis de Bourlemont, was initially nominated in early 1679, but by early 1681 he was archbishop of Bordeaux.

This brief comparison of episcopal patronage in the principal *pays d'états* reveals that in the early decades of the personal rule even the most historically distinctive provinces were hosts to a genuine mix of native and outsider bishops, with the latter dominating in those where they might not be expected to have – Provence. This was a continuation of patterns already evident under Richelieu and Mazarin. We should be careful not to exaggerate the extent of ecclesiastical localism in an age when royal control of the benefice system was secure and clerics were long accustomed to obtaining benefices well before the episcopate in parts of the realm with which they would have been unfamiliar. If there is a distinguishing feature of these dioceses in relation to the rest of the realm, it is perhaps in the higher levels of episcopal mobility there, but that can be explained partly by the presence of numerous small or under-endowed sees and the desire of many bishops, natives as much as outsiders, to move to less peripheral dioceses. A fascinating insight

---

77 Antoine Le Comte, briefly bishop of Grasse 1682–3, was nephew of René Le Clerc, bishop of Glandèves 1626–51.

78 BN, Mélanges Colbert 7, fos 126–81, Aubert's *factum* on the family benefice which led him to become embroiled with Colbert who wanted it for his son. Colbert is never mentioned by name and is referred to throughout as 'un grand ministre'.

79 For Poncet, who had originally been offered Fréjus in 1674 before the nomination to Bourges, see Retz, *Oeuvres*, xi, 142–4, letter to Cardinal Barberini, 5 Jan 1675. For Potier, see BN, MS Fr 7652 (*bienfaits du roi*), fos 39 and 200.

into contemporary attitudes on precisely this subject is provided by the Norman René Le Sauvage who, as we saw in the previous chapter, owed his nomination to Lavaur in 1673 to Cardinal Bouillon. His views are worth dwelling upon because such explicit statements have so rarely survived. Writing to his patron a few years later, in 1676, when his health had seriously deteriorated, he claimed that he would only leave Lavaur for one of two reasons – if his health or Bouillon's service required it, since his dependence on the cardinal was absolute. 'I am held in honour and loved in my diocese, I am the absolute master here, comfortably provided for in the most beautiful *pays* of the kingdom.' Significantly he ruled out a move to Mende or any other Languedoc diocese, 'since the volume of business that one is engulfed by in the dioceses of Languedoc is not something that suits me. A bishop in these parts, especially if he is liked and respected, has not a minute's rest; all the affairs, both public and private, of the diocese come to him, and the burden is intolerable unless one is of the right disposition.' Claiming that a damper climate would suit him better than Languedoc, Le Sauvage concluded that, of the northern sees to which he could aspire, Soissons was the best, since it was not too exalted in status for him (unlike its titled neighbours like Laon or Reims) and it was in the proximity of Paris. But the bishop of Soissons, who had often talked about resigning it in return for 'simple benefices', knew perfectly well he could strike a good bargain, and Le Sauvage informed Bouillon that another Languedoc bishop with ministerial connections, Phélypeaux of Uzès, would certainly make a move to get Soissons if he heard of its bishop's willingness to give it up. Le Sauvage's lack of personal means also led him to wonder how he could survive in Soissons, a poorly endowed diocese, with relatively heavy fixed charges, and where life was seriously expensive compared to the much cheaper Lavaur.[80] Le Sauvage, who was to die within months of writing this letter, covered most of the major angles regarding a change of diocese in a few pages. What he had to say, and the supporting arguments he used, make it clear that, in the minds of both the dispensers and beneficiaries of royal church patronage, the episcopal map of France was increasingly an integrated one, in which it was possible to envisage movement in numerous directions. But just as crucially, they knew that the map was not a homogeneous one, and that some dioceses were more or less attainable, depending on one's status, ambitions and connections.

V

The language used by Le Sauvage was the conventional coin of ecclesiastical patronage of almost any historical period, but it is significant that, writing in 1676, he *also* alluded at least twice to the likely implication of specifically

---

80   R du Coudrey, 'Un Granvillais oublié; René Le Sauvage, évêque de Lavaur 1630–1677', in *Le Pays de Grandville*, 5 (1909), 27–8, letter to Bouillon, 29 Dec 1676.

religious factors in certain episcopal nominations. He argued that the Jansenist bishop of Saint-Pons in Languedoc, Percin de Montgaillard, one of Louis XIV's earliest nominations, would never be moved to a see where the Jesuits were powerful, while the bishop of Noyon's pro-Jansenist sentiments would require the nomination of a successor with different opinions.[81] There is good reason to think that Le Sauvage's fellow-bishops would have reasoned along similar lines by the 1670s. A generation earlier, such an outlook would not have had much foundation; a generation later, in the run-up to *Unigenitus*, it had become a commonplace. The early decades of Louis XIV's rule witnessed the beginnings of a 'climate of opinion', for want of a better term, in which theological and ecclesiological preferences could be important in determining who did or did not join the episcopate. It deserves close attention at this point.

During the half-century after 1661, the appointment, transfer and promotion of bishops could never quite be divorced from considerations which to some degree or another involved what historians conveniently label as 'Jansenism' and 'gallicanism'. Both of these terms have attracted enough historical interest to fill an entire library, so that only a brief sketch, sufficient to understand the context of the present study, need be provided here. It would be a mistake to define either term too tightly, since it was their imprecision and mutability, as well as their capacity to come together in particular circumstances, which made them so historically enduring. Jansenism, the more recent of the two, was formally condemned for the first time only in 1653, and it was no accident that France's bishops were intimately involved with it from the outset. The first papal condemnation, in the bull *Cum Occasione*, was delivered in response to pressure from France first triggered by a letter signed by eighty-five of its bishops, though this statistic should not be taken to mean that the remaining twenty-eight or so bishops were somehow pro-Jansenist.[82] But to confine Jansenism to the content of the five propositions singled out by Innocent X's bull would be to misunderstand the place of 'Jansenist' opinions in the moral and theological culture of the day. Many of those accused of being Jansenists, then and later, were far less concerned with theological issues arising from Jansen's *Augustinus*, than with applying the moral rigour of the early church, which they revered as a fixed point in the Christian empyrean, to the penitential, sacramental and religious observances of their own time. As one historian has recently put it, 'the Jansenist project remained fundamentally the same as that of the Counter-Reformation, and brought to it a refusal to compromise and the certainty that the narrow road of asceticism was the only one for Christians'.[83] It is surely symptomatic

---

81   *Ibid*; he returned to some of these questions in a subsequent letter to Bouillon, pp 30–1, letter of 13 Feb 1677. Le Sauvage died only three months after this second letter. For his background, see above, pp 84–5.

82   There are numerous historical studies of early French Jansenism. There is a clear and detailed account in Pierre Blet, 'Louis XIV et les papes aux prises avec le jansénisme', *Archivum Historiae Pontificiae*, 31 (1992), 109–92; 32 (1993), 65–148.

83   Nicole Lemaitre, ed, *Histoire des curés* (Paris 2002), 209.

of its evolution that when Clement XI condemned Jansenism again in 1713 he should have singled out the French Oratorian spiritual writer Quesnel's widely read and admired *Réflexions morales*, and not a dense and rarely read Latin treatise on grace by a Flanders university theologian. At any rate, the 1653 condemnation was followed in France by energetic anti-Jansenist moves to copper-fasten the pope's decision by making it part of the law of the land and, more to the point, by imposing a profession of orthodoxy, the celebrated Formulary conceived initially by the assembly of clergy, on large sections of the clergy. Plans for implementing this were still being finalised by an assembly in the final months of Mazarin's ministry.[84] As we saw, it was to ensure that this campaign would not falter that Michel Le Tellier convinced Louis XIV to prefer Pierre de Marca over Péréfixe as the new archbishop of Paris in early 1662, since Marca had emerged during the 1650s as the real hammer of Jansenism. His successor Péréfixe inherited the problem, but was prevented from taking any action in his new diocese until 1664 for the simple reason that Rome refused to grant him his bulls for Paris until 1664 – an excellent example of how wider conflicts between Rome and France could suspend actions that both sides agreed were necessary. While Péréfixe's violent handling of the recalcitrant, anti-Formulary nuns of Port-Royal made most of the headlines, the episcopate itself also gave both the crown and the papacy cause for concern. Although successive assemblies of French clergy, dominated by the bishops, played a key role in moves to suppress Jansenism, problems appeared within their own ranks from the outset. For all the efforts of the successive assemblies, it was not until 1665 that bishops themselves were finally obliged to sign the Formulary – and even then it was by virtue of a papal bull, and not a collective decision of the clergy in assembly or a royal decree. If Jansenism in the episcopate was to exercise Louis XIV and his advisers down to 1715, the most prominent episcopal Jansenists of his early years had been placed in office by either Richelieu or Mazarin. During the 1650s, Gondrin of Sens, Choart of Beauvais and Choiseul of Comminges had been threatened with a full-scale trial before a commission of fellow-French bishops for publishing pastoral instructions which seemed to undermine the papal condemnation of Jansen. It took considerable courage to take an independent stance on such an issue, since it meant contradicting fellow bishops, so the refusing bishops often defended their decisions in terms of their inalienable pastoral responsibilities as bishops and the protection afforded by the gallican liberties against reprisals. If there was one key reason for the difficulty of disposing of the Jansenist problem it was precisely the increasing strength of gallican sentiments by the beginning of Louis XIV's personal rule, when they proved to be an important source of opposition to the papacy's plans to deal with recalcitrant bishops in particular. A convinced gallican might well detest Jansenists, yet be severely torn by the attempts made to eliminate the threat they posed, since the latter often seemed to

84   Blet, *Le Clergé de France et la monarchie*, ii, 300ff.

involve direct papal intervention in the affairs of the French church, precisely what the 'liberties' were meant to limit to a strict minimum. At nearly every turn, whenever Louis XIV and the pope, together or separately, attempted to extinguish the threat of Jansenism, they came up against gallican-inspired forms of opposition. When proper account of this is taken, the 'Jansenism' of many of those, bishops or otherwise, who were accused under Louis XIV of holding condemned views, was a variable mixture of rigorist morality, Augustinian-Thomist theology, and gallican sentiments. It was this admixture, the ingredients of which varied from one individual and situation to another, which enabled several bishops, actual and future, to participate in the acrimonious debates of 1663–4 in the Paris theology faculty which led to the censorship of defences of papal power and the adoption of the six articles which would be the precursors of the famous four Gallican Articles of 1682, the impact of which on episcopal tenure and recruitment we shall see in the next chapter. The poor state of Franco-papal relations up to, and even beyond the Treaty of Pisa of 1664, did little to help to smooth over such problems, and Alexander VII's bull of 1665, issued at Louis XIV's express request and imposing the signature of the Formulary by French bishops, led to an impasse: king and pope were effectively stymied by the resistance of four bishops (five initially, but the bishop of Noyon dropped out later), whose protest revived the threat of a commission of fellow bishops sitting in judgement upon them. But the more pressure Rome applied for action, the more the crown hesitated, fearing that it would make martyrs among the episcopate – especially as the four bishops enjoyed undisputed reputations as irreproachable pastors – and that others might well rally to them out of 'gallican' rather than Jansenist convictions. This came a step closer when yet another letter – very different from that of 1651 – was signed and despatched to Rome by nineteen rather than eighty-five bishops in support of their four recalcitrant colleagues in 1668. Interestingly, only two – Joly of Agen and Percin of Saint-Pons – of the signatories were bishops elevated since Mazarin's death: it was as if the newer arrivals generally were afraid to take the risk of counter-measures from Rome which such a gesture initially seemed to invite. The upshot was the negotiations, dominated by ministers and diplomats orchestrated by Lionne rather than by the French clergy, which led to what is known as the 'Peace of the Church' of early 1669. During the negotiations the threat of many more French bishops waiting in the wings to defend the four recalcitrants was effectively deployed to move the papacy towards a negotiated settlement. Yet the nature of the negotiations did not prevent one major historian of the problem from declaring the Peace 'a triumph of the episcopal order'.[85] By allowing individuals signing the Formulary to maintain a 'respectful silence' as to whether the condemned propositions were in the *Augustinus* or not, the Peace drew a line under the previous persecution of the Jansenists, but it enraged

85   Martimort, *Gallicanisme de Bossuet*, 298.

the anti-Jansenists by failing to elicit a clear statement of orthodoxy from the recalcitrants – a fudge that left them free to continue as before. For ten years their resentfulness bubbled away under the surface until the Peace itself collapsed around 1679 – by which time a more identifiably 'gallican' crisis arising from the extension of the *régale* had blown up.

It would be surprising if these developments did not have some impact on episcopal patronage during the 1660s and beyond. As we saw earlier, the papal nuncio, Bargellini, claimed in 1668 that Louis XIV had disbanded the *conseil de conscience* at the height of his quarrel with Alexander VII, and at the prompting of the Jansenists, happy to muddy the waters via a quarrel which opportunely took the pressure off them.[86] This explanation, based as it is on later testimony, has so far not been corroborated, but the nuncio could be forgiven for seeing the same names at work during these successive crises. Examples of individual bishops moving either towards or away from Jansenist affiliation are not hard to find, as the example chosen by Le Sauvage above, Clermont-Tonnerre of Noyon, make clear. He was initially one of five bishops to issue a pastoral instruction undermining the whole basis of the 1665 Formulary, but he soon withdrew it, yet that did not prevent the likes of Le Sauvage from thinking that he was still 'really' a Jansenist. Elsewhere, bishops felt to be of Jansenist inclinations could be subjected to different types of influence and pressure – some of which had probably been instrumental in securing episcopal office for them in the first place – to bring them back into line. For example, on Marca's translation from Toulouse to Paris in 1662, marshal Plessis-Praslin, brother of Choiseul of Comminges, pressed the king, via his patron the duc d'Orléans, to give Toulouse to Choiseul, to which both Louis and Anne of Austria replied sharply that his Jansenism made such a promotion out of the question. Praslin then rounded upon his brother for his proclivities that were ruining the prospects and affairs of his family – neatly illustrating the kind of 'private' pressures that aristocratic bishops in particular would normally find it difficult to ignore.[87] In the same year, nine possible choices for the vacant archdiocese of Bourges were listed, but only two of them elicited any sort of comment – Choiseul himself was noted as a 'Jansenist', and Barthélemy d'Elbène, bishop of Orléans, as 'suspected of Jansenism'.[88] Neither man became archbishop of Bourges, but it is impossible to be certain if they were excluded on precisely these grounds. Choiseul would never attain the archiepiscopal rank that his brother so clearly wanted for him, but his translation to Tournai in 1669 was rendered possible by his role in the gallican debates of the Paris theology faculty in 1663 and later as a mediator in the Peace of the Church, both of which lifted some of the

---

86 Blet, 'Louis XIV, les papes et le jansénisme', part ii, 94.

87 *Ibid*, part i, 175 quoting the *mémoires* of the Jesuit historian of Jansenism, René Rapin.

88 BN, MS Naf 5132, fo 32. This document was in Colbert's possession, but its precise purpose or significance cannot be fully explored in the absence of contextual information.

suspicion weighing on him since the 1650s.[89] What these cases do show, however, is that considerable suspicion of anyone tarred with the label 'Jansenist' not only existed by the 1660s, but that it was a potential basis of a veto against individual bishops. Such suspicion would rise and fall in subsequent decades, but however vigilant the king and the successive guardians of his conscience might be, they never quite managed to bar entry to the episcopate to 'Jansenists'. Apart from the elusiveness of the term itself, there was another reason for this failure: it was much easier to determine the views of those who were already bishops and therefore trapped 'on-stage', whereas clerics in search of high church office had a better chance of keeping their real convictions to themselves.

The Paris controversies of 1663–4 saw younger clerics like Percin de Montgaillard or Armand de Monchy d'Hocquincourt, both almost certainly much more gallican than Jansenist at this point, play roles which soon brought them royal attention and, with it, episcopal nominations. As bishop of Saint-Pons, Percin would infuriate colleagues, popes and even Louis XIV, something which, as we saw above, would not have surprised Le Sauvage of Lavaur, but in 1664 Percin got his bulls speedily enough, while Hocquincourt had to wait for over two years – and for a new pope – before finally receiving his in 1668. Two new bishops from the mid-1660s with somewhat similar profiles, albeit radically different backgrounds, were du Cambout de Coislin, great-nephew of Chancellor Séguier, nominated to Orléans in 1666, and Claude Joly, nominated to Agen in 1664. Joly was more of an episcopal gallican who created a storm by his attempts to control the pastoral and sacramental activities of the regulars in his diocese, while du Cambout, a favourite of Louis XIV who would later be made a cardinal, was at least 'permissive' in his attitude to Jansenism. The 'Peace of the Church', which came into effect early in 1669, put a temporary end to the war of attrition of the previous years. If Antoine Arnauld could go to court and be presented to the king, and his nephew, Pomponne, succeed Lionne as foreign minister in 1671, then the prospects of those with broadly similar views on religious affairs seemed to have improved dramatically. Port-Royal's reputation had never been higher than around 1670, and it left an enduring imprint on a new generation of high-flying clerics who gravitated around it, some of whom also frequented the Oratory or Saint-Thomas-du-Louvre, where Bossuet, Le Tellier, Le Plessis-Brunetière (later bishop of Saintes) and others were also in the habit of gathering.[90] Over the next few years, a small group of bishops would be seated whose rigorism ensured they were closer to the Jansenists than to their Jesuit opponents – which was often enough for them to be accused of Jansenism! Charles-Maurice Le Tellier, full archbishop of Reims after 1671, was already seated and his enduring hostility, like that of his family, to the Jesuits and their moral

89 Desmons, *Etudes historiques, économiques et religieuses sur Tournai*, 17ff for his early career.
90 Martimort, *Gallicanisme de Bossuet*, esp 294ff.

theology was no secret.[91] Among the new faces appearing after Le Tellier were Bossuet, Barillon, bishop of Luçon, Le Camus, bishop of Grenoble, and Sève, bishop of Arras, all of whom were to become distinguished figures in the French church over the next generation. Others who had frequented Port-Royal during the 1660s were probably among those appointed in the 1670s, but it is impossible to be sure how numerous they were, given that such affiliations were not exclusive and may have been either short-lived or opportunistic.[92] It may be surprising to see Bossuet mentioned in such company, but when he was nominated to Condom – Le Camus being passed over for it – the papal nuncio denounced him for supporting the publication of a new French translation of the Bible – the kind of venture which Rome disliked but which Port Royalistes would have supported. Bargellini even suggested that if Rome made Bossuet wait for his bulls (he did not go as far as to suggest outright refusal), then quite a few people in Paris would not be unhappy. The nuncio returned to the attack in 1671 in order to prevent Le Camus from obtaining his provisions for Grenoble, but with no more success.[93] His friend Barillon alleged that the royal confessor, Ferrier 'tried to discredit my opinions and my behaviour' in the hope of denying him episcopal promotion to Luçon later that year.[94]

However, the fact that all of those just named were appointed within a year or two of the Peace of the Church says much for the more relaxed climate it introduced. Yet with a combative confessor like Ferrier advising the king on episcopal nominations, it was unlikely that anyone of openly Jansenist sentiments would be successful. Some time after his death, the new confessor, La Chaize, and Harlay of Paris were ordered to conduct 'detailed enquiries' into candidates for benefices and alert the king if any of them were 'suspect of an inclination to Jansenism', since he wished to prevent them from 'obtaining graces'. According to the nuncio, this order was triggered by royal dissatisfaction with Arnauld of Angers and Pavillon of Alet over the signature of the Formulary rather than with recent nominations. Initially the order to La Chaize and Harlay was kept secret, but Harlay later wrote to the king to argue that it would be better to make it public, since it would act as an effective warning to individuals but also to parents to distance their offspring from

91 Lesaulnier, *Port-Royal insolite*, 214, which reports that Le Tellier learned of Jesuit opposition to him as soon as he was nominated coadjutor of Reims, and that he had a frosty interview with Annat, the confessor. The rest of his career was punctuated with similar hostility.

92 *Ibid*, 310, Guillaume de Meschatin de la Faye frequented Port-Royal around 1670, while still completing his theology studies in Paris. Nominated to Gap in 1675, he died young in 1679.

93 Martimort, *Gallicanisme de Bossuet*, 305. Bargellini's diplomatic style involved more personal initiatives than either Rome or Paris would have wished, and they were frequently disowned, their author reprimanded. See Blet, *Les Nonces du pape à la cour de Louis XIV*, ch 3, 'le nonce Bargellini et Hugues de Lionne', for a portrait of him that is more circumspect than Martimort's as to the exact reasons for Bargellini's disgrace and recall.

94 BN, MS Lat 18389, fo 289, Barillon's 'vie autobiographique', for the reference to Ferrier 'qui voulut décrier mes sentiments et ma conduite.'

sources of Jansenist teaching.[95] But the fact that some of the bishops nominated only a few years later, such as Noailles of Cahors and La Broue of Mirepoix, would become major figures in the later Jansenist quarrels, shows how
impossible it was successfully to screen all candidates for benefices. It also
serves as a reminder that the spiritual or theological preferences of individual
bishops were not always set in stone before they accepted the mitre.

VI

It would, however, be simplistic to see Port-Royal and its wider constituency
at this time as a pressure group simply attempting to pack the episcopate
with its own followers. It is all too easy to overlook the fact that one of its
most unusual features was its highly ambiguous attitude to the episcopate,
effectively warning clerics *against* being candidates for the mitre. Doubts over
the search for such office and its compatibility with the pursuit of an individual's salvation were hardly new, having been voiced by preachers and
moralists for centuries. But Port-Royal gave them a new lease of life, sharp-
ening the tension between the life of retreat, where compromise with worldly
values could be avoided, and a life of action and responsibility, which exposed
one to sin and damnation. From Saint-Cyran, *alias* Petrus Aurelieus's writings on the subject during the 1630s to the clandestine *Nouvelles Ecclésiastiques*
of the 1670s and 1680s and beyond, the Port-Royal and Jansenist view of
episcopacy per se was exceptionally elevated, based as it was on their uncon-
ditional reverence for the early church. No less important was its incorporation of key gallican maxims about bishops owing their office directly to God:
bishops were the lynchpin of the church, its indispensable doctors and pastors.
The responsibilities such office entailed were correspondingly awesome, and
only a small number of individuals were fit for the task. In contemporary
context, this translated into a sharp difference between the 'évêque de cour'
and the resident pastor-bishop – itself not a new distinction. In its disapproval
of careerists, it criticised bishops who would abandon their first diocese for
another – a form of episcopal 'separation' which should only occur in rare circumstances.[96] But while it might glory in being associated with some of
France's most revered bishops – Vialart of Châlons, Pavillon of Alet, Arnauld
of Angers and others – it was just as likely to inspire sentiments of withdrawal and retreat among those in line for nomination to the episcopate. An
influential figure like Rancé, abbot of La Trappe, who would normally have
entered the episcopate had he so wished, added his powerful and intransigent
voice to this particular chorus. But even Rancé's own initial turning away

---

95   ASV, Nunz Fr 154a, fo 154, Varese to Cardinal Cibo, 12 June 1676.
96   See the brief but rich sketch by René Taveneaux, 'L'Évêque selon Port Royal', *Chroniques de Port
     Royal*, no 32 (1983), 21–38 (reprinted in Taveneaux, *Jansénisme et Réforme catholique* (Nancy
     1992), 75–87).

from the episcopate was due in part to the advice of Vialart, Pavillon and Choiseul, so we should be careful not to see these ideas as originating or circulating purely outside the episcopate.[97]

It is virtually impossible, as one might expect, to know just how many refusals of the mitre were genuinely motivated by such sentiments. A case in point is François d'Aligre, the eldest surviving – and brightest – son of the second Chancellor Aligre, who refused Avranches in 1668 and every other offer thereafter, as the Port-Royal chroniclers noted. What cannot be determined is how far his refusal was a matter of temperament rather than of conviction.[98] It is, as might be expected, the 'near-misses' which are the best documented, since they provided the most dramatic illustrations of the verities in question. Thus Le Camus's refusal of Bazas in 1667 on the advice of Rancé and perhaps others led him to radically change his lifestyle and remove himself from court altogether for three years. Two years later, Rancé produced one of his more nuanced statements on the question, also *à propos* of Le Camus: 'it would be better if M le Camus did *not* wish to become a bishop, and it is a crime to want to do so, but he should not distance himself from it to the point that he excludes himself altogether . . . you know that it does not suffice merely to be called to the apostolate'.[99] When the successful Grenoble nomination followed in 1671, Le Camus sought and received advice from 'a great number of people possessed of piety and knowledge, all of whom gave me the same answer', after which he handed over the entire matter to Vialart of Châlons as judge of last resort, 'who knows my faults and the perils of the episcopate'.[100] Similarly extensive consultations occurred in the case of Le Camus's close friend, Barillon de Morangis, before he accepted Luçon, later in 1671. Of the many letters of congratulation Barillon received, there was one from Gondrin of Sens declaring that his nomination and the circumstances in which it arose 'serve as a consolation for so many other irregular promotions which infringe the holy laws'.[101] In their correspondence in subsequent

---

97 See Alban J Krailsheimer, *Armand-Jean de Rancé, abbot of La Trappe* (Oxford 1974), 13–15, who has much to say about the wider circles in which French bishops moved during these decades.

98 Lesaulnier, *Port-Royal insolte*, 389. Sturdy, *The D'Aligres de la Rivière*, 211.

99 Rancé, *Correspondance*, i, 277, to Pontchâteau, 28 Aug 1668, 'on ne voudrait pas que M Le Camus désirât d'être évêque, c'est un crime de le desirer, mais il ne faut pas qu'il s'en éloigne de sorte qu'il s'en exclue . . . vous savez que ce n'est pas tout que d'être appelé à l'apostolat'. Rancé was admitting that Le Camus had the qualities to be a good bishop. By this time both Grenoble and Condom were vacant, and Le Camus was in line to succeed to one or the other of them.

100 *Lettres du cardinal Le Camus* (ed Ingold), no 16, pp 37–8, to Pontchâteau, 28 Jan 1671, 'une infinite de gens de piété et de science qui m'ont répondu la mesme chose'; and for Vialart, 'lui qui connait mes miserères et les perils de l'épiscopat'; no 18, to Antoine Arnauld, early August 1671, still torn by doubts and scruples, Le Camus asks whether twenty years of dissipation followed by five years of retreat and 'éloignement' from the episcopate are sufficient signs of a genuine vocation.

101 *Documents pour l'histoire de Luçon*, no 1110, letter of 23 Oct 1671, '[qui] consolent de tant d'autres promotions irregulières qui blessent toutes les plus sainctes lois'.

decades, Le Camus and Barillon often discussed the prospect of resigning their dioceses outright in order to attend to their personal salvation.

But the real target for disapproval in these years was not so much those entering the episcopate, as those abandoning their first diocese for another. The criticism made by Gondrin came towards the end of 1671, a year which witnessed not merely a record number of episcopal nominations, but also of transfers of bishops, many of them only recently ensconced in their first dioceses.[102] In this he was echoing the hard-line stance of 'the ancient discipline of the canons' rather than the more generous provisions of the 'law of the decretals'.[103] After those of 1661–2, there had been a modest number of transfers during the 1660s, but Gondrin and those with similar views were probably angered less by those transfers that were promotions to archbishoprics than by the more dubious 'sideways' movements to, and from, lesser dioceses. These were on the whole uncommon under Henri IV and Louis XIII, and for much of the 1660s the picture did not change much. Only in 1670 and 1671 did such transfers suddenly become more visibly numerous than previously. But in addition to this, the late 1660s were a period during which it seemed to take several years to fill a number of vacant sees, with refusals, changes of mind and several instances of bishops nominated to one vacant see waiting for a considerable period before pressing for, and often obtaining, a more recently vacated but more attractive see. The king and his confessors, Annat and Ferrier, seemed to indulge candidates who were in no great hurry to press for the despatch of their papal provisions. Several of the thirteen bishops nominated in January 1671 were given dioceses that had been vacant in some cases since 1668 or 1669. Gondrin's letter to Barillon, quoted above, was targeting these practices as unacceptable, and in doing so he was adding his voice to others who had spoken before him. By the time he was writing, the story of how Colbert had manoeuvred his brother Nicolas into leaving Luçon for Auxerre by intercepting letters of advice counselling him *not* to do so, was probably known.[104] The nuncio picked up these murmurs in early 1671 when reporting that 'some zealots' found episcopal translations were too frequent and the pope was becoming party to an abuse.[105] The most intransigent critic was Rancé, who served as spiritual advisor of several of the bishops we have just encountered, and whose hard-line views on episcopal vocations and translations were no secret. Nor would they change over the next thirty years, even when bishops who were spiritually close to

---

102   1671 had no fewer than twenty-two nominations, nine of them transfers, a very high proportion.

103   BN, MS Baluze 112, fos 72–3, memorandum on the resignation of bishops, probably drafted by Pierre de Marca, which contrasts 'l'ancienne discipline canonique' with the 'droit des décrétales'.

104   BN, MS Fr 23509, fos 319–21, *Nouvelles Ecclésiastiques*. ASV, *Lettere de Vescovi* 57, fos 200–1, Nicolas Colbert to Clement X, 13 Aug 1671, explaining his dilemma, the steps he had taken to seek the appropriate advice, and leaving the ultimate decision to the pope.

105   ASV, Nunz Fr 144, fo 130, to secretary of state, 20 Feb 1671.

him were involved.[106] So much so that in 1680, when Louis XIV summoned
the bishop of Saint-Pol-de-Léon in Brittany to court in order to persuade him
to accept the Pyreneean see of Alet, the bishop deliberately avoided stopping
off to see Rancé on his way to court, knowing perfectly well that if, having
done so, he then refused Alet, he would be accused of allowing Rancé to tell
him what he could or could not do.[107] He duly went to court and refused it
anyway.

Even though the rate of transfers, especially of a 'sideways' kind, dipped
appreciably during the remainder of the 1670s, the criticism of crown practice had taken root. By this point, the first generation of *Nouvelles Ecclésiastiques*, compiled by Louis Fouquet, had taken up the theme of unfounded
episcopal translations, not to mention that of individuals obtaining bishoprics
without a proper vocation. It is ironic that in a very early *cahier*, obviously
unaware of his thoughts on leaving Lavaur, the *Nouvelles* should have singled
out René Le Sauvage's *amende honorable* shortly before his death, when he apol-
ogised to his chapter for having accepted episcopal office even though he had
not actively sought it.[108]

But perhaps the most unexpected feature of these early decades was the way
in which the role played by the papacy shifted. The 1660s, marked by the
Jansenist and gallican affairs, by Rome's prolonged unwillingness to grant the
indults for the provinces recently acquired by Louis XIV, and the various incidents in Rome which badly soured Franco-papal relations, ensured that papal
influence on episcopal patronage would be negligible. True, as already noted,
the days when Rome worried about the worthiness of episcopal nominations
in France were over – since the 1620s – and incoming nuncios no longer
received the briefing that had once been a regular feature of their instructions.[109] Successive nuncios tried to intervene over particular nominations, but
their influence was severely limited. In 1664, Nuncio Roberti tried to prevent
an Italian based in France, Alessandro Fabri, from becoming bishop of Orange,
but his arguments – that a diocese as full of Protestants as Orange needed a
bishop-theologian – were brushed aside, even though Fabri had to wait until
1667 for his bulls.[110] This was not the only instance from the mid-1660s when
Rome made future bishops wait for years for their provisions. As we saw,
Nuncio Bargellini made efforts around 1669–71 to delay rather than undo
nominations like those of Le Camus and Bossuet, with a view to making them
appreciate the value of papal goodwill. Considering how sensitive Rome was

106 For an example: Rancé, *Correspondance*, i, 359, to Louise Roger, 29 Jan 1671 about the new
     bishop of Lombez; iv, 25–6, to Barillon of Luçon, 21 Jan 1690 arguing against his transfer
     to another diocese, however much his health might benefit from leaving Luçon.
107 *Ibid*, ii, 471–2, Rancé to Pierre Le Neboux de la Brousse, 18 Dec 1680.
108 BN, MS Fr 23506 fo 240, *Nouvelles Ecclésiastiques*, n d, 1677. By way of underlining Le
     Sauvage's virtues, the *Nouvelles Ecclésiastiques* then incorporated a copy of his testament: fos
     240v–41v.
109 See *Correspondance du nonce Spada*, 94–10 (instructions of Jan 1674).
110 Blet, *Les Nonces à la cour de Louis XIV*, 37–8.

on Jansenist-gallican questions during these years, it is striking how little success Bargellini had. On a far bigger scale were the delays which accumulated in the mid-1670s, during the last two years of Clement X's pontificate, when two out of every three of Louis XIV's new bishops had to wait between a year and two years for their bulls. Part of the reason for it may simply be that, once again, Franco-papal relations soured from late 1674 through the summer of 1675, and that episcopal patronage was caught in the cross-fire.[111] But it seems unlikely that this is a complete explanation. Strangely, there is scarcely any reference to the problems in the nuncios' correspondence, with the exception of a comment in early 1677 that the king was taking steps to ensure that French nominees in no hurry to obtain their provisions would be penalised for their tardiness.[112] One or two of these newcomers were seeking reductions in the cost of bulls for dioceses long exposed to war damage (Toul, Boulogne), while some of the other nominations were also linked, as we have seen previously, to transfers of existing bishops – transfers which were sometimes complicated and delayed.[113]

The election of a new pope, Innocent XI, in September 1676 did not see the backlog cleared immediately, and some nominees had to wait another full year before their provisions arrived. Whatever the precise chain of events and influences, within a year or two of his election, Innocent was voicing his own disapproval of what he regarded as unacceptable practices in France – the unnecessary transfers of bishops, the nomination of underage clerics to abbeys and priories, the granting of pensions off bishoprics to third parties, the accumulation of too many benefices by individuals, and by bishops in particular, as well as the granting of coadjutorships to blood relatives of reigning bishops.[114] The circulation of such complaints is of particular interest since, as we have seen as far as the French church was concerned, they originated in the late 1660s mostly among supporters of the Port-Royal and Jansenist-rigorist causes, some of whom were based in Rome by the early years of Innocent's reign. The pope's reception of their ideas must have seemed a vindication of their criticisms, especially concerning unnecessary transfers of bishops.[115] At any rate, from early 1678, the papal nuncio was under instruction to raise these subjects at court, and to convince

---

111 *Correspondance du nonce Spada*, 50–68, 88.
112 ASV, Nunz Fr 155, fo 131, nuncio to Cardinal Cibo, 19 Feb 1677. The problem, as it was perceived then, was that the arrangements in force for the *régale* guaranteed that the revenues of dioceses during vacancies were assigned to bishops anyway, so there was no hurry to seek their bulls.
113 ASV, Nunz Fr 154a, fo 127 (Toul); fos 406–7 (Boulogne).
114 ASV, Nunz Fr 160, fo 102, Lauri to Cibo, 3 Feb 1679 (on coadjutorships).
115 Bruno Neveu, *Sébastien Joseph du Cambout de Pontchâteau (1634–1690) et ses missions à Rome, d'après sa correspondance et des documents inédits* (Paris 1969), the best study of these Roman connections. See also his important essay, 'Culture religieuse et aspirations reformistes à la cour d'Innocent XI', in Neveu, *Érudition et religion aux xvii* et xviii* siècles* (Paris 1994), 235–76.

La Chaize of the need to lift the burden such practices placed on the king's conscience.[116] But these issues lay at the heart of the crown's church patronage, and seeking to reform any one of them on its own was problematic. The nuncio, Varese, did make a start on these questions with the confessor, but he then died inopportunely in early November 1678, and France would be without a nuncio for the next five years. It is not surprising that during the interim a lower-rank diplomat, the auditor Lauri, without access to either the king or his ministers, could not achieve much, although he did clearly follow the instructions given to Varese and pressed La Chaize on some of the issues involved.[117] This loss of impetus did not deter Innocent and his advisers from acting as they saw best in particular cases. The records of the consistorial congregation show that bishops resigning their sees were quizzed on their motives, and attempts were made at independent enquiries.[118] One of these concerned the bishop of Nantes, La Baume le Blanc, who resigned in 1677 in favour of his nephew, whom Louis XIV obligingly nominated as his successor, but the pope refused all entreaties to confirm him until he had reached the minimum age for the episcopate, while insisting on receiving detailed information about his precise reasons for resigning – doubtless because Innocent himself was suspicious of uncle-nephew successions.[119] But there were, inevitably, limits to such severity. The rapid nomination and transfer of Louis de Bourlemont to Fréjus, Carcassonne and finally Bordeaux in 1679–80, was exactly the kind of abuse that Innocent's circle disapproved of, yet because Bourlemont had spent most of his career as an Auditor of the Roman Rota and enjoyed Innocent's respect, his transfers were in the end not blocked, despite known papal reluctance to grant them.[120] Likewise, the coadjutorship of Rouen, which Colbert lined up for his son by early

116 ASV, Nunz Fr 157, fo 373, nuncio to Cardinal Cibo, 18 Feb 1678, referring to instructions of 1 Feb from Rome. Further reports on discussions of particular issues with La Chaize in *ibid*, fo 519v–20, 21 Oct 1678.

117 ASV, Nunz Fr 160, fo 417–18, Lauri to Cibo, 17 April 1679, reporting on discussion with La Chaize on papal demand that only those over twenty-three be nominated to abbeys and priories. La Chaize did not think the king would respond well, and the nuncio wondered what the impact of Roman refusals would be. *Ibid*, fo 658, Lauri to Cibo, early June 1679, for a second discussion with La Chaize on this subject, in which he again objected that the Concordat of Bologna referred only to 'regular' abbots, not to 'commendatory' ones, and thus that Roman arguments were poorly supported. But he did claim that Louis XIV was more demanding than his predecessors, refusing to give abbeys to children, and promised to raise the matter with the king again.

118 ASV, Acta congregationis consistorialis, 1676, fos 34–5 (Montpellier); 1678–9, fos 260–2 (Lisieux), fos 401–2 (Nantes), fos 432 (Troyes); 1680–1, fo 372 (Carcassonne); 1682 (vol 1), fos 127–30 (Dax).

119 ASV, Nunz Fr 160, fo 68, Lauri to Cardinal Cibo, 21 Jan 1679; fos 488–9, same to same, 5 May 1679; fo 761, same to same, 30 June 1679.

120 ASV, Nunz Fr 163, fos 1027–8, Lauri to Cibo, 9 Dec 1680. Bourlemont claimed he was mortified by opposition to his transfers, but Lauri pointed out that to be given three dioceses in succession within a year was unprecedented, and the pope wanted to take his time to reflect and make sure that it was 'expedient' that he should be given his provisions.

1680, had been vigorously denied for virtually a year before that, partly for fear of the damage Roman opposition to it might do.[121] But when it did reach the agenda, it had to be handled carefully, at a time when Franco-papal relations were worsening. It helped, of course, that Jacques-Nicolas Colbert was no relative of the reigning archbishop, but the fact that he was still fractionally under age meant that Lauri felt obliged to say to him directly that the coadjutorship needed to be justified in accordance with the church's 'sacred canons'.[122]

Even though Franco-papal relations were heading towards crisis by the early 1680s, there is little doubt that the change in Roman attitudes did register within the French church. A bishop contemplating a transfer in early 1682 confessed to Favoriti, Innocent XI's confidant, that 'extraordinary graces' were not to be expected under this pope.[123] An even better indication of this shift is that a prelate as senior as Forbin-Janson, transferred by Louis XIV from Marseille to Beauvais in August 1679, found himself drafting a full-blown defence of the decision – beginning with the fact that since he had not sought the move, it could not *but* be canonical.[124] Like pro-Jansenist and anti-*régale* forces in France generally, the first generation of the *Nouvelles Ecclésiastiques* warmly welcomed Innocent X, and their early *cahiers* made much of his intention of restoring old church discipline where bishops were concerned – including his emphasis on his own functions as bishop of Rome. They reported his disapproval of the frequent translations of bishops in the gallican church as early as 1677.[125] They also picked up echoes of the nuncio's negotiations at court about translations, pluralism and pensions,[126] and offered a detailed account of discussions, probably early in 1679, between the king and archbishop Harlay, especially on transfers.[127] Their conclusion was not especially optimistic: the 'evil of translations' would only end when Rome itself led by example, but Rome was badly

---

121　ASV, Nunz Fr 160, fos 334–5, Lauri to Cibo, 24 March 1679. La Chaize, when questioned by Lauri, absolutely denied the truth of the project and that Colbert's age, which he put at twenty-three, was likely to encounter 'difficoltà insupportibili' in Rome: fo 445v, same to same, 21 April 1679.

122　ASV, Nunz Fr 163, fo 349, Lauri to Cibo, 15 April 1680.

123　ASV, Acta congregationis consistorialis 1682, vol i, fos 580–1, N (signature illegible) to Favoriti, Avignon, 23 Jan 1682. The bishop of Grasse, nominated to Saint-Paul-Trois-Châteaux, a diocese of equivalent revenue, wished to retain a benefice which required a papal dispensation, hence the comment, reported indirectly here.

124　ASV, Nunz Fr 161, fos 200–1, Lauri to Cibo, 20 Aug 1679; fos 206–7, text of Janson's memorandum. Of course, Janson was also looking to obtain a reduction in the cost of his provisions, so his motivation was hardly unmixed.

125　BN, MS Fr 23506, fo 371v, *Nouvelles Ecclésiastiques*.

126　BN, MS Fr 23508, fo 32v-33, 'les transférés ressemblent un peu aux commissaires et aux amovibles: sur quoy l'on dit que le Saint-Siège fait de profondes réflexions'.

127　*Ibid*, fo 181r. Harlay, who confessed that, having himself moved from Rouen to Paris, he was not best placed to cast stones, agreed 'qu'il estoit incontestable que les translations estoient tout affait opposés à l'esprit et aux lois de l'église'.

informed about the state of affairs in France.[128] That particular verdict, which would have been shared by someone like Mme de Sévigné, was to be borne out by the development of the conflict which would disrupt episcopal patronage for a full decade.[129]

128 *Ibid*, fo 182v.
129 Sévigné, *Correspondance*, vii, 263, letter to *président* Moulceau, 1 June 1684, 'je ne m'amuserai point à vous conter le remue-menage de tous les évêques; cela blesse et fait mal au coeur'.

CHAPTER 7

A Decade of Crisis

THE 1680s OCCUPY an uncertain place in the long history of Louis XIV's reign. In virtually every domain, from the political and military to the economic and demographic, its record seems to be of limited interest compared to other decades – at best as a period of calm before the storms of the final decades. However, the storm was already blowing in the religious domain, where the twin peaks of the Gallican Articles of 1682 and the Revocation of the Edict of Nantes of 1685 stand out. Not surprisingly, the thesis of a 'general crisis' of the reign occurring during the 1680s relies heavily on these religious issues, and their wider consequences, for its evidential ingredients.[1]

Within the French church itself, the events leading up to the 1682 articles and the long stand-off with the papacy which followed stand in sharp contrast to the pattern that obtains for the rest of post-1661 decades. Even the previous contretemps between the crown and the papacy in the early 1660s and the mid-1670s had not much involved the French church and clergy; that of the 1680s was very different, since assemblies of clergy and their episcopal leaders played an important part in triggering the crisis, which in turn led very quickly to the cessation of provisions to newly nominated French bishops for a full decade. In its duration and severity, this particular crisis had only one 'recent' historical precedent – that of the period from 1589 to 1596, at the height of the last war of religion. At that point, nominations of bishops by rival parties in the royal succession, and a ban by the Paris parlement on nominees seeking their provisions from Rome, led by 1596, when the ban was finally lifted and Henri IV was reconciled with Rome, to a situation in which up to forty dioceses were vacant.[2] But the similarities with the 1680s end there – except perhaps for the number of vacant dioceses – since the latter decade witnessed no such power vacuum or loss of royal control. The source of the crisis was radically different, but its unexpected

---

1   Andrew Lossky, *Louis XIV and the French Monarchy* (New Brunswick 1994), ch 9, 'The General Crisis of Louis XIV's Reign'.
2   Bergin, *Making*, 366–83.

duration, virtually ten years, meant that it was bound to have a serious impact on the body most directly affected by it – the French episcopate. The present chapter will focus essentially on that impact, but it needs to be prefaced by as brief a contextual analysis of the conflict as such a complex subject permits, if particular issues for subsequent discussion are to be intelligible. It spawned intense polemic then and later, and historians themselves have rarely been immune from its effects, especially in France where generations of gallicans and ultramontanes, clericals and anticlericals fought out their own battles with explicit reference to it.[3]

I

The first point to make is that the crisis had several strands, which were in principle distinct from each other, but which in practice became almost inextricably entwined. The Jansenist question was *not* among them, unless we are to regard the sympathy for Jansenist, rigorist and anti-Jesuit forces showed by Innocent XI and his entourage – itself a huge irony considering the early history of the Jansenist affair – as a contributory factor.[4] The main trigger was the *régale* affair, which began with two royal edicts in 1673 and 1675 extending the *régale* as historically practised in the northern and central dioceses of France to those of the southern provinces, even though the French church's reaction to the crown's espousal of the parlement's long-held theory of the *régale* as a universal and inalienable royal prerogative was largely one of passive compliance and acceptance. This was partly because since Richelieu, the 'temporal' *régale*, which in principle meant that the revenues of vacant bishoprics went to the crown, had been virtually emasculated: the revenues in question were in fact kept 'in reserve' for those nominated to them, and the royal *économes* entrusted with managing the temporalities during the vacancy were to account directly to the new bishops when the *régale* was formally terminated. The 'spiritual' *régale*, whereby the crown filled a certain number of benefices if they fell vacant during an episcopal vacancy, was still more 'real' than its temporal counterpart, but it only involved a limited number of benefices without cure of souls, such as posts of canons in cathedrals and collegiate chapters. As such, it clearly provided some additional but temporary royal patronage within the French church, which was attractive to ambitious clerics, but it bore no comparison with what was available, for example, to the Spanish crown.[5] Consequently, the *régale* was not an issue over which the

---

3 The standard late nineteenth-century works by Charles Gérin, Eugène Michaud and other scholars were highly partisan. The major revisionist works are those of Latreille, Martimort, Neveu and Blet, whose numerous contributions are listed in the Bibliography.

4 See Neveu, 'Culture religieuse et aspirations réformistes à la cour d'Innocent XI', 235–76, esp 241ff.

5 Christian Hermann, *L'Église d'Espagne sous le patronage royal (1476–1834)* (Madrid 1988).

vast majority of French bishops were prepared to man the barricades; even those who considered the royal argument to be groundless, like Le Camus of Grenoble, were still ready to see the problem resolved by means of the grant of a papal indult enabling the king to extend the *régale*.[6] Their attitude was not affected by the only serious change made to the temporal *régale* since Richelieu, namely the earmarking, by two decrees of 1677, of one-third of the revenues during vacancies to the cause of converting France's remaining Huguenots – hardly something to which the French clergy could seriously object.[7]

Only two of the fifty-nine southern bishops affected by the extension of the *régale*, Pavillon of Alet and Caulet of Pamiers, veterans of the Jansenist anti-Formulary wars of the 1650s and 1660s, protested against the king's decision. Their refusal to register their oath of fidelity to the king meant that their dioceses were considered vacant and therefore 'fallen into régale' (*tombés en régale*), which in turn meant that both they and the crown nominated to benefices as they fell vacant. Excommunications of 'intruders' (*régalistes*) followed, as did appeals by the latter to the archbishops of Narbonne and Toulouse, both of whom ruled against their recalcitrant suffragan bishops. By these means conflict began to spiral and by the time Caulet died in 1680 (Pavillon died a few years earlier, in 1677), the situation in Pamiers was chaotic. Both Caulet and Pavillon had in any case appealed to Innocent XI in 1677 and, to the increasing dismay of the French court, Rome came to their defence. Already touched by Caulet's predicament (his revenues sequestrated, some of his canons exiled), Innocent and his advisers viewed the *régale* less as another local difficulty than as a chapter in the greater *regnum-sacerdotium* quarrel which could not be ignored. As a result, he pressed Louis XIV to withdraw his edicts with three successive briefs of 1678, 1679 and 1680, each more threatening in tone than its predecessor.[8] Louis XIV and his ministers were uncertain as to how to respond to Rome's belated and surprising intervention against the *régale*, and it seems that their preference was for normal diplomatic action. Bringing the French clergy into the dispute would only make it more public and, consequently, more likely to get out of control. But this is what happened when the deputies of the 'little' Assembly of 1680, prompted by Archbishop Harlay, signed a letter to Louis XIV protesting that their place was alongside him in this affair. This provocative gesture generated consider-

---

6 Le Camus of Grenoble, who was close to Caulet and Pavillon, the principal opponents of royal policy over the *régale*, wrote that 'je ne sais pas si St Thomas de Cantorbery eût voulu mourir pour cela. Au moins vous savez que S Augustin ne l'eût pas fait': *Lettres du cardinal Le Camus* (ed Ingold), 278, to Pontchâteau, 22 Oct 1676. Le Camus was prepared to see the extension of the *régale* validated by a papal indult, but the king and his advisers were not prepared to entertain this idea, convinced of the 'surabondance de droit' of the crown in the matter: see Pierre Blet, 'Le Camus et le conflit de la régale', in Jean Godel, ed, *Le Cardinal des montagnes. Étienne Le Camus évêque de Grenoble (1671–1707)* (Grenoble 1974), 78.

7 Orcibal, *Louis XIV et les Protestants*, 44–5.

8 Blet, *Les Assemblées du clergé et Louis XIV*, chs 4–8 for the most fully documented exposition.

able indignation, not least in Rome, and by the time Cardinal d'Estrées finally began negotiations there in early 1681, attitudes had hardened so much that further papal briefs, whose language was less than diplomatic, only exacerbated matters to the point at which the crown was finally ready to accept the idea of an extraordinary general assembly of the clergy – with veiled hints of it turning into a gallican national council. The fact that the representatives of the French clergy, largely hand-picked by the crown and sitting between November 1681 and May 1682, formally accepted, in February 1682, the extension of the *régale* in return for royal agreement to reform certain features of its 'spiritual' dimension which they disliked, was quickly forgotten, overshadowed by the more momentous outcome of their deliberations a mere month later – namely, the celebrated four Gallican Articles.[9]

It is not necessary to trace the genealogy of the Four Articles here, beyond recalling the earlier history of the Six Articles of the Paris theology faculty of 1664, which had raised the tension between France and Rome at the time. But there were significant differences between 1664 and 1682 which went well beyond the number of articles involved. However pivotal the role of the Paris faculty might be in the formation of France's ecclesiastical elite, its pronouncements could no longer rival those of an assembly of clergy, regardless of how many members of the latter might be graduates of the faculty.[10] Moreover, in 1664, the faculty only went as far as identifying what its own maxims were *not*, which was the time-honoured format of doctrinal censure and which allowed for considerable freedom of opinion as to what the proper maxims might be.[11] The 1682 Articles, despite being more moderate and less antipapal than a first reading would suggest, did indeed purport to declare precisely what the maxims of the entire gallican church *were*, and that intention was placed beyond doubt by the royal edict which immediately made the teaching and profession of the articles obligatory within the realm.[12] Such a gesture was bound to create a storm, irrespective of whether there were other bones of contention between France and Rome.

For his part, Innocent XI stopped short of a full-blown censure of the Four Articles and left the door at least partially open for further negotiation.[13] But from the outset, the unfolding drama involved a number of familiar figures in the French episcopate – Choiseul, Harlay, Le Tellier, Bossuet, all gallicans to different degrees and enjoying the kind of royal protection that made them unassailable from Rome. In such circumstances, it was hardly surprising that

---

9 The key texts are reprinted in Léon Mention, *Documents rélatifs aux rapports du clergé avec la royauté de 1682 à 1705* (Paris 1893), nos 2–4, pp 6–32.

10 Thirty-four of the seventy members of the famous Assembly of 1682 were Paris theology graduates. Sixteen of them were already bishops, while ten of them would become so later: Grès-Gayer, *Gallicanisme de Sorbonne*, 251.

11 The most reliable study is Grès-Gayer, *Gallicanisme de Sorbonne*, esp chs 2–3, on the controversies of the mid-1660s.

12 Mention, *Documents*, no 5, pp 33–6, royal declaration of March 1682.

13 Blet, *Assemblées du clergé et Louis XIV*, esp 395ff.

Rome would train its sights on the members as much as on the maxims of the 1682 Assembly. Among them, the most vulnerable to papal reprisals were the second-order deputies with aspirations to episcopal office themselves. In Rome, the special ad hoc congregation of cardinals dealing with the *régale* (and associated questions) was divided over what should be done, and some extreme proposals, such as refusing provisions to all French nominees or all signatories of the articles, were tabled for consideration. But the more moderate case for denying bulls for benefices to any deputy of the 1682 Assembly who had signed the Four Articles was well supported, and by late July 1682 it became official papal policy. It was first put into effect at the consistory of 28 September, which should have confirmed two new French bishops. Augustin de Maupeou and Claude de Saint-Georges, nominated to Castres and Clermont respectively, had both been second-order deputies only a few months earlier, and been nominated bishops within days of the last of the assembly's meetings.[14] It is idle to speculate how this particular problem might have been resolved, since it was immediately transformed into a far broader and more intractable difficulty by the response of the d'Estrées brothers, the duke and the cardinal, France's principal representatives in Rome. They countered the pope's refusal of provisions to Maupeou and Saint-Georges by declaring that so long as they were denied their bulls, *no* French nominees at all, and not merely those associated with the 1682 Assembly, would be 'proposed' for confirmation in consistory. The d'Estrées' initiative, taken without prior consultation, was essentially intended as a tactic in order to make Innocent XI back down; it was supported by the argument that the refusal of provisions would be in breach of the Concordat of Bologna which made no mention of the grounds now being invoked by the pope. But Innocent was not intimidated, and the Estrées' manoeuvre quickly became even more of a roadblock when it received the king's firm approval within less than a week of his being informed of it. It was *this* decision, which raised the stakes a notch higher, rather than papal intransigence over individuals present at the 1682 Assembly, that was to lead to virtually ten years of deadlock. At the time, such brinkmanship did not seem a fateful move, as both Rome and Versailles were engaged in continuing negotiations. Needless to say, it put the exercise of episcopal patronage by Louis XIV back under the microscope.[15]

The halt in the granting of bishops' provisions came at a time when royal nominations were, in fact, encountering few delays in Rome, and when the delays which did occur were mostly explicable in terms of the continuing problems with newly acquired dioceses like Saint-Omer or Perpignan, which in turn had a knock-on effect on a few connected nominations.[16] The often lengthy delays of the mid-1670s were by now a distant memory, and even

14 Maupeou was nominated on 3 July, Saint-Georges on 17 July. The assembly disbanded on 1 July.
15 Blet, *Assemblées du clergé et Louis XIV*, 410–20.
16 See p 34 above.

Innocent XI's discontent with the rapid transfers of reigning bishops to other dioceses did not lead to a repeat of those earlier go-slows. French bishops were still being granted their provisions up to July 1682. The last of Louis XIV's choices to obtain his provisions before the trap shut later that year, Charles-François de Salettes, bishop of Oloron, had been nominated in January 1682 and received his provisions a mere three months later, itself a good index of how quickly such matters could be resolved in normal circumstances. But Mathurin Savary, nominated to Sées in May 1682 and not a deputy to the 1682 Assembly, was less fortunate. His papers seem to have been prepared with all due diligence, and in normal circumstances he would probably have been confirmed without difficulty a few months later.[17] But by that point, the d'Estrées brothers had played their card, and the unfortunate Savary was made to wait almost ten years for his bulls. In the intervening decade only one exception was made, in 1687, but it was for a French cleric nominated by Louis XIV to the see of Quebec. What the pope probably did not know was that Louis had offered the abbé de Saint-Valier the choice between Quebec and a French diocese, Aire, and that he had opted for the former.[18]

Of course, some hint of the trouble to come over vacant dioceses had already been provided by the diocese at the centre of the *régale* affair. Pavillon's death in 1677 had come early enough during the conflict for his succession at Alet not to cause serious difficulty, and his successor Louis Alphonse de Valbelle, the polar opposite of everything Pavillon represented, was quickly nominated and confirmed by Rome.[19] But by the time Caulet of Pamiers died in August 1680, there was open conflict in his diocese between pro- and anti-*régale* forces, so that finding a willing successor to him was far less straightforward.[20] Moreover, Innocent XI's attempts at direct intervention in the affairs of the diocese and the succession there infuriated many within the French church, and also ensured a difficult transition.[21] A month after Caulet's death, the bishop of Lombez, Cosme Roger, formerly superior-general of the Cistercian Feuillants, was nominated his successor, but he turned down the offer no fewer than three times in a row before it was then put to another reigning bishop, Le Neboux de la Brousse of Saint-Pol-de-Léon in northern Brittany, who also

---

17 Nominated on 20 May 1682, his enquiry *de vita et moribus* was conducted on 3 June by Archbishop Harlay of Paris: ASV, PC 86, fos 354, 355–60. The interruption of papal consistories during the high summer probably did not help him either, since by the time consistories resumed the confrontation with d'Estrées was imminent.

18 BN, MS Fr 23498, fo 9, *Nouvelles Ecclésiastiques*, 3 Feb 1685. Sourches, i, 174, 20 Jan 1685. Saint-Valier belonged to the Grenoble parlementaire dynasty of La Croix de Chevrières which had produced a bishop of Grenoble under Henri IV.

19 ASV, PC 77, fo 281, letter of nomination, 24 Dec 1677. His bulls were dated 14 March 1678, but he was not consecrated until Aug 1680, suggesting that he was less than anxious to embark on residing in and governing Alet in person.

20 See J-M Vidal, *Jean Cerle et le schisme de la régale du diocèse de Pamiers 1680–91* (*Histoire des évêques de Pamiers*, vi) (Paris 1938), is the most detailed account of events in Pamiers after Caulet.

21 Blet, *Assemblées du clergé et Louis XIV*, 197.

rejected it.[22] The reasoning behind these royal choices is hard to pinpoint, since Roger was known as a preacher, and Neboux as an able administrator; perhaps, it was felt that a consecrated, experienced bishop would encounter fewer objections and, above all, that he would be able to move quickly into Pamiers and deal with the problems there.[23] It is also possible that other reigning bishops subsequently declined this poisoned chalice, since it was not until July 1681, almost a year after Caulet's death, that a candidate willing to accept Pamiers was finally found, François de Bourlemont, nephew of two recent archbishops whose Roman connections augured well for as smooth a succession as could be expected in Pamiers.[24] But with Innocent XI effectively supporting the Caulet camp and the 1682 Assembly criticising the pope for the manner of that support, Bourlemont's provisions were not forthcoming before the guillotine fell in September on the granting of provisions to French dioceses. And it is worth noting that in late 1682, it was, understandably, the Pamiers succession rather than the bulls for the Assembly members, Maupeou and Saint-Georges, which was the French priority in negotiations in Rome: Pamiers, after all, had caused the biggest problems to date and only a confirmed bishop seemed capable of resolving them.[25] But, as we shall see, subsequent royal choices over Pamiers were no more inspired, with one of them bedevilling relations with Rome to the extent of impeding the final resolution of the wider conflict.[26]

The Pamiers succession was untypical for its time which was, as already noted, characterised by the speedy delivery of papal confirmation to royal nominees. An important consequence was that only two other sees, Saint-Omer and Ypres, remained unfilled by mid-1682, and that was only because of the continuing absence of a papal indult enabling Louis XIV formally to nominate to those dioceses.[27] He had, of course, made his choice for Saint-Omer, but not Ypres, as long ago as 1677 in the person of the bishop of Tarbes,

22 AN, O¹ 24, fo 249v, *brevet de nomination* for Roger, 6 Sept 1680. ASV, Nunz Fr 163, fos 871, 942, Lauri to Cardinal Cibo, 11 Oct and 4 Nov 1680 respectively. Rancé, *Correspondance*, ii, 471–2, Rancé to Le Neboux de la Brousse, 18 Dec 1680; ASV, Nunz Fr 165, fo 32, Lauri to Cibo, 20 Jan 1681 (Le Neboux). Lauri thought in Jan 1681 that Pamiers might be offered to Léon Bacoué, a regular (Franciscan) like Roger, who was then bishop of Glandève in Provence. Four years later, in 1685, Pamiers would be given to Bacoué's intended coadjutor and successor at Glandèves, François de Camps, with whom Bacoué would take up residence in Pamiers once he had resigned Glandèves outright.

23 As the provincial intendant, Foucault, argued: *Correspondance des intendants avec le contrôleur-général des finances 1676–1689*, ed Annette Smedley-Weill, 3 vols (Paris 1989–91) ii, 333–5, letters to Colbert, *contrôleur-général*, 4 Sept 1680 and 19 Dec 1680.

24 ASV, Nunz Fr 166, fos 254, 306, Lauri to Cardinal Cibo, 254, 11 July and 22 Aug 1681 respectively. Lauri added that the recent marriage of Bourlemont's sister to a former *premier valet de chambre* of Louis XIV had also helped to secure the nomination to Pamiers.

25 Blet, *Assemblées du clergé et Louis XIV*, 379–82, 410–20. See also Vidal, *Jean Cerle, passim*, and *idem, Jean-Baptiste de Verthamon (1693–1735) Histoire des évêques de Pamiers*, vii (Toulouse 1945), 5.

26 See below, p 259 for the fate of François de Camps and his behaviour while in Pamiers.

27 See chapter 1 above.

Table 7.1   *Episcopal vacancies 1682–91*

Year	Death	Resign	Total	Vacancies
pre 1682	3	0	3	3
1682	5	0	5	5
1683	1	0	1	1
1684	4	2	6	6
1685	5	0	5	5
1686	0	0	0	0
1686	6	1	7	7
1688	2	0	2	2
1689	4	0	4	3
1690	2	0	2	2
1691	2	0	2	1
Total	34	3	37	35

Note. The discrepancy between the 'total' and 'vacancies' columns is explained by two coadjutors succeeding their predecessors in 1689 and 1691.

who was, however, destined to remain at Tarbes for another fifteen years.[28] But by the time the granting of provisions was actually suspended in September 1682, the number of vacant sees was beginning to rise again through the deaths and resignations of ruling bishops. The overall scale of this thinning of the ranks in subsequent years is summarily conveyed in the accompanying table (7.1), while the dioceses which were vacant by early 1692, when the suspension of provisions was finally lifted, can be identified in the related map. Moreover, given the vagueness that surrounds the actual numbers of deaths and of dioceses vacant in many accounts, it is important to put the record straight on this point. As the map indicates, thirty-five dioceses (just over one-quarter of the total) were without a bishop in January 1692, though the most recent vacancy had arisen as recently as a few days before Christmas 1691.[29] Moreover, the timescale of these developments deserves attention. As table 7.1 shows, the highest proportion of deaths and resignations occurred in 1682 and the years immediately after it, down to 1687, which between them accounted for two-thirds of the vacancies thereby created, despite extremely 'lean' years like 1683 and 1686. An important consequence of this pattern was that dioceses experiencing long vacancies of between five and ten years were in the majority. After 1687, resignations disappeared altogether

28   Anne-Tristan de La Baume de Suze remained active in his first diocese, Tarbes, through the late 1680s, despite his nomination to Saint-Omer and, in 1684, to Auch. Smedely-Weill, *Correspondance des contrôleurs-généraux*, ii, 269, 273, letters to Le Peletier, *contrôleur-général*, 11 July, 7 Nov 1688. No nomination seems to have been made to Ypres until 1689.

29   Hugues de Bar, bishop of Lectoure, died on 22 Dec 1691.

Legend:
- Vacant diocese
- Bishop transferred elsewhere

4   *Impact of crisis on French dioceses 1682–92*

while deaths of reigning bishops settled at comparatively low figures. It is impossible to know if episcopal resignations were, given their likely consequences, strongly discouraged during these years. The fact that there were only three in all would certainly suggest such discouragement, but the last recorded one, that of Jacques Séguier, bishop of Nîmes, in 1687, does raise some doubts on this point, as he was to all intents and purposes forced out because of his inability to deal with the local Huguenot population.[30] His may have been a special case, precisely because of the Huguenot problem, to which we shall return later. There is no doubt, however, that the papacy of Innocent XI continued to be exacting in its dealing with requests by bishops to retire.[31] Finally, the virtual disappearance of coadjutor-bishops since mid-century ensured that there would be little or no 'insurance' in the event of reigning bishops dying or retiring during this decade. Only two such cases actually occurred, at Arles and Rouen, where the death of two aged and incapacitated archbishops enabled their long-serving coadjutors to replace them in 1689 and 1691 respectively.[32] It is clear that with such low figures for coadjutorships and resignations, the pattern of episcopal mortality was the decisive factor during this decade.

II

The suspension of papal provisions should not lead us to imagine that there was also a corresponding interruption in royal nominations as dioceses became vacant. In this regard, it was unquestionably 'business as usual' for the king and his advisors, candidates and their patrons throughout the entire decade. The *Gazette*, the letter-writers (Sévigné, Huxelles) and the diarists (Dangeau, Sourches) as well as the *Nouvelles Ecclésiastiques* continued to record episcopal nominations in their habitual fashion, as if nothing was amiss. But the bare statistics of dioceses without confirmed bishops in 1692 give no real sense of the scale of ecclesiastical patronage in the intervening years. If anything, the overall volume of patronage was more substantial than usual, thanks to the growing numbers of dioceses vacant and subject to the *régale*, in which the king could provide to a range of attractive positions. Obscured, for understandable reasons, by the well known Franco-papal confrontations of these years, this business-as-usual attitude was based, especially in 1682 and imme-

---

30 BN, MS Fr 23498, fo 58r, *Nouvelles Ecclésiastiques*, 25 Jan 1686; fo 168v, 15 Feb 1687. His opposition to the Four Articles of 1682 was also cited as a reason, but that seems less likely.

31 ASV, Acta congregationis consistorialis, 1682, vol i, fos 127–32; vol ii, fos 142–3, for papers and enquiry into proposed resignation of Paul-Philippe de Chaumont-Quitry as bishop of Dax, 1681–2. He did not resign until mid-1684. Léon Bacoué, bishop of Glandèves in Provence, initially obtained the nomination of a coadjutor in 1682, but then resigned Glandève outright in 1684.

32 Jean-Baptiste d'Adhémar de Grignan had been coadjutor of Arles since 1667, and Jacques-Nicolas Colbert of Rouen since 1680.

diately afterwards, on the assumption that the stand-off with Rome over provisions was only temporary, all the more so as pope and king had agreed *not* to press their more important demands and grievances.[33] This point is not undermined by the fact that, with one exception, no nominations at all were made between those of Maupeou and Saint-Georges in July 1682 and late May 1684, when a total of eight were announced on one day. Harlay of Paris explained to the papal nuncio that a 'wait-and-see' policy over episcopal nominations was the reason for this extended hiatus, but that as Rome had not responded by confirming the king's existing nominees, that policy had now been abandoned. Harlay even hinted that the next Assembly of Clergy might take up the cause of those being unjustly denied their provisions by Rome.[34] A few weeks later, La Chaize confirmed this message, telling Nuncio Ranuzzi that the king had decided not to ask that any provisions be granted until the major disputes between France and Rome were settled.[35] For its part, whenever it was challenged to respond to French overtures, Rome habitually replied that it could only grant provisions to men of 'proper doctrine' – a thinly veiled reference to deputies of the 1682 Assembly.[36] The stalemate which had finally set in by 1684 would become much worse by 1687–8 when new clashes saw Franco-papal relations reach their nadir in the final years of Innocent's pontificate.[37]

Meanwhile, in France itself, the death of Colbert in 1683 ushered in a phase of Le Tellier domination of the ministry, and their robust anti-Jesuit and gallican sentiments, especially of the Archbishop of Reims, were no secret.[38] La Chaize, the royal confessor, firmly supported the king and his ministers in their dealings with Innocent XI. Deprived of Colbert's protection, Archbishop Harlay set about bolstering his position within his diocese and in the king's favour.[39] There was a new nuncio, Angelo Ranuzzi, from 1683 onwards, but during the next six years he rarely received visits from French prelates, scarcely ever mentioned or recommended new nominees to bishoprics, and was generally kept far removed from matters of ecclesiastical patronage. The French bishops as a whole took the king's side in the dispute with Rome, whatever they may have felt privately, while those holding pro-Roman views were

33 Blet, *Assemblées du clergé et Louis XIV*, 410, 420.
34 *Correspondance du nonce Ranuzzi*, i, no 768, Ranuzzi to Cardinal Cibo, 3 July 1684.
35 *Ibid*, no 785, Ranuzzi to Cibo, 17 July 1684.
36 *Ibid*, ii, no 2353, Casoni to Ranuzzi, 3 Dec 1686; no 2388, Ranuzzi to Casoni, 30 Dec 1686.
37 See Blet, *Assemblés du clergé et Louis XIV*, ch 15; Lossky, *Louis XIV and the French Monarchy*, 213–17; *Correspondance du nonce Ranuzzi*, i, esp 142–67.
38 Blet, *Assemblées du clergé et Louis XIV*, 352–60, 409, for a discussion of this point in the context of the authorship of the 1682 articles and declaration.
39 Le Gendre, *Mémoires*, 56ff. See also BN, MS Fr 23510, fo 61r, *Nouvelles Ecclésiastiques*, 22 Aug 1682; fos 64v–5r, 10 April 1683. On the death of Archbishop La Mothe-Houdancourt of Auch in 1684, Harlay also added the provisorship of the college of Navarre to that of the Sorbonne which he already held (fo 261, 25 March 1684; fos 265v–6r, 15 April 1684), thus strengthening his grip on the theology faculty.

understandably reticent to air them. The crown also ensured that its policy of refusing to put episcopal nominees forward for papal provisions was not undermined by individual initiatives. At one point, Rome seems to have virtually invited the great scholar, Daniel Huet, to seek his bulls for Soissons, implying that he only needed to ask for them and they would be despatched, but Huet confessed that he dared not step out of line.[40] It is likely that others in a similar position, especially those who were pro-Jesuit and pro-Roman, acted no differently. Every effort was also made to discourage the king's nominees who might become tired of waiting for their bulls from returning their *brevet de nomination*; it was not wholly successful, but its purpose was to deprive Rome of any hope of believing that delaying tactics would triumph over French patience.

It was in this admittedly unusual context that the business of making new bishops was conducted after 1682. As already noted, deaths and resignations led to thirty-four dioceses becoming effectively vacant by ten years later. In response to this, an estimated total of sixty-four nominations of all kinds were made to those thirty-four dioceses between late January 1682 (date of the last nomination to be approved by Rome before the suspension of later that year) and the end of 1691.[41] In addition, as we saw in the previous chapter, there are instances where it is impossible to know if an actual nomination or merely an offer of a diocese was made to an individual who then turned it down. What is not in doubt is that total nominations far outstripped the number of dioceses effectively available. Why the disproportion? It would be tempting to imagine that high mortality rates afflicted the king's nominees during these years, but this was not the case. On the contrary, only one of these men died before 1692, and he had already returned the *brevet* (for Poitiers) to the king in late 1685.[42] One of the key reasons, as will be evident from the breakdown of the figures in table 7.2, was the relatively high ratio of nominations of individuals to second and even third dioceses while still waiting for their provisions from Rome to their first see. Claude de Saint-Georges, whom we have already encountered, is the best example of this pattern. His initial nomination in 1682 was in fact not to Clermont, but to Mâcon, whose bishop initially accepted, but then turned down, a move to Clermont, which was then offered to Saint-Georges in July 1682.[43] Five years later, he was nominated to Tours, but he was still waiting for his provisions in 1693 when Lyon,

40 BN, MS Fr 23498, fo 236v, *Nouvelles Ecclésiastiques*, 30 Oct 1687, '. . . mais il ne le veut pas ou ne l'ose pas faire en seul. L'on veut que tous les nommés ayent leurs bulles en meme tems.'
41 The dioceses include Pamiers and Saint-Omer because, although both were vacant pre-1682, they continued to attract new nominations after 1682.
42 Sources, i, 372, April 1686, for nomination of a new bishop of Poitiers arising from abbé de Quincé's refusal of several months earlier.
43 AN, O¹ 26, fo 330v, nomination of Cassagnet of Mâcon to Clermont. BN, MS Fr 23510, fo 52r, *Nouvelles Ecclésiastiques*, 25 July 1682, 'Mgr de Mâcon enfin n'a point voulu de l'évêché de Clermont après y avoir envoyé des meubles et fait les adieux à Mâcon, il en a rendu le brevet. M de St Georges nommé à sa place à l'église de Clermont.'

Table 7.2   Episcopal nominations 1682–91

Year	1st nom	2nd nom	3rd + nom	Translation
pre-1682	1			1
1682	5	1		1
1683	0	0	0	0
1684	6	0	0	3
1685	7	1	0	2
1686	3	2	1	2
1687	8	1	2	3
1688	3			
1689	5	2		
1690	3			1
1691	1			
Total	42	7	3	12

where he had long been a canon of Saint-Jean, fell vacant. As a 'grand ami' of La Chaize, the confessor with close personal ties to Lyon, Saint-Georges had little reason to fear competition, and it was as archbishop of Lyon that he was finally confirmed by Innocent XII in October of that year.[44] He had thus been the recipient of *brevets de nomination* to four different dioceses but, as he only held the last of them, no trace of his successive nominations survive in the standard record of the episcopal successions of Mâcon, Clermont or Tours.[45] Saint-Georges may have been an extreme case, but seven nominees accepted a second diocese and three a third diocese during these same years. It took no fewer than six nominations between May 1684 and April 1686 to fill the Provençal sees of Grasse, Vence and Glandèves, even though there were only three individuals involved from beginning to end. Finally, it will be no surprise to learn that existing bishops were involved in episcopal patronage during these years – a total of eleven nominations affected nine of them.

No doubt, the suspension of papal provisions made it easier for such changes to be made and accepted by those involved, since they did not entail the crippling expense that papal provisions for a second or third diocese normally did. With no end to the crisis in sight, some of the nominations must have seemed far more provisional than normally to those involved, whether to the confessor or the nominees themselves, all of which left the door open to subsequent changes of diocese. Most of the nominations to second or third

---

44 Sourches, iv, 258, 13 Sept 1693 comments that Saint-Georges got Lyon 'comme on se l'étoit toujours imaginé'. Lyon had been among the dioceses not granted in the 'distribution des bénéfices' on 8 Sept, and Sources claimed then that 'on ne douta pas qu'il ne le gardât *in petto* pour quelque prélat de l'assemblée du clergé de 1682' (iv, 255).

45 *Hierarchia Catholica*, v, 161, 261, 395. Strictly speaking, the *Hierarchia* is not an official record, but its data are derived from the archives of the papal consistory.

dioceses were not as complex as those of Grasse, Vence and Glandèves, and they did not involve the exchange of sees. But the fact that nominations were by now mostly confined to a few feastdays per year and usually involved filling several dioceses, suggests that efforts were made to coordinate nominations but also to satisfy at least some of candidates with dioceses which were, as La Chaize put it to one of the lucky candidates, 'à leur bienséance'[46]. The exchange of Soissons and Avranches dioceses between Daniel Huet and Fabio Brûlart was another example of such *bienséance*, as contemporaries immediately noted.[47]

III

Yet it is hard to believe that the crown had no objectives during this period beyond the convenience or preferences of candidates for the mitre. This is not to argue that it was in any way 'systematic' in the kind of bishops it was seeking to promote, if only because its decision-making remained closely tied to patronage considerations of a familiar kind. Certainly, considering the care it had devoted at the time to ensuring the election of deputies in 1682 who would support it against Innocent XI, it would be surprising if it did not reward some of them in subsequent years. But it would also be misguided to imagine that the services rendered by the deputies then were a guarantee of promotion in subsequent years, or that Louis and his advisors were bent on packing the episcopate with them. Out of the thirty-six 'second-order' deputies of the 1682 Assembly, ten were nominated to vacant dioceses over the following decade, while the remaining three waited until well after 1692 before entering the episcopate.[48] None of the many assemblies of clergy held under Louis XIV came remotely close to this score. On the other hand, of the twenty-seven 'ordinary' bishops attending the Assembly only five were transferred to another diocese during the same years, a figure that has to be seen in context, since the overall total of such transfers was itself relatively low.[49] By definition, all of the deputies singled out for nomination or promotion had signed the Four Articles in 1682 and were thus *personae non gratae* in Rome; and in the climate of Franco-Roman hostilities during the 1680s, the more of them who secured such preferment, the more likely Rome was to see the crown's use of episcopal patronage as adversarial.

---

46   AN, 109 AP 14, no 125, La Chaize to Gourgues of Bazas, 31 May 1684.
47   Sourches, iii, 170, 1 Nov 1689. Huet was from Caen, so Avranches was virtually his *pays natal*, while Soissons suited Brûlart since it was half-way between Paris and the family château of Sillery.
48   This figure includes François de Camps, who never received papal confirmation, but not Pierre-François de Beauvau, future bishop of Sarlat, who was initially elected by the province of Tours, but was too ill to attend the Assembly.
49   The total number of transfers was twelve, but only nine of them took effect.

At the same time, during the 1680s, the crown was almost certainly looking to replace 'difficult' bishops by more tractable successors: essentially, this meant replacing those held to be of Jansenist and rigorist sympathies with men who were closer to the Jesuits. By the early to mid-1680s, La Chaize was sufficiently dominant in selecting bishops for this to be possible, though he could not expect to win on every occasion. His attempt to promote a well-known protégé of his, Le Goux de la Berchère, bishop of Lavaur since 1678, to the politically important archiepiscopal see of Aix in 1685 soon came unstuck. Aix had long been governed by the rigorist and out-of-favour Cardinal Grimaldi, but by 1687, the move was judged to have been 'premature', and Le Goux was transferred to Albi instead; his ultimate reward would come years later when he succeeded Cardinal Bonsi at Narbonne.[50] In 1687, Aix went instead to another reigning bishop of long standing, Daniel de Cosnac of Valence, a former favourite of Gaston d'Orléans and not the most reputable prelate of his age. His own immediate reaction was to regard this 'promotion' as a disgrace, since he had Albi, richer and less troublesome than Aix, in his sights, but the king clearly judged him as possessing both the will and the political skills to dominate the Estates of Provence.[51] Two other dioceses of major importance were Sens and Tournai, whose previous incumbents, Gondrin and Choiseul, had both been regarded as Jansenists: both were succeeded by non-Jansenist rather than overtly anti-Jansenist candidates.

For all their importance, these individual cases should not lead one to imagine that the 1680s were years in which the Jansenist issue was of central importance in the choosing of bishops. The Peace of the Church may have broken down in or after 1679, but it did not immediately give rise to 'war' on all fronts. If there was a major issue by then, it was increasingly the Huguenot one. Needless to say, dealing with it in an age of *dragonnades* was not the exclusive domain of French bishops, but the crown's policy of forcible conversion of Protestants and their incorporation into the Catholic church thereafter could hardly work without the full cooperation of the episcopate; as the years passed and the initial results proved unsatisfactory, the crown even sought to moderate the methods employed by the intendants and to increase the role of bishops and clergy.[52] To find itself with an episcopate that was depleting from year to year was not an ideal situation to be in before or after the Revocation of 1685. And there was no predicting which dioceses would be visited by the death of their bishops, as a look at map no 6 shows. In northern and central France, Vannes, Saint-Omer or Toul had relatively few Protestants, but Sées and Chartres had substantial Protestant populations. It was, of course, in the great crescent running southwards and eastwards from

50 Sourches, ii, 6–7, 8 Jan 1687. Cosnac, *Mémoires*, ii, 126–7.
51 Cosnac, *Mémoires*, 123–8. In his account of his audience with Louis XIV, Cosnac states that Louis himself admitted that Le Goux had been unable to get on with the Provençaux, and that there was already 'beaucoup de désunion', which he implied it would be for Cosnac to repair.
52 Pérouas, *La Rochelle*, 336–7, citing Foucault, *Mémoires*, 161–70, 209.

La Rochelle to Grenoble that these populations were at their most numerous and recalcitrant. As we saw earlier, one response to these problems was the decision, taken in the late 1680s, to create two new dioceses, Blois and Alès, and to separate those of Valence and Die which had long been held as one. But as responses to the Protestant problem these decisions were limited in scope and something of an afterthought.

On the other hand, as the conversion crusades reached their pinnacle during the 1680s, no fewer than twenty southern dioceses stretching from Bayonne to Gap and Riez would fall vacant. The identity of those nominated to them is likely to be a better indicator of the crown's understanding of the kind of bishops that such dioceses needed at this juncture. Three of these dioceses were archbishoprics – Toulouse, Auch and Albi – and as was to be expected, there was no change in the king's long established habit of promoting reliable sitting bishops. In any case, Auch and Toulouse did not have large Huguenot populations, while Albi, which had rather more of them, was given in 1687 to Le Goux de la Berchère of Lavaur when his promotion to Aix fell through. But the picture for the dioceses in the Huguenot heartlands which fell vacant in these years – Gap, Nîmes, Viviers, Die, Montauban – is quite different. Each one was given to a nominee with experience, sometimes extensive, of preaching or of missions to the Huguenots – or both. The largest of the missions of the 1680s were organised by the crown itself, so that those who participated in them were closely observed by the confessor and royal ministers. Foucault, the intendant of Béarn in the mid-1680s, claims that it was he who sang the praises of Bernard Abbadie to Archbishop Harlay and La Chaize, which earned him the nomination to Dax in 1690.[53] We can assume that Basville, the intendant of Languedoc, who was even closer to La Chaize than was Foucault, and in whose bailiwick many of the dioceses most involved in the Huguenot affair were located, acted in a similar manner. Easing the elderly Jacques Séguier out of Nîmes, whose Protestant population was among the most intractable of the region, was regarded as an indispensable prelude to serious action there, though Séguier took a long time to comply. When he finally did so, in 1687, Nîmes was given to the prominent preacher, Fléchier, already nominated to succeed Le Goux at Lavaur in 1685, but on condition that he agreed to the creation of a new diocese of Alès within that of Nîmes, whose elongated shape and difficult terrain were regarded as major obstacles to tackling the Huguenot population there.[54] Commenting on Fléchier's nomination, the court diarist Sourches tersely wrote that he 'was not seen as one of those with ambitions of becoming a bishop'.[55] And the nominee for Alès was a much more experienced missionary, Chevalier de Saulx, who might not otherwise have attracted the

---

53 Foucault, *Mémoires*, 117.
54 Fléchier had some experience of dealing with the Huguenots, having accompanied the duc de Chaulnes to Brittany for that purpose in 1685, when the royal missions were launched: Sourches, i, 321, Oct 1685.
55 Sourches, i, 327, Nov 1685, 'on ne le comptoit pas parmi ceux qui prétendoient à être évêques'.

attention of the court.[56] It is interesting to note that when dioceses elsewhere in France with substantial Huguenot populations fell vacant during the 1680s, the crown tended to view the succession in much the same way. The vast diocese of Poitiers was a huge challenge, so it was given in 1685 to a reigning bishop with a high reputation as a preacher, Bishop Baglion of Tréguier in Brittany.[57] A few years later, when plans were made to divide the equally sprawling diocese of Chartres in order to create a diocese of Blois, the choice for the first bishop of Blois, David-Nicolas de Bertier, was known for his long involvement with Huguenot converts. By the mid-1680s, Louis XIV even seemed willing to let it be known that he would in future choose his bishops from those who had that kind of experience. According to one source, the king became exasperated by his confessor's behaviour in choosing a successor to Baglion for Tréguier in 1686. La Chaize's 'sin' was, apparently, to suggest a string of 'abbés de qualité', and in the end he found himself being harangued by the king in terms that were directed to all potential candidates for the mitre. 'Tell all those young *abbés* that they would do far better to go and reside in their benefices, conduct missions, and instruct the poor rather than to stay here [at court], and that I shall remember them all the better for not seeing them. I have a very good memory'.[58]

Without minimising the king's evident intentions at this juncture, we should not expect a sudden or systematic change in the familiar patterns of episcopal patronage: these were not about to disappear just because of the Huguenot problem. The elderly bishop of La Rochelle made more than one attempt to secure a coadjutor who was *not* a family member during these years, doubtless because he felt unable to deal with the Huguenots in his large diocese; he even suggested the names of men whose reputations would soar in later years – Godet des Marais and Fénelon – but his appeals fell on deaf ears.[59] Sées, whose bishops had always had problems with their Protestant population, was given in 1682 to a royal almoner with little administrative or pastoral experience in a classic piece of court intrigue.[60] Two southern

---

56   BN, MS Fr 23498, fo 213r, *Nouvelles Ecclésiastiques*, 25 Aug 1687, Chevalier de Saulx was nominated 'à cause des témoignages que l'on a rendu en Poitou de sa capacité pour les conversions. Il est docteur de Sorbonne et homme de condition.'

57   He moved to reside in Poitiers by 1688 at the latest, according to the provincial intendant, Foucault, *Mémoires*, 220, 224.

58   BN, MS Fr 23498, fo 95, *Nouvelles Ecclésiastiques*, 20 April 1686, 'dites à tous ces jeunes abbés qu'ils fairont mieux d'aler à leurs bénéfices faire des missions et instruire les pauvres que d'estre icy, et que je me souviendray plutot d'eux en ne les voyant qu'en les voyant. J'ay très bonne mémoire.' The chronicler adds that La Chaize, mortified by the king's outburst, 'y a fait de profondes réflexions'.

59   BN, MS Fr 23510, fo 71v, *Nouvelles Ecclésiastiques*, 15 May 1683, for mention of Godet and an abbé de Saint-Luc d'Espinay; MS Fr 23498, fo 252r, 7 Dec 1687, for refusal of coadjutorship for Fénelon, possibly because of negative reports on his approach to dealing with Huguenots while serving in the area in previous years. On this point, see also Fénelon, *Correspondance*, i, 165–7.

60   BN, MS Fr 23510, fo 30, *Nouvelles Ecclésiastiques*, for a detailed account of an intrigue in which

dioceses were given to *agents-généraux* of the French clergy at the end of their term in 1685, although the dioceses they received, Riez and Aire, were neither prominent nor home to large numbers of Huguenots. Nor had those nominated to similar dioceses with a similar profile – Bazas, Grasse, Sarlat – previously been known for the kind of preaching or missions to the Huguenots which would have brought them to the notice of the king and his advisors. Their understanding of how important a factor this qualification should be in deciding whom to nominate to a particular diocese was obviously variable, and we can only make a rough guess in several instances. It might be thought that it was not infallible in every case – after all, Valence, with its large Huguenot population, was given in 1691 to Bochart de Champigny, whose experience of such problems was virtually nil, while Lodève was given to a similarly inexperienced member of the Phélypeaux ministerial dynasty a few years earlier. Moreover, preachers or missionaries, however renowned, did not necessarily transmute into capable bishops once given the opportunity, as the experience of Fléchier at Nîmes was to demonstrate.[61]

Such a realisation still lay in the future during the 1680s, when the problem was of a different order. Even supposing that vacant dioceses and royal nominees were a perfect 'fit', what purpose did that serve if the papacy would not confirm the king's choices and allow them to govern their dioceses as consecrated bishops? Why nominate at all when there was no solution in sight? As we saw above, for almost two years after mid-1682 no nominations were made, but that interlude ended in May 1684. It was during this period, when the drive to convert the Huguenots was still gathering momentum, that one of the most significant developments of the decade took shape. As early as July 1683, the *Nouvelles Ecclésiastiques* reported a strong rumour that those nominated to vacant dioceses had been instructed to 'go and stay' ('aller demeurer') rather than formally 'reside' there, which would mean they could not be regarded as 'intruders engaged in governing dioceses without being either elected, confirmed or consecrated by the church'. The author concluded that this rumour was a manoeuvre designed to secure papal provisions for the king's nominees.[62] If it was, it clearly failed in that purpose, but the idea itself was not allowed to vanish for all that. It is not possible to pinpoint exactly when it ceased to be merely an idea and began to be translated into action.

clients of Colbert and Mme the Guise, Louis XIV's cousin, were eased out of the competition for Sées by inviting Marie-Thérèse, the queen, to press for it to be given to Mathieu Savary, one of her long-serving almoners. Sourches, i, 107, does not allude to the circumstances of Savary's promotion.

61 Sauzet, *Réforme et Contre-Réforme*, 416–17.
62 BN, MS Fr 23498, fo 92, *Nouvelles Ecclésiastiques*, 3 July 1683, 'le bruit est grand que ceux qui sont nommés aux évêchés à qui Rome refuse des bulles ont ordre d'y aller demeurer plustot que resider car ne seroint ils point intrus de ne se mesler par quelque detour que ce fût du gouvernement de l'église sans y estre ni elu ni confirmé ni sacré par l'église. Mais il y a apparence que cette nouvelle ne se répand que pour faciliter les bulles indistinctement de tous les nommés.'

It was a potentially explosive step to take, as church tradition was frankly hostile to unconfirmed or unconsecrated bishops becoming involved in governing their future dioceses – they were regarded as 'intruders', as the *Nouvelles Ecclésiastiques* and others recognised. But a way was duly found to enable this objection to be overcome. During a vacancy, a diocese was normally governed by vicars-general elected by the cathedral chapter which, as the bishop's 'church', took his place until a confirmed successor arrived.[63] The solution to the 'intrusion' problem was to ensure that the king's episcopal nominee would be one of the vicars-capitular, as they were called, chosen by the chapter to govern the vacant diocese. No innovation or institutional subversion was involved: instead of the usual two vicars-capitular, there would now be three. It is likely that measures along these lines were gradually introduced during late 1683 and 1684. Of course, they could only work if cathedral chapters were prepared to cooperate with the crown, and it seems that the provincial intendants were regularly employed for that purpose. As far as is known, all of those asked to do so complied, but only local studies of the dioceses concerned could establish how willingly they did so and with what results. At any rate, by October 1684 at the latest, a relatively ingenious but simple 'system' was firmly in place, one which by then even enabled reigning bishops whom the king had nominated to a new diocese to operate as vicars-capitular in their new dioceses. Le Camus of Grenoble described how it worked to Innocent XI's confidant, Casoni:

> The (reigning) bishops are despatched to the diocese to which they have been transferred, and carry out their functions there without having their provisions, thanks to the cathedral chapter which appoints them as vicars-general *sede vacante*. They leave behind their dioceses where they appoint as their vicars-general the *abbés* who have been nominated to be their (next) bishop. The bishop transferred to another see collects its revenues because the king makes him a gift 'en régale' of its temporalities, while the nominated *abbé* collects those of the other diocese 'en régale' because the transferred bishop cedes them to him. This is how they hope to overcome the absence of bulls. It looks like a case of intrusion because, after all, a consecrated bishop should not desert his spouse to go and serve in another church.[64]

For all his disapproval of his mitred colleagues' behaviour, Le Camus was describing a mechanism which seemed to be in place by 1684. There was no general outcry against it from within the French church, contrary to the impression given by anti-gallican historians of subsequent generations, and

---

63   Only two dioceses in France, Lyon and Autun, did not follow this general rule. By ancient custom, if Lyon was vacant, it was administered by the bishop of Autun – and vice versa.

64   Quoted in *Correspondance du nonce Ranuzzi*, i, 91–2, letter of 11 Oct 1684.

contemporaries did not hesitate to call the king's nominees 'Monseigneur' or 'Monsieur l'évêque de . . .'. Nicknamed 'black bishops', since they could only wear the normal black clerical garb and not that reserved for consecrated bishops, they were reported as referring to 'our diocese' or 'our episcopal palace' in their administrative acts.[65] Equally significant was the fact that the 1685 Assembly of clergy received Saint-Georges and another *évêque nommé* as deputies enjoying episcopal rank, while the 'small' Assembly of 1690 was dominated by a combination of such *évêques nommés* and reigning bishops transferred to new dioceses, but still awaiting their provisions.[66] In some parts of France, reigning bishops, doubtless unhappy at the prospect of being overlooked as potential deputies to the assemblies themselves, seem to have tried to prevent such elections, which led one *évêque nommé* to write to another to protest that 'it would be unjust for the consecrated bishops to add to the misfortune of the delay of our provisions from Rome by depriving us of the honours of the episcopate which His Majesty has agreed that we should enjoy'.[67] However, in the current state of research, it is impossible to say if all, or even most, of these new or 'transferring' bishops behaved exactly as Le Camus suggested. Needless to say, the crown encouraged them to reside in those dioceses where they were entitled to play an important role in the provincial estates; all the signs are that they did so, presiding over the estates and participating in local administration.[68] In Provence, one of the most important of the remaining *pays d'états*, the presidency of the Assembly of the Communities was awarded to the unconfirmed archbishop of Aix, Daniel de Cosnac, over the long-serving archbishop of Arles.[69] But political considerations might also militate against some bishops moving to their new dioceses: La Baume de Suze, nominated to Saint-Omer in 1677 and to Auch in 1684, does not appear to have set foot in either diocese during this period, but to have remained in his first one, Tarbes, where he continued to preside over the Estates of Bigorre.[70]

If there was a general problem with the new dispensation, it was probably about the extent to which the cathedral chapters were willing to allow one of their vicars-capitular, the *évêque nommé*, effectively to govern the diocese and in doing so reduce his fellow vicars to purely supporting roles. There are

---

65 BN, MS Fr 23501, fo 147, *Nouvelles Ecclésiastiques*, Nov 1691.

66 Blet, *Assemblées du clergé et Louis XIV*, 447–50 (1685), 506–9 (1690).

67 AN, 109 AP 14, no 248, François de Poudenx, *évêque nommé* of Tarbes, to Jean-Jacques de Gourgues, *évêque nommé* of Bazas, 4 July (no year given).

68 Pamiers, whose bishop presided over the estates of Foix, is a good example. The *évêque nommé*, François de Camps, corresponded assiduously with the *contrôleur-général* during the late 1680s and also figures frequently in the correspondence of the intendant: Smedley-Weill, *Correspondance des intendants*, ii, 366, 368–76.

69 BN, MS Fr 23498, fo 153v, *Nouvelles Ecclésiastiques*, 21 Dec 1686. Smedley-Weill, *Correspondance des intendants*, ii, 451ff, for numerous references to Cosnac's activity in the Assembly of the Communities of Provence.

70 Smedley-Weill, *Correspondance des intendants*, ii, 310 (1684), 268, 273, 367 (1688).

indications that some *évêques nommés* went too far for the chapter's liking in their new role. Mathurin Savary of Sées did so, offended the local clergy, and soon found himself so isolated that he retreated altogether to Paris to wait for his papal provisions.[71] In some dioceses, the crown almost certainly intervened to ensure the *évêque nommé* had full powers to govern unhindered, but that probably depended to some extent on local circumstances. We know that the diocese of Nîmes was visited intensively in the late 1680s by its *évêque nommé*, Fléchier, and by the vicar-general who was already earmarked as bishop of the new diocese of Alès, Chevalier de Saulx. It is likely that similar activity occurred in other dioceses, especially those with Protestant populations, but in others too, like Saint-Omer and Toul.[72] At Sens, which fell vacant in 1685, the king and his advisers were keen to see the consequences of the two previous episcopates (Jansenism and neglect respectively) tackled without delay, and nominated Bishop Fortin of Poitiers as the new archbishop. The Sens chapter had already elected its four vicars-capitular, and initially refused to revoke them so that Fortin could be the sole vicar-capitular. However, the threat of *lettres de cachet* was sufficient to make them change their mind, and to give Fortin the powers which king and confessor felt he needed.[73] But the reticence may also have been on the other side – the *évêque nommé* may, in some cases at least, have been unwilling to assume the primary responsibility for running a diocese while still without his provisions, even though the cathedral chapter was either willing or anxious for this to happen.

Needless to say, the ensuing variations in behaviour and attitudes were considerable, so it may be worth briefly looking at the experiences of an 'ordinary' diocese during these years. Jean-Jacques de Gourgues, son of a Bordeaux *parlementaire* family which boasted provincial intendants, was among the first batch of bishops nominated in May 1684. News of his nomination to Bazas, a diocese near Bordeaux which did have some Huguenots communities, was conveyed to him on the day itself by La Chaize, who had accompanied Louis XIV on the Luxemburg military campaign that spring. Addressing Gourgues as 'Monseigneur', the confessor wrote:

> at last, the king, convinced of your merit, has nominated you to Bazas. You know there is a lot of work to be done there, and that is why a workman of your strength was required. For the king to have placed you in a diocese that is so convenient for you, he must have for your person the kind of

---

71   H Fisquet, *La France pontificale, Sées* (Aix-en-Provence 1866), 71–3. According to Fisquet, the Sées chapter took offence, it seems, at a *mandement* published by Savary as if he enjoyed full episcopal powers. His absence from Sées seems to be confirmed by the pastoral visitation records, which were conducted by local officials or clergy until 1693, when Savary himself became involved in them: *Répertoire des visites pastorales de la France (anciens diocèses)*, iv, 254–5.

72   For evidence of the new bishops' conduct of visitations in their dioceses in the late 1680s, see *Répertoire des visites pastorales*, iv, 187 (Saint-Omer), 434 (Toul).

73   BM Sens, MS 77, p 1181. BN, MS Fr 23498, fo 136v, *Nouvelles Ecclésiastiques*, 2 Nov 1686.

regard that you deserve. I cannot express to you my joy at seeing you in this employment.[74]

It was understood, if never actually mentioned, that Gourgues would make his way to Bazas and become one its vicars-capitular, which he did without delay.[75] But unsure of how to deal with the chapter, he asked Augustin de Maupeou, whose nomination to Castres in 1682 had been instrumental in triggering the refusal of papal provisions, to advise him in the light of his own experience at Castres. Maupeou's reply provides both specific and general insight into the problems faced by the *évêques nommés* of these years. When he arrived in Castres, the chapter promptly removed jurisdiction from its three vicars-capitular, and asked him to govern the diocese alone. Maupeou turned down this offer, he told Gourgues, and asked for the restoration of the vicars on condition that they should do nothing without consulting him first, 'not because I wanted to limit their powers, but in order to benefit from their lights as to the nature of the diocese'. The chapter agreed to restore the vicars, provided they obeyed Maupeou while he was in Castres and confined themselves to routine matters when he was in Paris. In this way, Maupeou continued, he would be master of the diocese's business and would also 'oblige' the vicars-capitular who were all 'people of some consideration'. Beyond that, in ceremonial matters, the chapter treated him as if he was a consecrated bishop, 'so that the only problem I had was to protect myself against their civilities, with which they overwhelmed me'.[76] Precisely what Gourgue did with this advice we do not know, but incoming letters over the next few years show clearly that he was resident in Bazas, and treated as 'Monseigneur de Bazas' by his correspondents, ministerial and otherwise. He engaged in extensive and detailed correspondence with the provincial intendant and the secretary of state, Châteauneuf, as he attempted to rebuild churches, ban the *courses des taureaux*, and so on.[77] The Huguenot problem also demanded attention, as Gourgue discovered in late 1685 when Châteauneuf, replying to his request to spend some time in Paris because of a lawsuit involving family matters, explained the king would not like to see a bishop petitioning to leave his diocese at this juncture, only weeks after the Revocation, since he desired that bishops reside in them in order to instruct the 'new' Catholics in their religion.[78] Clearly, the crown's 'business-as-usual' approach to episcopal patronage was meant to be adopted by its *évêques nommés* in their dioceses, regardless of when their provisions might arrive from Rome.

---

74   AN, 109 AP 14, no 125, letter of 31 May 1684, from Valenciennes.
75   *Ibid*, no 108, Bishop of Aire to Gourgues, 17 Sept 1684, apologising for his slowness in writing to welcome him to the province of Bordeaux to which they both belonged.
76   *Ibid*, no 194, letter of 23 Aug (1684?).
77   *Ibid*, nos 19–39, twenty-one letters from Bazin, the intendant, and nos 60–74, fifteen letters from Châteauneuf, the secretary of state.
78   *Ibid*, no 61, letter of 1 Dec 1685.

IV

Gourgues would have to wait over nine years in all until October 1693 before being confirmed by Rome as bishop of Bazas, his first and only diocese. It is unnecessary here to examine the detail of the tortuous negotiations which led to this long-delayed outcome – it has been done with exemplary thorough-ness and clarity by Pierre Blet. But a number of questions deserve attention for the light they throw upon the predicament of the French episcopate during these years, and the nature of the final dénouement. To begin with, Gourgues was only one of many 1682 Assembly deputies who, having signed the Four Articles, was made to wait almost two years longer than many of those who had not attended the before receiving his provisions. The French refusal to seek provisions for *any* royal nominee had the effect of lumping all royal nom-inees together, thereby protecting those present at the 1682 Assembly from reprisals from Rome, but that held only until the granting of provisions resumed. In any case, for as long as Innocent XI lived, the prospects of a nego-tiated solution were slim. Each time overtures were made, by La Chaize or others, about episcopal provisions, the reply was the same: the *régale* must be withdrawn. Not even the Revocation of the Edict of Nantes could induce a change of heart.[79] La Chaize's suggestion, made in late 1686, that the 1682 deputies nominated to bishoprics might sign a declaration of satisfaction to the pope was promptly rejected on the grounds that there was no room for compromise on matters of doctrine.[80] In one particularly heated discussion in 1687, according to the *Nouvelles Ecclésiastiques*, the nuncio's complaints about dioceses being governed by vicars-general without bulls were met by the retort that France would not tolerate being treated like the Portuguese, who had been left for decades without bishops, and that in extreme necessity there was no reason why bishops could not be consecrated without papal bulls.[81] By 1688, relations with Rome worsened so badly that the prospect of papal censures against the king seemed imminent, which in turn triggered the pre-cautionary appeal by the *avocat-général* of the Paris parlement to a future general council of the church – a potentially provocative tactic condemned by a long series of papal decrees since the fifteenth century.[82] Needless to say, France's bishops were not consulted about this move, but Archbishop Harlay was ordered to convene an ad hoc assembly in late September 1688 to inform

79 *Correspondance du nonce Ranuzzi*, i, no 1517, Ranuzzi to Cibo, 10 Nov 1685, no 1739, Cibo to Ranuzzi, 15 Jan 1586.

80 *Ibid*, i, no 2313, Ranuzzi to Cardinal Cibo, 11 Nov 1686; no 2353, Casoni to Ranuzzi, 3 Dec 1686; no 2388, Ranuzzi to Casoni, 30 Dec 1686.

81 BN, MS Fr 23498, fo 213v, *Nouvelles Ecclésiastiques*, 25 Aug 1687. The reference to the Por-tuguese here concerns the dioceses left vacant between the revolt of 1640 against the Spanish monarchy and the confirmation of Portuguese independence in 1668.

82 For the background to this, see *Correspondance du nonce Ranuzzi*, i, 142–54 (editor's introduc-tion); Blet, *Assemblées du clergé et Louis XIV*, 487–8; Jean Orcibal, *Louis XIV contre Innocent XI. Les appels au future concile de 1688 et l'opinion française* (Paris 1949).

those present of what had already been done. On a strict interpretation of events, they laid themselves open to the censures against such appeals ordained by Pius II and his successors in the wake of the great schism and conciliar crisis of the early fifteenth century. Of the twenty-six prelates present at that Assembly, two were bishops who had been nominated to new dioceses since 1682, and six were *évêques nommés*, four of whom had also attended the 1682 Assembly. The bitter recriminations generated by this gesture included threats that France would renounce the Concordat of Bologna and that its bishops would be elected, confirmed and consecrated under the terms of the Pragmatic Sanction of 1439. This threat was no more than a stick with which to beat the pope, since the king and his advisers knew, but could not openly admit it, that the crown's prerogatives concerning church patronage were far more solidly based under the concordat than under any available alternative.[83] In any case, less than a year later, Innocent XI was dead, having refrained, despite the bitter recriminations on all sides, from taking any concrete action that would have made a negotiated solution impossible.[84]

It was not until Alexander VIII succeeded as pope in October 1689 that negotiations for an end to the deadlock could really begin.[85] With both sides willing to leave the question of the *régale* until later, the main issue was the provision of the vacant dioceses, which in turn depended on a declaration of satisfaction to the pope signed by the incoming bishops who had participated in the 1682 Assembly. But none of the successive drafts prepared and negotiated line-by-line in Versailles and Rome went far enough to satisfy Alexander who on his deathbed, in late January 1691, actually quashed the decisions of the 1682 Assembly – a futile gesture indeed. His successor Innocent XII was not elected until July 1691, but negotiations resumed immediately. Within two months it seemed that an agreement was secured, but high-level opposition in Rome insisted on not making concessions to France without simultaneously demanding satisfaction over the *régale*. The ensuing deadlock was only broken in late November–December 1691 when Louis XIV finally allowed the *évêques nommés* who had *not* been at the 1682 Assembly to seek their provisions, and in doing so overrode opposition from his own advisers who now feared for the fate of the 1682 deputies. Rome had no objections to this, on the contrary, but Innocent XII also faced continuing opposition within the curia, especially to the effect that some of the *évêques nommés* of the southern dioceses must, in administering their dioceses, have actually consented to an extension of the *régale*. Yet he agreed to take up the unexpected

83   Orcibal, *Louis XIV contre Innocent XI*, esp 13–47. Grès-Gayer, *Gallicanisme de Sorbonne*, 314–16.
84   *Correspondance du nonce Ranuzzi*, i, 123 (editor's introduction).
85   Towards the end of Innocent XI's reign, there were signs of a less intransigent attitude in Rome: the pope would prefer that the king replaced those deputies to the 1682 Assembly with different nominees, but that if that was not forthcoming, then he would be willing to envisage some form of 'reparation'.

lead provided by Louis XIV. After years of stalemate, intense activity over provisions now followed. The enquiries *de vita et moribus* into the king's nominees conducted immediately after their nomination being long out of date, new ones had to be hastily organised in either Paris or Rome.[86] With Innocent XII's election, the nuncio, Niccolini, reported repeated visits from the king's nominees, clearly hoping a change of climate would benefit them at last, but also confessing to knowing as little about what was happening as the nuncio himself.[87] In September 1691, the *agents-généraux* of the French clergy wrote to alert them to be prepared to seek their provisions, and in particular to ensure that the *banquiers expéditionnaires*, who handled the administrative and financial business of obtaining provisions, should have received the monies needed to pay for papal bulls. Despite this, not all were ready when the granting of provisions resumed in early 1692. When Cardinal Forbin-Janson, who was French ambassador and was entrusted with handling the matter, summoned the *banquiers* to report to him, some of them claimed that individual candidates for whom they were agents had not sent the funds needed, and had even instructed them *not* to proceed unless they could obtain a partial or total remission of the normal cost of bulls.[88] This egregious as well as familiar manifestation of business-as-usual partly explains why Forbin-Janson picked particular individuals to propose in consistory first, leaving the unready or undecided to wait their turn. Nevertheless, the process of repopulating France's dioceses began with the preliminary 'proposal' of the first four bishops in consistory on 2 January 1692. As Blet has shown, a pattern was established for the next few months – four candidates would be put forward on each occasion, two for northern dioceses where the *régale* had always existed, two for southern dioceses where it had not. By May 1692, the last of the king's twenty nominees who had *not* attended the 1682 or 1688 assemblies had been granted their provisions.[89]

For all the objections from within the Roman curia – some motivated by the fear that the pope's current policy effectively disowned those who had fought against the *régale* under his predecessors – this was the quicker as well as the easier part of the operation. It remained to deal with those who had attended the 1688 and the 1682 Assemblies, the membership of which only slightly overlapped. The greater of the two 'offences' from Rome's point of view was, undoubtedly, membership of the earlier assembly. So it was decided

---

86　ASV, PC 86. The huge volume consists exclusively of enquiries *de vita et moribus* of the French bishops confirmed in 1692–3, with the original papers and enquiries alongside those conducted in Rome in 1692–3.

87　ASV, Nunz Fr 180, fos 344, 352–3, Niccolini to Cardinal Spada, secretary of state, 24 Sept 1691; fos 517–18, same to same, 12 Nov 1691.

88　Aix, Bibliothèque Méjanes, MS 625, pp 461–2, 463, 465, 467, 475, memoranda and declarations, mostly addressed to Cardinal Forbin, Jan–Feb 1692. News of this lack of preparedness circulated and was picked up the *Nouvelles Ecclésiastiques*: BN, MS Fr 23502, fo 29, Feb 1692.

89　Blet, *Assemblées du clergé et Louis XIV*, 540–5.

by Cardinal Forbin-Janson to propose the 1688 Assembly members first, as being less likely to cause trouble. He had, after all, been present there himself, and Alexander VIII had made him a cardinal since then – a powerful argument that he readily used to counter those who tried to prove that those present at the meeting had actively 'adhered' to the appeal rather than, as they themselves and Forbin-Janson asserted, being merely informed of something that had already taken place. However, Innocent XII was not completely satisfied by Forbin-Janson's logic, and suspended the confirmations in consistory until he could investigate what those involved had done – or thought they had done – at the 1688 Assembly. The nuncio was instructed to interview the nominees concerned and report on their behaviour and attitudes; they all replied, not without some evasiveness, to the effect that they had merely 'applauded the king's zeal' on that occasion.[90] Needless to say, this took several months and it was not until October 1692 before the obstacles to the promotion of a further four *évêques nommés* were finally lifted.[91]

There only remained the most difficult problem of all, one which had been set aside nearly a year earlier – that of the deputies to the 1682 Assembly, five of them already consecrated bishops seeking provisions for their new dioceses, and twelve first-time *évêques nommés*. As we saw, the precise wording of the formula of satisfaction which they would have to sign before obtaining their provisions had defeated diplomats and advisers alike during 1691, and work on it had to be resumed in late 1692. In the end, diplomacy and grammar became inextricable – with disputes over the use of the conditional (the French) or indicative tense (Rome) in the agreed text separating the two sides, essentially because the French would not countenance anything which smacked of a retraction of the Four Articles. Once again, it took Louis XIV, now anxious to put the quarrel with Rome behind him as he confronted stark economic conditions at home and a European coalition on the battlefields, to overrule his own advisers in August–September 1693 and to impose a declaration whose tortuousness bore all the marks of its long gestation. Accompanied by the king's own letter to Innocent XII undertaking to put the Gallican Articles and the decree enforcing them into mothballs, it was enough to remove the last remaining obstacle.[92] The deputies of the 1682 Assembly still without bulls duly signed the agreed declaration, and most of them were confirmed in a single consistory in October 1693, as if to underline the one quality that these reigning bishops and *évêques nommés* shared.[93] The last of the

---

90 ASV, Nunz Fr 181, fos 232, 233, 234, 246, 250, 254–7, letters, some originally in code, from nuncio to Cardinal Spada, Sept–Oct 1692, recounting his efforts to meet the individuals concerned and their responses to the questions he put to them.

91 Blet, *Assemblées du clergé et Louis XIV*, 549–91.

92 The king's letter and the text which the bishops were required to sign are both in Mention, *Documents*, nos 11–12, pp 45–7.

93 Blet, *Assemblées du clergé et Louis XIV*, 552–76, for a meticulous account of these negotiations. Nine were confirmed on 12 Oct, the five others at other dates.

consistories in question, held on 7 December, confirmed Augustin de Maupeou to the see of Castres. It is hard to believe that the choice of Maupeou or the timing of this last act was anything other than deliberate, since it was his nomination (and that of Saint-Georges) which had triggered the suspension of provisions over eleven years earlier. He was not the only individual to be singled out for retribution by Rome. Bishop Colbert of Montauban was nominated to Toulouse in 1687 and had evidently incurred Innocent XI's displeasure for 'abandoning' Montauban at that point.[94] He was made to wait for a year longer than his successor at Montauban for his bulls in 1692–3, when the normal pattern would have been to grant provisions in the *reverse* order.[95]

The different 'categories' into which these French bishops were grouped and the sequence in which they were confirmed by Rome – as well as the undertakings demanded of them – all testify to a steely and, in many ways, effective determination on the papacy's part in the face of the French crown's high-pressure tactics. As for the *régale* which lay at the origin of the crisis, there was no such resolution. When in another surprising gesture in late 1693, Louis XIV renounced the controversial *parlementaire* theory of the *régale* as an inalienable right of the crown, and declared that he was willing to exercise it by virtue of a papal indult, as had originally been suggested before the crisis blew up, it was Innocent XII who shied away from bestowing a 'grace' which would have both appalled the convinced gallican and spectacularly underlined the king's continuing need of papal support.[96] He was far more concerned to ensure that incoming French bishops in dioceses where the *régale* had not traditionally obtained would receive and acknowledge a special papal brief urging them to abstain from doing anything that would extend it.[97] In sharp contrast to the isolated Ranuzzi during the 1680s, few papal nuncios can have been as much in contact with France's bishops as those of 1692–3, Niccolini and Cavallerini, as they interviewed, interrogated, and urged them to close the 'état d'exception' of the preceding decade.

94   Sourches, ii, 169, 26 May 1688, reporting the censure. *Correspondance du nonce Ranuzzi*, ii, no 3153, Casoni to Ranuzzi, 28 June 1686, denying the rumour (which Ranuzzi had picked up: no 3119, 7 June) that the pope had sent Colbert a formal reprimand, but adding that he could not understand how bishops could desert their diocese for another ('per andar a governar in grado di vicarii quelle che non gl'appertengono'). BN, MS Fr 23502, fo 25v, 29v-30r, *Nouvelles Ecclésiastiques*, Feb 1692, also claims that other royal nominees were in similar difficulties, while Colbert himself was desperately trying to pretend he was really still residing in Montauban when everyone knew that his successor, Henri de Nesmond, was installed there.

95   BN, MS Fr 23502, fo 176, *Nouvelles Ecclésiastiques*, Nov 1692, Nesmond of Montauban granted his bulls 'au grand préiudice de l'archevesque de Toulouse nommé'.

96   Blet, *Le Clergé de France, Louis XIV et le Saint-Siège*, 4–12. The king's offer remained opened in subsequent years, but Innocent XII declared he would not deal with the *régale* while war was still in progress. He was also fearful that even a *régale* exercised by virtue of a papal indult might encourage other powers to make the same demands.

97   Blet, *Assemblées du clergé et Louis XIV*, 542–3, for the text of the brief.

V

However long Maupeou – and many others – had had to wait for their bulls, the outcome was at least positive for them. Remarkably, given Rome's known dislike of the behaviour of some of the king's nominees since 1682, only *one* of the latter failed outright in his efforts to become a bishop. A brief account of that failure may serve as an appropriate coda to the prolonged crisis, since it brings us back to its genesis. François de Camps, whose early career began at Port-Royal, subsequently made his mark as secretary and protégé of Archbishop Serroni of Albi, who was instrumental in securing his nomination as coadjutor of Glandèves in 1682, and then as full bishop when its elderly bishop, Léon Bacoué, resigned outright two years later. But when François de Bourlemont finally tired of waiting for his provisions to Pamiers in late 1685, de Camps accepted that nomination instead – an apt illustration of the shuffling of nominations occurring during these years.[98] He took up residence in a diocese whose cathedral chapter and clergy were bitterly divided between regalists and anti-regalists and which, counting de Camps himself, had three competing vicars-general. Supported by the provincial intendant and the metropolitan, Archbishop Montpezat of Toulouse, de Camps attempted to govern Pamiers as if he were a confirmed bishop, rebuilding its cathedral and episcopal palace, presiding over the estates of Foix, and so on.[99] But the hostility he provoked, both locally and in Rome, was commensurate with the harsh treatment meted out to Caulet's supporters since his death in 1680. Unremitting trench warfare, punctuated by pamphlets and broadsides, ensued, so much so that by 1690 Alexander VIII, for all his desire to settle the French bishoprics problem, was said to have demanded de Camps's perpetual exclusion from the episcopate, allegedly on the grounds that he had actively pressed his clergy to adhere to the 1688 appeal to a general council.[100] By late 1691, the exclusion of de Camps was apparently agreed to by France's cardinals in Rome so that the other nominations could go through.[101] Amid rumours that Louis XIV himself was ready to abandon him for the sake of a deal over the remaining dioceses, de Camps battled on for another eighteen months, probably because he enjoyed the crucial support of the king's confessor, and inundated the other bishops, as one source put it, 'with big parcels in the post'.[102] But he finally quit 'voluntarily' in May 1693, since the king did not wish to

---

98   BN, MS Fr 23500, fo 29, *Nouvelles Ecclésiastiques*, Jan 1690. Louis Blazy, 'Sur la part de l'abbé François de Camps dans les travaux éxécutés à la Cathédrale de Pamiers', *Bulletin Historique des Diocèses de Pamiers, Couserans et Mirepoix*, 5 (1930), 318–20.
99   Smedley-Weill, *Correspondance des intendants*, ii, 366, 368–76.
100 BN, MS Fr 23500, fo 79, *Nouvelles Ecclésiastiques*, Feb 1690.
101 BN, MS Fr 23501, fo 136v, *Nouvelles Ecclésiastiques*, Oct 1691.
102 ASV, Nunz Fr 181, fo 282, nuncio to Cardinal Spada, 10 Nov 1692; Nunz Fr 184, fo 19, same to same, 5 Jan 1693. There are several reports and attached documents from the nuncio during Feb 1693 about the situation in Pamiers at fos 119–23, 133–7. BN, MS Fr 23502, fo 163r, *Nouvelles Ecclésiastiques*, Oct 1692; MS Fr 23503, fo 10, Feb 1693, 'Mr de Camps

lose face by abandoning him publicly in the face of Roman hostility, and was compensated for the loss of his remote Pyreneean see with an exceptionally wealthy abbey.[103]

In sharp contrast, de Camps's 'successor' Jean-Baptiste de Verthamon, nominated in September 1693, only had to wait two months for his provisions, which were granted while some of the last of the 1682 deputies were still waiting for theirs.[104] Rapidly executed and attracting no attention in despatches, his succession – and that of a dozen new bishops nominated by Louis XIV since early 1692 – symbolised the end of one of the most highly charged chapters in the history of the French episcopate and the prospect of a return to the more normal routines of episcopal patronage.

continue de régaler les evesques de gros paquets par la poste', no doubt a reference to the tracts and other documents he circulated to defend his position.

103   ASV, Nunz Fr 185, fo 17, nuncio to Spada, 7 July 1693; fo 30, same to same, 13 July; BN, MS Fr 23503, fos 78r, 96v, *Nouvelles Ecclésiastiques*, May 1693.
104   ASV, PC 87, fos 71–80. Vidal, *Jean-Baptiste de Verthamon (1693–1735)*, ch 1.

CHAPTER 8

New for Old?

By THE TIME the papacy had finally cleared the backlog of episcopal nominations in late 1693 – and in a manner which demonstrated its continuing ability to defend its role in the making of France's bishops – the wider world of Franco-papal relations had changed perceptibly.[1] The French crown, which had regularly outmanoeuvred its foreign opponents since the 1660s, was now involved in an unexpectedly expanding European war, more isolated than before and thus unable to force a quick conclusion.[2] The peace of Ryswick (1697) offered only a brief respite before more all-embracing conflagration that began in 1702. The astronomical costs of keeping successive coalitions of European powers at bay for so many years could scarcely have come at a more unfortunate juncture. The 'normal' pressures of war were exacerbated by the onset of major epidemic and famine in 1693–4, which in turn heralded a pattern of demographic and economic misery that would endure until virtually the end of the reign.[3] The days when each new war seemed to bring territorial gains and new dioceses were over and, as we saw in chapter 1, France would even have to contemplate surrendering some of those earlier acquisitions. Louis XIV's efforts to present himself as the champion of Catholicism were unlikely to convince many people while he was openly at loggerheads with the pope, and that proved to be a major reason for his willingness to make the concessions to Innocent XII in 1691–3. It may be somewhat of an exaggeration to say that settling the dispute with Rome was 'the most urgent task facing Louis XIV in the internal government of the realm' because it 'threatened to ruin the king's administrative machine, which

---

1 Jean Meuvret, 'Les aspects politiques de la liquidation du conflit gallican (juillet 1691 -septembre 1693)', *Revue d'Histoire de l'Église de France*, 33 (1947), 257–70.
2 The Nine Years' War (or War of the League of Augsburg), which grew out of the piecemeal expansion of France during the 1680s, has attracted widely differing interpretations. See, among many others, Lossky, *Louis XIV and the French Monarchy*, ch 10, 'France in the System of Europe 1688–97'; John A Lynn, *The Wars of Louis XIV* (London 1999), ch 6, 'The Great Miscalculation'; Ranghild Hatton, ed, *Louis XIV and Europe* (which includes Geoffrey Symcox, 'Louis XIV and the Outbreak of the Nine Years' War', 179–212) (London 1976).
3 Marcel Lachiver, *Les Années de misère* (Paris 1991), 93ff.

needed the cooperation of church authorities to function properly', but there is no doubt that the temper of Franco-papal relations would be markedly different for the remainder of the reign.[4] At any rate, the combative gallicanism of the 1680–2 Assemblies of Clergy had been quickly reined in during subsequent years, as the crown tried to ensure that their 'humours' would not undermine its dealings with Rome, which explains why the French clergy were largely kept in ignorance of the negotiations which led to the resolution of the crisis in 1692–3.

I

Other changes, the significance of which we shall revisit later in this chapter, also occurred within France itself during these years. Louis XIV himself had secretly married Mme de Maintenon in 1684 and, with the aid of allies inside and outside of the church, she was soon trying by every means she could find to secure his 'conversion'. The court, finally installed at Versailles after 1683, was still evolving in the direction of greater complexity and faction, due in part to the tri-generational 'layering' of the royal family itself which the long reign would produce by its last decades. The marriages of the king's offspring, legitimate and legitimised, and the ensuing creation of new royal households, inevitably sharpened the competition for place and favour within both church and monarchy. Factions and cabals, famously chronicled by Saint-Simon and others, were one significant outcome of these changes, particularly towards the last years of the reign.[5] The disappearance of Chancellor Le Tellier in 1685 and especially of his son, Louvois, in 1691, also led to a rebalancing of the ministry, with the introduction of the independent Phélypeaux de Pontchartrain as *contrôleur-général* in 1691 (and chancellor in 1699), but also with the entry into the *conseil d'en haut* of the likes of the duc de Beauvillier, Colbert's son-in-law, whose *dévot* credentials made him a potential ally of Maintenon.[6] The latter's influence is also evident in the tenure of both the finance and the war ministries by Michel Chamillart from 1699 and 1701 respectively until his replacement by yet another Maintenon protégé, Voysin, as war minister in 1709. The foreign secretary, Colbert de Croissy, who died in 1696, was briefly replaced by Arnauld de Pomponne, and he in turn was succeeded on his death in 1699 by *his* son-in-law, Colbert de Torcy, who also happened to

---

4 Lossky, *Louis XIV and the French Monarchy*, 279.

5 See the successive analyses of these phenomena, especially through the eyes of Saint-Simon, by E Le Roy Ladurie, *Saint-Simon ou le système de la cour* (Paris 1997), ch 4. This work summarises and expands the author's earlier essays.

6 The duc de Chevreuse, brother-in-law of Beauvillier and married to another of Colbert's daughters, never became a minister, but he was a trusted informal adviser of Louis XIV – as near to ministerial status as was possible. He and Beauvillier were close, both of them *dévots* imbued with a Fénelonian piety. It was as a result of conversations with him at his château of Chaulnes that Fénelon would later draft his *Tables de Chaulnes*, a programme for the reform of government after Louis XIV's death.

be Croissy's son. And the influence of the Colbert clan would be further reinforced by the return from disgrace of Nicolas Desmarets in 1703, when he
was made a *directeur des finances* before succeeding his superior, Chamillart, as
contrôleur-général in 1708.

Nowhere is the 'small world' character of ministerial office under Louis XIV
quite as palpable as in these changes. Such continuity was personified no less
strikingly by two of the most durable figures of the reign, at least as far as
ecclesiastical affairs were concerned, Harlay and La Chaize, even though they
were increasingly elderly by the early 1690s. Neither was seriously challenged
during the 1680s, so there was nothing to blunt the vigour of their mutual
rivalry. Contemporaries closely observed them, and tried to gauge their respective places in the king's favour. Their conclusions were not always reliable
because they tended to assume that as one rose in favour, the other must
somehow fall, when what was probably happening was a shift in roles and
functions. Many concluded that when Archbishop Le Tellier of Reims became
a *conseiller d'état d'église* in 1683 and president of the *bureau* handling ecclesiastical cases coming before the royal council, the days of Harlay's dominance
were numbered: he was a Colbert client and after 1683, men like him could
no longer expect to wield the same influence as previously. The fact that he
and La Chaize no longer met the king together in regular meetings also tended
to be viewed as a loss of influence on Harlay's part. But in fact, these suppo-
sitions were premature or misguided, and Harlay survived the potentially
troublesome post-Colbert years with sufficient adroitness to obtain the king's
nomination for the red hat in 1689, a decision that confounded as well as
enraged his many detractors. If there was a shift in roles, it was that La Chaize
probably extended his grip on ecclesiastical patronage at Harlay's expense
during the 1680s. Yet we should be careful not to conclude that Harlay was
excluded from such matters merely because his part in distributing place and
favour in the church is so difficult to establish. Apart from the fact that his
control of the assemblies of clergy was undiminished, which would have
enabled him to aid and abet those deputies with episcopal ambitions, his part
in the Revocation of the Edict of Nantes and in subsequent dealings with the
Huguenots provided him with opportunities to assist or block particular
clerics. For the same reason, it is not hard to see that the king would particularly value his advice on 'senior' nominations. By his own account, Daniel
de Cosnac's promotion from Valence to Aix in 1687 occurred largely because
of Harlay's repeated intercession on his behalf with Louis XIV.[7] And when
Harlay replied to Fénelon around the same time – 'you want to be overlooked?
Well, just wait and see, you will be overlooked' – it was hardly an idle remark,
and no one hearing it would have regarded it as anything other than a

---

7 Cosnac, *Mémoires*, ii, 106–23. Cosnac does not mention Harlay in connection with the nomination itself, but he acknowledges that he owed his emergence from his long disgrace to the archbishop, who ensured he would attend the assemblies of clergy of 1682 and 1685.

real threat from a man who, if he chose, could make or break those with episcopal ambitions.[8]

But Louis XIV's instinctive unease about giving his total confidence to any adviser meant that neither Harlay nor La Chaize could entirely eliminate competitors for the king's ear where church patronage was concerned. From the mid-1690s a rather different challenge to the confessor's influence emerged – and from a surprising quarter, one that had not previously counted for much – the king's own consort. Anne of Austria had vigorously promoted her clients until her death in 1666, but while former almoners of Queen Marie-Thérèse had become bishops after 1661, there is little or no evidence that it was due to intervention on her part. The only recorded instance of lobbying by her concerned the nomination of Mathurin Savary to Sées in 1682, but even then it seems that she was manoeuvred into doing so by others rather than on her own initiative.[9] When her *premier aumônier*, Simiane de Gordes, had been made bishop of Langres a decade earlier, her response was one of genuine regret at having to part with him.[10] Successive royal mistresses, especially La Vallière and Montespan, were more likely to obtain favours for ecclesiastics belonging to their families – and these included one or two bishoprics. This was no more than contemporaries would have expected in any age, but no hints survive that either mistresses or other personal favourites of Louis XIV managed to do more than just that over the years. The activities of the king's own brother, Philippe, remain uncertain in this regard. Louis's own secret marriage to Françoise d'Aubigné de Maintenon in 1684 did not radically alter this pattern of the limited influence of the immediate royal entourage. Her first success was probably securing the diocese of Lavaur for Victor de Mailly in 1687, less than a month after a Mailly-Aubigné marriage, so it can be seen as a purely conventional operation.[11] The next one, a landmark in retrospect, is evidence of the way in which Maintenon's own activities were gradually broadening her ambitions. Chartres was a crucial diocese for her, since her major project by that time, the royal convent-cum-school for the daughters of poor nobles at Saint-Cyr, was located within its borders; having a sympathetic or dependent bishop was vital to the future of the whole enterprise, especially as Rome had not yet granted its approval of the foundation. Obtaining Chartres for Godet des Marais in 1690, less than a month after it fell vacant in January 1690, fitted the bill perfectly.[12] A product of Saint-Sulpice, he had participated in the missions to the Huguenots in the mid-1680s, and had become Maintenon's

---

8   Fénelon, *Correspondance* i, 165 and note 11.

9   BN, MS Fr 23510, fo 30, *Nouvelles Ecclésiastiques*, 30 May 1682.

10   He remained her *premier aumônier* and came to court at regular intervals, where his gambling was well known and led to criticism from the king himself at a later date. Saint-Simon, ii, 364–5, 417–18. Sources, v, 83, 25 Dec 1695, '. . . on avoit rendu auprès du Roi de très mauvais offices à l'évêque qui venoit de mourir'.

11   Sources, ii, 75–6, 15 Aug 1687. AN, L 735, pièce 1, Lavaur, no 1.

12   Announcing the king's decision to Godet, Maintenon denied all responsibility for it – 'Ne m'en remercié point: je n'y ay aucune part. Vostre mérite et le Roy ont tout fait. L'église a besoin de

own director of conscience as recently as 1689. He was also among the first of the *évêques nommés* to get his bulls from Rome in early 1692, possibly because of Maintenon's good offices during the crisis of the previous decade.[13] Overcoming the ill health and discouragement which led him to make several efforts to resign outright in 1694, he remained at Chartres until his death in 1709. It was largely through him that Maintenon, who had experienced little except court life for many years, came into touch with a generation of ecclesiastics like him – some of them already bishops – who had attended one of the major Parisian seminaries, served on the royal missions to the Protestant areas of France, or were actively engaged in preaching or other enterprises. Fénelon was merely the most famous of them, but there were many others who were brought to her attention by Godet – Bossuet, Noailles or Tronson, the superior of Saint-Sulpice. A kind of pattern emerged in subsequent years whereby such individuals were then invited to preach at Saint-Cyr and, depending on the impression they made, might be retained for educational or pastoral activities. Some of them were recruited over the years to educate the younger generation of royal children, an activity in which Maintenon, given her own earlier history, had a particular interest. Echoing her royal husband, she would complain in her correspondence of not knowing this or that person who was proposed to her for preferment, but these disclaimers should not be misconstrued: the number of those she *did* know grew constantly, and many of them were candidates for high positions in the church.

It would be all too easy, with the benefit of hindsight, to chart the confluence of these different concerns in such a way as to suggest that, sooner or later, a drive to determine episcopal patronage was ineluctable.[14] Yet it would be difficult to pinpoint the moment when Maintenon herself admitted to holding such an ambition, if only because she had a healthy fear of going too far and incurring the royal disgrace. From her early years at court, she formed a low opinion of La Chaize's approach to his responsibilities as confessor, accusing him only a year after his appointment of being too half-hearted in his efforts to persuade the king to jettison Mme de Montespan.[15] Later on, Louis XIV certainly warned her to keep out of matters of government generally,

bons pasteurs et surtout le diocèse de Chartres' – *Lettres de Maintenon* (ed Langlois), iii, no 626, letter of 4 Feb 1690. See also Fénelon, *Correspondance*, iii, no 147a, notes.

13 *Correspondance du nonce Ranuzzi*, i, 63. See also Marcel Langlois, 'Madame de Maintenon et le Saint-Siège', *Revue d'Histoire Ecclésiastique*, 25 (1929), 33–72.

14 Maintenon's role at court and in politics remains severely under-researched. The publication of the Ph D dissertation (London) by Mark Bryant will contribute significantly to a major revision of her influence and activities. I wish to thank Dr Bryant for his advice about the location of surviving Maintenon papers, given that neither of the major modern editions of her voluminous correspondence (by Lavallée and Langlois) got beyond 1705 and 1701 respectively. Completing their work would itself advance our understanding of the last decade of the reign considerably.

15 *Lettres de Maintenon* (ed Langlois), i, no 106, to Mme de Saint-Géran, [26 July] 1676, '. . . le P de la Chaise est un honneste homme, mais l'air de la cour gaste la vertu la plus dure et adoucit la plus sévère'.

and in particular to leave the matter of choosing bishops to La Chaize, as she herself recognised in 1691.[16] Writing in mid-1692 to her relative by marriage, the comte de Caylus, who had obviously sought her good offices on behalf of his son, the future bishop of Auxerre, she prudently recommended him to approach La Chaize before the king's next *grandes dévotions*; disclaiming any role in these matters, she even advised Caylus to wait longer to enable his son 'to fortify himself in the duties of his profession before seeking the goods of the church for him'.[17] Apart from its frank acknowledgement of La Chaize's continuing importance, this reply also clearly indicates some readiness on her part to take a loftier view of church patronage than mere family advancement would require or suggest. Yet her supporters among the *dévots* who shared her misgivings about the existing approach to episcopal patronage did not believe she should be so reticent: in a wide-ranging letter of counsel, probably from early 1690, Fénelon explicitly raised the question of episcopal nominations: 'until such time as you can do good in the choice of bishops, try to reduce the harm'.[18] She did not, therefore, lack for prompting or support on that particular issue. And her letters in subsequent years announcing that the king had given benefices to relatives and acquaintances revealed rather than disguised her growing role as a 'point of contact' between those seeking and those granting church benefices.[19] It is not irrelevant to note that when Maintenon finally persuaded Louis XIV to dismiss Aquin, his powerful *premier médecin*, it was when Aquin annoyed the king by pressing him too hard to give his son the archbishopric of Tours in 1693.[20]

Moreover, a careful look at the new faces entering the episcopate in the early 1690s shows that Maintenon and the wider circle of *dévots* secured episcopal office for several of their candidates since Godet's nomination to Chartres in 1690. Among the twenty-one new faces from 1690 (Godet) to 1695 (Fénelon), alongside the usual relatives of ministerial or high-robe figures, court and military nobles, at least nine had significant *dévot* connections, having also served in most cases as missionaries in Huguenot areas, as vicars-general at Strasbourg or Pontoise, and so on. Fénelon, for example, was instrumental in gaining a mitre for Louis Milon, his successor as superior of the Nouvelles Catholiques house in Paris, even though he himself had to wait until early 1695 for his own much delayed promotion to Cambrai. The man designated to be the first bishop of the new see of Blois, David-Nicolas de

16 *Ibid*, iii, no 691, p 550, to duchesse de Ventadour, 30 Oct 1691.
17 *Ibid*, iv, no 737, p 58, letter of 24 June 1692. The comte de Caylus had not been asking for a bishopric for his son, more likely an abbey or a royal almonership.
18 Fénelon, *Correspondance*, ii, no 96, p 147 [?Jan 1690], 'en attendant que vous puissiez faire du bien par le choix des pasteurs, tâchez de diminuer le mal'.
19 *Lettres de Maintenon* (ed Langlois), iv, no 765, p 95, to Mlle d'Aubigné, 20 Oct 1692; no 781, p 115, to Claude-Maur d'Aubigné, 9 Jan 1693.
20 This was widely reported at the time: Saint-Simon, i, 286, 381–2. It was Aquin's refusal to take no for an answer which most angered Louis XIV, who was not in the habit of giving archbishoprics to men who were not already bishops.

Bertier, was from exactly the same milieu. But such neat categorisations ought not to be overdone: even a Le Peletier, who succeeded Arnauld de Pomponne's uncle at Angers in 1692 and who obviously appears as a 'ministerial' nomination, was from a family that was extremely close to Tronson and Saint-Sulpice.[21] As we saw in an earlier chapter, several of these bishops were products of Saint-Sulpice, Missions Étrangères or Saint-Magloire, whose directors were beginning to emerge as informal but influential 'referees' for individual ecclesiastics whose names were being proposed for advancement. A Godet or a Fénelon, who fitted into this pattern of formation, was in turn an ideal intermediary between the court circles around Maintenon or Beauvillier and the changing ecclesiastical world from which episcopal hopefuls were continually emerging. It is also plausible to suggest that groups like these were involved in the criticism of particular patronage practices, such as the frequent or rapid transfers of bishops from diocese to diocese, which resurfaced in the 1690s. In mid-1694, the *Nouvelles Ecclésiastiques* reported discussions at court on these questions, and that it was resolved that only transfers 'for canonical and legitimate causes' would be made henceforth. Promotions of existing bishops to archiepiscopal sees remained legitimate, though it seems that even they were subjected to criticism, since Louis XIV himself had to defend transferring the bishop of Die to Vienne, his metropolitan see, in 1694.[22] It seems unlikely that the king would have broken at this time with his long-established habit of not giving an archiepiscopal see to someone without prior episcopal experience, had such criticism *not* made some impression on him. According to the *Nouvelles Ecclésiastiques*, it was Fénelon himself, in the months before his nomination to Cambrai, who had been explaining the church's traditional canons on translations, and to good effect.[23] Yet there was probably even greater surprise and comment when Léon Potier, the future cardinal de Gesvres, was made archbishop of Bourges in mid-1694, and Fénelon archbishop of Cambrai six months later, neither

---

21 *Correspondance de Tronson*, iii, 305–6, Tronson to abbé Michel Le Peletier, 5 Jan 1690, advising him on what to do over the see of Blois, which had been offered to him but which his father had turned down on his behalf. ASS, Correspondence des supérieurs-généraux, iii, no 19, Tronson to Le Peletier, *contrôleur-général*, 19 Oct 1693, in response to Le Peletier's request for Tronson's advice as to a possible transfer of his son from Angers to Tours, and had his ambitions for his other son to succeed to Angers. The bishop of Angers's brother, the abbé de Saint-Aubin, became superior-general of Saint-Sulpice in 1725, while Tronson's immediate successor in 1700 would be François Leschassier, from the same family as the *contrôleur-général*'s mother!

22 BN, MS 23504, fo 103, *Nouvelles Ecclésiastiques*, June 1694, for a long disquisition on translations, and especially Claude de Saint-Georges's nomination to Lyon in 1693, his third diocese to date.

23 BN, MS 23505 fo 16v, *Nouvelles Ecclésiastiques*, Feb 1695, 'vous scavez peut estre que M de Cambray depuis quatre mois enseigne au Roy l'ancienne discipline de l'église fort ennemie des translations, luy lit tous les canons que Sa Majesté goute, et luy en explique tous les jours trois ou quatre des principaux. Il s'est fort appliqué surtout à faire remarquer au Roy combien les canons etoient fermes sur l'obligation des Evesques à résider dans leurs églises et qu'il n'y a presque jamais aucune raison ecclésiastique qui les en puisse dispenser.'

having any episcopal experience.[24] Another notable feature of these years was a short-lived 'movement' in which some of those nominated to bishoprics made a point of giving up the abbeys or priories they held *in commendam*. Fénelon's gesture in doing so was only the best known, but others, including a relative of Maintenon herself, had preceded him in doing so.[25] These acts of renunciation also attracted much comment: welcomed by rigorists championing the 'ancient' church discipline, they annoyed senior and extremely well-beneficed bishops like Le Tellier of Reims or Clermont-Tonnerre of Noyon, who were anxious about the impact of such practices and the awkward position it put men like themselves. Le Tellier was predictably blunt in his response, but as metropolitan of Reims he already had reasons to disapprove of the new archbishop of Cambrai, whose status he set about contesting as soon as he was nominated.[26]

II

If ever there was a chance to transform these ad hoc successes into something more permanent and significant, as well as to challenge La Chaize's position, it came when Archbishop Harlay died suddenly and without the last sacraments, on 6 August 1695.[27] Once again, the circumstances suggest that the succession was not absolutely settled in advance. Harlay's long and masterly tenure of Paris, on which opinion was sharply divided, meant that the significance of the king's choice of a new archbishop was not lost on contemporaries, Maintenon included. Moreover Harlay died just over a week before the king's *grandes dévotions* on the feast of the Assumption (15 August), which only increased the sense of anticipation. There were several other dioceses to be filled at the time, but as we saw Louis XIV was not averse to deferring nominations to sees which fell vacant too close to these great feastdays, especially if they involved major positions. On the other hand, past experience also suggested that the decision to fill Paris should be taken fairly quickly,

24 *Ibid*, fo 12r, 'Il est bon de remarquer par cet example, par le choix que le Roy fit de son chef pour les archevechez de Vienne et de Bourges, et pour celuy que l'on vouloit faire pour Lyon, que les maximes on entierement changé sur les grandes places.'

25 Claude-Maur d'Aubigné had returned one of his abbeys to the king 'par scrupule'. *Lettres de Maintenon* (ed Langlois), iv, no 781, p 115, letter to Aubigné, 9 Jan 1693.

26 AN, L 729, pièce 1, Cambrai, no 23. He contested the validity of Cambrai's status as an archbishopric, largely because the dioceses which made up its 'province' had been extracted from that of Reims in 1559. Undoing that change would bring significant benefit to Reims. For the tussle between Fénelon and Le Tellier, see Philippe Guignet, 'Évangélisation et apaisement d'un conflit séculaire avec l'archevêché de Reims: les engagements contrastés mais cohérents d'un jeune archevêque de Cambrai (1695)', in Gilles Deregnaucourt and Philippe Guignet, *Fénelon, évêque et pasteur en son temps (1695–1715)* (Lille 1996), 43–55.

27 Dangeau, v, 255, 6 Aug 1695. JRULM, MS French 90, fo 254, Huxelles to La Garde, 18 Aug 1695, who asserted that Harlay was 'mort de pure defaillance de nature, ne s'estant trouvé ni abcez ny nulle cause de sa fin'.

because delay virtually invited an array of major church figures and their supporters to push their claims on the king (as they had done in 1671). For once, it is possible to reconstruct some of the issues, personalities and manoeuvres surrounding such a major decision, even though some key questions remain unanswerable.

Straining to uncover the chain of events leading to the final decision, diarists and letter-writers from Sourches to Mme d'Huxelles noted that La Chaize was summoned to Versailles in the normal manner on the eve of the Assumption, while Maintenon herself organised public prayers to inspire the choice of a new archbishop.[28] Sourches noted on 15 August that Cardinal Bouillon, who was then at court, was doing everything he could to capture Paris, over twenty-five years after Louis XIV rejected his first attempt to do so. But at least six other potential successors were also mentioned: Bossuet was strongly supported by the Dauphin, his former pupil; Fénelon, despite his recent nomination to Cambrai, also had his backers, while Cardinal Forbin-Janson and the archbishops of Auch (Maupeou) and Sens (Fortin de la Hoguette) were also in the lists. Noailles of Châlons-sur-Marne was the last among those to be mentioned.[29] Some of these figures (but others too) had already been 'mobilised' earlier that year when Cambrai, then reputed to be the richest diocese in France, was given to Fénelon after months of waiting and speculation.[30] Numerous other bishops were in Paris since a 'major' Assembly of Clergy had just ended when Harlay died.[31] So the list of potential successors and active candidates for Paris was probably a fairly long one, and most were hovering around the court by then. But although various items from Harlay's substantial portfolio of honours were re-distributed to senior bishops on 15 August, no decisions on vacant dioceses, Paris included, were made on that day: the king had gout, and so did not perform his devotions![32]

28 JRULM, MS French 90, fo 254, Huxelles to La Garde, 18 Aug 1695: 'On est aux escoutes sur le successeur qu'on promit au people aujourdhuy ou demain, le père de la Chaise alla hier à Versailles, et Mme de Maintenon fait prier Dieu partout pour ce choix'.

29 Sourches, v, 32, 15 Aug 1695.

30 Fénelon, *Correspondance*, i, ch xi, 'La Nomination de Fénelon à Cambrai'. This account, written by the editor of the correspondence, Jean Orcibal, shows in detail the circumstances of Fénelon's elevation. Cardinal d'Estrées, the archbishops of Auch and Embrun, and the bishop of Noyon were among those angling for Cambrai, which became vacant in mid-November 1694. The need for a papal indult to make the nomination led Louis XIV to defer announcing his decision from Christmas 1694, which would have been the normal date for such an announcement, until early Feb 1695.

31 Sourches, v, 29, 12 Aug 1695. Blet, *Le Clergé de France, Louis XIV et le Saint-Siège*, 57–60. Many had attended the funeral of Harlay on 10 Aug, but several had declined to deliver the traditional funeral sermon because of Harlay's dubious morals.

32 Sourches, v, 30. Harlay's title of *commandeur* of the Order of the Holy Ghost went to the Bishop of Noyon, Clermont-Tonnerre. Bossuet and Le Tellier were made provisors of the colleges of Navarre and the Sorbonne respectively. Bishop Coislin of Orléans replaced Harlay as Louis XIV's nominee for the red hat. JRULM, MS French 90, fo 252, Huxelles to La Garde, 15 Aug 1695, who alone mentions that the king was suffering from gout and did not perform his *grandes dévotions* on 15 Aug.

More likely, however, the decision over Paris was not sufficiently finalised to be publicly announced then, so the royal illness may have been more 'diplomatic' than real.

It was not until five days later that the court learned that Noailles of Châlons was to be the next archbishop of Paris. Sources even recorded the hour that the news broke, but he had neither gossip nor 'inside' information with which to explain it.[33] The impression conveyed by these sources – whose authors rate among the best informed of their day – is one of slowness and secrecy, and perhaps even indecisiveness. But even allowing for the initial surprise caused by Harlay's death, the charge of indecisiveness would not stick. It seems probable that Maintenon and her supporters moved quickly to persuade Louis XIV to choose Noailles, whom he reportedly did not know personally, although several Noailles family members were held in the highest esteem by him.[34] The future cardinal was a widely admired *dévot* bishop, who belonged to a generation of clerics who had frequented the Sorbonne, Saint-Sulpice and Saint-Cyr, while Maintenon herself had sought his opinion on the Quietist affair only a year before, in 1694.[35] She and her supporters, both lay and clerical, desired an 'anti-Harlay' in Paris, and Noailles certainly fitted the bill. The fact that La Chaize was not consulted about the final decision indicates that, not for the first time, Paris was too important to be left to the confessor's judgement. The first offer of Paris to Noailles was probably made on, or just before, 12 August, but Noailles refused it, saying he was 'married' to Châlons. As we have seen, such a conventional response, however sincere, was never taken at face value on its first enunciation. As a second messenger galloped off on 14 August to summon Noailles to court, Maintenon secretly urged him, in uncompromisingly direct terms, to think again: he must not decide purely with reference to himself, but rather to consult 'les gens de bien' around him, who would surely agree that this translation was thoroughly justified, because in the wider interest of the church.[36] She got her way:

33   Sourches, v, 41–2, 20 Aug 1695.
34   *Lettres de Maintenon* (ed Langlois), iv, no 993, p 420, quoting Louis XIV's letter to French ambassador, 24 Aug 1695: 'outre la vertu et le mérite personnel de ce prélat, je considère aussi beaucoup les services que le feu duc de Noailles son père, le maréchal de Noailles son frère, et tous ceux de sa famille m'ont rendu et continuent de me rendre tous les jours'. Indeed when Louis XIV translated Noailles from Cahors to Châlons in 1680, he wrote to him personally, 'j'ay resolu de vous y nommer sans autre solicitation que celle de vostre vertu et des services de vostre famille. Je m'asseure que vostre zele pour la pureté de la foy n'y sera pas d'un moindre secours que dans vostre premier diocèse': BN, MS Fr 6919, fo 173, letter of 22 June 1680.
35   *Lettres de Maintenon* (ed Langlois), iv, no 896, p 283, letter to Noailles, 22 June 1694. Noailles was asked to keep his report secret and not to date it!
36   JRULM, MS French 90, fos 225–6, Huxelles to La Garde, 22 Aug 1695, for date of courier. *Lettres de Maintenon* (ed Langlois), iv, no 990, letter of 13 Aug: 'Sy l'on vous offre la place vacante, la refuserés vous, Monsieur, sans consulter les gens de bien? En trouverés vous qui ne vous disent pas qu'il faut souffrir les maux desjà faits, dans la veue de tout changer à l'advenir? Y eut-il jamais une cause de translation plus forte que le bien de l'église et le salut du Roy? Est-il permis de préférer le repos au travail, et de refuser une place que la Providence nous donne, sans que nous y ayons contribué?'

Noailles accepted the offer at the third time of asking, before coming to court some days later. Bossuet, whom Louis XIV reputedly rejected for Paris on the grounds of his 'petite naissance', was aware of the comings and goings, and declared himself delighted by the choice of Noailles for Paris.[37]

Only when the desired outcome was secure did Maintenon reveal to Noailles – but not, alas, to posterity – something of what had happened over the Paris succession, adding that she could understand Noailles's fears about 'the weight and importance of the burden that the king wishes to impose on you'. Far more eye-raising was another confession contained in the same letter: 'it is sometimes necessary to deceive the king in order to serve him, and I hope that God will give us the grace to do so again in the future for the same ends and with your cooperation'.[38] What the 'deception' in question was remains unknown, but her success in 'persuading' Louis XIV to give Noailles the see of Paris was evidently something she hoped to repeat henceforth for other individuals and dioceses in coming years; she also expected Noailles to use all his credit with the king in a good cause from which, by implication, La Chaize would be either wholly or partly excluded.[39] The mystery may have been connected to discussions of the role of post-Harlay Paris which occurred *before* Noailles was chosen, as a result of which Louis XIV apparently agreed to some important changes: the new archbishop would deal purely with the affairs of his diocese, and would not have Harlay's regular weekly meeting with the king nor Harlay's oversight of the affairs of the religious orders or of the dioceses of the kingdom.[40]

If this outcome, which seemed to make the archbishop of Paris look like any other French bishop, was not what Maintenon and her allies aimed at, all the signs are that little attention was subsequently paid to it. What mattered to her was that this great coup was just the beginning of a new chapter in church politics and patronage. The Noailles interest was already immensely

---

37 Bossuet, *Correspondance*, vii, no 1266, p 190, Bossuet to M d'Albert, 16 Aug, 'il passa hier à 2 heures après midi un courier qui dit qu'il allait porter de bonnes nouvelles à M de Châlons'.

38 *Lettres de Maintenon* (ed Langlois), iv, no 991, p 418, to Noailles, 18 Aug 1695, 'Voicy une lettre d'un de vos amis, qui sait une partie de ce qui se passé. Vous nous garderés le secret à tous. Il faut quelques fois tromper le Roy, pour le servir; et j'espère que Dieu nous fera la grace de le tromper encore, à pareille intention, et de concert avec vous. '

39 *Ibid*, no 1000, pp 427–8, to Noailles, 9 Sept 1695, 'Dieu instruit le Roy, malgré luy (La Chaize); et je vis hier des dispositions qui vous raviroient, si je pouvois vous les confier dans une lettre . . . je n'eus jamais de sy grandes esperances que celles que j'ay depuis hier, et je n'ay pu vous les taire'.

40 JRULM, MS French 90, fo 255–6, letter to M de la Garde, 22 Aug 1695, '. . . le Roy ne vouloit plus qu'un archevesque de Paris se meslast d'autre chose que des affaires de son diocèse, sans avoir de vendredy, ni d'inspection sur tous les moines en général comme sur les affaires des autres diocèses, qui venoient au deffunt'. The phrase 'sans avoir de vendredy' refers to the weekly meetings with the king, since they were held on Fridays. Writing only days later from Brussels, Quesnel also wrote that the next archbishop would have no other business than governing his diocese: *Correspondance*, i, 370–1, to du Vaucel, 26 Aug 1695.

powerful, and it would be fortified by the marriage in 1698 of marshal Noailles's heir to Maintenon's niece and sole heiress.[41] Initially it did not seem to matter that Noailles himself, who would be a cardinal by 1700, was not the dominant figure that Harlay had been. Within days of his nomination, he was being bombarded by Maintenon with letters and questions on all aspects of church affairs, letters which also reveal her opinions and interventions over episcopal nominations as, for example, when she begged Louis XIV not to give Châlons to a Clermont-Tonnerre purely to satisfy the vanity of the bishop of Noyon who wanted three of the ecclesiastical peerages for his family.[42] Other cases could be more difficult to handle. With the king's *grandes dévotions* of 15 August 1695 deferred until September, the curé of Saint-Sulpice approached her to obtain one of the then-vacant dioceses, probably Châlons, for the abbé de Béthune-Charost, but when Maintenon replied nervously that the abbé and his family were all suspect of ties with the disgraced Quietist, Mme Guyon, as well as being relatives of Fouquet, it was agreed that Béthune should be interrogated by Tronson, the superior of Saint-Sulpice.[43] Despite Tronson's reassurance about his orthodoxy, Béthune did not become a bishop, either then or later. The curé of Saint-Sulpice had other names for Maintenon's attention although, so she informed Noailles, he was less enthusiastic about them than about Béthune.[44] At any rate, the four episcopal nominations deferred to early September 1695 were evidently to her satisfaction, and she reported to Noailles that the king's dispositions on that occasion were everything she could have wished for.[45] Noailles's own succession at Châlons was still not settled, however, and it was complicated by the fact that from the outset his younger brother, Gaston, was among the candidates whose names were put forward. Young and inexperienced, he had left Saint-Sulpice only fairly recently to live at Châlons with Noailles, who was evidently embarrassed by the prospect of such a succession.[46] So Maintenon took it largely upon herself to push his brother's claims on the king, who replied at one point that he would not decide on Châlons without first conferring with the new archbishop

41   As early as Oct 1695 (i.e. only weeks after the Paris succession was settled), rumours were already circulating about the possibility of such a marriage, Sourches, v, 65, 15 Oct 1695. The Paris nomination may well have been intended to pave the way for a Noailles family agreement to a marriage alliance with Maintenon's family.

42   *Lettres de Maintenon* (ed Langlois), iv, no 994, p 421, Maintenon to Noailles 29 Aug 1695, 'je priay le Roi de préférer un bon choix à cette simétrie'.

43   His mother, the duchess, the only child of Nicolas Fouquet, the disgraced *surintendant*, by his first wife, was also a close friend of Mme Guyon and one of her earliest disciples.

44   *Lettres de Maintenon* (ed Langlois), iv, no 998, pp 425–6, Maintenon to Noailles, 8 Sept 1695.

45   *Ibid*, no 1000, pp 427–8, to Noailles, 9 Sept 1695, 'je vis hier des dispositions qui vous raviroient, si je pouvois vous les confier dans une lettre . . . je n'eus jamais de sy grandes espérances que celles que j'ay depuis hier, et je n'ay pu vous les taire.'

46   *Ibid*, no 998, pp 425–6, 'sur Mr l'abbé de Noailles, il ni aura qu'à dire que vous ne le nommeriés pas, sy vous en cognoissiés un meilleur, et que vous le trouvés trop jeune, pour le proposer, à tout autre evesché que Chaalons.'

of Paris.[47] In the end the nomination was made, despite some resistance from La Chaize, on the understanding that Gaston de Noailles would seek guidance from his predecessor.[48] It took until Christmas 1695 for the Châlons succession to be announced, and for several years thereafter, the archbishop of Paris virtually governed Châlons by correspondence, regularly answering detailed questions put to him by his brother on every conceivable aspect of diocesan rule.[49]

III

For all its remaining secrets, the Paris succession of 1695 sheds a light on ecclesiastical decision-making at the highest level, as well as on the *modus operandi* of those involved, that is unrivalled by any other during Louis XIV's reign. For Maintenon at least, the Noailles succession was a key step in putting together – or, better still, extending – a network of advisers and informants who would enable her to draw worthy ecclesiastics to the king's attention when bishoprics were available, but who would also brief her so that she could reply to questions and objections when put to her. She was enough of a realist to see that she could not achieve much in this particular domain, especially when faced by La Chaize, unless counselled by those she trusted. Her incessant letters to Noailles after August 1695 testify eloquently to this need: so many names are proposed to her, but she knows little about them and fears that if she makes mistakes, she will lose the initiative and the king will inevitably turn again to familiar figures like La Chaize. Because of the continuing danger of falling foul of her husband – ever suspicious of cabals around him – she informed Noailles that their liaison was to be secret, and she even sent him a cipher for use in case of necessity.[50] Such caution was all the more essential since her animosity to La Chaize deepened during this same period: she was especially incensed by his alleged jibes about *dévots* being good for nothing, especially governing dioceses. Only someone holding Noailles's elevated rank and favour could effectively counter such sentiments, and influence the king in a different direction. By New Year 1696, she was ready for battle, having been assured by Godet of Chartres that, provided she contributed to selecting 'good bishops', he would overlook everything else

---

47 *Ibid*, no 1015, p 450, Maintenon to Noailles, 6 Oct 1695, 'le Roy ne veut point vous donner un evesque à Chaalons que vous ne soyés icy, et, quand j'ai voulu luy dire que vous auriés des mesures à prendre avec luy, il m'a respondu qu'il faudra tousjours bien que vous les preniés à Paris, et, que quand vostre successeur seroit nommé, il n'iroit pas sitost à Chaalons. Je n'ay guère insisté, parce que j'ay cru qu'il estoit bon que cette affaire se conclust avec vous'.

48 *Ibid*, no 1039, p 476, to Noailles, 25 Dec 1695.

49 See the extensive surviving correspondence between the two brothers in BN, MSS Fr 23206 and 23483.

50 *Lettres de Maintenon* (ed Langlois), iv, no 1026, pp 461–4, to Noailles, 15 Nov 1695.

about her behaviour.[51] Within two weeks, she was asking Noailles to draw up a list of the good bishops already in place so that, whenever the occasion arose, she could support their cause with the king or submit cases requiring investigation to them to the exclusion of others deemed less worthy; she would even copy the list in her own hand and destroy the original, so that nothing could be traced back to Noailles.[52] Around the same time, it seems that the duc de Beauvillier, perhaps independently of Maintenon, asked Hébert, curé of Versailles and later bishop of Agen, to compile a list of desirable candidates for the episcopate.[53] If these and possibly other moves are connected, then it would seem that concerted efforts being made to marginalise if not actually to oust the confessor at this point.[54] Maintenon could hardly have put it more bluntly to Noailles in late January 1696: 'as long as La Chaize remains in post, we shall achieve nothing'.[55]

But sidelining the experienced La Chaize was never going to be easy. Louis XIV might occasionally scoff at him, or berate him on particular issues, but he had, as with other advisers, become more dependent on him than he would have admitted.[56] Having kept Harlay at bay for two decades, La Chaize's own political skills were hardly negligible. He had also been critical of Noailles's role in the Quietist debate only a few months before his nomination to Paris, and some of the delay in choosing Noailles may have arisen from those objections, even if he was not involved in the final decision over the Paris succession.[57] Moreover, a covert partnership between Maintenon and Noailles on ecclesiastical affairs carried its own dangers – especially that of alienating a king allergic to string-pulling behind his back – and was hardly the ideal basis for making the confessor redundant. La Chaize sensed the challenge to his position, and was soon courting Maintenon, whose suspicions of him showed no sign of abating in the following years.[58] As we have seen, La Chaize's influence over episcopal decisions certainly did not evaporate at this

---

51 *Ibid*, no 1041, pp 478–80, to Noailles, 27 Dec 1695.
52 *Ibid*, v, no 1049, pp 12–13, to Noailles, 14 Jan 1696.
53 *Lettres de Mme de Maintenon* (Amsterdam edn 1766), iv, 88–9, editorial note. This is the sole uncorroborated source of Hébert's mission. Hébert was highly regarded by Noailles, Fénelon and other figures in the French church, so Beauvillier's choice of him for this purpose was consistent. The editor adds that this list provided the names of candidates who were acceptable to the king until Beauvillier himself became suspect of Quietist opinions, and that during that time La Chaize was no longer master of the *feuille des bénéfices*.
54 *Lettres de Maintenon* (ed Langlois), v, no 1106, pp 94–5, to Noailles, 4 Sept 1696.
55 *Ibid*, no 1054, pp 17–18, to Noailles, 31 Jan 1696.
56 *Ibid*, no 1097, p 81, to Noailles, 5 Aug 1696, in which Maintenon relates a recent conversation she had with Louis XIV who said, 'je m'en vais voir un homme que vous croyés bon homme, mais sans esprit, et me nomma le Père de la Chaise. Je luy répondis: 'Vous le croyés encore plus que moy, car vous le voyés plus souvent.'
57 *Ibid*, iv, nos 981–2, pp 404–8, letters of 18 and 25 May 1695.
58 *Ibid*, no 1039, pp 476–7, to Noailles, 25 Dec 1695; v, no 1076, pp 55–6, to Noailles, 23 April 1696, recounting one such encounter and her disagreement with La Chaise over what the 'love of God' amounts to in the case of a king like Louis XIV; v, no 1328, p 404, to Noailles, 3 Jan 1699, 'ceux qui aiment l'épiscopat ont quelque chose à souffrir.'

point, and his objections to Gaston de Noailles receiving Châlons were probably instrumental in delaying that decision during the final months of 1695.
Some of the bishops chosen in September 1695 were close to the Jesuits and
even to La Chaize's own family. Maintenon's own dismay at the decision to
nominate a Clermont-Tonnerre – 'un homme sans piété', as she put it – to
Langres at Christmas 1695 was directed primarily against the confessor.[59]
After that there was not much immediate opportunity to sideline La Chaize,
at least as far as episcopal nominations were concerned, since scarcely any were
made thereafter until Christmas 1697.

In any case, the prospect of a unified *dévot* 'team' gathered around
Maintenon was itself increasingly problematic, as some of its most prominent
members were falling out among themselves. The Quietist affair, which blew
up in 1693 and only ended with the papal condemnation of Fénelon in 1699,
had already set some of Maintenon's most influential associates against each
other – in particular Fénelon against Godet, Bossuet and Noailles. Although
his nomination to Cambrai was not the immediate signal for his disgrace,
Maintenon was certainly relieved to have Fénelon removed from her presence.[60] The support that Fénelon was rumoured to have for the Paris succession in 1695, and the successful opposition to it, may both be seen in this
context.[61] His formal disgrace only came later, in 1697, after the publication
of his *Maximes des Saints*, but much damage was already done. In subsequent
years, animosity would deepen between him and Bossuet, who proved an
implacable and ruthless adversary over Quietism, but even more so between
Fénelon and Noailles. The Quietist affair was also a precursor of the Jansenist
one after 1702 in the sense that by dividing some of the French church's
leading figures, both affairs forced them into sometimes unexpected realign-
ments, and these in turn influenced episcopal patronage. Thus Fénelon, denied
episcopal office in the mid-1680s on allegations that his ideas seemed close
to Jansenism, became an ally rather than a friend of the Jesuits and especially
of La Chaize's successor, Tellier, and a determined back-stage orchestrator of
anti-Jansenist campaigns in the last years of the reign.[62] Many other reigning
bishops were to do likewise over the years. Noailles, whose family were

---

59 *Ibid*, iv, no 1041, pp 478–80, to Noailles, 27 Dec 1695, 'n'en dirés vous rien au P de la Chaize?'
    The curé of Saint-Sulpice was the source of her view of Clermont-Tonnerre as being 'sans piété.'
60 Fénelon was to remain preceptor to the duc de Bourgogne, the king's grandson, on the under-
    standing that he would spend three months of the year at court, but Maintenon hoped that his
    involvement with Saint-Cyr itself, where the Quietist affair had begun, would cease entirely.
61 Fénelon, *Correspondance*, v, appendix 2.
62 There is no satisfactory modern study of Fénelon, but the recently completed critical edition
    of his correspondence is a mine of information on which future work will have to be built; each
    volume of letters is accompanied by a volume of notes, while the first volume consists of studies
    of Fénelon before his elevation to Cambrai by Jean Orcibal, the doyen of Fénelon scholars. See
    Fénelon, *Correspondance*, i, ch 5, 'Le Jansénisme de l'abbé de Fénelon', esp pp 165–6. See also
    Henk Hillenaar, *Fénelon et les Jésuites* (The Hague 1967), for a very balanced account of Fénelon's
    relations with the Jesuits.

traditionally close to the Jesuits, moved in the opposite direction to Fénelon and became the principal target of the anti-Jansenist camp during Louis XIV's last years. By then, he too would have lost Maintenon's support and patronage – though she would continue to write to, and berate him for his obduracy in the Jansenist affair in the 1710s.[63] Of course, no one had any inkling of this during Noailles's early years in Paris. Even though he was attacked in print as early as 1698 for his 'inclinations' towards Jansenism, he went on to become cardinal and successfully presided over a major Assembly of Clergy, both in 1700. Without anticipating later developments, the evidence we have suggests how difficult any attempt like that envisaged by Maintenon of gathering together a *dévot* party opposed to the Jesuits and capable of promoting its view of what made an acceptable episcopate, might be.

IV

Before attempting to measure how well or badly the *dévots'* ambitions fared, there are some broader features of episcopal patronage in these years which are indispensable to a balanced perspective on any attempt to reshape the episcopate. Firstly, it should be said that while competition for episcopal office acquired additional layers of complexity from the mid-1690s onwards, it did not radically alter. The record of nominations does not show the outright dominance of any particular 'tendency'. Neither the Quietist nor the Jansenist controversies ever come close to suppressing established conventions, which continued to be respected, so that former or serving *agents-généraux* of the clergy, tutors to members of the royal family, or royal almoners were still regarded as perfectly 'natural' candidates for the mitre. Indeed, as we saw in an earlier chapter, at no time were the first two groups more successful in gaining such preferment as in the last decades of the reign.[64] Royal ministers and officials just below ministerial office expected to advance their relatives – and with names like Colbert, Desmarets, Chamillart, Phélypeaux, Fleuriau, Argenson figuring among the new appointees or securing promotion to an archbishopric, it is clear that they were successful. Great nobles in favour at court, or benefiting from their enhanced military prestige at a time when France was almost constantly at war, could expect similar rewards for family members or clients. As we saw, Fénelon himself remarked in 1690 that in wartime the king was more likely than ever to give benefices to clerics whose fathers and brothers served in his armies, and he probably did not exclude bishoprics from this assessment. It was this kind of circumstance which enabled the Villeroy family to regain Lyon for one of theirs as late as 1714, a

---

63   Maintenon's correspondence after 1705, when Lavallée's final unpublished volume ends, has not been systematically collected and published. A substantial corpus of her post-1710 letters to Noailles are in BN, MS Fr 23483, fos 27 *et sqq*.

64   See p 127ff.

year after Beauvillier finally placed his half-brother at Beauvais.[65] It seems highly improbable that a much more modest figure like Frétat de Boissieu, who became bishop of Saint-Brieuc in 1705, would have gained his prize without his sister's marriage into the Villars family some years previously – and this at a time when the long-standing presence of Villars members in the episcopate (at Vienne) had come to a close.[66] Nor should it be forgotten that as well as pursuing her crusade for a *dévot* episcopate, Mme de Maintenon herself continued to sponsor relatives of her own in search of a mitre. She was directly instrumental in promoting François de Mailly to Arles (1697), Claude-Maur d'Aubigné first to Noyon (1701) and then to Rouen (1707), and the most notorious of them all, Caylus, to Auxerre in 1704. Finally, even if Noailles, a cardinal after 1700, did not have La Chaize or Harlay's regular 'vendredy' with the king, his rank and myriad connections made him a natural patron for many of those seeking office, while Louis XIV often seems to have turned to him when he entertained doubts about particular names put to him. It was Noailles who vouched for the orthodoxy of Colbert de Croissy when he was being considered for Montpellier in 1697 – hardly an auspicious start, given Croissy's hardline Jansenist position during his long episcopate.[67] It was Noailles's persistence which obtained Fréjus from Louis XIV for Fleury in 1698 when every other effort by his patrons had failed utterly in the face of prolonged royal intransigence, which led the king to predict that Fleury would one day be Noailles's nemesis.[68] There were almost certainly other cases where his intervention during these years was of decisive importance to epis-copal patronage – as Louis XIV's own request for his advice during the scandal of the abortive nomination to Poitiers of abbé Coëteletz, also in 1698.[69] It was thus no accident that in 1703, the ageing Bossuet, whose own patronage had been indispensable, either directly or indirectly, in the making of several bishops, and who was desperate to secure Meaux for his nephew, finally decided to entrust the affair to Noailles.[70] He continued to fulfil this kind of role for several years thereafter. The king's promise of 1695 that Noailles would simply govern Paris was long forgotten, and the cardinal's tirade of

---

65 Maintenon expressed her doubts about the wisdom of this: 'l'archevêché de Lyon est comme héréditaire dans cette maison, et toutes les autorités dans la province, ce qui n'est pas trop bon en bonne politique; car tous les Villeroy ne seront pas peut-être tels que ceux que nous con-noissons. Quant à l'abbé de Villeroy, je ne le connois point assez pour me mêler de son étab-lissement': *Lettres inédites de Mme de Maintenon et de Mme la princesse des-Ursins*, ed Bossange, 4 vols (Paris 1826), iii, 86–7, 16 July 1714.

66 The first Villars bishop (of Mirepoix) had taken office as long ago as 1561, while the last of the four Villars archbishops of Vienne died in 1693.

67 Valentin Durand, *Le Jansénisme au xviiie siècle et Joachim Colbert évêque de Montpellier (1696–1738)* (Toulouse 1907), 366–7, letter of Colbert de Torcy to his sister, 18 Dec 1737, relating this incident.

68 Saint-Simon, vi, 45–52 and notes.

69 See below, p 284

70 Ledieu, *Journal*, i, 421, 428–9, 444, 464–5 (May–Aug 1703). Bossuet had enabled several future bishops to take service as tutors to younger members of the royal family over the years.

1706 arising from his having been kept in the dark by the king and confessor, but especially by Maintenon herself, over the nomination of a new bishop of Orléans, a suffragan of Paris, shows just how accustomed he had become to participating in episcopal patronage.[71]

These and other cases indicate that access to high church patronage remained relatively 'open', and that Louis XIV and his confessor received recommendations from a wide range of supplicants and patrons. The ageing monarch's now well established habit of reserving decisions for major feast-days provided the time, often amounting to several months, to consider, enquire, and weigh up the merits of individuals, and that could either be done in formal sessions with La Chaize, who still kept the *feuille des bénéfices*, or in private encounters with Noailles or other interested parties. Not every episcopal succession could expect equal attention from diarists, correspondents or gossips as that of Paris, but there is no doubt that they were watched with greater interest than at any time during the reign, though we cannot always be certain of how well informed their reflections actually are. For obvious reasons, the nomination of archbishops continued to attract close competition and attention. They were, in certain circumstances, the ones that could involve the longest delays, as if the king and his advisers needed more time to make up their minds, or were divided over what to do. It was, therefore, not uncommon for such nominations to be held over from one feastday to the next. It was in the 1690s that Louis broke, albeit briefly, with his rule of only nominating reigning bishops to such sees. Fénelon was one of them, but most of the comment at the time was devoted to the other two cases, the future cardinals Potier de Gesvres, nominated to Bourges in 1694, and François de Mailly, who was given Arles in 1697. Gesvres was thought to have missed out on an early red hat on account of Franco-papal clashes of the late 1680s, so it was felt that something more than an 'ordinary' diocese should be offered to a man whose father was governor of Paris and *premier gentilhommme* of the bedchamber.[72] Mailly was a relative by marriage of Mme de Maintenon, who had secured a Languedoc diocese, Lavaur, for his brother a decade earlier. Both Mailly and Gesvres became cardinals in 1719, and Fénelon would doubtless have achieved similar rank were it not for his disgrace in 1697.[73] These three

71 *Lettres de Mme de Maintenon* (Amsterdam edn 1766), iv, 280–4, Noailles to Maintenon, no date (early April 1706), 'l'humiliation a été très complète pour moi, Madame. Pendant que j'étois à Versailles, où je ne pus rien apprendre de la destination de l'évêque d'Angers [Le Peletier, nominated to Orléans on 3 April], le P de la Chaise en disoit publiquement à son audience la nomination: et le soir, M de Bourges m'étant venu voir, trouva que je l'ignorais absolument . . . ainsi tout le monde a vu que je ne l'ai apprise qu'avec le public.' Noailles may only be complaining here about being left to discover a major decision at the same time as the general public, but behind the long and bitter pages that follow, it is not hard to see what his expectations amounted to.

72 Saint-Simon, xiii, 107–9. According to Saint-Simon, Potier senior tried to prevent the king from giving Bourges to his son, but not because he thought him unfit or unprepared for such a position.

73 *Ibid*, iv, appendice xvi, 516–19, for a 'fragment inédit' on Mailly.

cases proved exceptional, for after 1697 the king reverted to his previous practice; it is plausible to think that the eyebrows raised and the comment elicited by them were responsible for him closing this brief interlude.[74]

The other seventeen archiepiscopal nominations made after 1693 were more conventional, though the first two – to Lyon and Tours during 1693 – involved ecclesiastics who had not been consecrated bishops in their previous dioceses.[75] At last, Louis XIV had the opportunity to fill major sees that had not previously fallen vacant since Mazarin's death. Not all of the archbishoprics in question were regarded as equally important by the crown: Arles, Embrun, Auch and Vienne came well below Aix, Narbonne, Bordeaux, Rouen or Reims on account of the political responsibilities or the status attached to the latter. Saint-Georges received Lyon in 1693 partly because of his role in the 1682 Assembly, partly because of his ability and his connections to Lyon itself, at a time when the Villeroy family did not have a possible successor to Camille de Villeroy; but when Saint-Georges died in 1714, the Villeroy tenure of Lyon, interrupted in 1693, simply resumed almost as inevitably as before. Hervault of Tours was a staunch gallican who had served as France's Auditor of the Rota in Rome during the crisis of the 1680s. As we have seen already, Daniel de Cosnac had been chosen for Aix in 1687 because the crown clearly wanted a different sort of archbishop to the rigorist and independently minded Cardinal Grimaldi. Cosnac's political skills, not to mention his readiness to fight his corner, were put to the test soon after Rome confirmed him in 1693.[76] Moreover, his value to the crown in this role enabled his nephew to become bishop of Die in 1702, and explains why Cosnac was instrumental in other episcopal nominations in Provence. When he died in 1708, Aix went to a man with a long career still ahead of him – Charles-Gaspard de Vintimille, already bishop of Marseille, but who would end his career as Noailles's successor at Paris. In nominating Vintimille to Aix, Louis XIV ignored the claims of Fleury, bishop of the neighbouring diocese of Fréjus; instead he took his advice from Cardinal Forbin-Janson who, although no longer based in Provence, was playing, not for the last time, the role of 'bishop-maker' for his native province.[77] His last opportunity to do that came in 1711 when his own nephew was given the see of Arles, but paradoxically it was the king, and

---

74 With one exception – the nomination of Jacques de Forbin-Janson to Arles in 1711.

75 Claude de Saint-Georges, had been nominated to Poitiers and Tours in the 1680s, Mathieu Ysoré d'Hervault to Condom in 1693, which meant that neither of them was regarded at the time as lacking episcopal experience, though in Hervault's case, it was really nonexistent.

76 See Saint-Simon, vii, 271–8, and the extensive documentation of the accompanying notes.

77 JRULM, MS French 95, fo 25, Huxelles to La Garde, 6 Feb 1708, 'on donne à Mr l'Evesque de Fréjus généralement parlant l'archevesché d'Aix; fo 30, same to same, 12 Feb, 'c'est Mr l'Evesque de Marseille qui a l'archevesché d'Aix, et Mr le Cardinal de Janson qui a opéré ce changement auprès du Roy, dont on luy fait compliment.' Needless to say, the Vintimille du Luc and Forbin-Janson families were closely interrelated, whereas Fleury was an outsider from Languedoc.

doubtless other Forbin family members, who insisted on the nomination, while the cardinal himself strenuously resisted it on the grounds that his nephew was simply not fit for the post.[78]

In terms of its political importance, Aix was probably superseded only by Narbonne, where Cardinal Bonsi's thirty-year reign ended with his death in 1703. Having lost political favour at court in the mid-1680s and failed to recover it thereafter, his place as the dominant bishop in the Estates was taken during the 1690s, it seems, by Phélypeaux of Lodève, whose ministerial connections need hardly be underlined. Bonsi made strenuous efforts to place his nephew, the abbé de Castries, in either Albi or Narbonne itself, even pleading that his great age meant he needed a coadjutor, but his successive pleas went unheard.[79] Maintenon confessed to Noailles that she did not know who to propose to Louis XIV as Bonsi's successor for Narbonne in 1703, but La Chaize (and probably the intendant Basville) certainly did: it was the confessor's *mignon*, as contemporaries called him, Archbishop Le Goux de la Berchère of Albi, who got the nomination in due course.[80] Maintenon was to make up for such slips in later years when Rouen was awarded to her cousin, Aubigné of Noyon, and Reims to Mailly of Arles, another relative of hers, in 1707 and 1709 respectively. By the latter date, Louis's bishops in the Flanders dioceses were in a highly exposed position, and it was with a view to compensating one or more of them should France lose these dioceses in a peace settlement that he kept Toulouse, Arles and later Auch vacant for extended periods – well over two years in the case of Toulouse. Observers noted the king's failure to fill them as the major feast-days came and went, but evidently had no real idea of the reasons.[81] In the event only one of these archbishoprics was needed for that purpose: René-François de Beauvau was given Toulouse early in 1713, just in time to ensure a pro-French bishop could be installed in Tournai, one of the rare occasions when the fate of a diocese of the 'interior' depended on international politics.[82]

But, as noted in a previous chapter, not all archbishoprics were equally attractive, and in some cases Louis XIV often had to seek out successors. Bourges, which along with Tours was the least well endowed of France's archdioceses, saw its financial position improve as a result of the creation of that of Albi, and this may well have facilitated its acceptance by Potier de Gesvres

---

78 Saint-Simon, xx, 79–80.
79 JRULM, MS French 90, fos 78–9, Huxelles to La Garde, 20 July 1694, recounting one of Bonsi's highly complex proposals involving several bishops changing diocese. *Lettres de Maintenon* (ed Langlois), v, no 1404, to Noailles, 25 Nov 1700, 'Cardinal de Bonsi presse pour avoir un coadjuteur; j'en presse le Roy aussy, parce que je croy qu'il y va de sa conscience, mais je ne scay sur qui ce choix devrait tomber'.
80 Dangeau, ix, 268–9, 14–15 Aug 1703.
81 Sourches, xii, 263, 11 July 1710; 272, 14 July 1710; 322, 15 Aug 1710; 391, 31 Oct 1710; 418–19, 24 Dec 1710; xiii, 79, 5 April 1711; 477, 15 Aug 1712; 521, 1 Nov 1712; 552, 24 Dec 1712. Dangeau, xiv, 251, 1 Nov 1712; 414, 4 June 1713.
82 See pp 38–9 above.

in 1694.[83] As always, the precise motives of those refusing and accepting promotions remains elusive. When Bordeaux fell vacant in 1697, Noailles apparently suggested giving it to one of its longest-serving suffragans, the now elderly Bishop Barillon of Luçon, but the idea got short shrift from Louis XIV, who had no doubt been briefed, possibly by La Chaize, about Barillon: he was a Port-Royalist and rigorist, a correspondent of Rancé and Le Camus, and therefore no friend of the Jesuits, all of which offered ample scope for tainting him with Jansenism in the king's eyes.[84] With Maintenon afraid formally to propose Barillon, Louis offered Bordeaux to the future Cardinal de Bissy, Henri de Thyard, then bishop of Toul in Lorraine. But having come to court to discuss the move with the king, he duly declined it. Various reasons were given for this by observers: one was that he could not afford the bulls for Bordeaux, as his father refused him financial assistance; another was his desire to remain 'wedded' to Toul; yet another that Bordeaux was too far away and he would prefer to wait until something closer to the court became available.[85] The upshot was that Bordeaux was offered three months later to a third candidate, Armand Bazin de Bezons, bishop of Aire in Gascony, a highly pro-Jesuit figure.[86] In the circumstances, Bazin could hardly complain of his lot or hold out, like Bissy, for a better offer later. Given the location of his existing diocese, Bordeaux was a major step upwards for him, while the king and his advisers finally found the right 'fit' of diocese and successor, not least because Bazin's brother had been intendant at Bordeaux since 1686. Similar comments could be made about the manner in which Auch was twice filled in Louis's last years when it was given to a Maupeou (1705) and a Desmarets (1714), or Embrun, given to a d'Argenson in 1714: all three men moved from relatively placid and minor dioceses to well-endowed but less than major archbishoprics. All three may have been related to ministers, present or future, but in the competition for the most attractive 'senior' sees, it seems as if their connections and patrons were much less influential than those of competitors like Aubigné, Mailly, Le Goux or Villeroy.

Of course, archiepiscopal nominations only accounted for a small proportion of all episcopal patronage in the years from 1692 to 1715. Strictly speaking, there were only fourteen such promotions in this period, which was relatively small compared to the 111-strong cohort of new bishops – five of them archbishops *ab initio* – entering the episcopate in the same period.[87] Nor, as we saw earlier, can they be divorced entirely from the bulk of decisions

83 AN, L 729, pièce 1, Bourges, no 15, Père Léonard's account of Potier de Gesvres's record as archbishop, and his success in ensuring that the additional revenues derived from the see of Albi agreed in 1676 were effectively paid. The upshot was that its income virtually doubled, though that still left it some way behind France's richest dioceses.

84 *Lettres de Maintenon* (ed Langlois), v, no 1243, to Noailles, 20 Nov 1697.

85 JRULM, MS French 92, fos 16v–17r, Huxelles to La Garde, 3 Feb 1698; fo 18, same to same, 5 Feb 1698.

86 AN, L 729, pièce 1, Bordeaux, no 4, Père Léonard papers.

87 This figure does not include Daniel de Cosnac, who was nominated to Aix in 1687.

about ordinary dioceses, if only because most archiepiscopal appointments involved promoting existing bishops, whose places had to be filled at the same time or shortly afterwards. As always, the exception here was the five vacant dioceses which were not archdioceses but nevertheless carried peerages with them.[88] Their attractiveness probably exceeded that of several archbishoprics, not least because they were also located within striking distance of the court and capital. Sees like Laon and Noyon were poorly endowed, but this prospect would only deter candidates who were either of undistinguished origins or who were poorly endowed with benefices in the first place, both increasingly unlikely. Madame de Maintenon may have argued against giving Châlons-sur-Marne to a Clermont-Tonnerre in 1696 when Noailles moved to Paris, but the ambition of the bishop of Noyon to have three ecclesiastical peerages in one family was not as quixotic as it sounds. A Clermont de Chaste relative had succeeded to Laon as recently as 1694, and a Clermont-Tonnerre would obtain Langres (a ducal peerage like Laon) only months after failing to secure Châlons.[89] Cardinal Forbin-Janson's preference for Beauvais over an archbishopric in 1679 – over a decade before he obtained his red hat – clearly underlined the relative attractiveness of this set of elite dioceses, and it is hardly surprising that when he died in 1713 it should have passed to one of the Beauvillier family. As we saw earlier, Noyon was given in 1701 to Maintenon's own relative, Claude-Maur d'Aubigné, and when, in an unusual move, he left it in 1707 for an archbishopric, that of Rouen, his successor, Châteauneuf de Rochebonne, was a member of the chapter of Saint-Jean of Lyon, the most prolific 'seminary' in France for aristocratic bishops. Aubigné underlined the special status of these bishoprics by securing the privilege of retaining his title of 'évêque et pair' despite his move to Rouen – and was imitated by others making similar moves later in the century.[90] Aubigné might have failed to gain entry to Saint-Jean had he sought it, but he had Maintenon's patronage to offset the limitations of his genealogy. As for the other bishops-cum-peers, their pedigree and, often, their close connections and service to the royal family itself ensured they would keep these dioceses beyond the reach of social outsiders.

V

Yet the persistence of such familiar features of episcopal patronage during the *grand siècle* should not obscure the fact that the latter years of the reign witnessed some noteworthy shifts in the profile of those entering the episcopate.

88   Paris and Reims were both archbishoprics. Beauvais, Laon and Noyon were comital peerages; Langres and Châlons-sur-Marne had ducal peerages.

89   The bishop of Noyon, whose genealogical vanity was legendry, was reluctant to recognise Clermont-Chaste of Laon as a blood relative: Saint-Simon, viii, appendice v, 442.

90   Jean-Pierre Labatut, *Les Ducs et pairs de France au xvii* siècle* (Paris 1972), 70.

Some of the most important of them have already been noted individually in earlier chapters, so it may be useful to recall them together here: the almost total dominance of theology graduates, especially from Paris, among new-comers to the bench; the gradual rise in the number of those who had once frequented major seminaries like Saint-Sulpice; the increased presence of men with experience of diocesan government as vicars-general or *officiaux* or who had participated in preaching or missions to Protestant areas. Moreover, these were not alternative or competing claims to preferment, but were increasingly *combined* in the same curricula vitae. When royal almoners who might also be sons of aristocratic families with names like Villeroy and Beauvillier not only took doctorates in theology, but also took up posts of vicars-general, it was obvious that a minor revolution in attitudes was taking place. One side-effect of this change was, as we also saw, that as soon as non-graduates became candidates for the mitre, they promptly set about gaining a degree, either in law or from a provincial theology faculty. In 1709 Louis XIV finally consented to allow Godet des Marais's nephew to become his coadjutor and successor at Chartres, but even though he was an active vicar-general in Chartres, it was agreed that the nomination could not be made until he had returned to the Sorbonne and completed his theology licence.[91] The cumulative effect of these trends was to ensure that the pool of potential candidates for episcopal office would be increasingly defined and particularised.

Change of this nature was gradual, but it picked up serious pace from the 1690s onwards. Assigning credit for it to particular individuals or groups risks creating artificial time sequences of a 'before' and 'after' type. It would be absurd to deny some of the credit to La Chaize and Harlay, both of whom in their different ways were looking for bishops with some record of activity. But the acceleration of change in the decades after the crisis with Rome points, as suggested earlier in this chapter, to the growing influence of the *dévot* networks allied to Mme de Maintenon, Godet des Marais, Bossuet and Noailles, once he was installed in Paris. Until his loss of favour Fénelon also played a part, if reports of his sessions with Louis XIV on 'the ancient discipline of the church' are true. Each of these individuals had their own circles of relations, which overlapped to a greater or lesser extent. Maintenon herself relied very heavily on Godet of Chartres, and it was mainly through him that the influence of Saint-Sulpice took shape. But while the evidence for Maintenon's ability to obtain bishoprics for clients of hers until the very end of the reign is not in doubt, the question remains as to whether the outcome came close to the plans she and her supporters had outlined in the 1690s. Predictably perhaps, the answer cannot be a simple 'yes' or 'no'. For one thing, one of Maintenon's prerequisites at that time, namely the removal of La Chaize as confessor, did not happen. Not only did he survive

---

91 BN, MS Fr 19212, fo 225r, Père Léonard, 'mémoires ecclésiastiques', n.d., 'Il l'auroit esté plustost nommé s'il avoit soustenu ses actes de licence'.

that 'external' threat, but the confessor also saw off the 'internal' challenges from his own Jesuit confrères, some of whom wanted to see him replaced by a confessor who would defend them more robustly against their critics inside and outside of the episcopate during these stormy years when their moral teachings and their stance over the Chinese rites put them on the defensive.[92] And when he made his own attempts to retire, as in 1704, it was the king who insisted that he stayed on – which he did until his death, aged eighty-five, in January 1709. The upshot of this was that competing influences and interests would continue to determine episcopal nominations either side of 1700. For much of the time, it seems that La Chaize was on the defensive. As already noted, he was able to discredit Barillon of Luçon as a candidate for Bordeaux in 1697, when Barillon enjoyed Noailles's support, but whether the elderly bishop would have accepted it anyway is highly doubtful.[93] At Easter 1698, when the abbé Coëteletz was 'revoked' as the nominee for Poitiers, it was La Chaize's turn to be very publicly mortified when an angry Louis XIV refused to sign off the *feuille des bénéfices* in question, and accused the confessor of allowing himself to be duped and, therefore, of duping the king in turn.[94]

A further possible reason for the furore was that the Coëteletz nomination was intended, along with others before it, to signal the king's desire to seek new bishops from outside the charmed world of the *abbés de cour*. It was probably the reason the king believed he had done the right thing in the first place by nominating Coëteletz, an archdeacon from Vannes in Brittany and unknown at court.[95] When precisely this particular 'turn' in episcopal patronage was first articulated remains unknown, but it could well have been early in 1698 after a series of nominations in previous years that had favoured court-based clerics and well connected families, some of them ministerial. It came at a time when the king's aversion to transfers and coadjutorships was also

92 *Lettres de Maintenon* (ed Langlois), v, no 1292, p 356, to Noailles, 12 July 1698, referring to La Chaize administering a coup de grace to Père le Valois. *Lettres de Germain Vuillart*, no 148, pp 359–60, 11 July 1700, 'le pauvre Père Confesseur est pillé et mangé par ses confrères de les laisser aujourd'hui et actuellement si indéfendus. Mais que voulez-vous que je face, leur dit-il, après les measures si justes et prises de si loin contre nous par l'archevêque de Reims et les autres.' The latter was a reference to Archbishop Le Tellier's role in the anti-Jesuit (and anti-regular) measures discussed by the 1700 Assembly of Clergy.

93 BN, MS Lat 18389 ('Vie autobiographique de Monsieur de Barillon, évêque de Luçon'), fo 310r, 'J'ai appris qu'on avoit encore songé à moi à Paque pour l'archeveché de Bordeaux. Dieu n'a pas permis que cela eut de suites. Je l'en remercie de tout mon coeur. L'état dans le quel j'étois et mon incapacité pour un fardeau aussi grand m'auroit obligé de le refuser.'

94 *Lettres de Germain Vuillart*, no 54, 10 May 1698, making the La Chaize-Coëteletz-Harlay connection. JRULM, MS French 92, fo 42, Huxelles to La Garde, 2 April 1698; Sourches, vi, 21, 29 March 1698. The nomination was reported to have been secured by the Jesuits in order to repay *premier président* Harlay, whose daughter had married into the Coëteletz family, for his good offices towards them in a recent dispute with Archbishop Le Tellier of Reims: AN, L 740, pièce 1, Poitiers, no 36, Père Léonard papers.

95 BN, MS Fr 6919, fo 178, letter to Noailles, 8 April 1698. JRULM, MS French 92, fo 42 (see p 178 above).

widely known.[96] At any rate, the king was reported in November 1698 as having just '*renewed* the declaration he had made [previously] not to give bishoprics to courtier clerics'. This 'renewal' coincided with the nomination to Alet of an archdeacon of Sens, Nicolas Taffoureau, who was known to Beauvillier for his work in Sens diocese, but who was recommended neither by La Chaize nor by his archbishop.[97] During 1698 and subsequent years, there is considerable supporting evidence for some such a commitment on Louis's part. The new bishops nominated to Poitiers and Boulogne earlier in 1698 were both associates of Bossuet who had obtained tutorships to members of the royal family for them, but both had subsequently moved to non-court activities rather than, say, seeking to become royal almoners.[98] Over the next few years, a steady stream of nominations followed the same pattern and, as in the case of Coëteletz, they were portrayed by those reporting them as 'unknowns'. In November 1702, Maintenon herself wrote to Noailles to say that the king had given Saint-Pol-de-Léon and Sarlat to two men 'whom he does not know', adding, as if in some trepidation, 'may God grant that he has made the right choices'. Evidently, nominating unfamiliar faces to bishoprics remained unsettling and 'unnatural'.[99] It was not the last time she would express such sentiments, which would sometimes be accompanied by a claim that there were no or scarcely any fit candidates for the episcopate.[100] Two years earlier she had admitted she had 'never heard' of the new bishop of Bayonne, even though the abbé Beauvau was from a prominent family with ancient Bourbon connections.[101]

96 As late as 1705, that aversion was still given by La Chaize as the reason why the king was reluctant to nominate a coadjutor for Quebec, even though its reigning bishop was being held prisoner in Farnham, England! In the end, after several discussions with Leschassier of Saint-Sulpice (and doubtless others), La Chaize persuaded Louis to change his mind: ASS, Correspondance des supérieurs-généraux, iii, no 1070, Leschassier to Bishop Saint-Valier, 18 Mar 1705. BM Versailles, MS G 329, fos 76–7, Bishop Turpin of Rennes to Maintenon, 5 Aug 1714, who claimed, in relation to Bissy of Meaux and Aubigné of Rouen (two of her closest friends in the episcopate), 'que s'ils ne scavoient pas l'eloignement que le Roy a pour les translation d'évêchés, ils me proposeroient pour celuy de Lisieux.'

97 JRULM, MS French 92, fo 155, Huxelles to La Garde, 7 Nov 1698. *Lettres de Maintenon* (ed Langlois), v, no 1322, p 395, to Noailles, 2 Nov 1698. Sourches, vi, 2 Nov 1698, notes that courtiers were intrigued by such a strange name as Taffoureau, but he himself observes curiously, 'mais la personne pouvoit avoir plus de mérite que le fils d'un duc et pair.' Dangeau, vi, 453, 2 Nov 1698, says the king nominated Taffoureau 'by reputation only and that no one had recommended him'. He ordered La Chaize to enquire of Archbishop Fortin if reports of Taffoureau were true.

98 Antoine Girard, nominated to Poitiers, was a former tutor to the comte de Toulouse who succeeded Fénelon's friend, Louis Milon, as superior of the Nouvelles Catholiques in Paris; Pierre de Langle, also a tutor to Toulouse, had become *agent-général* of the clergy in 1697 after Colbert de Croissy's son was nominated to Montpellier.

99 Maintenon, *Correspondance* (ed Lavallée), v, no ccxcv, p 227, letter of 2 Nov 1702. Lavallée incorrectly dated this letter to Nov 1703, but no episcopal nominations were made at that date.

100 For example: BN, MS Naf 13634, fo 38, Maintenon to Aubigné of Rouen, 29 July 1710: 'jamais je n'ai moins cognu les Evesques qu'à cettre promotion'.

101 *Lettres de Maintenon* (ed Langlois), v, no 1395, pp 516–17, to Noailles, 8 Nov 1700.

Needless to say, the search for outsiders who were not 'listed' on the confessor's *feuille* was bound to upset the more 'natural' aspirants for bishoprics. At various times in 1702, a bumper year for episcopal patronage when seven out of the eleven new bishops nominated could be classed as outsiders, Mme d'Huxelles picked up and reported echoes of the 'disputes' in question. One concerned Béziers, which was apparently being competed for by different *abbés de cour* with names like Estrées, Pomponne and Castries, whose claims to it seemed to enjoy support from La Chaize. The king, 'fed up of arguing over these men of quality', apparently asked him for the name of a vicar-general and the prize went to abbé du Rousset, vicar-general of neighbouring Carcassonne.[102] Later, in November 1702, the same source claimed that the *abbés de cour* 'were roughly treated, particularly over the bishoprics', with the result that several of them had left court to bide their time.[103] It seems that some of the more familiar anecdotes about Louis XIV tripping up La Chaize during their working sessions and asking him for the names of individuals on the *feuille des bénéfices* who were not based at court, date from precisely these years.[104]

It would be mistaken to take this search to mean that one type of bishop was about to supplant another. It may well be that, at a time when there were continuing problems with how to deal with nominally converted Huguenots and the establishment of *hôpitaux-généraux* in many cities, 'hommes de terrain' whose eyes were not fixed on the court, were regarded as more likely to become active bishops. The intention was to ensure access to the episcopate was not confined to court-based insiders, and the consequences of that could cut across social rank and extraction. Not every court cleric was of high noble status, nor every vicar-general from the provinces of commoner stock: in some cases, it could be the precise opposite. There was no question of setting aside conventions or applying one set of criteria to all dioceses. In November 1698 Taffoureau's nomination to Alet caused widespread comment, but he shared the limelight on that occasion with the celebrated Hercule Fleury, a royal almoner of similarly modest background who was simultaneously nominated

---

102 JRULM, MS French 94, fo 101, Huxelles to La Garde, 12 May 1702. Castries was nephew of Cardinal Bonsi. The new bishop of Béziers was related to the Grignan family, to which Huxelles's correspondent also belonged, and had been vicar-general of Carcassonne, then held by Louis-Joseph de Grignan! This would explain Huxelles's close interest in the Béziers succession.

103 JRULM, MS French 94, fo 233, Huxelles to La Garde, 27 Nov 1702, '[ils] ont eu sur les oreilles particulièrement pour les Evêchés'.

104 *Lettres de Mme de Maintenon* (Amsterdam edn, 1766), iv, 284–5 (April) 1706, Maintenon to Noailles, 'depuis long-tems il (Louis XIV) avoit mis Mr l'abbé de Genetine sur son mémoire, après l'avoir fait sur le témoignage de plusieurs personnes: qu'il est vrai que le p de la Chaise n'a point parlé pour lui: et que c'est de son seul mouvement qu'il a cherché un homme de condition qu'il a d'ailleurs cru bon. Il n'a pas encore signé la feuille: et je crois qu'il ne la signera pas sans faire quelque information.' The 'abbé de Genetine' (Antoine Charpin de Génétines) in question was nominated to Limoges on 3 April 1706. He was a native of Forez, like La Chaize, so the confessor's silence about him is intriguing.

to Fréjus. François Hébert, parish priest of Versailles, would surely have escaped the royal gaze entirely had he not been closely tied to Noailles and Bossuet who were instrumental in gaining Agen for him in 1703. On the other hand, when Evreux was rumoured vacant in 1699, the king made it clear that he wanted 'un homme de condition' for a successor, but without indicating why.[105] Three years later, it was accepted that Poitiers, too, ought to be confided to a bishop with genuine noble status, given how difficult it was for anyone else to govern it effectively.[106] The new bishop, La Poype, was from an old Dauphiné-Lyonnais family and a *chanoine-comte* of Saint-Jean of Lyon, while fellow nominees of these years bore names like Pas de Feuquières, Beaupoil de Saint-André, Voyer d'Argenson, Nettancourt, Caylus. And Maintenon pointed out that Charpin de Génétines was the 'homme de condition' that the king desired for Limoges in 1706.[107]

It would be tempting to regard the search for 'outsiders' and 'non-candidates' as evidence of the growth of the Maintenon-Godet-Noailles network's influence over episcopal patronage, and the decline of the confessor's long ascendancy in these matters. There is no doubt that many of those becoming bishops in the late 1690s and early 1700s were connected to the *dévots*, but it would be anachronistic to see this question in crude binary terms – with La Chaize, the gentleman-Jesuit and patron of 'abbés de qualité', on the opposite end of the spectrum. As suggested in an earlier chapter, the confessor was as well placed as his *dévot* 'opponents' to look for 'outsiders', and he did not lack for advice from friendly reigning bishops about vicars-general, missionaries, and the like who would make suitable bishops. Coëteletz, after all, was one such outsider, and it was La Chaize who proposed him. When unfamiliar individuals became bishops, contemporaries were just as likely to conclude that they were protégés of the Jesuits as of the *dévots*. If we were to list the patrons of incoming bishops chronologically during, say, the decade after 1695, what we would find is an alternation of *dévots* and Jesuits, with the former more prominent, especially in the later years. But equally we would find regular instances where the two interests combined to sponsor particular bishops; and there is no reason to imagine that there was anything unnatural about that. One example among many is that of Étienne de Champflour, who as bishop of La Rochelle after 1702 would play a peculiar part in the pre-*Unigenitus* conflicts. Like his contemporary Godet of Chartres, he had long been attached to Saint-Sulpice, having joined the 'Compagnie'

---

105 *Lettres de Maintenon* (ed Langlois), v, no 1352bis, p 444, to comte d'Ayen (Noailles), ca 5 Dec 1699. Maintenon gave no reason for the king's wish. Evreux did not become vacant until 1709, and its new bishop was almost as far from being 'un homme de condition' as was possible. But by then times had changed, and it was anti-Jansenism which now mattered most.

106 This was because of the large number of noble families resident in the diocese and who, it was thought, were unlikely to respect a bishop of low status or who was otherwise unable to sustain the 'dignité' of his office.

107 See n 104 above.

itself, but he was also closely connected to the Jesuits, having two brothers in the Society.[108] Yet it may be doubted whether without the Sulpician connection, he would have become a candidate for the mitre.

Although rivalry and competition over episcopal patronage continued unabated, it may be suggested that some of the edge was taken off it by the relative unimportance of 'ideological' problems while La Chaize remained confessor and, no less importantly, by the fact that both sides were ready to patronise the same types of candidate for the episcopate. If there was a major religious issue around 1690–1700, it was not Jansenism specifically, but the conflict between laxist (associated with the Jesuits) and 'rigorous' (or 'severe') moral theology. When the Jansenist issue flared up again in the last decade of the reign, it affected episcopal nominations more than it had ever done in earlier decades. In their different ways, both questions helped to boost the role and place of Saint-Sulpice in the episcopate. Not only did its alumni tend to become vicars-general and the like rather than court almoners, but the seminary had acquired a reputation for sure-footedness in theological and ecclesiological matters. Ever since Saint-Simon's bilious tirades against the entry of 'dirty beards' and 'flat-footers' into the episcopate of his day, the question of Saint-Sulpice's influence within the higher echelons of the French church has exercised historians, especially those of the eighteenth century. But that influence should be seen in its context. We noted some features of this 'peculiar institution' in an earlier chapter, which in itself showed how substantially different individual experiences of Saint-Sulpice could actually be. For much of Louis XIV's reign, as we also saw, it was only one of a cluster of similar institutions based in the capital, and if well-informed observers like Père Léonard are to be believed, it was not always the one that was most favoured by those in high places. However, it did enjoy some advantages over rivals like Saint-Magloire or Missions Étrangères de Paris. At a crucial period of its development, Louis Tronson, its long-serving superior-general (1676–1700), became a highly respected figure; related by blood to several prominent robe families of the capital, he served as director or adviser to ministers like Seignelay and Le Peletier in the 1680s and 1690s, but also to numerous bishops as they struggled with problems in their dioceses.[109] Just as crucial, from the perspective of this chapter, was his ability and that of his successor, Leschassier, to keep Saint-Sulpice well clear of entanglement with the Gallican Articles, Quietism or Jansenism, so that it was seen as less compro-

108   Lucien Ceyssens, 'Autour de la bulle Unigenitus. Jean-François de Lescure évêque de Luçon et Étienne de Champflour, évêque de La Rochelle', *Augustiniana*, 38 (1988), 149–204. P Delattre, *Établissements des Jésuites depuis quatre siècles. Répértoire topo-bibliographique publié à l'occasion du quatrième centenaire de la fondation de la Compagnie de Jésus, 1540–1940*, 4 vols (Enghien 1949–57), ii, cols 1012–14.

109   See *Correspondance de Tronson*. This selection of Tronson's correspondence is arranged under various headings. Letters to bishops are in the first section of vol iii, pp 1–172, with another section of 'lettres à divers laiques', pp 367–451, most of them to members of the Colbert family, especially to Seignelay.

mised than rival institutions like Saint-Magloire. In the final years of the reign, with religious controversy re-igniting, this feature of Saint-Sulpice would appeal just as much to a Jesuit confessor looking for bishops who would avoid 'heterodox' opinions as it would to Maintenon and her circle, who would also oppose Jansenism but who wanted bishops untainted by the moral laxism of which the Jesuits were accused. For her part, in addition to Godet, Maintenon also employed succesive curés of Saint-Sulpice parish, especially Joachim de La Chétardie, as her confessor for many years, and it is clear, as we saw above in relation to abbé Béthune-Charost, that she either solicited or received advice from him on particular candidates for the mitre. She even obtained the bishopric of Poitiers for La Chétardie himself in 1702, but he decided against taking it. After his death, she would turn for her confessor to his successor Jean-Baptiste Languet, brother of the notoriously anti-Jansenist bishop of Soissons, for whom she also obtained episcopal office in early 1715.[110] It was to curé Languet that she revealingly wrote, also in 1715, that his 'parish was as important as a diocese'.[111] When her own dissolute brother needed surveillance and assistance in his last years, it was to a priest of the parish community of Saint-Sulpice, Madot, that she turned, and for that he was successively rewarded with the dioceses of Belley (1705) and Chalon-sur-Saône (1711).[112]

Prior to the 1690s, the number of former residents or 'associates' of Saint-Sulpice entering the episcopate had been quite small – between four and six per decade – and it had even dropped during the 1680s, possibly because Tronson's determination to keep Saint-Sulpice clear of involvement in the gallican crisis of the time did not endear it to the king and his advisers of the day. But from the 1690s this began to change, though the pace of the change ought not to be exaggerated, nor is it fully conveyed by mere statistics. Nine new bishops of the 1690s and fourteen from the 1700s had connections to Saint-Sulpice. But while this increased tally is important, it is not the most

110 Théophile Foisset, 'Quarante-six lettres inédites de Madame de Maintenon', *Le Correspondant*, 1 (1859), 641–92. The correspondance begins in late June 1714 on La Chétardie's death, and much of it reflects Maintenon's involvement in the post-*Unigenitus* Jansenist affair. Bishop Languet finished his career as archbishop of Sens, and was responsible for collecting Maintenon's letters, many of which remain unpublished in the Bibliothèque municipale of Versailles. His *Mémoires de la vie de Madame de Maintenon*, based on the letters, are a major source of information about her and her doings.

111 Foisset, 'Quarante-six lettres inédites de Mme de Maintenon', no xxiii, p 38, 1 Jan 1715.

112 Maintenon, *Correspondance* (ed Lavallée), v, no cdxxvii, p 430, Maintenon to Madot, 22 Oct 1705. 'Lettres inédites de Mme de Maintenon', ed Henri Courteault, *Revue des Etudes Historiques* (1900), 401–13, for her letters to Madot. Her brother, whose daughter married Noailles's son, the comte d'Ayen, died at Bourbon in 1703. Her last letter to Madot (pp 412–13, 12 June 1712), written after his transfer to Chalon, conveys a sense of the war-weariness of the king's last years: 'c'est une grande consolation pour les gens de bien de voir de tels ministres de Jésus Christ en état d'augmenter son royaume et surtout dans un temps de si affligeantes contradictions . . . le Roi n'eut jamais plus de santé ni plus de courage pour soutenir la bonne doctrine, et pour rétablir ses peuples.'

significant change: whereas earlier Sulpician bishops had been scattered about France, from the 1690s onwards, a small number of them were able to play key roles in determining episcopal patronage. Godet of Chartres is the best known and most enduring of them, because of his closeness to Maintenon, but Fénelon's influence was cut short by Quietist controversy. The younger Noailles, Gaston, bishop of Châlons, may also have been instrumental in bringing younger 'Sulpicians' to the attention of the court. The simple fact that the duc de Beauvillier's half-brother was resident in Saint Sulpice for most of the decade after 1700 ensured that the duke, who followed his brother's progress with some anxiety, was in regular touch with the superior-general, which probably proved a useful channel for exchanges about church patronage.[113] An energetic figure like Bishop La Poype of Poitiers attracted younger Sulpicians into his service, and was almost certainly instrumental in bringing their claims to episcopal office to Maintenon's attention.[114] Two of Maintenon's own episcopal relatives, Aubigné and Caylus, were also former residents of Saint-Sulpice, and the first of them both received queries from, and freely gave advice to her about certain episcopal nominations.[115]

The upshot, therefore, was a steady rise in the number of Sulpician 'gradu-ates' entering the episcopate, especially in the early 1700s. This did not pass unnoticed, especially from 1702–3 onwards. The new superior-general, Leschassier, found himself explaining to Godet, *his* patron, that 'people write to me as someone who enjoys great credit with your lordship' – and imme-diately went on to explain to him how the Bishop of Autun was aiming to secure his nephew as his successor.[116] Indeed, Leschassier had to rebut charges that Saint-Sulpice wielded excessive influence over nominations, notably in

---

113 ASS, Correspondance des supérieurs-généraux, iii, nos 534, 610, 650, 877, 1106, 1357–8, for some of Leschassier's letters to Beauvillier, 1700 to 1708. In 1709, the abbé de Beauvillier left Saint-Sulpice to serve as vicar-general at Orléans.

114 BM Versailles MS G 329, fos 63–4, Rousseau de la Parisière, bishop of Nimes, to Maintenon, 12 March 1712, reference to 'M de Poitiers lorsqu'il eut la bonté de me presenter à vous'; fo 65, Châteauneuf de Rochebonne, évêque nommé of Noyon, to Maintenon, 22 April 1708, 'Monsieur l'Evesque de Poitiers a bien voulu me dire toutes les obligations que je vous ay'. La Poype had a sister who was a nun at Saint-Cyr, and thus an additional link to Maintenon. Some of his voluminous correspondence with Maintenon is in BM Versailles, MS G 331, fos 1–27 (for the years 1711–17 only).

115 BM Versailles, MS P 67, pp 244–6, Aubigné to Maintenon, 5 March 1710, expressing his views on how Evreux should be filled. Maintenon's own replies to him on Evreux (and other issues) are in BN, MS Naf 13634, fos 29, 31–2, 36. As metropolitan of Evreux, Aubigné did have a particular interest in the succession, but by 1710 there was also a Jansenist dimension to it. BM Versailles, G 329, fos 91–2, Aubigné to Maintenon [early 1712], expressing his wish to see Bishop Sanzay to obtain a transfer from Rennes, which is too impoverished for him, to Le Mans; fos 76–7, Bishop Sanzay of Rennes to Maintenon, 5 Aug 1714, on his need for a transfer or some additional resources.

116 ASS, Correspondance des supérieurs-généraux, iii, no 768, letter of 22 June 1702. The uncle-nephew succession at Autun went through in the following weeks; no 769, Leschassier to Godet, 24 June 1702, sending him the Bishop of Autun's letter outlining his reasons for resign-ing Autun to Bernard de Sénaux, his nephew, who had recently been nominated to Saintes.

that of Étienne de Champflour to La Rochelle in 1702: 'many people were strangely surprised and some conclude as a result that it would be best to withdraw altogether'.[117] He was heavily involved in discussions for a coadjutor-bishop of Quebec in 1705, when he and La Chaize were clearly at cross pur-poses.[118] Quebec might not belong to the 'French' church in the conventional sense, but the nomination rights belonged to the crown, and the candidates for the position included Sulpicians like Languet de Gergy who would become bishops in France in due course. Leschassier also had to admit that the choice of Pierre Sabatier for Amiens in 1706 'has raised an outcry against Saint-Sulpice', although he claimed that they had not been involved in it, and indeed were about to lose one of the Company's most valuable full members.[119] As he put it, 'he [Sabatier] was not expecting it, nor were many others either. Many will be mortified by this choice for a diocese so near to Paris'.[120] Inevitably, Leschassier's disclaimers were not believed, and the 'all powerful-ness' of Saint-Sulpice in the distribution of benefices, great and small, gradu-ally gained currency and was shared by well-placed ecclesiastics themselves in coming years.[121]

V

The growth in Saint-Sulpice's influence was something more than a new round in the endless competition for favour and office, as is clear from the impact of the Jansenist controversy during the king's last years. Moreover, the Jansenist issue also offers some of the best evidence for the limitations of the crown's capacity to select and promote only those clerics who would act as docile and doctrinally sound bishops. The king's early and well-known equa-tion of Jansenists with rebels need hardly be rehearsed here, and the fact that he 'inherited' from Mazarin a number of bishops who were openly sym-pathetic to Port-Royal rather than to a strictly theological Jansenism did nothing to diminish such sentiments. That some of them, such as Pavillon and Caulet, subsequently defied him over the Formulary and the *régale* affair, and even secured the highly public support of the philo-Jansenist Innocent

---

117 *Ibid*, no 845, n d (but early Jan 1703) to 'Monseigneur': 'plusieurs ont esté estrangement surpris et quelques uns . . . concluent de là qu'il faut prendre le parti de la retraitte pour toutes sortes de raisons.' Who precisely he has in mind in the second part of this sentence, and what the 'parti de la retraitte' refers to remain mysterious.

118 *Ibid*, nos 1060, 1067, 1089, letters to Bishop Godet, 27 Feb, 12 March and May 1705 respec-tively; nos 1070, 1084, to Bishop of Quebec, 18 March and 2 May 1705.

119 *Ibid*, no 1180, to Bishop La Poype of Poitiers, 17 Sept 1706, '. . . fait crier contre Saint-Sulpice'.

120 *Ibid*, no 1174, Leschassier to Bishop Fleuriau of Aire [Aug 1706].

121 *Ibid*, no 1223, Leschassier to Godet, 15 April 1707, claiming that the future Cardinal Polignac, while in Lyon on his way to Rome, made this assertion and led the vicar-general of Lyon to petition for a pension for a third party.

XI, was bound to strengthen those royal convictions further. But for as long as the Peace of the Church of 1669 – itself negotiated against a background of substantial episcopal support for bishops refusing to sign the anti-Jansenist Formulary which the crown and the papacy were trying to impose throughout France – endured, Jansenist-related problems would involve individual bishops rather than the episcopate generally. Thus when the eight or nine early Jansensist bishops died, mostly during the 1670s and 1680s, due care was taken to ensure that their successors would not only be irreproachably orthodox, but also willing to undo the damage done within their dioceses by their Jansenist predecessors. For this reason, 'adversarial' exercises of epis-copal patronage of this type were an episodic feature of the early decades of Louis's reign – as the choice of successor to Gondrin of Sens, Pavillon of Alet, Caulet of Pamiers, Choart of Beauvais and several others shows. Indeed, Louis seems to have told Bossuet to his face that he passed him over for Beauvais in 1679 because he was not convinced he would tackle the Jansenist problem there.[122] The Pamiers succession, as we saw, was rejected by more than one sitting bishop, doubtless because the prospect of restoring 'order' there was too unattractive.

The 'turn' towards greater severity in moral theology by the French church, which Bossuet himself exemplified, could also mean rigorist bishops being depicted as Jansenists, not least because their policies often brought them into conflict with the Jesuits and other regulars in their dioceses. Le Camus of Grenoble was *persona non grata* at court well before his independent elevation to cardinal's rank by Innocent XI on account of his repeated altercations with the local Jesuits, against whom he even appealed to Louis XIV in person.[123] But as the case of Le Camus itself suggests, Louis and his advisers were ulti-mately no more successful than Mazarin in filtering out 'Jansenists' from the *feuille des bénéfices*. During the two decades after 1661, fifteen or so bishops of varying degrees of Jansenist, rigorist or Port-Royal affiliation took office, followed by about thirteen more in the decades after 1692. Even these numbers are highly approximate, since the behaviour of individual bishops varied over time, and some of them probably did not genuinely discover their real preferences until well *after* they entered the episcopate. Some, like Le Tellier of Reims, Roquette of Autun or Coislin of Orléans were rigorists who were regarded as allowing too much latitude to Jansenists in their dioceses; others like La Broue of Mirepoix or Percin of Saint-Pons were

---

122 Quesnel, *Correspondance*, i, 26–7, letter to abbé Nicaise, 2 Nov 1680, recounting Chancellor Le Tellier's response to the refusal to give Beauvais to Bossuet in 1679: 'qu'on n'avoit eu garde de le lui donner, parce que l'on ne le croyoit pas assez ennemi du jansénisme'. Quesnel repeated this story when Bossuet was a candidate for Paris in 1695: p 364, letter to du Vaucel, 12 Aug 1695, 'qu'il ne serait pas homme à pousser à bout les jansénistes'.

123 *Lettres du cardinal Le Camus* (ed Ingold), no 152, pp 306–11, Le Camus to Louis XIV, 18 June 1678. Le Camus also wrote to Innocent XI to the same effect, but also asking his permission to resign as bishop: *Lettres du cardinal Le Camus* (ed Faure), no 98, pp 168–75, letter of 22 Nov 1678.

more openly Jansenist. At various times during the later Jansenist crisis, Fénelon would mercilessly identify some of the most anti-Jansenist of his episcopal contemporaries as having been Jansenists or pro-Jansenist in their earlier years, only to shift to safer ground for *politique* or careerist reasons. It was with such uncertain and unfixed 'material' that the king and his advisers had to deal when filling episcopal vacancies, so it is hardly surprising that their assessment of those they promoted was to be disproved later in numerous instances. It was during the last seventeen years of the La Chaize confessorship (1692–1709) that all of the thirteen 'Jansenist' bishops of the final decades of the reign mentioned above were nominated. Few would have predicted at the time that Colbert de Croissy of Montpellier and Pierre de Langle of Boulogne, both serving *agents-généraux* of the clergy when they were made bishops in 1696–8, would become unyielding Jansenists and authors of the 1717 appeal to a future general council against the bull *Unigenitus*. But the same might be said in respect of others, such as Hervault of Tours, a former Auditor of the Roman Rota, or the celebrated Oratorian and Harlay-man, Soanen of Senez. All of them had occupied positions from which they were relatively easy to observe and evaluate, yet nobody predicted their subsequent affiliations.[124] Others again, such as Verthamon of Pamiers or Desmarets of Saint-Malo (brother of the *contrôleur-général des finances*) would pass through a Jansenist phase before returning to more orthodox positions. The last on this list of Jansenist bishops, André Dreuillet, was nominated to Bayonne at Easter 1707. Much more needs to be known about the religious affiliations of their families and their early milieux before making judgements about why 'Jansenism' appealed to these men: Croissy of Montpellier was not merely a Colbert, he was also related to the Arnauld family; and it will hardly come as a surprise that Gaston de Noailles of Châlons followed in his brother's pro-Jansenist footsteps.

Counter-balancing this numerically modest influx of Jansenists into the episcopate were the continuing attempts made during the 1690s and 1700s to ensure that 'Jansenist' bishops were replaced by men with anti-Jansenist credentials. This was especially evident at Angers (1692), La Rochelle (1693 and 1699) and Luçon (1699), whose bishops, the 'three Henries', had published a famously 'rigorist' catechism. If Maintenon's relative, Aubigné, was persuaded to leave the peerage-bishopric of Noyon for Rouen, it was to combat the supposed Jansenist legacy of Jacques-Nicolas Colbert there. The Jansenism of Louis Fouquet of Agde was too well known for his Oratorian nephew to have much hope of succeeding him in 1702, which in turn makes the nomination in 1697 to Metz of Henri du Cambout, nephew of the pro-Jansenist Cardinal Coislin, even more puzzling. The difference was, no doubt,

124 That there were some questions about whether Colbert of Montpellier's anti-Jesuit sentiments amounted to Jansenism is clear from the fact that Noailles was called upon to certify his orthodoxy before his nomination in 1697: Durand, *Le Jansénisme et Joachim Colbert*, 365–6.

that the Coislin were in favour, the Fouquet definitely not – and such considerations, it need hardly be repeated, were not insignificant.[125] However, when Cardinal Coislin himself died in 1706, Orléans was given in quick succession to two proven anti-Jansenist bishops, Le Peletier of Angers (who died shortly after) and then to his cousin, Fleuriau of Aire under whom the ensuing repression was severe enough to prompt some of the late cardinal's closest supporters to take shelter at Metz.[126] The following decades would witness much more of this kind of episcopal activity, sometimes anticipating, sometimes following royal policy, but often supported by a liberal use of *lettres de cachet*.

By this point, the last decade of the reign, the politico-religious context had begun to change significantly. We need only dwell here on those aspects of it which are necessary for an understanding of church patronage during these years.[127] The early attacks, especially that of 1698, on Noailles himself for having approved and recommended the exiled Oratorian Pasquier Quesnel's *Réflexions morales*, did little immediate damage: even if they did make the king have doubts about his orthodoxy, they were not enough to prevent him from becoming a cardinal in 1700, let alone exclude him, as already noted, from playing his part in episcopal nominations.[128] Moreover, Quesnel's work had been read, admired and recommended by figures as diverse as Bossuet, La Chaize, and Clement XI himself when still Cardinal Albani. But attacks like this were signs of what was to come, and would soon overlap with other incidents. In 1703, the seizure and subsequent partisan use of Quesnel's correspondence by the Jesuits, revealed the spectre of a vast Jansenist conspiracy with links inside and outside of France, one which seemed to involve even some French bishops; under a king as convinced as

---

125 Louis XIV's actual dislike of the nephew was well known, but he greatly esteemed the uncle. According to Saint-Simon, the nomination to Metz was made in order to placate his uncle who had recently been involved in a serious quarrel at court with the duc de la Rochefoucauld. Saint-Simon, iv, 121–3.

126 BN, MS Fr 19212, fo 236, 1 July 1709, Père Léonard, 'mémoires ecclésiastiques', referring to new bishop of Orléans's measures, including changing the epitaph on his predecessor's tomb in Orléans cathedral to remove mention of Cardinal Coislin's rigorist policies. See also E Fleur, *Essai sur la vie et les oeuvres de Henri-Charles du Cambout duc de Coislin évêque de Metz 1697–1732*, vol i (Nancy 1933), 125–7, an account based largely on Saint-Simon, xiii, 250–6.

127 The bibliography of the Jansenist crisis of these years is vast, and the account that follows is based mainly on Blet, *Le Clergé de France, Louis XIV et le Saint-Siège*; Lucien Ceyssens and J G A Tans, *Autour de l'Unigenitus* (Louvain 1987), a series of connected essays by Ceyssens, some of which will be cited individually in subsequent notes; McManners, *Church and Society*, ii, chs 35–6; Catherine Maire, *De la cause de Dieu à la cause de la nation. Le Jansénisme au xviii*ᵉ *siècle* (Paris 1998), 51–85; Marie-José Michel, *Jansénisme et Paris* (Paris 2000), ch 4.

128 There are relatively few serious studies of Noailles. Ceyssens, 'Le Cardinal de Noailles (1651–1729)', in *Autour de l'Unigenitus*, 649–733, focuses mainly on the Jansenist question. Marcel Fossoyeux, 'Le Cardinal de Noailles et l'administration du diocèse de Paris', *Revue Historique*, 114 (1913), 261–84; 115 (1914), 34–54, provides some broader perspectives. The portrait of Noailles by Pierre Chaunu in Pierre Chaunu *et al*, *Le Basculement religieux de Paris aux xviii siècle* (Paris 1998), ch 4, is a tirade lacking in historical sense and proportion – in sharp contrast to the following chapter, by Françoise de Noirfontaine, on Noailles post-1715.

Louis XIV of the connection between Jansenism and subversion, such revelations were dangerous, although the bishops concerned were spared the rigours imposed on lesser ecclesiastics rounded up and *embastillés*.[129] Simultaneously in France, polemic and censure grew apace, particularly after the famous *Cas de Conscience* of 1701 that led to the issue in 1705, at Louis XIV's express request, of a papal bull, *Vineam Domini*. Although it did formally end the equivocation built into the Peace of 1669 by condemning the 'respectful silence' as to the presence of the Five Propositions in Jansen, *Vineam Domini* failed to resolve any of the underlying issues.[130] For precisely that reason, it opened the door to a new chapter of pressure, harassment and persecution of those suspected of heterodox views, as illustrated most evidently – and notoriously – in the dispersion of the remaining nuns of Port-Royal (1709) and the brutal razing of the abbey (1711). Louis XIV and his advisers finally decided to press for a more exhaustive and definitive papal pronouncement on the Jansenist problem, and their persistence resulted in the celebrated bull of September 1713, *Unigenitus*, with its condemnation of 101 propositions from Quesnel's *Réflexions morales*.

What is worth noting here is the nature of the role played in this phase of the Jansenist conflict by France's bishops, by contrast with that of fifty years previously, when their role was essentially reactive and largely confined to assemblies of clergy. The first formal censure of Quesnel's *Réflexions* dates from 1703 and was the work of Foresta-Coulongue, the openly pro-Jesuit bishop of Apt in Provence, while others, such as the archbishop of Besançon and the bishop of Nevers, would follow suit in 1707.[131] The very 'gallican' format of the reception of the bull *Vineam Domini* by the 1705 Assembly of Clergy incensed Rome and the anti-Jansenists, whose ire was increasingly directed at Noailles, the architect of this very public exhibition of gallican ecclesiology, as much as Quesnel.[132] Noailles's subsequent refusal to offer Rome

129 See Lucien Ceyssens, 'Les Papiers de Quesnel saisis à Bruxelles et transportés à Paris en 1703 et 1704', *Revue d'Histoire Ecclésiastique*, 44 (1949), 508–51; *idem*, 'Pasquier Quesnel', in *Autour de l'Unigenitus*, 583–648. Bishops whose letters were discovered and broadcast included Le Tellier of Reims, Sève of Arras (and other anti-Jesuits). Le Tellier was in semi-disgrace as a result, while Sève, already out of favour, tempered his anti-Jesuit actions, a step apparently taken by other confreres. BN, MS Fr 19212, fo 82, Père Léonard 'mémoires ecclésiastiques', 3 Sept 1704 (Sève); fo 131v, 26 Jan 1705 (Le Tellier).

130 Blet, *Le Clergé de France, Louis XIV et le Saint-Siège*, chs 6–9, is the most detailed account of the genesis, reception and fate of the bull, based mainly on French and papal diplomatic sources. See also Lucien Ceyssens, 'La Bulle *Vineam Domini* (1705) et la jansénisme français', *Antonianum*, 64 (1989), 398–430.

131 BN, MS Fr 19212, fo 55, for Apt's censure, which threatened anyone reading the *Réflexions* with automatic excommunication. Ceyssens, *Autour de l'Unigenitus*, 635–8, for these and other attacks on Quesnel.

132 Blet, *Le Clergé de France, Louis XIV et le Saint-Siège*, ch 8. The 1705 Assembly refused to accept the bull 'purely and simply' as a papal decree, but insisted on associating itself with the pope in the act of deciding and condemning. The idea of French bishops acting as co-judges with the pope was anathema in Rome, since it seemed to subordinate papal judgements to the approval of the French clergy. Noailles, having presided at the 1705 Assembly, was held

any satisfaction on this point even had the effect of Rome deliberately slowing down the granting of provisions to new bishops around 1709–10.[133] In 1710, it was the turn of the bishops of La Rochelle and Luçon to relaunch the attack on Quesnel – but in reality on Noailles, since their pastoral instruction was placarded all over Paris – and in the ensuing fray other bishops not merely took opposite sides but publicly confronted each other.[134] A war of attrition, in which episcopal ordinances served as heavy artillery, ensured that 'parties' of a sort began to form within the episcopate, with Noailles's mostly gallican rather than outright Jansenist supporters denouncing the anti-Jansenist bishops as tools, wittingly or otherwise, of the Jesuits and of ultramontanes like Fénelon. Along the way, assemblies of clergy, pastoral instructions, and pamphlets raised the stakes, and not even *Unigenitus* when it did finally appear could restore calm. By the time Louis XIV died in September 1715, the bull had split the French episcopate in a manner that was unprecedented: most accepted it, but a substantial minority did not, or only did so with qualifications, despite the enormous pressure brought to bear upon them.[135] Had a projected national council convened while the king was still alive, Noailles himself risked disgrace and formal deposition as cardinal and as archbishop of Paris for having refused to accept *Unigenitus*.

VI

It is not hard to imagine the side-effects of this long-drawn out affair on the episcopate and those entering it during these years. As noted earlier, the last of those bishops who would openly reject *Unigenitus* and appeal to a future council, Dreuillet of Bayonne, was nominated as late as 1707. The influence of the orthodox Saint-Sulpice on nominations was at its height in the early 1700s, so it is not surprising that some of the most prominent anti-Quesnel and anti-Noailles bishops, such as Luçon and La Rochelle, were themselves Sulpicians. Polemic and censure were, it seems, forcing potential candidates for episcopal office into taking positions in a way that the Peace of the Church had hitherto rendered at least avoidable. But potentially the most significant

responsible for this provocation, and in the coming years he would become the main target of the anti-Jansenists, some of whom were anxious to use the affair to promote the thesis of papal infallibility.

133   ASV, Nunz Fr 219, fos 31–33, 69–70, 256, 282–3, 374, nuncio to secretary of state, 29 March 1707, 6 June 1707, 10 Aug 1708, 28 Sept 1708, and 1 July 1709 respectively; Nunz Fr 221, fo 245, nuncio to secretary of state, 20 May 1709, for further suggestions about delaying bulls for new bishops. Maintenon was aware of the difficulties in obtaining provisions from Rome in 1710: *Lettres inédites Maintenon-Ursins* (ed Bossange), ii, 49, letter to Ursins, 17 March 1710, 'nos affaires ne manquent pas de difficultés a Rome aussi bien qu'ailleurs'.

134   Lucien Ceyssens, 'Autour de la bulle Unigenitus. Jean-François de Lescure évêque de Luçon et Étienne de Champflour, évêque de La Rochelle', 149–204, esp 170ff.

135   AM Saint-Malo, GG 290, no 25, 'La Tour de Babel'.

factor was the arrival of a new royal confessor following the death, after thirty-five years of service, of the aged La Chaize in January 1709. It took a month to find a successor, but little is known of how exactly the decision was reached. In the absence of supporting evidence, one can but note Saint-Simon's account that the search for a confessor was confided, even while La Chaize was still alive, to the ducs de Chevreuse and Beauvillier, but nothing had been decided before the confessor's death, whereupon Maintenon ensured that Godet of Chartres and the curé of Saint-Sulpice would participate in their discussions and thus swing the decision in a fateful direction.[136] As usual there were several Jesuits on the list, some of them suggested by La Chaize himself before his death.[137] Maintenon and Noailles supported the same candidate, Père La Rue, but he was among those passed over. She claimed that the king was searching for 'a straight man who would not bend' and who would, therefore, be the opposite of La Chaize, whose affability and nonchalance were thought to have 'spoilt' too many affairs.[138] But if the choice of Michel Tellier, only recently installed as provincial superior of 'France', fitted well into such a putative royal design, it was less calculated to restore calm to the French church: Tellier had been deeply embroiled in many of the major religious controversies – the Chinese rites, the polemic over 'philosophical' sin, the Quesnel affair – over the previous twenty years, and in which he neither took nor gave much quarter.[139] Doctrinaire and intransigent, his accession to the confessorship was a victory for a particular tendency within the Jesuits. Few characters have been as blackly painted as Tellier in Saint-Simon's vast portrait gallery, and the duke's stinging verdict, from which Tellier's reputation has never recovered, included references, *inter alia*, to his partisan handling of episcopal patronage.[140]

Only five years younger than Louis XIV himself, Tellier was certainly more enterprising than La Chaize had ever been, and more determined to press the king into agreeing with him.[141] He was no less firmly convinced of the need

---

136 Saint-Simon, xvii, 52–7. Saint-Simon claimed that his source for this was Mareschal, the king's *premier chirurgien*, who recounted the story to the duke and his wife.

137 Hillenaar, *Fénelon et les Jésuites*, 254.

138 Lucien Ceyssens, 'Madame de Maintenon (1635–1719)', in *Le Sort de l'Unigenitus*, 47–100. Père La Rue, a well-regarded preacher, was probably seen as too close to Noailles to be made confessor. See Hillenaar, *Fénelon et les Jésuites*, appendix xx, p 368 ('Extraits d'un mémoire adressé en mai 1720 à un jésuite de Rome'): 'Le Père de la Rue a toujours eu presque le mesme dévouement pour M le cardinal de Noailles que le P Gaillard, et la mesme opposition pour le zèle du P Le Tellier'.

139 Ceyssens, 'Le P Michel Le Tellier 1643–1719', in *Autour de l'Unigenitus*, 333–400, is the only extensive study, ancient or modern, of Tellier, but it is strongly influenced by the author's visible antipathy towards the man and the Jesuits of the day generally.

140 Saint-Simon, xvii, 57–61. For an attempt to defend Tellier against Saint-Simon, see P Bliard, *Les Mémoires de Saint-Simon et le Père Le Tellier confesseur de Louis XIV* (Paris 1891).

141 Saint-Simon, xx, 82–9, for his success in persuading Louis XIV to grant a bishopric (Autun) to abbé Maulévrier de Langeron, something La Chaize had failed to do, despite Langeron's connections and his position of *agent-général* of the clergy.

to destroy the Jansenist hydra, and this particular mission was not separate from the nurturing of an anti-Jansenist episcopate. But however anxious he may have been to dominate church patronage, we ought not to assume that he was given carte blanche on this question. As always, other long-standing interests were involved and could not be ignored. In this, as in other matters, Tellier knew perfectly well that he had to work hard to win the cooperation if not the respect of the *dévot* circles around the ducs de Bourgogne, Beauvillier and Chevreuse, who looked certain to govern France after the king's death, and for that he used the likes of the absent Fénelon and even Saint-Simon himself.[142] Clearly, many quarrels, past and imminent, with Noailles ensured that the two men could not seriously cooperate in guiding the royal choice of new bishops. But Maintenon still saw herself as 'mother of the church', despite the failure of Noailles to match up to her expectations. The death of her principal adviser on ecclesiastical matters, Godet of Chartres, only months after La Chaize in 1709, deprived her of a trusted conduit to ecclesiastical circles. His nephew and successor at Chartres, Mérinville, was too young and inexperienced to take his place, which went to another anti-Jansenist, Bissy, bishop of Meaux since 1704, who would become one of Père Tellier's main supporters in the coming years. Unlike Godet, he was not a product of Saint-Sulpice, but Maintenon retained close contacts there via her successive confessors, La Chétardie and Languet. Moreover, by 1709, she had supporters or clients within the episcopate who could help her to exercise some sway over appointments. Her anti-Jesuit sentiments might not have disappeared completely, but the anti-Jansenist struggle of Louis XIV's final years ensured that she and Tellier were more often allies than rivals.

One of Saint-Simon's criticisms of Tellier has particular point here – namely, his introduction into the episcopate of obscure dependents who owed him everything and who knew that they would have to accept his direction. For the duke, Tellier's bishops were even more objectionable than the 'dirty beards' of Saint-Sulpice. Worse still, Tellier used contemptible tricks which enabled him to surprise candidates and interested parties, for example by making episcopal nominations at dates other than those of the major feast-days of the year. Given how often the charges have been recycled ever since, it is essential to look closely at them. Some of the issues are more straightforward than others, and there is no need to argue either for or against the duke's view of the substandard bishops whom Tellier was responsible for making during his short confessorship. During his six-year term, thirty new bishops entered the episcopate, while five existing bishops were promoted to archbishoprics (although one of them, François de Mailly, was already archbishop in a lesser see). This level of 'turnover' corresponds very closely to the average for the personal rule as a whole, though Tellier might have fared

---

142   Saint-Simon, xvii, 63–4, for Saint-Simon's account of his first encounters with the intimidating confessor.

slightly better had Louis XIV been willing to make further nominations in his last months. In purely arithmetical terms, what this means is that just below one-quarter of the episcopate was replaced during the Tellier confessorship, and any evaluation of his activity must bear this in mind. Appointments were also scattered unevenly across the six years after February 1709, but there was nothing especially unusual about that and, with one possible exception to which we shall return later, there was no untoward delaying or 'bunching' of nominations.

What then is the veracity of Saint-Simon's charge that Tellier deliberately wrong-footed candidates and interested parties by making nominations in advance of the usual feast-days when the king was accustomed to distributing benefices? First of all, it should be noted that while two new bishops were nominated after Easter 1709, less than two months after the new confessor entered service, these were the only nominations of the entire first eighteen months of his tenure. The first newcomer to have the honour was the famous Belsunce of Marseille, nephew of Lauzun, and if his nomination took place a few days after Easter 1709, it was for the simple reason that the king was indisposed the previous week and had postponed his *grandes dévotions*.[143] Godet des Marets's successor at Chartres was nominated three weeks later again, but as this initially entailed a coadjutorship, it was manifestly a special case, the timing of which was of no general import and may not have involved the confessor except in a nominal way. Saint-Simon's memory of Tellier's 'skulduggery', however, derived mainly from the next set of nominations, which took place in mid-July 1710, a month before the normal date of 15 August, and which involved no fewer than eight vacant dioceses. The timing itself might well not have loomed so large in the duke's mind had fewer nominations occurred at that date.[144] Two of the dioceses involved, Autun and Evreux, had been vacant since April and October 1709 respectively, but in fact nominations had been made to each one without delay: what could not be foreseen was that the *évêque nommé* of Evreux would die in February 1710 and his counterpart for Autun would, after long reflection, simply return the *brevet*.[145] All of the other six sees had fallen vacant between February and late June 1710, so filling them in July 1710 was hardly proof of deplorable insouciance. At first sight, it is more difficult to establish why some at least of these decisions were not made at the usual dates of Easter or Pentecost, or at least not delayed until the *grandes dévotions* of mid-August. Curiously, neither Dangeau nor

---

143 BN, MS Fr 19212, fo 222, Père Léonard, 'mémoires ecclésiastiques', 4 April 1709. Easter Saturday, when nominations would normally have been decided, fell on 30 March.

144 Saint-Simon, xx, 75–89, for an extended account of these nominations.

145 Sourches, xi, 338 and Dangeau, xii, 417, 18 May 1709 (for Autun); Sourches, xii, 109 and Dangeau, xiii, 57, 1 Nov 1709 (Evreux). The nominee for Autun was the abbé de Maulevrier-Langeron who had twice served as *agent-général* of the French clergy, and he had previously declared that he had no great desire to be a bishop, not least because his revenues from the *agence* and his benefices were easily the equivalent of those of a bishopric: BN, MS Fr 19211, fo 77r, Père Léonard, 'mémoires ecclésiastiques', 27 Dec 1703.

Sourches comments at all on the timing of these nominations, though both were aware of the backlog that had been building up in previous months.[146] The most plausible reason that can be given for both the initial delay and the 'out of season' timing of the nominations of July 1710 is that only two weeks earlier an important assembly of clergy, which met during May-June, had finally dispersed, and that with the return of the Jansenist question, the crown reverted to Mazarin's tactics in order to control the assembly.[147] Of the seven new bishops chosen in July 1710, five had been members of the assembly.[148] But there is really no evidence that a precedent was being deliberately set for the years to follow, as a close look at the timetable of subsequent nominations makes clear. Between 1710 and 1715, a small handful of nominations were made which did *not* occur on the conventional feast-days, but there is independent evidence in at least some cases that this was because an original nominee had second thoughts about entering the episcopate, which in turn triggered a replacement nomination either some days or weeks later. The most unusual instance of this dates from Easter 1712 when Louis XIV nominated the abbé de Vassé to Le Mans. How – or indeed why – this particular nomination happened at all is not clear, since the abbé, reputedly of 'great piety', was aged eighty, easily the oldest nominee to a bishopric of the whole century! He at least had the good sense to return the honour, leaving the king to make a second nomination two weeks after Easter.[149] When no nominations were made at Christmas 1714, Dangeau merely noted that they were promised for two weeks later – and that promise was duly honoured.[150] Whatever else Père Tellier may have been trying to do, springing surprises of the kind alleged by Saint-Simon was, with the one possible exception of July 1710, not among them. What probably annoyed Saint-Simon most about the mid-1710 nominations is that it was made known in advance that Père Tellier alone was to be consulted over the nominations.[151]

None of this, of course, accounts for the other objectives Tellier may have pursued in the choice of new bishops. Saint-Simon's case against the confessor for packing the episcopate with obscure dependents relies heavily on the

---

146　Sourches, xii, 238, 7 June 1710. Dangeau, xiii, 205–6, 11 July 1710, for a list of the bishoprics and abbeys then vacant and which he calculated were worth nearly 450,000 *livres* a year in revenues – an inviting prospect for benefice-seekers of all stripes.

147　ASV, Nunz Fr 222, fo 267, 'news from Paris' sent by nuncio to secretary of state, 14 April 1710, where the postponement of nominations is explained in terms of the large number of candidates for them.

148　AN, G⁸, vol 89, *procurations* to 1710 Assembly. For its history, see Blet, *Le Clergé de France, Louis XIV et le Saint-Siège*, 293–324.

149　Sourches, xiii, 336–7, 26 March 1712, for nomination; 353, 11 April 1712, for his 'remerciement au roi' a few days previously, which opened the way to the immediate nomination, on 8 April, of Rogier du Crévy to Le Mans.

150　Dangeau, xv, 315, 24 Dec 1714; 341, 12 Jan 1715. The nominations were actually decided on 11 Jan, when Tellier met the king, but were not announced until the following day.

151　*Lettres inédites Maintenon-Ursins* (ed Bossange), ii, 70, to Ursins, 25 May 1710, referring to the forthcoming *distribution des bénéfices* 'dans laquelle personne ne sera appelé que le P le Tellier'.

mid-1710 nominations, so a brief look, under a number of headings, at what actually happened then may serve as a point of departure for a more general assessment of all nominations under his confessorship. Three of the seven new bishops nominated then were indeed of relatively modest social origins, though only one of them (Le Normand of Evreux) was born a commoner; both Rousseau of Nîmes and Lobière of Comminges were from recently ennobled families. But the other four newcomers were of more ancient noble stock, and included a Montmorin de Saint-Hérem and a Turgot. Montmorin of Aire already had an uncle who was a well respected archbishop of Vienne, while Turgot, whose family was of 'old' noble status long before it took up robe officeholding, was an *agent-général* of the clergy and almoner to the duc de Berry. All seven nominees were either vicars-general to reigning bishops or held equivalent-status positions, so they were neither untried nor obscure within the ecclesiastical world of the day.[152] One consequence of this was that with the exception of Turgot, none of them was court-based; three of them served as far away as Vienne, Rodez and Mende. Attendance at the 1710 Assembly probably helped to offset this occupation-induced *éloignement* and brought them to the attention of the court. But as we do not know how much pressure was exerted upon the provinces to elect pliable second-order delegates already known to the court, distinguishing cause and effect here is problematic.

This brief group portrait seems largely representative of the bishops of Louis XIV's final years. A further six of those nominated between 1709 and 1715 had either commoner origins or had nobility that was itself recent or somewhat obscure. But here, too, we should not jump to conclusions: their social status was compensated for by their activities and connections. One of them was the son of the king's favourite physician, the great Fagon; another, Malezieu, was tutor and son of a tutor to the king's son, the duc du Maine and his children. Vicar-generalships were also widely shared among them, with the exception of Jean du Doucet, who was no more than a curate in Saint-Sulpice parish when nominated to Belley – the parish which Maintenon would claim was an important as a diocese. These were precisely the kind of nominations which Saint-Simon would regard as demeaning the episcopate, but it is worth noting that a sense of proportion was observed in the choice of dioceses for these men. Competition for sees like Belley, Lombez, Lavaur or Saint-Paul-Trois-Châteaux was always infinitely less intense than for those with better revenues and location, which was why they were frequently offered to members of religious orders or the new congregations of the seventeenth-century. The exception among the dioceses given to 'obscure men' (in Saint-Simon's terms at least) in the 1710s was probably Soissons: although

152 The five were vicars-general of Laon (two), Rodez, Mende and Vienne. Turgot and Le Normand were the two exceptions, but Turgot's rank of royal almoner and *agent-général*, and Le Normand's post of *official* and *promoteur* of Paris under Noailles made them more rather than less prominent figures.

poorly endowed, its proximity to Paris meant that it could always attract bishops with private means or with an income derived from other benefices. In early 1715, after the death of Brûlart de Sillery, it was given to Languet de Gergy, a former protégé of Bossuet and son of a financial family from Dijon. Interestingly, only Languet and Fagon were later to move from their first dioceses to better ones, doubtless because of their connections and services.

It will be clear from what we have just seen that even the most obscure of the 'Tellier' bishops enjoyed patronage and protection from well-placed patrons, which in turn brings us back to the question of how far the confessor alone 'made' bishops in the way the historiography, relying on Saint-Simon, usually contends. When the focus of attention shifts from the marginal bishops discussed above to their more 'distinguished' contemporaries, by birth at least, it becomes evident that up to two-thirds of the 'Tellier' bishops were not 'dependents' of the confessor. Sons or relatives of ministers (Phélypeaux, Trudaine, Beauvillier), of great nobles (Belsunce, Villeroy, Brancas, Crillon, Forbin-Janson, Dromesnil), and courtiers (Sourches, Fagon), to name just some, would not have been reduced to soliciting Père Tellier to make their case for preferment. Laval de Montmorency, the short-lived bishop of Ypres in 1713, was 'obscure' only in the sense of being part of Fénelon's circle at Cambrai, but his patron's close ties with Tellier, Beauvillier and Chevreuse did more than remedy this defect. Likewise, it is hard to imagine Père Tellier persuading Louis XIV to give episcopal office to the eighty-year old abbé de Vassé, so the case for offering him Le Mans, one of France's largest dioceses, must have been made by someone else. The same impression emerges from the promotions to archbishop made during this period. Tellier is usually credited with moving François de Mailly from Arles to Reims in order to spite Noailles, but Maintenon was right behind this advancement of a relative. As we saw earlier, Arles itself was given to a nephew of the *grand aumônier de France*, Cardinal Forbin-Janson, who allegedly objected, on the grounds that his nephew was unfit for such a position.[153] Three of the remaining archiepiscopal promotions went to scions of ministerial families – Desmarets, Villeroy, Argenson – while Toulouse, as we saw, was reserved for Beauvau of Tournai. On this kind of evidence, it can be said that Tellier's influence over the king was, in numerous instances, perhaps more nominal than real: episcopal nominations still had to go via the confessor, but he either bowed to pressures emanating from the circles noted above, or was ready to satisfy their ambitions in many cases.

If this suggestion is well founded, it would help explain the continuing role of Maintenon and her circle in episcopal patronage. As we saw, she herself was far from abandoning her interest in it during these years, and was no more willing to see it monopolised by Tellier than by his predecessor. Nor is it hard

153 Saint-Simon, xx, 79–80.

to imagine her playing her part in more than one of the nominations just discussed. Bishop Hébert of Agen wrote specifically to thank her for her role in the very first episcopal nomination after La Chaize's death, that of Belsunce of Marseille.[154] The record of nominations itself is supported by the evidence, patchy and episodic though it is, of her surviving correspondence. Ensuring that Chartres would remain in safe hands after Godet's death was of the greatest importance to her, on account of Saint-Cyr, even though she understood the dangers of having an inexperienced bishop there.[155] The deferential Des Montiers de Mérinville never acquired his uncle's influence over her, so she sought advice from elsewhere, notably from her own relative, Aubigné, archbishop of Rouen from 1707. Whether the nomination of the abbé Sublet de Heudicourt to Evreux, a suffragan and immediate neighbour of Rouen, in 1709, was done at their instigation or not, they had every reason to welcome it.[156] Sublet's sudden death early in 1710 spurred Maintenon and Aubigné into action. She wrote to him: 'I am really upset at the death of Evreux, not so much on his account but on that of the king, who will find it difficult to replace him . . . maybe you will get a successor who will not suit you, but I hope that you will be consulted a little on this. I had thought of proposing abbé Languet, but I did not want to do so without knowing what you think'.[157] Aubigné responded by outlining the qualities needed in a new bishop, apparently 'in relation to the difficult character of the people of this *pays*', but he may not have mentioned individual candidates at this point. However, he agreed with her pessimistic assessment of the immediate prospect for episcopal nominations: 'there are so many dioceses vacant and so few satisfactory subjects with which to fill them; it is to the master of the harvest that we should turn for them'.[158] Six months later, Louis XIV found a new bishop for Evreux in Jean Le Normand, although Aubigné had apparently lobbied for abbé Dromesnil who, according to Maintenon, would indeed have been nominated had Autun

---

154 BM Versailles, G 329, fo 3, letter of 25 April 1709. Belsunce had been vicar-general at Agen under Hébert, formerly curé of Versailles and confidant of Maintenon.
155 BN, MS Naf 13634, fo 23–4, Maintenon to Aubigné, 14 Oct 1709, 'je crains que bien des gens ne veulent gouverner son diocèse sous pretexte que l'experience lui manque'; Victor Glachant, 'Quelques lettres de la vieillesse de Mme de Maintenon 1708–16)' *Revue de l'Histoire de Versailles et de Seine-et-Oise*, 27 (1925), no 17, to Aubigné, 14 Dec (year unknown); no 21, same to same, 2 Aug 1713.
156 BM Versailles, MS G 330, fo 8, Des Monstiers to Maintenon, 10 Feb 1710, regretting Heudicourt's death as that of a close friend with whom he had frequented Saint-Sulpice for several years.
157 BN, MS Naf 13634, fo 29, Maintenon to Aubigné, 10 Feb 1710. Mme Heudicourt, who died in early 1709 was one of Maintenon's oldest and closest friends: *Correspondance de Madame de Maintenon et de la princesse des Ursins: 1709, une année tragique*, ed Marcel Loyau (Paris 2002), 93–4, Maintenon to Ursins, 27 Jan 1709; 116–17, Ursins to Maintenon, 18 Feb 1709, asking her to intercede with Louis XIV to grant favours to members of the Heudicourt family; 131, Maintenon to Ursins, 4 March 1709, recounting the king's generosity towards them.
158 BM Versailles MS P 67, p 245, Aubigné to Maintenon, 5 March 1710. Earlier and later items of this correspondence are missing, hence the need to surmise some elements of its content.

not been vacant and Dromesnil not been given it instead.[159] This combination of satisfaction and dissatisfaction rolled into one was eminently typical of nominations made when several dioceses were available at the same time. However, Le Normand, another of Saint-Simon's *bêtes noires*, was in one respect at least to Aubigné's taste, as Maintenon acknowledged – he was, despite his years of service to Noailles in Paris, a vehement anti-Jansenist.[160] Nor would Languet, her original suggestion for Evreux, sink without trace: he might have to wait until 1715 before the episcopate beckoned for him, against thanks to Maintenon, but in the meantime, he moved to Autun to serve as vicar-general to Dromesnil, an experience which presumably made his claims to royal attention all the more persuasive at a later date.[161]

But the Aubigné-Maintenon exchanges were not merely about Rouen and its suffragans. Her wider concerns were still at work. She may well have wanted Aubigné promoted from Rouen to Reims in 1711, but she cannot have been displeased at François de Mailly's good fortune.[162] She certainly wanted Aubigné's opinion on Mailly's promotion to Reims – 'does this choice have your approval? I can assure you as to the king's intentions' – not because the decision was reversible, but in order to feel it was the correct one.[163] When Aubigné himself put forward the claims of Christophe de Turpin for a diocese in 1710, she replied that they would depend on which diocese would be rendered vacant when Reims was filled, but she noted that Nîmes and Lombez were still available. Nothing came of this, but Turpin was rewarded in 1711 with Rennes, a poorly endowed diocese from which he was soon vainly attempting – again with Aubigné's backing – to escape.[164] There were, as always, limits to the marquise's influence, but that did not dissuade Turpin from making a direct appeal to her in 1714, an appeal which is particularly interesting for its explicit acknowledgement that Louis XIV's dislike of 'sideways' episcopal transfers was as firm as ever: Turpin was now ready to

159　BN, MS Naf 13634, fo 38, Maintenon to Aubigné, 29 July 1710.

160　*Ibid*, fo 36, Maintenon to Aubigné, 27 July 1710. Le Normand's surviving papers, BN, MSS Fr 7026–7, are concerned almost exclusively with the theological issues surrounding Jansenism.

161　BM Versailles MS G 329, fos 101–2, Languet to Maintenon, 19 Jan 1715, 'je croy devoir à l'honneur de votre protection la grace que je viens de recevoir du Roy, et je ne dois pas perdre un moment à vous en tesmoigner ma profonde reconnaissance; elle doit rester d'autant plus vive que je méritois moins la place dont on m'honore, et encore une place distinguée'. Languet certainly did a great deal to preserve Maintenon's memory, collecting her letters and writing the *Mémoires de Madame de Maintenon*.

162　BM Versailles MS P 67, p 244, Aubigné to Maintenon, 5 March 1710, 'si par hazard, Madame, vous m'entendés nommer parmi ceux qui désirent ou qui demandent d'avoir part aux dépouilles de feu Mr l'archevesque de Reims, soyés je vous supplie bien persuadée que c'est entièrement à mon insu, et le seul effet de quelque office bon ou mauvais que je désavoue absolument'.

163　BN, MS Naf 13634, fo 36, Maintenon to Aubigné, 27 July 1710.

164　BM Versailles, MS G 329, fo 92v, Aubigné to Maintenon, 20 May 1712. Aubigné had someone to recommend to her for Rennes if Turpin moved to Le Mans.

remain at Rennes but asked for 'quelque secours' that would enable him to do so.[165] He was, assuredly, not the only bishop still prepared to beat a path to the door of the 'protectress of bishops' as a *confrère* had described her some years earlier.[166]

VII

This examination of episcopal patronage in Louis XIV's last years may be completed by returning to the impact of the Jansenist storm both before and after *Unigenitus* was issued in September 1713. Doing so also brings the role of the confessor back into focus, since Père Tellier's main claim to succeed La Chaize was undoubtedly his long experience and combativeness in the theological disputes of his day. Probably the real reason for assuming that he was sole 'dispenser of benefices' was his single-minded pursuit of Jansenism in all its forms. Of course, in seeking to do that and to counter Noailles, he could count on vigilant defenders of orthodoxy like Maintenon and Saint-Sulpice. For example, although Tellier is generally credited with moving Mailly from Arles to Reims in order to keep the pressure on Noailles, Maintenon also confessed to her 'malign joy' at the decision for the same reason.[167] No doubt, Tellier's incoming correspondence was as voluminous as Maintenon's, but its surviving scraps do not relate, unfortunately, to his role in church patronage. That he, too, was not bereft of advice is clear from the efforts of one his major allies in the anti-Jansenist offensive, the still disgraced Fénelon, who made explicit connections between the Jansenist problem and episcopal patronage in a memorandum-letter destined to reach the confessor indirectly. Writing nominally to Chevreuse, but in fact to Père Tellier, in late 1709, Fénelon began with brief 'warts and all' (au naturel) portraits of some of his episcopal colleagues (Bissy of Meaux, Beauvau of Tournai, Aubigné of Rouen), alleging that all of them had been, and perhaps still were, partial towards Jansenist ideas, even though they might have changed their behaviour in recent years. He followed with a truly withering verdict:

> these people are not good at the core. All of them will support whoever is the strongest, so you cannot rely on them. Where can we find better people? I have no idea. We have allowed the wellsprings of public studies to be poisoned. The indolence of the late Archbishop of Paris [Harlay] and the

---

165 *Ibid*, fos 76–7, letter of 5 Aug 1714. The letter claimed that Bissy and Aubigné, her main advisers, would have proposed his transfer to Lisieux were the king not so averse to transfers, yet the timing of Turpin's letter, ten days before episcopal nominations were due to be made, suggests that he had not himself given up hope of such a transfer.

166 *Ibid*, fo 70, Bishop Rochebonne of Noyon to Maintenon, 20 Dec 1714, asking for her intervention with Louis XIV for an abbey to supplement the meagre revenues of Noyon. He had given her the title of 'protectress' in 1709; fos 66–7, letter of 16 Nov 1709.

167 BN, MS Naf 13634, fo 38, Maintenon to Aubigné, 29 July 1710, 'je vous advoue que jay eu une maligne joye de sa nomination à Reims par raport à M le Cardinal que j'en croy fasché.'

excessive goodness of Père de la Chaize were the cause of this. Cardinal Noailles has completed the job, and evil is at its height.

But rather than leave his analysis hanging on such a hopeless note, Fénelon resumed with at least one clear recommendation:

> it seems to me essential that P Le Tellier seeks out and examines the candidates [for the episcopate] in depth. It is better to select them from Saint-Sulpice, on condition that they be pious and soundly educated, than to allow the Jansenist party to prevail within the episcopate . . . it is the bishops who ruin everything, thanks to their partiality towards the [Jansenist] party. They all avoid upsetting Cardinal Noailles.[168]

Sentiments like these would have reinforced the confessor's existing convictions, even though there was one item of Fénelon's advice that Tellier did not especially take to heart – the look for new bishops from among the alumni of Saint-Sulpice. Of the thirty new bishops nominated during his confessorship, only seven were products of the seminary, a lower proportion than for his predecessor's final years. Moreover, an examination of their backgrounds suggests that most of them were far closer to Maintenon's circle than to the Jesuits. Although such differences of affiliation ought not to be exaggerated – both would have been firmly anti-Jansenist – resentment was occasionally expressed by Maintenon and others at what they perceived as Jesuit domination.[169] At any rate, the record of episcopal nominations between 1709 and 1715 does show that Tellier was indeed highly successful in preventing the entry of Jansenists of any kind from entering the episcopate. As far as is known, not one of these new bishops rejected *Unigenitus* in 1713 or later, and scarcely any of them played a part in the subsequent moves to 'explain' or supersede it with successive 'accomodations'.[170] And, needless to say, the same care was exercised when it was a matter of promoting bishops to archdioceses. In his opposition to *Unigenitus*, Noailles would have the support of only one other archbishop – the former Roman Rota Auditor, Hervault of Tours, whose real motives were probably as gallican as those of Noailles himself. As we saw earlier, the business of selecting successors to bishops who were either Jansenist, or generally sympathetic to Jansenist-rigorist ideas, was a delicate and important one. It was thus doubly vital to ensure that an archiepiscopal see like Reims was in safe hands, after the long reign of the viscerally anti-Jesuit and rigorist Maurice Le Tellier, and François de Mailly was certainly such a choice. But the number of such 'Jansenist' dioceses to fall vacant after

---

168 Fénelon, *Correspondance*, xiv, no 1340, pp 177–80, letter to duc de Chevreuse, 19 Dec 1709.

169 Foisset, 'Quarante-six lettres de Mme de Maintenon', no 31, to Languet, curé of Saint-Sulpice, 24 March 1715, 'il est certain que les Jésuites gouvernent absolument, et qu'ainsi il faut malgré qu'on en ait, compter avec eux'.

170 AM Saint-Malo, GG 290, no 25, 'la Tour de Babel' (1721) for an extensive tableau of the actions of France's bishops from 1713 to early 1721.

1709 was actually quite small – no more than four or five – and that of itself severely limited what the crown could do against Jansenism in several other dioceses. Whether Louis d'Aquin, bishop of Sées, was anything more than a rigorist who disliked the Jesuits is hard to know for certain, but the successor nominated in 1710, Turgot, was an anti-Jansenist for whom, it appears, Tellier's fellow Jesuits had strongly lobbied.[171] The best known, but also the smallest of the 'Jansenist' dioceses that did become vacant was Saint-Pons in Languedoc, whose bishop, Percin de Montgaillard, died after a fifty-year term in 1713. It was he rather than Quesnel who was originally singled out for censure in the campaign to condemn Jansenism in 1711–13.[172] His successor at Saint-Pons, a Crillon, was certainly a safe choice, having been groomed for the episcopate by his uncle, the bishop of Vence who was also on the verge of promotion to the archdiocese of Vienne in 1714. Finally, Embrun and Soissons, though very different in location and status, were held for many years by two Brûlart cousins, who died within weeks of each other in November 1714. And as each of them was suspected of holding Jansenist opinions, their successors were chosen accordingly. Archbishop Brûlart de Genlis of Embrun, whose 'Jansenism' was probably inflated because of his dislike of the Jesuits, was followed by the frankly pro-Jesuit François-Elie d'Argenson, bishop of Dol.[173] Brûlart de Sillery of Soissons had courted the Jesuits at various times for pragmatic reasons, but in the assembly held in October 1714 for the reception of *Unigenitus*, he showed himself to be favourable to Noailles. He died suddenly a few weeks later, amid rumours about his remorse for having betrayed his real convictions during his episcopate.[174] His successor at Soissons, Languet de Gergy, would become known as the 'athlete of the Constitution' on account of his indefatigable efforts to defend and impose *Unigenitus* in subsequent decades.[175]

171 Delattre, *Établissements des Jésuites*, i, 124–9 (Alençon).

172 Blet, *Le Clergé de France, Louis XIV et le Saint-Siège*, 325ff. Ceyssens, *Autour de l'Unigenitus*, 709–10. Percin's dispute with Fénelon had led the latter and the confessor to agree to appeal to Rome to have him censured.

173 In 1711, Genlis criticised the pastoral instruction of his suffragan, Berger of Gap, declaring the 'incomparable doctrine of Saint Augustine on grace and predestination' was the only correct one: see Fénelon, *Correspondance*, xiv, no 1481F, p 418, Jacques-Philippe Lallemant, Jesuit, to Fénelon, 16 Aug 1711. Genlis also made a declaration of orthodoxy in May 1714, a few months before his death: AD Hautes-Alpes, G 223. See G 224, for similar statements about his true opinions.

174 Foisset, 'Quarante-six lettres de Mme de Maintenon', nos 18–19, Maintenon to Languet, curé of Saint-Sulpice, 20 and 24 Nov 1714. Saint-Simon, xxv, 137–42, memorably depicts him as selling himself to the Jesuits and then execrating the bull *Unigenitus* on his deathbed. But his own incomplete journal of the Assembly of Oct–Nov 1714 shows him in a very different light – *ibid*, appendix viii, pp 453–9.

175 See the studies, based on research on Languet's large collection of letters and papers in the municipal library of Sens, conducted by Nelson-Martin Dawson and his students in *idem*, ed, *Crise d'autorité et clientélisme: Mgr Jean Joseph Languet de Gergy et la bulle Unigenitus* (Sherbrooke 1997); *idem*, ed, *Clientélisme ecclésiastique et antijansénisme* (Sherbrooke 1998); *idem*, ed, *Fidélités ecclésiastiques et crise janséniste* (Sherbrooke 2001).

By the time Languet, the last of Louis XIV's nominations bar one, was consecrated at Saint-Sulpice in late June 1715, the reign was within weeks of ending. The furore over *Unigenitus*, in which Noailles – whose political ineptitude in previous years had not lost him his support of Paris, the parlement and gallican opinion generally – defied pope and king, had not died down. Louis XIV and his ministers were preparing for a national council which would obliterate this opposition once and for all. But the king's death, coming quickly after a short illness, radically changed the immediate political and religious prospect. Instead of Noailles being humiliated and ejected from Paris, it was Père Tellier, whom Noailles had once banned as confessor in the Paris diocese, who was sent into internal exile, while his closest associates in the anti-Jansenist struggle, Cardinals Bissy and Rohan, were 'thanked' for their past services, as Philipe d'Orléans, the regent, abruptly abandoned the late king's policies and plans. In his very first exercise of bishop-making in January 1716, Orléans, with large numbers of petitioners to satisfy, was in the happy position of having a correspondingly large number of benefices to distribute, thanks to Louis XIV's refusal, despite his confessor's insistence, to do so during his last months.[176] Maintenon, for her part, continued to correspond in her last few years with bishops and other figures, expressing both her desires and anxieties about the French church. Only two months after her husband's death, she wrote wearily to her confessor, Languet, curé of Saint-Sulpice: 'I am more disappointed than surprised that the *conseil de conscience* did not decide to ratify what the king had done. If these poor people obtain something, they will owe it to you. As for me, you know well enough that I can no longer do anything, and I have no hope at all that Cardinal Noailles will grant them benefices'.[177] Now she had quit the court, she could share the sentiments of many lesser mortals when negotiating the labyrinthine benefice-system which remained wholly untouched by the recent changing of the guard.

---

176   Saint-Simon, xxvii, 253–4, for a characteristically hostile account of Tellier's last 'vendredy' with Louis XIV, on 23 Aug 1715; xxix, 332–3.
177   Foisset, 'Quarante-six lettres inédites de Mme de Maintenon', no 42, 30 Oct 1715.

CHAPTER 9

Full Circle

HAVING EXAMINED LOUIS XIV's bishops from so many different but converging angles, it is now feasible to propose an overview of some of the key elements which define the lifecycle and activity of a corporate group such as the episcopate. In order to understand the evolution of the episcopate as a whole during the king's personal rule, the present chapter will pull together strands that were either implicit, or only briefly mentioned in previous ones. For reasons that will be obvious to anyone familiar with the research done since the 1950s on the religious history of seventeenth-century France, especially at the local and regional level, what follows will not attempt to show how well, badly, or otherwise French bishops performed their duties as bishops within their dioceses; it will also be obvious that, apart from its own inherent flaws, such an exercise would have no organic connection to the preceding chapters of the present study. The more modest aim of this chapter is to follow Louis XIV's bishops collectively from their point of entry into the episcopate towards their final exit, examining along the way the kinds of issue – age at entry, duration of careers, rates of change and promotion, resignations, retirements, deaths and so – which determined the degrees of stability and longevity that characterised the 'first order of the kingdom'.

I

It will be abundantly clear from the preceding chapters that the legend which depicts *ancien-régime* bishops as being chosen at an impossibly early age finds little support in the episcopate of Louis XIV. That quite a number of precocious promotions had occurred in previous reigns is well documented, but they were confined to the century or so following the Concordat of Bologna. With the minimum age for an incoming bishop set at twenty-six years by the Concordat, the French church already enjoyed a privilege which the rest of Europe did not, since the minimum age elsewhere was twenty-nine.[1] For the period from the later Wars of Religion to 1661, under-age nominations clustered heavily in the early decades, down to about 1620.[2] After that they dropped substantially, not least because in both France and Rome there was increasing unwillingness to accept such practices any longer. The last decade of Mazarin's ministry witnessed three underage nominations, but they were significantly different from those of a half a century earlier, when candidates several years short of the already abnormally low required age for French bishops were not unknown. The last of the three cases involved a bishop who is familiar from previous chapters – Louis Fouquet, nominated to Agde in 1657 and one of the most long-suffering bishops of Louis XIV's reign. In 1657, his 'youth' (he was only a few months short of twenty-six years old) was clearly an embarrassment: anticipating a frosty welcome in Rome, a memorandum was compiled for despatch to Rome comparing Fouquet's nomination to past cases of bishops who, like him, were only a few *months* short of the required age, and which was a far cry from the underage bishops of the previous century.[3] He would have only three 'successors' of this type while Louis XIV was king. The average age of incoming bishops on a decade-by-decade basis between 1589 and 1661 offers the clearest evidence as to why it seemed so necessary to defend the Fouquet nomination in 1657. From a minimum of barely over thirty-one years for the 1610s, itself a decade when young candidates probably fared better than at any time since the Concordat of Bologna, the average age of new bishops rose quickly and substantially to the high thirties where it remained during the 1630s and 1640s, before moving to just below forty-one during the 1650s. The hardening of attitudes towards episcopal promotions reflected by this trend shows just how out of season the easy-going habits of earlier generations had become as Louis XIV was on the verge of taking the reins of power for himself. Would the next fifty years witness any further change to what seemed by then like a well-set pattern, one which ensured that future bishops would have, on average, a pre-episcopal career of somewhere between ten and twenty years, depending on the studies they had undertaken and the age at which they completed them?

The accompanying table (table 9.1) tells a reasonably straightforward tale. The overall average age for incoming bishops during the half-century after 1661 moved up by a single point, to just under forty-two years. During the first decade of Louis's rule, when nominations were on the relatively low side, the average had already reached that figure, before dropping back again to below forty in the 1670s, which is not surprising for a decade when nominations were more plentiful than ever. But the average having begun to rise

---

1 The Concordat clearly stipulated that candidates be in their twenty-seventh year (i.e. that they be twenty-six years of age), a difference which historians have not always appreciated.
2 The remainder of this paragraph is based on the discussion in Bergin, *Making*, 296–303.
3 ASV, Nunz Fr 110a, fo 36. See also Bergin, *Making*, 542.

Table 9.1   Age and career durations of French bishops

Decade	Nominations	Average age	Career duration	Age at career end
1661–9	35	42.3	23.8	66.1
1670–9	55	39.3	27.1	66.4
1680–9	44	40.3	21	61.3 (64.8)
1690–9	42	40.8	23.7	64.5
1700–9	45	45.1	23.8	68.9
1710–15	29	43.8	25.2	69
Totals	250	41.9	24.1	66

Note. The figure for career duration and career end for bishops seated in the 1680s is significantly lower on account of the refusal of papal provisions down to 1685, which had the effect of reducing the average career by 3.5 years – hence the figure in brackets in the column to that effect.

again during the 1680s, there can be no doubt of which way the curve was moving during the final decades of the reign, and it may well be that the average for the decade after 1700, which stands at just over forty-five years, was an absolute record for the whole early modern era. Certainly, it seems that under Louis XV the average age dropped back again to around forty, which is the figure adopted by Michel Péronnet for the eighteenth-century episcopate.[4] For our purposes here, and taking the figures simply as they are, it is clear that by the latter stages of Louis XIV's reign, future bishops could expect to wait longer – up to five years – before being promoted to the bench, which in turn had obvious implications for pre-episcopal careers spanning possibly twenty years or more. Despite that, incoming French bishops remained notably younger than their counterparts in other parts of Europe, both Catholic and Protestant.

But however useful, these long-run aggregates inevitably hide a number of developments which have a direct bearing on the careers of future bishops as well as revealing something about the kind of 'policy' adopted by the crown with regard to nominations. Firstly, the bar with regard to the minimum age for nominations was gradually allowed to rise until under-age candidates simply disappeared altogether. As already noted, only three bishops were under the canonical age of twenty-six on receiving their *brevet* from Louis XIV – one per decade from the 1660s to the 1680s. As we might expect, each of them was in a position where such an exception does not come as an utter surprise – a Le Tellier in the 1660s, a Beauvau in the 1670s, and ending with a Colbert in early 1680. Charles-Maurice Le Tellier was only two weeks short of the canonical age when nominated coadjutor of Reims in 1668 but, as we

4   Péronnet, *Évêques de l'ancienne France*, i, 451.

have already seen, it was not his age which caused a stir at the time. Beauvau was being pushed with great haste by his family into succeeding his uncle at Nantes; the former favour of his cousin, Louise de la Vallière, meant he could count on royal support at a time when the pope was extremely reluctant to confirm an underage candidate. And Innocent XI made Beauvau wait for two years and ordered an enquiry into the circumstances of his nomination before finally confirming him as bishop.[5] The last of the three, Jacques-Nicolas Colbert was also the youngest of them, barely twenty-five in early 1680 when nominated coadjutor of Rouen. But a combination of ministerial descent and the fact that he was only being proposed for a coadjutorship blunted objections from Rome, especially as the coadjutorship was presented as a form of episcopal apprenticeship with limited initial responsibility for a diocese.[6] Interestingly, his father consulted the superior of Saint-Sulpice, Tronson, as to whether there were any valid objections to the move. The answer he got was masterly: 'with all the sincerity I can muster, there is nothing in him to make him unsuitable . . . and he can render service to the church'.[7] Yet Tronson's carefully chosen language itself shows just how strong sensitivity to criticism of underage nominations had grown by then.

Further evidence for this sensitivity may be found in the fact that the numbers of those acceding to the episcopate while still under thirty also took a real tumble, especially from the 1680s onwards, when the happy few in this category were spread extremely thinly. As might be surmised, they, too, consisted largely of men who were close to the fount of favour, either by birth or by family positions in government or at court. All in all, the 'under-thirties' among Louis XIV's bishops, numbering twenty-five in all, accounted for no more than 10 per cent of the total, a spectacular reduction from the impressive 40 per cent for the period from 1589 to 1661. The reduction in question takes on even greater significance when broken down decade-by-decade: it had begun in the 1620s and 1630s, then levelled off for several decades before falling to around 5 per cent of nominations from the 1680s onwards. What this means is, as will be evident from table 9.2, that the 'big battalions' were increasingly drawn from the thirty–forty-five age group, which provided over 58 per cent of all of Louis XIV's bishops; the table also shows that each five-year cohort within that group was fairly well represented, although those in their early thirties were more prominent than those in their early forties. Also significant is the proportion of new bishops who were older, and sometimes considerably so, than the majority. The numbers of those over

5   For the nuncio's letters to Cardinal Cibo, the papal secretary of state, on this succession, see ASV, Nunz Fr 158, fo 735, 17 June 1678; Nunz Fr 159, fo 145r, 29 July 1678; Nunz Fr 160, fo 68, 27 Jan 1679; 201–2r, 24 Feb 1679; fos 488–9, 5 May 1679; fo 761, 30 June 1679. See also the material on the case in ASV, Acta congregationis consistorialis 1678–9, fos 401–2.

6   Rome's reluctance was conveyed to Colbert by Lauri, ASV, Nunz Fr 163, fo 349, letter to Cardinal Cibo, 15 April 1680, reporting on conversation with Colbert.

7   *Correspondance de Tronson*, iii, 389–90, letter to Colbert, 29 Aug 1679.

Table 9.2   Age profile of Louis XIV's bishops at nomination

Decade	Under 26	26–29	30–35	36–39	40–44	45–49	50–54	55–59	Over 60	Noms
1661–9	1	8	6	1	6	1	6	4	2	35
1670–9	1	5	19	11	7	5	3	2	2	55
1680–9	1	3	16	4	9	1	5	4	1	44
1690–9	0	3	9	10	10	4	4	2	0	42
1700–9	0	1	5	7	12	7	8	5	0	45
1710–15	0	2	4	5	5	5	3	4	1	29
Total	3	22	59	38	49	23	29	21	6	250

forty-five fluctuated strongly in the early decades of the reign, falling from 37 per cent in the 1660s to just under 24 per cent in the 1690s. But in the years after 1700 candidates in their mid-forties and above fared far better than at any time since 1661, accounting for nearly 45 per cent of nominations. Their presence is undoubtedly the main reason why the overall average age of new bishops rose so markedly in the latter decades of the period.

II

The implications of such shifts in the age-profile of incoming bishops since the 1620s and 1630s for the duration of episcopal careers as well as for the exercise of episcopal patronage by the crown hardly need to be emphasised. The ways in which episcopal careers ended will be studied later in this chapter, but in order to understand the constraints that a combination of age-at-entry and subsequent career-durations placed on royal patronage we need to introduce another element at this point, namely the age at which those careers terminated. Here, too, the pattern of the decades between 1589 and 1661 provides the necessary context. The average age of death for bishops over that period as a whole was 62.6 years, but the trend per decade was upwards, especially from the 1620s onwards, with the 1650s recording the highest average of all at 67.4 years. The average length of careers for the same period was 23.7 years, but it too fluctuated from one decade to the next, while also reaching its highest decennial figure, that of 25.6 years, in the 1650s.[8]

Each of these trends is significant, since during the following half-century the *maxima* recorded for the 1650s were not significantly improved upon. At first sight, this may cause surprise, but the reason for it is, as we have just seen, that the age at which bishops were nominated was itself moving

8   See Bergin, *Making*, 303–4.

upwards, whereas the already quite respectable life expectancy for bishops did not rise accordingly (table 9.1). For example, no decade before the 1700s saw the average age at death noted above for the 1650s overtaken, and even when it did happen, the difference was not enormous (68.9 against 67.4). Needless to say, an average figure for the duration of episcopal careers between 1661 and 1715 disguises the enormous disparities in the length of those careers. A less one-dimensional idea of what lies behind the aggregates is provided by table 9.1 which gives a breakdown of the data by a series of time-spans. The overall pattern that emerges from the table is distorted by the figures for the bishops nominated during the 1680s whose careers as *confirmed* bishops were, it should be recalled here, seriously affected by the long delays – over 3.5 years on average, but up to ten years in some cases – in obtaining provisions by Rome. Nevertheless, table 9.1 clearly shows the variations in the duration of Louis XIV's bishops' careers. Only a handful came close to rivalling the king's own long government of the kingdom, and without the benefit of ruling their dioceses from their early twenties onwards! Taken together, just under 60 per cent (59.6) of all bishops reigned in excess of twenty years, and one-third for over thirty years. At the other extreme, very short reigns of less than five were more numerous than expected, and some of them lasted only a year or two – too short, it may be assumed, to have had much of an impact of the dioceses they had obtained. Scarcely any of these short reigns were a consequence of nominating elderly bishops: they were much more likely to be individuals in their prime, victims of sudden illness or accidents for the most part. Even though instances of individual bishops dying during out-breaks of plague are recorded, there is little evidence to indicate that more bishops died in crisis years like 1693 or 1710, especially when those dying during these years were already elderly.[9] Yet the averages for the age of bishops at the end of their careers given in table 9.1 seem to indicate that the bishops seated from the 1660s to the 1690s died younger than their predecessors from the 1650s or their successors from 1700 onwards, who presumably benefited from the improved conditions of post-Louis XIV France.[10]

III

The demographics of the episcopate were, it need hardly be said, the prime determinant of the scale of royal patronage, dictating which would be its fat or lean years. Like the conduct of government generally, Louis XIV had left

---

9   Of the nine bishops to die between early 1693 and mid-1694, only two could be said to be in mid-career, all of the others were aged seventy and over. For the problems of the last decades of the reign, see Marcel Lachiver, *Les Années de misère. La famine au temps du grand roi 1680–1720* (Paris 1991).

10 The figure for the bishops of the 1680s is fictitious, since it does not take account of the 3.5 years average cut in the duration of the careers because of the suspension of papal provisions.

Table 9.3 *Yearly averages for episcopal nominations per decade*

Decade		Noms
1661–9	35	4.8
1670–9	55	5.5
1680–9	44	4.3
1690–9	42	4.2
1700–9	45	4.5
1710–15	29	4.8

episcopal patronage entirely in Mazarin's hands until his death in early March 1661. The formal record shows the king making his last nominations at Easter 1715, but in reality early in January that year.[11] When he died eight months later, in September 1715, he left only three recently-vacated dioceses (Cambrai, Bayeux and Clermont) without a nominated successor, despite the efforts of his confessor. What kind of overall pattern can we detect in the 250 nominations which occurred between these terminal dates? The most elementary analysis of the figures shows that the ranks of the episcopate were renewed twice over during the king's personal rule. Secondly, there were on average 4.6 nominations of new bishops per year, compared with that of 4.9 for the period from 1589 to 1661. The drop may seem relatively small, but it reflects, *inter alia*, the greater political stability, the improved economic circumstances of France's bishoprics, despite the dip just noted, and the gradual rise in the age at which careers ended – all of which made for greater episcopal longevity.[12] However, such an average is useful only as a general guide to how much or little episcopal patronage was available to the crown over the period as a whole: the last thing we should expect is that it would have been uniform across over half a century. Thus the decade-by-decade figures, which can be construed as relatively neutral since they do not derive from preconceived 'turning-points', give a somewhat better idea of where the 'lean' and 'fat' periods may have occurred.

The trends displayed in table 9.3 clearly indicate a low point for episcopal patronage coming in the 1680s and 1690s, no doubt in part as a consequence of the all-time peak of the 1670s, easily the most 'productive' decade of those represented here. But the 'slump' of the 1680s and 1690s was, as we saw, also connected to the crisis of the 1680s, when large numbers of nominees had to

11 The letters of nomination of Louis's last two bishops, Sourches of Dol and Languet of Soissons, are clearly dated 20 April 1715, but Dangeau's diary (xv, 341) includes them among the bishops chosen and announced on 12 Jan 1715.

12 This is evident from a comparison with the figures for the period 1589 to 1661 in Bergin, *Making*, 304, table 8.4.

wait for up to ten years for confirmation by Rome; for some, the confirmation never came, and they either died or gave up the chase altogether. On the other hand, the last fifteen years of the reign were increasingly more bountiful for episcopal hopefuls. Coinciding as they also did with the revival and escalation of the Jansenist dispute, it is not surprising that the nominations of these years, especially with the arrival of a new confessor in 1709, were subject to intense competition and, sometimes, recrimination.

But the above figures do not account for the total volume of episcopal patronage during these years. They were constantly interwoven with decisions to transfer and promote existing bishops to new dioceses. It is here that the overlap between any generation of bishops already 'en place' and newcomers is most apparent. This, as we saw in a previous chapter, was particularly so under Louis XIV when the major sees – the archbishoprics – were largely ruled out of bounds to newcomers, something which his predecessors had not envisaged. Thus the first generation of bishops seated after 1661 had to wait for longer than was customary before reaching the heights of the episcopal hierarchy itself. In some cases, of course, the wait did *not* prove an especially long one, and we should avoid thinking in terms of an obligatory long stay in one's first diocese or of a patronage system so rigid as to preclude any form of 'leap-frogging'. It was, in fact, its ability to combine both of these factors which accounts in some part for its 'originality'. In earlier chapters we encountered the rapid promotion to an archdiocese of the likes of Michel Amelot, Louis de Bourlemont and Mathieu d'Hervault from their first diocese, in which they had hardly set foot, let alone acquired much experience of episcopal office. The most ambitious and complex exercises in episcopal patronage usually involved some synchronising of such promotions and first-time nominations. The calculations that lay behind a given set of decisions could be thrown into disarray if one of those involved preferred to stay in his existing diocese, or if a newcomer declined the offer of a particular diocese vacated by a promotion. The effect of such responses was to spread out decisions across several doubtless busy days or indeed across the intervals between major feast-days, as we have already seen. Sometimes the synchronisation of decisions involved a measure of prior participation and consent by those concerned, since even the ambitious were not willing to jeopardise their interests any more than they felt was tolerable. For example, Georges d'Aubusson de la Feuillade, archbishop of Embrun since 1649, negotiated a move to Metz in 1669, while insisting as a condition of vacating Embrun that he be allowed to keep his title of archbishop and the *pallium* that went with it.[13]

---

13 ASV, Nunz Fr 134, fo 623, Vibo to Rome, 4 May 1668; fo 124 for the arguments of Aubusson for his course of action; Nunz Fr 135, fo 254, 13 July 1668, Nuncio Bargellini to Rome, 13 July 1668. ASV, PC 66, fo 103, 24 June 1668, Aubusson's procuration before notary to resign Embrun 'in favour of' Genlis, while retaining the 'denomination of former archbishop of Embrun, its rank and honours' as well as a pension of 6,000 *livres*.

If we return to the episcopate as it stood in 1661, we can fit Louis XIV's record on transfers and promotions into a broader context. Of the 105 bishops in office at Mazarin's death, nineteen had already moved from their first diocese, though only four of them to an archbishopric; two of these nineteen were to move again under Louis XIV, to a higher-status rather than a same-status see. A further nineteen of the 105 were to move to another diocese *after* 1661, and three of them were to do so twice. Thus, under Louis there were twenty-four transfers of pre-1661 bishops involving twenty-one individuals. One significant departure from the pattern of the preceding period is that eleven of the twenty-one individuals moved upwards to the rank of archbishop. Taken together, slightly over a quarter (27.6 per cent) of the surviving pre-Louis XIV episcopate moved from their first diocese; half of them did so before 1661, and it seems that the longer they had to wait for a move, the more likely it was to be upward rather than sideways. Furthermore, the mobility experienced by the episcopal 'generation of 1661' was noticeably out of line with that for the period 1589–1661 as a whole, when only 17.7 per cent of all bishops moved from their first diocese. Did they set a pattern which would be followed by the 250 bishops seated after 1661? Fifty-four of the latter moved from their first diocese, sometimes quite quickly, as noted above, raising the possibility of further movement later. However, a mere ten moved a second time, with just one individual claiming the undisputed record of holding four dioceses – René de Beauvau, whose career, as we saw, began modestly in Bayonne in 1700. By 1713 he was installed as archbishop of Toulouse, the reward for his wilderness years at Tournai from 1707 onwards.[14] It is interesting to note that only a quarter of the *grand roi*'s bishops to leave their first diocese managed to do so *after* his death, which stands in contrast with their own pre-1661 counterparts, who, as we saw, fared rather better under Louis XIV than under Mazarin.

With fifty-four bishops moving at least once in their careers, it is clear that the bishops seated under Louis XIV were less mobile than those in office in 1661 – 21.6 per cent against 27.6 per cent. Now, this pattern of falling episcopal mobility was far from visible to contemporaries, some of whom argued that never had the abuse of transfers been as rampant as under Louis. The virulence of the polemic of the 1670s and 1680s on the subject, which we noted in previous chapters, at least suggests the need for a closer look at patterns of mobility, to see if the latter differed significantly at any point of the reign. If we amalgamate the figures for both the pre- and post-1661 bishops from the preceding analysis on a decade-by-decade basis, we may be able to judge whether there was any factual basis for the criticism levelled at the crown and the extent to which it may have responded to it.

14 He would, like several archbishops of Toulouse before him, end his career as archbishop of Narbonne.

Table 9.4   Episcopal transfers as total of nominations

Decade	Nominations	Transfers	Total	%
1661–9	35	14	49	28.5
1670–9	55	21	76	27.6
1680–9	44	19	63	30
1690–9	42	4	46	8.6
1700–9	45	9	54	16.6
1710–15	29	7	36	19.4
Total	250	74	324	22.8

The data in table 9.4 give a first impression of how significant the movement of bishops between dioceses was in relation to the entry of newcomers into the episcopate. They refer to movement between dioceses, and not to the numbers of individuals involved in them, since what matters at this point is the *proportion* of transfers within the overall distribution of episcopal patronage. It is clear that the highest percentages are concentrated in the first three decades after 1661, though it should be made clear that the figures for the 1680s, the highest of all, were almost certainly inflated by the crisis of episcopal tenure during that decade. By contrast, it looks as if the last three decades, especially the 1690s, witnessed something of a reaction against episcopal movements, followed by a partial recovery after 1700, but one which remained well short of the figures for the earlier decades. Thus the last generation of Louis XIV's bishops were much less likely to change diocese than their predecessors. If criticism of the crown for moving bishops around was to be made at any time, then it was most likely to happen in the 1660s and 1670s rather than later.

The question of episcopal mobility also needs to be approached from an angle which corresponds as closely as possible to contemporary assumptions about its permissibility. All but the most austere voices under Louis XIV accepted that moving to an archbishopric was justifiable as a useful service to the church. As we saw, 'horizontal' mobility by contrast tended to be looked at askance, and the motives for doing so held to be dubious. A comparison between 'vertical' and 'horizontal' of the kind provided by table 9.5 will help us to grasp the relative importance as well as the chronological spread of these forms of mobility.

The figures in table 9.5 would seem to confirm what the preceding analysis could only suggest – namely that a decline in the overall levels of movement by bishops tended to coincide with a tendency to limit it to 'vertical' mobility into archbishoprics. Here too, the troublesome 1680s seem to be the exception that proves the rule. 'Horizontal' mobility was increasingly

Table 9.5   Episcopal mobility/promotion under Louis XIV

Decade	Transfers	Promotions	Promotions as % of all movement
1661–9	14	6	42.8
1670–9	21	10	47.6
1680–9	19	6	31.5
1690–9	4	3	75
1700–9	9	5	55.5
1710–15	7	5	71.4
Total	74	35	47.9

being squeezed out of the system during the last decades of the reign. But there were always more plausible ad hoc reasons than we might expect as to why there would continue to be exceptions to this pattern of movement. In some cases, as we saw in chapter 1, it might be the need to despatch experienced bishops to govern newly acquired dioceses like Tournai or Saint-Omer; in others it might be the need to do the same in dioceses with strong Protestant populations or which were thought to have been infiltrated by Jansenist influences: most of these dioceses, as it happened, were 'ordinary' rather than archiepiscopal sees. The very last 'sideways' move saw this same logic being employed in 1713 when it was necessary to 'parachute' the bishop of Ypres into an ordinary French diocese, Viviers, just as Ypres was about to come under Austrian sovereignty.[15] Once again, it was early during the personal rule that sideways movement was easiest and most common, so the objections of the purists to bishops abandoning their dioceses would seem to have an objective basis in fact. Of course, contemporaries would not have consulted statistics before reaching for their pens on such a subject: they were just as likely to have been spurred into action by individual instances of rapid nominations to a second or third diocese of the kind noted above. Mme de Sévigné's disapproval of a batch of nominations in 1684 which involved some such musical chairs demonstrates how widely held such views could be.[16]

But the historian's analysis of episcopal mobility does not need to be restricted to – or by – the concerns of some of Louis XIV's subjects. Overall,

15 Martin Ratabon was given Viviers in April 1713 at a time when Auch, Toulouse and Alès were unfilled. Toulouse had been earmarked for Beauvau of Tournai by then, but Auch was not filled until mid-1713. Ratabon's record as a bishop was decried by some, of whom Fénelon was possibly one, so promotion to an archiepiscopal see was probably ruled out: Saint-Simon, xxiii, 356–7.

16 Sévigné, *Correspondance*, vii, 263, letter to *président* Moulceau, 1 June 1684, 'je ne m'amuserai point à vous conter le remue-menage de tous les évêques; cela blesse et fait mal au coeur'.

the amount of mobility seems relatively contained, bearing in mind the king's self-imposed rule, broken in only four cases in all, not to grant archbishoprics to ecclesiastics without some prior episcopal experience.[17] And the increase in the number of archbishoprics during Louis's XIV reign, from fifteen to eighteen, was itself too modest to significantly widen this avenue of vertical mobility. But there is another side to the story, and it is that we should be wary of *over*-estimating the willingness of French bishops to move to another diocese. Undoubtedly, there were some, possibly many, who wished to do so and who, like Richelieu in his time, found that their dioceses were among 'les plus crottés de France', but their desires were for the most part simply ignored. However, others again were not inclined to move at all, and that for a variety of motives. We saw that filling dioceses left vacant by bishops who had been Jansenist was likely to elicit refusals from sitting bishops when they were offered the nomination; dioceses with large communities of Protestants or Nouveaux Catholiques were not always attractive either; others still had reputations for being troublesome or hard to govern because of unresolved conflicts with cathedral chapters or the royal courts. And it was virtually axiomatic at the time that 'a second diocese ruins you', in that the cost of new papal bulls would be prohibitive. Bishops with excellent family, court or ministerial connections were all the more likely to angle for promotion or transfer to better dioceses during their careers, precisely because their chances of obtaining substantial reductions in, or even complete waivers, of these costs were so good. The Roman curia could, of course, dig in its heels on requests for graces of that kind, even when supported by the king and his ministers, for however much the pope might wish to grant such favours for diplomatic reasons, they were always deeply unpopular among its resident cardinals and officials. Archbishop Fortin de la Hoguette of Sens, who did not enjoy *that* kind of favour in high places yet was promoted twice, declared in his will that a major reason for his lack of means at the end of his life was the cost of three sets of episcopal provisions.[18] The future Cardinal Bissy, reluctant to accept the offer to move from Toul to Bordeaux in 1697, adduced his own lack of means and his father's unwillingness to assist him financially, even though the real reason was that he wanted a diocese closer to Paris more than an archbishopric.[19] Bissy's rejection of a major see like Bordeaux was not as quixotic as it may sound, as others would have shared both his argument and his ambition. When he finally moved in 1704, it was to succeed Bossuet at Meaux, a small and reasonably endowed see, but within striking distance of

---

17   The first of these nominations, that of Brûlart de Genlis to Embrun in 1668, may actually have
      occurred before Louis XIV made his resolution only to offer archbishoprics to reigning bishops.
18   AD Yonne, G 177, testament of 28 Nov 1715. He was bishop of Tréguier and Poitiers before
      moving to Sens. He did also confess that he was not a *bon mesnager*.
19   JRULM, MS French 92, fos 16v–17r, Huxelles to La Garde, 3 Feb 1698, '[il] balance
      d'accepter Bordeaux, disant n'estre pas assés riche et Mr son pere ne le voulant point aider, il
      eut hier là dessus, a ce que l'on presume, une longue conference avec le Roy'.

the court: it did indeed prove eminently suitable for him while Louis XIV lived, allowing him to play a major role in the Jansenist affair and obtain the red hat in due course. In addition to Meaux, other small or poor dioceses around Paris, such as Orléans or Senlis, were similarly attractive to ecclesiastical politicians, for whom a distant archbishopric did not have the same pulling power. To that extent, ambition and 'promotion' cannot be viewed purely in hierarchical terms. Tenure of Meaux and Orléans was, after all, no obstacle to either Bissy or Coislin (Orléans) becoming cardinals. This is evident in other ways, too. Five of the six sees with a peerage were *not* archbishoprics (Reims being the exception here), and they, too, experienced extremely low levels of movement, incoming or outgoing, under Louis XIV.[20] Only Reims, Beauvais and Châlons-sur-Marne witnessed bishops who were moving into them from their first see, and it only happened once in each case, while Châlons and Noyon were the only two to 'export' a bishop to another see. This limited range of movement is underlined by the fact that, in the case of Châlons, the inward and outward movement involved the same person – the future Cardinal Noailles.[21] Similarly, an indeterminate proportion of 'ordinary' dioceses – with neither ecclesiastical nor 'feudal' prestige attached to them – were desirable enough for their bishops *not* to be unduly tempted to change places. It would be impossible to itemise all the possible reasons for this, and even if we did, we would not have accounted for the similarly indeterminate number of Louis XIV's bishops who were in principle opposed to moving between dioceses at all.

IV

The preceding discussion leads naturally to the related question of how far the pattern of episcopal tenure may have varied from diocese to diocese under Louis XIV. A brief analysis of the problem from this perspective will also shed some light on the possibilities for reshaping the episcopate enjoyed by the crown after 1661. The figures in table 9.6 indicate one important set of parameters for royal policy.

Extraordinary as it may seem, given the duration of Louis's personal rule, one diocese escaped him altogether: he never nominated a bishop of Bayeux, whose incumbent, François de Nesmond, was one of Mazarin's last nominees and who died less than four months before the king. As we shall see, Nesmond's longevity was to be matched by a number of the bishops seated after 1661. It would be easy to assume, on the strength of the opinion current at the time, that numerous dioceses saw too many bishops come and go in

---

20 That figure should be raised to seven after 1674 when Louis XIV created the peerage of Saint-Cloud for the archbishop of Paris.
21 Noailles moved to Châlons from Cahors in 1680, and left it for Paris in 1695.

Table 9.6   Patterns of episcopal tenure of dioceses

Bishops per diocese	No of dioceses	% of dioceses
0	1	0.8
1	10	8.0
2	57	45.6
3	37	29.6
4	8	3.2
5	6	4.8
6	1	0.8

Note. The percentages in the final column are based on a total of 125 dioceses.

short periods of time, and Louis himself was reported to have complained that there were five ex-bishops of Digne still alive at one point.[22] But a close look at the diocese with nominally the highest turnover of bishops under Louis, Fréjus rather than Digne, shows how problematic the stereotype of bishops with an itch to move elsewhere can be. After the death of the Mazarin fidèle, Bishop Ondedei, in 1674, Fréjus was given to Michel Poncet who was indeed moved upwards to Bourges before his bulls for Digne were even granted. The diocese was then held by an active young bishop, Clermont-Tonnerre, but he died of consumption within two years.[23] His nominal successor, Louis de Bourlemont, never set foot there but, like Michel Poncet, was immediately moved to Carcassonne and then Bordeaux. Both were royal decisions. Bourlemont's two immediate successors, the Aquin, uncle and nephew, also made highly unusual exits – the uncle was pressured into resigning in 1697, only to effectively prevent his nephew, to whom Louis XIV had given the see, from taking possession of it the following year. And their successor was none other than the future Cardinal Fleury, who resigned Fréjus in 1714 in order to become Louis XV's preceptor. Only four of these seven individuals were ever bishops of Fréjus in any real sense, although six of them held formal title to it. Between the extremes represented by Bayeux and Fréjus, as table 9.6 shows, we find that the great majority of dioceses had two or three rather than four or five bishops nominated by Louis XIV. The group of nine to which the king nominated a bishop only once includes four dioceses that were either acquired (Cambrai, Ypres, Besançon) or created (Blois) well into his personal rule, which naturally provided few opportunities to make more than one nomination.

22   BN, MS Fr 23508, fo 181r, *Nouvelles Ecclésiastiques*, ca. 1679.
23   Espitalier, 'Les évêques de Fréjus', 87ff.

There are a number of ways in which we can interpret figures like those in table 9.6. The first is to think in terms of episcopal continuity within dioceses. That ten dioceses had only one bishop nominated by Louis XIV was due mostly to the longevity of pre-1661 incumbents. Those dioceses with two or three bishops represent over three-quarters of the French church, while the high-turnover dioceses with four or more bishops represent about one-eighth only. This snapshot of episcopal (dis-)continuity at diocesan level can be enlarged by a study of inward and outward movement of bishops from, or to, other dioceses. Forty-five dioceses – well over one-third of the total – experienced no such movement at all. Their bishops were newcomers whose entire episcopal career was played out in their first and only diocese. For that reason, it would be highly tempting to regard this group as containing the least desirable dioceses of France: given to bishops who were unable to obtain a better diocese elsewhere because they lacked ambition or good connections, these dioceses, when they fell vacant, could not attract bishops wanting to move into them from their existing dioceses. Apart altogether from the inevitably subjective basis of the notion of 'desirable' dioceses, such assumptions would be clearly misleading in respect of many of these dioceses, beginning obviously with those to which they king only nominated a single bishop: no one would suggest that Chartres, Langres, Le Mans or Lisieux, to name just a few, were anything but desirable sees whose bishops had every reason to remain content with their lot. But it is equally true that about fifteen of these thirty-seven dioceses may be counted among France's least desirable sees. In between the two ends of the spectrum we have a small cluster of sees that cannot be unequivocally placed among either the desirable or undesirable.

This analysis can be taken a stage further if we identify those dioceses which *attracted* bishops from elsewhere. Making allowances for a small number of anomalies, it emerges that forty-two – one-third of all dioceses – fit into this category, with twenty-four of them 'importing' a bishop on just one occasion.[24] The figures here confirm, from yet another angle, the gradual squeezing out of sideways mobility among reigning bishops. Among the eighteen dioceses attracting two or more reigning bishops from elsewhere, twelve were archbishoprics; and where such movement occurred three times or more, it was exclusively in the direction of archbishoprics. Toulouse holds the absolute record in this regard – all five of its archbishops under Louis XIV came from other dioceses, and all but the last of them moved from another diocese in Languedoc. This is perhaps the closest we get to the sense of a 'systemic' logic at work in episcopal patronage. It remains the case, however, that eighty-four dioceses, a full two-thirds of the total, did not attract bishops in search of new pastures. For them, clearly, each new bishop was an unknown quantity, whose abilities and preferences as a bishop would only surface when confronted with

---

24 Five transfers have been discounted as being purely nominal, since the bishops involved had not got beyond obtaining papal provisions to their first dioceses.

local realities. That too represented a challenge to the king, his confessor and other advisers when deciding which *episcopabile* should be given which diocese.

By comparison, the number of dioceses whose bishops moved to another one elsewhere is higher, if not extravagantly so – fifty-one for 'outward' compared to forty-two for 'inward' episcopal migration for the 1661–1715 period.[25] Only six of them were archbishoprics, and in all but one instance, their incumbent moved to a 'better' archbishopric, while the sixth moved to a see, Metz, that was highly attractive because still formally a prince-bishopric of the Holy Roman Empire. It is also significant that thirty-seven of these fifty-one dioceses only 'exported' one bishop during the Louis XIV period. As it happens, Digne *does* hold the record here, exporting three of its bishops to other dioceses, so there is a clear basis in fact for its reputation at the time. What is also noteworthy is that in France under Louis XIV, unlike Spain since the age of Philip II at least, the practice of seeing certain dioceses as suitable for episcopal beginners and from which they could expect to move after a relatively brief apprenticeship, did not really take root. That, of course, did not prevent a considerable number of dioceses from being seen as 'évêchés crottés' by contemporaries, bishops included, but it is likely that the severity of the comments made about particular French dioceses owes more to the limited prospects of ever moving from them to something better than to objective reality.

V

The gradual reduction of mobility within the French episcopate should not prevent us from looking for other, possibly less immediately significant, developments. In preceding generations, it was not unusual for two bishops to negotiate a straightforward exchange of dioceses and then lobby for royal and papal approval. Not a single instance of this occurred under Louis XIV, and there are no indications of efforts being made to do so, but failing. However anxious bishops might be to move, a straight swap of dioceses with a *confrère* was not among the possibilities open to them. At best, exchanges of nominations to vacant dioceses *prior* to the despatch of papal provisions might be authorised, but as the only known instances of this date from the 1680s, they may be regarded as exceptions to the normal pattern.

More significant, however, is the drastic reduction in the number of coadjutorships which, as we saw, had been the classic way under Henri IV and Louis XIII of ensuring the transmission of a diocese within a family or passing it on to a dependent cleric. Having become more difficult to obtain under Richelieu, they reappeared under his successor, Mazarin, partly because of Mazarin's own political weakness at different times during his ministry. As

25   The figures exclude any transfers that occurred after Louis XIV's death.

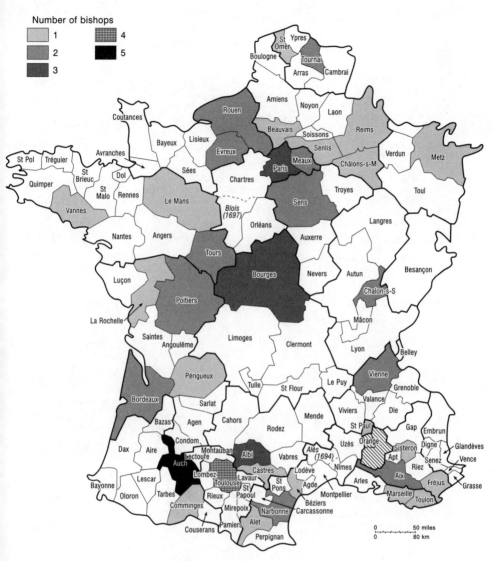

Number of bishops

- 1
- 2
- 3
- 4
- 5

St Pol, Tréguier, St Brieuc, Quimper, St Malo, Dol, Rennes, Vannes, Nantes, Angers, Luçon, Poitiers, La Rochelle, Coutances, Avranches, Bayeux, Lisieux, Sées, Le Mans, Rouen, Evreux, Chartres, Blois (1697), Orléans, Amiens, Beauvais, Noyon, Laon, Soissons, Senlis, Paris, Meaux, Sens, Troyes, Reims, Châlons-s-M, Verdun, Metz, Toul, Langres, Auxerre, Nevers, Bourges, Autun, Besançon, Chalon-s-S, Mâcon, Lyon, Belley, Saintes, Angoulême, Limoges, Clermont, Périgueux, Tulle, St Flour, Le Puy, Vienne, Grenoble, Valance, Die, Bordeaux, Sarlat, Bazas, Agen, Cahors, Rodez, Mende, Viviers, St Paul, Uzès, Orange, Gap, Embrun, Dax, Aire, Condom, Montauban, Lectoure, Albi, Vabres, Alès (1694), Nîmes, Sisteron, Apt, Digne, Glandèves, Senez, Vence, Auch, Lombez, Castres, Lavaur, Lodève, Agde, Arles, Aix, Riez, Fréjus, Grasse, Bayonne, Lescar, Oloron, Tarbes, Toulouse, St Papoul, Rieux, Mirepoix, St Pons, Béziers, Carcassonne, Montpellier, Narbonne, Marseille, Toulon, Comminges, Couserans, Pamiers, Alet, Perpignan

0 — 50 miles
0 — 80 km

5 *Dioceses attracting reigning bishops*

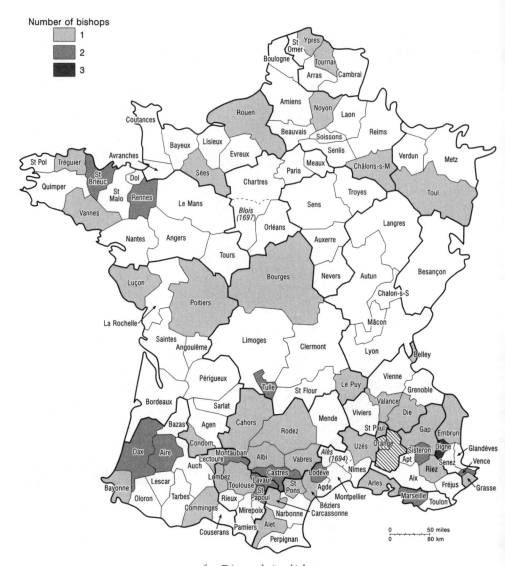

Number of bishops
- 1
- 2
- 3

St Pol
Tréguier
Quimper
St Brieuc
Vannes
St Malo
Dol
Rennes
Coutances
Avranches
Bayeux
Lisieux
Sées
Evreux
Le Mans
Nantes
Angers
Tours
Blois (1697)
Orléans
Chartres
Paris
Meaux
Senlis
Sens
Troyes
Auxerre
Nevers
Bourges
Langres
Autun
Besançon
Chalon-s-S
Mâcon
Lyon
Belley
St Omer
Ypres
Boulogne
Tournai
Arras
Cambrai
Amiens
Noyon
Laon
Beauvais
Soissons
Reims
Châlons-s-M
Verdun
Metz
Toul
Luçon
La Rochelle
Saintes
Angoulême
Poitiers
Limoges
Clermont
Périgueux
Tulle
St Flour
Le Puy
Vienne
Grenoble
Valence
Die
Viviers
St Paul
Gap
Embrun
Bordeaux
Sarlat
Bazas
Agen
Cahors
Rodez
Mende
Uzès
Orange
Sisteron
Digne
Glandèves
Vence
Dax
Aire
Condom
Montauban
Lectoure
Auch
Albi
Vabres
Alès (1694)
Nîmes
Apt
Senez
Riez
Grasse
Bayonne
Lescar
Oloron
Tarbes
Lombez
Toulouse
Castres
Lavaur
St Papoul
Lodève
St Pons
Agde
Arles
Aix
Fréjus
Toulon
Marseille
Rieux
Mirepoix
Béziers
Carcassonne
Montpellier
Narbonne
Comminges
Pamiers
Alet
Couserans
Perpignan

0   50 miles
0   80 km

6   *Dioceses losing bishops*

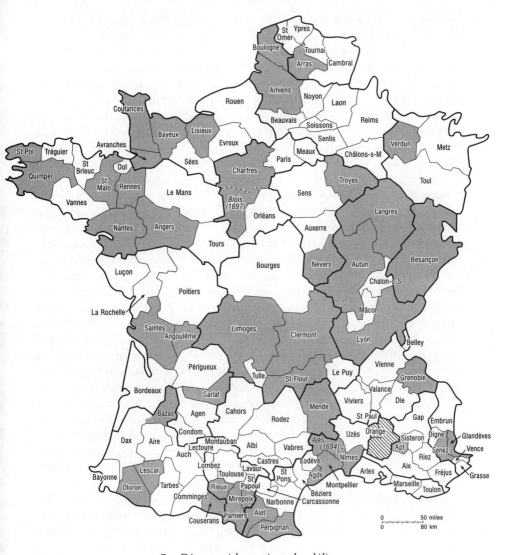

7   *Dioceses without episcopal mobility*

early as April 1661 it was claimed by Michel Le Tellier in a reply to the elderly bishop of La Rochelle, who had requested royal consent to taking one of his nephews as his coadjutor and, therefore, successor, that Louis XIV himself was averse to such arrangements. While wishing he could help the bishop, Le Tellier wrote that from what he had learned from the king's ecclesiastical advisors, Louis's unwillingness to nominate coadjutors was on the verge of becoming a general rule.[26] The bishop's suit went unheeded, and the *conseil de conscience*'s views on coadjutorships, as Le Tellier hinted, were indeed as unfavourable as one would expect. Furthermore, they were taken to heart by the young king and Le Tellier's hunch was to be very largely borne out during the remainder of the reign. La Chaize and others had occasion to remind petitioners that Louis XIV was determined not to permit coadjutorships, especially when they seemed contrived largely to satisfy family ambition. It may, therefore, come as something of a surprise that a total of ten coadjutorships were sanctioned by the king in the half-century after Le Tellier's assertion. They do shed a distinctive light on episcopal patronage during these years. Of the ten, only six actually took effect: three of the remaining ones were rendered unnecessary by the death of the reigning bishop and the automatic succession of the designated coadjutor, while the selection of François de Camps for coadjutor of Glandèves in 1684 was overtaken by his subsequent nomination to Pamiers.[27] That the six 'successful' coadjutorships all occurred between 1666 and 1680 might suggest that they only became impossible to attain in later decades. In fact three further coadjutorships were decided upon after 1680, the last of them as late as 1709. Even allowing for this, the record remains one of growing royal parsimony in this regard. Another significant difference with past practice is that only three of the ten intended coadjutorships entailed uncle-nephew successions, and that was because they involved elderly bishops who enjoyed, by one means or another, enough royal esteem to win such a concession – Grignan of Arles, Bosquet of Montpellier and Godet des Marais of Chartres. Despite the role of family interests here, all three coadjutorships were based on genuine rather than feigned need for assistance on the part of aged, infirm bishops, and there is no evidence of contemporary criticism of the case for them: in two instances, the reigning bishops themselves either died before the coadjutorship had been approved by Rome (Chartres, 1709) or almost immediately afterwards (Montpellier, 1676). The third, François de Grignan of Arles, was virtually blind by 1666, when his nephew became coadjutor, but he actually lived the longest of all, only dying in 1689. We have already seen, in their political context, two of the successful bids for a coadjutorship – Charles-Maurice Le Tellier at Reims and Jacques-Nicolas Colbert at Rouen. Neither involved family ties to the existing archbishops,

---

26   SHAT, Archives de la Guerre, A¹ 168, no 273, 15 April 1661. The bishop of La Rochelle, Jacques Raoul, himself successor to his uncle in 1631, was aged seventy-two at this point, and would die a month after Le Tellier's letter.

27   BN, MS Fr 20969, fo 35r, 10-3-1684 (Glandèves); fo 44r, 9 Nov 1685 (Pamiers).

but represented a more typical attempt by ministerial families to join the upper clergy at the highest entry-level possible: the great advantage of a coadjutorship was that individuals could be pushed forward for them while still too young or inexperienced to be serious candidates for a 'full' bishopric.

This evidence suggests that royal parsimony over coadjutorships was never so absolute as to deter efforts to secure them. Two cases from the final phase of the reign will illustrate both the reasons for, and the difficulty that it entailed. As in the past, bishops and their families were not averse to trying their luck and mobilising their patrons and supporters at court or in the church itself. This is what the famous Gabriel Roquette, bishop of Autun, attempted on discovering that his nephew and vicar-general, Bertrand de Sénaux, had been nominated to Saintes at Whit 1702 – unbeknown, it seems, to Roquette. But when he came to court to plead his need for a coadjutor, he was firmly told that if he wanted Sénaux at Autun, he should resign outright.[28] He promptly did so, and Sénaux's nomination was switched accordingly. It would probably be going too far to regard this as just a ploy in which uncle and nephew played out their respective roles in order to secure Autun for Sénaux. Nearly ten years later both Rome and the crown agreed that the elderly archbishop of Embrun, Brûlart de Genlis, badly needed help in dealing with the 'disorders' in his diocese, but they soon disagreed on the best solution. A name was chosen by Louis XIV, but the papacy rejected the move, arguing that there was no precedent for a suffragan bishop at Embrun, even though it had no problem about accepting one for Lyon at that time. But when it countered by saying it would look favourably on a coadjutor with succession rights at Embrun, it was the French turn to put a prompt stop to the discussion.[29]

As the Autun succession indicates, outright resignations by reigning bishops were historically associated with family politics. How many episcopal reigns under Louis XIV ended in this way, whether or not they involved family interests? What can we know about the circumstances and motivations that led to such decisions? There were twenty-five definitive episcopal resignations during Louis's personal rule, eight of which involved bishops from the Richelieu-Mazarin era. Twelve of Louis's own nominees did likewise in the

28 JRULM, MS French 94, fos 115 and 155, Huxelles to La Garde, 5 June and 28 July 1702 respectively. ASS, Correspondance des supérieurs-généraux, iii, no 768, Leschassier, superior-general to Godet, bishop of Chartres, 22 June 1702: 'On s'adresse encore à moy comme à un homme d'un grand crédit auprès de Vre Grandeur. Mons d'Autun voyant M l'abbé de Senaux nommé Evesque de Xaintes souhaitte ardemment de lui faire donner l'Evesché d'Autun. Il est si persuadé qu'il gouverneroit très bien un grand diocèse où il est connu et fort estimé qu'il ne feroit point de scrupule de l'oster s'il pouvoit à Xaintes pour le donner à Autun où il y a 200,000 ames plus que dans le diocèse de Xaintes. Vous avez esté Msgr assez informé du mérite de M l'abbé de Senaux sans qu'il soit besoin d'en faire un nouvel éloge. Je crois aussi que Mgr d'Autun n'aura pas manqué de vous marquer dans sa lettre qu'il ne demande pas un coadiuteur mais qu'il est prest de donner sa démission de l'Evesché d'Autun.' See also AN, L 744, pièce 1, nos 26–7, Saintes.
29 ASV, Nunz Fr 223, fos 180, 345, 460, 584, nuncio to secretary of state, 30 March 1711, 22 June 1711, 10 Aug 1711, 5 Nov 1711 respectively.

years after 1715, bringing the number of retirees who had entered the episcopate under him to twenty-nine (11.6 per cent of the total). This is virtually identical to the proportion for the years from 1589 to 1661 when, as we
have seen, coadjutorial successions were also easier to obtain.[30] Twenty-five
resignations scattered unevenly from 1661 (Artus de Lionne, father of the
royal minister) to early 1715 (the future Cardinal Fleury) constitute a steady
if small trickle, but not enough to open up a glut of unexpected opportunities for the crown or episcopal hopefuls. Of course, that depended largely on
who were the beneficiaries of the resignations. Eight of the twenty-five did
indeed involve episcopal successions within particular families, with five of
them arising during the years down to 1681 – a proportion and a chronology which echo almost perfectly those of the coadjutorships discussed above:
coadjutorships were, after all, deferred rather than immediate transfers. These
eight resignations, as we might expect, concerned bishops with substantial
court connections, and ranged from Cardinal d'Estrées to the Matignon
(twice), Beauvau (twice), Aquin and Bouthillier families. In purely formal
terms, Roquette of Autun was the last to obtain such a concession, but in
reality that honour should be reserved for Mme de Maintenon's favourite
bishop, Godet des Marais who, having secured his nephew's nomination as
his coadjutor in 1709, then died before the coadjutorship could take effect,
thereby ensuring that his nephew would succeed him immediately.

The seventeen remaining resignations cannot be readily grouped together
under one or two headings. Despite that, they suggest something of the range
of grounds for resignation. At least two or three are known to have occurred
on account of illhealth among bishops who were not especially elderly. This
is not wholly surprising. The Norman René Le Sauvage, bishop of Lavaur,
who was not one of them, confessed that a humid northern diocese would suit
him far better than Languedoc, but the steadily deteriorating health which
characterised his four-year episcopate ended in an early death rather than
transfer or promotion.[31] Louis Abelly, another northerner, was more fortunate
– or determined – in quitting Rodez after only two years on such grounds,
as he survived for another twenty-five! But ill health was also probably used
to strengthen, or even disguise, problems of a kind that the crown and especially the papacy would find it hard to accept – Daniel Huet of Avranches
was not well suited for the episcopate and was anxious to return full-time to
his scholarly pursuits.[32] Paul-Philippe de Chaumont of Dax also declared he

30   Bergin, *Making*, 304–6.
31   Daniel Rivals, 'Un prélat modèle du xviie siècle: René Le Sauvage, évêque de Lavaur', *Revue du Tarn*, 117 (1985), 73–4, letter to Cardinal Bouillon 29 Dec 1676.
32   *Lettres inedites de Pierre-Daniel Huet évêque d'Avranches à son neveu, M de Charsigné*, ed Armand Gasté (Caen 1901), 13–14, 20 April 1699, 'Vous serez bien surpris, mon cher neveu, quand vous apprendrez par cette lettre que je ne suis plus évêque d'Avranches. J'ay remontré au Roy que l'air et les eaux de ce lieu là sont entierement contraires à ma santé et m'ont souvent donné de cruelles coliques et des rumes continuels, et l'ai supplié de me décharger de cet Evesché. Il a eu la bonté de me l'accorder, et m'a donné pour dédommagement l'Abbaye de Fontenay.'

wanted to finish his study of Christianity, but an independent Roman enquiry discovered that the real trigger for his resignation was that he had fallen foul of some of the local nobility.[33] Three successive bishops of Tulle under Louis XIV abandoned the see for other dioceses on account of bitter disputes with their chapter and, possibly, their clergy, but only one of them resigned outright rather than moving to another diocese.[34] Here, too, there is simply too little evidence to explain why these particular individuals managed to have their pleas to resign heard at court, since many more bishops were still encountering problems, which could sometimes lead to physical threats or even injuries, than these few resignations would suggest. They were, it seems, either more stoic or more determined – or both – than those who opted to quit the episcopate outright.

It would certainly be mistaken to think of all of these resignations as death-bed efforts by infirm or elderly bishops. The most obvious exceptions are the only two bishops to make a comeback under Louis XIV – Louis Thomassin who quit Vence in 1680 only to be nominated to Sisteron in 1681 and, more famously, Bossuet who quit Condom in 1672 in order to act as preceptor to the Dauphin, before resuming his episcopal career at Meaux in 1681. Fleury, of course, was to imitate him in 1715 by resigning Fréjus for the preceptorship to Louis XV, but his subsequent good fortune dispensed him from returning to episcopal service. Bossuet and Fleury were the only bishops to resign in order to enter royal service: as we saw, movement was usually in the opposite direction.

At other end of this particular spectrum we ought to place the equally few bishops who resigned because of the pressure – itself a highly extensible notion ranging from exhortation to threats of action – exerted upon them by the crown. The most famous of them, of course, was that of Retz in 1662, though his past made that resignation unique in many respects: once he had resigned Paris, his Fronde was essentially buried and forgotten. In sharp contrast, Luc d'Aquin of Fréjus was forced to resign in 1697 by a combination of no less formidable pressures: the anger and discontent of his diocesans to start with; the ambition of his own family to put a nephew in his place; and, finally, the king's ultimatum that failure to resign could prompt legal action that might lead to his deposition. He was bounced into complying, especially after conferring with Archbishop Noailles, but quickly changed his mind and created such a furore by appealing to Rome that his nephew never managed to take 'peaceful possession' of Fréjus and had to accept a move elsewhere. However, the uncle's fury did not benefit him beyond that, and indeed only

33 ASV, *Acta congregationis consistorialis* 1682, vol i, fos 127–30; 1682, vol ii, fos 142–3 for the enquiry.

34 Humbert Ancelin resigned in 1702. His predecessors Guron de Rechignevoisin and Mascaron had moved to Comminges and Agen respectively. His successor, Beaupoil de Saint-André would also resign and retire to Périgueux seminary in 1722. Tulle was hardly more successful than Digne or Fréjus in retaining its bishops.

prompted successive *lettres de cachet* exiling him to deepest Brittany.[35] Royal *rigueur* also led to successive internal exiles for Charles Hervé of Gap between 1702 and his final resignation in 1705, but it remains unclear as to whether the allegations of immorality against him were fabrications or not.[36] The resignation of Jacques Séguier of Nîmes in 1687 was, as we saw, of a different order again: his age meant he was incapable of dealing with the Huguenot problem there after the Revocation of 1685, and he was induced into giving up his diocese so that Fléchier could be nominated to replace him.[37] It ought perhaps to be added in this context that from the outset of the king's personal rule, the crown also resorted to disciplinary action against individual bishops in the form of *lettres de cachet* ordering them either to stay within their diocese or removing them from it altogether. The Fouquet brothers were the earliest and best known victims of this practice, which was used more widely than ever before at the height of the Jansenist affair in the years after 1700, yet it did not induce either of them to resign their office. As far as we know, only in the case of Hervé of Gap did it lead directly to such an outcome, though whether that was the intention, it is impossible to say.

With so few cases of resignation occurring for reasons of extreme old age or incapacity, it seems that most of the bishops involved did so out of a desire to end their lives 'en retraite'. For scholars like Huet or Chaumont, the 'retraite' in question was to be another, more sedentary form of activity. Gilles de La Baume le Blanc of Nantes stepped down in order to become a Jesuit, even though it took him nearly thirty years to actually take the final step. Some of those resigning in the latter part of the reign retreated to the seminary they had been instrumental in founding or to Parisian seminaries which they had frequented in earlier years. But two exceptions are especially noteworthy, since resignation for them proved to be the opposite of 'retraite'. Once they had secured their nephews as their successors – nephews who had previously been their vicars-general – both François Bouthillier of Troyes (1697) and Gabriel Roquette of Autun (1702) simply took over the vicar-generalships vacated by

---

35   This particular affair created quite a stir and was public knowledge. The chorus of local complaints against Aquin at Fréjus was dismissed while his brother was Louis XIV's *premier médecin*, but not in subsequent years. See the substantial file of material collected by Père Léonard in AN, L 730, Fréjus, nos 22–28. JRULM, MS French 92, fo 30, Huxelles to La Garde, 25 Feb 1698.

36   AN, L 730, Gap, no 30, Père Léonard's papers. *Gallia Christiana Novissima*, i, cols 524–6. See the far more favourable account, based on a detailed knowledge of the local sources, in the *Inventaire-sommaire des archives départementales des Hautes-Alpes, série* G, t. iii (Gap 1897), xx–xxi.

37   BN, MS Fr 23498 fo 58r, *Nouvelles Ecclésiastiques*, 25 Jan 1687, 'vous estes à portèe de savoir les vrayes raisons pour lesquelles on a engagé pour ne pas dire obligé M de Nixmes à quitter son evesché pour l'abbaye de Lire en Normandie . . . Il s'est déclarée contre les quatres propositions du clergé, et l'on veut establir un nouvel evesché à Alaix au milieu des Sevennes pour les contenir (Huguenots) . . .'. *Sourches*, i, 471, 31 Dec 1686, makes no mention of these issues, but it certainly seems that Séguier was too old to tackle the Huguenot problem in Nîmes. See Sauzet, *Contre-Réforme et réforme catholique*, 408, who shows that some pressure of an unspecified kind was used to persuade Séguier to retire.

their nephews which enabled them to act as mentors and right-hand men to their successors. Bouthillier, who enjoyed the king's graces, wanted to resign Troyes, so he told Louis XIV he wished to do so in order to atone for his worldly existence and neglect of his diocese during his episcopate; the atonement began with the sale of his Paris townhouse and continued with him living in the Troyes seminary and serving as vicar-general.[38]

VI

With virtually nine out of ten bishops dying in office, answering the question of how most careers ended is a straightforward matter. There is simply not enough reliable information for a discussion of the causes or circumstances of death, even supposing that such a discussion were of genuine value here. In any case, the deaths that we know something about are, not surprisingly, the sudden, sometimes violent ones – but too few in number to form the basis of a worthwhile discussion. In attempting to complete the analysis of episcopal 'exits' there is one source which may enable us to reach beyond the realm of objective and quantifiable patterns into the more subjective one of attitudes and intentions. Episcopal wills, usually drafted fairly close to the testators' death, are a potential window into the minds of bishops as they contemplated their exit from both office and life. Since the heyday of the *Annales*-inspired 'histoire sérielle' approach to the mentalities of a given historical period, region or group, historians have learned to decode testaments in ways that take account of their formulaic structure as well as their self-presentational purposes.[39] The purpose of the analysis that follows is not to reopen the methodological discussions: it sets itself the more modest task of highlighting a limited number of themes that we might expect the leading figures in the French church to address as they made their last will. It is based on a highly random sample of thirty-eight testaments of bishops seated under Louis XIV (15.2 per cent of the total), even though many of them were obviously drawn up years, sometimes even decades, after the king's death; for comparative purposes, a small number of testaments of earlier bishops who

38 For the Troyes succession, AN, L 746, no 1, Troyes, Père Léonard's papers. JRULM, MS French 91, fo 83, Huxelles to La Garde, 3 Aug 1696; fo 220, same to same 12 April 1697. See the portrait of him in Saint-Simon, iv, 363–5, 453–6 (a separate 'fragment' from the text of the *Mémoires* themselves). François Bouthillier would become a member of the council of the regency after Louis XIV's death, and that enabled him to continue serving his nephew in yet another way, since the latter was made archbishop of Sens in 1716.

39 The classic studies in this field are Michel Vovelle, *Piété baroque et déchristianisation en Provence au xviii* *siècle. Les attitudes devant la mort d'après les clauses des testaments* (Paris 1973); Pierre Chaunu, *La Mort à Paris, xvi*, *xvii*, *xviii* *siècles* (Paris 1978). More recently: Marc Bouyssou, *Réforme catholique et déchristianisation dans le sud du diocèse de Chartres. Les testaments ruraux du Blésois et du Vendômois, xvi*–*xviii* *siècles*, 2 vols (Chartres 1998), i, 106, 'les testaments constituent sans doute la meilleure de ces sources' – for popular religious attitudes over time in this case.

died during the king's personal rule have also been pressed into service in order to track certain developments over time. It should be noted that contemporaries were often keenly interested in these documents, whose contents could attract widespread comment, especially where a large fortune was being distributed among testamentary beneficiaries.[40] As a result, some were printed at the time, while others appear to have circulated in manuscript – with either the full text or the essential details finding their way into the *Nouvelles Ecclésiastiques* or the hands of some of the correspondents of the day.[41] The testament of the redoubtable pro-Jansensist archbishop of Sens, Gondrin, was probably unique in attracting attention from as far away as Rome: the papal nuncio was instructed to procure and despatch a copy there for scrutiny in order to see if it contained any reprehensible utterances on religious matters.[42]

At the outset, it should be said that most of the episcopal testaments are not fundamentally different in layout and content to those of other social groups. Some of them are extraordinarily short, like that of Bossuet, as if the fear of immediate death left them too unprepared to make a more substantial testamentary effort.[43] We know that yet other bishops made no will, leaving the law of the land to decide the fate of their estate, while a few managed to draft their will only to die before reviewing and signing it. Like most testators, bishops saw the purpose of making a will to be that of putting their affairs in order well in advance of the hour of death, so that when the latter arrived they could, as one of them bluntly put it, 'be solely occupied by the important matter of my salvation'.[44] But apart from the obvious 'duties of their rank' (*devoirs d'état*) which they were honour-bound to perform as bishops

40 See Saint-Simon's reference to the scandal caused by the testamentary legacies of Cardinal Le Camus, a man whose original conversion and austere lifestyle otherwise had his approval: xv, 266–72, 497–8. His will is in AN, MC, CXI, 35, 23 March 1706. AN, L 730, pièce 1, no 52, for a printed 'État des donations et des legs' made by Le Camus. See Edmond Esmonin, 'La Fortune du cardinal Le Camus', in his *Etudes sur la France des xviie et xviiie siècles* (Paris 1964), 383–96.

41 The manuscript *Nouvelles Ecclésiastiques* contains copies of six episcopal testaments from the late 1670s – BN, MS Fr 23506, 23508–9.

42 *Correspondance du nonce Spada*, nos 517, 546, 549, 609, for correspondence between Spada and Cardinal Altieri in Oct–Nov 1674 about the testament. Gondrin, archbishop of Sens since the 1640s, had been a major critic of the methods used to condemn Jansen in the 1650s, when Rome wished to put him on trial. He was also an uncle of Madame de Montespan who, as Louis XIV himself admitted, feared nobody and was capable of answering the king to his face.

43 Bossuet, *Correspondance*, xiv, appendice v, 252–5. The testament contains only five clauses, two of them formulaic. After the conventional references to his burial and the payment of his debts (unspecified), the only substantive clause was that making his nephew, abbé Bossuet, both *héritier universel* and executor, with the request that the other Bossuet family members accept him as such. Bossuet family dissensions and jealousies, which the testament barely disguises, are chronicled by Bossuet's secretary, Ledieu, in his *Journal de Bossuet*, especially for the years 1703–4. The will of Daniel de Francheville of Périgueux, written after he had suffered sun-stroke, was shorter again, and dealt purely with disposal of his patrimonial property in Brittany and his church-derived *biens* on the other hand: see the text in L Entraygues, *Mgr Daniel de Francheville évêque de Périgueux* (Périgueux 1923), 163.

44 AD Gers, I 2283, testament of Augustin de Maupeou, archbishop of Auch, 7 April 1712.

– for example, legacies to their cathedral and their principal servants and so on – there are fewer clauses than we might expect concerning their calling as bishops. The specifically religious references which they contain are largely those of individuals preparing to die as Christians rather than as dignitaries of the church, though the latter motif is evident, albeit indirectly, in the clauses in which they specify their preferences about the nature and place of their burial. We should not expect to find here profound or explicit statements into episcopacy in general, least of all in the preamble where, in customary fashion, they invoke God's mercy and the intercession of Christ and the saints. Yet the testaments are full of substantial if often implicit evidence of significant shifts in ideas about what it meant to be a bishop at this time, and it is that which is of interest here.

As already indicated, the testaments contain few clues as to the theological or related leanings of their authors. Only nine of the thirty-eight studied here record their desire to 'die in the bosom of Catholic, Apostolic and Roman church'. Such a declaration – which could be accompanied by a phrase such as 'and in allegiance to the Pope' – was confined to those who had experienced the Jansenist crisis of Louis XIV's last years and the regency that followed, and who (with one exception) found themselves publicly defending Rome and doctrinal orthodoxy during their careers.[45] The most detailed testamentary *apologia* of this kind came in 1749 from Archbishop Languet of Sens, whose career and writings were overwhelmingly devoted to combating Jansenism wherever Languet saw it at work.[46] But this kind of discourse was exceptional: as it turned out, there was nothing whatever that Rome could have objected to in the testament of his distant predecessor at Sens, Gondrin.[47]

Perhaps the first real surprises in these testaments are to be found in the instructions about the funeral and burial of the testators. Nine of the thirty-eight made no mention at all of either subject, while sixteen referred to their burial but not to the kind of funeral service they wished. We can assume that these bishops were happy to follow the custom of the day, which meant allowing heirs, executors and the cathedral chapter to decide how much ceremony and display they thought fit for the occasion. Of the twenty-two leaving

---

45 Colbert (Auxerre), Baudry (Mende), Aquin (Sées), Maupeou (Auch), Grignan (Carcassonne), Berger (Gap) and Languet de Gergy (Sens). The exception mentioned above is Archbishop Brûlart de Genlis of Embrun, who had been accused of pro-Jansenist sentiments, and who used his will as well as other means to defend himself against the charge – AD Hautes-Alpes, G 223, 18 April 1714. See also his separate declaration in AD Hautes-Alpes, G 224, an *état général* of his affairs and estate written for his heirs and other interested parties. In discussing his notes and writings, which he declares unpublishable, he affirms that 'en celles de la religion, je me suis uniquement attaché à ce que l'église Catholique et Apostolique et Romaine reconnoit estre de foy . . .'

46 Louis Jarrot, 'Le Testament de Jean-Joseph Languet de Gergy, archevêque de Sens, membre de l'Académie française', *Bulletin d'Histoire et d'Archéologie Religieuse du Diocèse de Dijon*, 18 (1900), 217–22, 257–8, 278–82.

47 AD Yonne, G 177, testament of 18 Sept 1674.

instructions for their funeral service, fourteen explicitly asked for them to be modest affairs, 'sans pompe ni solennité excessives' and only costing a limited sum of money.[48] Bishop Valbelle of Saint-Omer felt that a cathedral canon's funeral would be appropriate for him, after which they could bury him in the midst of the poor of the *hôpital-général*, while Taffoureau of Alet put a truly drastic tariff of 200 *livres* on his funeral.[49] Of the remaining eight, one left it entirely up to his heir and executor, who happened to be his elder brother.[50] The other seven wanted as modest funeral as either *la bienséance* or their dignity as a bishop would allow – a condition that seems to have been used largely by archbishops and bishops dying well into Louis XIV's reign, when it would seem that episcopal self-deprecation was less common than later.

Twenty-two of the twenty-nine specifying their desired form and place of burial chose, not surprisingly, their cathedral; some of them explicitly asked to be buried beside their predecessors generally, or even beside a particular predecessor to whom they were devoted and who might also be a family member. A few of those desiring a cathedral burial declared that they would leave it to the chapter to decide where precisely it should be. Two bishops wished to be buried in the chapel of the seminary, doubtless because they had built one or both of them, while three opted for burial in a cemetery. Berger of Gap asked to be buried among the poor of the local *hôpital-général* in a chapel he intended building in the town cemetery, but sensing that the chapter might well veto this, he also asked for a particular spot within the cathedral.[51]

Two further items may offer further enlightenment about episcopal behaviour here. Only six of the thirty-eight testators refer to the question of an epitaph or inscription over their place of burial and/or a funeral oration at their burial. It would seem, therefore, that over three-quarters of the bishops in our sample were either indifferent to these matters or, as suggested already, were tacitly consenting to church custom as executors and cathedral chapters might choose to interpret it. Three of the six who mentioned epitaphs forbade them absolutely, while the other three insisted that they be restricted to a simple inscription, the exact words of which some of them prescribed themselves. Two of these six stipulations were accompanied by a similar veto on the use of lead coffins for their burial. On the other hand, the six testaments which mentioned funeral orations all did so in order to ban them unequivocally! These rejections were part of a pattern of behaviour on the part of their authors who also

---

48 'Baroque' episcopal funerals and burials could be expensive affairs. In 1721 that of Cardinal François de Mailly, archbishop of Reims, cost 11,556 *livres*, a year's revenue for some of France's most poorly endowed bishops: AN, V[7] 88, liasse 62.

49 H Laplane, *Messieurs de Valbelle, évêques de Saint-Omer, 1684–1754* (Saint-Omer 1872), 25, testament of François de Valbelle, 7 Aug 1727. BM Sens, MS 245, fos 81–9, for a defective copy of Taffoureau's will.

50 AN, MC, XCI, 659, 1 Oct 1719, testament of Roland Kerhoent de Coëtanfao, bishop of Avranches.

51 AD Hautes-Alpes, G 1389, testament of 25 March 1735.

invariably asked for a modest funeral and a simple burial. It might be thought that rejections of funeral orations would only emanate from bishops governing important dioceses with a major town or city – and thus likely to, and capable of hosting a grand funeral oration; but apart from Cardinal Le Camus of Grenoble, this was not so, as a similar veto by the bishops of much smaller sees like Alet, Saint-Omer and Carcassonne all demonstrate. Although they only involve under a quarter of our sample, it is nevertheless remarkable to observe individual bishops penning such categorical refusals of one of the recognised glories of Louis XIV's reign – the *oraison funèbre*, the most admired of which were also delivered by French bishops.

It would be relatively easy to dismiss this kind of soul-searching in the face of death as yet another variation on a familiar theme were it not for the emergence during roughly the same period of an unexpected but key characteristic of the testaments studied here. At first sight, however, the two topics may seem to have little in common. As late as 1707, Bishop Baudry of Mende chose to open his testament by explicitly invoking the canonical tradition that the poor were the rightful heirs of the church's bishops, but that too often they were neglected in favour of their relatives.[52] He was not the first to make such an observation, but lying behind it and giving it effect was a clear distinction between patrimonial goods inherited from one's family and church goods deriving from benefices and other offices. Since the distinction itself was hardly new, it may be futile to try pinpointing its first appearance in episcopal testaments. What was new was the growing awareness of it, and the manner in which that awareness began to affect bishops' behaviour. In an admittedly small sample of late sixteenth and early seventeenth century testaments, there is no trace of it at all, even on the part of bishops who made otherwise generous legacies to religious and charitable institutions. When it came to designating ('instituting') their *héritier universel*, the key moment of any testament as they themselves regularly declared, they invariably picked a family member, and made no allusion to, let alone any provision for, keeping the twin sources of their wealth distinct. But that distinction becomes increasingly evident, if not always explicitly mentioned, in episcopal wills from the mid-seventeenth century onwards.[53] For a long time, however, invoking and applying it seems to have been a genuine source of anxiety for some bishops. It is clear from their often pathetic appeals to their families that they did not expect them to swallow the idea or its implications easily, and that it involved a genuine shift in attitudes, which might be interpreted as the abandonment of a long tradition of *pietas* towards one's family.[54] Another manifestation of

52 AD Lozère, F 396, testament of François-Placide de Baudry de Piencourt, 7 Dec 1705.

53 The first explicit example to date is in the will of Octave de Bellegarde, archbishop of Sens, who died in 1646: AD Yonne, G 117, 29 May 1646.

54 Languet de Gergy went further than that in his testament, compiling a list of the contents of his residual estate in order to prove that none of it could be claimed by members of his family: Jarrot, 'Le Testament de Languet de Gergy', 217–22, 257–8, 278–82.

this principle took the form of testators claiming that they had either inherited nothing from their families, or had subsequently 'returned' that inheritance to them, usually in the form of equivalent gifts to nephews and nieces
on their marriage and that, as a result, they were under no further obligation
whatever towards family members.[55] In some instances, the point was underlined even more spectacularly by the making of legacies of a purely nominal
monetary value – ten *sous* or ten *livres*, for example – to family members.[56]
But not all bishops adopted this distinction under Louis XIV and later, and
the evidence so far indicates that resistance to it was at its strongest in tightly-
knit families, mostly but not exclusively aristocratic in character, for whom
the elevation of an individual member to the episcopate was – and was felt
to be – as much a consequence of family 'credit' and reputation as of individual merit or achievement. Bishops with names like La Mothe-Houdancourt, Villeroy, Aubusson de la Feuillade, Coislin and Coëtanfao, but also from
less elevated circles of the robe, Parisian or provincial, like Pajot, Bossuet,
Le Camus, Maupeou or Gourgues, went on to choose brothers or nephews as
their 'universal' heirs. Perhaps the easiest resolution of such a dilemma was
that achieved by bishops who at the time of making their wills had secured
a nephew as their coadjutor-successor: making them their *héritier universel*
satisfied both family and episcopal principle in one stroke. But as we saw
above, the rarity of coadjutors under Louis XIV ensured that this option was
only available to a tiny minority.[57] Of a larger sample of forty-eight testaments,
which includes a number of bishops seated in the Richelieu-Mazarin period,
no fewer than thirty-four acted upon the distinction, as is evident most clearly
in the selection of two sets of *héritiers universels*, one for patrimonial property
– which might, of course, be located in a part of France far removed from
the diocese they governed – and another for their church-derived wealth.
Moreover, when the sample is looked at chronologically, it becomes clear that,
for all the exceptions mentioned above, episcopal will-making increasingly
respected the distinction.

What were the practical consequences of this development? Apart from
those few bishops who 'instituted' their coadjutor-successors or vicar-general

---

55   AD Doubs, G 949, testament of François-Joseph de Grammont, archbishop of Besançon, 1 May
      1707, 'et comme nous nous somes desia dépouillés cy devant en faveur de nostre famille des
      biens qui nous en estoient escheus, à la réserve de quelques droits, qu'ainsy les biens qui nous
      restent proviennent presque tous de l'église et qu'il est des règles de la justice comme du bien
      de nostre ame de rendre à l'église ce que nous en avons, nous espérons que nos frères et parens
      voudront bien approuver que nous sacrifions en cela nostre bon Coeur et nos amitiés pour eux,
      aux engagements et devoirs de nostre conscience . . .'

56   An example is Joseph Revol of Oloron's first testament of 1732, in which he left 10 *sols* to his
      nephew and blood heir, the marquis de Revol: Jacques Staes, 'Deux testaments de Monseigneur
      Joseph de Revol, évêque d'Oloron (1732 et 1735)', *Documents pour servir à l'histoire du
      département des Pyrénées-Atlantiques*, 7 (1986), 142.

57   It was was taken up by Grammont of Besançon (1681), Godet des Marets of Chartres (1709),
      Grignan of Carcassonne (1721), Revol of Oloron (1735).

as their *héritier universel* and those whose testaments omit any mention of such
an heir at all, it is clear that a small number of institutions were the main
beneficiaries of the shift. In an age which saw the Catholic Reformation reach
its apogee, it is not surprising that bishops might select their seminary as
their *héritier universel*. But there are fewer cases of their doing so than one
might imagine – only five out of twenty such testamentary 'institutions' went
to seminaries. It is evident enough from the other clauses of numerous testaments that bishops had already devoted money and effort towards their completion and that, while they often made additional legacies to them in their
wills, they were less willing to leave them the residue of their estate. Some
of the decisions to do so are not hard to understand. François Hébert of Agen
made the Lazarist directors of his seminary his *héritier universel*, but then
he had himself been a Lazarist and seminary director.[58] The obsessive anti-
Jansenist warrior, Languet of Sens, was convinced that only by endowing his
two seminaries could 'the most pressing need of the diocese which is the
proper education of the clergy' be met.[59] At Embrun and Gap, Brûlart and
Berger 'instituted' their cathedral clergy as their *héritiers universels* because of
the lack of endowment of the cathedrals.[60]

There is little doubt, however, that the prime object of episcopal testamentary goodwill was either the 'poor of the diocese' in general, or specific
institutions dedicated to dealing with the poor. Twelve out of the twenty
recorded *héritages universels* were decided in their favour. Sometimes, the
héritage universel would be split between two or more such institutions, most
commonly the *hôtel-dieu* or the newer *hôpital-général*. Bishop Champflour of La
Rochelle split his between four institutions, Briqueville of Cahors between
three.[61] Yet another, Langle of Boulogne, split his in a slightly different way
still, between the *hôpital-général* and his seminary.[62] A chronological analysis
of these wills shows that the broad movement of episcopal testamentary
provision for the poor tended to move away from the 'poor of the diocese' in
a general, undifferentiated sense, and towards the selection, jointly or singly,
of the *hôpital-général* or a similar institution. Of course, we simply do not know
how substantial a benefit this kind of action was in financial terms, since our
knowledge of the overall value of the episcopal estates in question *and* of the
existing endowment of charitable institutions is still very slight. And it is
possible that by the time legacies, debts, wages to servants and so on were

---

58 *Testament de feu messier François Hébert évêque et comte d'Agen* (Agen 1728), 5. A copy of this printed
    version is in the *archives municipales* of Agen.
59 Jarrot, 'Le Testament de Languet de Gergy', 217–22, 257–8, 278–82.
60 AD Hautes-Alpes, G 223 (Brûlart, 1714 – the *fabrique* of the cathedral was to share the *héritage
    universel* with the *hôpital-général*); G 1389 (Berger, 1735).
61 AD Puy-de-Dôme, 9 F 61, no 53 (Champflour 1715). L Combarieu, 'Testaments de trois
    évêques de Cahors', *Bulletin de la Société d'Étude du Lot*, 6 (1880), 38–42 (Briqueville 1740).
62 C Landrin, *Un prélat gallican. Pierre de Langle évêque de Boulogne (1644–1725)* (Calais 1905),
    307–10.

paid, the residue of an estate was not a princely sum.[63] Even allowing for that, it seems that episcopal largesse made quite a difference to many of the *hôtels-dieu* or *hôpitaux-généraux* that they sponsored in this way. The pattern observed here certainly supports the contention of Olwen Hufton that 'all the *hôpitaux* in the diocesan centres, Clermont, Dijon, Mende, Montpellier, Bayeux, Rennes, Rouen, were main beneficiaries under the testaments of their bishops in the period 1680–1740'. France's bishops were among the most enthusiastic respondents to the crown's demands to build up and support institutions like the *hôpital-général*, especially in the difficult decades towards the end of the century, and it would seem from the evidence of the testaments examined here, that their sponsorship of them lasted longer than that of the other groups which had initially helped to fund them.[64]

This exploration of episcopal behaviour and attitudes as refracted by the testaments of France's bishops covering a period of over sixty years from the mid-1670s onwards is tentative and provisional, but its underlying conclusion seem inescapable. The manner in which they put their affairs in order before death, even where there was no grand rhetorical effort involved, clearly shows the extent to which they had experienced the imprint of some of the deeper currents of the French Catholic Reformation, an imprint which is not always easy to pinpoint as convincingly from other sources. Nor should we assume that bishops who did *not* choose their seminary, *hôtel-dieu*, or *hôpital-général* as their *héritier universel* turned their back on the needs of their dioceses, as the evidence of individual legacies shows.[65] By disposing of their estates in the ways we have seen here, they were applying the rhetoric of preachers and the strictures of reformers in a sphere where there had always been powerful reasons, deeply embedded in social mores, especially those of family *pietas*, for resisting it. Such a gesture was tangible proof of their devotion to the diocese – or more unusually, dioceses – that they had governed during their long careers.[66]

63   This could only be done on the basis of local archival studies, beginning with the *inventaire après décès* of the individual bishop, followed by the subsequent *partage* and other documents. Evidence of designated heirs only accepting a will on certain conditions (*sous bénéfice d'inventaire*) would be a first sign of suspicion that the estate might not be worth enough to pay all the debts and legacies.

64   Olwen Hufton, *The Poor of Eighteenth-Century France 1750–1789* (Oxford 1974), 152–3. The quotation is on p 153, n 1.

65   The most spectacular instance of this was the huge legacy of 170,000 *livres* which Augustin de Maupeou extracted from his estate, and which he earmarked for the poor of Auch diocese and other places where he held church benefices. AD Gers, I 2283, testament of 7 April 1712. Michel Cassagnet de Tilladet of Mâcon set aside 50,000 *livres* for the poor of the diocese even though his will made the *hôtel-dieu* and *hôpital-général* of Mâcon his *héritiers universels*: AD Saône-et-Loire, J681, testament of 7 Nov 1725.

66   For a broader but also more hagiographical account of the charitable activities of eighteenth-century bishops, see Sicard, *L'Ancien clergé de France, les évêques*, 375–421, 'les évêques et la charité'. See also McManners, *Church and Society*, i, 289–96.

CONCLUSION

IT WILL BE apparent by now that the French episcopate under Louis XIV was shaped in subtle and numerous ways by the changes occurring within the French church during the seventeenth century. The evidence for this is much easier to recognise if, as this study has attempted to do, we think in terms of the successive cohorts of new entrants to the bench rather than of the episcopate as a single, immobile aggregate during the half century after 1661. This is particularly clear from the discussion of their studies and of pre-episcopal careers, which provided the most direct insight into the nature, scale, and chronology of such change. That discussion showed the impact of change to have been piecemeal, and that in some respects it was not being fully felt until the 1680s or the 1690s. Although these two chapters seemed to deal with distinct subjects, it became clear that studies and early careers often overlapped, and that during both of them ties of friendship, service and patronage/clientage increasingly developed in such a way as to make future bishops part of a wider milieu which by the end of the reign was widely recognised as the seedbed of the episcopate. Among the signs of change we must also include the patterns of episcopal testamentary behaviour outlined in the previous chapter, even though it was evidence which confirmed and extended the conclusions suggested in earlier chapters rather than a last-minute surprise.

It would be all too easy, by adding further brushstrokes, to end up painting a portrait of an episcopate which verged on collective sainthood. Their contemporaries, whom we have so often observed straining to obtain information about matters of episcopal patronage and behaviour generally, were acutely aware of the failings of its members. Nor were they slow to comment, in tones that varied from amusement to outright hostility, on the lapses of individual bishops or the survival of practices from the past – their vanity, profligacy, neglect of the duties of their office, and so on. In recounting how a particular bishop never left his diocese for fear of dying outside it, Mme de Sévigné could not help adding that there were others where death would be have to move quite smartly in order to catch them *inside* their dioceses – a

complaint that was hardly new.[1] The sexual indiscretions of men like
Cardinal Bonsi or Archbishops Harlay and Le Tellier were no secret – or were
at least widely rumoured. Commentators immediately 'knew' the meaning of
Le Tellier's decision to leave most of his huge fortune to his favourite niece.[2]
When Harlay died without the sacraments in 1695, the opportunity of deliv-
ering his funeral sermon was promptly declined by a long list of preachers,
some of them bishops, who evidently shared the opinion of contemporaries
that there were only two obstacles to a eulogy of Harlay – his life and his
death.[3] The refusal of the hardline bishop of Montpellier, Colbert de Croissy,
to allow the ailing Bonsi to be absolved in confession unless he renounced his
liaison with Mme de Ganges, was reported and applauded, albeit with a
frisson, in Paris and elsewhere.[4] The accusation of atheism levelled against
Bishop Beaumanoir of Le Mans (1649–71) was to be repeated later in respect
of Bishop Phélypeaux of Lodève (1694–1732), whose morals were not spared
either[5]. Equally, bishops regarded as exemplars of their office received
commensurably fulsome praise, and nowhere more than in the *Gazette*, which
was probably the main source of information for many diarists, letter- and
memoir-writers. Yet even the negative verdicts to be found in writers from
Sévigné to Saint-Simon should be read as evidence that contemporaries were
more exigent than before in what they expected of bishops, rather than of
their being of an 'objectively' lower calibre than in the past. In this context,
the influence of Port-Royal and related currents of Augustinian thinking
should not be minimised at a time when the image of the 'good bishop' was
increasingly derived from the idealised early church.[6] Saint-Simon was not
alone in echoing such thinking when he referred to one or two of Louis XIV's
bishops as not deserving the mitre 'according to the mores of the present time'
but whose family's influence overrode such considerations.[7]

1   Sévigné, *Correspondance*, ix, 43, Sévigné to Mme de Grignan, 9 May 1689, 'il y en a d'autres qu'il
    faudroit que la mort tirât bien juste pour les y attraper.' The resident 'saint évêque' to whom
    she referred was Froually du Tessé, bishop of Avranches.
2   Saint-Simon, xix, 42–8, and appendix 4, pp 494–6, 'enfin par son testament, il n'a suivi, ni la
    nature, ni les lois, ni la religion'.
3   Sévigné, *Correspondance*, xi, 305, Mme de Coulanges to Mme de Sévigné, 12 Aug 1695.
4   JRULM, MS French 93, 213v, Huxelles to La Garde, 12 Dec 1700, 'Je croy, Monsieur, que vous
    scavez ce qui s'est passé a Montpellier au sujet de l'administration des sacrements a Mr le
    Cardinal de Bonzi, ou l'Evesque a fait son devoir à toute rigueur, les gens d'icy disent qu'ils ne
    veulent point aller mourir là.' *Lettres de Germain Vuillart*, no 173, 16 Dec 1700, 'que de pareils
    pasteurs et de pareils prélats sont necessaires au monde . . . dans un siècle où la discipline est si
    déchue et la vigueur sacerdotale si rare'.
5   See E Appolis, *Le Jansénisme dans le diocèse de Lodève au xviii*ᵉ *siècle* (Albi 1952), ch 1.
6   René Taveneaux, 'L'Évêque selon Port Royal', in Taveneaux, *Jansénisme et Réforme catholique*,
    75–87. For the case of Saint-Simon, see E Le Roy Ladurie, *Saint-Simon ou le système de la cour*
    (Paris 1997), ch 6, esp 338ff.
7   One of them was François-Paul de Villeroy, archbishop of Lyon in 1714, whose father's influence
    more than compensated for his son's inadequacy: Saint-Simon, xxv, 80–1, 'ses moeurs et son
    ignorance, l'un et l'autre parfaitement connus'; 358, 'l'abbé de Villeroy, selon les moeurs

It is equally obvious that the role of the crown was central to evolution of the episcopate under Louis XIV. Its responsiveness to the changes within the ecclesiastical circles from which bishops were drawn in turn enabled the episcopate to continue to reflect that wider (if also narrow) world. As always, identifying what might be called the crown's 'policy' in this domain remains highly problematic, and the best that can achieved is an 'external' verdict based upon the tabulation and subsequent interpretation of its decisions to nominate, transfer, and promote particular bishops. The inner workings of its decision-making elude us because of the secrecy encompassing it, but that should not lead to the conclusion that only a particular type of candidate could be considered, as the myth of an episcopate reserved for *abbés de cour* would suggest. The king and his advisers remained relatively 'accessible' to pleas on behalf of individuals who did not necessarily belong to any charmed circle, and we noted several occasions in which Louis XIV, feeling cornered perhaps even by his own confessor, deliberately sought to demonstrate his independence by promoting 'outsiders'; in doing so, he was also trying to make a point to all those with designs on a mitre. Decisions of this kind may not have been especially numerous, but there were just enough of them – and they continued to be made until the last years of the reign – in order to ensure that the bishop-making process was not closed off. What has been observed in relation to military patronage at this time is directly pertinent to its episcopal counterpart: 'constructing a model of patronage for the French officer corps is complicated by the plurality of people who were accepted, after 1661, as having the right to suggest candidates to the king. Even if there was some restriction caused by career structures . . . that did not mean that Louis XIV did not welcome suggestions from many sources'.[8]

The evidence provided in the chapters devoted to royal patronage also highlighted the care and time taken over episcopal patronage, regardless of whether the king formally consulted a *conseil de conscience* or just his confessor. We saw that the 'identikit' for what constituted a typical bishop only took shape over several decades, and that the preference for doctors of theology who had served as vicars-general or related posts was slow to make its mark. The gradual restriction, especially from the early 1680s onwards, of nominations to certain dates was bound to lead to closer *comparative* scrutiny of the candidates inscribed on the *feuille des bénéfices*. The concomitant 'bunching' of nominations which this entailed reduced the ad hoc character of individual nominations, and frequently led contemporaries to comment more on the 'distribution' of dioceses arising from the exercise as a whole rather than on individual nominations within it.

présentes, se trouvoit bien éloigné d'être évêque; mais la situation et l'intéret du père suppléa à tout'.
8 Rowlands, *Dynastic State and the Army*, 354.

Yet it would be naive to assume that because episcopal patronage was gradually institutionalised along these lines, decision-making became more and more exclusively focused on 'religious' considerations. As we saw, a steady number of nominations were promotions to the rank of archbishop, which under Louis XIV nearly always involved transferring a reigning bishop, and thus opened the way to a second nomination – which in turn might be only one of several decisions pending by then. The leeway that this offered the king and his advisers was appreciable, and it enabled them to match candidates and dioceses in a way which suited the crown's interests, while making it extremely difficult for successful candidates and their patrons to do anything more than grumble when given dioceses that they had not especially wanted. The 'remue-ménage des évêques' that Mme de Sévigné decried in May 1684, was the result of one such set of nominations, when eight decisions were made simultaneously, and three of them involved the sideways rather than upward movement of existing bishops. In fact, as we saw, what she was criticising was far less common than previously, and it was triggered by two especially difficult problems – the recently acquired diocese of Saint-Omer and the need for a consecrated bishop to take over Pavillon's diocese of Alet. Not all exercises of episcopal patronage had to deal with factors like these, but 'one-off' problems caused by an individual bishop or diocese were never far away in a church the size of France. In such instances, making bishops was far less concerned with weighing up the 'absolute' merit of candidates than with deciding which of them was best suited to deal with a particular set of circumstances. As we saw in chapter 1, these considerations emerged most clearly in the choice of bishops for recently acquired dioceses: the crown adjusted according to circumstances, sometimes installing reigning bishops from elsewhere, sometimes preferring natives, or near-natives, to outsiders, depending on how successfully or not integration into France was proceeding.

That kind of flexibility was 'political' by any definition of the word, but we should not imagine that it was reserved for frontier dioceses. The most striking examples of this concerned archbishoprics like Paris, Narbonne, Aix, Reims, Lyon and possibly others: who should move into them was the kind of decision that could not be made in the course of a royal confessor's 'vendredy' at Versailles. Above all, in a church whose numerous dioceses varied so considerably in their attractiveness to candidates for preferment, royal decision-making could not escape being highly pragmatic. In normal circumstances the guidelines for episcopal patronage elaborated in Louis XIV's *mémoires* for 1662 sufficed, especially when accompanied by the king's own instinctive reluctance to depend on a single source of advice. That line of action was faithfully echoed at the very end of the reign by Mme de Maintenon à propos of one of Louis XIV's last major and most evidently political acts of episcopal patronage, the nomination of abbé Villeroy, a man with no prior episcopal experience, to the archiepiscopal and primatial see of

Lyon in 1714. Clearly showing her own continuing interest in these issues Maintenon – who was uneasy about the Villeroy succession despite confessing to knowing nothing that would debar the abbé Villeroy himself from preferment – concluded: 'positions in the church involve to some degree the conscience of those who grant them, but we have enough sins of our own without having to answer for those of others'.[9] It was when issues such as Jansenism, real or alleged, arose that the king's touch became much less sure. But it was his instinctive readiness to associate it with subversion rather than his ignorance of religious questions per se – one of the most absurd charges levelled against him by generations of historians – that left him open to manipulation by his confessors and others.[10]

II

The richness and variety of contemporary responses to the condition of, and changes to, the episcopate could form the point of departure for a separate study of the development of an 'ideology', for want of a better term, of episcopacy itself during Louis XIV's reign. Research to date has focused on the preceding half-century or so, but it has shown how much scope for a full-blooded 'défense et illustration' of episcopacy was provided by the gallican tradition and framework. The more recent influences associated with Borromeo and de Sales, but also with Bérulle and the 'French school', were being continually reworked and enriched, to enhance the pastoral and ecclesiological status of episcopacy.[11] Much of that reworking was done by authors who, from Bérulle to Bossuet, were themselves important actors within the French church. Even a figure as apparently detached from those affairs as the 'tempestuous abbé' of the austere Cistercian monastery of La Trappe, Rancé – who as a Bouthillier could have followed his uncles relatively easily into the episcopate – enjoyed enormous influence; his unwavering, hardline views on

---

9   *Lettres de Mme de Maintenon et de la princesse des Ursins* (ed Bossange), iii, 86–7, Maintenon to Ursins, 16 July 1714, 'les places dans l'église intéressent un peu la conscience de ceux qui les donnent, et l'on a bien assez de ses péchés sans avoir à répondre de ceux des autres. Cependant je ne sais rien qui lui donne l'exclusion.' This last phrase is a giveaway, since there were reservations, echoed by Saint-Simon and others, about the suitability of abbé Villeroy, as Maintenon's subsequent correspondence clearly indicates: iii, 98–9, 100–1, letters to same, 12 and 19 Aug 1714; iv, 425, 461, Ursins to Maintenon, 2 July and 27 Aug 1714. See above, n 7.

10 François Hébert, *Mémoires*, ed G Girard (Paris 1927), 154–8, for Hébert, bishop of Agen's account of his efforts while still curé of Versailles to persuade Louis XIV that Bishop Sève of Arras, to whom Hébert had been confessor and director of conscience, was not an insubordinate Jansenist.

11 See Alison Forrestal, ' "Fathers, Leaders, Kings": Episcopacy and episcopal reform in the seventeenth-century French school', *The Seventeenth Century*, 17 (2002), 24–47, for a brief, up-to-date summary, which will be more fully elaborated in the same author's book on the subject. I would like to thank Dr Forrestal for sharing her ideas with me during many conversations on the subject.

clerical ambition and episcopal obligation ensured that his advice, as we have seen, was sought by many bishops – potential and actual – for over thirty years down to his death in 1700.[12]

The impact of such ideas and influences was not locked away in individual consciences. Indeed, they help to explain why France's bishops should have shown themselves to be, individually and collectively, far more assertive than the conventional image of a subservient church under a dominant monarch like Louis XIV usually allows for. It is worth briefly speculating in these concluding pages about the effect of this on the character of the French church. Obviously, no clear distinction can be drawn between individual and collective action, since each constantly prompted – and was prompted by – the other. What may look like individual action within dioceses was often a response to impulses coming from elsewhere, sometimes from assemblies of clergy, which in turn often took up causes pressed by individual bishops.

In the early decades of the seventeenth century papal nuncios were regularly reporting on the inadequacies of bishops and the scandals they often caused, whereas by the 1660s they were far more likely to worry about their 'entreprises', some of which were prompted, or at least supported, by the crown itself. Only the most prominent of them need be itemised here. The first was the attempt made during the mid-1660s to reduce the number of obligatory religious days of rest – a project dear to Colbert, its real instigator – with several bishops being reported by name to Rome by the nuncios for their unilateral action.[13] This complaint overlapped with others about similar 'entreprises' concerning liturgical books and practices, the most notorious being the publication by Pavillon in 1667–70 of the *Rituel* of Alet diocese, which was condemned by Rome despite winning the approval of a large number of Pavillon's colleagues in France.[14] The row over the *Rituel* and the ensuing confrontations between Pavillon and his episcopal detractors and supporters was a sign of similar displays of episcopal independence to come. Rome, as we saw in the case of Bossuet when he became bishop of Condom in 1671, also worried about possible episcopal support for vernacular translations of the Bible, notably the 'Mons' Bible published in 1666, a project that Port-Royal and its supporters actively pursued. These issues arose during the tense years between the anti-Jansenist Formulary of 1665 and the Peace of the Church of 1669, when it was the behaviour not just of the four recalcitrant bishops, but the willingness of an undefined number of others to intervene by writing to the pope in their defence, which proved to be a major factor in producing a negotiated outcome.

12   A brief sketch of that influence is given by Krailsheimer, *Rancé Abbot of La Trappe*, ch 10.

13   For examples, see ASV, Nunz Fr 134, fos 629 and 768, nuncio to secretary of state, 4 and 22 May 1668, singling out the bishops of Saintes and Périgueux; Nunz Fr 141, fos 386–9, same to same, 27 June 1670, for a long account of the nuncio's negotiations with ministers and churchmen over the problem.

14   BN, MS Fr 23506, fo 396, for a list of the twenty-eight bishops who approved of the *Rituel*.

At virtually the same time, the centuries-old regulars-versus-seculars quarrel resurfaced in a manner that, while different from that of the 1620s and 1630s, was no less spectacular. This was initially exemplified by the famous *arrêt d'Agen*, issued on appeal by the royal council itself in March 1669 in support of the bishop of Agen, Claude Joly, in his attempts to impose his authority on the preachers and confessors of his diocese. Although described by one historian as 'a clear breach of the privileges granted to the regulars by the papacy and which Richelieu and Chancellor Séguier had obliged the prelates of the kingdom to observe',[15] the *arrêt* was not decisive enough to put an end to such disputes, but the evidence of royal support for episcopal claims that it provided emboldened many bishops to imitate Joly. Increasingly personified by the Jesuits, who were still expanding their activities and who could expect high-level protection from royal confessors now more influential than any of their predecessors since Richelieu's time, the regulars did not disarm after 1669, but engaged in protracted and often bitter rows with bishops like Le Camus of Grenoble and Percin of Saint-Pons, who clearly saw themselves as following in the footsteps of an earlier generation of rigorist bishops like Vialart of Châlons-sur-Marne, Grimaldi of Aix, and Gondrin of Sens. Of course, ambitions to control pastoral activities within one's diocese were not confined to bishops with Port-Royal, rigorist or Augustinian affiliations, but they tended to have a natural affinity, so it is hardly surprising that several of them attracted, despite the Peace of the Church, the label of 'Jansenist' over the years. Intertwined with other issues and punctuated by ordinances and lawsuits, these conflicts formed the background to the far more substantial royal edict of 1695 which, despite the subsequent royal watering-down of the clauses most unpalatable to the regulars, further secured episcopal jurisdiction within dioceses while publicly signalling the crown's continuing support for the episcopate.

By that point tensions at the diocesan level had risen further as the Jesuits began, from the 1680s onwards, to accept the management of seminaries within France. Soon there was an impressive queue of bishops seeking their assistance, since the Jesuits were a guarantee of doctrinal and political orthodoxy, and with the Jansenist affair reviving after 1702, these considerations mattered even more in the thinking of numerous bishops and the crown itself.[16] But it would be wrong to see what was happening as one-directional, since the Jesuits themselves, with high-level support at court in many cases, were actively seeking to replace existing seminary directors, whether they were seculars or regulars, suspected of being 'Jansenist'. It is impossible to know how many bishops moved in the direction of 'Jansenist' positions in response to such pressures, but there is evidence that some of them decided

15 Blet, *Assemblées du clergé et Louis XIV*, 38.
16 See Degert, *Histoire des séminaires français*, i, 326–77; Pierre Delattre, 'Les Jésuites et les séminaires', *Revue d'Ascétique et de Mystique*, 20 (1953), 20–44, 160–76.

to confide their seminary to the Jesuits in order to defuse suspicion and secure a form of insurance against further pressure.[17] This kind of conflict, involving an issue of crucial interest to bishops, had all the features of a power struggle, and it certainly reinvigorated accusations made against the Jesuits of an excessive desire for power.[18] By 1700 it, too, overlapped with yet other disputes which, it might be thought, were only remotely connected to it – the best example being that of the 'Chinese rites'. But even that issue turned out to be the 'rigorists versus accomodationists' confrontation in yet another guise, which helps to explain why so many French bishops were eager to engage in the struggle against the *morale relachée* that gathered new momentum during the final decades of the century. Matters came to a head at the Assembly of Clergy of 1700, where Noailles, Le Tellier and Bossuet took the lead in censuring a large number of laxist propositions as well as of the Jesuit attempts to accommodate the Chinese rites to Christian tenets.[19]

Conflicts like these should not be dismissed as mere clerical infighting, though they were that too: they were far more closely concerned with the religion of French people than of the Chinese than we might initially suspect. For they also reflect episcopal activity within dioceses at a time when the Catholic Reformation was running at full tilt. The scope of reforming action within dioceses had moved well beyond that of the early decades of the century: synodal legislation and pastoral instructions became increasingly frequent and at times encyclopaedic, showing a far greater ambition than previously to regulate religious and related behaviour. Bishops who were themselves theology graduates and who consulted their former mentors when preparing their instructions, were engaged in extending and 'reprogramming' religious reform in an age which had moved beyond the earlier and more ad hoc phase. This kind of activity, which only gradually took shape in the second half of the century, had important implications for the character of the French church. Its bishops were, whether they liked it or not, never more busy than under Louis XIV, faced with a long line of major issues of doctrinal, pastoral or political content, from the *régale*, the Four Articles of 1682, and the Huguenots to the Quietist and Jansenist issues. It is hardly an accident that many of them drafted their own private theologians into their service, and relied heavily – too heavily, according to some critics – on them by the early eighteenth century.

---

17 One of these was Archbishop Brûlart of Embrun whose original wish to confide his seminary to the Oratorians was flatly rejected by Louis XIV; only then did Brûlart turn to the Jesuits, whom he was well known to dislike! See AN, L 730, pièce 1, Embrun, no 13, Père Léonard's notes. See also Compère-Julia, *Les Collèges français*, i, 276; Delattre, *Établissements des jésuites*, ii, 356.

18 For one of many cases of such tension, Saint-Omer, see L Mahieu, 'L'Orientation doctrinale des évêques de Saint-Omer sous la domination française (1677–1796)', *Bulletin Historique de la Société des Antiquaires de la Morinie*, 16 (1944), 481–515, at 487, 490.

19 There is a characteristically shrewd analysis of the context of these disputes in Robin Briggs, *Communities of Belief* (Oxford 1989), 214–26.

III

This, as it happens, is one of several points at which local and national, individual and collective action by France's bishops intersects. The claim to govern their dioceses in a very gallican way – that is, without substantial restriction by the privileges of regulars, cathedral chapters or other exempt groups or, *a fortiori*, by intervention from Rome – derived part of its force from the conviction that as bishops they were primarily responsible for the doctrinal and pastoral state of their dioceses, which could simply not be left to others. Staking such a claim was not confined to bishops intending to institute penitential regimes delaying absolution for sinners, or to take stern action against usury, the theatre, lotteries and so on. Perhaps the best evidence for it is to be found in the successive assemblies of clergy, especially those concerned with deliberating and pronouncing on doctrinal questions. Despite the fact that most of the second-order deputies to the assemblies were doctors of theology and, increasingly, vicars-general to ruling bishops, they found themselves being firmly denied anything like a deliberative voice in such discussions during the assemblies.[20] And that episcopal exclusiveness extended well beyond individuals and the chambers of the assemblies, since it ultimately included the Paris theology faculty itself (and the others by implication). The muzzling of the faculty by the crown during Louis XIV's reign already helped to weaken a doctrinal authority to which bishops themselves had readily deferred a century earlier. It seems paradoxical that bishops who were themselves increasingly graduates of that faculty should also be intent on reducing it from a body enjoying a distinctive and long-standing *magisterium* in its own right to a purely consultative convenience. The paradox is merely apparent, but the reasons why that is so tell us something important about the evolution of the episcopate under Louis XIV.[21]

Dealing with this issue points us in the direction of gallican ecclesiology. The successive 'affairs' in which the French clergy had been involved since at least the Estates General of 1614, with its celebrated attempt to define a fundamental law of royal sovereignty had, despite continuing differences between gallicans and 'ultramontanes', sharpened ideas about the role of the episcopate within the church. The principal forum for such reflection was the regular assemblies of clergy, but the wider contexts in which these ideas were formulated were political, since they would typically involve rebutting accusations or claims by bodies like the parlements, not forgetting the claims of papal power that were never far away either. And such formulations might be made during 'small' as much as the 'great' assemblies: all depended on the immediate political context rather than the status of the assembly in question.

20   BN, MS Fr 19212, fo 164r, Père Léonard's discussion of clashes at 1700 and 1705 Assemblies.
21   Jacques M Grès-Gayer, 'The Magisterium of the faculty of theology of Paris in the seventeenth century', *Theological Studies*, 53 (1992), 424–50, brings out the importance of this theme.

Not all of these statements were formally adopted yet alone publicised, as Blet's studies of the assemblies have shown, but they sedimented over time as a body of ideas of growing precision as to the centrality of the episcopate's self-understanding as 'the principal part of the mystical body of the church', in the words of the 1670 Assembly of Clergy. That same assembly of clergy's vigorous reply to the parlement may be taken as typical of such thinking:

> the episcopate is as one in the body of the universal church, even though it belongs jointly to all of the bishops, each one of whom rules that portion of the church entrusted to him by the Holy Spirit under the authority of the Holy See, so that everywhere in the church, the bishops have a character and a power that are inseparably attached to their person and which, through the bond of the spirit and of charity, embeds them in the unity of a single episcopate'.[22]

The last of the Gallican Articles of 1682, which subordinated papal authority to a general council of the church, was an affirmation of episcopal authority of a kind which only the French episcopate was capable of making in later seventeenth-century Europe. The text may read like a historical fossil from the conciliar era, but its reiteration in 1682 was not an expression of pure nostalgia or defensiveness.[23] Indeed, by the time of the Jansenist crisis of the last decade of Louis XIV's reign the French bishops' sense of rightfully participating in the definition and defence of true doctrine was stronger than ever before, sharpened by the experience of censures deliberated on, and voted by, previous assemblies. Such a stance was far removed from a purely defensive dislike of papal 'interference' within the affairs of the French church: it entailed a more inclusive view of the nature of the universal church than the post-tridentine papacy could stomach. The most public and deliberate illustration of this stance came in 1705 with the acceptance of the anti-Jansenist bull, *Vineam Domini*, by the Assembly presided over by Noailles, which insisted that its reception of the bull was not passive and purely declaratory, but active and judgemental – and, by implication, that without it the papal bull had no force in France. This move, and its ecclesiological presuppositions, so enraged Rome that it proved willing a few years later to target the man it held to be mainly responsible for such a public exhibition of gallican thinking, Cardinal Noailles. Indeed, when *Unigenitus* was finally published in September 1713, it was with a solemn promise from Louis XIV that there

---

22   Quoted in Blet, *Assemblées du clergé et Louis XIV*, 24: '[l'épiscopat] est un dans tout le corps de l'Église universelle, bien que possédé solidairement par tous les évêques, dont un chacun en particulier régit sa portion où le Saint Esprit l'a établi sous l'autorité du Saint Siège Apostolique, de sorte que en tous les endroits de l'Église, les évêques ont un caractère et un pouvoir inséparable attaché à leur personne qui par le lien de l'esprit et de la charité les constitue dans l'unité d'un seul épiscopat.'

23   *Ibid*, 350, 'la substance des quatre articles n'a pas été dictée par la cour: ils traduisent un courant issu des temps du grand schisme et qui avait cheminé pendant tout le siècle à travers les séances des Assemblées du Clergé de France.'

would be no repeat of the 'conditional' acceptance by the assembled clergy of 1705.

IV

Rejected by Rome, this vision of doctrinal collegiality involving the pope and the episcopate as partners was also finer in theory than in practice within France itself. From the early days of the Jansenist question, especially over the imposition of a Formulary, recalcitrant bishops had challenged the claim that an assembly of clergy could act as a council of bishops with power to impose their views on the French church as a whole. The opposition to the Formulary spoke the language of the individual bishop as the guide and doctor of faith for his diocese. Partly because neither the crown nor the papacy wished to see assemblies of clergy become real national councils, the potential conflict between these two strands of gallican thinking was never resolved, so that circumstances and context would dictate which of the two seemed the more dominant and appropriate. During the fierce disputes of the years immediately preceding the publication of the *Unigenitus* bull, when Noailles was under intense pressure to retract his censure and ban of the anti-Quesnel instruction of the bishops of La Rochelle and Luçon, Bissy of Meaux, his suffragan and future tormentor, constantly urged him not to damage 'the unity of the episcopate', the foundation of which was respect for the pronouncements of fellow bishops within their dioceses.[24] From Bissy's point of view, worse was to follow since the promised 'reception-without-examination' of *Unigenitus* collapsed almost as soon as Noailles and some fellow bishops read the text of the bull.[25] And when a carefully hand-picked, unelected assembly was duly convened in late 1713-early 1714 to receive *Unigenitus*, the crown proved unable to prevent a minority, led by Noailles, from refusing to accept it without further explanation from Rome; as for the majority, they felt sufficiently unsure of the outcome that, after several months of examination, which itself angered Rome, they drafted their own explanation of the bull, the 'Instruction pastorale des Quarante'. All forty of its signatories were bishops, needless to say, since there was no question of any other ecclesiastic, even a doctor of the Paris theology faculty, being publicly party to such a decision. Indeed, when the doctors of the faculty offered their assistance to Noailles in a particularly difficult juncture, the only reply that they received was that each one should confine his attention to what concerned him.

---

24 BN, MS Fr 23483, fos 173–8, 179–82, Bissy to Noailles, 24 and 27 June 1711. Bissy recommends Noailles to change his approach 'sans qu'on puisse vous reprocher d'avoir rien fait contre l'unité de l'épiscopat, qui ne permet pas qu'un évêque condamne le mandement d'un de ses confrères.'

25 Le Gendre, *Mémoires*, 300. Le Gendre was at this point working closely with Père Tellier, the confessor.

To many contemporaries and later historians, the hair-splitting, equivocation and chicanery involved in these confrontations ranked among the most egregious instances of *odium theologicum*, but buried underneath them lay some deeply entrenched convictions about the nature and character of episcopal office. The immense pressure exercised by the crown to secure the publication of *Unigenitus* in every French diocese, ensured there would be relatively little open defiance while Louis XIV himself lived, so that the *mandements* issued across France in 1714–15 employ a largely shared vocabulary. Those accepting the bull pointed towards their duty as bishops to protect their flocks from the poison of heresy, while the nine bishops requesting further papal explanations before accepting the bull explicitly did so in terms of their episcopal rights and responsibilities.[26] The king's death enabled some of the 'accepters', like Caylus of Auxerre, to change their initial stance, with many others changing their minds again in later years. By 1720 the situation had already become so confused that the French episcopate was cleverly depicted by a Jansenist as a genealogical tree with the unflattering title of 'the tower of Babel'.[27] It would take nearly two decades to deal with the problem of Jansenist affiliations within the episcopate. Only one bishop, Soanen of Senez, effectively lost his see in the process, but the furore that his treatment generated would ensure that it would not be repeated. With sitting bishops unassailable, attention had to be turned elsewhere, and there is no small irony in the fact that this involved two *revenants* of the previous century, each closely involved with the exercise of episcopal patronage – a cardinal-minister in the shape of Dubois and then Fleury, and a revamped *conseil de conscience*.[28]

Cardinal Bissy's plea for respect for the unity of the episcopate in 1711 came at a moment when such unity was at its most elusive. France's bishops seemed to have established their dominance within the church, only to turn on each other. The secular clergy, notably the chapters, had been largely brought under episcopal control, or at least rendered relatively harmless. The regulars were better equipped to defend their exempt status but they, too, had been forced to give ground, especially in the sphere of pastoral activities. In only a small number of French dioceses did regulars enjoy the kind of role in diocesan government that was common in other early modern Catholic countries, and that, too, depended entirely on the leanings of individual bishops. But the theologically literate and experienced episcopate which came to the

---

26 *Recueil des mandemens et instructions pastorales de Messeigneurs les Archevêques et Évêques de France pour l'acceptation de la Constitution de Notre Saint Père le Pape Clement XI* (Paris 1715), contains the complete texts of all the *mandements*, letters and other relevant documents, including those of Noailles and his supporters.

27 'La Tour de Babel, ou la division des Evesques de France qui ont eu part à la constitution Unigenitus, depuis l'année 1714', in AM Saint-Malo, GG 290, no 25.

28 Antoine, *Le Conseil du roi sous Louis XV*, 82, 109–13, 128–31. The *conseil* had largely disappeared again by the early 1730s, when the *ministre de la feuille*, a bishop, was ready to take its place.

fore in the second part of Louis XIV's personal rule would discover in the next century that its exclusivism bred other enemies which it could scarcely have foreseen. As early as the 1679, however, Jean Le Noir, *théologal* of Sées and scourge of the courtier bishop, was already denouncing what he called the 'heresy of episcopal domination that is being established in France'.[29]

---

29   Jean Le Noir, *Lettre à Son Altesse Royale madame la duchesse de Guise, sur le sujet de l'hérésie de la domination épiscopale, qu'on établit en France* (Cologne [sic], 1679).

APPENDICES

ADDITIONAL ABBREVIATIONS

This list should be completed by that on p xi

abp	archbishop	Nom	nominated, nomination
AC	Assembly of Clergy	OSA	Order of St Augustine
admin	administration,	OSB	Order of St Benedict
	administrator	O Cist	Order of Cîteaux (Cistercians)
ag-gén	*agent-général*	OFM	Order of St Francis (Franciscans)
bacc	baccalaureate	O Prem	Order of Prémontré
bp	bishop		(Premonstratensians)
c	century	parlt	parlement, parlementaire
ca	circa	phil	philosophy
cath	cathedral	*pr prés*	*premier président*
coadj	coadjutor	*prés*	*président*
coll	college	*proc-gén*	*procureur-général*
consec	consecrated/consecration	prov	provincial
cons	*conseiller*	provs	provisions
cons-clerc	*conseiller-clerc*	*rec-gén*	*receveur-général*
contr-gén	*contrôleur-général*	resign	resigned, resignation
dioc	diocese	sec of state	secretary of state
doct	doctor(ate)	sgr	seigneur
fac	faculty	SJ	Society of Jesus, Jesuits
gov	governor	SR	*secrétaire du roi*
gr conseil	*grand conseil*	St	Saint
gr-vic	grand vicar	sup-gen	superior-general
hum	humanities	theol	theology
in comm	*in commendam*	*trés de France*	*trésorier de France*
in utr	*in utroque jure*	*trés-gén*	*trésorier-général*
lic	licence/licentiate	univ	university
lieut	lieutenant	vic-gen	vicar-general
lt-gen	lieutenant-general	vic-cap	vice-capitular
MR	*maître des requêtes*		
ND	Notre Dame	(Sens)	refers to particular dioceses

Note: The biographical notices contained in this appendix are designed, as were those in my previous study, *The Making of the French Episcopate*, to provide an outline of the background and (mostly) early careers of Louis XIV's bishops, with a view to understanding the reasons why they succeeded in joining the episcopate. A great deal is known, or is knowable, about Louis XIV's bishops, though that should not be exaggerated: these notices will show how many of them continue to remain obscure. The structure of the individual notices 'shadows' in some respects the structure of the early chapters of the book. Only where bishops were transferred or promoted to other dioceses do these sketches devote much space to their episcopal careers, though exceptions have also been made for those bishops who became well known for their activities, mishaps, conflicts and so on, especially where the latter seem to be of interest to historians.

I have adhered as far as possible to the format adopted for the notices in *The Making of the French Episcopate*. Because of the greater amount of material available, I have resorted to abbreviating a substantial number of recurring words or terms, but I have endeavoured to avoid excessive abbreviation and the irritation which it can so easily engender. Readers unfamiliar with the subject matter may well find themselves none the wiser as they confront terms like 'official', 'vicaire capitulaire', or 'théologal', since even their English-language equivalents will not be immediately intelligible to them. Some of these terms no longer figure in either French or English dictionaries, but I have tried to explain their meaning or provide an English equivalent to them when they first arise in the text of the book.

APPENDIX A

Dioceses and their Bishops under Louis XIV

Names in italics are those of bishops who entered the episcopate before 1661

AGDE
Fouquet, Louis 1657–1702
Pas de Feuquières, Philibert-Charles
  1702–26

AGEN
Delbène, Barthelemy 1636–63
Joly, Claude 1665–78
Mascaron, Jules (from Tulle) 1680–1703
Hébert, François 1704–28

AIRE
Bernard de Sariac 1659–72
Fromentières, Jean Louis, 1673–84
Bazin de Bezons, Armand J-B, 1693–8
  (to Bordeaux)
Fleuriau d'Armenonville, Louis-Gaston,
  1698–1706 (to Orléans)
La Mer de Matha, François-Gaspard,
  1707–10
Montmorin de St-Hérem, Joseph-Gaspard,
  1710–23

AIX
Grimaldi, Hieronimo 1655–85
*Cosnac, Daniel de (from Valence) 1693–
  1708*
Vintimille du Luc, Charles-Gaspard (from
  Marseille) 1708–29

ALBI
Daillon, Gaspard de 1636–74
Hyacinthe Serroni (from Mende) 1676–87
Le Goux de la Berchère, Charles (from
  Lavaur) 1693–1703 (to Narbonne)
Nesmond, Henri de (from Montauban),
  1703–22

ALÈS
Chevalier de Saulx, François, 1694–1712
Hénin-Liétard, Jean-François, 1713–20

ALET
Pavillon, Nicolas 1639–77
Valbelle de Tourves, Louis-Alphonse,
  1678–93 (to St-Omer)
Méliand, Victor-Augustin (from Gap)
  1692–8 (resign)
Taffoureau de Fontaine, Charles-Nicolas,
  1699–1708
Maboul, Jacques, 1710–23

AMIENS
Faure, François 1654–87
Feydeau de Brou, Henri 1692–1706
Sabatier, Pierre, 1707–33

ANGERS
Arnauld, Henri 1650–92
Le Peletier, Michel 1692–1706
Poncet de la Rivière, Michel 1706–30

ANGOULÊME
Péricard, François de 1647–89
Bénard de Rézay, Cyprien 1692–1737

APT
Villeneuve des Arcs, Modeste de 1629–70
Gaillard, Jean 1671–95
Foresta-Coulongue, Joseph-Ignace
  1696–1723 (resign)

ARLES
Adhémar de Grignan, François 1643–89
Adhémar de Monteil de Grignan,
  Jean-Baptiste (coadj) 1667/89–97

Mailly, François 1698–1710 (to Reims)
Forbin-Janson, Jacques 1711–41

ARRAS
Moreau, Etienne 1668–70
Sève de Rochechouart, Guy 1670–1724

AUCH
Henri de la Mothe-Houdancourt (ex-Rennes)
    1664–84
La Baume de Suze, Anne-Tristan (from
    Tarbes) 1692–1705
Maupeou, Augustin de (from Castres)
    1705–12
Desmarets, Jacques (from Riez) 1714–25

AUTUN
Doni d'Attichy, Louis 1652–64
Roquette, Gabriel, 1666–1702 (resign)
Senaux, Bertrand 1703–9
Hallencourt de Dromesnil, Charles-François
    1711–22

AUXERRE
Broc, Pierre de 1639–71
Colbert, Nicolas (from Luçon) 1671–6
Colbert, André 1678–1704
Caylus, Louis-Daniel de 1705–54

AVRANCHES
Boislève, Gabriel de 1653–76
Froulay du Tessé, Gabriel-Philippe
    1668–89
Huet, Pierre-Daniel, 1692–9 (resign)
Kerhoënt de Coëtanfao, Roland 1699–1719

BAYEUX
Nesmond, François de 1661–1715

BAYONNE
Dolce, Jean 1643–81
La Roque-Priélé, Gaspard 1681–8
La Lanne, Léon, 1692–1700
Beauvau du Rivau, René-François 1701–7
    (to St-Omer)
Dreuilhet, André 1707–27

BAZAS
Martineau, Samuel 1646–67
Boissonade, Guillaume 1668–84
Gourges, Jacques-Joseph 1693–1724

BEAUVAIS
Choart de Buzenval, Nicolas 1650–79
Toussaint de Forbin-Janson (from Marseille)
    1679–1713
Beauvillier de St-Aignan, François 1713–28

BELLEY
Passelaigue, Jean de 1629–63
Belin, Jean-Albert 1665–77
Du Laurens, Pierre 1678–1705
Madot, François 1705–12
    (to Chalon-sur-Saône)
Du Doucet, Jean 1712–45

BESANÇON
Grammont, Antoine-Pierre de 1663–98
Grammont, François-Joseph 1698–1717

BÉZIERS
Bonsi, Pierre de 1660–71 (to Toulouse)
Rotundis de Biscarras, Jean-Armand (from
    Lodève) 1672–1702
Des Alries du Rousset, Louis-Charles
    1702–44

BLOIS
Bertier, David-Nicolas 1697–1719

BORDEAUX
Béthune, Henri de 1648–80
Bourlemont, Louis d' Anglure de (from
    Carcassonne) 1681–97
Bazin de Bezons, Armand J-B (from Aire)
    1698–1719

BOULOGNE
Perrochel, François 1645–75 (resign)
Ladvocat-Billiad, Nicolas 1677–81
Le Tonnellier de Breteuil, Claude 1681–98
Langle, Pierre de 1698–1724

BOURGES
Ventadour, Anne de Levis de 1651–62
Montpezat de Carbon, Jean (from St-Papoul)
    1665–75 (to Sens)
Poncet de la Rivière, Michel (from Sisteron)
    1675–7
Phélypeaux de la Vrillière, Michel (from
    Uzès) 1679–94
Potier de Gesvres, Léon 1694–1729 (resign)

CAHORS
Sevin, Nicolas 1659–79
Noailles, Louis-Antoine (to Châlons-sur-
    Marne) 1679–81
Le Jay, Henri-Guillaume 1681–93
Briqueville de la Luzerne, Henri
    1693–1741

CAMBRAI
Fénélon, François de la Mothe-Salignac de
    1695–1715

CARCASSONNE
La Valette-Nogaret, Louis de 1656–79
Bourlemont, Louis de 1680–1 (to Bordeaux)
Adhémar de Monteil de Grignan, Louis-Joseph 1681–1722

CASTRES
Bourlemont, Charles d'Anglure de 1659–64 (to Toulouse)
Tubeuf, Michel (from St-Pons) 1664–82
Maupeou, Augustin de 1693–1705 (to Auch)
Quiqueran de Beaujeu, Honoré 1705–36

CHALON-SUR-SAÔNE
Maupeou, Jean de 1659–77
Tassi, Henri Felix de (from Digne) 1678–1711
Madot, François (from Belley) 1712–53

CHÂLONS-SUR-MARNE
Vialart, Félix 1640–80
Noailles, Louis-Antoine (from Cahors) 1681–95 (to Paris)
Noailles, Gaston 1696–1720

CHARTRES
Neufville de Villeroy, Ferdinand de 1657–90
Godet des Marais, Paul 1692–1709
Mérinville, Charles-François Desmontiers de 1710–46

CLERMONT
d'Estaing, Louis 1651–64
Vény d'Arbouze, Gilbert 1664–82
Bochart de Saron, François 1692–1715

COMMINGES
Choiseul, Gilbert de (to Tournai) 1646–70
Guron, Louis de Rechignevoisin de (from Tulle) 1677–93
Brisay de Denonville, Jean-François 1693–1710
Lobière de Bouchet, Olivier-Gabriel 1711–39 (resign)

CONDOM
Lorraine-Guise, Charles de 1659–68
Bossuet, Jacques-Bénigne 1670–1 (resign)
Goyon de Matignon, Jacques 1672–93 (resign)
Milon, Louis 1693–1734

COUSERANS
Marmiesse, Bernard de 1654–80

St-Estève, Gabriel 1680–1707
Verthamon, Jean-Jacques 1708–25

COUTANCES
Le Clerc de Lesseville, Eustache 1659–65
Loménie de Brienne, Charles-François 1667–1720

DAX
Le Boux, Guillaume 1659–66 (to Périgueux)
Bar, Hugues de 1667–71 (to Lectoure)
Chaumont-Quitry, Paul-Philippe 1671–84 (resign)
Abbadie d'Arboucave, Bernard 1692–1732

DIE (held by bishops of Valence before 1692)
Montmorin, Armand 1692–4 (to Vienne)
Pajot du Plouy, Séraphim 1694–1701
Cosnac, Gabriel 1702–34 (resign)

DIGNE
Forbin-Janson, Toussaint 1657–68 (to Marseille)
Vintimille du Luc, Jean 1670–6 (to Toulon)
Tassi, Henri Felix de 1676–8 (to Chalon-sur-Saône)
Le Tellier, François 1678–1708
Puget, Henri de 1708–28

DOL
Thoreau, Mathieu 1661–92
Chamillart, Jean-François 1692–1702 (to Senlis)
Voyer d'Argenson, François-Elie 1702–15 (to Embrun)
Sourches, Jean-Louis du Bouchet de 1716–48

EMBRUN
Aubusson de la Feuillade, Georges 1649–69 (to Metz)
Brûlart de Genlis, Charles 1669–1714
Voyer d'Argenson, François-Elie (from Dol) 1715–20

EVREUX
Boutault, Gilles 1649–61
Maupas du Tour, Henri (from Le Puy) 1664–80
Grignan, Louis-Joseph d'Adhémar 1681–2 (to Carcassonne)
Potier de Novion, Jacques (from Sisteron) 1682–1709
Le Normand, Jean 1710–33

FRÉJUS
Ondedei, Zongo 1658–74

Clermont-Tonnerre, Antoine-Benoît
1676–8
Bourlemont, Louis Anglure de 1679–80 (to
Carcassonne)
Aquin, Luc (from St-Paul-Trois-Châteaux)
1681–97 (resign)
Aquin, Louis 1697 (failed to take up see)
Fleury, André-Hercule 1699–1715
(resign)
Castellane, Joseph-Pierre 1715–39

GAP
Lionne, Artus de 1639–61 (resign)
Marion, Pierre 1662–75
Meschatin de la Faye, Guillaume 1677–9
Méliand, Victor-Augustin 1680–92 (to
Alet)
Hervé, Charles-Bénigne 1692–1705
(resign)
Berger de Malisolles, François 1706–38

GLANDÈVES
Ithier, Dominique 1654–72
Bacoué, Léon 1673–84 (resign)
Villeneuve de Vence, Charles 1694–1702
Sabran, César 1702–20

GRASSE
Bernage, Louis de 1653–75
Aube de Roquemartine, Louis 1676–82 (to
St-Paul-Trois-Châteaux)
Le Comte, Antoine 1682–3
Verjus, François 1692–1710
Mesgrigny, Joseph-Ignace 1711–26

GRENOBLE
Scarron, Pierre 1620–68
Le Camus, Étienne 1671–1707
Alleman, Ennemond 1708–19

LA ROCHELLE
Raoul, Jacques 1649–61
Laval-Boisdauphin, Henri de (from Rennes)
1661–93
Frézeau de la Frézilière, Charles-Madeleine
1694–1702
Champflour, Étienne de 1703–24

LANGRES
Barbier de la Rivière, Louis 1655–70
Simiane de Gordes, Louis-Marie-Armand
1671–95
Clermont-Tonnerre, François-Louis
1696–1724

LAON
d'Estrées, César 1655–81 (resign)

Estrées, Jean 1681–94
Clermont de Chaste, Louis-Annet
1695–1721

LAVAUR
Tulles, Jean de 1647–68
Amelot de Gournay, Michel 1671–3 (to
Tours)
Le Sauvage, René 1673–77
Le Goux de la Berchère, Charles 1677–93
(to Albi)
Mailly, Victor-Augustin 1692–1712
Malezieu, Nicolas 1713–48

LE MANS
Beaumanoir de Lavardin, Philibert-Emmanuel
1649–71
Lavergne de Montenard de Tressan, Louis
(from Vabres) 1672–1712
Rogier du Crévy, Pierre 1712–23

LE PUY
Maupas du Tour, Henri 1643–64 (to Evreux)
Béthune, Armand 1665–1703
La Roche-Aymon, Claude 1704–20

LECTOURE
Caset de Vautorte, Louis 1655–71 (to Vannes)
Bar, Hugues de (from Dax) 1672–
91
Polastron, François-Louis 1692–1717

LESCAR
Saliès, Jean du Haut de 1658–81
Desclaux de Mesplès, Dominique
1681–1716

LIMOGES
La Fayette, François de 1627–76
Lascaris d'Urfé, Louis 1676–95
Carbonnel de Canisy, François 1696–1707
(resign)
Charpin de Genétines, Antoine 1706–29
(resign)

LISIEUX
Matignon, Léonor I de 1646–74 (resign)
Matignon, Léonor II 1675–1714
Brancas, Henri-Ignace 1714–60

LODÉVE
Harlay de Césy, Roger de 1657–69
Rotundis de Biscarras, Jean-Armand
1669–72 (to Béziers)
La Garde de Chambonas, Charles-Antoine
1671–92 (to Viviers)
Phélypeaux, Jacques-Antoine 1692–1732

LOMBEZ
Séguier de la Verrière, Jacques 1662–71 (to Nîmes)
Roger, Cosme 1672–1710
Fagon, Antoine 1712–20 (to Vannes)

LUÇON
Colbert, Nicolas 1661–71 (to Auxerre)
Barillon, Henri 1672–99
Lescure de Valderiès de, Jean-François 1699–1723

LYON
Neufville de Villeroy, Camille de 1654–93
St-Georges, Claude 1693–1714
Neufville de Villeroy, François-Paul 1714–31

MÂCON
Lingendes, Jean de 1651–65
Colbert de St-Pouange, Michel 1666–76
Cassagnet de Tilladet, Michel 1677–1731

MARSEILLE
Puget, Etienne de 1644–68
Forbin-Janson, Toussaint (from Digne) 1668–79 (to Beauvais)
Étampes de Valançay, Jean-Baptiste 1682–4
Vintimille du Luc, Charles-Gaspard 1692–1708 (to Aix)
Poudenx de Castillon, Bernard-François 1708–9
Belsunce, Henri de 1710–55

MEAUX
Ligny, Dominique de 1659–81
Bossuet, Jacques-Bénigne (ex Condom) 1681–1704
Thyard de Bissy, Henri-Pons (from Toul) 1705–37

MENDE
Serroni, Hyacinthe (from Lavaur) 1661–76 (to Albi)
Baudry de Piencourt, François-Placide 1677–1707
Baglion du Saillant de la Salle, Pierre 1708–23

METZ
Aubusson de la Feuillade, Georges (from Embrun) 1669–97
Du Cambout de Coislin, Henri-Charles 1697–1732

MIREPOIX
Ventadour, Louis Hercule de Lévis de 1655–79
La Broue, Pierre 1679–1720

MONTAUBAN
Bertier, Pierre de 1651–74
Colbert, Jean-Baptiste-Michel 1675–93 (to Toulouse)
Nesmond, Henri 1692–1703 (to Albi)
Nettancourt d'Haussonville, François, 1704–29 (resign)

MONTPELLIER
Bosquet, François 1656–76
Pradel, Charles 1675–96
Colbert de Croissy, Charles-Joachim 1697–1738

NANTES
Beauvau, Gabriel de 1636–67 (resign)
La Baume de Blanc de la Vallière, Gilles 1668–79 (resign)
Beauvau du Rivau, Gilles 1679–1717

NARBONNE
Fouquet, François 1659–73
Bonsi, Pierre de (from Toulouse) 1674–1703
Le Goux de la Berchère, Charles (from Albi) 1703–19

NEVERS
Chéry, Eustache de 1659–67 (resign)
Vallot, Edouard 1667–1705 (resign)
Bargedé, Edouard 1706–19

NÎMES
Cohon, Anthime-Denis 1657–70
Séguier de la Verrière, Jacques (from Lombez) 1671–87 (resign)
Fléchier, Esprit 1692–1710
Rousseau de la Parisière, Jean-César 1710–36

NOYON
Clermont-Tonnerre, François de 1661–1701
Aubigné, Claude-Maur 1701–8 (to Rouen)
Châteauneuf de Rochebonne, Charles-François 1708–31

OLORON
Maytie, Arnaud II de 1659–81
Salette, Charles-François 1682–1704
Revol, Joseph 1705–35 (resign)

ORLÉANS
Delbène, Alphonse 1647–65
Du Cambout de Coislin, Pierre 1666–1706

Fleuriau d'Armenonville, Louis-Gaston
(from Aire) 1706–33

PAMIERS
Caulet François-Etienne 1645–80
Verthamon, Jean-Baptiste 1693–1735

PARIS
Gondi-Retz, Jean-François-Paul (coadj)
1643/54–62 (resign)
Péréfixe, Hardouin de Beaumont de (from
Rodez) 1662–71
François II de Harlay (from Rouen) 1671–95
Noailles, Louis-Antoine (from Châlons-sur-
Marne) 1695–1729

PÉRIGUEUX
Villers la Faye, Cyrus de 1653–65
Le Boux, Guillaume (from Dax) 1666–93
Francheville, Daniel 1693–1702
Clément, Pierre 1702–19

PERPIGNAN
Margarit, Vicent 1668–72
Habert de Montmort, Louis 1682–95
Bazan de Flamanville, Jean-Hervé
1695–1721

POITIERS
Clérambaut, Gilbert de 1658–80
Fortin de la Hoguette, Hardouin (from
St-Brieuc) 1680–92 (to Sens)
Baglion du Saillant, François-Ignace (from
Tréguier) 1693–98
Girard de la Bournat, Antoine 1698–1702
La Poype de Vertrieu, Jean-Claude
1702–32

QUIMPER
Louet, René du 1641–68.
Coetlogon-Méjusseau, François de (coadj)
1666/8–1706
Ploeuc de Timeur, François-Hyacinthe
1707–39

REIMS
Antonio Barberini 1668–71
Le Tellier, Charles-Maurice (coadj)
1668/71–1710
Mailly, François (from Arles) 1710–21

RENNES
La Vieuville, Charles-François de 1660–76
Beaumanoir de Lavardin, Jean-Baptiste
1677–1711
Turpin de Crissé de Sanzy, Christophe-Louis
1712–24

RIEUX
Bertier, Antoine-François 1662–1705
Charrite de Ruthie, Pierre 1705–18

RIEZ
Valavoire, Nicolas de 1652–85
Desmarets, Jacques, 1693–1713 (to Auch)
Phélypeaux d'Herbaut, Louis-Balthazar
1713–51

RODEZ
Péréfixe, Hardouin de Beaumont de 1648–62
(to Paris)
Abelly, Louis 1662–6 (resign)
Voyer d'Argenson, Gabriel 1667–82
Lézay de Lusignan, Paul-Louis 1693–1716

ROUEN
Harlay, François II de 1651–71 (to Paris)
Rouxel de Médavy, François (from Sées)
1671–91
Colbert, Jacques-Nicolas (coadj)
1680/91–1707
Aubigné, Claude-Maur (from Noyon)
1708–19

SAINTES
Bassompierre, Louis de 1646–76
La Brunetière, Guillaume du Plessis
1677–1702
Chevriers de St-Mauris, Alexandre 1702–10
Le Pileur, Henri-Augustin 1711–15
(resign)

SARLAT
Fénélon, François de La Mothe-Salignac
1659–88
Beauvau du Rivau, Pierre-François
1692–1701
Chaulnes, Paul de 1702–21

SÉES
Rouxel de Médavy, François 1651–71 (to
Rouen)
Forcoal, Jean 1672–82
Savary, Mathurin 1692–8
Aquin, Louis 1698–1710
Turgot de St-Clair, Dominique 1710–27

SENEZ
Duchaine, Louis 1623–71
Aubert de Villeserin, Louis-Antoine
1671–95
Soanen, Jean 1696–1727 (deposed)

SENLIS
Sanguin, Denis 1651–1702

Chamillart, Jean-François (from Dol)
1702–14
Trudaine, François-Firmin 1714–54

SENS
Gondrin, Louis-Henri de 1645–74
Montpezat de Carbon Jean de (from Bourges)
1675–85
Fortin de la Hoguette, Hardouin (from
Poitiers) 1692–1715

SISTERON
Bargemon, Antoine Arbaud de 1648–66
Poncet de la Rivière, Michel 1667–7 (to
Bourges)
Potier de Novion, Jacques 1677–82 (to
Evreux)
Thomassin, Louis (from Vence) 1682–1718

SOISSONS
Bourlon, Charles 1656–85.
Brûlart de Sillery, Fabio 1692–1714
Languet de Gergy, Jean-Joseph 1715–31

ST-BRIEUC
La Barde, Denis de 1642–75
Fortin de la Hoguette, Hardouin 1676–80
(to Poitiers)
Coëtlogon-Méjusseau, Louis-Marcel
1681–1705 (to Tournai)
Frétat de Boissieu, Louis 1705–20

ST-FLOUR
Montrouge, Jacques de 1647–64
La Mothe-Houdancourt, Jérôme 1664–93
d'Estaing, Joachim-Joseph 1693–1742

ST-MALO
Villemontée, François de 1659–70
Guémadeuc, Sébastien 1671–1702
Desmarets, Vincent-François 1702–39

ST-OMER
Valbelle de Tourves, Louis-Alphonse (from
Alet) 1693–1708
Valbelle de Tourves, François 1710–27

ST-PAPOUL
Montpezat de Carbon, Jean 1658–64 (to
Bourges)
Montpezat de Carbon, Joseph 1665–75 (to
Toulouse)
Barthélemy de Grammont, François
1677–1716

ST-PAUL-TROIS-CHÂTEAUX
Ruffier, Claude 1658–74
Aquin, Luc 1674–1681 (to Fréjus)

Aube de Roquemartine, Louis (from Grasse)
1682–1713
Maurel du Chaffaut, Joseph 1714–17

ST-POL-DE-LÉON
Visdelou, François de 1662–8
Le Neboux de la Brousse, Pierre
1672–1701
La Bourdonnaye, Jean-Louis 1702–45

ST PONS
Tubeuf, Michel 1654–64 (to Castres)
Percin de Montgaillard, Pierre-Jean-
François 1665–1713
Berton de Crillon, Jean-Louis 1713–27

TARBES
Malier du Houssay, Claude 1649–68 (resign)
Malier du Houssay, Marc 1668–75
La Baume de Suze, Anne-Tristan de
1677–92 (to St-Omer)
Poudenx, François 1692–1716

TOUL
Du Saussay, André 1656–75
Fieux, Jacques de 1676–87
Thyard de Bissy, Henri-Pons 1692–1705
(to Meaux)
Blouet de Camilly, François 1705–21

TOULON
Pingré, Pierre 1658–62
Forbin d'Oppède, Louis 1664–75
Vintimille du Luc, Jean (from Digne)
1676–82
Bonnin de Chalucet, Armand-Louis
1692–1712
La Tour du Pin-Montauban, Louis-Pierre
1712–37

TOULOUSE
Marca, Pierre de 1654–62 (to Paris)
Bourlemont, Charles-François de (from Castres)
1664–9
Bonsi, Pierre de (from Béziers) 1671–4
Montpezat de Carbon, Joseph (from
St-Papoul) 1675–87
Colbert, Jean-Baptiste-Michel (from
Montauban) 1693–1710
Beauvau du Rivau, René-François
(from Tournai) 1713–21

TOURNAI
Choiseul, Gilbert de (from Comminges)
1670–89
Caillebot de la Salle, François 1692–1705
(resign)

Coëtlogon-Méjusseau, Louis-Marcel (from
 St-Brieuc) 1705–7
Tournai, Beauvau du Rivau, René-François
 (from Bayonne) 1707–13 (to Toulouse)
Laval-Montmorency, Guy 1713

TOURS
Bouthillier, Victor 1630–70
Rosmadec, Charles de (from Vannes) 1672
Amelot de Gournay, Michel (from Lavaur)
 1673–87
Hervault, Mathieu Isoré d' 1693–1716

TRÉGUIER
Grangier, Balthasar 1646–79
Baglion du Saillant, François-Ignace
 1679–93 (to Poitiers)
Le Sénéchal de Carcado, Eustache 1692–4
Jégou de Kervilio, Olivier 1694–1731

TROYES
Malier du Houssay, François 1641–78
Bouthillier, François 1679–97 (resign)
Bouthillier, Denis-François 1697–1718

TULLE
Guron, Louis de Rechignevoisin de 1653–71
 (to Comminges)
Mascaron, Jules 1672–80 (to Agen)
Ancelin, Humbert. 1681–1702 (resign)
Beaupoil de St-André, André-Daniel Tulle
 1702–20 (resign)

UZÈS
Grignan, Jacques d'Adhémar de 1660–74
Phélypeaux de la Vrillière, Michel 1676–8
 (to Bourges)
Poncet de la Rivière, Michel 1678–1728

VABRES
Habert, Isaac 1645–68
Lavergne de Montenard de Tressan, Louis
 1670–2 (to Le Mans)

Baradat, Louis-Daniel 1673–1710
Le Filleul de la Chapelle, Charles-Alexandre
 1710–64

VALENCE-DIE (united until 1693)
Cosnac, Daniel de 1655–1693
Bochart de Champigny, Guillaume
 1693–1705
Catelan, Jean 1705–25

VANNES
Rosmadec, Charles de 1647–71 (to Tours)
Caset de Vautorte, Louis (from Lectoure)
 1671–87
Argouges, François d' 1692–1716

VENCE
Godeau, Antoine 1639–72
Thomassin, Louis, (coadj) 1671/2–82 (to
 Sisteron)
Allart, Théodore-Germain 1682–5
Cabanes de Viens, Jean-Balthazar 1693–7
Berton de Crillon, François 1697–1714 (to
 Vienne)
Moret de Bourchenu, Ennemond 1714–27
 (resign)

VERDUN
Monchy d'Hocquincourt, Armand 1668–79
Béthune, Hippolyte 1681–1720

VIENNE
Villars, Henri de 1653–93
Montmorin Armand de (from Die)
 1694–1713
Crillon, François Berton de (from Vence)
 1714–20

VIVIERS
La Baume de Suze, Louis de 1621–90
La Garde de Chambonas, Charles-Antoine
 (from Lodève) 1692–1713
Ratabon Martin de (from Ypres) 1713–23

APPENDIX B

Biographical Dictionary

Abbadie d'Arboucave, Bernard. Dax 1692–1732.   Henri IV had recognised the fidelity of the Abbadie family to Catholicism since Jeanne d'Albret by nom Jean-Pierre bp of Lescar (1599–1609). Since then they had strengthened their ties to other members of Béarn elite and, through his mother, bp of Dax was related to a family that produced several bps under Louis XIV.

Born Maslacq, 1654, son of Daniel Abbadie d'Arboucave and Anne Poudenx, sister of François Poudenx bp of Tarbes (1692–1716), married in 1647. He studied initially at coll of Lescar, later canon law and theol at Toulouse and Bordeaux, where he took doct of theol. Also appears to have studied 'sacra litteraria' and church history in Oratorian seminary of St-Magloire for over 3 years, where he took major orders. Was archpriest-cum-curé of St-Jean-de-Maslacq for 10 years, and engaged in attempts to convert local Huguenot populations in Lescar and Oloron diocs. He was also made vic-gen of Tarbes *sede vacante* in order to confront Huguenots during 1680s. Foucault, intendant of Béarn, recommended him strongly to Abp Harlay and La Chaize in mid-1680s on these grounds, pressing them to promote him. A model resident bp, on good terms with cath canons, with whom he resolved predecessor's litigation. Dep to 1705 AC, his anti-Jansenism was marked, but he oscillated for a while (1718–28) in favour of Jansenists.

Nom 1-11-1690. Provs 5-5-1692. Consec 26-10-1692. Died 14-12-1732.

Sources: ASV, PC 86, fos 398–445. Quesnel, *Correspondance*, i, 237. Foucault, *Mémoires*, 116–17. Bluche, *L'Origine*, 55, DBF, i, 51–2. Chaix d'Est-Ange, *Dictionnaire des familles*, xvi, 348–50. Bergin, *Making*, 562.

Abelly, Louis. Rodez 1664–6 (resign).   Although Parisians, family history is relatively obscure, though bp of Rodez was probably from same family as Antoine Abelly, a Parisian Dominican, well-known preacher, director of conscience and protégé of Catherine de' Medici who wanted to give him a dioc before her death in 1589. Other family members were wine merchants before moving into service of the queen mother, which in turn probably led to involvement in financial affairs. Bp's own father, Pierre, rose higher still, and was a *rec-gén des finances* at Limoges from 1604 to 1617 when he went bankrupt and his assets were sold off, while a brother of his was *avocat* in Paris parlt.

Born Paris, June 1604, baptised at St-Gilles-St-Leu. Son of Pierre and Marie Dechars, from a Parisian merchant family. Nothing known about studies, except he was a bachelor of theol, possibly from Paris, by 1630, and only took doct in theol years later, at Bordeaux, in 1639. Ordained priest in 1628, he was almoner to Bp Loménie of Marseille (a man with Limoges origins) by 1630, but moved into service of Abp Gondi of Paris. Above all, he was early disciple of Vincent de Paul, and one of founders of *retraites* de St-Lazare in 1633. De Paul arranged for him to become vic-gen to Bp François Fouquet at Bayonne in 1639, but did not follow him when he later moved to Agde. He was also vic-gen of Bayeux for a time. Succeeded Pierre Méliand as curé of St-Josse, Paris in 1644, he tried to turn it into a model parish, like Olier at St-Sulpice, founding a parochial community of priests. Membership of Compagnie du St-Sacrement brought further responsibilities, such as directorship of *hôpital-général* in 1657. Earliest works published in late 1620s, later biographer of de Paul and theorist of episcopacy, his *Enchiridion sollicitudinis* becoming standard text. Delay in obtaining provs induced by delay of those for predecessor, Péréfixe, for Paris, granted 24-3-1664. After rapid resign on grounds of ill health and attack of apoplexy, he returned to St-Lazare, where he continued to write and publish extensively.

Nom 18-4-1662. Provs 9-6-1664. Consec 24-8-1664. Resign 1666. Died 4-10-1691.

Sources: ASV, PC 62, fos 411–36; AN, Y 171, fos 429–30, 11-7-1630. Bergin, *Making*, 660–1. DBF, i, 130–40.

Adhémar. *See* **Grignan.**

Allart, Théodore-Germain. Vence 1682–5.   Relatively little known about background of one of Louis XIV's most short-lived bps. Family resided in Sézanne, north-west of Troyes, where they are best described as small town notables, some of whose members held office of various if modest status in local tax admin (*élection, grenier à sel*). Father was an *élu* at Sézanne when he married in 1599, and wife's family were of virtually identical status and activity, municipal councillors in more important (and episcopal) town of Châlons-sur-Marne. His own career owed most to his activities among the Récollets, the religious order to which he belonged for several decades, and which brought him into regular contact with king and entourage. It seems as if Bontemps, king's influential *premier valet de chambre*, was instrumental in obtaining his promotion, paying for his consec etc.

Baptised Théodore, he took name of Germain in religion. Born in 1617, son of Nicolas Allart and Marguerite Clément. Entered Récollets (offshoot of Franciscans) in 1636, and took vows of religion 23-2-1637 in Paris convent (province of St-Denis) before being ordained priest in 1642. Studied phil and theol, but no mention of degree, though he later taught both subjects in Récollet houses. For next 30 years he held a string of major offices in his order. 'Guardian' of houses at Corbeil 1648–9, Rouen 1650, St-Denis 1657–9, he was provincial superior 4 times, twice Visitor, and also *commissaire-général* over all French provinces of Récollets order for a 3-year period. Also played minor political role in service of Louis XIV, which involved uniting the Récollet provinces of Paris and (post-conquest) Artois. King sent him to Canada in late 1660s where he restored Récollets to missionary activity, returning to France in 1670, where he continued to hold high office within his order, and to be busy on several fronts, some of them involving royal orders and service. Brief and peaceful episcopate at Vence.

Nom 30-5-1681. Provs 8-6-1682. Consec 12-7-1682. Died 13-12-1685.

Sources: ASV, PC 81, fos 665–81. BN, PO 39, no 807; Doss bleus 12 (Allart); MS Fr 23510, fo 48v (4-7-1682). DBF, ii, 134–6. *Dictionary of Canadian Biography*, i, 55.

Alleman de Montmartin, Ennemond. Grenoble 1708–19.   The Alleman were among oldest and most prominent surviving noble families in 17th c Viennois-Dauphiné region, tracing their origins back to 13th c and counting an impressive array of bps among their number, not to mention military posts and provincial governorships, inc that of Dauphiné itself. In 17th c, they kept a foot in both robe and sword camps, as their marriage alliances with parlt families show. But as far as bp's career is concerned, their ties to their fellow Viennois, the Villars (who inc abps of Vienne to 1693), may well have been the most important of all.

Ennemond born Vienne, 1660, son of Gaspard, comte de Montmartin, and Marguerite Duprat. Advanced studies in Paris, where he took MA in July 1683, 72nd place in 1690 lic, followed by doct on 8-4-1690. Ordained priest in 1689. A canon of Vienne while a student, he later became *grand chantre* of the chapter, then vic-gen of Vienne in 1699, where he served until 1707.

Nom 1-11-1707. Provs 12-3-1708. Consec 6-5-1708. Died 28-10-1719.

Sources: ASV, PC 101, fos 132–44. BN, MS Lat 15440, p 308; MS Lat 16573, p 38 (1689). Fénelon, *Correspondance*, xvii, 117, n 15. Virieux, 'Parlement de Grenoble', 115–16. Vindry, *État major, gendarmerie*, 12, 22.

Amelot de Gournay, Michel. Lavaur, 1671–3, Tours 1673–87. This family originated in Orléans where they were *bons bourgeois* in early 16th c, and remained commoners thereafter. But a younger son, Jacques, moved to Paris in 1504, acquired a reputation as an *avocat*, which in following generations led descendants to robe officeholding and *lettres de noblesse* in 1583. 16th c marriages to Vialart and St-Germain within Parisian *robe* gave way to later marriages to Saux-Tavannes, Caumont-la Force, Nicolay, Vitry and others, even though they remained faithful to robe offices. Several presidencies in *gr conseil, cour des aides,* and parlt followed, combined with posts as MR and prov intendants under Richelieu and later, culminating in the *honneurs de la cour*, 'avec dispense de preuves', in 18th c. They subdivided into several branches (Chaillou, Châteauneuf, Gournay), distinguishing themselves in church, robe, Malta, and ministerial office – a keeper of the seals, a minister of foreign affairs, an ambassador to Spain and Portugal under Louis XIV, a sec of state.

Baptised in St-Jean-de-Grève, Paris, 15-8-1624. 2nd son of Jean (1577–1644), *prés* in *gr cons*, later MR, and Catherine de Creil, dame de Gournay. Studies at Univ of Paris, coll of Beauvais, where he took MA 7-6-1642. Studied some theol, but took doct of canon law 20-4-1651, possibly because of change of career, as he was *cons* in Paris parlt from Jan 1648. Ordained priest by Claude Auvry in Jesuit church of St-Louis, Paris, *extra tempore*, 15-2-1671, *after* his nom to Lavaur. Also held 3 abbeys in Le Mans dioc: St-Calais (1648), where he introduced Maurist reform, and which he resigned in 1671 on nom to Lavaur; Evron, received in 1657 and resigned to a nephew in 1681; and Gué de Launay, which he retained until death. He only took possession of Lavaur in June 1672, but 6 months later he was transferred to Tours.

Nom 5-1-1671. Provs 22-6-1671. Consec 2-8-1671. Nom to Tours, 16-1-1673. Provs 11-9-1673. Died 17-2-1687.

Sources: ASV, PC 70, fos 1130–58; PC 71, fos 795–813. BN, MS Fr 7655, fos 21–22 (*bienfaits du roi*). BSG, MS 942, f 43r (MA). Tallemant des Réaux, *Historiettes*, ii, 459–64. Lacger, *Etats administratifs*. Bluche, *L'Origine*, 60. Trani, 'Conseillers du grand conseil', 99–101. Chaix d'Est-Ange, *Dictionnaire des familles*, xv, 369–71.

Ancelin, Humbert. Tulle 1681–1702 (resign). Son of Perrette Dufour, wet-nurse of Louis XIV since 1640, married to Étienne Ancelin, a *voiturier* from Poissy. She later became *première femme de chambre* of Anne of Austria and Marie-Thérèse, while her husband became *maître d'hôtel du roi* and *contr-gén* of queen's household. In 1653 they obtained *lettres de noblesse héréditaire*, and monopoly on coaches between certain major cities. Losing their positions on queen's death in 1683, they got substantial pensions as reward and meanwhile their children also prospered – one of future bp's brothers succeeding their father as *contr-gén* of queen's household, another, Henri-Charles, becoming abbot *in comm* of St-Vincent-de-Metz.

Born Paris, Humbert was baptised in St-Eustache, 1648. Studied phil, theol for 3 years as far as bacc, which he took in Paris, March 1668. Ordained priest 10-6-1675 by bp of Coutances. Almoner in service of Queen Marie-Thérèse, also abbot *in comm* of Marcillac, which he resigned in 1685. Gallican at outset of his episcopate, but apparently changed to more ultramontane line in later years. He encountered numerous problems and became involved in bitter, prolonged disputes in his dioc with hospital, his canons, St-Sulpice (over running of seminary), leading to his resign in 1702, in return for which he got abbey of Ham.

Nom 4-10-1680. Provs 17-3-1681. Consec 18-5-1681. Resign before 25-9-1702. Died 26-6-1720.

Sources: ASV, PC 80, fos 695–707. AN, O^1 46, fos 88–90 (confirm of noble status, 1702). St-Simon, xxviii, 521–31 (valuable documentary appendix on Ancelin family). Fénelon, *Correspondance*, xi, p 166, n 6. Sourches, vii, 234. Dangeau viii, 351. DBF, ii, 787–9.

Anglure. *See* **Bourlemont**.

Anselin. *See* **Ancelin**.

Aquin, Luc. St-Paul-Trois-Chateaux 1674–1681, Fréjus 1681–97 (resign).   The 2 Aquin bps, uncle and nephew, owed their success to their family's favour at court as physicians to royal family. They were descended from a Jewish family from Carpentras, where first bp's grandfather, originally named Mardochée, was born, ca 1578. Expelled from his synagogue, he fled to Italy, and was baptised as Philippe at Aquino, hence adopted family name, Aquin. Settling in Paris, possibly in entourage of Concini and Marie de' Medici, he published a *Dictionnaire hébreu-chaldéen-thalmudique rabbinique* (1629) and a 'lament' for Cardinal Berulle in Hebrew and Latin, in 1629, finishing his career as professor of Hebrew at the Coll de France. His son, Louis-Henri, was both orientalist and physician, who served as *premier médecin* to Marie de' Medici, and later *médecin ordinaire* to young Louis XIV (1653). It was his son, Antoine, brother of Luc, who transformed family's fortunes: the *survivance* of his father's post in 1656 and marriage into family of Vallot, the *premier médicin*, 'made' him – *médecin ordinaire* (1660), *premier médecin* (1667) to Maria Thérèse and to Dauphin, ennobled by Louis XIV in 1669. He duly succeeded Vallot as king's own *premier médecin* in 1671, thanks to protection of Mme de Montespan. Powerful and dangerous, 'plus courtisan que médecin' for some, finally brought down in 1693 by Mme de Maintenon, anxious to promote her client and Aquin's main rival, Fagon. Aquin pushed family's interests energetically, even for some years after 1693, by which date office in Paris parlt, accompanied by prov intendancies, had already materialised, not to mention preferment within the French church.

Luc may have been born in London, 1641, where his father was physician to Henrietta Maria, queen of England. Younger son of Louis-Henri and Claire Lopez, brother of Antoine, *premier médecin*, and Louis-Thomas, dean of St-Louis-du-Louvre. Studies in Paris, where MA in Aug 1657, followed by doct in canon law. Ordained priest in 1667, canon of Toul for 10 years before episcopate. Dep to AC of 1675. Avaricious and arrogant, he soon fell out with diocesans, but his connections made him a dangerous adversary. Took opportunity to move to Fréjus when vacant in 1680. Very active in preparation of 1682 AC and Four Articles, as he was energetically gallican. His behaviour at Fréjus no better than at St-Paul, but problems only arose after brother's fall from favour: admonished by Louis XIV himself in 1696, he was persuaded to resign by/in favour of nephew in 1697, with handsome payoff in pensions and benefices. His continuing obstinacy drove king to exile him to Carhaix, but he later allowed him to return to Paris.

Nom 6-4-1674. Provs 11-6-1674. Consec 12-8-1674. Nom to Fréjus 6-9-1680. Provs 17-3-1681. Resign 5-1-1697. Died 2-3-1718.

Sources: ASV, PC 73, fos 359–76. *Journal de la santé du roi*, xxii–xxix. Bluche, *L'Origine*, 65. DBF, iii, 190–3. Chaix d'Est-Ange, *Dictionnaire des familles*, i, 265–6. Tiersonnier, 'Les Origines juives d'un intendant du Bourbonnais', *Bulletin de la Soc d'Émulation du Bourbonnais*, 15 (1907), 228–30.

Aquin, Louis. Fréjus, 1697–98, Sées, 1698–1710.   2nd last of 10 children of Antoine, Louis XIV's *premier médecin*, and Marguerite-Geneviève Gayant, daughter of long established Parisian family, and niece of Antoine Vallot, previous *premier médecin* to king. Born 20-5-1667, but baptised 11-11-1669, when he was held over font by Grand Condé and Queen Marie-

Thérèse. Educated at coll de la Marche and later at coll du Plessis, Paris. Took MA in Paris, July 1684, 5th place in theol lic of 1692, and doct at Sorbonne, 29-3-1692. Ordained priest 15-1-1690. Received, through father's favour, a clutch of desirable benefices, inc abbeys of ND de Moreilles and St-Serge of Angers (1678) and St-Denis-de-Reims (1685). Entered entourage of Harlay of Paris while studying theol, and that patronage probably ensured his election in 1690 as *ag-gén*, a relatively sure avenue to episcopate. Nom to Fréjus in 1697 to replace disgraced uncle, Luc, but latter's protests against his forced resign made it impossible for nephew to enter his dioc, so tenure of Fréjus was purely nominal. He soon quit and accepted Sées in 1698, where he was a resident, active and conscientious bishop, and friend of the ageing Rancé, so accusations of pro-Jansenism surfaced from time to time.

Nom 6-1-1697 to Fréjus. Provs 27-3-1697. Consec 16-6-1697. Nom to Sées 1-11-1698. Provs 30-3-1699. Died 17-5-1710.

Sources: AN, MC, LXXXII, 51, 11-1-1697 (Fréjus); L 744, no 43 (Pére Léonard). BN, MS Fr 19212, fo 105r; Naf 9651 (Louis Aquin papers). *Gall Chr Nov*, Fréjus, 411–12. St-Simon, i, 286; vi, 43–5. DBF, ii, 186–8. L-V Dumaine, *Mgr Louis d'Aquin évêque de Sées*.

Arbouze. *See* **Vény.**

Argenson. *See* **Voyer.**

Argouges, François. Vannes 1692–1716. The Argouges were one of oldest noble families of Normandy, originating from near Bayeux, where their *noblesse* was confirmed several times between 1463 and 1666. Bp's family claimed descent from them via a branch settled in Touraine and Vendomois in 15th c (producing 2 mayors of Tours in 1483 and 1526), but that connection seems baseless, and the Argouges of Tours were probably quite separate, having their origins in bourgeoisie of later medieval Tours. Florent, great-grandfather of bp, settled in Paris in 16th c, engaged in trade and later became *trés-gén* of *gabelles*, sec of the *chambre du roi* and *intendant général* of Marie de' Médici's household. Henri IV forgave this *dérogeance* which enabled Argouges to be declared 'noble de race' in 1609 by *cour des aides*. Bp's father, François (d 1695), was successively *cons* at *gr conseil* (1645), intendant of household and finances of Anne of Austria, MR (1665), with Colbert's support he became *pr prés* at Rennes parlt (1661–75), but 1675 Breton revolt exposed him to failure. Replaced as *pr prés*, he was made a *cons d'etat et des finances* (1685). Bp's elder brother Florent, MR, was intendant at Moulins (1686) and Dijon (1688).

Born Sept 1653, son of François and Anne Hodicq, daughter of a *prés* in the Paris parlt. Studied mainly in Paris where MA in Sept 1672, 85th place in 1680 lic in theol, doct 5-3-1683. Ordained priest in August 1682. Abbot *in comm* of Valasse near Yvetot (Rouen) in 1678. Anti-quietist and anti-Jansenist, he was an active bp.

Nom 24-12-1687. Provs 4-2-1692. Consec 3-3-1692. Died 15-3-1716.

Sources: ASV, PC 86, fos 153–75. St-Simon, ii, 85; vii, 230. Saulnier, *Parlement de Bretagne*, i, 40–1. Bluche, *L'Origine*, 65–6. Béguin, *Condé*, 397. Boisnard, *Touraine*, no 65. DBF, iii, 595–602.

Aube de Roquemartine, Louis. Grasse, 1676–82. St-Paul-Trois-Châteaux 1682–1713. Aube (or Albe) was an old Provençal noble family, whose Roquemartine title belonged to them for generations. They had long had a foot in both robe and sword nobles circles, but also in church and Order of Malta. Connected by marriage to some of Provence's most established families, some of which themselves counted bps among their ranks – Sabran, Villeneuve, Castellane. But by later 17th c, they were approaching extinction, as the bp's only brother, Claude, was childless. Their father had played a part in Provençal politics during and after the Fronde, being sacked as first consul of Aix in 1659 for opposition to Mazarin and his local ally, Oppède, *pr prés* of Aix parlt. Roquemartine, the family's principal seigneurie, was elevated to status of marquisat in 1671, while family was adjudged noble for 12 generations by *réformation de la noblesse* of 1667. Its members were also well established in cath chapter of Arles since at least mid-16th c, the bp himself being 5th family member to be provost of cath since then.

Born in Roquemartine château (Avignon dioc) 9-12-1630, baptised on 5-3-1634. Son of André, sgr (later marquis) of Roquemartine, and Marie de Tinelis du Castellet. Godson of Louis de Paule, *prés* in Aix parlt, and Marguerite de Lubières, baronne de Croze. Studied with Jesuits, took bachelor's degree at precocious age, on 2-11-1644 at Avignon, but proceded no further until returning to Avignon to take lic 27-11-1675, 2 months *after* nom to Grasse. Tonsured 20-1-1641, took minor orders 17-12-1644, ordained subdeacon and deacon, 16/17-3-1652, and priest 17-3-1655. Canon and provost of Arles in Dec 1649 (a post he was allowed to retain while bp until finally obliged to resign it in 1703!). Elected to 1665 AC, but ceded his place to abbé Grignan, whose *titre* was better, though he was allowed to remain in assembly without a vote. Moved from Grasse to St-Paul when Aquin left it for Fréjus. He took tough line with local Protestants during 1680s and 1690s, but was subject of repeated complaints and rebukes, even at ACs of 1695 and esp 1700, about his laxity in ordaining large numbers of clerics without letters of permission (*dimissoires*), who seemed to flock to St-Paul from all quarters. Suspicion was that he was making money out of this, to offset poverty of his dioc. Yet he was a capable and tireless admin, 'né pour etre évêque' according to one source.

Nom 17-9-1675. Provs 16-11-1676. Consec 17-1-1677. Nom to St-Paul, 21-3-1681. Provs 25-5-1682. Died 19-9-1713.

Sources: ASV, PC 75, fos 233–57; PC 81, fos 588–611. BN, PO 117, no 2482. BM Aix, MS 257, p 241–2. AD Vaucluse, D 36, fo 246; D 137, fo 210v. Blanc, 'Origines', 52–3. *Gallia Chr Nov* (Arles), cols 1203–5, 1208–11, 1215–18, 1220–5, 1395–7; *ibid* (St-Paul), cols 623–53. DBF, iii, 1476–7. Pillorget, *Mouvements insurrectionnels*, 869, n 14.

Aubert de Villeserin, Louis-Anne. Senez, 1671–95.　　A common name and unspectacular family history makes it difficult to identify the milieu from which this bp emerged, but which does not seem related to the Aubert de Tourny family who achieved some fame thanks to the 18th c intendant of Bordeaux. A 16th c connection with Orléans is possible, but various family members seem to have held offices of SR at different times from Francis I to Louis XIV inclusive. Bp's father briefly did so (1635–7), having been previously an artillery officer, but he spent most of his career until his death in the late 1650s as a *maître* in *chambre aux deniers*, i.e. a financial official in king's household. On mother's side, bp was descended from a family which, in her own generation and the preceding one, included a *trés-gén* and a *rec-gén* in Picardy, as well as *officiers* in 3 Parisian sovereign courts. Through his grandmother, Jeanne Bourlon, he was related to another Parisian robe family with solid connections and which produced Mathieu, bp of Soissons 1651–85. If, however, Louis XIV and Anne of Austria were indeed his godparents, as his 1st names suggest, then both royal almonership and mitre seem less difficult to explain.

Born 1635, baptised in St-Merry church, Paris. Son of Renaud, sr de Villerserin, *maître* in the *chambre aux deniers*, and Marie Bouvot, d of Claude, *trés-gén* in Picardy. He actually succeeded father as *maître* in *chambre aux deniers* in late 1650s, but had probably resigned by 1661, though financial litigation arising from his and his father's activities continued to surface until at least 1690. Ordained priest at St-Victor, *extra tempore*, 3-1-1662. Took doct *in utr* at Orléans, 13-6-1668. Abbot *in comm* of Ardenne (Sept 1669), prior of Houdreville OSB (Evreux), he was almoner to Louis XIV before 1669. One of the more obscure members of episcopate, he was, according to one account, 'spirituel et lettré', while his record at Senez was one of an active organiser of an admittedly small dioc. He may have missed out on promotion to Toul in 1674 because he fell foul of Colbert arising from an Aubert family row over a lucrative benefice.

Nom 12-4-1671. Provs 1-7-1671. Consec 9-8-1671. Died 7-2-1695.

Sources: ASV, PC 70, fos 1012–36. BN, PO 120, no 2533; MS Fr 7651, fo 231 (*bienfaits du roi*); Mélanges Colbert 7, fos 126–81 (Aubert *factum* re family benefices). Tessereau, *Chancellerie*, i, 85, 93, 354, 404, 406, 537. Bergin, *Making*, 582–3 (Bourlon). Popoff, *Prosopographie*, no 736, p 369. DBF, iv, 78–9.

Aubigné, Claude-Maur. Noyon 1701–8, Rouen 1708–19.   The exact background of bp's family is shrouded in some mystery since bp and family claimed descent from same family as Agrippa d'Aubigné, the Huguenot soldier-poet – but above all of his grand-daughter, Françoise d'Aubigné, marquise de Maintenon! One possibility is that a Théodore Aubigné from Loudun, but no relation to Agrippa, managed to graft himself onto same family tree and, with connivence of Maintenon, obtained confirmation of their noble status over 8 generations on basis of falsified documentation. St-Simon's mockery of Maintenon-Aubigné connection led to other criticisms of bp's own qualities, and he also suffered from well-known *frasques* of his own brother.

Born parish of Tigny, near Saumur, 7-6-1658. Son of Urbain, sgr de la Touche and Tigny, and Marie Gabriau de Riparfont, daughter of *cons* at Poitiers *présidial*. Younger brother of Louis, marquis de Tigny. Attended coll de Dainville, then studied theol in Paris, where he took 107th place in 1688 lic and doct 14-7-1688. Ordained priest by Forbin-Janson, bp of Beauvais,13-4-1686. Served as vic-gen of Luçon, Beauvais and finally Chartres. It was he who persuaded Mme de Maintenon that they were related, and she duly made his career. Obtained pension of 2,000 off see of Sens (Nov 1685), he became abbot *in comm* of Pothières OSB (Langres) in 1686 and La Victoire OSA (Senlis) in 1692, but he resigned the former out of scruples over holding 2 abbeys at same time. Excellent bp, active and capable, he was last abp of Rouen to visit his dioc. Anti-Jansenist, both Fénelon and St-Simon had serious doubts about his intellectual abilities.

Nom to Noyon 26-3-1701. Provs 6-6-1701. Consec 24-7-1701. Nom to Rouen, 24-12-1707. Provs 27-2-1704. Died 22-4-1719.

Sources: ASV, PC 94, fos 581–95; PC 103, fos 651–63. BN, Cab d'Hozier 17, no 383. St-Simon, viii, 77–9. Fénelon, *Correspondance*, xiv, no 1340; xv, 134–5, n 9. Port, *Dictionnaire du Maine-et-Loire*, i, 148–50. Boisnard, *Touraine*, no 85. Compère and Julia, *Collèges français*, ii, 501. Dinet, *Religion et société*, ii, 468. DBF, iv, 159–61.

Bacoué, Léon. Glandèves, 1673–84 (resign).   Born in Castelgeloux, in duchy of Albret, Bazas dioc, 1607. Son of Jean, *lieutenant principal* of *sénéchaussée* of Castelgeloux in 1590s, and Anne Bérault, both Calvinists. Bacoué was himself a Calvinist until 18th year, after which he entered reformed Franciscan observance in the *grand couvent* of Toulouse, where he also read theol, but took no degree because of OFM rules against it. Translated the Spanish Franciscan Villalobo's treatise on moral theol in 1650, taught theol within his order, preached widely, esp the Lenten and other stations, in Agen and other cities, held disputations with former co-religionists, esp in Montauban. Served as 'guardian' of Franciscan houses in Toulouse and Bordeaux and as prov superior of 'Aquitaine', and was also appointed *commissaire* of both sup-gen and pope within his order. He composed several *carmina panegyrica* dedicated to Louis XIV and Clement IX in the 1660s. His offer of 1653 to help with Louis XIV's education by composing *annotations politiques et chrestienes* on the Old Testament chronicles was not taken up by Péréfixe, king's tutor and future abp of Paris, but nearly 20 years later, he tried again, approaching Colbert to offer his services for Dauphin's education. The ensuing educational treatise, published in 1671, did not lead to appointment, but probably ensured he was well enough known to be considered for episcopate instead. He obtained nom of François de Camps as coadj in early 1682, but by then crisis with Rome intervened, blocking the move. He resigned Glandèves outright in 1684 and took up residence in conflict-ridden dioc of Pamiers where de Camps was nom bp in 1685!

Nom 15-10-1672. Provs 27-11-1673. Consec 24-6-1674. Resign 1684. Died 13-2-1694.

Sources: ASV, PC 72, fos 406–35. BN, PO 164, no 3401; Mélanges Colbert 176bis, fos 877–8. St-Simon, xxxviii, 255. Andrieu, *Bibliographie de l'Agenais*, i, 37. Chapelain, *Lettres*, ii, 560 (panegyrics of Louis XIV).

Baglion du Saillant, François-Ignace. Tréguier, 1679–93, Poitiers 1693–8. Beginning with Pietro, a Florentine merchant who settled and married in Lyon in 1539, the Baglioni were among the leading Lyon-based Italian merchant houses of 16th c, branching out into various commercial activities, but also gravitating towards consular office and urban notability. This was already evident in elections as *échevins* of Lyon from 1550 onwards, culminating in 1617 with Léonor de Baillon (sic), baron de Joux en Dauphiné, *gentilhomme ordinaire du roi* like his father, marrying the granddaughter of an even more successful Lyonnais, Chancellor Bellièvre, with extensive connections in high Paris robe circles (e.g. Harlay). Léonor himself was *prévôt des marchands* of Lyon in 1640 and one of his brothers a *cons* in Paris parlt. But they also moved in direction of military nobility, thanks initially to Godi-Retz connections in 1560–70s: La Salle became a *comté* in 1635, and by the time François, brother of bp of Mende, married in 1686 he was captain in a company of light horse and 'commandant' of the nobility of the Lyonnais, Forez and Beaujolais. His father had been one of the *élus* of Estates of Charolais in 1662, thanks to the support of Condé, in whose household he was a leading *commensal*. A 3rd bp would follow relatively quickly, with elevation of Pierre's nephew, François, to Arras in 1725.

François-Ignace was son of Léonor, *maitre d'hotel* to Louis XIII, and Françoise Henry, daughter of Denise Bellièvre and Artus Henry. Born Lyon, where baptised 1-8-1632. After initial education, he served in royal cavalry and probably succeeded father as *gentilhomme du roi*. But he changed course and entered the Paris Oratory on 5-7-1655, studying phil and theol for a time, but not taking his degree, the doct in canon law, until March 1679, *after* his nom to Tréguier. Ordained priest 20-4-1658. Superior of Oratorian house in Montmorency near Paris in 1659, followed by 6 years as assistant to Oratorian sup-gen, Sénault, and then as superior of Paris house in 1672. He held other offices, inc the important one of *proc-gén* of the Oratory, and was Abp Harlay's candidate as successor to Sénault as sup-gen in 1672, but bid was foiled. He also worked closely with Harlay (to whom he was related via Bellièvre family) to produce Oratorian statement of theological orthodoxy in 1679, year of his episcopal nom, by which time he was well known in king's entourage, not least to his fellow Lyonnais, La Chaize, who held him in high esteem, entrusting him with tasks which would advance his episcopal prospects. While an Oratorian, he established reputation as preacher, and in Tréguier he apparently learned to preach in Breton. Nom to Poitiers, possibly in preference to Fénelon, then active as missionary in western France (Batterel), after Armand de Quinçay returned his nom to king in March 1686. St-Simon regarded him as an ideal, residential bishop.

Nom 24-2-1679. Provs 12-6-1679. Consec 23-7-1679. Nom to Poitiers 26-4-1686. Provs 23-11-1693. Died 26-1-1698.

Sources: ASV, PC 78, fos 576–87. Batterel, *Mémoires domestiques*, iv, 120–30. *L'Intendance du Lyonnais, Beaujolais, Forez*, 70. Vindry, *État major, gendarmerie*, 217. St-Simon, v, 78–9. Fénelon, *Correspondance*, iii, 134, n 21. Béguin, *Princes de Condé*, 180. Chaix d'Est-Ange, *Dictionnaire des familles*, ii, 198–201. Poncet, *Bellièvre*, 342. Gascon, *Grand commerce*, i, 205, 208; ii, 788. Minois, *La Bretagne des prêtres*, 141–2.

Baglion du Saillant, Pierre. Mende 1708–23. Nephew of François-Ignace above. Born 1661, son of François, comte de la Salle, *premier gentilhomme* of prince of Condé, and Marie de Percy, his 2nd wife. Seems to have studied hum and phil, followed by theol in Paris, taking doct in theol in 1683, but not in Paris (possibly in Poitiers). Priest for many years before episcopate. Grand archdeacon of Poitiers cath, also vic-gen of Poitiers, thanks to uncle, for over 20 years, during which he also took substantial part in Poitiers theol fac affairs. Also served as *official* of Poitiers, and metropolitan judge for province of Bordeaux during same time. Abbot of Bonneval O Cist (Poitiers) since 1693.

Nom 24-12-1707. Provs 30-4-1708. Consec 24-6-1708. Died 27-9-1723.

Sources: ASV, PC 101, fos 182–95. BN, MS Fr 20969, fo 86v.

Balbe de Berton. *See* Crillon.

Bar, Hugues de. Dax 1667–72, Lectoure 1672–91.   The original patronymic of this family was Moulceu or Monceu, while Bar was an early seigneurie of theirs which gradually replaced their original name. Natives of the Limousin, where they were minor landed gentry since later 14th and 15th c. Intermarriage with other local nobles and, possibly, service to Turenne family during the following generations oriented them towards military activity, but they remained relatively anonymous until the 17th c. Bp's father, possibly under the influence of wife's family, embarked on military career in 1620s, serving successively as guards capt for Richelieu and especially for Mazarin, who trusted him sufficiently by 1650 to confide to him governorship of Vincennes, a key fortress during Fronde since Frondeur princes were held there in 1650. He later operated under Turenne in Picardy and Flanders, and was rewarded with post of lt-gen in army and governorship of Amiens in 1654, confirmed (despite his apparent links to Fouquet) by Louis XIV in 1661, and inherited by his son after father's death in 1695.

Born in Tulle, 1632, 2nd son of Guy, sgr de la Faurie, and Jeanne de Genesse, his 2nd wife, daughter of a *prés* in Bordeaux parlt. Studied phil at coll of Navarre, taking the MA in August 1650, followed by theol, which he did not pursue beyond bacc, taken in Jan 1654. Only ordained priest in 1665, a year before nom in 1666. Dep to 1665 AC. Well before then he had obtained 2 abbeys *in comm*, St-André-de-Vienne OSB (1655) and ND des Vertus (Châlons-sur-Marne) which he exchanged for Pontaut O Cist (Aire) in 1668. A resident and respected bp, esp in Jansenist-leaning circles, he took a strong Augustinian stance on sacraments and religious practice, which created strong opposition in Dax and led to his transfer to Lectoure. Wealthy, he was also remembered for his charity in years of distress.

Nom to Dax 12-5-1666. Provs 7-3-1667. Consec 10-4-1667. Nom to Lectoure 28-1-1671. Provs 2-5-1672. Died 22-12-1691.

Sources: ASV, PC 65, fos 66–83, PC 71, fos 463–85; Misc Arm XII, 151, fo 13v (ND des Vertus). BN, Doss bleus 55, no 1279; MS Fr 22834, fo 88r (tentativa); MS Fr 7651, fo 205 (*bienfaits*). AN, O[1] 11, fo 91 (Vincennes, 1650); L 735, pièce 1, no 2 (Lombez). Pinard, *Chronologie*, iv, 149–51; vii, 109–10. *Lettres de Turenne*, 26. *Mémoriaux du conseil de 1661*, i, 48. M Bordes, 'Le Jansénisme dans le diocèse de Lectoure', *Actes du 96ᵉ Congrès National des Sociétés Savantes* (Toulouse 1971), ii, 107–35, esp 110–12.

Baradat, Louis-Daniel. Vabres 1673–1710.   The Baradat were originally a family established in Navarre-Armagnac area. Guillaume, a *gentilhomme* in service of Catherine de' Medici, settled near Epernay, Champagne, where he married in late 16th c. Bp of Vabres was his grandson, and nephew of Henri Baradat, bp of Noyon under Louis XIII. Bp's parents were married in exile in Brussels in 1632, where he had joined with Gaston d'Orléans in revolt against Louis XIII, but Baradat was allowed to return to his estates soon afterwards, and later served briefly in French armies until 1643, when he retired for good. None of his 8 children left any offspring, 2 were clerics, 2 knights of Malta.

Born Damery, 5-1-1640, but not 'ceremonially' baptised until 1652, when Louis XIV and Anne of Austria held him over the baptismal font. Son of François, marquis de Damery, lt-gen in Champagne, and Gabrielle de Coligny. Took lic in canon law, Paris, date unknown. Succeeded his uncle Bp Baradat as prior of Essarts and abbot of Clermont O Cist (Le Mans), both benefices being virtually family heirlooms. Ordained priest by his diocesan, Bourlon of Soissons, in Paris 8-3-1664, who also involved him in organising missions in Soissons dioc. An uneventful episcopate in a rather anonymous dioc, which he did reorganise early during his reign.

Nom 16-1-1673. Provs 12-6-1673. Consec 31-12-1673. Died 17-3-1710.

Sources: ASV, PC 72, fos 764–84. Anselme, *Histoire*, ii, 442–5. Pinard, *Chronologie*, vi, 288–9. Bergin, *Making*, 567–8. *Répertoire des visites pastorales*, iv, 553. *Revue Historique du Rouergue*, 4 (1917), 139–40.

Bargedé, Edouard. Nevers 1706–19.   Little known about this Nivernois who rose to govern his native dioc, where he had long been active. His family were natives of Corbigny, north-east of Nevers, but seem increasingly resident in Auxerre by early- to mid-17th c. Such a move may have coincided with officeholding of limited scale at *présidial* court of Auxerre, where some family members were *cons*, and later a *prés*, under Louis XIII and Louis XIV, while others still were barristers – as in case of bp's own father whose title of *bailli* of the abbey of St-Léonard-de-Corbigny should not be over-rated. A church presence is also evident with Gaspard, canon and chantre of Auxerre cath, in the 1620s. Judging by the numbers of clerics and nuns in every generation in this period, they were a highly *dévot* family, and bp may have had 2 brothers who also became ecclesiastics.

Born Corbigny, dioc of Autun, 10-3-1651, son of Gaspard, bailli of Corbigny, and Marguerite Goussot. Studied initially at Nevers. Doct of theol 4-4-1680, possibly from Bourges. Priest since September 1682. Wide experience at Nevers, initially as curé of Montreuillon and later of St-Arigle in the town of Nevers itself, before bp Vallot made him successively his vic-gen and *official* in 1694, then canon and *grand chantre* of the cath in 1701. Vallot died before his intention of taking Bargedé as his coadj, for which royal nom was granted in Aug 1705, could be implemented. He received abbey of Beaulieu at same time as nom as coadj of Nevers, supplemented in 1710 by that of St-Cyran. St-Simon claimed he obtained Nevers because he behaved very firmly and diplomatically in dispute over marriage of duke of Mantua and Mme de Pompadour in 1704. Published a strong *mandement* against Quesnel in 1707, showing him to be hard-line anti-Jansenist, which after 1713 incited some of his clergy, esp cath canons, to sign the appeal to a future council of 1717 and later. His last years were ones of animosity and conflict.

Nom 3-9-1705. Provs 22-3-1706. Consec 2-5-1706. Died 20-7-1719.

Sources: ASV, PC 99, fo 397–409. BN, PO 196, no 4258; Doss bleus 57, no 1382. AD Cher, D 9, D 17. Fisquet, *France pontificale*, Nevers, 92–5. Dinet, *Religion et société*, i, 131. Dinet, *Vocation et fidélité*, 27, 36–7. St-Simon, xii, 244–5. Fénelon, *Correspondance*, xvii, 118, n 21. Victor Guéneau, *Dictionnaire biographique du Nivernais* (Nevers 1899), 10.

Barillon, Henri. Luçon 1672–99.   Natives of Issoire in Auvergne, the Barillon were ennobled in early 16th c via an office of SR. They owed their ascent to the patronage of fellow Auvergnat, Duprat, chancellor under Francis I, who married a cousin of his to Jean Barillon, whom he made his *premier commis*. Entry into parlt followed in subsequent generation through Jean, Antoine, and Jean-Jacques. The latter, father of bp, briefly succeeded his brother Antoine, in Rennes parlt in 1620, before entering Paris parlt in 1623 as *cons*, becoming *prés* in *Enquêtes* chamber, 1628. But he fell foul of both Richelieu and Mazarin for his independence of mind and tongue, enduring several periods of exile from 1631 onwards and dying in confinement at Pignerol 1645. Their fortunes recovered later under Mazarin and Louis XIV, when bp's uncle (who also brought him up after father's death) Antoine III, sgr de Morangis, became *directeur des finances* from 1648 until 166s, and his brother, Antoine IV, married daughter of another Chancellor, Boucherat. Antoine III was an influential early member of Compagnie du St-Sacrement, with close ties to *dévot* and Port-Royal circles, which bp himself inherited and maintained.

Born Paris parish of St-Jean-de-Grève, 4-3-1639 during father's exile at Amboise. Son of Jean-Jacques (d 1645) and Bonne Fayet, daughter of a *prés* in *Enquêtes*, Paris parlt. Began studies with Oratory at Juilly in 1645, finished them at coll des Grassins, Paris (hum, phil and theol) with MA in May 1660, going on to theol doct, 30-6-1666, having taken

81st (and 2nd last) place in licentiate of same year. Tonsured 23-9-1651, initially destined for Order of Malta, but changed his mind in 1660 and opted for church, influenced by Le Camus, Rancé and other close friends at the time. Ordained deacon 19-9-1665 and priest by bp Ligny of Meaux in Paris 9-6-1666. He held priory of Boulogne, which his friend Rancé, who regarded him very highly from early years, resigned to him, 1663. Close to the Oratory, having spent several periods of retreat at St-Magloire from the mid-1650s onwards. Le Camus had a hand in his episcopal nom. A widely respected bp of rigorist disposition, he gave his approval to several works from Port-Royal, was joint author (with Arnauld of Angers and Laval-Boisdauphin of La Rochelle) of the 'Catechism of the three Henris', close to the Oratory, former members of which served him as vic-gen and *théologal*. Proposed at various times for more prestigious sees than Luçon – Tours in 1687 when La Chaize failed to persuade Louis XIV, Bordeaux, and even Paris in 1695, where he died after an operation for gallstones.

Nom 17-10-1671. Provs 8-2-1672. Consec 5-6-1672. Died 6-5-1699.

Sources: ASV, PC 71, fos 514–32. BN, MS Lat 15540, p 228; MS Lat 18389, fos 285–312, *vie autobiographique*. AN, L 735, pièce 1, n 13. *Documents pour l'histoire du diocèse de Luçon*, nos 1103–1377. Bossuet, *Correspondance*, xiii, 57. St-Simon, vi, 182–4. Saulnier, *Parlement de Bretagne*, i, 53–4. *Lettres de Séguier*, ii, 1185–6. Antoine, *Coeur de l'état*, 235, 294. Poutet, 'Docteurs', 295, no 494. Bluche, *L'Origine*, 75–6. Chaix d'Est-Ange, *Dictionnaire des familles*, ii, 339–40. *Lettres de Germain Vuillart*, 221–2, 224, 236–7. Krailsheimer, *Rancé*, 231–5. DBF, v, 466–74.

Barthélemy de Grammont de Lanta, François. St-Papoul 1677–1716.   This well-known Toulouse robe family originated in Mur de Barrez, near Aurillac, where their ancestor Pierre, an *avocat*, was resident in early 16th c. But within a generation, they had entered Toulouse parlt, initially (1543) as *cons*, but soon (1554) followed by a presidency in the *Enquêtes* chamber, which remained in their hands for several generations. Like other Toulousains of similar ambition, they were tempted by office in Paris – the *gr conseil*, MRs – but that proved short-lived. Intermarriage, esp via daughters, with existing parlt families consolidated their position in Toulouse, so that by mid-17th c, they were among its most prominent robe dynasties. Acquisition of barony of Lanta gave entry to Estates of Languedoc, in which bp's uncle played a major role in 1650s, developing connections to Gaston d'Orléans, prov governor, and famously confronting Mazarin directly over royal policies in 1657. Although involved in Catholic League in Toulouse, there are relatively few signs of ecclesiastical interests until next century, when an uncle of the bp, also François, was *cons* in the parlt and abbot *in comm* of Eaunes. His father evidently had intellectual interests, writing continuation of de Thou's *History* down to 1629.

Born Toulouse 16-2-1638, youngest of 10 children of Gabriel, *prés* in *Enquêtes* in Toulouse parlt, and Anne de Malecoste. Most of his studies seem to have been in Paris, where he was student at coll of Harcourt by 1652. Took MA there in July 1655, but did not take bacc in theol until April 1661, followed by 74th place in 1666 lic exams, but not the doct. Probably returned to Toulouse, and acquired 2 abbeys *in comm*, Calers O Cist (Rieux) and Eaunes O Cist (Rieux), the latter from an uncle. Canon and archdeacon of Tarbes before 1670, which enabled him to obtain election by Auch province as *ag-gén* in 1670. Diligent and strongly resident bp, he was on close and good terms with Basville, the prov intendant.

Nom 13-9-1675. Provs 11-10-1677. Consec 5-12-1677. Died 26-2-1716.

Sources: ASV, PD 55, fo 163–5. AN, O^1, vol 19, fos 233–5 (*brevet* and letters of nom, 1675). BN, MS Fr 7651, fo 209 (*bienfaits du roi*). Navelle, *Familles nobles et notables*, ii, 23–9. Trani, 'Conseillers du grand conseil', 106–7. Etchéchoury, *Maîtres des Requêtes*, 203–4. Vindry, *Parlementaires du xvie siècle*, ii, 172, 174, 196. Beik, *Absolutism and Society*, 216–18 (uncle).

Baudry de Piencourt, François-Placide. Mende 1677–1707.   Several families of this name existed in various parts of Normandy. Bp of Mende was son of a relatively anonymous family originally from the Evreux area, where they were gentry since mid-15th c, but by 17th c, they lived near Les Andelys. Their claims to a crusading past under Godefroy de Bouillon elicited the sarcastic reply from Hozier, the royal genealogist: 'j'en scay grand nombre qui ne se croiroint pas bien gentilhommes silz ne se faisoient descendre de Loys le Gros!' None of the bp's brothers produced male heirs, so the Piencourt land and title entered house of La Rocheaymon via marriage of a niece of bp in 1680. It was their ecclesiastical activities which, perhaps unexpectedly, opened way to episcopate to him in an age when Benedictine bps were exceptionally rare.

Born 1630, son of Henri, sgr de Piencourt, and Charlotte de Lamotte, from a Breton family, married in 1621. Studied in Paris, took 16th place in lic in theol of 1658, followed by doct 30-10-1659. He entered Benedictine abbey of La Croix St-Leufroy (Evreux) in his teens, taking monastic orders and becoming its coadj-abbot 1653, finally succeeding an uncle and great uncle before him as abbot in 1669, and reformed it after that date, before resigning it outright on nom to Mende. Ordained priest at Evreux in 1656. Dep to 1665 and 1682 ACs. It was alleged that Claude Pellot, *pr prés* of Rouen parlt and relative of Colbert, used his influence to obtain Mende for Baudry on understanding that Pellot *fils* would get Ste Croix.

Nom 4-7-1677. Provs 11-10-1677. Consec 16-1-1678. Died 13-12-1707.

Sources: ASV, PC 76, fos 578–96. BN, PO 222, no 5011; Doss bleus 64, nos 1555, 1558; Cab d'Hozier 30, no 720; Carrés d'Hozier 69; Nouv d'Hozier 29, no 586; MS Fr 7655, fo 72; MS Lat, 15440, p 203; MS Lat 16573, p 7. AD Creuse, E 452 (Rocheaymon papers). *Gallia*, xi, col 637 (La Croix St-Leufroy). Pellot, *Notes*, 220. Poutet, 'Docteurs', 271, no 282.

Bazan de Flamanville, Jean-Hervé. Perpignan 1695–1721.   The Bazan were among the most prominent and wealthy noble families of northern Cotentin, lower Normandy, with Flamanville becoming a marquisat in 1654. Bp's father's 2 marriages convey some idea of their connections: his 1st wife was an Argouges de Ranes (no relation to the bp of Vannes above), his 2nd a Molé, daughter of a top Parisian robe family, and whose sister was married to Georges de Monchy, marquis d'Hocquincourt. Bp's eldest brother served in cavalry for several decades, ending career as lt-gen in 1704, having married Marie-Anne le Camus, niece of the Cardinal of Grenoble, in 1690.

Born 16-2-1660 in château of Flamanville, Coutances dioc. 3rd son of Jean-Hervé, marquis de Flamanville, *grand bailli* of Cotentin, and Agnès Molé de Champlatreux, his 2nd wife. May have studied in Paris, but only took lic *in utr* in 1692 at Angers when already in service of bp there – which was almost certainly because he had entered St-Sulpice on 1-11-1682, joined its *petite communauté* 5-1-1683, and then exercised ministry in parish. He may also have been associated with Missions Etrangères seminary during this period. Priest since 24-9-1687. After studies, he was *chapelain* of St-Sauveur d'Octeville (1687), and later vic-gen of Bp Le Peletier of Angers, where he ran seminary for young clerics and taught religious articles to the young, also involving himself in reform of female monasteries in Angers dioc. Vic-gen of Castres in 1694 under its new bp, Augustin Maupeou. Failed to get bulls for abbey of St-Michel-de-Cuxa in 1701, given ND la Royale instead, which was then incorporated into see of Perpignan to boost its revenues.

Nom 8-9-1695. Provs 12-12-1695. Consec 12-2-1696. Died 5-1-1721.

Sources: ASV, PC 89, fos 222–30. Arch MEP, 9, pp 478–81. Pinard, *Chronologie*, iv, 550–2. Tronson, *Correspondance*, i, 44; iii, 253. Stewart, *Assimilation*, 159. Pellot, *Notes*, 318. *Intendance de Caen*, 240.

Bazin de Bezons, Armand-Jean-Baptiste. Aire 1693–8, Bordeaux 1698–1719, Rouen 1719–21.   Family originally from Méry-sur-Seine, north-west of Troyes, where they moved into local muncipal offices, but also the *élection* of Troyes in 16th and early 17th c, where they were related by marriage to Pithou family and other local notables. Bp was descended from a

Parisian offshoot, which obtained letters of ennoblement in early 17ᵗʰ c, by which time they were poised to begin an impressive ascent into high *robe* of the capital, but also into *épée*, since bp's brother was made marshal of France in 1709. Louvois patronage seems to have been crucial along the way. Before that their main claim to attention was that of long-serving prov intendants – e.g. bp's father and brother. Church preferment may have come late but it was also impressive – bp had 3 Le Blanc nephews in the episcopate by the 1720s!

Son of Claude (1617–74) and Marie Targer, born at Montpellier, 29-12-1654, when father was long-serving intendant of Languedoc (1653–73). Held by Conti and marquise de Castries, sister of Cardinal Bonsi, over baptismal font. Studied in Paris, MA in Aug 1674, 5ᵗʰ place in theol lic of 1682, and doctor 17-12-1682. In 1667, he obtained abbey of Ressons, adding La Grasse in 1705. In 1680, while only bachelor of theol, he became *ag-gén* of French clergy. Priest for 12 years before episcopate. Dep to 1695 AC. When Thyard de Bissy refused move from Toul to Bordeaux in 1697, Louis XIV turned to Bazin. By that point his brother was an influential, long-serving prov intendant in Bordeaux itself (1686–1700). Regent appointed him to *conseil de conscience* in 1718, in 2nd place after Noailles. This was possibly the reason why Rouen seemed most sensible next move.

Nom to Aire 15-8-1685. Provs 12-8-1693. Consec 22-11-1693. Nom to Bordeaux 4-4-1698. Provs 15-9-1698. Nom to Rouen 4-5-1719. Provs 18-9-1719. Died 8-10-1721.

Sources: ASV, PC 87, fos 809–30. BN, MS Lat 15440, p 272; MS Lat 16573, p 29. St-Simon, xviii, 306–8, Moréri, *Grand Dictionnaire*, ii, 229–30. Anselme, *Histoire*, vii, 682–3. Chaix d'Est-Ange, *Dictionnaire des familles*, iii, 129–31. Peyrous, *Réforme à Bordeaux*, ii, 729–32. Kuno Böse, *Amt und soziale Stellung*, ii, 21–6. Degert, *Histoire des évêques d'Aire*.

Beaumanoir de Lavardin, Jean-Baptiste. Rennes 1677–1711.   From same family that held Le Mans from 1610–37 and 1649–71, bp of Rennes was born in family château of Lavardin, Le Mans dioc, ca 1642. 2ⁿᵈ son of Claude, vicomte de Lavardin, and Renée de la Chapelle. Further studies in Paris, where he took MA in Sept 1660, 76ᵗʰ place in 1668 theol lic, and doct on 21-2-1669. Brief sojourn in St-Sulpice (June-July 1661) when he was sub-deacon. Canon and archdeacon in Le Mans cath from early age, he was elected its dean in 1666, and subsequently became vic-gen to his increasingly absentee uncle. Dep to 1675 AC, initially nom to Dol in Aug 1676, when Thoreau, bp of Dol, was offered Rennes, which he refused, remaining at Dol. Rennes then given to François Bouthillier, but he too renounced it in hope of getting Poitiers instead, opening way to Beaumanoir! Obtained abbey of Montieramey OSB (Troyes) in 1696. Unpopular as bp, it seems, also at odds with intendants, but Beamanoir family ties in Brittany and at court provided ample protection.

Nom 26-11-1676. Provs 8-11-1677. Consec 20-2-1678. Died 23-5-1711.

Sources: ASV, PC 76, fos 780–800. BN, MS Fr 7657, fo 19 (*bienfaits du roi*). Levesque, 'Liste des élèves', no 667. *La Bretagne à la fin du xviiᵉ siècle d'après le rapport de Béchameil de Nointel*, ed Jean Bérenger and Jean Meyer (Paris 1976), 159. Bergin, *Making*, 570–1.

Beaupoil de St-Aulaire, André-Daniel. Tulle 1702–21 (resign).   This family claimed to have been highly prominent in Brittany in the 13–14ᵗʰ c before being obliged by political difficulties and confiscation of their lands to settle in Limousin. Hozier and others challenged this legend, so that earliest members in Limousin may well have been both local and commoner in origin. But no doubt that from mid-15ᵗʰ c they entered nobility of province, intermarrying to good effect with local nobles, as well as with those of neighbouring provinces (Auvergne and Périgord). Several branches developed, though connections between them are not easy to disentangle, so that relation of bp's immediate family to wider network remains elusive. Mother's family was influential and well-connected in Auvergne, and counted Veny d'Arbouze family among their kin. One of his sisters married marquis de Fénelon, while his elder brother was a political and literary figure elected to Académie Française in 1706.

Born château of St-Aulaire, Limoges dioc, 16-6-1651, bp was 2nd of 3 sons of Daniel and Guyonne de Chauvigny le Blot, his 2nd wife, married in 1643. Little known about his studies, except that he took doct in theol at Bourges. Tonsured Limoges 8-11-1666, he was ordained priest in 1682. Resided at St-Sulpice for some time, but was mostly involved with seminary in Limoges. Archpriest in 1693 of la Porcherie (Perigueux), he was also made vic-gen of Périgueux and superior of its seminary by bp Daniel de Francheville, and had long experience of missions before nom to Tulle. After resigning as bp in 1721, he retired to live with missionaries de Périgueux and died there in 1734, where buried.

Nom 15-4-1702. Provs 25-9-1702. Consec 29-10-1702. Resign 8-9-1721. Died 18-11-1734.

Sources: ASV, PC 95, fos 448–63. BN, PO 249, no 5463; PO 1645, no 38,210. Fénelon, *Correspondance*, xvii, 117. Nadaud, *Nobiliaire de Limoges*, i, 144–65. Champeval, *Dictionnaire des familles nobles de la Corrèze*, ii, 23–50. St-Simon, xviii, 167. Béguin, *Condé*, 400–01.

Beauvau de Rivarennes, Gilles. Nantes 1679–1717.   From same extended and complex family as his great-uncle and predecessor but one, Gabriel de Beauvau, bp of Nantes (1636–67) and his own immediate predecessor at Nantes, Gilles de la Baume Le Blanc (1668–77 – see below). The different branches of family intermarried to a significant degree, while their continuing presence in the episcopate under Louis XIV owed much to the consequences of the king's liaison with their cousin, Louise de la Vallière, whose daugher by Louis XIV later became princess of Conti.

Son of François, marquis de Beauvau-Rivarennes, and Louise de La Baume le Blanc (younger sister of Gilles la Baume le Blanc, bp of Nantes, and daughter of a Beauvau du Rivau), married in 1646. Born 1652. Doctor in canon law from Orléans. Priest since 3-4-1677. Obtained abbey of Tréport in 1702. Innocent XI refused to confirm royal nom until Beavau had reached canonical age for French bps. A long uneventful career, he died leaving substantial debts.

Nom 5-7-1677. Provs 17-7-1679. Consec 24-8-1679. Died 7-9-1717.

Sources: ASV, PC 78, fos 409–22. St-Simon, xxxi, 346. Sévigné, *Correspondance*, viii, 27. Anselme, *Histoire*, ix, pt II, 662–77.

Beauvau du Rivau, Pierre-François. Sarlat 1692–1701.   Born ca 1638, son of Jacques II, sgr du Rivau and lt-gen of Poitou, and Isabeau de Clermont-Tonnerre, his 2nd wife. Further studies at Univ of Paris, where he matriculated in 1654 and took MA in July 1655. Theol studies leading to 58th place in 1660 lic, followed by doct 18-7-1661. Dep to 1660 AC, but health reasons prevented attendance at that of 1682. Canon of Nantes, thanks to Bp Beauvau, before 1660. Prior of St-Patrice OSB (Tours), he obtained abbey of Turpenay OSB (Tours) in Feb 1668. Encouraged charitable works and protected Jesuits. He was offered Bayonne by Louis XIV in 1701 but refused it, so his nephew (below) got it instead.

Nom 15-8-1688. Provs 15-10-1692. Consec 25-1-1693. Died 23-10-1701.

Sources: ASV, PC 86, fos 711–19. AUP, reg 97, fo 29v. BN, MS Fr 7651, fo 191 (*bienfaits*). Pinard, *Chronologie*, iv, 158–60; vi, 350. Poutet, 'Docteurs', 275, no 327.

Beauvau du Rivau, René-François. Bayonne 1701–7, Tournai 1707–13, Toulouse 1713–21, Narbonne 1721–39.   Nephew of Pierre-François above. Born Lemeré in Tours dioc, 4-11-1664. Son of Jacques, marquis du Rivau, capt of Swiss guards of Gaston d'Orléans, and Diane Marie de Campet. Univ studies in Paris, where MA in July 1687, 112th place in 1692 theol lic, followed by doct 13-5-1694, the year he was also ordained priest. Obtained canonicate in Sarlat cath via *régale*, 9-4-1689 when still a simple clerc of Tours, and was appointed *official* and vic-gen of Sarlat in uncle's service before 1696. Previously canon of Nantes cath, he became abbé *in comm* of St-Victor-de-Calais OSB (Rouen) in 1685. Resigned priory of Pardaillan (Agen) when nom to Bayonne. Dep to 1693 AC. An 'honnête homme selon le monde', Fénelon did not think he was really capable of dealing with problems of Tournai (inc Jansenism there). Later, as bp in Languedoc, he was one of sponsors of Benedictines' *Histoire du Languedoc*.

Nom to Bayonne 1-11-1700. Provs 18-4-1701. Consec 17-7-1701. Nom to Tournai 23-4-1707. Provs 19-12-1707. Nom to Toulouse, 29-7-1713. Provs 11-12-1713. Nom to Narbonne, 5-11-1719. Provs 28-5-1721. Died 4-8-1739.

Sources: ASV, PC 86, fos 711–26; PC 94, fos 314–27; PC 100, fos 446–58. BN, MS Lat 15440, p 319; MS Lat 15673, p 51; MS Fr 20969, fos 76v, 158v. Fénelon, *Correspondance*, xiv, 178; xv, 134, n 7. St-Simon, xvi, 295, n 6. Sourches, ii, 199.

Beauvillier de St-Aignan, François. Beauvais 1713–28 (resign). One of the most favoured of aristocratic families under Louis XIV, the Beauvillier originated in the Beauce near Chartres, but with presence in Touraine from 14ᵗʰ c onwards. Their nobility was declared to be of 'extraction chevaleresque' and traceable to 1220 by 17ᵗʰ c *recherches*. Well before then, military activity, positions at court and governorships, accompanied by some substantial marriages (e.g. Rohan, Babou), brought them gradually into the ranks of the higher nobility, confirmed by the *duché-pairie* in 1663. This pattern would continue under Louis XIV, with marriages into ministerial families like Servien and Colbert. Bp's elder half-brother, Paul (1648–1714), was a *ministre d'état* from the 1690s onwards who, along with his brother-in-law, Chevreuse, was a leading *dévot* figure in court politics.

Son of François, duc de St-Aignan (1610–87), and 2nd wife, Françoise Géré de Rancé, he was born 6-10-1682. Entered St-Sulpice 10-7-1700, a few weeks after taking MA at Univ of Paris. Went on to take 1ˢᵗ place in Paris theol lic of 1708, and became doctor there 31-3-1708, having on Louis XIV's explicit orders defended the 1682 Gallican Articles in Sorbonne, which caused Rome to delay granting him his bulls for Beauvais for a time. Ordained priest ca 1707. Abbot *in comm* of St-Germer-de-Fleix OSB (Beauvais) in May 1701, which he resigned on becoming bp. In 1709, he left St-Sulpice to become gr-vic-of Orléans, but when nom to Beauvais, was regarded as an inexperienced, if model, seminarian – no doubt because of his age. But his half-brother's earlier worries about his character (impetuous, obstinate, 'vivacious'), which apparently led him to press Louis XIV not to nom him to episcopate, were subsequently borne out, and he was forced to resign in 1728 because of scandalous behaviour, threatened with deposition, and was placed under arrest by *lettre de cachet* at Cîteaux and later Prémontré, where he died.

Nom 1-4-1713. Provs 30-8-1713. Consec 1-10-1713. Resign 10-4-1728. Died 19-8-1751.

Sources: AN, MC, LXXXII, 122, 30-4-1713. BN, MS Lat 15440, p 373; MS Fr 22832 (list of 1708 graduates). *Hierarchia Catholica*, v, 117, 'Bellovacen', n 3. St-Simon, x, 369ff; xiv, 123; xv, 342; xxiii, 373–6; xxxiii, 348–57 (appendix of documents). Fénelon, *Correspondance*, xvi, no 1711; xvii, p 162, n 1. Sévigné, *Correspondance*, xi, 78. Barbier, *Journal*, i, 251. *L'Intendance de Caen en 1700*, 15–20. Vindry, *État major, gendarmerie*, 475, 488–9.

Belin, Jean-Albert, OSB. Belley 1665–77. The Belin family emerged into the political limelight in Besançon after mid-17ᵗʰ c and retained their political and social importance until the Revolution. But their early history is difficult to elucidate – even identity of bp's own parents is not perfectly clear. Before settling in Besançon by first half of 16ᵗʰ c, they had moved from Salins, their likely place of origin, to Gy and then Vesoul, where bp's grandfather was lawyer in service of Philippe II and, in 1588, a *cons* in Dole parlt. One of his sons, Claude, became a doct of medicine, practising in Besançon after 1606, where other members of the same family, it seems, were already resident, practising as apothecaries etc. Claude Belin repeatedly held municipal office during 1620s and 1630s, while his brother, Jean (d 1637), probably bp's father, began as a notary in 1607, was regularly elected to muncipal office, and finished his career as city treasurer (1633–7). Both were outdone by Hugues (1608?–85), probably bp's brother, who was also a doct in law, held major municipal office for virtually

30 years after 1646, and became a key figure in city and prov politics before and during French conquest of Franche-Comté, participating in delegations to courts of Vienna, Madrid, Brussels and, finally, Paris after first French conquest of the Franche-Comté. Having helped to ensure transition to French rule, when Hugues was 1ˢᵗ 'French' mayor of Besançon, office in parlt of Besançon followed naturally, and Belin comfortably belonged to robe elites of 18ᵗʰ c Besançon.

Born Besançon, ca 1612, he was (probably) son of Jean, city treasurer, and Claude Brun, daughter of a *cons* in the parlt. Early studies in Besançon, took theol degree at Bourges. He entered Benedictine abbey of Faverney (Besançon dioc), belonging to reformed observance of St-Vanne of Lorraine, possibly following a family tradition, and was professed there 29-12-1629. His pre-episcopal career was closely bound up with internal affairs of Benedictines – St-Vanne, St-Maur, Cluny – and conflicts they generated. By early 1630s he left St-Vanne for Cluny, settled mainly in leading Parisian priory of St-Martin-des-Champs (where dom Ildefonse Belin, probably a relative, resided in 1630s), and went on to hold various positions within order, inc that of grand prior of Cluny (which his immediate successor at Belley, Pierre du Laurens, also held!). From early 1640s he published a number of spiritual and other works, inc ones on alchemy, talismans, emblems of the Eucharist (1647), proofs of the truth of Christianity (1666). Latter was dedicated to Colbert, whose patronage he had managed to secure before his nom to Belley, '[que] vous avez eu la bonté de me procurer comme lieu de séiour'.

Nom 24-4-1664. Provs 7-12-1665. Consec 14-2-1666. Died 29-4-1677.

Sources: ASV, PC 63, fos 115–22. BN, Mélanges Colbert 139, fo 77–8. Pidoux de la Maduère, *Officiers du parlement de Dôle*, iii, 409–11. Lurion, *Nobiliaire de Franche-Comté*, 73–4. Dom E Martène, *Histoire de la congregation de St-Maur*, iii, 159–60. Godefroy, *Bibliothèque des bénédictins*, 15–16. P Denis, *Richelieu et la réforme des bénédictins* (Paris 1912), pp 454, 486. Guilhermo Carvalho and Jean-Yves Kind, *Besançon 1290–1676. Dictionnaire des gouverneurs et des notables* (Loray 1994), 45–7 (Belin)

Belsunce, Henri de. Marseille 1710–55.   Connected to some celebrated figures of (often Huguenot) aristocracy – Candale, Turenne, Lauzun, La Force – through his mother, bp established his own distinctive claim to fame through a long and respected career in Marseille. His ancestors, traceable to 13ᵗʰ c, were natives of lower Navarre, and subsequently served Foix and Albret dynasties, which in turn led to adoption, in generation of bp's grandfather, of Protestantism. Then and later, their marriages were with major Huguenot dynasties of the southwest who, like the Belsunce, gradually moved back into Catholic fold in following century. Bp's branch, known as Castelmoron, were settled in Agenais, of which his father became *sénéchal* in 1697, and close to La Force family lands in Périgord.

2nd son of Armand, marquis de Castelmoron, and Anne de Caumont, sister of Louis XIV's troublesome and episodic favourite, the duc de Lauzun, and granddaughter of Huguenot marshal-duc de la Force. Both parents were still Protestants when bp was born at La Force 9-12-1670, where he was baptised in Protestant faith on 21-12-1670. After his mother's conversion in 1679 (and father's in 1685), he studied with Jesuits in Paris, and subsequently entered SJ in 1691, teaching in Paris and Amiens colls, but ill health made him leave by 1701, after which he entered Périgueux seminary in 1703, where Mascaron was bp. Took MA at Cahors, 22-8-1704, followed by bacc and doct in theol the next day! *Dimissoires* for tonsure 1687, for subdeacon on 2-6-1703. Ordained priest on Quatre Temps Saturday 1703. Since 21-12-1704, he was also vic-gen of Hébert at Agen. Obtained abbey of La Réole (Lescar) on 15-8-1688, which he resigned later when bp, though by then he held abbey of Chambons O Cist (Viviers). Dep to AC 1710, he refused see of Laon in 1723, Bordeaux in 1729, and even candidacy for cardinalate! Accepted abbey of Montmmorel instead, exchanged it for St-Arnoul-de-Metz in 1729. St-Simon regarded him as a *saint évêque*, but too docile towards his Jesuit mentors, hence his involvement in persecuting Jansenists, esp Soanen at Embrun in 1727. Within Marseille itself he was resident, active, pastoral and charitable bp, esp in 1720 plague.

Nom 3-4-1709. Provs 19-2-1710. Consec 30-3-1710. Died 4-6-1755.

Sources: AN, MC, LXXXII, 102, 1-6-1709. BIUT, MS 96, fo 43v; MS 97, fo 34v. BN, MS Fr 20969, fo 68 (La Réole). Pinard, *Chronologie*, viii, 83–4. St-Simon, xvii, 227. Fénelon, *Correspondance*, xvii, 118, n 17; Anselme, *Histoire*, ix, part ii, 960–6. Albanès, *Armorial et sigillographie des eveques de Marseille*, 174–6. Chaix d'Est-Ange, *Dictionnaire des familles*, iii, 320–4. Bérengier, *Vie de Mgr Henry de Belsunce évêque de Marseille*, 2 vols.

Bénard de Rézay, Cyprien-Gabriel. Angoulême 1692–1737.   Bénard (sometimes misspelled Bernard) family origins lay in Tours, where they belonged to upper *bourgeoisie* in early 16th c, and provided a lt-gen in *bailliage* as early as 1470. Formal ennoblement came via an office of SR in 1534, while next generation held office in the parlts of Rennes and Paris successively. Thereafter their activities centred on Paris, where bp's grandfather and father were both parlementaires, with the latter securing an office of MR and serving as a prov intendant in the 1630s. By then they were connected to robe families such as the Forget and Fortia, while his father's marriage to Françoise Méliand made the bp of Angoulême a cousin of Victor Méliand, bp of Gap and Alet.

Born 1650 Paris. Son of Cyprien, MR, *cons d'état* in 1682, and Françoise Méliand, daughter of a *maître des comptes*, married in 1645. Studied in Paris, MA in July 1668, 7th place in 1676 theol lic, doct of theol 25-5-1682. Also ordained priest in 1682. Prior *in comm* of St-Aigulphe OSB (Sens) when nom to Angoulême. As bp, he completed building of seminary largely from personal resources, confiding it to Lazarists. He was strongly opposed to Jesuits and in 1718 adhered to appeal against *Unigenitus*, possibly under pressure from Jansenist clergy in dioc. Reputed an able theologian, his writings were burned after his death 'par des ordres supérieurs'.

Nom 1-11-1689. Provs 10-3-1692. Consec 24-8-1692. Died 5-1-1737.

Sources: ASV, PC 86, fos 245–69. BN, MS Fr 7655, fos 90–1. AN, Y 229, fo 19-2-1645 (c.m. of parents). Lapeyre and Scheurer, *Notaires et secrétaires du roi*, i, 29–30. Bluche, *L'Origine*, 81–2. Fénelon, *Correspondance*, xvii, 313, n 17. Bonney, *Political Change*, 201. Saulnier, *Parlement de Bretagne*, i, 79–80.

Berger de Malisolles, François. Gap 1706–38.   The Berger were a relatively obscure family from the Viennois-Dauphiné, of whom virtually nothing is known until bp's generation. He was one of 10 children, 3 of them became nuns, one an officier in French army, one a *cons* in Grenoble parlt from 1692 onwards. 2 sons entered the church, François and Claude, who became a canon of Die cath, where the future bp also served for a number of years as gr vic – all of them were regarded as strongly pro-Jesuit.

Born Vienne 1668. Son of François, sgr de Moydieu, 'vi-bailli' of Vienne, and Anne de Tarnésieu. Seems to have studied in Vienne or Valence, where he took doct in theol in 1695, the year he was ordained priest. He had spent several years first at St-Magloire and then at Missions Etrangères seminary in Paris, associating with St-Sulpice in subsequent years, suggesting a streak of opportunism, since the curé of St-Sulpice was apparently instrumental in obtaining mitre for him, according to one source. Even if true, that is probably only a small part of his success, since as canon and dean of Die before 1701, and as vic-gen during and after vacancy in 1702, he showed a talent for organisation and pastoral activity in recently restored dioc previously subsumed into Valence, while attendance at the 1705 AC may have enabled him to impress a wider audience. He appears to have refused succession to Le Camus at Grenoble in 1707, despite unspecified *démarches* and *voeux*. He was a resident, hyper-active and conscientious bishop, known as the 'saint of the Alps'. Strongly anti-Jansenist, one of 1st bps to issue *mandement* versus *Réflexions morales*.

Nom 3-4-1706 (after resign by Hervé). Provs 15-11-1706. Consec 2-1-1707. Died 21-8-1738.

Sources: ASV, PC 99, fos 579–92. BN, PO 296, nos 6453–5. AN, L 730, pièce 1, no 30. AD Hautes-Alpes, G 1355. *Inventaire-sommaire des A D antérieures à 1790. Hautes-Alpes*, série G, vol iii (Gap 1897), xxi–xxii. St-Simon, xx, 349. *Gall Chr Nov*, Gap, cols 526–7. Virieux, 'Parlement de Grenoble', 136.

Bertier, Antoine-François. Rieux 1662–1705.   3 members of this distinguished Toulou-sain parlt family had become bps under Henri IV and Louis XIII, 2 of them holding Rieux from 1602 to 1662, the other that of Montauban 1651–74. Their continuing prominence in Toulouse and excellent *dévot* connections made them capable of attracting further royal patronage.

Antoine-François was son of Jean, sgr de Montrabé, *prés* in Toulouse parlt (1611–52), and Marie-Louise Lecomte, born Toulouse 1-8-1633. Canon of Toulouse, *cons-clerc* at parlt from early age, elected dep to 1655 AC. His uncle, Jean-Louis, bp of Rieux, resigned abbeys of Lezat OSB (Rieux) and La Capelle O Prem (Toulouse) as well as *prevoté* of St-Etienne cath (Toulouse) to him. At end of 1655–7 AC, uncle also secured Mazarin's agreement to nom him as his suc-cessor at Rieux. But papal concerns about effects of Jansenism among French clergy, and terms of uncle's resignation and pension off the see, delayed bulls, and Antoine-François, himself sus-pected of Jansenist sympathies, was made to wait until uncle's last months before obtaining provs. A wealthy 'évêque grand seigneur', with a splendid residence and library in Toulouse, he was highly learned, esp in canon law, and regarded as a capable bp, close to Charles-Maurice Le Tellier, Pavillon, Percin de Montgaillard and Caulet, and hostile to Jesuits – hence endur-ing suspicions of Jansenism, evidenced by preference for Oratorians to run Rieux seminary from 1675 onwards.

Nom n.d. (1657/1661). Provs 17-4-1662. Consec 25-6-1662. Died 29-10-1705.

Sources: ASV, no PC file. AN, G 8* 653 (*in fine*, no folio no); L 740, pièce 1, Rieux, no 85. *Gallia*, xiii, col 197. Contrasty, *Histoire de la cité de Rieux-Volvestre*, 297–308.

Bertier, David-Nicolas. Blois 1697–1719.   Cousin of André-François above, and nephew of Pierre, bp of Montauban (1651–74). Son of Jean-François, sgr de St-Geniès, *cons* in Toulouse parlt, 1641–80, and Antoinette de Flory. Born Vabres, 1652, raised Toulouse, but seems to have been entrusted to bp of Montauban, where he completed early studies under Louis Bruel, his preceptor. After taking MA and bacc in theol at Toulouse in 1670, he moved to Univ of Paris where he was MA in Oct 1670. Studied theol at Sorbonne, taking 92nd place in 1676 lic, but delayed taking doct until 22-8-1697, i.e. *after* his nom to Blois. Priest since about 1676. Dep to 1675 AC for Toulouse, when abbot *in comm* of Belleperche O Cist (Montauban). Resided in St-Sulpice's *petite communauté* at same time as Fénelon, to whom he was close and whom he joined (as did Louis Milon and others) on missions in western France after Revocation of 1685. Also preached in Paris, and esp at Nouvelles Catholiques convent, while Fénelon was superior, in 1685 and 1688. Regarded as something of a specialist 'en controverse', Godet of Chartres made him vic-gen in 1690 with special responsibility for *nouveaux convertis* of Blois and Vendôme parts of dioc, but also with a view to subdivision of Chartres dioc and creation of see of Blois,which Rome took several years to approve. As suffragan of Paris and protégé of Godet, he was later involved in *Maximes des Saints* and Jansenist affairs. Obtained abbey of Relecq O Cist (St-Pol-de-Léon) in 1706.

Nom 21-3-1693. Provs 1-7-1697. Consec 15-9-1697. Died 29-8-1719.

Sources: ASV, PC 91, fos 39–59. Fénelon, *Correspondance*, iii, 59–60, n 1. Dangeau, iv, 176. Sourches, iv, 156. St-Simon, xvi, 151, n 2. Bergin, *Making*, 574–6.

Berton. *See* **Crillon**.

Béthune, Armand. Le Puy 1665–1703.   Few families of French aristocracy can have been as ubiquitous and enduring as Béthunes, whose internal religious differences did not hinder their progress. Bps of Le Puy and Verdun were nephews of Henri de Béthune, abp of Bordeaux 1646–80. Their father's marriage firmly secured their position at court under Louis XIV where the Beauvillier family played a major role over 2 generations.

Born Paris 7-8-1635, son of Hippolyte, comte de Chelles, and Anne-Marie de Beauvillier de St-Aignan, married in 1629. Initial studies at Benedictine abbey of Pontlevoy, while 'educated' in church affairs by his uncle, Abp of Bordeaux, who also made him canon of St-André cath. Studied phil and theol for 6 years, but took doct in canon law from Bourges ca 1658–9. Abbot *in comm* of La Vernusse OSA (Bourges) at early age, which he exchanged for St-Martin-de-Villemardy OSB (Chartres) soon after confirmation as bp of Le Puy. Dep to 1660 AC. One of earliest post-Mazarin noms, initially to Evreux, then to Le Puy, but provs were delayed until 1665 by combination of circumstances which affected other nominees at this time.

Nom 19-8-1661. Provs 22-4-1665. Consec 12-7-1665. Died 10-12-1703.

Sources: ASV, PC, 63, fos 38–51. Bergin, *Making*, 576. DHGE, viii, 1254–5.

Béthune, Hippolyte. Verdun 1681–1720.   Younger brother of Armand, above. 6th child of his parents, born in 1646, baptised in St-Paul parish church, Paris. Studied phil and theol, and followed his brother by taking degrees, esp the doct in theol, at Bourges, but he also enrolled in Paris canon law fac, where he took bacc in canon law, July 1669. Ordained priest 12-4-1671 by brother, Bp of Le Puy, whose patronage had already secured for him post of dean of Le Puy cath. Abbot *in comm* of Beaupré O Cist (Toul) in Sept 1666 thanks to resign of an elder brother, he also became *aumônier* of Queen Marie-Thérèse in 1660s. At Verdun, he continued philo-Jansenist policies of his predecessor, Hocquincourt, during his long episcopate. Hostile to *Unigenitus*, he banned Jesuits in dioc, 1715.

Nom 6-9-1680. Provs 23-6-1681. Consec 3-8-1681. Died 24-8-1720.

Sources: ASV, PC 80, fos 726–40. AN, MM 1059, p 285; MM 1115, fo 85r (bacc in canon law, 16-7-1669). BN, MS Fr 7651, fo 147 (*bienfaits du roi*). St-Simon, xxix, 299. DHGE, viii, 1257–8. Taveneaux, *Jansénisme en Lorraine*, 177–9.

Bezons. *See* **Bazin.**

Biscarras. *See* **Rotundis.**

Bissy. *See* **Thyard.**

Blouet de Camilly, François. Toul 1705–21, Tours 1723.   Originating among the bourgeoisie of 16th c Caen, the Blouet family gradually moved into officeholding in finance and lower law courts there. Bp's great-grandfather, Tassin, was ennobled for services unspecified in Jan 1589, as was bp's grandfather, Pierre, a *contrôleur des tailles* in Caen *élection*, in 1610. But they remained relatively obscure until bp's own father, Augustin, became a *cons* at Rouen parlt in 1656 – his marriage in 1658 to daughter of a *procureur du roi* at Pont-Audemer confirms their limited social advance, although bp's 2 brothers took up military/naval rather than robe careers, with one of them becoming vice-admiral of the Levant. Blouet family members were prominent in *dévot*-reformist circles in Normandy (Eudes, Bernières, Renty, du Fossé), with bp's grandfather financing some of early missions of Jean Eudes, while an uncle, Jean-Jacques, succeeded Eudes as sup-gen of Eudist congregation in 1680; another uncle was *théologal* of Bayeux. Along the way, they picked up wider connections in French church, and it was the Eudist Jean-Jacques who first introduced future bp to Tronson of St-Sulpice, enabling him to develop his own ties with major figures like Brisacier.

Born Rouen 22-5-1664, son of Augustin and Catherine Grossin, married in 1654. Studied in Paris: MA in Aug 1682, 10th place in 1692 theol lic, during which he was prior of Sorbonne, followed by doct 30-9-1692. Priest since 1692. He spent about 2 years at St-Sulpice from Nov 1683 onwards, and later resided in Missions Etrangères seminary. Abbot *in comm* of

Val Richer O Cist (Bayeux) in 1693 and St-Pierre-de-Dives (Sées) in 1699. *Official* and vic-gen of Strasbourg in 1694, in succession to Martin Ratabon, nom bp of Ypres, but unable to become canon of the grand chapter, given his 'petite noblesse'. His relatively long stay at Strasbourg revealed both his organisational and reformist abilities. St-Simon claimed that it was Camilly's *tours de souplesse* which enabled future Cardinal de Rohan to become coadj of Strasbourg, which brought him his own reward in due course. At Toul, he also showed peacemaking skills after the clashes of Bissy years, refusing to countenance open Jansenism after *Vineam Domini*, but leaving discreet Jansenist activity in his dioc unharmed. His promotion to Tours was shortlived.

Nom 11-5-1704. Provs 7-9-1705. Consec 22-11-1705. Nom to Tours, 10-1-1721. Provs 20-1-1723. Died 17-10-1723.

Sources: ASV, PC 98, fos 593–603. BN, MS Fr 20969, fos 88–9, 150 (for abbeys); PO 373, no 8152. St-Simon, vii, 79; xl, 255. Frondeville, *Conseillers au parlement de Normandie 1641–1715*, 307–8. Vergé-Franceschi, *Officiers généraux de la marine*, vii, 47–8. Taveneaux, *Jansénisme en Lorraine*, 213ff. Châtellier 'Le Vicaire général François Blouet de Camilly', 75–92. Gatz, *Bischöfe*, 33–4. Berthelot du Chesnay, *Missions de Jean Eudes*, 327–8.

Bochart de Champigny, Guillaume. Valence 1693–1705.   Family originally from Vézelay in Burgundy, present in Paris in 15th c, where Jean was ennobled by an office in Paris parlt in 1466. 2 generations later (in 1548), Claude Bochart was 1st wife of François de La Porte, Richelieu's maternal grandfather, from whom La Porte de la Meilleraye family descended. By then Bochart family was well entrenched in highest robe circles of Paris, related to families as distinguished as Briçonnet, Tronson, Allegrain, Vigny and others, and reinforced after 1600 by marriages with Molé, Le Charron and Luillier families. One branch embraced Protestantism and persevered with it until well into 17th c. Richelieu's ministry saw Jean V (d 1630), bp's great-grandfather, briefly hold ministerial office – as did his nephew, Sublet des Noyers, after his death. Thereafter, the Champigny and Saron branches continued to remain faithful to their robe-parlt traditions, though the Champigny branch preferred the sword to robe in 18th c. Fathers of the 2 bps were both *cons* in the parlt, MRs and prov intendants! Without ever quite reaching same heights as in 1620s, they remained among best connected and most *dévot* of Parisian robe families, as evidenced by continual presence of several members in cath chapters (notably ND de Paris), religious orders and convents.

Born ca 1648, Guillaume was son of Jean VII, sgr de Champigny, *cons* in parlt, MR (1645), intendant, *cons d'état*, and Marie de Boyvin, his 1st wife, daughter of a Rouen parlt family boasting a bp of Avranches under Louis XIII and related to Péricard bps of Evreux and Angoulême. Studied hum, phil and theol in Paris, taking his MA in July 1666, 19th place in 1674 theol lic, and finishing with doct 16-5-1676. Priest since 4-4-1676, ordained by Bp Péricard of Angoulême. Canon, then archdeacon in Rouen cath for 14 years before episcopate, also vic-gen and *official* in Pontoise, a uniquely valuable springboard towards the episcopate. Dep to 1675, 1682 and 1685 ACs.

Nom 5-10-1691. Provs 12-10-1693. Consec 30-11-1693. Died 4-7-1705.

Sources: ASV, PC 87, fos 778–90. BN, MS Lat 15440, p 250; MS Lat 15673, p 22. Bluche, *L'Origine*, 95–6. Dubé, *Intendants*, 280–6. Bayard 'Jean Bochart de Champigny (1561–1630)', 39–52. Bonney, *Political Change*, 79–80. Bergin, *Making*, 577, 681–2.

Bochart de Saron, François. Clermont 1692–1715.   Son of François, *cons* in *gr conseil*, MR (1634), intendant, *cons d'état*, and Madeleine Luillier, from an equally distinguished and well-connected Paris robe family.

Born 1633 Paris where he studied hum under a tutor who was a disciple of Gassendi, and took bacc in theol, 1661. Priest since Easter 1668. Canon and *chambrier* of ND chapter in Paris. Dep to several ACs (1660, 1665) before nom to Clermont, which he obtained 'à la sollicitation de son frère gouverneur de Péronne', once Claude de St-Georges moved to Poitiers.

Initially used services of Étienne Champflour, future bp of La Rochelle, as vicar *in spiritualibus*, but he was directly involved in admin of Clermont from 1688. Anti-Noailles in 1711 along with royal confessor Tellier.

Nom 18-5-1687. Provs 10-3-1692. Consec 31-8-1692. Died 11-8-1715.

Sources: ASV, PC 86, fos 222–43. AN, Y 169, fo 45v (c.m. of parents 31-8-1629). AN, L 730, pièce 1, no 3. *Lettres de Séguier*, ii, 1186–8. St-Simon, xxii, 213. Welter, *La Réforme ecclésiastique à Clermont*, 239, 242–3.

Boissieu. *See* **Frétat.**

Boissonade d'Ortie, Guillaume. Bazas 1668–84. This family's origins are difficult to discern, but they were resident in Agen, where they had achieved the status of town-hall notables by mid-16th c, if not earlier. Their ranks also included medical practicioners and, increasingly lawyers. Officeholders of varying types, virtually all based in or near Agen itself, only really emerged from early 17th c onwards, in course of which intermarriage with similar families consolidated their status. Over several generations after 1605, family members served as *juges-mages* and *pres* in *présidial* court of Agen, initially thanks to bp's father's marriage into Ortie (or Orty) family, which enabled him to succeed his father-in-law as *juge-mage*. Ortie marriage connected them to better-placed local families, some of whom held office in Bordeaux parlt. The only significant departure from such local rootedness was represented by military career of bp's elder brother, Antoine, known as 'capitaine d'Ortie' whose extended service from early 1640s onwards earned him, albeit belatedly, promotion to governorship of Bapaume (1672) and rank of *maréchal de camp* in 1677, having married a Beaumanoir de Lavardin (a sister of Jean-Baptiste, bp of Rennes 1677–1711) en route, in 1659.

Born Agen ca 1622. Son of Antoine, *prés* and *juge mage* of Agen, and Françoise d'Ortie, daughter of *prés* in Agen *présidial*, married in 1605. Probably studied initially in Agen, and later at Cahors, where bachelor in theol in 1658, and finally at Toulouse, where he took lic in law. Within months of nom to Bazas, he took doct in canon law in Paris (Dec 1667). Priest for 9–10 years before nom as bp. Initially a canon in *collégiale* of St-Capraise in Agen, he was later canon and cantor in Agen cath. Nom to Bazas subsequent to refusal by Étienne Le Camus, June 1667. Relatively uneventful episcopate during which he laid foundations of new seminary, which he confided to Barnabites, shortly before death.

Nom 27-7-1667. Provs 30-1-1668. Consec 29-4-1668. Died 22-9-1684.

Sources: ASV, PC 67, fos 803–19. BN, PO 395, no 8730; Doss bleus 108, no 2640; MS Fr 7652, fo 28; 7657, fo 208. AN, MM 1115, fo 59v (canon law doct, 29-12-1667). AD Lot-et-Garonne, B 35, fos 292–9 (c.m. of bp's parents 17-4-1605). Pinard, *Chronologie*, vi, 434. *Hierarchia Catholica*, iv, 405, n 4. Compère and Julia, *Collèges français*, i, 117–18.

Bonnin de Chalucet, Armand-Louis. Toulon 1692–1712. The Bonnin were a relatively anonymous family of established nobility, with branches in Poitou and Brittany. Marriage with Urbaine de Maillé-Brézé (a relative of Richelieu) in 1634 prompted bp's father to move to Brittany, where he was made lt-gen of city and county of Nantes under governorship of Richelieu's cousin, La Meilleraye, and was later elected to represent Nantes nobility at planned 1651 Estates-General. Also served regularly in royal armies from mid-1630s, he was still gov of Nantes when Retz was imprisoned there, and was succeeded there by his son after his death in 1670. It seems likely that bp's sister Anne-Louise's marriage to famous intendant of Languedoc, Basville de Lamoignon, in 1672, guaranteed the Bonnin some additional connections to court and admin circles in later years, since bp's 2 brothers died childless.

Born and baptised in parish of Ste Radegonde, Nantes, 1641. 3rd and youngest son of Jean-François, marquis de Chalucet, and Marie Urbaine de Maillé-Brézé. Univ studies in Paris, matriculated in 1655, MA in June 1659, but did not proceed beyond bacc in theol, although his bulls say he held lic in canon law. Priest since 1675. *Official* of Nantes for one year *sede vacante*. Abbot *in comm* of Vaux de Cernay, 1673. Also seems to have engaged in converting Huguenots in Poitiers and region. Acted energetically and firmly during 1707 siege of Toulon, and left personal fortune to hospital of Toulon which he had done much to found and finance. Nom 31-5-1684. Provs 4-2-1692. Consec 25-3-1692. Died 10-7-1712.

Sources: ASV, PC 86, fos 134–51. BN, PO 413, no 9199. AUP reg 97, fo 37r. AN, MC, LXXV, 160, 9-4-1672 (c.m. of Mlle Bonnin and Basville); MC, LXXII, 121, 23-3-1713 (for bp's testament). Lefèvre d'Ormesson, *Journal*, ii, 630. Antoine, *Gouvernement*, 143–4. Beauchet-Filleau, *Dictionnaire*, i, 620–5. Chaix d'Est-Ange, *Dictionnaire des familles*, v, 295–6. Retz, *Mémoires*, 955. Tallemant, *Historiettes*, 329, 330. *Gall Chr Nov*, v, cols 673–8.

Bossuet, Jacques-Bénigne. Condom 1670–1, Meaux 1681–1704.   *L'aigle de Meaux* was descended from a family of wheelwrights based in Seurre, Burgundy, in early 15th c. Bourgeois of Seurre by 1460, notables and mayors by early 16th c, they gradually changed their name to Bousseut/Bossuet. A century later, they had begun moving to Dijon and, initially, to office in *chambre des comptes*, with early marriages to families that would later figure prominently in local and national politics – such as Le Goux de la Berchère. Their *noblesse* begins with Antoine, *auditeur aux comptes* in 1540s. Bp's grandfather, Jacques, was their 1st parlt, a royalist during the League, who married Claude Bretagne, from a more powerful parlt family. Eldest son, Claude, was also *cons* in parlt, *maire* of Dijon in 1647; the 2nd son, Benigne, bp's father, moved to Metz as a *cons* in the parlt, where his uncle Antoine de Bretagne was made *pr prés* by Richelieu. His father even succeeded his most famous son as dean of Metz cath in 1665, having taken orders in widowhood. Another uncle, François Bossuet, 'le Riche', *secrétaire du conseil*, was destroyed by fall of Fouquet and *chambre de justice*. Bp's brother, Antoine, enjoyed Condé's favour, and became *rec-gén* of Estates of Burgundy in 1652, held it until 1674 when he became MR, and prov intendant at Soissons in 1685.

Born Dijon where baptised 27-9-1627, 7th child and youngest surviving son of Bénigne, then *avocat* in Dijon, later *cons* in parlt of Metz (1638–58), and Marguerite Mochet, daughter of a fellow *avocat* in the parlt, married in 1618. Early studies in SJ coll des Godrans at Dijon, moved to Paris in 1642 where he took MA at Univ, July 1647, and 3rd place in 1652 theol lic. A 'Navarriste', he was made doct of theol 16-5-1652. Tonsured in Dec 1635, he was ordained priest 16-3-1652. Canon of Metz cath in 1640, thanks to father's move to parlt there, later *grand archidiacre*, a post in which his widowed father succeeded him, when he became dean of Metz in 1665, and where he resided and preached for 4 years. Influenced by Vincent de Paul and St-Lazare in early days in Paris, whose salons he also frequented, he developed ties to Port-Royal during 1660s. By time of nom to Condom, such ties had diminished, though he remained a defender of a rigorist theol for rest of his career. Nom preceptor to Dauphin in Sept 1670, after confirmation as bp of Condom (Aug 1670), he abandoned see within 2 years, only rejoining episcopate in 1681.

Nom to Condom 13-9-1669. Provs 2-6-1670. Consec 21-9-1670. Resign 31-10-1672. Nom to Meaux 2-5-1681. Provs 17-11-1681. Died 12-4-1704.

Sources: ASV, PC 68, fos 206–24. Bossuet, *Correspondance*, xv, 431–516 ('Chronologie de la vie de Bossuet'). Dessert, *Argent, pouvoir et société*, 544–5. Béguin, *Princes de Condé*, 403–4. Boisnard, *Les Phélypeaux*, 165. Thomas, *Les Bossuet en Bourgogne*.

Bouchet. *See* **Lobière.**

Bourchenu. *See* **Moret.**

Bourlemont, Louis Anglure de. (Fréjus 1679–80, Carcassonne 1680–1), Bordeaux 1681–97.   Younger brother of Charles-François, bp of Aire (1650–9), Castres (1659–64), and abp of Toulouse (1664–9). Born Bourlemont (Toul) 30-8-1618, son of Claude, and Angélique d'Adjaceto. Studied canon law at Pont-à-Mousson, and took doct *in utr* there in

April 1658. By then he had certainly attracted attention of Mazarin who chose him in 1658 to be France's Auditor of the Roman Rota. This move probably explains timing of his degree and also his clerical orders, up to that of deacon, all taken in quick succession during 1658. The lateness of his tonsure (1656 or 1657) suggests that a church career may not have been intended for him initially. Served during tense years of Franco-papal relations, esp after 1662, and helped negotiate Treaty of Pisa ending the standoff, acting as France's *chargé d'affaires* at various times in Rome. Obtained 2 wealthy abbeys of La Grace and L'Isle de Medoc. Louis XIV tried to lure him back to France with offers of bishoprics (Tournai 1668, Lavaur 1669), but he declined. Only 10 years later did he accept Fréjus, but did not take possession of it, as he was nom to Carcassonne instead in Jan 1680. Having obtained bulls for Carcassonne, in July 1680, Abp Béthune of Bordeaux died, and Louis XIV nom him as successor. In reality, he only ever had one dioc. His record at Bordeaux not easy to characterise but he seems to have been a good admin, suspicious of extremes, and pacifier of disputes.

Nom 24-2-1679. Provs 17-7-1679. Consec Rome 1-10-1679. Nom to Carcassonne 12-1-1680. Provs 15-7-1680. Nom to Bordeaux 10-9-1680. Provs 28-4-1681. Died 9-11-1697.

Sources: ASV, PC 78, fos 176–85; Sacra Romana Rota, *Processus in admissione auditorum*, vol 81. BN, MS Fr 7652, fos 44, 64. Cerchiari, *Capellani Pape et Apostolicae Sedes auditorum causarum sacri palatii apostolici seu Sacra Romana Rota*, ii, 177–8. St-Simon, v, 36. Peyrous, *Réforme à Bordeaux*, ii, 725–7.

Bouthillier, François. Troyes 1679–97 (resign).   Although their maker and protector Richelieu had long since disappeared, and Mazarin had destroyed their ministerial ambitions, by Louis XIV's time the Bouthilliers were securely entrenched within highest echelons of robe and sword, esp through numerous marriages of daughters.

Born and baptised in parish of St-Paul, Paris, 14-9-1642. 5th son of Léon, comte de Chavigny, former sec of state under Richelieu, and Anne Phélypeaux de Villesavin, niece of 2 secs of state. Studied at Univ of Paris, MA in Aug 1658, 82nd (and last) place in 1666 theol lic, with doct following 7-6-1666, Bossuet presiding. Became royal almoner a few days later. Ordained priest 28-3-1666, with papal dispensation *de defectu aetatis*. Obtained benefices early in career – abbeys of Oigny in Burgundy, Sellières in Chapagne, later the priories of Beaumont-en-Auge, Pont-sur-Seine, Chaoisy au Bac previously held by uncle, Victor, abp of Tours. Canon and archdeacon of Tours, also thanks to uncle. Dep to 1670 AC, and *cons d'état* before episcopate. Nom to Rennes in 1676, but resigned it after receiving bulls, and moved to Troyes in 1678. Resigned Troyes to nephew in 1697, and retreated into isolated existence – out of remorse for his worldliness during episcopate, according to contemporaries. Came out of retirement in 1715 and was made member of *conseil de regence*.

Nom to Rennes, 3-2-1676. Provs 22-6-1676. Nom to Troyes 17-10-1678. Provs 6-2-1679. Consec 9-4-1679. Resign before 9-3-1697. Died 15-9-1731.

Sources: ASV, PC 75, fos 545–55; PC 78, fos 565–73 (Troyes). BN, MS Lat 15440, p 228; MS Lat 15673, p 13; MS Fr 7651, fo 142 (*bienfaits du roi*). Poutet, 'Docteurs', 295, no 495. St-Simon, iv, 115–19; iv, 363–4. Sévigné, *Correspondance*, v, p 17–18. Béguin, *Princes de Condé*, 405–6. Prévost, *Diocèse de Troyes*, iii, 1–26.

Bouthillier, Denis-François. Troyes 1697–1718, Sens 1718–30.   Nephew of François. Born in Paris 23-6-1665. 4th son of Armand Bouthillier de Chavigny and Elisabeth Bossuet. Studied in Paris, where he took MA in Aug 1684, 8th place in 1692 lic, with doct at Sorbonne 10-4-1692, of which he was a *socius* by then. Appears to have been a *habitué* of Missions Etrangères during 1680s, though he did not take priestly orders until 22-3-1692. Canon of Troyes in 1684, he was also abbé of Pont, then of Chavigny, Bassefontaine O Prem (Troyes) in Nov 1687, followed by Oigny in 1697, Mortemer (1703) and St-Loup-de-Troyes (1709), partly to compensate for mediocre revenues of Troyes itself. Vic-gen of Troyes under his uncle with title of archidiacre of Sézanne, from 1693. Dep to ACs of Clergy of 1693, 1695, 1702, 1705,

1710. His uncle, a member of Regency council from 1715, got him see of Sens in 1716. A respected figure whom St-Simon thought might have become abp of Paris after Noailles in 1729.

Nom 7-4-1697. Provs 10-3-1699. Consec 2-4-1699. Nom to Sens 21-1-1716. Provs 11-5-1718. Died 9-11-1730.

Sources: ASV, PC 92, fos 486–504. BN, MS Fr 20969, fo 61rv. Arch MEP, vol 8, pp 153–8; vol 9, pp 479–81. Bossuet, *Correspondance*, viii, 233. St-Simon, iv, 118, 453–6. Prévost, *Diocèse de Troyes*, iii, 26–48.

Brancas, Henri-Ignace de. Lisieux 1714–60.   Like many other families, the Brancas claimed a glorious descent – in their case from the famous Brancaccio family of Naples, but no evidence exists for this. They were ennobled through commensal office in service of René d'Anjou in 15ᵗʰ c, while the Céreste, which were the senior branch, obtained a Spanish grandeeship in 1730 and French ducal status under Louis XVI. Meanwhile, they could boast an impressive roll call of high officials, including cardinals and bps, among their ranks from later medieval period onwards. Heavily involved in miltary and political events in Provence during Wars of Religion, a tradition sustained under Louis XIV, when their military activities were impressive. One of bp's brothers became a marshal of France, the other abp of Aix.

Born Pernes, Carpentras dioc, 6-11-1684, Henri-Ignace was 4th son of Henri, baron, later marquis de Céreste, and Dorothée de Cheylus. Having taken Paris MA in 1705, he began theol studies there, taking bacc in Jan 1706, 5th place in 1710 lic, completed by doct 16-5-1710. Ordained priest in 1710. Vic-gen of Meaux for 4 years before nom to Lisieux. Also *aumônier du roi* since Feb 1710. Abbot *in comm* of St-Gildas-des-Bois OSB (Nantes) in 1706, Chambre-Fontaine O Prem (Meaux) in 1712.

Nom 15-8-1714. Provs 19-11-1714. Consec 13-1-1715. Died 31-3-1760.

Sources: ASV, PC 103, fos 419–30. AN, 0¹ 55, fo 14v. BM Aix, MS 257, p. 265. St-Simon, xxi, 87; xxix, 77–9. Vindry, *État major, gendarmerie*, 390. Boisnard, *Touraine*, no 420. *Encyclopédie des Bouches-du-Rhône*, iv, part ii, 102–3. Chaix d'Est-Ange, *Dictionnaire des familles*, vi, 352–7. Antoine, *Gouvernement*, 54. Labande, *Avignon au xvᵉ siècle*.

Brienne. *See* **Loménie**.

Briqueville de la Luzerne, Henri. Cahors 1693–1741.   This old noble family from lower Normandy embraced Calvinism during the 16ᵗʰ c, and several of its members played an active role in Normandy and elsewhere during Wars of Religion. Bp's great-great-grandfather, a strong supporter of Henri IV, was the 1ˢᵗ of them to become a *maréchal de camp*, abjuring Calvinism in 1628; his son held the same rank after him. Their military traditions flourished under Louis XIV, and they produced a vice-admiral of France under Louis XV. Their family alliances improved correspondingly from mid-17ᵗʰ c, and they added those of Condé, Tourville and Chateaurenault families to existing ones like Harcourt, Madaillan and Monchy. Bp's own father, having been gov of Mont-St-Michel and lt-gen of Caen, became governor of Louis XIV's illegitimate son, the comte de Vermandois, admiral of France, from 1680 to 1683. Bp's sister married the comte de la Chaize, nephew of king's confessor, making their connections all the stronger.

Born in parish of St-Gregoire, Isigny, Bayeux dioc, in 1658, son of Louis-Gabriel, marquis de Briqueville and gov of Mont-St-Michel, and Marguerite de Bonvoust, married in 1656. Studied in Univ of Paris, where he was MA in Aug 1677, and then theol at coll of Navarre, taking a very honourable 2ⁿᵈ place in 1686 lic, finishing off with doct in Paris 23-4-1686. Priest since 1686. Abbot *in comm* of Chantemerle (Troyes) in Nov 1680, *aumônier ordinaire* of Dauphine in 1686 in succession to Fléchier. Also given abbey of Garde-Dieu O Cist (Cahors) in 1706.

Nom 31-5-1693. Provs 28-9-1693. Consec 28-10-1693. Died 16-6-1741.

Sources: ASV, PC 87, fos 191–201. BN, MS Fr 7657, fos 56–7 (*bienfaits du roi*); MS Fr 20969, fo 27; MS Fr 23498, fo 87; MS Lat 17025, fo 24. Pinard, *Chronologie*, vi, 60–1, 164–5, 413, 570–1. Pellot, *Notes*, 13, 251. St-Simon, xvi, 397, n 5; xvi, 397. Chaix d'Est-Ange, *Dictionnaire des familles*, vii, 76–9. Vergé-Franceschi, *Officiers généraux de la marine*, vii, 58–9.

Brisay de Denonville, Jean-François. Comminges 1693–1710. An old noble family, the eldest branch of which disappeared in 16th c, the Brisay were originally from area around Mirebeau in Poitou, but a junior branched settled in Beauce, where marriage of bp's *trisaieul* enabled them to take place of Hémard de Denonville family which was dying out by mid-16th c. With close connections to the Longueville-Rothelin family, the next 2 generations were committed Huguenots, with bp's grandfather, a Sully client, playing important part in local and national Huguenot politics until the 1610s. But bp's parents converted to Catholicism in 1636, some years before his birth. Father seems to have entered Mazarin's service, and opened up avenues for his children, the eldest of whom, Jacques-René, the marquis of Denonville, after years of military service, was successively gov of French Canada (1685) and, on his recall in 1689, quickly installed as *sous-governeur* of children of Monseigneur, Dauphin of France, which in turn entailed close relations with the influential duc de Beauvillier, their governor.

Born Denonville in Chartres dioc, 4-10-1641, one of 13 sons of Pierre and Louise d'Alès de Corbet. Early education in Jesuit coll, and remained strongly pro-Jesuit thereafter. Lic *in utr* from Orléans, but no degree in theol, even though he studied it for up to 5 years. Priest since 1671. Archdeacon of Blois in Chartres dioc (1659) and canon of Chartres from 1663 to 1676, when he became *chambrier*, an office he resigned to nephew on nom to Comminges. Vic-gen of Chartres in 1677, he was also *official* there for some years. This brought him into close contact with Maintenon and her confidant Godet, bp of Chartres, and he was involved with affairs of St-Cyr on her behalf. Obtained abbeys of La Bussiere O Cist (Autun) in 1686 (resigned in 1693) and St-Pierre-de-Caunes OSB (Narbonne) in 1689. At Comminges, he had the reputation of being an energetic bp, with strong anti-Jansenist streak.

Nom 31-5-1693. Provs 5-10-1693. Died 12-4-1710.

Sources: ASV, PC 87, fos 224–34. AN, L 730, pièce 1, no 6. Merlet, *Dignitaires de l'eglise ND de Chartres*, 90. Pinard, *Chronologie*, vi, 477–8. Chaix d'Est-Ange, *Dictionnaire des familles*, vii, 125–9. St-Simon, xx, 94–5. Prince-Falmagne, *Un marquis du grand siècle*. Boisnard, *Touraine*, no 457. Contrasty, *Histoire des éveques de Comminges*, 380–7.

Brulart de Genlis, Charles. Embrun 1669–1714. The Brûlart were originally from Champagne, where they claimed descent from medieval counts of Champagne, but it was through Parisian municipal office in 16th c that they initially made their mark, and obtained noble status. One of them, Pierre, sgr de Genlis, served as sec of state under Henri III before the great dismissals of 1588, but the Genlis branch was subsequently, if temporarily, eclipsed by rise of the Sillery branch under Henri IV whose political demise after 1624 under Louis XIII and Richelieu was equally sharp and terminal. If they were not wholly eclipsed by mid-17th c, when both branches had ceased to hold ministerial or other office, it was largely thanks to the extensive and valuable aristocractic connections which they had, and were still, acquiring (Hallwin, Chabot, La Rochefoucauld), and which saw them heavily involved in military service to crown. 3 of the abp of Embrun's brothers died in service in 1670s.

Charles was born in family château of Genlis near Noyon. Born 16-3-1633, son of Florimond, marquis de Genlis, and Charlotte de Blicourt. Relatively little known about early years or studies, and only took lic in canon law, Paris, in July 1668, the week *following* his nom to Embrun – but soon enough for it to be mentioned by witnesses in his *de vita et moribus* enquiry. He spent a few months at St-Sulpice seminary in 1658. Priest for 7 years before nom, and had some experience of preaching, notably in Paris parish church of St-Gervais et Prothais.

A royal almonership was a more useful route to advancement, which also included gift of abbey of Genlis in 1666, though he held abbey of Joyenval (Chartres), which he surrendered in order to succeed Aubusson at Embrun, since 1649. A resident and conscientious as well as scholarly bishop, with a large library, he tried to keep clear of clerical politics, rarely attending ACs. He defended the doctrine of St Augustine when his suffragan Berger of Gap published his anti-Jansenist *mandement* in 1711, leading to suspicions of Jansenism, but Brûlart openly declared his orthodoxy in 1714 after publication of *Unigenitus*.

Nom 30-6-1668. Provs 15-7-1669. Consec 1669. Died 3-11-1714.

Sources: ASV, PC 66, fos 101–34. AN, MM 1115, fo 66r (3-7 and 4-7-1668). ASS, Bertrand *fiches*. Levesque, 'Liste des élèves', 34, no 496. Pinard, *Chronologie*, iv, 281–4; vi, 207–8, 362, 491–3. St-Simon, xxvi, 98. Fénelon, *Correspondance*, xv, 326, n 6. Lapeyre and Scheurer, *Notaires et secrétaires du roi*, i, 64–5. *Lettres de Séguier*, ii, 1191. Boisnard, *Touraine*, no 476. *Gallia*, iii, 1099. DBF, vii, 490.

Brulart de Sillery, Fabio. Soissons 1692–1714. Bp of Soissons was great-grandson of Noël Brûlart de Sillery, chancellor of France 1607–24 and grandson of Pierre (d 1640), marquis de Puysieux, sec of state under Louis XIII, who lost out politically with the arrival of Richelieu. Extremely well-connected with high robe (e.g. Villeroy, Bellièvre) and aristocratic (Étampes de Valançay, later La Rochefoucauld and Luxembourg) families. Unlike them, however, the Brûlart did not seek, or at least obtain, high church office until Louis XIV's reign. Yet chancellor's brother, the *commandeur* de Sillery, was a collaborator of Vincent de Paul, and founder of Canada mission bearing his name, while Jean-Baptise (1570–?) was a celebrated Capuchin. All of bp's father's siblings were either in Order of Malta or the church! Bp's father and eldest brother both followed military rather than robe careers.

Born in chateau of Pressigny near Loches (Tours dioc), 28-10-1655, but resided in Paris since early school days. 4th of 7 sons of Louis-Roger, marquis de Sillery (1619–91), and Catherine de la Rochefoucauld (1622–98), daughter of 1st duc and sister of author of *Maximes*, married in 1639. Received name of Fabio from his godfather, the papal nuncio Piccolomini, in honour of reigning Pope, Alexander VII (Fabio Chigi). Studies coll de la Marche, Univ of Paris, MA in July 1676, followed by theol at Sorbonne where he obtained 100th and last place in 1682 theol licence, with doct 23-7-1682. Ordained priest during Lent, 1682, by Charles-Maurice Le Tellier of Reims, who also made him dean of his cath. Obtained abbey of St-Basle (Reims) from elder brother in 1663, and added Le Gard O Cist (Amiens) in 1693 and Mas Granier in Aug 1710, finishing with St-Pierre-de-Chézy in 1711. Dep to 1685 AC, he was initially nom to Avranches in 1689, but exchanged it in 1690 for Soissons with Pierre-Daniel Huet, previously nom to Soissons. Member of Academy of Inscriptions in 1701, of Académie Française 1705. Frequented Sceaux and court of duc du Maine, and may have aimed at Le Tellier succession at Reims in 1710. Chosen as commissioner for the reception of *Unigenitus* by assembly of 1713–14, he was rumoured (unfairly) as dying of remorse for betraying his real convictions by supporting the bull.

Nom to Avranches 10-6-1689, to Soissons 1-11-1689. Provs 22-1-1692. Consec 23-3-1692. Died 20-11-1714.

Sources: ASV, PC 86, fos 36–55 (Soissons); PC 101a, fos 247–54 (St-Pierre). BN, MS Fr 7651, fo 65 (*bienfaits du roi*); MS Fr 12986, fos 4–7, 102–6 (Sillery's papers); MS Fr 20969, fo 87. St-Simon, v, 85–6, 419; xxv, 137–42, 362–3, 453–67 (appendix, no vii, for 1713 journal). Boisnard, *Les Phélypeaux*, 166. DLF, 1182.

Cabanes de Viens, Jean-Balthazar. Vence 1693–7. In late 15th-early 16th c, the Cabanes family were apothecaries in Trets, east of Aix, but then moved into the medical profession in generation of bp's grandfather, with Claude, bp's grandfather, becoming a royal *médecin ordinaire* in 1590 and his son or nephew, Nicolas, was still one of Louis XIII's physicians in 1610s.

The next generation combined law and military service, passing themselves off as nobles and getting away with it, thanks to grant of membership of royal order of St-Michel in 1634, which effectively put their recent commoner status behind them, though it was not enough to get a female relative of future bp into St-Cyr in 1691! Bp's sister married into the Sabran family (see below).

Born 1654, 2nd son of Balthasar, baron de Viens, *prés* in *chambe des comptes* of Provence since 1639, and Madeleine de Vallavoire-Volx, sister of Nicolas Valavoire, bp of Riez. Took doct in theol at Avignon, 10-3-1674. Priest since ca 1680. Abbot *in comm* of ND de Clusonne (Gap) in 1683. Thanks to his uncle, he was canon of Riez from an early age, and later served as his vic-gen for several years. Won contested election to 1680 AC, also attended 1682 Assembly. Nom to Grasse in Nov 1685, but preferred Vence when it fell vacant soon afterwards.

Nom 26-4-1686. Provs 26-4-1693. Consec 29-11-1693. Died 9-5-1697.

Sources: ASV, PC 87, fos 800–7. BN, PO 564, no 12860; Doss bleus 147, no 3660. AD Vaucluse, D 137, fo 163v. Griselle, *Etat*, no 1828 (Nicolas). Chaix d'Est-Ange, *Dictionnaire des familles*, viii, 37. Clapiers-Collongues, *Chronologie*, 203.

Caillebot de la Salle, François. Tournai 1692–1705 (resign).   St-Simon was disparaging about this bp's origins, claiming his grandfather had sold clogs at Senonches, but although they were not nobles by the 15th c, when resident at Beuvron in Normandy, their condition had changed considerably a century later – as military service under the Harcourt, fellow Normans, and a marriage to Jacqueline d'O in 1558 testify. Bp's grandfather was captain in royal guards in 1590s and was a *gentilhomme ordinaire* in Louis XIII's household, while his father (d 1682) was *maître de la garderobe* (1679) and *cons d'état*, having served in several military and gubernatorial capacities since 1640s. Bp's brother succeeded father in royal *garde-robe* and was closely connected to Colbert de Seignelay.

Born Rouen dioc, 1655, François was elder of 2 sons of Louis, marquis de la Salle, and Marie Madeleine de Martel de Montpinçon. Studied hum and phil at coll du Plessis, Univ of Paris, where he took MA in June 1676, 1st place in 1684 theol lic, followed by doct 20-5-1684. Royal almoner in 1685. Abbot *in comm* of Plainpied OSA Bourges (1666–83), Rebais OSB Meaux (1672–1736), where he became involved in running jurisdictional disputes with Bossuet as bp of Meaux. Obtained abbey of La Couture (Le Mans) when resigned see of Tournai in 1705. Signatory of the appeal against *Unigenitus* of 1717, he also accepted miracles of Jansenist deacon, Paris.

Nom 21-5-1690. Provs 5-5-1692. Consec 31-8-1692. Resign March 1705. Died 21-12-1736.

Sources: ASV, PC 86, fos 373–96. BN, PO 570, no 13088; Doss bleus 148, no 3722. AN, L 745, pièce 1, no 18 (Tournai). Pinard, *Chronologie*, iv, 151–2. St-Simon, vi, 159; xxiii, 163–71, 483–91 (appendix viii). Fénelon, *Correspondance*, iii, 460, no 287, n 4. Bossuet, *Correspondance*, vi, 75–6. Chaix d'Est-Ange, *Dictionnaire des familles*, viii, 91–3.

Carbonnel de Canisy, François. Limoges 1696–1706 (resign).   The Carbonnel de Canisy family was from lower Normandy, with an ancestry that went back to Crusades and a clear filiation since later 14th c. Their nobility was confirmed by 1463 *recherches*. Several branches developed later, of which Canisy was one of most important. Good connections to other long-established noble families in province were crowned by a marriage in 1588 to a daughter of powerful marshal Matignon, whose family included several bps in 17th c – and which clearly benefited bp of Limoges in years before episcopate. Bp's father and brother were both lts-gens in lower Normandy, governors of Avranches, and military commanders through century. They were also related to Briqueville de la Luzerne family, one of whom had married niece of royal confessor, La Chaize.

Born Avranches, ca 1656, son of Hervé, governor of Avranches, and Catherine de Jugé. Studied phil in Paris for 2 years, theol for 3 years, and took bachelor's exam in theol, Feb 1678. Ordained priest in 1683. Dean of native Avranches cath in 1680, he later became canon and *grand chantre* as well as vic-gen of Lisieux under his relative, Bp Matignon, for 2 years. Dep to 1690 AC. Active, discreet but charitable bp, spending large amounts of money helping his impoverished dioc in 1690s and engaging in defiant correspondence with Mme de Maintenon over state of France on account of wars. He made more than one attempt to resign from Limoges, esp 1704–5, which Louis XIV finally (and reluctantly, it seems) accepted in 1706. He retired as bp-abbot of Montebourg near Valognes in lower Normandy which he had obtained in 1699, to which Louis XIV added that of Belval in 1706.

Nom 8-9-1695. Provs 23-1-1696. Consec 25-3-1696. Resign 1706. Died 28-10-1723.

Sources: ASV, PC 90, fos 280–88. AN, L 735, no 3, p 4 bis. BN, MS Fr 20969, fo 149 (Montebourg). Pinard, *Chronologie*, vi, 111–12. St-Simon, xli, 365. Limouzin-Lamothe, *Le Diocèse de Limoges*, 34–5.

Cassagnet de Tilladet, Michel. Mâcon 1677–1731. The Cassagnet, sgrs de Tilladet and Fimarcon, were natives of Gascony, settled in Vic Fezensac near Auch in the early 15th century. They were extremely active militarily under Henri II and his successors, and related to important *épée* families like Roquelaure. In the 1560s, Antoine, 'capt Tilladet' was colonel of the *bandes des légionnaires* raised in Guyenne. Less than a century later, when the Tilladet and Fimarcon branches were both clearly established, Gabriel, bp's father, was a *maréchal de camp* and gov of Bapaume, having been briefly banished during last months of Richelieu's ministry. Enduring fortune came of his brief marriage (1645–9) to Madeleine Le Tellier, sister of Mazarin's war minister. By his death in early 1660s he was a lt-gen in army, while his eldest son, having begun as a guards officer in 1654, would, thanks to Louvois patronage, become a lt-gen in 1678, col-gen of the Cent Suisses in 1679, gov of Cognac 1688 and lt-gen of Artois in 1689. Le Tellier patronage extended into church too, and bp was a prime beneficiary of it over many years.

Born Paris, 1646, son of Gabriel and Madeleine Le Tellier (d 1649). Studied phil and theol at Univ of Paris. MA in July 1664, followed by 87th place in 1674 theol lic. Doct of theol 27-5-1678, the week before his episcopal consec. Ordained priest on 13-12-1676, less than a week before nom to Mâcon. Abbot *in comm* of ND de la Honce O Prem (Bayonne) before 1663. Dep to 1670 AC (Le Tellier of Reims patronage) and 1675 AC for Lyon (Colbert of Autun patronage). Offered move to Clermont in 1682 but changed his mind, doubtless because provs unlikely to be granted by then.

Nom 18-12-1676. Provs 4-11-1677. Consec 4-6-1678. Died 5-9-1731.

Sources: ASV, PC 76, fos 542–60. BN, PO 609, no 14320; Doss bleus 156, no 4069. St-Simon xiii, 151; xxiii, 167. Pinard, *Chronologie*, iv, 84–5, 309–11, 325–6; v, 8–9; vi, 25, 131, 192–3. Anselme, *Histoire*, ix, pt i, 286–7. Rowlands, *Dynastic State and Army*, 43.

Castellane, Joseph-Pierre. Fréjus 1715–39. One of the oldest, most prolific and best-connected of all Provence's noble families, who by 17th c numbered up to 14 different branches – one of which was that of Adhémar de Grignan, which entered the Castellane 'galaxy' in 16th c. There was virtually no noble family of any significance to whom they were not related. Consequently, its members were to be found in virtually ever sphere of public life, lay and religious, civil and military, of region.

Son of Horace, baron de Norante, and Anne de Bonne, born in Norante, Senez dioc, ca 1661. Nothing known about early career, and timescale of his orders and studies raises questions about it. Lic in theol Paris, 7-2-1710. Ordained priest 2-6-1708. Availed of *régale* to obtain royal nom to canon's stall at Aix cath in 1687, when he was still just a tonsured cleric. Vic-gen of Aix under Abp Vintimille, and renewals of his powers in 1711 and 1713 show that he was specifically responsible for oversight of clergy and of the poor of Aix. Dep to 1710 AC.

Fréjus became vacant when reluctant Louis XIV agreed to nom future Cardinal Fleury as Louis XV's preceptor.

Nom 12-4-1715. Provs 29-5-1715. Consec 30-6-1715. Died 21-3-1739.

Sources: ASV, PC 104, fos 209–20. AD Bouches-du-Rhône, 1 G 1273, fos 499v–502v; 1 G 1281, pp 304–5; 1 G 1282, fos 147v–48r. St-Simon, xii, 430, n 2. *Gallia Chr Nov*, Fréjus, 414–15. Blanc, 'Origines', 153–9. Boisnard, *Touraine*, no 541.

Catelan, Jean. Valence 1705–25.   The legend of a family of Florentine origin, taking refuge in France after Pazzi conspiracy, and then migrating from Avignon to Toulouse, seems without foundation. Their origins were more prosaically Languedocian, with first clearly identifiable ancestor of bp elected *capitoul* of Toulouse in 1530. From there they migrated into parlt, initially as SRs in *chancellerie*, then as *cons* by the generation of bp's grandfather, François, who was *doyen* of the *cons* by the time of his death (1645). Bp's father, Jacques, sgr de la Masquere, and brother were successively *prés* in *Enquêtes* chamber. Marriages along the way to established families like Vedelli, Puget and Guilhermin secured their position within Toulouse, and probably helped to obtain some important positions within church there. A nephew, Fançois de Catelan, was vic-gen of Toulouse, canon of St-Etienne; another, Jean-Baptiste, was *grand chantre* of St-Etienne, while Jean-Marie, became bp of Rieux in 1740s. Bp's own career owed much to an uncle, Pierre de la Broue, bp of Mirepoix, and a close friend of Bossuet.

Born Toulouse, 30-3-1659. Son of Jacques, *prés* in parlt, and Catherine de Puget. Further studies in Paris, mostly in coll of Navarre, where MA in Aug 1683, 5th in 1690 theol lic, and the doct 3-5-1690. Ordained priest in February 1690. His uncle, bp La Broue of Mirepoix, hoped to become preceptor of duc de Bourgogne, but lost out to Fénelon, instead his nephew got post of *lecteur* to duc de Berry, in 1693, and later to Bourgogne himself. Dep to ACs of 1700 and 1705, he obtained abbey of Boulancourt O Cist (Troyes) in March 1701. Vic-gen, *théologal* and sacristan of Mirepoix under uncle for several years before 1705, but also moved in Bossuet circle. He seems to have been a capable and intellectual bp, publishing remarkable *Instructions pastorales* to new converts in dioc (1722–3), and the *Antiquitez de l'église de Valence* (1724).

Nom 15-8-1705. Provs 14-12-1705. Consec 21-2-1706. Died 8-1-1725.

Sources: ASV, PC 98, fos 604–16. BN, Doss bleus 158, nos 4135–6. Bossuet, *Correspondance*, vi, 86; xii, 172–4. O'Gilvy, *Nobiliaire de Guienne*, iii, pp 547–56. Villain, *France moderne*, 236–42. Ledieu, *Journal*, ii, 456, 464.

Caylus, Charles Daniel Gabriel de Thubieres de Lévis de. Auxerre 1705–54.   The 'daisy-chain' name of this family illustrates their successive turns of fortune and their geographical mobility. Caylus, 50 km south-west of Villefranche-de-Rouergue, was a seigneurie in Lévis family which was scattered via its marriages across Gascony and Languedoc, but by early 17th c it had moved, again via marriage of heiresses, through successive families until estate and name belonged to the Thubières de Grimoard family from Quercy. They participated in Thirty Years' War and bp's father's marriage to daughter of marshal Fabert was important in securing their position. They already had strong ties with Noailles before bp's brother's marriage to a Villette-Mursay relative of Mme de Maintenon brought them even closer to the fount of favour. An uncle of bp was a highly active Sulpician missionary in Canada until his death in 1677.

Born 20-4-1669 Paris. Son of Charles-Henri de Thubières de Grimouard de Pestels de Lévis, marquis de Caylus, and Claude Fabert, married in 1663. Early studies with Jesuits. Took 7th place in 1696 theol lic, doct of theol of Paris 9-8-1696. Ordained priest 26-2-1695. Abbot *in comm* of St-Jean-de-Laon in 1687 (or 1697?). Also appointed royal almoner in April 1696 (successor to Clermont-Tonnerre). Gr-vic to Noailles of Paris, who probably secured his election to attend 1701 and 1702 ACs, and associated with Bossuet. Maintenon seems to have been instrumental in obtaining Auxerre rather than Toul, as originally mooted, for him in 1704.

She even attempted to oversee his admin of Auxerre in early years and to vet his appointments – did she already suspect him of Jansenist leanings? Initially accepted *Unigenitus*, then appealed against it in 1717 and remaind firmly Jansenist therafter. Longest serving French bishop at time of death in 1754.

Nom 15-8-1704. Provs 26-1-1705. Consec 1-3-1705. Died 3-4-1754.

Sources: ASV, PC 91, fos 183–93. BN, Cherin 43, no 902. Maintenon, *Correspondance* (ed Lavallée), iii, 339; v, 243–5, 304. *Lettres de Le Camus* (ed Ingold), 618–26. Pinard, *Chronologie*, iv, 466–7. St-Simon, xii, 158, n 2. Bossuet, *Correspondance*, xiii, 253, n 3. Vergé-Franceschi, *Officiers généraux de la marine*, vii, 259–60. DBF, vii, 1518.

Cercado. *See* Le Sénéchal.

Chambonas. *See* La Garde.

Chamillart, Jean-François. Dol 1692–1702, Senlis 1702–14.   Originally from Berry, where their status was modest enough (they included a *chapelier*). Bp's great-grandfather was a receiver of *tailles* at Sens, his grandfather a successful *avocat* in Paris parlt who was involved with admin of Mazarin's benefices. More substantial officeholding began with father of bp, Guy (1624–75), who was successively *avocat-général* of gr conseil, MR, intendant at Caen, *proc-gén* of *chambre de justice* in 1662. Guy's career secured their position in influential robe circles of Paris, but future finance minister, Michel, who was initially designated for an ecclesiastical career, owed his ascent to Mme de Maintenon, who employed him at St-Cyr and in many other capacities from the mid-1680s onwards (St-Simon alleged that his skills as a billiards player were the making of him at court!). By 1692 he was also connected to the Colbert, Beauvillier, Chevreuse families, which facilitated his brother's promotion to the episcopate, but fact that he himself had only one son limited his scope for further direct family patronage within church. Their uncles, Gaston and Michel, were both prominent docts of Paris theol faculty, where Gaston served as royal professor and syndic of faculty until his death in 1679.

Born 1657, son of Guy, then *avocat général* of gr conseil, and Catherine Compaing. Studies at Univ of Paris, where he took MA in August 1676, 99th place in theol lic of 1684, and doct 10-1-1685. Ordained priest 1686. Prior of Isle-Adam, abbot *in comm* of Fontgombault in 1687. *Premier aumônier* to duchesse de Bourgogne in 1704, on death of Bossuet. According to St-Simon, a *sot* of the kind a minister must advance but preferably to distant dioc like Dol in Brittany. Obtained Baume O Cist (Besancon) on same day as transferred to Senlis, possibly to compensate for revenue loss.

Nom 5-4-1692. Provs 6-10-1692. Consec 30-11-1692. Nom to Senlis 15-4-1702. Provs 31-7-1702. Died 16-4-1714.

Sources: ASV, PC 86, fos 666–76. BN, MS Lat 9155, fo 129v; MS Fr 20969, fo 163. Chamillard, *Correspondance et papiers*. Bossuet, *Correspondance*, ii, 425. St-Simon, ii, 193, n 3; vi, 292, 303, n 7. Dangeau, viii, 495; xv, 125–6. Bayard, *Dictionnaire des surintendants*, 102–5. Favre-Lejeune, *Secrétaires du roi*, i, 335–6. Antoine, *Coeur de l'état*, 355–64.

Champflour, Étienne de. La Rochelle 1703–24.   The Champflour family, originating in bourgeoisie of Clermont in early 15th c, became prominent there, partly because they were so numerous, in following centuries, although their social advance and professional activities were in no sense spectacular. Ennoblement came slowly, and only in generation of bp's grandfather and father, both of whom held office in *cour des aides* at Clermont. Another branch of family held office in the Clermont *sénéchaussée* court. Their presence, male and female, in church was no less impressive, esp in bp's own generation, which included Gérard, the eldest cleric, dean of Clermont cath from 1659, an Oratorian (Jean-Baptiste), 2 Jesuits (Antoine and Pierre), and several nuns. A classic *dévot* family with active and well-placed second-order clergy up to bp's generation.

Son of Jean and Marie Fayet married in 1639, born in Clermont 19-5-1646, where began studies with Jesuits, before entering St-Sulpice seminary 8-10-1664. MA in Univ of Paris in Aug 1669, 72nd place in 1674 theol lic, when also admitted to Compagnie de St-Sulpice. Soon afterwards he became director of Sulpician *solitude* of Issy, devoted to clerical formation in broadest sense. Sent to Limoges to run seminary and teach moral theol in 1681, he also acted as virtual gr-vic to Bp Lascaris of Limoges, who knew him well from St-Sulpice. In 1679, his uncle resigned his benefices, inc that of *abbé* ('dean') of Clermont chapter, in his favour, but despite intense family pressure, he refused to accept it until 1682 when uncle died. When bp Arbouze of Clermont also died that year, cath chapter elected him to admin Clermont dioc *sede vacante*. Despite his unconcealed ultramontane views, which saw him exiled briefly to Pontorson (near Avranches) for opposing a royal nom to chapter of Clermont under the terms of *régale*, which he contested, his admin lasted 10 years, with a further 10 years as vic-gen of Bp Bochart of Clermont down to 1702. His anti-Jansenist zeal compensated for earlier anti-gallican views to win nom to La Rochelle, but his age and experience may have made him less dynamic than his short-lived predecessor at La Rochelle, Frézeau; he was also a more doctrinaire and admin than pastoral bp (Pérouas). Heavily involved against Jansenists by 1702, he is best known for his attacks on Quesnel and Cardinal Noailles of Paris in particular, his pro-Jesuit stance triumphing in 1713 with *Unigenitus*.

Nom 31-12-1702. Provs 14-5-1703. Consec 10-6-1703. Died 26-11-1724.

Sources: ASV, PC 96, fos 511–23. BN, MS Lat 17028, fos 111r–13v (ms biography, 1703). AD Puy-de-Dôme, 9F, vol 61 (personal papers). Fénelon, *Correspondance*, xiii, 32–3, n 32; xv 99, n 4. St-Simon, x, 401; xx, 339–49; xxii, 145–9. *Recherche générale de la noblesse d'Auvergne de 1656 à 1724*, 142. Tronson, *Correspondance*, i, 389–409. A de Lantenay-Bertrand, *Mélanges de biographie et d'histoire* (Bordeaux 1885), 139–81. Bertrand, *Bibliothèque Sulpicienne*, iii, 92–137. Welter, *Réforme ecclésiastique*, 243–5. Pérouas, *Diocèse de la Rochelle*, 356–9.

Charpin de Genétines, Antoine. Limoges 1706–29 (resign).   The Charpin were a family from Forez region, whose nobility was sufficient to enable bp and his brother, as well as relatives before him to gain entry to the socially exclusive chapter of St-Jean at Lyon. His father commanded *arrière-ban* of Lyonnais, not the most redoubtable challenge, but a clear sign of status and authority within nobility, while his mother was daughter of a long-established noble family from Vivarais with solid connections to high-status families of region.

Born 16-3-1669, baptised at St-Romain d'Urfé 2-5-1669. Son of Jean, sgr de Génetines, and 1st wife Marie de la Rivoire, married in 1657. Little known about his studies except that he took doct of theol at Bourges 3 years before nom to Limoges. Tonsured in Lyon, April 1688, where he became a canon-count of St-Jean in July 1689. Ordained deacon in May 1695, priest ca 1702. By 1706 he was *official* and vic-gen at St-Flour, where a former fellow-canon of St-Jean, Joseph d'Estaing was bp. Obtained abbey of Pebrac in Auvergne at same time as Limoges in 1705, followed by La Crète in 1711. Fragile in health, he had bp of Tulle conduct ordinations and visitations after 1718, and from 1725 onwards, he took a suffragan bp, Charles-Antoine de la Roche-Aymon, later cardinal and abp of Reims. After that he resided less than before, while remaining active in running of dioc. But his financial admin disastrous, and was main reason for his resignation in 1729, when he retired to native Forez where he died in 1739. Held strong gallican views, and was anti-Jansenist, but encountered little trouble in his dioc.

Nom 3-4-1706. Provs 13-9-1706. Consec 23-1-1707. Resign Dec 1729. Died 21-6-1739.

Sources: ASV, PC 99, fos 312–29. BN, PO 687, no 16020; Doss bleus 170, no 4515. AN, L 735, n 3, Limoges. Beyssac, *Chanoines de Lyon*, 217. Villain, *France moderne* (Ardèche and Drôme), 554–6. Chaix d'Est-Ange, *Dictionnaire des familles*, x, 43–6. *Intendants du Lyonnais*, 698. Nadaud, *Nobiliaire de Limoges*, ii, 289–90. Limouzin-Lamothe, *Diocèse de Limoges*, 67–9.

Charrite de Ruthie, Pierre. Rieux 1705–18.   Unravelling the antecedents of this bp is particularly hazardous, as neither Père Anselme nor his successors managed to establish a clear family history. This is compounded by the different spellings of name Ruthie, which is also rendered Urruty. Of Basque origin from Aussurucq in the pays de Soule, close to Spanish frontier, they can be traced back to 15th c. Bernard de Ruthie was successively *premier aumônier* and *grand aumônier de France* under Henri II (1552–6) and other family members held positions at court or were govs of châteaux or towns (Soule, Bayonne), but this did not lead to increased status or visibility. Within a generation, the direct family line disappeared, and a St-Martin family seems to have acquired their lands and title of Ruthie by later 16th c. They resumed a position as local nobles, though bp's grandfather's marriage in 1605 to Jeanne Deschaux, a relative of Bertrand, later abp of Tours, may have contributed towards later position within local clergy.

Son of Pierre Charitte de Ruthie and his cousin Marguerite de Ruthie, born at Aussurucq ca 1655. Took bacc, lic and doct in theol at Toulouse, 20 and 24-5-1673, where he studied for 5 years. Priest since about 1685. Canon and grand archdeacon of Comminges from early age. Both Guron and Brisay de Denonville, successive bps of Comminges, employed him as their vic-gen and *official* for many years, making him the senior sub-episcopal figure of dioc. Dep to 1705 AC. His relatively brief episcopate was apparently uneventful.

Nom 24-12-1705. Provs 13-9-1706. Consec 31-10-1706. Died 7-9-1718.

Sources: ASV, PC 99, fos 481–89. BIUT, MS 10, fo 266v. Anselme, *Histoire*, viii, 267–9. Contrasty, *Histoire de Rieux-Volvestre*, 343–7. Lamant, *Armorial de Bayonne, pays Basque et sud-Gascogne*, 2 vols (np 1981–4), i, 356; ii, 95–9, 243–5.

Châteauneuf de Rochebonne, Charles-François. Noyon 1708–31, Lyon 1731–40.   A well connected noble family originally from the Vivarais, where present since late 14th c and where they still had lands in 17th c, but whose centre of gravity shifted to Beaujolais and Lyonnais by 16th c, reinforced by marriage of bp's parents in 1668. They were already related to bishop-producing families like La Baume de Suze, but direct line died out in bp's generation, with several of its members being killed in service during Louis XIV's wars. They were well represented since earlier in 17th c in highly noble chapter of St-Jean in Lyon, where bp was one of an impressive line of canons over 3–4 generations; some of them held offices of influence within chapter and elsewhere in Lyon, sometimes with joint canonicate in equally noble chapter of St-Pierre of Mâcon. As *commandant pour le roi* in the Lyonnais in 1690s and 1700s, bp's father was also close to Villeroy family which dominated the province. Bp's mother was a Grignan, but other alliances with prov nobility were just as impressive – La Baume de Suze, des Serpents, etc. One of bp's brothers, Louis-Joseph, was bp of Carcassonne in 1720s, where he succeeded their Grignan uncle.

Born Lyon 6-1-1671, baptised there in Ste Croix church 11-1-1671. Son of Charles, marquis de Rochebonne, and Thérèse d'Adhémar de Grignan (sister-in-law of Mme de Sévigné's daughter), married Oct 1668. Further studies in Paris where he was MA in March 1694. Took theol bacc exam in Dec 1694, 99th place in 1700 lic and doct on 22-4-1701. On Fénelon's recommendation, he entered St-Sulpice as a deacon 3-4-1696, left 4-1-1697, though he had previously spent some time in St-Irénée seminary in Lyon in 1695. Tonsured cleric in Sept 1676, he was ordained deacon in March 1695, priest ca 1699. Canon of St-Jean (Lyon) chapter in Nov 1687, holds post of cantor from 1705 onwards, while a Rochebonne uncle occupied major position as *chamarrier*. He served his fellow Lyonnais, La Poype de Vertrieu, as vic-gen of Poitiers for 6 years before episcopate and was consec bp by him at Poitiers. Dep to 1707 AC, episcopal nom followed soon afterwards. Obtained abbeys of Elan in 1710, St-Riquier in 1717. Strongly anti-Jansenist bp at Noyon, like Aubigné his predecessor. Returns to Lyon as Abp in 1731.

Nom 24-12-1707. Provs 26-3-1708. Consec 29-7-1708. Nom to Lyon 26-7-1731. Provs 19-11-1731. Died 28-2-1740.

Sources: ASV, PC 101, fos 219–28. BN, MS Lat 5496, p 3 (theol bacc). Beyssac, *Chanoines de Lyon*, 200, 204–5, 210, 216–17. St-Simon, xxx, 382; xxiii, 331, n 4. Fénelon, *Correspondance*, iv, no 357a, p 79; v. 92, n 1. Sévigné, *Correspondance*, iii, 154–7. Anselme, *Histoire*, ii, 456–8. Chaix d'Est-Ange, *Dictionnaire des familles*, x, 129–30.

Chaulnes, Paul de. Sarlat 1702–21, Grenoble 1721–5.   When bp's father's exemption from the *taille* – and by implication, his nobility – was challenged by *consuls* of Grenoble in 1641, he claimed he was descended from a Burgundian family which had always lived nobly and which could be traced to Jean de *Chaoniis*, who made a donation to a church in Tonnerre, Burgundy, in 1270! The *consuls* were less sure, given absence of proofs, which Chaulnes explained were due to fire which destroyed relevant documents in Tonnerre in 1556 – a not uncommon recourse by families like them during *recherches de noblesse*. There was, it seems, more substance to his claim to have blood ties to prominent Parisian robe family of same name, though the point of contact is obscure. In fact his grandfather and a brother moved to Grenoble by mid- to late-16ᵗʰ c, where their activities and milieu into which they married were relatively diverse and unspectacular – notaries, *procureurs*, SRs in some cases. Bp's immediate forebears, father and grandfather, held offices in royal financial admin, with his grandfather inching his way upwards from a *trésorier provincial des guerres* and of the fortifications of Dauphiné around 1600, to SR in 1604, and finally to a *trés de France* by 1615, before ending his career as *prés* of *trésoriers* of Grenoble – an office in which bp's father naturally succeeded him in 1629. By then, the Chaulnes had become far more solidly connected in robe circles, thanks to advantageous marriages. Bp's father, who served as an army intendant more than once, was, in addition, a *savant* and *bel esprit*, educated by Jesuits of Tournon coll along with Abel Servien and others, a writer of 'libertine' works, who enjoyed connections with ministers like Fouquet, Lionne. At the same time, he and related families were at heart of a powerful and active *dévot* movement within Grenoble.

Born Vif near Grenoble, 23-10-1647, baptised in Grenoble 20-12-1649. Son of Claude, *prés* of *bureau des finances*, and Marguerite de Chissé de la Marcousse, married in July 1631. Doct of theol, Valence, in 1695. Obtained abbey of Pessans OSB (Auch) in April 1689, when still subdeacon, ordained priest in 1692. In 1689, his fellow-Dauphinois Abp La Baume de Suze of Auch took him as his vic-gen, which enabled him to represent clergy of Auch province at AC in 1695, 1701 and 1702. At Grenoble, he was hostile to Oratorians patronised by predecessors Le Camus and Alleman, but failed to evict them from management of seminary.

Nom to Sarlat 1-11-1701. Provs 6-2-1702. Consec 26-3-1702. Nom to Grenoble 8-1-1721. Provs 16-6-1721. Died 20-10-1725.

Sources: ASV, PC 95, fos 396–410. BN, PO 714, no 16399; Doss bleus 178, no 4637; MS Fr 20969, fo 75v. AN, L 744, pièce 1, nos 28–31. AC Grenoble, CC 725, fos 26–7, CC 424 (dossiers on noble status, 1601 and 1641); GG 49 (baptism). Mousnier, *Séguier*, i, 129–35. H-J Martin, *Les Registres du libraire Nicolas*, i, p 165. Martin, *La Compagnies pour la propagation de la foi*, 308.

Chaumont-Guitry, Paul-Philippe. Dax 1671–84 (resign).   Under Louis XIV this bp's family alleged they were descended from the kings of Austrasia, while a more sceptical St-Simon traced them back to Gisors in Normandy, where they were present from 13ᵗʰ c onwards, with evidence of royal service, but neither their offices, alliances nor lands distinguished them from other nobles. One of them, Jean, was a *chambellan* to duc d'Alençon-Anjou in 1570s and a capt in royal guards. A century later, the chevalier de Chaumont achieved some celebrity as Louis XIV's ambassador to Siam. In between, the branch to which future bp belonged established itself in court and literary *milieux*, thanks in part to marriages which connected them to major robe families like the Séguier, Bailleul and Habert de Montmort. Bp's own career owed nearly everything to these activities – even its last decade or so was a tribute to them, since he resigned as bp in 1684 in order to complete a book finally published in 1692–3. The marquis de Chaumont-Guitry (d 1672), a relative of bp, was one of Louis XIV's favourites in the 1660s and had as his mistress a sister of Mme de Montespan!

Born and baptised in parish of St-Germain-l'Auxerrois, 1635. 4th and youngest son of Jean, sgr de Boisgarnier, keeper of king's private library, and Marie de Bailleul, daughter of Nicolas and Marie Habert de Montmort. Matriculated in 1651 at Univ of Paris, where he studied phil and later some theol at Sorbonne, but took doct in canon law in Paris. Ordained priest ca 1663. Failed to have election to 1665 AC upheld. Abbot *in comm* of St-Vincent-de-Bourg OSA (Bordeaux), while very young, he may have held a benefice with cure of souls in Rouen dioc, but probably did not reside there. He spent much of his time before episcopate working under direction of Chancellor Séguier, dealing with family affairs and helping administer Chancellor's literary patronage. In 1667 he succeeded his father as keeper of king's private library, and was soon made *lecteur du roi*, residing in Louvre until his nom to Dax. Also an active preacher, he was elected young to the Académie Française in 1654, probably because of Séguier and Habert patronage. He resigned Dax in 1681, partly on health grounds, partly because of hostility of certain 'powerful persons' who included his chapter, elements of clergy and magistrates, but promising to pursue his scholarly work on the heresies of his time. His 2-vol *Réflexions sur le christianisme dans l'église catholique* appeared a decade later.

Nom 17-5-1671. Provs 14-12-1671. Consec 1-5-1672. Resign 1684. Died 24-3-1697.

Sources: ASV, PC 70, fos 71–93. BN, Doss bleus 178, no 4642; Carrés d'Hozier 179. AUP, reg 97, fo 7. ASV, Acta congregationis consistorialis 1682, i, fos 127–30; ii, fos 142–3 (resign enquiry, 1682). Pinard, *Chronologie*, vi, 132, 416–17. St-Simon, iii, 81, 395–6. Chaix d'Est-Ange, *Dictionnaire des familles*, x, 162–5. Kerviler, *Le Chancelier Séguier*, 537–49.

Chevalier de Saulx, François. Alès 1694–1712. 'Cest un gentilhomme de Poitou' – that was practically all that contemporaries seemed to know about the 1st bp of Alès. Numerous families of this name existed in Poitou – and elsewhere. Bp's ancestors apparently originated in St-Maixent, where they were probably *bourgeois* at the outset, but by mid-14th c they had abandoned such ties and begun to merge with local landed noble families. Over the generations, they provided knights of Malta, abbots of St-Maixent abbey itself, as well as various *officiers* and *gentilhommes* in the royal households, esp in 16th c. Their activities during 17th c seem more obscure, and the 'de Sceaux/Saulx' suffix was only added thanks to bp's mother's dowry in 1630. It is not easy to see how family status or relations per se did much to advance future bp's career, although Père Léonard's claim that they were related by marriage to Abp Péréfixe of Paris and esp to Mme de Basville, wife of the influential intendant of Languedoc, might help to explain why he rather than the many other missionaries of the Cévennes was brought to the attention of Louis XIV, La Chaize and others in Paris.

Born Poitou 1643, 3rd son of Philippe Chevalier and Louise de Marcirion, dame de Sceaux, married ca 1630. Higher studies in Paris, MA in July 1667, bachelor of theol in 1670, taking 20th place in 1676 theol lic, doct 31-3-1678. He obtained priory of Availlé before 1667, and that of Chizé before 1670. Briefly superior of Sens seminary in 1679–80, he was active in Cévennes missions in mid-1680s but, with exception of his mentor Tronson, his connections at that time remain obscure. His record as missionary secured him nom in 1687 as 1st bp of the planned new dioc of Alès, in the heart of the Cévennes, the need for which Cardinal Bonsi impressed on Louis XIV. Made vic-gen of Nîmes in 1687, he prepared for the creation of Alès by a general visitation of parishes concerned in 1688, 1690 and 1692. Given abbey of Psalmody (Nov 1689) with view to incorporation into temporalities of new dioc. He was also known to be pro-Jesuit before episcopate, and confided his seminary, founded in 1704, to SJ, also founded *petit séminaire* in 1708.

Nom 15-8-1687. Provs 17-5-1694. Consec 29-8-1694. Died 28-10-1712.

Sources: ASV, PC no file. BN, MS Lat 17021, fo 121; Cab d'Hozier 92, no 2452. AN, L 727, Alais, no 24. AAE, MD France 972, fos 221–2. Tronson, *Correspondance*, iii, 104, 205–7.

Sourches, ii, 76. Sauzet, *Réforme et Contre-Réforme*, 489–90. Beauchet-Filleau, *Dictionnaire des familles de Poitou*, ii, 430–7. *Archives Historiques du Poitou*, xxii, 96–7; xxiii, 105–6, 342.

Chevriers. *See* **St-Mauris**

Clément, Pierre. Périgueux 1702–19.   Clément was descended from a franc-comtois family who moved from their native village of Cléron into Besançon in later 16th c. Although their nobility was upheld in 1702, when the *chef de famille* was a *cons* in *présidial* of Besançon, they should be regarded as relatively modest in their status and attainments. Bp himself may well have obtained his initial *coup de pouce* from powerful Grammont family which held archiepiscopal see of Besançon for 3 successive generations. Thereafter, remaining in Paris, he moved into the service of Colbert family, first as tutor/mentor to minister's son, Jean-Nicolas, future abp of Rouen, while he was still a theol student in Paris in the late 1670s, and then as one of his subalterns when he became coadj of Rouen in 1680.

Born either Besançon or Ornans in 1646. Son, it seems, of Jean-Simon, lawyer and city co-*gouverneur* in 1651, and Jeanne-Françoise Gillebert. He may have studied for a time at Avignon before moving to Paris, where he entered St-Sulpice along with Jean-Joseph de Grammont, future abp of Besançon, on 24-2-1666, leaving in 1679. Meanwhile, he took MA in July 1673, 4th place in 1678 theol lic, doct in theol 10-6-1678, and was ordained priest in same year. Accompanied J-N Colbert to Rouen where he was initially curé of St-Maclou, then canon and archdeacon of cath, finally vic-gen and *official* of Rouen for 10 years before episcopate. His performance as right-hand man to Abp of Rouen was not universally appreciated, and Colbert effectively relieved him of his powers after some time. This may explain why it was Jesuits and Godet des Marais, with whom he had been close since their days together at St-Sulpice, who were really behind his nom to Périgueux. Consec in Rouen cath by Abp Colbert and bps of Sées and Boulogne, all 3 suspected of pro-Jansenist views! He defended Cardinal Noailles, published an 8-vol work, the so-called 'théologie de Périgueux', which became the standard seminary theol manual for next century.

Nom 3-6-1702. Provs 25-9-1702. Consec 29-10-1702. Died 8-1-1719.

Sources: ASV, PC 95, fos 329–39. BN MS Lat 17028, fo 36. AN, L 744, pièce 1, no 28. AD Vaucluse, D 136, fo 143v (1664). Levesque, 'Liste des élèves', no 898. Fénelon, *Correspondance*, ix, 49–50, n 6. Bertrand, *Bibliothèque sulpicienne*, iii, 216, 220, 241. Lurion, *Nobiliaire de Franche-Comté*, 218.

Clermont-Tonnerre de Crussy, Antoine-Benoit. Fréjus 1676–8.   Son of an old noble family of Dauphiné, which already had a bp – of Noyon – in episcopate in 1676.

Son of Roger de Clermont, marquis de Crussy, and Gabrielle de Berne. Born in family chateau at Raviers, Langres dioc, 1644. Student at coll of Navarre, where he studied phil (to 1662), taking MA in Aug 1662, before continuing with theol and taking 84th (and last) place in 1672 lic. Ordained priest in same year. Was active on missions, confessing, etc before episcopate. Initially, bp Poncet of Sisteron was given nom to Fréjus, but he declined it when offered see of Bourges. Provs delayed by poor Franco-papal relations, so he only entered Fréjus 2 years after original nom. An active bp of great promise for reform of dioc, he was apparently physically attacked by a local *seigneur* while on visitation, and never recovered, while a 'saignée imprudente' by his doctors hastened his end, in Aug 1678.

Nom 21-11-1674. Provs 23-3-1676. Consec 26-4-1676. Died 24-8-1678.

Sources: ASV, PC 75, fos 208–22. *Gallia Chr Nov*, Fréjus, 408–9. Foucault, *Mémoires*, 7. Bergin, *Making*, 597–8.

Clermont de Chaste de Roussillon, Louis-Annet. Laon 1695–1721.   From same extended family as Clermont-Tonnerre bishops, though bp of Noyon refused to accept their claim to be cousins 'au second degré connu' and they did not prove their case. Their family roots remained in the Dauphiné and Rhone valley, and 'Roussillon' refers to a small town there rather than the frontier province. Bp's brother was a favourite of Monseigneur and his wife, Mlle de Choin, which brought him church preferment well before his nom to Laon, while his brother's marriage to a sister of Bp Caillebot de la Salle of Tournai enabled him to become gr-vic of that dioc in 1692.

Born at Charpé, dioc of Valence 16-4-1662. Son of François, comte de Clermont et de Chaste, and Roussillon, *grand bailli* of Velay, and Claire d'Agout de Morges, his 2nd wife. MA at Univ of Paris, July 1679, where he remained to study theol, taking 107th and last place in 1684 lic, but waited until after nom to Laon before taking doct 14-7-1695. Ordained priest in 1687. Abbot *in comm* of Landevennec 25-12-1693, of St-Valery in 1695, which he exchanged for St-Martin-de-Laon in 1701 so that it could be 'united' to his see of Laon, but it did not work as Premontré canons successfully blocked it, and king then gave it to him *in comm* instead, 'sa vie durant'. Dean of chapter of Tournai, and gr-vic of bp of Tournai for 2 years before nom to Laon. Initially one of most anti-*Unigenitus* bishops, denouncing pope himself as a 'prevaricateur de la foi', he was one of 8 bishops to reject *Unigenitus* in 1714 AC, but he soon changed his mind – which meant neither side respected him thereafter, not least because he subsequently changed positions twice again! Nom 24-12-1694. Provs 19-9-1695. Consec 6-11-1695. Died 5-10-1721.

Sources: ASV, PC 89, fos 274–82. Fénelon, *Correspondance*, xvii, 248, n 7. Anselme, *Histoire*, ii, 132. St-Simon, ii, 186, n 2. Sars, *Laonnais féodal*, ii, 85.

Clermont-Tonnerre, François-Louis. Langres 1696–1724.   Relative not just of other Clermont-Tonnerre bps, but also of immediate predecessor, Simiane de Gordes.

Born 1658, son of Jacques, comte de Tonnerre and Clermont, 'premier baron, connétable et grand-maître du Dauphiné', and Virginie de Fléard de Pressins. Not much is known of his early studies, as he did not take a degree at the time: his doct in canon law, from Paris, was taken in a hurry *after* his nom to Langres at end of Dec 1695 and early Jan 1696, and at request of chancellor. Ordained priest at Christmas 1689. Abbot *in comm* of Thenailles O Prem (Laon) in 1691 and of St-Pierre-de-Bèze in 1706. *Aumônier du roi* in Sept 1692, he was in service to Monseigneur when news of his episcopal nom was announced. Also vic-gen of Noyon since 1691, where his uncle was bp, and who would have preferred he got see of Châlons-sur-Marne. Dep to 1695 AC, he also played important role in ACs of 1700, 1707, 1710, 1716, where his eloquence impressed. Initially supported Noailles in *Unigenitus* affair, but was apparently persuaded by Cardinal Rohan to change sides and accept the bull, after which he remained steadfastly orthodox. Nom 24-12-1695. Provs 23-7-1696. Consec 14-10-1696. Died 12-3-1724.

Sources: ASV, PC 90, fos 297–305. AN, MM 1098, fo 10r; MM 1099, p 42, 31 Dec 1695–2 Jan 1696 (Paris law fac). BN, MS Fr 20969, fo 128. St-Simon, ii, 366, n 2. Fénelon, *Correspondance*, xvii, 248, n 8. Abbé Roussel, *Le Diocèse de Langres*, 122.

Coëtanfao. *See* **Kerhoent.**

Coëtlogon-Méjusseau, François de. Quimper coadj 1666/8–1706.   A well-established noble family of Brittany, whose origins go back to 12th c, their presence was attested at *réformations* et *montres* of diocs of St-Brieuc, Treguier and St-Malo 1426–1543, and they were dispensed outright from *preuves de noblesse* in 1666. Militarily active in 16th c when they married into similar families. Mejusseaume, near Rennes, became a *vicomté* in 1573, while Coëtlogon itself became *marquisat* in 1622. Bp's father, Louis, vicomte de Mejusseaume, became *cons* in Rennes parlt (1619), and was the 1st parlementaire of the family, according to Saulnier, marrying the daughter of a *prés* in Rennes parlt. La Meilleraye got him commission as intendant in Brittany in 1645, which led to clashes with prov interests, and protest by Estates against his use of title of intendant there. Bp was one of 15 children who included Guy, *doyen of cons* of Rennes parlt; René, marquis de Coëtlogon (via marriage to heiress of senior branch), an active and influential gov of Rennes (brother in law of d'Oger marquis de Cavoie, Seignelay's favourite). He was uncle of Alain-Emmanuel, a long-serving naval commander who became vice-admiral and marshal of France (d 1730).

Born 3-6-1631 in St-Brieuc dioc. 3rd son of Louis and Louise le Meneust, married in 1613. Early education in hum with Jesuits, then progressed to phil and theol, matriculating at Univ of Paris and taking MA in 1655, and lic in canon law, also from Paris, in Dec 1665. Ordained priest in mid-1664. In 1665, the existing coadj of Quimper and later bishop of St-Pol-de-Léon, Visdelou, who was closely related to the Coëtlogon family, opted to take vacant see of St-Pol-de-Léon rather than remain at Quimper as coadjutor, and struck a bargain with Coëtlogon for the Quimper coadjutorship, which involved Coëtlogon paying him a sum of money and resigning a priory he held *in comm* – as near to simony as one could get, and which some accused him of doing. In Sept 1665, possibly at Coëtlogon's request, Estates of Brittany petitioned king to nom him as coadj of Quimper.

Nom as coadj 21-11-1665. Provs 1-3-1666. Consec 18-4-1666. Succeeds du Louet 11-2-1668. Died 6-11-1706.

Sources: ASV, PC 64, fos 165–83. AUP, reg 97, fo 32r. AN, MM 1115, fo 34 (law degree). Saulnier, *Parlement de Bretagne*, i, 244–7. Carné, *Chevaliers bretons de St-Michel*, 109–12. Vindry, *État major, gendarmerie*, 62, 155. Chaix d'Est-Ange, *Dictionnaire des familles*, xi, 143–7. Colbert de Croissy, *La Bretagne en 1665*, 168, 194, no 18. St-Simon, i, 268; x, 52. Villette-Mursay, *Mes campagnes*, 281–2. Bonney, *Political Change*, 300, 368. DHGE, xiii, 196–7.

Coëtlogon-Méjusseau, Louis-Marcel. St-Brieuc 1681–1705, Tournai 1705–7.   Nephew of François above. Born Rheu, dioc of Rennes, 1648. Son of René, marquis de Coëtlogon and gov of Rennes, and Philippe de Coëtlogon, his 1st cousin and *fille d'honneur* of Queen Marie-Thérèse after 1661. Univ studies in Paris, where took MA in June 1666, 2nd place in 1674 theol lic, and doct on 22-3-1674. Ordained priest in 1674. Obtained abbey of ND de Begard O Cist (Tréguier) in early 1676. Dep to AC in 1680.

Nom 6-9-1680. Provs 1-9-1681. Consec 14-12-1681. Nom to Tournai 1-4-1705. Provs 7-9-1705. Died 18-4-1707.

Sources: ASV, PC 77, fo 564–78; PC 80, fos 111–25; Misc Arm XII, 151, fo 16v. St-Simon, x, 52. DHGE, xiii, 197–8.

Coislin. *See* du Cambout.

Colbert de St-Pouange, Michel. Mâcon 1666–76.   No family quite matched the Colbert in their ability to secure episcpal office under Louis XIV, and their success was not confined to those bearing the Colbert name (see Desmarets, Beauvillier).

Michel was son of Jean-Baptiste Colbert, sgr de St-Pouange and cousin of Louis XIV's minister, and Claude Le Tellier, sister of chancellor. Born 1629, he studied in Paris where MA in Aug 1649, later becoming bachelor in theol, but possibly not in Paris. Ordained priest by Bourlemont of Bordeaux in 1659. Elected *ag-gén* in 1660 by Rouen province. Prior *in comm* of Ste-Marguerite-d'Eslincourt O Cluny (Beauvais) before episcopate.

Nom 12-5-1666. Provs 11-10-1666. Consec 12-12-1666. Died 28-11-1676.

Sources: ASV, PC 64, fos 361–76.

Colbert, Jean-Baptiste-Michel. Montauban 1675–93, Toulouse 1693–1710.   Brother of Michel, above. Baptised at St-Gervais and Prothais, Paris, 1640. Studied in Paris, where Bossuet presided over his bachelor's *tentativa* exam in theol in March 1662, taking 79th place in 1666 lic, which he followed up, not with doct in theol, but a law degree, since he became *cons-clerc* in Paris parlt. Ordained priest 5-10-1670. Royal almoner before elected to 1665 and 1670 AC. Foucault, intendant of Montauban, claimed he alerted Colbert, the *contr-gén*, as to the deteriorating condition of Pierre de Bertier, the previous bp in 1674, so likely to have paved the way for succession. Obtained abbey of Mas-Granier OSB (Toulouse) in 1686. Heavily criticised for behaviour in Toulouse during the 1680s.

Nom to Montauban 21-11-1674. Provs 15-7-1675. Consec 28-10-1675. Nom to Toulouse 15-8-1687. Provs 12-10-1693. Died 11-7-1710.

Sources: ASV, PC 74, fos 335–51 (Montauban); PC 87, fos 702–20 (Toulouse). Bossuet, *Correspondance*, xv, 440. BN, MS Fr 20969, fo 50; MS Lat 15440, p 227.

Colbert, André. Auxerre 1678–1704. Son of Charles, *prés* in *présidial* court of Reims, and Marguerite de Mévilliers. Born Reims, 1646, but resident in Paris since early 1660s, where he studied phil and theol, taking his MA Aug 1663. Prior of Sorbonne in final years, before taking doct in theol on 28-6-1672, having been ranked 2nd in 1672 lic. Priest since 1672, ordained by Bp Chaumont of Dax. Canon of Reims cath in 1663, he was made canon of *collégiale* of Appoigny (Auxerre) and archpriest in cath chapter by his uncle, Nicolas, bp of Auxerre, which doubtless paved way for deputation to AC of 1675. Succeeded uncle at Auxerre despite ambitions of nephew of previous bp but one, Pierre de Broc.

Nom 21-9-1676. Provs 6-6-1678. Consec 24-7-1678. Died 19-7-1704.

Sources: ASV, PC 77, fos 53–63. Poutet, 'Docteurs', 306, no 626.

Colbert, Jacques-Nicolas. Rouen coadj 1680/91–1707. Baptised in St-Eustache, Paris, 14-2-1655. 2nd son of Jean-Baptiste, royal minister, and Marie Charron. Studied phil in Paris, where MA in Aug 1672, followed by theol at Sorbonne, ranked 1st in 1678 lic and doct 14-4-1679. Entered St-Sulpice 1-12-1679, and was ordained priest 1-4-1679. Abbot *in comm* of Bec and prior of La Charité sur Loire when only 10 years old, adding Ambierle OSB (Lyon) in 1669. His father's prestige got him elected to Académie Française, also in 1678. Nom coadj of Rouen early in 1680, but moves had been afoot to that end for over a year previously. He effectively admin Rouen from early 1680s onwards, and displayed considerable organisational skills, but his dislike of Jesuits earned him unfounded suspicion of pro-Jansenism. He advocated moderation in treatment of Huguenots.

Nom 2-2-1680. Provs 29-8-1680. Consec 4-8-1680. Succeeds to Rouen, Jan 1691. Died 10-12-1707.

Sources: ASV, PC 79, fos 537–50. Bossuet, *Correspondance*, i, 393. Goujard, *Un Catholicisme bien tempéré*, 14–16. DHGE, xiii, 225–6. DBF, ix, 191–2.

Colbert de Croissy, Charles-Joachim. Montpellier 1697–1738. Son of Charles Colbert, marquis de Croissy, and Françoise Bérauld. Born Paris 11-6-1667, baptised in St-Eustache church, 16-6-1667. Educated at Jesuit coll of Louis-le-Grand and coll of La Marche, Univ of Paris, where he was MA in July 1684. Accompanied Cardinal Fürstenberg to 1689 conclave, was arrested and detained by Spaniards at Milan on way home. Completed studies on return, taking 1st place in 1692 lic and obtaining doct on 21-3-1692. Ordained priest 22-12-1691. Abbot *in comm* of Froidmont O Cist (Beauvais) in 1684. Vic-gen of his cousin at Rouen for Pontoise. Elected dep to 1693 AC and *ag-gén* in 1695, by Rouen province on both occasions. A rigorist who was suspected of Jansenist leanings from his early days, he was one of first 4 bps to appeal versus *Unigenitus* in 1717.

Nom 1-11-1696. Provs 14-1-1697. Consec 10-3-1697. Died 8-4-1738.

Sources: ASV, PC 91, fos 259–77. Bossuet, *Correspondance*, ix, 267. Durand, *Le Jansénisme au xviiie siècle et Joachim Colbert*. DHGE, xiii, 226–7.

Cosnac, Gabriel. Die 1702–34 (resign). Nephew of Daniel de Cosnac, bp of Valence and Die until 1687. Born Vic le Vicomte, Clermont dioc, 1-11-1650. Son of Armand, marquis de Cosnac and elder brother of Daniel, and Marie de Penacoit, heiress of the La Guesle and Veilhan families. Studied in Paris along with Jacques Demarests and others, where he took lic in theol. Ordained priest 29-6-1690. Canon of Aix, thanks to *régale* and uncle's goodwill as the 'nominated' archbishop, in April 1690, he duly became provost of Aix chapter a few years later, again with uncle's patronage, who also made him his vic-gen, and almost certainly used his political influence in Provence, which was considerable, to open ranks of episcopate to him. The deputation to 1695 AC, followed in 1700 by election as *ag-gén* by province of Aix, were key stages in this progression. Obtained St-Jean-d'Orbestier OSB (Luçon), also on resignation of uncle in 1701, on same day as nom to Die. His own nephew, Daniel-Joseph succeeded him at Die in 1734.

Nom 24-12-1701. Provs 12-6-1702. Consec 23-7-1702. Resign 15-4-1734. Died 26-10-1739.

Sources: ASV, PC 95, fos 132–44. BN, 20969, fo 161. AD Bouches-du-Rhône, 1 G 1273, fos 784–8r (canon of Aix). Champeval, *Dictionnaire des familles nobles de la Corrèze*, ii, 109–40. Cosnac, *Mémoires*, ii, 455–70. Chevalier, *Essai historique sur l'église et la ville de Die*, iii, 566–604. Bergin, *Making*, 600.

Crévy. *See* **Rogier.**

Crillon, François Balbe de Berton de. Vence 1697–1714, Vienne 1714–20. From same family as Henri IV's legendary 'brave Crillon' who had managed to capture a significant amount of church patronage in southern France thanks to his role in Henri IV's service in the early 1590s, but long before family members were in a position to benefit from it. In fact, Crillon family's roots were far more modest than this suggests. Natives of Piedmont, they moved to Avignon in 15th c, where they held municipal office in subsequent generations. Yet no more than *marchands bourgeois* of Avignon in mid-16th c when they bought the fief of Crillon near Carpentras and were ennobled and naturalised by Henri II. A century later, still firmly based in Avignon region, their status was much improved by royal service, esp military, which they sustained under Henri IV's successors. By now church office loomed large, with older and younger generations cooperating effectively, as is demonstrated by those becoming bishops under Louis XIV and Louis XV.

François, 4th son of Louis, sgr de Crillon, colonel of papal artillery, who had earlier served in French army, and Marie d'Albertas de Bertons, was born in 1640 in Avignon dioc, and baptised in collegiate church of ND de Principali on 17-3-1648. He took his doct of theol, at the Sapientia, in Rome, at an unknown date, and lic *in utr* at Avignon on 15-5-1687. Ordained priest 21-2-1671. Served as vic-gen of St-Paul-Trois-Châteaux for some years. Provost of Cavaillon cath chapter in 1667, thanks to his Roman connections, he obtained St-Liguaire of Niort before episcopate, followed by St-Florent-de-Saumur (1712).

Nom 25-5-1697. Provs 20-11-1697. Consec 29-12-1697. Nom to Vienne, 31-3-1714. Provs 17-9-1714. Died 30-10-1720.

Sources: ASV, PC 91, fos 524–43; PC 103, fos 813–24. AN, MC, LXXXII, 113, 27-1-1712 (St-Florent). BM Aix, MS 257, p 254. AD Vaucluse, D 138, fo 5v. Fénelon, *Correspondance*, xvii, 117–18, n 16. Pinard, *Chronologie*, vi, 469–70. Chaix d'Est-Ange, *Dictionnaire des familles*, iv, 131–4. Labande, *Avignon au xvᵉ siecle*. DBF, ix, 1249–51.

Crillon, Jean-Louis Balbe de Berton de. St-Pons 1713–27, Toulouse 1727–39, Narbonne 1739–51. Nephew of François above, he was born in Cavaillon dioc, 1-7-1685. 4th son of Philippe Marie, marquis de Berton, originally a knight of Malta, and Françoise de Saporta-Chateauneuf. His uncle, bp of Vence, took charge of his education and possibly his career. He studied mainly in Avignon, where he took his lic in theol on 24-5-1706, when still a mere tonsured cleric. Subdeacon in 1708, he was ordained priest in 1711. By then he was vic-gen to uncle in Vence dioc, who secured his election to 1710 AC. He also became abbot *in comm* of St-Etienne-de-Baignes (Saintes) in 1710. An experienced preacher before episcopate, he was offered Vienne in 1720 on death of uncle, but refused it, as he did post of French ambassador to Madrid. Accepted Toulouse in 1727, whence he moved to Narbonne in 1739. *Commandeur* of order of St-Esprit in 1742.

Nom to St-Pons, 22-4-1713. Provs 18-9-1713. Consec 15-10-1713. Nom to Toulouse 23-8-1727. Provs 22-9-1727. Nom to Narbonne 31-8-1739. Provs 14-12-1739. Died 5-3-1751.

Sources: AN, MC, LXXXII 118, 13-8-1710 (St-Etienne de Baigne); LXXXII 122, 7-6-1713 (St-Pons). BM Aix, MS 257, p 264–5. AD Vaucluse, D 140, fo 141. DBF, ix, 1251–2.

Crissé de Sanzay. *See* **Turpin.**

Des Alries du Rousset, Louis-Charles. Béziers 1702–44.   The bp's family seem to have originated in the Vivarais, but settled in the Dauphiné in 15th c, intermarrying with local noble families and following, as far as can be determined, military careers in next century or so. By mid-17th c, they were also allied by marriage to some parlt families of Aix (Fabri, Simiane). Bp's eldest brother was the 1st to hold parlt office in Grenoble, but 2 of his brothers were Knights of Malta. The line had died out by mid-18th c.

Born at Valréas in Vaison dioc, in 1663, son of Joseph des Alries, marquis de Rousset, and Gasparde de Roustain de Gerson. He took 42nd place in 1692 theol lic in Paris, but doct 6 years later on 9-8-1698, same year as his ordination. He became dean of Carcassonne cath in Jan 1700, as well as vic-gen there for over 3 years before nom to Béziers, thanks to patronage of bp, Louis-Joseph de Grignan, a fellow Dauphinois, who consec him in Carcassonne in due course. Elected to represent Narbonne province at 1701 AC which, as so often, brought him a step closer to episcopate. Not king's 1st choice for Béziers in 1702, but his services as vic-gen in Carcassonne were thought to have helped him when La Poype de Vertrieu was given Poitiers having rejected Béziers.

Nom 15-4-1702. Provs 25-9-1702. Consec 3-12-1702. Died 6-9-1744.

Sources: ASV, PC 95, fos 66–74. Virieu, 'Parlement de Grenoble', 117. Borricand, *Nobiliaire de Provence*, i, 64. Clapiers-Collongues, *Chronologie*, 86, 100.

Desclaux de Mesplès, Dominique. Lescar 1681–1716.   Relative of Jacques, bp of Dax (1638–58) and Dominique, Richelieu's confessor. Born Dax 1637, son of Sauvat Desclaux, *avocat* in parlt of Navarre and later *cons* in *présidial* of Dax, and Catherine de Bedbeder. In 1655, having taken doct *in utr* at Bordeaux to follow a legal career, he married Louise de Mesplès, daughter of *cons* in Navarre parlt and heiress of family title, and marriage contract bound him to add her family name to his. Her family ties were more impressive than his, and opened up new avenues. Their eldest son married Jeanne de Gassion, niece of the marshal and bp Pierre Gassion of Lescar (1648–52), and finished his career as *prés à mortier* in parlt of Navarre and *premier baron* of Estates of Béarn, a spectacular metamorphosis! Another son was *cons* in Pau parlt. Bp succeeded his father-in-law in parlt in 1657, and as baron of Dourmy was admitted to Estates of Béarn in 1670. His wife's death in 1670 led to change of direction: ordained priest in 1678, he became dean of Bidache chapter in Dax dioc, and participated in a mission against Calvinists of Bearn, which may well have brought him to royal attention subsequently.

Nom 30-5-1681. Provs 1-12-1681. Consec 19-4-1682. Died 23-1-1716.

Sources: ASV, PC 80, fos 395–416. Dufau de Maluquer, *Armorial de Béarn*, iii, 51–4. Labau, *Lescar, cite épiscopale*, ii, 87, 100–1. Lamant, *Armorial et nobiliaire*, ix, 274–6. Bergin, *Making*, 607, 627–8.

Des Marais/Desmarets. *See* **Godet.**

Desmarets, Jacques. Riez 1693–1714, Auch 1714–25.   Family originates from Le Plessis-Alleaume in Picardy, but by 16th c it was based in Laon where it belonged to the merchant-bourgeois class. Their origins were rather less modest than St-Simon claimed, but far less elevated than Desmarets family themselves asserted, i.e. descent from a gov of Laon. Grandfather of future *contr-gén* was a modest *procureur du roi* at the *baillage* of Vermandois in 1603, but his son Jean's marriage to Marie Colbert, sister of Jean-Baptiste, in 1634 later catapulted eldest branch of the Desmarets out of their obscurity, whereas the younger one remained commoner and provided a *fermier-général* and an inspector of royal manufactures in 18th c. Bp's father was ennobled by office of *trés de France* at Soissons from 1634. Nicolas, the bps' brother, on whom their fortunes depended after Colbert's death in 1683, suffered eclipse in subsequent years before making a comeback as Louis XIV's last *contr-gén des finances* 1709–15.

Born Soissons 1655, while his father was prov intendant, but lived in Paris virtually since birth. Son of Jean and Marie Colbert, sister of the 'grand' Colbert. Studies in Paris from hum and phil onwards, MA in July 1672, 9th place in 1680 theol lic, and doct in theol on 30-7-1681. Priest since ca 1679, when also becomes canon of ND de Paris. Abbot *in comm* of Landais (Bourges) in 1677. *Ag-gén* from 1678 to 1685, which normally opened way to episcopate, and *cons d'état*, 1680. Long episcopate at Riez unremarkable, while brother's return to office ensured transfer to a better see.

Nom to Riez 15-8-1685. Provs 7-12-1693. Consec 24-1-1694. Nom to Auch 21-7-1713. Provs 26-2-1714. Died 27-11-1725.

Sources: ASV, PC 87, fos 626–34 (Riez); PC 103, fos 66–78 (Auch). Bluche, *L'Origine*, 146–7. St-Simon, xxiii, 280–1. *Gall Chr Nov*, Riez, cols 642–3. Boisnard, *Touraine*, no 826.

Desmarets, Vincent-François. St-Malo 1702–39. Younger brother of Jacques. Baptised in St-Lodegard's church Soissons 11-6-1657, 3rd son of Jean and Marie Colbert. Initially known as M de Vouzy, he served first in French navy as *capitaine de vaisseau* and then obtained a company of French guards in 1680, but had quit service by ca 1687, when he began studies at coll du Plessis, Paris. On completing phil, he obtained lic in canon law, but not clear from which univ. He entered St-Magloire seminary in Sept 1692 and was ordained priest 22-12-1696. Gr-vic of abp of Rouen, his Colbert uncle, for Pontoise and Vexin by 1697. *Ag-gén* of clergy in 1698. Close to Oratorians in whose seminary chapel he says mass and assists at divine offices before episcopate. Abbot of St-Bénigne of Dijon in July 1710 (which made him *cons-né* in Dijon parlt), adding St-Nicolas-aux-Bois in Jan 1715. Joined the appeal against *Unigenitus* but renounced it in last years.

Nom 15-4-1702. Provs 31-7-1702. Consec 17-9-1702. Died 25-9-1739.

Sources: ASV, PC 95, fos 265–81. BN, MS Fr 23502, fo 158 (Sept 1692). Bossuet, *Correspondance*, xii, 335, n 6. Fénelon, *Correspondance*, xvii, 240, n 8. Couet, 'Mgr Desmaretz, seigneur-évêque de St-Malo', 467–87. Compère and Julia, *Collèges français*, ii, 649.

Des Montiers. *See* **Mérinville.**

Dreuillet, André. Bayonne 1707–27. Identifying the background of this bp is complicated by the various spellings of the name (Druillet, Dreuilhet, Druilhet), as well as the existence of unrelated families from Toulouse and elsewhere bearing similar names. But his family appear to have been established in Toulouse as *marchands* and *bourgeois* by mid-16th c, with some of them being suspected of Protestant sympathies in the 1560s and 1570s. Despite a marriage alliance with the Caulet family in 1594, until the 1620–30s they were at best lawyers and barristers in Toulouse, and bp's grandfather (d 1653) was 1st of them to enter the parlt of Toulouse, where he ended his career as a *prés* in *Enquêtes* chamber, a post also held by bp's father (1678–1718) and elder brother with whom the male line died out in 18th c. Both of bp's father's wives were daughters of *trés de France*, while the 2nd of them, Isabeau de Thomas de Montlaur, whose mother was a Lavergne de Tressan, was a social and literary figure in her own right whose connections were of vital importance in her stepson's church career.

Born 1-12-1664, in parish of St-Etienne, Toulouse. Son of Jacques, *prés* in parlt, and Marie Dupuy, his 1st wife. Further studies in Paris, where he took MA in Feb 1684, 94th place in

1690 theol lic, and doct on 23-1-1694. Priest since 19-12-1693. Already a *prébendier* of Conques and holder of other benefices while student in Paris, he was made canon of Le Mans cath in Nov 1692 by bp Lavergne de Tressan, a relative of his stepmother. He became vicegerent of the *officialité* and archdeacon of Montfort in 1694, and finally vic-gen in Oct 1695 of what was one of northern France's larger diocs. He preached a funeral oration for Philippe d'Orléans in 1703. Cardinal Noailles pushed his case for mitre, while Mme de Maintenon personally presented him with his bishop's staff. Devoted to Noailles, he proved to be fierce opponent of *Unigenitus*, being one of 4 bps to launch the 1st appeal against it in 1717.

Nom 23-4-1707. Provs 7-11-1707. Consec 8-1-1708. Died 17-11-1727.

Sources: ASV, PC 100, fos 107–19. St-Simon, xxxviii, 324. Dubarat and Daranatz, *Recherches sur la ville et l'église de Bayonne*, iii, 1333–5. O'Gilvy, *Nobiliaire de Guienne et de Gascogne*, i, 269–75. Villain, *France moderne*, ii, 2, 1813–14.

Dromesnil. *See* **Hallencourt**.

Du Bouchet. *See* **Lobière, Sourches**.

Du Chaffaut. *See* **Maurel**.

Du Cambout de Coislin, Pierre. Orléans 1666–1706.   Originating in 13th c in northern Breton dioc of St-Brieuc, the du Cambout moved south into county of Nantes after acquiring the Coislin title by marriage in 1537 – not uncommon among noble families. The next generation was marked by marriage to a great-aunt of future Cardinal Richelieu, in 1565, and acquisition of barony of Ponchâteau, in 1585, which included right to preside over the noble chamber in the Breton Estates, by which time du Cambout was gov of Nantes and *grand maître* of the Breton *eaux et forêts*. A generation later, Richelieu, himself woefully short of close relatives, utilised the services of, and advanced the fortunes in every sense of his Breton cousins, and laid the foundations of their rise into the peerage in 1660s. His death did them no damage – their Séguier connections as well as Louis XIV's own esteem for the younger generation (the new duc de Coislin and the bp of Orléans in particular) did the rest. But bp of Metz was the last of his line, inheriting the duchy of Coislin itself.

Born Nov 1636, 2nd son of César (1613–41), marquis de Coislin, col-gen of Suisses, and Marie Séguier, eldest daughter of Chancellor Séguier. Doctor in theol, Univ of Valence, no date, but he studied primarily in Paris. Deacon at time of nom to Orléans, ordained priest 16-8-1665 at St-Victor, *extra tempora*, by Abp Péréfixe of Paris. Abbot *in comm* of Jumièges, aged 6, in 1641, he exchanged it for St-Victor (Paris) in 1643. Also abbot *in comm* of St-Jean of Amiens, St-Gildas-des-Bois, and prior *in comm* of Argenteuil, Longpont, St-Pierre of Abbeville, etc. Canon of ND Paris, *premier aumônier* of king in 1657, *commandeur des ordres*, 1688, cardinal in 1697, *grand aumônier de France* in 1700. St-Simon had extremely high opinion of him, but was not alone, as king held him in highest regard. Despite court office, he was a resident and active bishop of Orléans, a rigorist whose sympathies were pro-Jansenist to all intents and purposes.

Nom 24-5-1665. Provs 29-3-1666. Consec 20-6-1666. Cardinal 22-7-1697. Died 5-2-1706.

Sources: ASV, PC 64, fos 54–71. St-Simon, i, 82; ii, 354–7. Vindry, *État major, gendarmerie*, 105–6. Neveu, *Sébastien Joseph du Cambout de Pontchâteau*. J. Debal, *Histoire d'Orléans*, 116–19.

Du Cambout de Coislin, Henri-Charles. Metz 1697–1732.   Nephew of bp of Orléans. Baptised in St-Sauveur parish church, Paris, 2-9-1664. Youngest of 5 sons of Armand (1635–1702), duc de Coislin, lt-gen in Lower Brittany, member of Académie Française in 1652, and Madeline du Halgouet, daughter of an old Breton family, married in 1654. Godson of Henri de Lorraine comte d'Harcourt, *grand ecuyer* de France, and Charlotte Séguier, dowager duchess of Sully, daughter of Chancellor Séguier. May have been initially intended for Order of Malta, but death of elder brother and influence of uncle led him towards church, against father's wishes. Studies at coll of Navarre, Paris where he took MA in highly public ceremony, July 1682, followed by 109th (and last) place in 1688 theol lic, and finishing with doct in Paris on 3-8-1694. Ordained priest by Abp Le Tellier of Reims on 7-6-1694. Also abbot *in comm* of Boscherville (Rouen) in 1684. *Premier aumônier* to Louis XIV in succession to uncle who obtained *survivance* for him. Also vic-gen at Orléans for 2–3 years before episcopate. The Cardinal, who was largely responsible for his career, persuaded a reluctant Louis XIV to give him Metz, where he became a model bp despite fears of a *vocation forcée*. *Commandeur* of Order of St-Esprit 1701, elected to Académie Française in 1710, he also inherited the famous Séguier library, which he left to abbey of St-Germain-des-Prés on death in 1732.

Nom 25-6-1697. Provs 11-11-1697. Consec 22-12-1697. Died 28-11-1732.

Sources: ASV, PC 91, fos 234–58; fondo Santini 210 (benefices). Bossuet, *Correspondance*, viii, 190. Taveneaux, *Jansénisme en Lorraine*, 221ff.

Du Doucet, Jean. Belley 1712–45. Belley rarely attracted bps of more than limited social origins or ambition, so relative obscurity of this bp is not surprising. It seems his family were originally from Anjou or Poitou, but settled in Cussac in the Limousin via marriage to daughter of the sgr of Le Puy de Cussac in 1549. Their tacitly acquired nobility was upheld in 1667 *recherches*, but little else is known about them. Bp's career was made elsewhere.

Born in parish of Cussac, 50 km south-west of Limoges, 3-10-1665. Son of Pierre, sgr of Le Puy de Cussac, and Marie du Rousseau de Ferrière. His early studies went no futher than bacc in theol, but he made good the defect by taking the doct of theol at Bourges in May 1711. He joined clergy of St-Sulpice where, after his ordination as priest on 11-3-1690, he served as curate under direction of famous Chétardie, its curé, for 16 years before 1712. And at Belley, he succeeded a fellow-Sulpician, Madot, transferred to Chalon-sur-Saône.

Nom 26-03-1712. Provs 5-10-1712. Consec 11-12-1712. Died 4-2-1745.

Sources: AN, MC, LXXXII, 115, 27-7-1712. Lamant, *Armorial et nobiliaire*, xix, 61.

Du Houssay. *See* **Malier.**

Du Laurens, Pierre. Belley 1678–1705. Nephew of 2 archbishops promoted by Henri IV, Honoré, abp of Embrun (1601–12), and Gaspard, abp of Arles (1608–30), who owed their good fortune to their brother, André, the king's *premier médecin*. Although that influence waned sharply after his death in 1609 – André's only son died childless and his brother Gaspard failed to obtain coadjutorship of Arles for a nephew – it kept next generation close enough to centre of power to consolidate their gains (e.g. 2 *cons* in Paris parlt), though Pierre's route to episcopal rank was wholly unlike that of his uncles before him. One of his sisters married the prov intendant, Jean de Balthazar, and their connections to the powerful Sanguin family also benefited them under Louis XIII and beyond.

Born in St-Nicolas-du-Chardonnet parish, Paris, ca 1620, son of Richard, sgr de Chevry, *avocat au conseil*, and Anne Robert. He entered OSB relatively young, since he was already a professed monk of St-Martin-des-Champs, Paris, while studying in Paris theol fac in early to mid-1640s. Took 1st place in lic exam of 1646, with doct in May 1646, he also became a *hospes* of Sorbonne, 28-4-1646. Ordained priest in 1648. Prior of coll of Cluny, Paris, and also grand prior of Order of Cluny as a whole under generalship of Conti and Mazarin, which enabled him to obtain several benefices for himself. One source claims that a favour he engineered for one of Mme de Montespan's children by Louis XIV was the real reason for his nom to Belley, where he took close interest in formation of clergy and ecclesiastical discipline.

Nom 18-6-1677. Provs 7-11-1678. Consec 12-2-1679. Died 17-1-1705.

Sources: ASV, PC 77, fos 80–92. AN, L 728, pièce 1, no 66. Poutet, 'Docteurs', 248, no 101. St-Simon, xl, 251, n 1. Popoff, *Prospographie*, 653. Bergin, *Making*. 613–14.

Du Luc. *See* **Vintimille**.

Estaing, Joachim-Joseph. St-Flour 1693–1742.   This bp was grandnephew of the 2 Estaing bps of neighbouring dioc of Clermont (1614–64), themselves nephews of Cardinal de la Rochefoucauld, previously bp of Clermont (1585–1610). It was through his marriage, in 1616, to Catherine du Bourg, dame de Saillans, that bp of St-Flour's grandfather (a brother to the bps of Clermont) acquired lands/title of Saillans (or Saillant) in Auvergne, which Louis XIV raised to *comté* status, and duly became the name by which his branch of this already extensive family were usually known. Extensive military service in armies of Louis XIV by bp's father and several brothers was complemented by the presence of other members in St-Jean chapter in Lyon. The Combourcier were related by marriage to the Montmorin and other prominent prov families.

Born in château of Ravel, Clermont dioc, 1654, baptised on 24-12-1656. 4th of 10 sons of Jean, comte de Saillans, and Claude-Marie de Combourcier, married in 1647. Little known about studies except he took bacc in theol, Univ of Valence, date unknown. Tonsured in Clermont, March 1676, he was elected canon of St-Jean Lyon in March 1677, where an elder brother was already a canon. He took remaining minor orders and subdiaconate in March 1679, the diaconate in Sept 1680, and priesthood in March 1682. Some activity in missions to new converts in 1680s. Prior of St-Irenée in June 1693. He was the *doyen* of French bps when he died in 1742.

Nom 8-9-1693. Provs 9-11-1693. Consec 3-1-1694. Died 13-4-1742.

Sources: ASV, PC 87, fos 245–53. AN, L 744, pièce 1, no 2. Remacle, *Dictionnaire des familles d'Auvergne*, ii, 90–1. Pinard, *Chronologie*, iv, 527–30, 573–5; vi, 283. Beyssac, *Chanoines de Lyon*, 213. Vergé-Franceschi, *Officiers généraux de la marine*, vii, 107–8. Bergin, *Making*, 620.

Étampes de Valançay, Jean-Baptiste. Marseille 1682–4.   From same extended family as Léonor d'Étampes de Valançay, bp of Chartres (1621–41), abp of Reims (1642–51). Their 17th c history saw them keep – or establish – a foot in several spheres at once – the army, diplomacy, robe officeholding and church. Their marriages also made them one of France's best-connected families.

Born at Neuvy in Orléans dioc, 1638. Son of Joseph d'Étampes, marquis d'Autry, and Louise Legrand. Studied mainly in Paris arts and theol fac, where matriculated in 1654, and later took 63rd (and last) place in the lic of 1662. Elected *socius* of Sorbonne, he became doctor of theol 14-2-1664. Nom bp and inquisitor of Perpignan in 1675, but with differences between Rome and France over Perpignan dioc delaying despatch of bulls, he opted instead for see of Marseille, for which bulls were also slow in coming. Episcopal dep to 1682 AC for Arles province, despite being neither confirmed by Rome nor consec. He took possession of Marseille *par procureur* in early June 1682, but died on 6-1-1684 suddenly, just when he seemed finally disposed to move there. 'D'un grand éclat pour le faste, d'un grand nom pour sa maison, d'un grand rang pour son caractère', he was a classic *abbé de cour* and a reluctant bp who was ill suited for such distant diocs.

Nom 3-9-1679. Provs 12-1-1682. Consec 22-2-1682. Died 6-1-1684.

Sources: ASV, no PC file. BN, MS Fr 32510, fo 223. AUP, reg 97, fo 30r. AN, G^{8}, vol 88 (1682 AC). *Lettres de Séguier*, ii, 1195–6. Albanès, *Armorial et sigillographie des évêques de Marseille*, 167–8. Poutet, 'Docteurs', 283, no 386. Boisnard, *Touraine*, no 909. Bergin, *Making*, 621–2.

Estrées, Jean. Laon 1681–94.   Nephew of Cardinal d'Estrées, his predecessor at Laon (1655–81). Born 1651, 3rd son of François-Annibal, gov of Ile-de-France, ambassador to Rome, and Catherine de Lauzières de Thémines. *Enfant d'honneur* of Louis XIV's son, the dauphin, he studied at Univ of Paris, where he was MA in June 1676, bachelor of theol, Dec 1676 under presidency of Bossuet, and went on to take 1ˢᵗ place in 1680 lic, followed by doct 9-4-1680. Already abbot *in comm* of Conches, in 1673 his powerful uncle seems to have little difficulty exercising a cardinal's prerogative of selecting him as his successor at Laon, where his own diplomatic responsibilities had reduced him to an infrequent visitor. Did much to assist poor in 1693, and was active in founding *conférences ecclésiastiques* and *maison de retraite* for clergy 1687 – a short but well-filled episcopate, he was not much tempted by glittering career of uncle, who outlived him by 20 years.

Nom 2-4-1681. Provs 2-6-1681. Consec 27-7-1681. Died 1-12-1694.

Sources: ASV, no PC file. BN, MS Lat 15440, pp 265–6; MS Lat 15673, p 26. Bossuet, *Correspondance*, v, 307. Sars, *Laonnais féodal*, 84.

Fagon, Antoine. Lombez 1712–20, Vannes 1720–42.   Family originated in Brittany, but moved to Paris by early 17ᵗʰ c at latest, where bp's great-grandfather was in household and financial service of *grands* like Guise and Condé, while his grandfather was a *commissaire des guerres* who married Louise de la Brosse, niece of Guy de Brosse, *médecin ordinaire* of Louis XIII, which opened the door to medical career for next generation under Louis XIV. Bp's father Guy-Crescent (1638–1718), godson of Guy de la Brosse, was initially employed by Vallot in the Jardin des Plantes, before becoming successively *premier médicin* of Dauphin's wife and Marie-Thérèse, finally replacing Aquin as king's *premier médecin* (1693). *Surintendant* of the Jardin royal (1699), where he was already an intendant and professor. Highly regarded for his learning, powerfully connected at court, where his rise was sponsored from the outset by Maintenon in her desire to get rid of Aquin. Eldest son an *intendant des finances* in later years of Louis XIV and subsequent Regency.

Born Paris, parish of St-Paul, probably 1665, younger of 2 sons of Guy-Crescent and Marie Nozereau, daughter of Paris silversmith. He studied in Paris with, *inter alios*, Jacques Forbin-Janson abp of Arles, with whom he travelled to Rome and with whom he later shared the position of vic-gen to Cardinal Janson at Beauvais. MA in Paris, with full public ceremony, in Aug 1688. Bossuet presided over his *tentativa* in coll of Navarre, Feb 1692, he obtained 8ᵗʰ place in 1696 lic, and took doct 24-5-1696. Ordained priest in 1698. His father's influence sufficed to gain him benefices relatively quickly: he was nom to Chatrices OSA (Châlons-sur-Marne), in 1687, followed by St-Méen OSB (St-Malo) in 1698, and a pension of 1,200 *livres* off St-Malo in 1701. Dep to 1705 AC for Paris, suggesting Noailles patronage, when he was dean of Notre Dame chapter.

Nom 5-4-1711. Provs 16-3-1712. Consec 22-5-1712. Nom to Vannes 29-8-1719. Provs 20-3-1720. Died 16-2-1742.

Sources: AN, MC, LXXXII, 112, 26-12-1711. BN, MS Fr 20969, fos 56, 142, 163; MS Lat 15440, p 330; MS Lat 15673, p 57. *Journal de la santé du Louis XIV*, xxix–xxxvi. St-Simon, i, 287, n 5. Bluche, *L'Origine*, 170–1. Brockliss and Jones, *Medical World*, 288, 301. Bossuet, *Correspondance*, v, 74. Antoine, *Gouvernement*, 99.

Felix de Tassy, Henri. Digne 1676–7, Chalon sur Saône 1677–1711.   His real family name was *Felix*, that of Tassy or Tassi being a seigneurial title only. Their origins were possibly Piedmontese, but by 17ᵗʰ c there were branches in Marseille and Avignon. Bp's father, François, was born in Avignon, but moved to Paris, became *premier chirurgien* to Louis XIV in 1653, died in 1676. Bp's elder brother, Charles-François (d 1703), obtained reversion of his father's office in 1662, and succeeded him in 1676. Both father and son were well respected, and were close to certain literary circles of the capital. Charles-François was ennobled by Louis XIV in 1690 for his services – well deserved, given that his dexterity had saved king's life by removing fistula in 1686, though the ennoblement was presented as confirmation of their original noble status. Other court offices followed in 1690s – one of 4 posts of *premier valet de la garde-robe* in 1690, and later one of *contr-gén* of *maison du roi*, which he passed to his son in 1698.

Born 23-7-1641, Henri was son of François, sgr de Stains, and Helene Barbier. Univ studies in Paris, MA in Sept 1665, 69th place in theol lic of 1670, and becoming doct there on 24-9-1670. Priest since 1664. Obtained archdiaconate in Auch cath in June 1662, almost certainly thanks to graduate rights. Treasurer of Ste-Chapelle of Vincennes in 1664, which he kept until 1689. Also seems to have been made royal almoner in 1660s. He preached in several churches of the capital. Initial talk of him getting Apt or Gap, but Digne materialised instead. Nom just before father's death. Transferred to Chalon-sur-Saône in 1677, where he reputedly showed the *douceur* and *sagesse* he inherited from father. Obtains ND de Mezières O Cist (Châlons) when bp of Chalon-sur-Saône, 17-4-1688.

Nom 17-9-1675. Provs 19-10-1676. Consec 6-12-1676. Nom to Chalon-s-Saône 18-6-1677. Provs 31-1-1678. Died 11-11-1711.

Sources: ASV, PC 75, fos 169–79. AN, O[1] 34, fo 65v (ennoblement letters, March 1690). BN, MS Fr 20969, fo 65, 119; MS Lat 15440, p 240; MS Lat 15673, p 17. Blanc, 'Origines', 234. St-Simon, viii, 239. Sévigné, *Correspondance*, iv, 141, 146. Poutet, 'Docteurs', 303, no 584. Fisquet, *France pontificale*, Digne et Riez, 117–18.

Fénelon, François de la Mothe-Salignac. Cambrai 1695–1715.   The most celebrated member of a family which had previously confined its episcopal ambitions to its local dioc, Sarlat, which they had held almost without interruption for a century before the wealthier and more prestigious see of Cambrai briefly took its place. Their 17th c history is paradoxical – prestigious alliances with aristocratic families, mainly from south-west France, accompanied by increasing levels of debt. The young Fénelon, son of a 2nd marriage, was entrusted after father's early death, to his *dévot* uncle, Antoine, marquis de Fénelon-Magnac, who patronised St-Sulpice and other good causes sponsored by the Compagnie du St-Sacrement to which he belonged. He owed far more to him than to his other uncle, bp of Sarlat (1659–88).

Born at château Fénelon, 6-8-1651, son of Pons, comte de Fénelon (1601–63), and his 2nd wife, Louise de la Cropte de St-Arbre, married in 1647. Early studies mainly in family residence, also possibly at coll in Cahors (1663–5), then at coll du Plessis (Univ of Paris), but he returned to Cahors to take MA ca 1669 and again for doct in theol on 26-3-1677. Tonsured in 1669, he frequented St-Sulpice in mid-1670s and engaged in pastoral activities under direction of Louis Tronson. Ordained priest possibly in March 1677, he was made (nominal) superior of community of Nouvelles Catholiques in 1679 on nom of L-A de Noailles to see of Cahors. Already well experienced as a preacher, which he pursued through 1680s mainly in Parisian churches, but also leading crown-sponsored missions to Protestants of Aunis-Saintonge in late 1685-early 1686 and 1687. Canon of Sarlat, where uncle was bp, in 1671, succeeds same uncle as dean of Carennac in 1681, and added priory of St-Avit-Sénieur OSA (Sarlat) in 1688. Nearly obtained Poitiers in 1685 and coadjutorship of La Rochelle in 1687, but was vetoed by Harlay of Paris. Preceptor of duc de Bourgogne, Louis XIV's eldest grandson (Aug 1689), Philippe d'Anjou (Aug 1690), duc de Berry (Aug 1693), thanks to links with Mme de Maintenon. Succeeds Pellisson in Académie Française 1693. Obtains abbey of St-Vallery OSB Amiens on 24-12-1694, but resigned it on nom to Cambrai. Compromised in Quietism affair by 1695, he was finally exiled to Cambrai, Aug 1697, his family and friends were banished from court 1698, he was deprived of post of preceptor to royal family and his *Maximes des saints* was condemned by Rome in 1699. Resident abp thereafter, but remains in contact with duc de Bourgogne's circle, whose death dashed his hopes of political reform after Louis XIV's death, but without diminishing his criticism of the king and his policies, nor his hostility to Jansenists.

Nom 4-2-1695. Provs 10-7-1695. Consec 10-7-1695. Died 7-1-1715.

Sources: ASV, PC 89, fos 99–108. Fénelon, *Correspondance*, 17 vols. *Oeuvres de Fénelon* (*La Pléiade* edn). Hillenaar, *Fénelon et les jésuites*. Bergin, *Making*, 698–9 (on Sarlat). DGS, 580–2.

Feuquières. *See* **Pas.**

Feydeau de Brou, Henri. Amiens 1692–1706. Family originally from La Marche region, where modest bourgeois in late 15th c. A century later, the main Parisian branch (Brou) was heavily involved in financial activities and officeholding, and survived bankruptcy of the great financier and tax-farmer Denis Feydeau (the bp's grandfather) in 1620s, moving with bp's father into judicial office in Paris parlt and rising further still to ministerial office in 18th c. They were connected to Phélypeaux family, also to prominent robe dynasties like Dugué de Bagnols, Le Camus, Lesrat, Maupeou, Bordeaux.

Son of Henri, *doyen* of *cons* in Paris parlt, and Marie Rouillé, daughter of a prominent robe family. Born and baptised Paris, 13-6-1653. All of studies in Paris – MA in July 1673, 6th place in 1678 theol lic, and doct on 2-8-1678. Ordained priest 18-12-1677. Dep to 1675 AC, when he was prior of St-Martin-de-Corras. *Aumônier du roi*, active as preacher, member of *petit concile* of Bossuet, whom he assisted at consecr of Fénelon as abp of Cambrai! St-Simon praised him highly – Feydeau de Brou 'fort distingué dans le clergé pour ses moeurs, sa piété, le gouvernement de son diocèse, sa science, sa capacité en affaires du clergé, son attachement aux maximes du Royaume et à la bonne morale, avec beaucoup de sagesse et discernement . . . et de ce qui étoit le plus éclairé dans l'épiscopat'.

Nom 18-5-1687. Provs 24-3-1692. Consec 31-8-1692. Died 14-6-1706.

Sources: ASV, PC 86, fos 324–30; PC 87, fos 31–43. BN, MS Lat 15440, p 261; MS Lat 15673, p 24. Fénelon, *Correspondance*, v, 199, no 404. St-Simon, iv, 93; xiii, 419–20. Boisnard, *Les Phélypeaux*, 169. Bluche, *L'Origine*, 175–7. Antoine, *Gouvernement*, 101–2.

Fieux, Jacques. Toul 1676–87. Natives of Brive and its environs in the Limousin, most of bp's family continued to reside there in 17th c and held secondary offices in local *présidial* court. It was, it appears, bp's father who moved to Paris early in century and who by the mid-1610s, at least, had begun to move in the capital's financial circles, as evidenced by activities as a *prête-nom* and *donneur d'avis* after 1617. He was successively *contrôleur* of the royal domain in the Soissonais (1621), SR (1623), RG at Rouen, and *intendant* and *contr-gén* of the *gabelles* in the 1630s. Services rendered to Richelieu during the La Rochelle campaign and later may have played a part in his advancement, which his son's marriage to Marie Charpentier, daughter of the cardinal's secretary, Denis, would seem to confirm. On his death in 1641, he was succeeded as SR by his eldest son, who went on to become an MR in 1653 and may have been attached in some way to the *conseil des finances* during these years, while other members of the family seem increasingly to have followed military careers. Bp's generation had strong Norman links, in both church and officeholding.

Born Paris, 1621, and baptised in St-Sulpice parish. Son of Etienne, marquis de Muis, and Marie Thévenin, daughter of a *prés* in parlt. All of his studies in Paris, initially at coll of Harcourt, where he was MA in July 1637, and then theol at Navarre, where he took lic exams in 1648 but was not 'presented' for his degree because not yet a deacon. Doctor of theol, Paris, 27-11-1656, having been contemporary of Bossuet, Harlay of Paris, and Monchy of Verdun, being particularly close to the latter in spirituality and his rigorist episcopal style. Priest for 16 years before episcopate. He preached widely and was superior of nuns of St-Sepulchre, Paris since late 1650s. Abbot *in comm* of Beaulieu O Cist (Langres), and Bellozane O Prem (Rouen) in Feb 1668. Initially intended as coadj to elderly Bp du Saussay at Toul, but latter's death in Sept 1675 made that unnecessary. A rigorist like Monchy of Verdun, he published work condemning usury in 1679, republished by successor, Bissy, in 1703.

Nom 29-6-1675. Provs 2-12-1676. Consec 17-1-1677. Died 15-3-1687.

Sources: ASV, PC 75, fos 761–81; Acta congregationis consistorialis, 1675, fo 284. BN, PO 1153, no 26195; Doss bleus 270, no 6983; Nouv d'Hozier 134, no 2923; MS Fr 7651, fo 191v; MS Fr 7656, fo 59 (*bienfaits du roi*). BSG 941, 123v, 17-7-1637 (MA). Poutet, 'Docteurs', 265, no 238. Taveneaux, *Jansénisme en Lorraine*, 195–6. Féret, *Faculté de Théologie*,

Époque moderne, v, 134–6. Champeval, *Dictionnaire des familles nobles et notables de la Corrèze*, ii, 198–201. Tessereau, *Chancellerie*, i, 345, 427, 480. *Inventaire des arrêts du conseil d'état de Henri IV*, no 13362. Bayard, *Le Monde des financiers*, 100.

Flamanville. *See* **Bazin.**

Fléchier, Valentin Esprit. Nîmes 1692–1710.   One of the glories of Louis XIV's episcopate, though not primarily for his episcopal record. Born in Perne (Carpentras dioc), baptised there 19-6-1632. Son of 'noble homme' Michel Fléchier, in reality a candle-maker – like the father of Cohon, one of his predecessors at Nîmes – and Marguerite Audiffret. Early studies at Tarascon in coll of Doctrinaires. Entered congregation of Doctrinaires at 15, where his uncle, Hercule Audiffret, was later to become sup-gen, and subsequently taught in Doctrinaire colls at Tarascon, Draguignan and Narbonne (where he preached his 1st major *sermon funèbre*, for Abp Rebé of Narbonne, 1659). Doctor of both theol (univ unknown) and canon law, Paris, though it was only after nom to Lavaur that he took law degree, in April 1686. Although leaving the Doctrinaires soon after his ordination as priest, ca 1665, he had already benefited substantially from uncle's Paris connections in Paris since early 1660s, frequenting the best literary salons, writing verses, and making connections that would serve his career. Successively preceptor in 1662 to Lefèvre de Caumartin (hence his presence in Auvergne for *grands jours* of 1665, in which Caumartin played important role as 'garde des sceaux') and Conrart families, he was recruited in 1668 by the duc de Montausier to assist in education of the Dauphin, for whom he wrote a life of Theodosius. But it was his preaching prowess which brought him renown, esp his funeral orations. Succeeded his uncle Audiffret's friend, Antoine Godeau in the Académie Française in 1672, he was made *aumônier ordinaire* of queen in 1680, then to the Dauphine in 1683. Montausier also obtained both abbey of St-Etienne-de-Baignes OSB (Saintes) and priory of Peyrat OSA (Perigueux) for him in Nov 1684. Selected along with Fénelon and Bourdaloue to conduct (pacific) conversion missions to Huguenots in 1685, on returning from which Louis XIV gave him Lavaur (where he obviously settled as vic-gen), but soon transferred him, despite his letter of refusal, to Nîmes, an even more intractable dioc, where he began residing in 1687–8. In Nîmes he was moderate, scholarly and a serious admin, probably too moderate and reasonable to understand passions of Camisards and pèlerins, but no friend either to Penitents and exaggerated meridional religiosity (despite his own Midi origins) – he championed a purified, reflective religion that avoided extremes. But he was not really 'up to' job of dealing with Huguenot problem in Nîmes, which required more than first-ranking preaching talents.

Nom to Lavaur, 9-11-1685. Nom to Nîmes, 15-8-1687 (renewed on 24-12-1689 after death of Séguier). Provs 21-1-1692. Consec 24-8-1692. Died 16-2-1710.

Sources: ASV, PC 86, fos 61–84. BN, MS Fr 20969, fo 36r. AN, L 737, pièce 1, no 47; MM 1120, p 190. Fléchier, *Oeuvres* (Paris 1782), v, 52. St-Simon, xix, 41–2. Sauzet, *Contre-Réforme*, 411–17. J de Viguerie, *Une Oeuvre d'éducation sous l'ancien régime* (Paris 1976), 248, 398. DLF, 489–95.

Fleuriau d'Armenonville, Louis-Gaston. Aire 1698–1706, Orléans 1706–33.   Originally a family of merchants and notables from Tours, where they engaged in business, along with their Bonneau and Drouyn relatives (and future financiers), until the 1630s when bp's father bought an office of SR (1634) and followed them into the world of Parisian royal finance and tax-farming, in which he prospered, escaping with a relatively light punishment from *chambre de justice* in 1665. His 2nd marriage in 1656 to Catherine Guillemin, daughter of a former *intendant de maison* of duchesse d'Orléans, illustrated his success, establishing kinship ties with Méliand and Bénard families among others. His eldest daughter's marriages would underline that success even more clearly – her 1st short-lived marriage (1652–5) was to a Fourcy, related to the Effiat and Ormesson families, her 2nd (1656–71) was to a then modest *cons* in parlt of Paris with a ministerial future, Claude Le Peletier, *contr-gén des finances* (1683–9).

Another sister, Marie, would be mother of Nicolas de Paris, bp of Orléans immediately after his uncle in 1733. It was Le Peletier (and later Phélypeaux de Pontchartrain) patronage that enabled bp's elder brother, Joseph Jean-Baptiste, to rise to a high rank in the financial admin from 1683 onwards, ending his career after 1715 as sec of state and keeper of the seals. Another brother, Thomas, was a well known Jesuit.

Born Paris, 15-6-1662. Son of Charles-François, sgr d'Armenonville, and Françoise Guillemin. Univ studies in Paris, where MA in July 1683, 47th place in 1688 theol lic. Doctor of theol, Paris on 4-2-1689. Ordained prest 20-9-1687. He entered St-Sulpice seminary in April 1681, moved to *petite communauté* in 1683, which he left in 1685, but maintained close links with Tronson and Leschassier as bp of Aire and Orléans. Canon of Chartres, 1684, treasurer of Ste Chapelle, 1687. Nom to ND de Moreilles in 1685 on resign of Louis Aquin. At Orléans, he reversed policies of his predecessor, Cardinal du Coislin, and conflicted with clergy.

Nom 29-3-1698. Provs 24-11-1698. Consec 18-1-1699. Nom to Orléans, 15-4-1706. Provs 15-11-1706. Died 10-6-1733.

Sources: ASV, PC 92, fos 30–48; PC 99, fos 56–69. BN, MS Fr Fr 20969, fo 57v, 147. Levesque, 'Liste des élèves', no 1438. St-Simon, xiii, 257. See Boisnard, *Les Phélypeaux*, 176. Boisnard, *Touraine*, no 953. Dubé, *Les Bigot*, 154–72.

Fleury, André-Hercule. Fréjus 1699–1715 (resign).   Louis XIV's best-known minister may have been described in his time as having descended from an 'old noble family of Languedoc', but in fact his origins belie such embellishment. Their roots lay in textile industry (maternal side) and, more recently, finances (paternal side) of Lodève and its environs, where they only began to acquire wealth and connections in mid-17th c. Royal and church finances were an obvious next target, with bp's father becoming a receiver of *décimes* of Lodève dioc, while a rich uncle, who paid for the young cleric's education in Paris, was *trés-gén des finances* at Montpellier and intendant of the *gabelles* of Languedoc. The modest nature of his father's office should not disguise his family's wider connections and advantages in lower Languedoc.

Born Lodève, not Montpellier, 22-6-1653, baptised 14-7-1653 in parish of St-Fulcran, he was 2nd son of Jean, sgr de Balquières, and Diane de Fougières. Thanks to an uncle, Pierre, canon of Montpellier cath, he was sent to study, first with SJ, then at coll of Navarre in Paris, ca 1666, and from there he moved to colls of Harcourt and Sorbonne. Took MA in July 1669, 67th and 3rd from last place in 1678 theol lic, but waited until nom to Lodève before taking doct on 27-6-1699. Tonsured 2-2-1666, followed by minor orders and subdeacon in Béziers Sept 1674, deacon and priest in Paris, July 1677. Frequented salons of certain important nobles from early in career, but vital early patronage comes mainly via Cardinal Bonsi, as well as Noailles and Castries families. Bonsi engineered his appointment as canon of Montpellier 1668, enabled him to purchase almonership to queen in 1675, before helping him to move to king's own chapel as almoner in 1680. Dep to ACs of 1680 and 1682, representing Bourges and Narbonne respectively – i.e. he was well beneficed and well connected! Accompanied Janson to Rome in 1690, gets abbey *in comm* of La Rivoure on return (Dec 1691) but Louis XIV unwilling to give him the mitre. Only through intervention of Mme de Caylus, niece of Maintenon, and Mme de Noailles, did he finally get Fréjus, where he initially encountered problems because of behaviour of Aquin, his predecessor. Very able bishop, widely liked and admired, strongly anti-Jansenist, but claimed also to have no love of Molinist positions, his unhesitating pro-*Unigenitus* position in 1713 brought him wider attention, esp at court. By 1715 he was anxious to quit and pursue a career there, which Louis XIV permitted by naming him preceptor of Dauphin, future Louis XV, who in turn rewarded him with red hat and 18 years as chief minister.

Nom 1-11-1698. Provs 18-5-1699. Consec 22-11-1699. Resigns 3-5-1715. Cardinal 11-9-1726. Died 29-1-1743.

Sources: ASV, PC 93, fos 194–212. BN, MS Naf 22404 (Fleury papers); MS Fr 20969, fo 129. AN, G[8], vol 88 (1680, 1682). St-Simon, vi, 46–9; xi, 138–45. *Gall Chr Nov*, Fréjus, 412–14.

Campbell, *Politics and Power in Old Regime France*, ch 1. A Vitalis, 'Fleury, les origines, la jeunesse', *Annales du Midi*, 18 (1906), 40–62. Ceyssens, *Sort de la bulle Unigenitus*, 439–75. DHGE, xvii, 476–9.

Forbin-Maynier d'Oppède, Louis. Toulon 1664–75.   The Forbin counted at least 7 major branches by mid-17th c, allied to virtually every family that mattered in Provence. Already represented in 17th c episcopate by Auguste, bp of Toulon (1627–38) and Cardinal Forbin-Janson, bp of Digne (1655–68), Marseille (1668–79), Beauvais (1679–1713), long-serving diplomat in Rome and elsewhere. The Maynier d'Oppède branch could claim to be the most powerful branch by mid-century, as bp's elder brother, Henri, became *homme fort* of Provence in aftermath of Fronde, *pr prés* of parlt in 1655 and, as *commandant pour le roi* after 1667, the pillar of Mazarin/Louis XIV's power there.

Son of Vincent Forbin-Maynier d'Oppède, *pr prés* of Aix parlt, and his 2nd wife, Aymare de Castellane-Esparron. Born Aix 8-11-1622, baptised on same day in Aix cath, where Louis XIII held him over font. Earliest studies in Paris, but studied phil in coll de Bourbon in Aix, followed by theol there, which he interrupted to take doct *in utr* at Aix. Further studies of theol in Paris, with suggestion of doct, possibly at Orange. Tonsured while student in Paris, 1630, but only took minor orders and priesthood shortly before episcopal nom, being ordained priest by Cardinal Grimaldi, with papal dispensation for ordination *extra tempora*, 1-3-1662. Prior of parish church of Laureis, where cure of souls was exercised by a vicaire, *chapelain* of St-Joseph's chapel in Aix cath, where he was made a canon in 1661 and later *théologal*.

Nom 28-2-1664. Provs 23-6-1664. Consec 28-9-1664. Died 29-4-1675.

Sources: ASV, PC 62, fos 597–634. *Gallia Chr Nov*, Toulon, col 665–8. AD Bouches-du-Rhône, 1 G 1271, fos 204v-13v. Blanc, 'Origines', 243–8. Pillorget, *Mouvements insurrectionnels*, 87–8. Bergin, *Making*, 625–6.

Forbin-Janson, Jacques. Arles 1711–41.   The last of the four 17th c bps from the vast Forbin family, and one of the few whom Louis XIV nom directly to an archiepiscopal see without prior experience as a bp.

Born on 23-4-1673 Paris, parish of Saint Sepulchre. 4th son of Laurent, marquis de Janson, who served in army in 1650s and later, also as *viguier* of Marseille 1653, gov of Antibes and Grasse, and Geneviève de Briançon de la Saludie. Studies in Paris, where he was MA in Nov 1691, taking theol bacc in Aug 1695, 40th place in 1700 theol lic, followed by doct on 15-3-1709. He was tonsured in Paris in Sept 1687, and ordained priest ca 1706. Spent some time in the Bons-Enfants seminary in Paris where he was contemporary of Paul Lefèvre d'Ormesson, almoner to his uncle, Cardinal Janson, bp of Beauvais. The cardinal duly made him vic-gen and canon of Beauvais (before 1705), but he had already been canon of Aix since 1691, thanks to *régale* and royal goodwill, and he also got abbey of St-Valéry in 1701. Accompanied uncle to 1700 conclave in Rome, where he stayed 3 years before returning to Beauvais. He was a conscientious abp, who proved very charitable in 1720 epidemic. He succeeded Abp Mailly at Arles on 5-4-1714, despite warnings of uncle that he was not fit for episcopate (St-Simon). Highly pro-Jesuit, he evicted Oratorians from teaching functions and from Arles seminary, 1720.

Nom 5-4-1711. Provs 1-6-1711. Consec 2-8-1711. Died 13-1-1741.

Sources: AN, MC, LXXXII, 110, 30-4-1711. AD Bouches-du Rhône, 1G 1273, fos 940–9 (Aix chapter). Pinard, *Chronologie*, vi, 577–8. St-Simon, xvii, 118; xx, 79–80; xxxiii, 372. Bossuet, *Correspondance*, viii, 17. DHGE, xvii, 1003–4.

Forcoal, Jean. Sées 1672–82.   Family originally from Cévennes, where they had adopted Protestantism, but bp's own father abjured at some point after settling in Paris, which enabled him to obtain office of SR in 1632 (in which his son succeeded him in 1651), though his financial activities doubtless predated that event. At the height of his career and influence as a financier he held strategically useful office of *greffier* of royal council, though he was posthumously severely fined by the *chambre de justice* of 1661–5.

Born ca 1621 Paris, probably in parish of ND des Champs, where family was resident. Son of Jacques, sgr de Sollies, and Marie le Roy. Studied in Univ of Paris where he took his MA in Dec 1645. Bachelor of canon law until nom, but in Nov 1670 he took lic from Paris (canon) law fac. Ordained priest by Bp Cohon of Nîmes, 21-9-1654. Prior of Moutiers OSB (Chartres), he served as royal almoner 'par quartier' since 1644. Abbot Rancé, a severe judge whose abbey lay in Sées dioc, had a high opinion of Forcoal, who appears to have encountered hostility for much of his episcopate.

Nom 31-10-1670. Provs 16-5-1672. Consec 24-8-1672. Died 27-2-1682.

Sources: ASV, PC 71, fos 695–715. BN, Doss bleus 275, no 7186; MS Fr 7854, fos 331r. AN, MC, XCIX, 198 (IAD of bp's father, 7-2-1658). Rancé, *Correspondance*, i, 643–4; ii, 620. Tessereau, *Chancellerie*, i, 375, 472, 570. Dessert, 'Finances et société au xviie siècle', *AESC*, 29 (1974), 875. Fisquet, *France pontificale*, Sées, 69–71.

Foresta-Coulongue, Joseph-Ignace. Apt 1696–1723 (resign).   A family of Genoese origin, which settled in Provence in later 15th or early 16th c with Christophe, who became a royal *médecin ordinaire* under Francis I, made a fortune, bought noble estates and discreetly brought the Foresta into the local nobility. They also figured *ab initio* among *cons* in Aix parlt, where they remained for over a century. Jean-Augustin Foresta was *pr prés* of Aix parlt by 1558, and they also provided a royalist *prés* in 1630s and 1640s whose loyalty to Mazarin brought rewards after the Fronde – inc a marquisate. Either bp's father, Scipion-Antoine or his uncle (named Scipion!) was admitted to Company of Holy Sacrament at Marseille in 1666, but the connection seems to go back to the beginnings of the Company in Marseille, ca 1639. No doubt that they were prominent in *dévot* circles, and also related by marriage to the Gaillard and Cabanes families, both of whom produced bps under Louis XIV.

Born Marseille, 14-5-1654, where baptised 8-6-1654. Eldest son, possibly, of Scipion-Antoine and Louise de Moustier, which may explain late entry into church when about 30 years old. He obtained canonicate in Marseille cath thanks to *régale*, and became its provost soon after. Studied at Toulouse, where took bacc in theol in 1686, having taken doct *in utr* in Avignon on 10-8-1672. Admitted to Marseille Compagnie du St-Sacrement, April 1689, director in Nov 1689, superior in 1693, by which time he was gr-vic of Marseille, having already assisted Vintimille who governed Marseille as *vic-cap* before 1692. He then became Vintimille's own vic-gen for several years after he got papal provs. A very active anti-Jansenist, he was first bp to launch attack on Quesnel. Founded Apt seminary 1706, confided it to Jesuits. Secured his nephew J-Bapt de Vaccon, son of Catherine Foresta, canon and vic-gen of Apt, as successor in 1723.

Nom 8-9-1695. Provs 23-1-1696. Consec 4-3-1696. Resign 10-5-1723. Died 18-10-1736.

Sources: ASV, PC 90, fos 52–60. BN, Carrés d'Hozier 265, Foresta. BIUT, MS 121, fo 155v. *Gallia Chr Nov*, Apt, 290–3. Blanc, 'Origines', 248–9. Chaix d'Est-Ange, *Dictionnaire des familles*, xviii, 333–7. *Encyclopédie des Bouches du Rhône*, iv, pt ii, 214–15. Clapiers-Collongues, *Chronologie*, 6, 19, 68–9, 81, 96, 107. Teulé, *Chronologie des docteurs*, 81. Pillorget, *Mouvements insurrectionnels*, 226–8. Kettering, *Judicial politics*, 219. Rebelliau, *La Compagnie du Très Saint-Sacrement à Marseille*, 6, 12.

Fortin de la Hoguette, Hardouin. St-Brieuc 1676–80, Poitiers 1680–92, Sens 1692–1715.
Usually described as a Norman family of *gentilshommes* from near Falaise, but bp's grandfather began as a bourgeois of Caen, later becoming a *prés* in *élection* of Falaise, ennobled in 1590 for services to cause of Henri IV. Bp's father (1585–1668) was initially preceptor of duc de Longueville's children, but then broke with family past to take up a military career, serving at siege of La Rochelle and later becoming capt of Blaye under governorship of St-Simon's father. Best known for his literary output – from the early tract against favourites (1620) to his famous

Testament, written for his children, and other works of moral and political phil – he was closely connected to Parisian intellectuals, esp Dupuy circle. Military careers were also adopted by bp's 2 brothers, both killed in action under Louis XIV, while their father's marriage brought high-level church patronage to future bp, whom St-Simon famously praised not just for his qualities as man and model prelate, but also for refusing the *cordon bleu* on account of his *petite noblesse*.

2nd son of Philippe, sgr de la Hoguette, and Louise de Péréfixe, sister of Hardouin de Péréfixe, abp of Paris (1664–71), born July 1643. Studied first at Oratorian coll of Juilly near Paris, then at Univ of Paris, where he was MA in July 1662, and took first place in 1670 theol lic, followed by doct 24-3-1670. Also ordained priest in 1670. Uncle's protection opened ecclesiastical doors to him early: canon of Paris since 1665, archdeacon of Josas in 1668, of Paris in 1670. Also abbot *in comm* of Sablonceaux 1671–1713, prior of Ste-Gemme 1671. More importantly, he was *ag-gén* of clergy in 1670. Moved from St-Brieuc to Poitiers in 1681, which he admin until 1685 when nom to Sens, which he admin as *vic-cap* until confirmation as abp in 1693. Refused *cordon bleu* in 1701, succeeded Bossuet as one of clerical *cons d'état* in 1704. Moderately pro-Jesuit, he pacified his troubled dioc after Jansenist period of Gondrin and laxism of his predecessor, Montpezat.

Nom 12-9-1675. Provs 23-3-1676. Consec 3-5-1676. Nom to Poitiers 2-2-1680. Provs 15-7-1680. Nom to Sens 9-11-1685. Provs 21-1-1692. Died 28-11-1715.

Sources: ASV, PC 75, fos 45–57. BM Sens, MS 77, 1181ff (history of abps of Sens). Fortin de la Hoguette, *Lettres*, ii, 855–7. Pinard, *Chronologie*, iv, 370–3. St-Simon, viii, 279–87. Bossuet, *Correspondance*, xii, 291–3.

Francheville, Daniel. Périgueux 1693–1702.   This family claimed Norman, English but esp Scots background, allegedly settling in Brittany in 1422 after marriage of its duke to Elizabeth of Scotland (Isabeau d'Ecosse), and serving in ducal entourage. Ennobled by duke in 1477. Later, several members of family held office in *chambre des comptes* at Nantes (1551) and then in Rennes parlt, beginning with Jean, sgr de Lainet, who became *cons* in 1594, having succeeded his father in 1575 as *proc-gén* of *chambre des comptes*. On the female side they had multiple connections to urban, officeholding elite of Nantes. Other members served in military capacities, and did not disdain relatively unpromising offices around Brittany, as witness that held by bp's own father. Family's noble status was upheld in 1669 and later. Bp's own early career was itself an accurate synopsis of their recent past.

Eldest son of Claude, *sénéchal* in *présidial* at Vannes, and Perrine Huart, daughter of a *cons* in Rennes parlt. Born Vannes 2-6-1648, baptised 17-9-1648. Studied in SJ coll at Vannes, later legal studies and degree, univ unknown, as he became *cons* in Rennes parlt 1678. Increasingly under influence of his aunt, Catherine, foundress of Filles de la Sainte Vierge des retraites de Vannes, who was his principal mentor. Changes direction and decides upon career in church, takes orders and finally resigns office to brother in 1691. Obtained doct in canon law, took all major orders in March 1682, and was immediately made vic-gen by Vautorte, bp of Vannes, while still holding and exercising his charge of *avocat-général*. Sent by king after Revocation of Nantes to preach/instruct Huguenots, esp in diocs of Dol and St-Malo. Personally wealthy, he used his resources to help poor, known as *le père des pauvres* while still in Vannes. Active resident bp at Sarlat, where he died after admin sacraments to a patient.

Nom 8-9-1693. Provs 17-11-1693. Consec 17-1-1694. Died 26-5-1702

Sources: ASV, PC 87, fos 546–54. AN, L 744, pièce 1, no 28. Saulnier, *Parlement de Bretagne*, i, 394–7. Chaix d'Est-Ange, *Dictionnaire des familles*, xix, 204–6. Entraygues, *Mgsr Daniel de Francheville*. Dujarric-Descombes, *Essai historique sur Mr Daniel de Francheville*. DHGE, xviii, cols 574–6.

Frétat de Boissieu, Louis. St-Brieuc 1705–20.   The Frétat de Boissieu family died out in 1739 with death of comte de Boissieu, maternal nephew of marshal Villars and able military officer, but their origins and attainments in previous generations were decidedly more modest. They can be traced back to merchants and notaries in 15th c at Chomélix in the Auvergne. A century later Pierre Frétat, an *élu*, was ennobled by Henri III in 1576 for his services, which may have been financial, during the civil wars, while one of his sons, Benoît, bp's great-grandfather, started the Boissieu branch, one of several to proliferate from late 16th c onwards around Clermont. Thereafter they settled among the officeholding notables of Clermont, and a son of one branch married a cousin of Blaise Pascal in the early 1640s, while a daughter married into another Clermont family, the Girard de la Bournat, which produced a bp of Poitiers in 1698. But it was marriage of Jean, the bp's brother, to Thérèse de Villars, sister of the marshal, in 1687, which was probably decisive in obtaining church preferment for bp of St-Brieuc, though another branch produced a bp of Tréguier and Nantes in next generation.

Born Clermont, where baptised 22-12-1662, Louis was youngest son of François, sgr de Boissieu, and Claude Françoise de St-Martial, married in 1643. Initially, he served as an officer in navy, when known as sieur de Duret, before entering Bons-Enfants seminary in Paris, possibly in mid to late 1690s, where he resided, it seems, for a few years, during which he became involved in missions to Protestants and also with the house of Nouvelles Catholiques. Obtained doct in canon law, Univ of Paris, by special dispensation and at royal request, in May 1705, shortly *after* nom to St-Brieuc. Priest for many years before nom.

Nom 11-4-1705. Provs 7-9-1705. Consec 11-10-1705. Died 30-10-1720.

Sources: ASV, PC 98, fos 131–45. BN, PO 1248, no 27933; Doss bleus 293, no 7444. Nouv d'Hozier 145, no 3171. AN, MM 1110, p 13 (doct). BM Clermont-Ferrand, MS 552, fos 192–222, *preuves de noblesse*, 1667. Anselme, *Histoire*, v, 106. Chaix d'Est-Ange, *Dictionnaire des familles*, xviii, 269–71. Remacle, *Dictionnaire des familles d'Auvergne*, ii, 164–76.

Frézeau de la Frézilière, Charles-Madeleine. La Rochelle 1694–1702.   Both Moréri and Chenaye-Desbois depict the family as very ancient, even Scottish ('Fraser') in ancestry, but no real proof of such lineage and distinction survive. Yet they were clearly a family of military nobility originating in Maine, residing near Chateau-Gontier, in Anjou, but also settled in Poitou and Touraine. Their 'extraction chevaleresque', which they traced back to 1335, was accepted in 1667 *recherche de noblesse*, by which time they had provided a gov of Niort and of Poitiers. Militarily active during the Wars of Religion, they contributed so much to 17th c wars that eldest branch died out altogether with Isaac, a prominent military officer killed at Hesdin 1639. His lands were only preserved, temporarily, when Isaac's daughter/heiress married her cousin, bp's father, in 1648. Latter became *lt-gén de l'artillerie de France*, in which he became the dominant figure in a long career, while 3 of his 4 sons died in service to Louis XIV, leading to the family's extinction in the early 18th c.

Born Poitiers 4-9-1654, son of François (1623–1702), marquis de la Frézilière, and his cousin, Charlotte Marie Frézeau, married in 1648. Early career was military and, following family tradition, he became colonel of regiment of dragoons, but aged 25, he entered seminary, ca 1680. Studies in Paris, where he was MA in April 1685, followed by 37th place in 1692 theol lic. Sometime after his ordination as priest, in 1689, chosen as vic-gen of Strasbourg, nominally by Louis XIV, but he only served briefly, as he was quickly nom to succeed Laval at La Rochelle in December 1693. Abbot *in comm* of St-Sever OSB (Coutances) before episcopate, which he resigned on, or shortly after, nom as bp. Young, authoritarian and demanding, he was the most energetic of La Rochelle's bishops of this period. Close to Jesuits, but not anti-Jansenist, steering well clear of doctrinal controversy. Worked himself into early grave, aged only 46.

Nom 24-12-1693. Provs 17-5-1694. Consec 27-6-1694. Died 4-11-1702.

Sources: ASV, PC 88, fos 392–400. BN, Doss bleus 293, no 7453; Nouv d'Hozier 145, no 3175; MS Fr 20969, fo 92r. Vindry, *État major, gendarmerie*, 187. Pinard, *Chronologie*, iv, 327–8, 638–9; vi, 118. St-Simon, iv, 166, n 2; x, 145–6; xvi 284–6. Boisnard, *Touraine*, no 1010.

Beauchet-Filleau, *Dictionnaire des familles nobles de Poitiou*, iii, 600–1. Gatz, *Bischöfe*, 131. Pérouas, *La Rochelle*, 353–6.

Fromentières, Jean Louis. Aire 1673–84.   Ancestors originated in Anjou and Maine, but were also present in Brittany and Touraine. *Maintenus nobles* in 1667 on basis of titles dating from 1542. In Maine, they settled in St-Denis-des-Gastines parish, and were allied to Froulay family, which produced Gabriel bp of Avranches under Louis XIV. Officeholding in Paris only seems to have come as a result of bp's father's marriage into a well-established Paris robe family. Bp's maternal great-grandfather, Nicolas Perrot, was chancellor of duc d'Anjou, his grandfather, Cyprien, a *prés* in the Paris parlt.

Born Paris and baptised at St-André-des-Arts, 30-10-1632. 3rd son of Jacques, sgr des Etangs Larchevêque, *cons* in *gr conseil* in 1612, and Marie Perrot, his 2nd wife, married in 1614. Initial studies at Oratorian coll of St-Ouen at Le Mans, prolonged in Paris from 1648 onwards, and coinciding with a sojourn in St-Magloire seminary run by the Oratorians. Studies were mainly theological, but did not take a degree, waiting until 1672, the eve of his episcopal nom, before taking doct in canon law in Paris, defending theses on the subject of transfers of bps from one dioc to another! Subdeacon on 2-5-1657, he was ordained priest in 1664. Lived for several years afterwards at St-Magloire, but did not join the Oratory, then or later. In 1663, he was made *théologal* of Le Mans, and also seems to have taught theol at Le Mans Oratory coll in 1660s, but he was largely non-resident, finally resigning it in 1672 when relations with Le Mans chapter had soured beyond repair. Trained as preacher at St-Magloire by influential Sénault, he preached frequently in Paris churches and at court, and was made *prédicateur du roi* in 1662. His oration for Anne of Austria (1666), a great devotee of his sermons, and for the religious 'clothing' of Louis XIV's former mistress, Louise de la Valière, in 1674, were among those which made his reputation at a time when there was some serious competition. Abbot *in comm* of ND du Jard OSA (Sens) in 1668, which helped him to gain election to 1670 AC, when he narrowly missed out on election as *ag-gén* to Fortin de la Hoguette, elected by Paris. Once he moved to Aire, he was a resident bp who devoted much energy to rebuilding a dioc badly damaged in 16th c wars and to imposing reforms on its clergy.

Nom 16-1-1673. Provs 11-3-1673. Consec 1-10-1673. Died 18-12-1684.

Sources: ASV, PC 72, fos 19–39. BN, Doss bleus 295, no 7484; MS Fr 7651, fo 205 (*bienfaits du roi*); MS Fr 20969, fo 36. Poutet, 'Docteurs', 321. Port, *Dictionnaire historique de la Mayenne*, ii, 234–5. Hurel, *Orateurs sacrés à la cour de Louis XIV*. Lehargou, *Messire J L de Feomentières évêque d'Aire* (Paris 1892). Boisnard, *Touraine*, no 1012. DHGE, xix, cols 169–71.

Froullay du Tessé, Gabriel-Philippe. Avranches 1668–89.   The bp was born into a junior branch of the Froullay family, based at Montflaux, which by then was more important than the senior Froullay line itself. The Tessé title was acquired by marriage in 2nd half of 16th c, and was elevated to *comté* status by Henri IV for René I who had supported him during the League. Marriage in 1596 to Marie de Sourdis brought him into major aristocratic circles, something which his son René II, who was made *maréchal de camp* in 1652, repeated when he married Madeleine de Beaumanoir-Lavardin in 1638, parents of marshal Tessé, who had a distinguished military and diplomatic career under Louis XIV. The Froullay branch was not entirely eclipsed, esp at court, where bp's brother, the comte de Froullay, held important post of *grand maréchal des logis*. Blood ties to families with major church connections (Sourdis, Beaumanoir, Beauvau du Rivau) also helped.

Born in family château of Monflaux, 1615. Son of René de Froullay, comte de Tessé and 2nd wife, Marie d'Escoubleau, sister of Cardinal de Sourdis, abp of Bordeaux (1599–1628), and cousin of Cardinal de Vendôme. Further studies in Paris, where he began *primum cursus* in theol in Aug 1640, and seems to have taken bacc exam in or soon after Dec 1640, but went no further. Priest for 'over 20 years' by 1666. His uncle, Henri de Sourdis, abp of Bordeaux, made him canon and vic-gen of Bordeaux in 1642, dean of St-Emilion in 1643, and may have been grooming him as successor, but he died in 1645. Uncle also enabled him to acquire additional benefices, inc priories of St-Astier (Agen) and Tiffauge (La Rochelle), as well as abbey of Ste-Croix-de-Anglis OSA (Poitiers). Represented Bordeaux province at 1645 AC. A case of delayed accession to episcopate, but his tenure of Avranches was that of a highly resident bp. Nom 13-4-1668. Provs 26-11-1668. Consec 20-1-1669. Died 27-4-1689.

Sources: ASV, PC 66, 54–88. BN, Doss bleus 295, no 7496; MS Clairambault 814, fo 245. Pinard, *Chronologie*, vi, 307–8, 359–60. St-Simon, iii, 128–32; vii, 24–7; xi, 145. Port, *Dictionnaire Historique de la Mayenne*, ii, 235–7. Bertrand, *La Vie de Messire Henri de Béthune*, i, 240–1. Peyrous, *Réforme catholique à Bordeaux*, ii, 717, 1031–2.

Gaillard, Jean. Apt 1671–95. Not related to an old Provençal noble of the same name. Bp was born into a Provençal branch of a Parisian financial family, originating in Blois area, where they held office in 15ᵗʰ c, and one of whose members, Michel, a financier, apparently, married an illegitimate sister of Francis I in early 16ᵗʰ c. 2 generations later they were still active in Parisian financial world, when in 1595 Jean settled in Provence as a *contr-gén des guerres*, and prospered sufficiently for his brother and later his nephew, Pierre, sgr de Ventabren, father of bp, to become a high-profile *trés-gén* of Estates of Provence in 1623, surviving bankruptcy during Fronde in 1651 and still in service until at least late 1650s. By then, the family was solidly connected to major Aix parlt families like Grimaldi-Régusse, Valbelle etc, while bp's mother was daughter of a prominent Marseille family originally from Berry but whose Provençal ancestor had settled in Marseille as a factor of Jacques Coeur whose niece he had married in mid-15ᵗʰ c! The Gaillard were Mazarinists during the Fronde in Aix, where Mazarin's brother was abp and where other family members were temporarily based. A vital role was played by bp's sister Madeleine, Mme de Venel, wife of a *cons* in Aix parlt; she initially entered Mazarin's service as governess to his nieces, first in Aix and then in Paris, and moved from that post to that of subgoverness of Louis XIV's children via household of Queen Marie-Thérèse in subsequent decades. Meanwhile, the Parisian Gaillards were in service of Gaston d'Orléans by the 1620s and 1630s. A cousin of bp, Honoré (1641–1727) was a distinguished Jesuit, preceptor of Turenne's sons, rector of coll de Clermont (1710), and a noted preacher, with many funeral sermons, inc one of Turenne, to his credit.

Bp was son of Pierre, sgr de Ventabren, and Marquise de Villages de la Salle. Born Aix 14-5-1634, tonsured in Aix 1646, but sent to Paris to complete hum and further studies, and from June 1650 to Sept 1653 he was resident at St-Sulpice. He went no further than bacc in theol, taken at Univ of Caen (his provs to Apt were granted *cum dispensatione gradus*). His move to Caen derived from sister's influence with Mazarin, to whom she introduced him and who was employed by Mazarin in some capacity in relation to Roman and Polish affairs. It brought Gaillard some rewards (as it did a brother of his who preceded him to Normandy) and he became both canon and archdeacon of Caen in Bayeux cath, while still a tonsured cleric, apparently via the *régale* during vacancy of Bayeux in 1659–60, which also seems to be how he became *théologal* in Coutances cath later again. Ordained priest by Bp Nesmond at Bayeux in 1662. Mme Venel had a keenly developed talent for promoting family members, though Apt's main attraction, as one of France's more obscure diocs, must have been its location in the family's native Provence. As bp he was anxious to restore splendour of liturgy and reform female orders, but local resistance to him was stiff. Apparently refused promotion to Limoges offered by Louis XIV in 1676. Interested in historical research and fathers of the church, he used his Mazarin-Colonna connections in Rome to obtain materials from Vatican Library. Moréri was his almoner and bp supported him and his *Dictionary*, which was dedicated to him. Some commentators believed Gaillard was himself real author of 1ˢᵗ edition of 1694, the year before his death.

Nom 5-1-1671. Provs 20-4-1671. Consec on 28-7-1671 in Bayeux. Died 10-2-1695.

Sources: ASV, PC 70, fos 48–70. BM Aix, MS 257, p 235; MS 1181 (MS life of Mme Venel and bp Gaillard). AD Bouches-du-Rhône, 1 G 1320, 1-7-1661 (*dimissoires* for ordination). *Gallia Chr Nov*, Apt, 288–9. *Encyclopédie des Bouches-du-Rhône*, iv, pt ii, 223, 489. Boisnard,

Touraine, no 1025. Blanc, 'Origines', 253–4. Clapiers-Collongues, *Chronologie*, 86, 93, 96, 107. Levesque, 'Liste des élèves', no 146. Michel Mollat, *Jacques Coeur* (Paris 1988), 13, 55, 111, 117. Kettering, 'The Household Service of Early Modern French Noblewomen', 55–85; Kettering, *Judicial Politics*, 74–6.

Génétines. *See* **Charpin.**

Genlis. *See* **Brûlart.**

Gesvres. *See* **Potier.**

Girard de la Bournat, Antoine. Poitiers 1698–1702.　　Unrelated to older Auvergnat noble family of Girard de Ste-Radegonde, bp's family were bourgeois/natives of Maringues, east of Riom, and settled in Clermont in early 17th c, holding office in *cour des aides* there before dying out in 18th c. Antoine, bp's grandfather, began life as a merchant in Lyon, and ended it as *cons* in *présidial* of Clermont, having acquired seigneurie of la Bournat in 1616, while his father, Joseph, became a respected figure in Clermont robe circles, hostile to Jesuits and connected to the Pascal-Périer circle. Ecclesiastics, both male and female, were prominent across the generations (inc canons of ND du Port and Clermont cath), with pro-Jansenist inclinations in some cases. His youngest sister's marriage made bp a brother-in-law of Louis de Frétat, bp of St-Brieuc (1705–20).

　　Born 9-6-1656 Clermont. Eldest son of Joseph, *cons* at *cour des aides*, Clermont, and Catherine Guerry, daughter of a *receiver des tailles* at Guéret. Tonsured 17-5-1674, by which time he had completed phil at Univ of Paris with the MA in Aug 1673. Studied theol, taking bacc in 1675, 10th place in 1680 lic, and finishing with doct 29-8-1680. Ordained priest 15-6-1680. Friendship with Bossuet was probably instrumental in obtaining post of preceptor to Louis XIV's illegitimate sons, first to comte de Vexin, who died very young in 1683, then to the comte de Toulouse, for which he was given abbey of Pontlevoy (Nov 1683). Louis ended the preceptorship abruptly in April 1691, when he and Toulouse both pensioned Girard for his services. He was an influential associate of Missions Etrangères seminary, where he may have resided in 1690s. He also succeeded Fénelon and Milon as superior of Nouvelles Catholiques, and became a director of Maintenon's community at St-Cyr, a highly useful *tremplin* to greater things. Initially nom to Toul (and not Toulouse, as sometimes asserted), then to Boulogne, when Thyard de Bissy refused to leave Toul for Bordeaux, but finally to Poitiers, 29-3-1698, a dioc with large Protestant population for which his experience of missions and of Nouvelles Catholiques was no doubt regarded as particularly useful. An energetic and respected bp but of precarious health, who worked himself, it seems, into an early grave.

　　Nom 29-3-1698. Provs 15-9-1698. Consec 19-10-1698. Died 8-3-1702.

Sources: ASV, PC 92, fos 411–27. BN, MS Fr 23510, fo 142r; MS Fr 20969, fo 34v. AN, L 740, pièce 1, nos 38–53. Arch MEP, vol 95, p 42. BM Clermont, MS 553. Bossuet, *Correspondance*, iv, 212–13. Pouzet, *Chronique des Pascal*, 227, 457–8, 590. Remacle, *Dictionnaire des familles d'Auvergne*, ii, 199–200. DBF, xvi, 141.

Godet des Marais, Paul. Chartres 1692–1709.　　'Fort peu de chose pour la naissance' according to St-Simon, conveniently ignoring the social cachet of bp's mother's family. His father, having served under Condé, was killed during the Fronde (1652), his mother remarried and established further connections which would assist her son during his career. An aunt of bp, Françoise Godet, was also close to Colbert, who helped to limit damage done to their financial interests by *chambre de justice* of early 1660s.

　　Son of François, sgr des Marais, and Marie de la Marck, illegitimate daughter of Louis de la Marck and Elisabeth Salviati. Born Talcy, Chartres dioc, 9-6-1648, baptised 24-6-1649. Studies at Paris Univ, where MA in June 1667, taking 17th place in 1676 theol lic, and the doct on

31-8-1677. Initially entered Bons-Enfants and later St-Sulpice seminary, joining the *petite communauté* formed there in 1672, of which he became leading member. Ordained priest by Louis Thomassin coadj of Vence shortly after Easter 1672. Obtained abbey of Igny (Reims) aged 14, previously held by a La Marck uncle. Director of seminary of the Trente-Trois after doct, active as preacher, closely linked to Tronson of St-Sulpice, his mentor, which in subsequent years led to ties to Fénelon and *dévots*, above all to Mme de Maintenon, who encountered Godet by late 1687, and within a few years he emerged as her confessor and principal confident, esp for *maison* of St-Cyr she had just founded. Laval-Boisdauphin seems to have wanted to have him as coadj of La Rochelle around 1683, but nothing came of it. When Bp Ferd de Neufville of Chartres died in Jan 1690, Godet was obvious (and Maintenon's) choice as successor, after Michel Le Pelletier turned it down, esp as Godet consented to part of his dioc being hived off into a new one, that of Blois. He helped bring down Guyon and Fénelon in Quietist affair, and opposed Noailles in the Jansenist disputes. His influence over episcopal noms seems to have derived largely from support from Maintenon and others rather than from his own (limited) powers.

Nom 4-2-1690. Provs 4-2-1692. Consec 31-8-1692. Died 26-9-1709.

Sources: ASV, PC 86, fos 110–32. AN, L 729, Chartres, no 81. Fénelon, *Correspondance*, v, 289–90. Sourches, iii, 193. St-Simon, xviii, 229ff; xiv, 119. Bossuet, *Correspondance*, ix, 294, n 7. Le Brun, 'Paul Godet des Marais', 47–78. Dessert, *Argent pouvoir et société*, 595. DBF, xvi, 456–7. DLF 542.

Gourgue, Jacques-Joseph. Bazas 1693–1724.   A Guyenne family of noble extraction, long settled in Bordeaux, where they held parlt office from later 16th or early 17th c, and where Marc-Antoine, bp's great-grandfather, was *pr prés* in 1617. Marriages with Séguier (1604), Lamoignon (twice) and Larcher families brought them into Parisian robe circles and, back in Bordeaux, with offices of MR following over several generations and, in the case of bp's father, prov intendancies (Limoges 1685, Caen 1686–9 – but sacked from latter post). Bp's brother, Jean-François-Joseph, was also an MR married to a Barillon de Morangis.

Son of Armand-Jacques de Gourgue (1643–1726), *prés* and lt-gen in Bordeaux *présidial*, MR (1677), and Elisabeth Le Clerc d'Aulnay, his 1st cousin. Born Bordeaux, 1649, but higher studies in Paris, where he took 83rd place in 1674 theol lic, followed by doct in Aug 1676. Already a priest by time of his brief sojourn at St-Sulpice (Oct–Dec 1672). Prior *in comm* of St-Caprais of Agen and dep to 1680 and 1682 ACs, which would have brought him to attention of royal entourage. St-Simon regarded him as 'le mépris de la Gascogne', possibly because of his closeness to Jesuits, but this seems a rather partial view of a bp known for good work in his dioc, where he conducted extensive visitations, promoted introduction of new religious orders and founded a seminary to which he left his estate.

Nom 31-5-1684. Provs 12-10-1693. Consec 15-11-1693. Died 9-9-1724.

Sources: ASV, PC 87, fos 791–99. Fénelon, *Correspondance*, v, 16, n 1. St-Simon, xxix, 191–2. Bluche, *L'Origine*, 202–3. Smedley-Weill, *Intendants de Louis XIV*, 48–9. Bertrand, *Histoire des séminaires de Bordeaux et de Bazas*, iii, 207–16 (testament). Trani, 'Conseillers du grad conseil', 147–8. Compère and Julia, *Collèges français*, i, 118.

Grammont, François-Joseph. Besançon 1699–1717.   'Ancienne maison', tracing origins back to 13th c. Jean-Gabriel des Granges, comte de Grammont/Fallon, lt-gen of Spanish troops in Franche-Comté, died in French conquest of Franche-Comté in 1674, but it seems other, younger members rallied to French service rapidly enough, though one was involved in a conspiracy in province in 1709. From 1704 until death in 1718, Jean-Ferdinand, comte de Grammont, was 'commandant pour le roi' in the province.

Born at family estate of Châtillon-Guyotte, Besançon dioc, 14-5-1646. Son of Laurent Théodule, baron of Melisey, and Jeanne-Françoise de Poitiers, and nephew of Antoine-Pierre, abp of Besançon (1663–1698). Tonsured and already a canon of Besançon, when entered St-Sulpice seminary on 24-2-1666, leaving on 6-2-1667. Took doct in law at Univ of Dole in Franche-Comté. Elected *grand archidiacre* of Besançon cath in July 1679, later becoming its *haut-doyen*, abbot *in comm* of Bithaine and Montbenoit, prior of Mortan and Champlitte and Jussey, all bar one in Besançon dioc. Priest for several years before uncle requests his appointment as auxiliary bp of Besançon in 1683, which papacy granted in 1686. An anti-Jansenist who later had problems with his own clergy.

Auxiliary of Besançon 18-3-1686. Consec 16-6-1686. Royal nom to Besançon 17-8-1698. Provs 7-9-1699. Died 20-8-1717.

Sources: ASV, PC 93, fos 64–75. St-Simon, xviii, 163; xxvi, 257; xxxii, 119. L Jadin, 'Procès d'information pour la nomination des évêques' *Bibliothèque de l'Institut Historique Belge de Rome*, 6 (1928), 299–300. DHGE, xxi, 1063–7.

Grammont de Lanta. *See* **Barthélemy.**

Grignan, Jean-Baptise d'Adhémar de Monteil de. Arles coadj 1667/89–97.   The Grignan family already had 2 well-placed bps in Provence (Arles and Uzès) since Richelieu and Mazarin's time. Enjoying considerable favour by the beginning of Louis XIV's reign, their political, matrimonial and religious 'capital' continued to accumulate in subsequent decades, enabling them to envisage high-level church careers until well into the next century. 3 brothers in generation of Jean-Baptiste were earmarked for such positions, with one of them, Gabriel, originally designated to succeed his uncle at Arles, but he died young soon after nom as coadj in 1666.

Son of Louis Gaucher de Grignan and Marguerite d'Ornano, born in 1638. Univ studies in Paris, where took MA in June 1661, and 78th place in 1666 theol lic. Doctor of theol 18-5-1666. Priest 20-3-1666. Abbot *in comm* of Aiguebelle (1663) and prior of Portes (St-Paul-Trois-Châteaux), his uncle made him archpriest and canon of Arles in 1663. Dep to 1665 AC. Taking place at Arles originally intended for brother Gabriel, he had far longer career as coadj than as full abp at Arles, even though his uncle was virtually blind and incapacitated by 1666. Royal generosity, mediated no doubt via his brother, who was king's 'commandant' in Provence, produced 3 abbeys for him in the meantime. Some talent as a preacher, but also active as a pastoral bishop.

Nom 31-7-1666. Provs 3-8-1667. Consec 11-12-1667. Succeeds to Arles 9-3-1689. Died 11-11-1697.

Sources: ASV, PC 65, fo 84–108. BM Aix, MS 257, pp 230, 232–3. Poutet, 'Docteurs', 295, no 492. *Inventaire des archives dauphinoises de Henri Morin-Pons*, ed U Chevallier and A Lacroix (Lyon 1878), 63. Blanc, 'Origines', 153–9. Bergin, *Making*, 634–5.

Grignan, Louis-Joseph d' Adhémar de Monteil de. Carcassonne 1681–1722.   Younger brother of Jean-Baptiste, above. Born 4-6-1650, *ondoyé* at that date, baptised 30-9-1660. Further studies in Paris, where MA 27-7-1671, bacc in theol, March 1672. By 1680, he had taken doct, but at another (unknown) univ. Ordained subdeacon with papal dispensation at St-Lazare, 31-5-1670, deacon on 11-4-1675, and priest in Paris Feuillants church 19-5-1675, with *dimissoires* and papal brief *extra tempora*. Obtained abbey of St-Georges-sur-Loire OSA (Angers) on death of uncle, bp of Uzès, in 1674, which he exchanged for St-Hilaire-de-Carcassonne OSA in 1684. Elected *ag-gén* by province of Arles in 1675. Nom to Evreux in 1680 at end of term as *agent*, but had not taken possession before he was given Carcassonne in 1681 – possibly because retiring bp wanted too hefty a pension. Obtained nephew, Châteauneuf de Rochebonne as coadj in 1720.

Nom to Evreux, 20-4-1680, renewed 6-9-1680. Provs 28-4-1681. Nom to Carcassonne 2-5-1681. Provs 22-9-1681. Consec 21-12-1681. Died 1-3-1722.

Sources: ASV, PC 80, fos 151–59; PC 80, fos 330–37. BM Aix, MS 257, p 245. *Inventaire Morin-Pons*, 66–9. Fénelon, *Correspondance*, xvii, 313. St-Simon, xl; 242. Léon Charpentier,

Un évêque d'ancien regime. Louis-Joseph de Grignan. Compère and Julia, *Collèges français,* i, 192.

Guémadeuc, Sébastien. St-Malo 1671–1702.   A long-settled noble family from northern Brittany near St-Brieuc, they were related to Sevigné and other prominent houses of similar noble rank, but they emerged from shadows with marriage of bp's aunt, Marie-Françoise, to François du Pont de Courlay in 1626: their son succeeded to Cardinal Richelieu's vast estate and title of duc de Richelieu in 1642. Possibly because her father had been executed for a sensational murder in 1616, the Geumadeuc do not appear to have benefited markedly from the Richelieu connection, though bp's brother was gov of St-Malo.

Born Pluemellet (Vannes) 1626. Son of Thomas, marquis de Guemadeuc, gov of Ploermel, and Gilette de la Fresnaye. Univ studies in Paris, coll of Navarre, where he was MA in July 1645. Doct of theol, also of Paris, 7-8-1664, and *socius* of Navarre. Reputed one of more propapal docts of Paris fac before episcopate. Ordained priest by Charles de Rosmadec 8-4-1662 in chapel of St-Germain-en-Laye. Abbot of La Noë O Cist (Evreux) and Jean-des-Prés OSA (St-Malo) in 1650, he was also canon of Vannes cath from 1643 to 1649, when he resigned, subsequently becoming canon and archdeacon of Rennes. *Aumônier ordinaire* to Anne of Austria in 1658. Dep to 1655 and 1660 ACs, elected *ag-gén* in 1665, and served as *promoteur* at 1670 AC. Nom to Lavaur in 1670, but waited until he got St-Malo later that year. Developed strong ties with Harlay of Paris, but his reputation at time of death appears as that of an indolent *seigneur* and *chasseur* who neglected his dioc.

Nom 31-10-1670. Provs 4-5-1671. Consec 5-7-1671. Died 2-3-1702.

Sources: ASV, PC 70, fos 618–40. BN, P O 1424, no 32262; Doss Bleus 336, no 8605; MS Fr 7652, no 49. Sévigné, *Correspondance,* ii, 317, n 3. Carné, *Chevaliers bretons de St-Michel,* 167–72. Poutet, 'Docteurs', 285, no 397. Lesaulnier, *Port-Royal insolite,* 517. Colbert de Croissy, *La Bretagne en 1665,* 91, 240.

Habert de Montmort, Louis. Perpignan 1682–95.   Bp was grandnephew of Pierre Habert, bp of Cahors (1627–36), the 1st member of this prominent family of Parisian officeholders and literary figures to enter the episcopate. In generation of bp's father and grandfather, their integration into these milieux was consolidated and extended by marriage to older noble families like Estrées, Aloigny and Frontenac. Bp's father and his 2 Habert cousins were founding members of Académie Française.

Born in parish of St-Nicolas-des-Champs on 14-12-1644. Son of Henri-Louis, marquis de Marigny, MR, and Henriette-Marie de Buade Frontenac. Univ studies in Paris, where took MA in July 1662. Doct of theol in Cahors, 28-8-1674. Ordained priest in 1671 by bp of Laon. Nom to Perpignan by virtue of indult of Clement IX to Louis XIV for Roussillon, and after Jean d'Étampes de Valançay had exchanged the nom for that of Marseille in 1679.

Nom 15-11-1680. Provs 12-1-1682. Consec 12-4-1682. Died 23-1-1695.

Sources: ASV, PC 81, fos 261–70. BIUT, MS 104 f° 4r. St-Simon, vi, 273, n 6. Chapelain *Lettres,* ii, 639–41, 750–52. *Lettres de Séguier,* ii, 1202–3. Bergin, *Making,* 637–8. DLF, 575–6.

Hallencourt de Dromesnil, Charles-François. Autun 1711–22, Verdun 1722–54. This Picard noble family of ancient lineage claimed clear filiation from 12th c onwards. Bp's generation and that of his father owed much to marshal Boufflers, whose aunt was grandmother of bp. Bp's father (1642–1724), a 2nd son of Louis, comte de Dromesnil and Francoise de Boufflers, served, as did his own eldest son, for a time in royal armies, and family line died out with him.

Born Neuville, Laon dioc, 24-10-1674. 2nd son of Louis-François, sgr de Neuville, and Françoise de Proisy, dame de Neuville, married in 1667. Studies in Paris, where MA in Oct 1694, took theol bacc in Jan 1700, followed by 1st place in 1704 theol lic, and doct on 3-3-1704. Priest since 1699. Vic-gen of Laon for few years, also royal almoner in 1704 (successor to Nettancourt). Abbot of Uzerche in 1701, of La Charité in 1706. Dep for Reims province to ACs of 1707 and 1710, which undoubtedly helped to obtain mitre, but St-Simon claims it was Boufflers who obtained Autun for him in 1710. In fact, Autun had been given previous year to abbé de Maulévrier, *ag-gén*, who finally turned it down. Hallencourt, having resigned Uzerche in 1710, obtained abbey of Homblières in 1717, moved to Verdun in 1721, where he built the most magnificent palace in France. Portrayed as a strange and dangerous character by St-Simon, close to Fénelon and Jesuits.

Nom 2-7-1710. Provs 23-2-1711. Consec 22-11-1711. Nom to Verdun, 11-2-1721. Provs 1-6-1722. Died at La Charité 16-3-1754.

Sources: ASV, PC 101a, fo 22–34; PC 100, fos 228–39. BN, PO 1466, no 33257; Doss bleus 344, no 8873. St-Simon, xx, 82–7. BN, MS 5496, p 247 (bacc theol). Sars, *Laonnais féodal*, iii, 33–4. Taveneaux, *Jansénisme en Lorraine*, 484–6.

Haussonville. *See* **Nettancourt.**

Hébert, François, Lazariste. Agen 1704–28.   One of the few of Louis XIV's bps to have served his time in a parish – though his was not an ordinary parish! His family were of Parisian *bourgeois* stock, his father an iron merchant, while his elder brother, Guillaume-André (d 1720) played many parts, being variously *premier échevin* of Paris, director of East India Company at Pondicherry, and generally acting as a royal agent in the region. He was also a chevalier of St-Lazare and Mount Carmel.

Son of André, bourgeois de Paris, and Marthe Marchand, daughter of a Paris merchant family. Although born in Tours during the Fronde on 13-9-1651, bp's family resided in St-Merry parish in Paris. Entered St-Lazare in 1667 where he trained under auspices of Louis Abelly, former bp of Rodez and a family friend, and became a member of Congregation of the Mission. Ordained priest in 1675, he began career as prof of theol at Sens seminary in early 1670s, became superior of seminary of Alet 1677, then of Arras. He seems to have taken doct in theol of Bourges, Jan 1704, only 3 weeks after nom to Agen. Rector of Les Invalides, Paris, before becoming parish priest of Versailles, a new parish, in 1686. He served as confessor to Fénelon, and was on particularly close terms with Bossuet, Noailles and many others who held him in high regard, and whose anti-Molinist convictions he shared. Had he not narowly missed being elected superior of Lazarists in 1703, his nom to Agen might not have happened at all! It was probably Noailles who obtained Agen for him despite the statutes of his congregation against seeking benefices. Subsequently he strongly supported Noailles against critics, inc fellow bps, during Jansenist controversies after 1710. Adhered to appeal vs *Unigenitus* in 1717, but signed accommodation of 1720 and accepted bull in 1721.

Nom 24-12-1703. Provs 11-2-1704. Consec 6-4-1704. Died 20-8-1728.

Sources: ASV, PC 97, fos 17–30. AN, L 727, Agen, no 11. AD Lot-et-Garonne, G/E 70, Hébert dossier. Hébert, *Mémoires*. Fénelon, *Correspondance*, iii, 258, no 119. St-Simon, xx, 348. Favre-Lejeune, *Secrétaires du roi*, ii, 693–4. DHGE, xxiii, 702–4.

Hennin-Liétard, Jean-François. Alès 1713–20, Embrun 1720–4.   Several branches of this family developed from later Middle Ages onwards in Artois-Hainaut, and subsequently scattered across Picardy, Champagne and Burgundy. The main (Hainaut) branch added 'Alsace' patronymic after 1660 and with it correspondingly grandiose claims of descent from an old Flanders-Artois family of counts of Alsace: the Cardinal of Alsace, abp of Malines in early 18th c, was one of them. Another branch was that of the princes of Chimay. Though allegedly related to Chimay branch, bp's family, sgrs of Roche etc, were probably a Burgundian offshoot of Champagne branch, modest in their wealth and distinction, acting as capt-govs of Chalon-sur-Saône over several generations. D'Artagnan married a half-sister of bp's father in 1659, while bp himself was apparently last male of his line.

Born Chalon-sur-Saône 11-5-1665. Relatively little known about his early years, but he studied in Paris, where he was MA in May 1684, and took bacc in theol. Took doct at Bourges only 2 months before his episcopal nom. Ordained priest ca 1700. He was a canon of Tournai cath, but for several years before 1713 he had been active as vic-gen of Bp Madot of Chalon-sur-Saône, his native dioc. Episcopal consec by 3 Jansenist bishops raised suspicions that he was one himself, but there is no independent evidence. His friend, the abbé Thésut, *secrétaire des commandements* of Regent, Philippe d'Orléans, and holder of the *feuille des bénéfices* after the *conseil de conscience* was discontinued, was instrumental in obtaining Embrun for him in 1719, but did not take possession until 1722. In poor health, he died in Paris waiting for an operation for gallstones

Nom 13-1-1713. Provs 28-4-1713. Consec 9-7-1713. Nom to Embrun 1-11-1719. Provs 27-5-1720. Died 26-4-1724.

Sources: AN, MC, LXXXII, 121, 12-2-1713. St-Simon, xxxvi, 372. Chesnaye-Desbois, *Dictionnaire de la noblesse*, i, 375–389. DBF, ii, 328–9; xvii, 900.

Hervault, Mathieu Isoré d'. Tours 1693–1716. An old Angevin family, whose nobility went back several centuries, fortified by its intermarriage with other provincial families. In later Middle Ages, they provided several *chambellans* to Louis XI and Charles VIII, a vice-admiral of Guyenne, as well as a gov of Blaye in 16th c, and successive 'lieutenants du roi' in Touraine. The abp belonged to senior branch, with Hervault lands becoming a marquisat in 1652. They claimed to be 1st cousins of Beauvilliers de St-Aignan, but although not true, the family connection, on the female side, went back 3 generations. It was apparently Cardinal d'Estrées, to whom they may also have been related, who was instrumental in obtaining Auditorship of the Roman Rota for future bp. Even if some family ties remain obscure, there is no doubting solidity of those which are documented – Babou de la Bourdaisière, Chamborant, Roncherolles, La Rocheposay.

Born 1647 at Boissy-sur-Claise. 3rd son of Georges (1606–78), marquis de Pleumartin and lt-gen of Touraine, and Marguerite de Roncherolles, daughter of Pierre, *premier baron de Normandie*. Univ studies in Paris, where MA in Aug 1666. He took 4th place in 1674 theol lic. Two docts from Paris – in theol, 13-2-1681; in canon law 10-3-1681. Nom Auditor of the Roman Rota by royal *brevet* of 15-1-1681, installed in his *charge* 15-12-1681, an appointment which caused some opposition and embarrassment in Rome, given his lack of experience as a lawyer. Ordained priest in 1678. Received abbey of St-Jean-d'Angely in Aug 1688. Nom to Condom on Sept 1693, but was almost immediately given archbishopric of Tours. Received St-Maixent OSB (Poitiers) on same day as nom to Tours as recompense for revenue difference between Tours and Condom. A firm gallican, close to Noailles over *Unigenitus*, he died having opposed the bull. St-Simon had highest opinion of him as a perfect match of pedigree and virtue.

Nom to Condom 8-9-1693. Nom to Tours 1-11-1693. Provs 22-12-1693. Consec 25-2-1694. Died 9-7-1716.

Sources: ASV, PC 87, fos 769–77. AN, MM 1120, pp 5–6 (law degrees). BN, MS Fr 7656, no 187; MS Fr 20969, fo 87. Boisnard, *Touraine*, no 1258. Fénelon, *Correspondance*, vii, 123, n 9. St-Simon, i, 286–7. Cerchiari, *Capellani Pape*, ii, 193–5. Beauchet-Filleau, *Dictionnaire des familles du Poitou*, v, 158 ff. DHGE, xxiv, 233–5.

Hervé, Charles-Bénigne. Gap 1692–1705 (resign). The Hervé were still active in Paris as *marchands-drapiers* in early 17th c, as evidenced by bp's grandfather's prominence in that capacity. His children, among them bp's father, moved into the world of robe and royal finance, marrying into families of similar background. Bp's father also established service ties with great aristocratic families like the Nemours and Montmorency, and then princes of Condé, becoming one of their principal agents of Condé in Paris parlt. His 1st wife, Marie Doujat, was from a family in service of Marie de' Medici and Gaston d'Orléans (as *avocat-général*), while his 2nd wife, Marie Le Ragois de Bretonvilliers, the bp's step-mother, was from a financial family of considerable standing, but also deeply involved in *dévot* circles.

Born Paris, 1651. Son of Charles (d 1697), *avocat*, later *cons* in Grenoble (1632–3) and Paris parlts, and Marie Doujat, his 1st wife. Studied hum, phil and theol in Paris for 6 years, then took lic in Bourges. Ordained priest on Easter Saturday 1675 by Bp Saint-Valier of Quebec. Led crown-sponsored missions to Huguenots in diocs of Laon, Saintes, Poitiers, and in Cevennes after 1683. Between nom to, and grant of papal provs for Gap, he was active there as vic-gen of his predecessor, Méliand, himself transferred to Alet in 1684. Difficult problems of rebuilding Gap dioc after its devastation in 1692 by Savoyard troops, with Hervé often travelling to Paris and elsewhere for financial support, which was never quite enough. But in 1702, Hervé was sent into internal exile 'pour l'honneur du roy', allegedly on account of personal behaviour, but real reasons may have been different. He spent periods in Condom seminary, and then in an abbey in Lower Brittany, before finally resigning Gap in Nov 1705 and receiving the rich benefice of *domnerie* of Aubrac in compensation. Retired to Paris, he continued to concern himself with the dioc in subsequent years, supporting his successor, Berger.

Nom 31-5-1684. Provs 15-10-1692. Consec 7-12-1692. Resign 12-11-1705. Died 27-6-1722.

Sources: ASV, PC 86, fos 692–706. BN, PO 1518, no 34513; MS Fr 19212, fo 33v. AN, L 735, pièce 1, n 30. *Inventaire-sommaire des archives des Hautes Alpes, Série G*, ed Guillaume, iii, xx–xxi. St-Simon, xli, 368–9. *Gallia Chr Nov*, Gap, cols 524–6. Béguin, *Princes de Condé*, 291, 417. Frondeville, *Conseillers*, 66. Virieux, 'Parlement de Grenoble', 208–9. DHGE, xxiv, 244–5.

Huet, Pierre-Daniel. Avranches 1692–99 (resign).   Probably the greatest scholar of all Louis XIV's bps, he was born in Caen 8-2-1630, baptised on 9–2. Son of Daniel, a *cons* in *élection* of Avranches, and Isabelle Piton de Berteville, both converts from Protestantism who died in mid-1630s. Studied initially with SJ at Caen, then law at Univ of Caen, where he took bacc, lic and doct *in utr* in Aug-Sept 1670. Before then he had settled in Paris, where he frequented major scholars of the day, travelled to Holland and Sweden with Bochart 1652. His learning got him the sous-preceptorate to Dauphin in 1670 (Bossuet was preceptor), and election to Académie Française in 1674. He also won good graces of Philippe d'Orléans, who was an effective protector to him. Although tonsured in 1656, he only took minor orders in 1671 and was ordained priest in 1676. Nom to abbey of Aunay in 1679. Given see of Soissons in early Nov 1685, he exchanged it with Brûlart for Avranches in 1690. He resigned for health reasons in 1699 in return for abbey of Fontenay, and then retired to Jesuit *maison professe* to continue his studies, for which he was admired across Europe. His episcopate was an interlude in a much longer career as an scholar, but he was a more active bp of Avranches than is commonly imagined.

Nom to Soissons, 9-11-1685. Nom to Avranches 5-10-1689. Provs 5-5-1692. Consec 5-9-1692. Resign 2-4-1699. Died 25-1-1721.

Sources: ASV, PC 86, fos 365–72. BN, MS Fr 20969, fo 25. St-Simon, iv, 92, n 6. Fénelon, *Correspondance*, xv, 111. Bossuet, *Correspondance*, i, 208–10. Fortin de la Hoguette, *Lettres*, ii, 848–9. E A Pigeon, *Le Diocèse d'Avranches* (Coutances 1888). DBF, xvii, 1431–3.

Isoré. *See* **Hervault.**

Jégou de Kervilio, Olivier. Tréguier 1694–1731.   Several families of this name existed in 17th c Brittany, all confirmed as noble *d'ancienne extraction de chevalerie* during 1668 *recherches de noblesse*, though they were not all related by lineage. Bp belonged to a family from Quimper dioc where they had been resident since 15th c. A foray into Rennes parlt proved very short-lived (1657–86), since it involved only 2 of bp's own elder brothers, Claude and René, both of whom predeceased him. Bp's father was 'captain' of the Quimper nobility, while on the his mother's side, he belonged to a family much more prominently represented in parlt, court and army, its most famous member being the comte de Guebriant (1602–43), *maréchal de France* in 1642.

Born at Paul (Cotes-du-Nord) 1643. Son of Gilles, sgr de Kervilio, and Marie Budes, married in May 1629. Further studies in Paris Univ: MA in Oct 1667, 17ᵗʰ place in 1674 theol lic, doctor of theol 5-9-1684. Priest since ca 1674. Successively *recteur* of Glomel and Ploermel before becoming canon and grand archdeacon in Quimper, the post he held at time of nom to Tréguier, his predecessor, Le Sénéchal, dying while on deputation to court in March 1694. Jégou proved to be an extremely active bp, visiting dioc intensively, virtually annually for over 35 years. A strong supporter of Noailles in Jansenist affair, refusing *Unigenitus* and subsequent compromises, he spared dioc by refusing to publish *mandements* or instructions raising doctrinal issues. All in all, a highy local career.

Nom 29-5-1694. Provs 3-10-1694. Consec 3-10-1694. Died 2-8-1731.

Sources: ASV, PC 88, fos 497–504. BN, PO 1578, no 36213; Doss bleus 369, no 9697. Fénelon, *Correspondance*, xvii, 313, n 19. Saulnier, *Parlement de Bretagne*, ii, 531–3. *Repertoire des visites pastorales*, iv, 500–2. DHGE, xxvii, 967–8. Minois, *La Bretagne des prêtres*, 142ff.

Joly, Claude. Agen 1665–78.   Not to be confused with Claude Joly, canon of ND of Paris, best known for his pamphlets during the Fronde and his role in Paris church politics under the Cardinal de Retz. From Lorraine, this Joly family were village notables rather than mere hard-working peasants – one of bp's uncles was curé of the parish of Buzy during his childhood, one was a local *bailli*, while another relative was canon of Verdun cath, a post which he passed on to Claude in due course. 2 of the bp's brothers settled in Paris by mid-century, and outlived him – which may explain the confusion of identity and background just mentioned.

Born in village of Buzy-sur-Orne in Verdun dioc, where baptised on 25-6-1610, Claude was 3ʳᵈ child of Nicolas and Catherine *alias* Comptesse La Charette. Tonsured young, there is no evidence of where he studied, but by 1635 he was a bachelor of theol, univ not given, whereas his doct in theol, date also unknown, was from Pont-à-Mousson, and not Paris as sometimes claimed. He may have served briefly as a curé in Verdun dioc before becoming one of the earliest disciples and companions of Olier in St-Sulpice parish, which he joined (July 1643) and where he participated in running the parish for several years, earning a reputation as a regular preacher. Non-resident canon of Verdun (1649–53), a benefice he passed on to a younger brother, and canon-treasurer of Beauvais cath (1651–3), which he exchanged in 1653 for the parish of St-Nicolas-des-Champs in Paris, where he was curé until 1664. His reputation grew while there, partly via his preaching (some of it in Languedoc at invitation of Pavillon bp of Alet), leading Mazarin to ask for his assistance on his deathbed, and Fouquet for his services as confessor when imprisoned after 1661. Such notoriety sufficed to bring nom to St-Pol-de-Léon in July 1661 but he returned the *brevet* 6 months later! At Agen, he caused a storm by revoking powers of all confessors, regulars and seculars, in 1667 with a view to reforming confessional practice, a decision which led to litigation in the royal council – which by the celebrated 'arrêt d'Agen' of 1669 judged in favour of bp and episcopal powers to control clergy and pastoral activities. His subsequent career showed him to be a determined reformer, anxious to restore the correct sacramental discipline to the French church. Rigorist, anti-regular, and friend of Port-Royal. 8 vols of sermons were published posthumously and, as befitted one with his Sulpician background, he was active in formation of clergy.

Nom 25-4-1664. Provs 12-1-1665. Consec 15-3-1665. Died 21-10-1678.

Sources: ASV, PC 61, fos 204–21. AN, L 727, Agen, no 10. ASS, Bertrand fiches. Abbé Gillant, 'Messire Claude Joly, évêque et comte d'Agen', *Semaine religieuse de Verdun* (1930), 157–60, 166–8, 175, 182–4 (partly based on local records destroyed in 1914). Lesaulnier, *Port-Royal insolite*, 182. DLF, 632–3. DHGE, xxviii, 739–40.

Kerhoent de Coëtanfao, Roland. Avranches 1699–1719.   According to Moréri, this bp was descended from an 'ancienne maison de Bretagne' which he traces back to early 12th c. 18 generations later, bp's grandfather founded the Coëtanfao branch, but subsequently recovered the lands and titles of the main branch. A 16th c marriage to a daughter of the Ploeuc family (see below) brought the Coëtanfao title with it. Their military activity, already visible by this date, became more prominent under Louis XIV, when bp's elder brother benefited from patronage of a fellow Breton, the prince de Soubise, who recognised him as a kinsman; he also became a friend of St-Simon, who helped him to obtain the post of *chevalier d'honneur* of the duchesse de Berry, 1715.

Son of Sebastien, marquis de Coëtanfao, and Marie-Renée de Kerhoet, married in 1654, born on 10-1-1662. Further studies in Paris, where MA in Aug 1679, taking 61st place in 1688 theol lic. Doct of theol, Paris, 2-5-1689. Priest since 1689. Dean and 1st dignitary of St-Pol-de-Léon cath, and then vic-gen of Dol for 5 years before nom. Obtained Avranches on resignation by Daniel Huet. Little known about his episcopate, but he seems to have had pro-Jansenist sympathies.

Nom 24-4-1699. Provs 5-10-1699. Consec 29-11-1699. Died 2-10-1719.

Sources: ASV, PC 93, fos 1–15. BN, PO 1607, no 37103; Doss bleus 373, no 9910. Pinard, *Chronologie*, iv, 643–4. St-Simon, xviii, 188; xx, 219; xxvi, 203. Moréri, *Grand Dictionnaire*, viii, 672–7 (Querhoent). Carné, *Chevaliers bretons de St-Michel*, 193–6. Compère and Julia, *Collèges français*, ii, 78.

Kercado. *See* Le Sénéchal.

Kervilio. *See* Jégou.

La Baume de Suze, Anne-Tristan. Tarbes 1677–92, Auch 1692–1705.   Nephew of Louis-François de la Baume de Suze, bp of Viviers (1618–90). The already formidably connected La Baume further expanded its kinship ties inside and outside of Dauphiné during 17th c, as witnessed by marriage of bp of Tarbes' own parents, an aunt (to La Garde de Chambonas, father of bp of Lodève and Viviers), and his eldest brother (to a Montiers de Mérinville, aunt of bp of Chartres) – not to mention others involving the Beaumanoir de Lavardin.

One of 3 sons of Anne, comte de Rochefort and Suze, and Catherine de la Croix de Chevrières, from a major parlt family of Grenoble, married in 1631, bp was born in Grenoble 1640. Seems to have studied mainly in Paris where he took MA in July 1656, followed by 73rd place in 1664 theol lic. Priest since 1669. He received provostship of Nîmes cath from Louis XIV in Sept 1666 when he was a deacon. Dep to ACs in 1665, 1670, 1675, thanks to extensive benefice-holdings and connections. Nom to St-Omer after French conquest but without a royal indult, his bulls were not forthcoming, and he renounced the nom in 1685 for that of Auch, the metropolitan of Tarbes. St-Simon thought well of him despite his closeness to Jesuits, and remarked that he was not liked at court, for which not really cut out.

Nom 12-9-1675. Provs 30-8-1677. Consec 10-10-1677. Nom to St-Omer, 25-10-1677 (no provs granted). Nom to Auch 31-5-1684. Provs 4-2-1692. Died 4-3-1705.

Sources: ASV, PC 76, fos 918–30; PC 86, fos 176–221. BN, MS Fr 7651, fo 147 (*bienfaits du roi*). St-Simon, i, 128. Vindry, *État major, gendarmerie*, 43, 80. Anselme, *Histoire*, ix, pt i, 72–3.

La Baume le Blanc de la Vallière, Gilles. Nantes 1668–77 (resign).   It was in 1635 that this family was allowed to add La Baume to its initial Le Blanc patronymic. Their origins lay in the Bourbonnais, where the senior branch continued to reside, and were related to the La Baume family which provided bps of St-Flour in the late 16th c. The future La Vallière branch moved to Touraine by early 16th c, where they provided several mayors of Tours from 1558 to 1637, acquiring the seigneurie of La Vallière, which is indissociably linked with Louis XIV's early mistress, Louise La Baume le Blanc, duchesse de la Vallière, of whom the bp of

Nantes was an uncle. Bp's mother descended from a family related by blood since 15th c to ruling Bourbons.

Born 22-11-1616 Tours, where baptised on 24-11-1616. 5th of 7 sons of Jean de la Baume le Blanc, sgr de la Valliere, and Françoise de Beauvau, married in 1609. Godson of Louis XIII's childhood gov, marshal Souvré. Studied phil and theol with Jesuits in Paris, but unable for that reason to take degree. Priest since ca 1648. Canon of St-Martin of Tours. He was originally intended as coadj to uncle, Gabriel de Beauvau, but latter died before papal provs granted. He himself resigned to make way for a Beauvau relative, Gilles, and in order to become a Jesuit – but that only happened in 1707 shortly before his death.

Nom as coadj 9-12-1667. Nom as bp of Nantes 1-2-1668. Provs 16-1-1668. Consec 25-5-1668. Resign 10-6-1677. Died 9-6-1707.

Sources: ASV, PC 67, fos 365–400. Anselme, *Histoire*, v, 489–96; ix, pt ii, 672–4. Boisnard, *Touraine*, no 186.

La Bourdonnaye, Jean-Louis. St-Pol-de-Léon 1702–45.　An old Breton family claiming a noble, chivalric pedigree as far back as 13th c. Several branches appeared and disappeared in subsequent centuries, and by 16th c, the Coëtion branch, from which the bp descended, was the principal one. Virtually exclusive military traditions until 17th c, when robe occupations make their appearance without fully replacing army, navy, Order of Malta. Bp's father (1630–99) the 1st of no fewer than 12 members to serve in Rennes parlt after 1650, and who included bp's half-brother, Yves-Marie, who was also a long-serving prov intendant in various parts of France (1689–1713). A relative, possibly an uncle, may also have been confessor to Philippe d'Orléans.

Son of Louis, vicomte de Coëtion, and Louise le Tresle, his 2nd wife, married in 1656. Born in parish of Ruffiac, Rennes dioc, 25-2-1667. Univ studies in Paris, where he took MA in Aug 1686, and 96th place in 1694 theol lic. Doctor of theol, Paris, 20-1-1695. Ordained priest 5-6-1694, having been at St-Sulpice from May 1693 to Aug 1694. For many years provost of Guérande, Nantes, as well as vic-gen in that dioc.

Nom 1-11-1701. Provs 6-2-1702. Consec 23-4-1702. Died 22-2-1745.

Sources: ASV, PC 95, fos 240–53. AN, L 744, dossier 1, no 24. Saulnier, *Parlement de Bretagne*, i, 131–2. Bluche, *L'Origine*, 222–3. St-Simon, xviii, 112.

La Broue, Pierre. Mirepoix 1679–1720.　The origins of this family remain unclear, as several families of same name existed in Auvergne, Languedoc, Angoumois and Poitou. Earliest sources trace bp's family to Aurillac around 1400, before settling in Gourdon in Quercy during 15th and 16th c, where they moved into legal profession, with some of them holding relatively modest offices at *sénéchaussée* court of Gourdon in later 16th c. Yet others were merchants and notables resident at Moissac in late 16th and early 17th c. Bp's father may well have been the 1st of them to enter Toulouse parlt, and his marriage to a Catelan would certainly have consolidated his position in Toulousain society. Bp's elder brother became a military officer in Louis XIV's bodyguard, married into the Crusy de Marsillac family (which produced a bp of Mende under Richelieu) and had his nobility upheld in 1668 on (dubious) claim that it went back to their Auvergnat origins in 13th c. Bp's own early career also extended these connections beyond Toulouse and its robe circles.

Born Moissac, Cahors dioc, on 6-2-1644 and baptised on 8-2-1644, though family was by then mostly resident in Toulouse. One of 3 children of Blaise (d 1650), *cons* in Toulouse parlt, and Jacqueline Catelan, eldest daughter of François, *doyen* of *cons* in the parlt. Studied phil and theol in Paris, where he took MA in July 1667, 26th place in 1672 theol lic, finishing with doct on 22-8-1680 – i.e. *after* episcopal nom. Priest since 8-6-1675. He preached widely in Paris and St-Germain in 1679, and for 1st time at court in early Feb 1679 – only 3 weeks before nom to Mirepoix! Some literary talent or activities, as he seems to have written some poetry. Prior of Bruniquel in succession to a family incumbent, he was regarded as a client of

Bossuet in Languedoc, but failed to obtain preceptorship to duc de Bourgogne ca 1689, though there was some compensation when his nephew, Jean de Catelan, future bp of Valence, was appointed *lecteur* to duc de Berry in Aug 1693. Bossuet was instrumental in his episcopal elevation, but might not have predicted that in 1717 he would be one of 4 bps to appeal to future general council against *Unigenitus*, having declared that Quesnel was as 'instruit de la doctrine de l'église' as Bossuet himself!

Nom 24-2-1679. Provs 17-7-1679. Consec 8-9-1680. Died 20-9-1720.

Sources: ASV, PC 78, fos 347–59. BN, PO 529, no 11948; Cab d'Hozier 68, no 1765. AC Moissac, GG 21, fo 28. Beauchet-Filleau, *Dictionnaire des familles du Poitou*, vi, 24–5. Fénelon, *Correspondance*, i, 191, n 4. Bossuet, *Correspondance*, ii, 202–11; vi, 86, n 11; xiv, 276–7. St-Simon, xxxviii, 10. DLF, 646.

La Brousse. *See* **Le Neboux**.

La Brunetière, Guillaume du Plessis. Saintes 1677–1702.   This bp's family seem to have been long settled in Anjou, of noble rank but relatively limited activity or *éclat*. Some members appear to have served under Condé during religious wars, so Protestant affiliations cannot be ruled out. Military activities dominate down to generation of bp's father, who was a captain in Brézé regiment. Bp's mother, Elisabeth Lasnier, was from a bourgeois family from Angers ennobled by holding mayoralty in 1560. Subsequent generations of Lasnier held office in local *présidial* court, but also in Rennes parlt under Henri IV and, above all, in Paris *gr conseil*, from Henri III to Louis XIV. These connections were certainly useful to future bp of Saintes, whose early career was exclusively Parisian and where his uncle, Guy Lasnier (1602–81) was highly esteemed by *dévots* and reformers.

Born in family chateau of le Plessis en Gesté near Angers 24-11-1630. Son of Antoine, sgr du Plessis de Gasté, and Elisabeth Lasnier. Attended SJ coll of La Flèche, then to Univ of Paris where MA in July 1648. Studied theol at coll of Navarre, where he was a contemporary of Bossuet, taking 4th place in 1656 lic exam, and doct on 27-7-1656. Ordained priest in 1655, he frequented Bossuet in *doyenné* de St-Thomas-du-Louvre, but influence of uncle Guy Lasnier was decisive for his early career. A friend of Vincent de Paul, archdeacon of Brie (Paris dioc) since 1643, Lasnier resigned that position to nephew in 1657. From early 1660s La Brunetière was vic-gen of both Péréfixe and Harlay, and also during the vacancy between the 2 abps. Involved in liturgical research and changes in Paris, esp for Breviary, but still unfinished when he became bp. He took major part in campaign against nuns of Port-Royal in 1664 over the anti-Jansenist Formulary. Proposed for Tulle in 1671 by Bossuet and Péréfixe but, unsuccessful, he remained vic-gen of Paris until 1676, when Harlay may have preferred to see him move to a bishopric elsewhere. Active in converting Protestants during episcopate. Well regarded by Bossuet, Fénelon, and Louis XIV, who is quoted as saying of him in 1676, 'I have made a man I have never seen a bishop, but I have never met anyone who did not speak well of him'. Died in odour of sanctity according to contemporaries, though Fénelon found him 'trop mou et trop crédule'.

Nom 9-8-1676. Provs 20-8-1677. Consec 30-11-1677. Died 2-5-1702.

Sources: ASV, PC 76, fos 1076–88. AN, L 744, Saintes, nos 26–7. Saulnier, *Parlement de Bretagne*, ii, 576–7. Trani, 'Conseillers du grand conseil', 166. Poutet, 'Docteurs', 264, no 226. Bossuet, *Correspondance*, i, 88, 504, 506; iii, 333–8; xi. 382; xiv, 410. Sévigné, *Correspondance*, v, 20. Ferté, *Vie religieuse*, 30.

Ladvocat-Billiad, Nicolas. Boulogne 1677–81.   The Ladvocat (or l'Advocat) seem to have been a Parisian merchant family, who can be traced at least as far as Nicolas, a silk merchant who in 1554 married Marie de Castille, whose family would rise more spectacularly in subsequent generations than the Ladvocat, though ensuring them some solid connections (e.g. Jeannin de Castille, Fouquet). Their eldest son was a receiver of *tailles* in Meaux around 1600, but offices of SR, and in *chambre des comptes* and *gr conseil* followed in generation before bp, whose own father and elder brother served in the *chambre des comptes*, albeit relatively modestly, for several decades. Bp's Ladvocat cousins seemed to have done better, which in differing ways helped his career. In particular his aunt, Catherine, married Arnauld de Pomponne, one of Louis XIV's foreign ministers, and distinguished member of celebrated Parisian family of lawyers, *dévots*, nuns and reformers, so bp's own encounter with Cardinal de Retz may have arisen from these connections. Catherine's brother, Jacques, became a royal almoner, while François, probably a cousin, was a canon of Notre-Dame who retired in 1646 in order to make room for Nicolas in the chapter early in his career. They were connected to other Parisian *dévot* groups, while Louis, sgr de Sauveterre, was a long-serving member of Condé clientele, serving as agent of the prince of Conti and his mother from 1646 onwards.

Born 25-3-1620, baptised in parish of St-Paul, Paris. Son of Louis, *maître* in *chambre des comptes*, Paris, and Madeleine de Billiad, daughter of Charles, a *prés* in Paris parlt. Studied in Univ of Paris, where took MA in April 1648, 1st place in 1654 theol lic, followed by doct 9-5-1654. Canon of ND de Paris in 1646, he was made vic-gen of Paris in 1654, initially in order to stymy Retz, but he duly accepted him. Later exiled to Auvergne for refusing to follow orders from Mazarin after Retz's arrest. Came to Lazarists in Paris to prepare for priesthood and was ordained priest with them in 1672. Active in admin sacraments on missions and in hospitals, he served as confessor at Paris hôtel-dieu. Also published several works on Assumption and virginity of mother of Christ. Bp Perrochel of Boulogne, a former Lazarist *compagnon* of Vincent de Paul, was seeking to retire so the exchange of Boulogne for canon's stall at ND between him and Ladvocat was agreed, esp as Boulogne was not especially sought-after. Retz, who had provided Ladvocat with some minor benefices, strongly recommended him to the nuncio in 1675 – 'Le sieur L'Advocat est un docteur en théologie de la maison de la Sorbonne, d'une érudition au dessus du commun'.

Nom 11-3-1675. Provs 8-2-1677. Consec 30-5-1677. Death 11-4-1681.

Sources: ASV, PC 76, fos 104–27; Nunz Fr 153, fo 186. BN, PO 1616, no 37369; Doss bleus 387, no 10423; MS Fr 7655, no 51; MS Fr 32139, pp 47–9. Retz, *Mémoires* (Pléaide edn), 1037–53. Rapin, *Mémoires*, ed Aubineau, ii, 505–9. St-Simon, vi, 351. Sévigné, *Correspondance*, x, 59, n 2. Poutet, 'Docteurs', no 184, 259. Golden, *Godly Rebellion*, 29, 35–8, 56–7. Mesnard, *Pascal et les Roannez*, ii, 776–7. Béguin, *Princes de Condé*, 254, 423–4.

La Faye. *See* **Meschatin.**

La Garde de Chambonas, Charles-Antoine. Lodève 1671–92, Viviers 1692–1713.   It was through his uncle, La Baume, bp of Viviers (1619–90), and the La Baume de Suze family connections that La Garde and his family advanced their fortunes under Louis XIV. Bp's elder brother, who obtained the elevation of Chambonas to marquisate status, was a favourite of Louis XIV's illegitimate son, duc du Maine – capt of his guards from 1688, *premier gentilhomme* in 1706 – not unimportant given that Maine was also gov of Languedoc.

Born in Uzès dioc, 1636. 2nd son of Charles-Antoine, sgr de Chambonas, and Charlotte de la Baume de Suze, both dead before 1671. Place of studies not known, but he took lic *in utr* at Orléans. Ordained priest 25-1-1671 in Montpellier by uncle, Bp La Baume de Suze of Viviers, who had made him a canon and vic-gen of Viviers during mid 1650s, and who also resigned his abbey of Mazan O Cist (Viviers) to him in 1688. Uncle and nephew both elected canons of Nîmes in 1659, with Chambonas becoming an archdeacon in 1661 against wishes of bp and chapter, and where his behaviour fell well short of edifying. Dep to 1665 and 1670 ACs. One of the most politically active bps in Languedoc, he frequently resided outside his successive diocs, esp Viviers, which he seems to have left in hands of his vic-gen, Puget, future bp of Digne. Dangeau hinted at a fortune amounting to 600,000 *livres*.

Nom 28-2-1671. Provs 28-9-1671. Consec 15-11-1671. Nom to Viviers 22-9-1690. Provs 5-5-1692. Died 21-2-1713.

Sources: ASV, PC 70, fos 510–36. BN, MS 20969, fo 69v, 116. St-Simon, x, 99; xxiii, 280. Sévigné, *Correspondance*, ii, 49. Dangeau, xiv, 354. Chaix d'Est-Ange, *Dictionnaire des familles*, xx, 133–6. Sauzet, *Contre-Réforme*, 344, 437. Joret, 'Basville et l'épiscopat', 435–64'. Bergin, *Making*, 645.

La Hoguette. *See* **Fortin.**

La Lanne, Léon. Bayonne 1692–1700.   The bp's family seems to have originated in the Landes in dioc of Dax, and was unrelated to the Navarre family of that name. Its best known branch was that of Villandraut, whose members served from mid-16th c in the parlt of Bordeaux, first as *cons*, then as *prés*, where they still figured a century later and where they intermarried with parlt families like the Pontac. An even brighter future seemed to open up for them when Sarran, bp's uncle, a *prés à mortier* in parlt in succession to his father, became Richelieu's lt-gen for admiralty of Guyenne in 1627, only to be disgraced and condemned to death for counterfeiting in 1640, a disgrace compounded by his flight abroad to escape retribution. Rehabilitated after cardinal's death, 1644. Of this generation, however, only bp's father produced male heirs. He also moved away from a parlt career, preferring a post in *artillerie de France*, and then a captaincy in guards of Gaston d'Orléans. A small number of ecclesiastics figured in this and related branches of the family in 2 generations before bp, and they managed to establish a solid enough foothold among better-connected chapters of region – notably St-Sernin and St-André of Bordeaux – but also in neighbouring chapter and dioc of Bazas. Louis de Lalanne, having been *cons* in parlt and dean of both St-Sernin and St-André, resigned his benefices *in comm* to his nephew, the future bp, before he died in 1667. Noel de Lalanne (1618–73), the noted pro-Arnauld Jansensist theologian, was son of a Parisian offshoot of this family.

Born ca 1642 in Bordeaux. Son of Alphonse, baron of Rouillan, and Jeanne de Tustal, his 1st wife, married in 1632. No information on place or duration of studies, merely that he was doctor of theol by 1688, though he probably took his degree in Bordeaux. Ordained priest in Bazas 9 years before nom to Bayonne. It appears he began career as *cons* in Bordeaux parlt and became dean of St-Sernin in 1651, which he then resigned in 1653. In exchange, he obtained several benefices scattered through neighbouring diocs, to which he later added the abbey of Ferme OSB (Bazas), which his uncle held before him, as well as 'simple' priories of Mons and St-Exupery-de-Belin (Bordeaux) in 1674. Gr-vic of Dax for some time before 1681 when bp Chaumont resigned it in his favour and with royal approval, but his provs were held up by crisis of 1682–92. In 1688, he renounced his title to Dax in return for nom to Bayonne.

Nom to Bayonne 1-11-1688. Provs 10-3-1692. Consec 24-8-1692. Died 6-8-1700.

Sources: ASV, PC 86 fos 266–88. ASV, Acta congreg consist 1682, vol i, fos 127–30. BN, MS Fr 20969, fos 67, 71r. Vindry, *Parlementaires*, ii, 8, 20. V Foix, *Lalanne. Essai généalogique sur les familles nobles ou titrés de ce nom* (Dax, n d). Grillon, *Papiers de Richelieu*, ii, no 185.

La Luzerne. *See* **Briqueville.**

La Mer de Matha, François-Gaspard. Aire 1707–10.   This family may have originated in Forez, but its principal base lay in lower Auvergne and Bourbonnais, where it had been present since at least 1420s and held several seigneuries. It was connected by marriage to many of the best-known noble families of the province (Langeac, Frédeville, St-Quentin, Canillac), but did not follow numerous families in developing collateral branches. Despite evidence of service to crown in 16th and early 17th c, they do not seem to have achieved more than a modicum of distinction, and finally died out by the mid-18th c. An elder brother of bp served as a capt in Tilladet regiment, which could suggest a Le Tellier connection.

Born 1660 in Clermont dioc, son of Gaspard, sgr de Matha, and Catherine de Montchannin, married in 1652. Higher studies in Paris, where he took his MA in July 1679, followed by successful theol studies, since he obtained 2nd place (after Michel Le Pelletier) in 1688 lic, followed by doct on 20-4-1688. He was by then a *socius* of Sorbonne, of which he was prior and to which he was strongly attached. Ordained priest 6-4-1688. Pére Léonard regarded him as a successful preacher in Paris churches, but he also spent some time as a missionary in Cévennes during 1690s. Obtained abbey of St-Cyran OSB (Bourges) in April 1700. Close to Jesuits, he was regarded as their protegé, probably owing his elevation to their patronage. His brief reign was terminated by infection while on visitation of his dioc.

Nom 1-8-1706. Provs 21-2-1707. Consec 10-4-1707. Died 30-6-1710.

Sources: ASV, PC 100, fos 1–13. AN, L 727, Agen, no 14. BN, MS Fr 20969, fo 152r. Sourches, xii, 262. Remacle, *Dictionnaire des familles d'Auvergne*, ii, 305–7.

La Mothe-Houdancourt, Jérôme. St-Flour 1664–93.   Younger brother of Henri, abp of Auch, and nephew of Daniel, bp of Mende under Louis XIII. Born 1621 at château of Houdancourt in Beauvais dioc. Probably studied mainly in Paris, but took doct of theol at Bourges, 1655 'as letters of that univ show' (ut patet ex litteris huius universitatis). He also appears to have frequented one or more Parisian seminaries, but it is not known which. His nom to St-Flour was almost certainly Anne of Austria's doing – St-Flour was within her dower lands, she had the rights of presentation, and the bp's uncle, Henri, abp of Auch, was her *premier aumônier* and confidant in ecclesiastical affairs.

Nom 1-5-1664. Provs 23-6-1664. Consec 17-8-1664. Died 29-5-1693.

Sources: ASV, PC 61, fos 373–87. Poutet 'Docteurs', 322. Bergin, *Making*, 649.

Langle, Pierre de. Boulogne 1698–1724.   Unrelated to long-serving Breton parlt family of same name, the de Langle (or Delangle) were natives of Evreux, where they were resident since later 16th and possibly much earlier. As office of *receveur des tailles* held by the bp's father and grandfather suggests, they were local notables involved mainly within the royal financial admin, and other family members in both previous and later generations held positions in Evreux *grenier à sel*, the *chambre des comptes* at Rouen, as well as in local *présidial* court by later 17th c. His father's ennoblement in 1661, as part of celebration of peace with Spain, was revoked some years later, but was confirmed in 1675, challenged again in 1698 but also upheld. His 1st marriage was to a 1st cousin of Longueil des Maisons, *surintendant des finances* and gov of Evreux during the Fronde, yet there was nothing especially remarkable about family's subsequent progress. Bp's own entry into ecclesiastical world was clearly helped by an uncle, Jacques de Langle, doct of theol (Paris), canon and penitentiary of Evreux by 1640s, who preceded him and his eldest brother, François, in Evreux chapter.

Baptised in St-Nicolas parish church, Evreux, 6-3-1644. 3rd son of Mathieu de Langle, sgr de Mosny, receiver of *tailles* in Evreux *élection*, and Marie de Resnel, married in 1630. Studied initially in coll at Evreux, then Paris at coll of Navarre, where he dedicated MA theses to Longuil des Maisons, and became doct of theol on 29-5-1670, having taken the bacc in 1666, followed by 11th place in 1670 lic, and attracted interest of Bossuet, a fellow Navarriste. After ordination as priest, also in 1670, he returned to Evreux where he became canon by 1674 and grand penitentiary in succession to uncle in 1678. By 1681 he was *official* and gr-vic under bp Potier de Novion. Thanks to Bossuet he was made tutor, in 1690, to Louis XIV's son, the comte of Toulouse, who seems to have interceded on his behalf for nom to Boulogne in 1698. Prior of St-Lo in Coutances in Dec 1695, he was elected *ag-gen* by province of Rouen in 1696, replacing Colbert de Croissy, recently nom to Montpellier, but he only served part of his term before own nom to Boulogne. He acquired a reputation for litigiousness in early years at Boulogne, but he was an austere and pious bp, organising massive charities in famine of 1709. One of 4 bps to appeal to a future council against *Unigenitus* in 1717, but he remained resident in his dioc, which suffered from the disputes between him and regulars esp over Jansenist and related moral theol issues.

Nom to Boulogne, 29-3-1698. Provs 15-9-1698. Consec 14-12-1698. Died 12-4-1724.

Sources: ASV, PC 89, fos 193–201 (St-Lo); PC 92, fos 187–201 (Boulogne). BN, PO 1640, no 38140; Doss bleus 381, no 10235; Nouv d'Hozier 202, no 4516. AN, L 729. Boulogne, no 5. AD Eure, E 2485–8, G 22. St-Simon, xxvi, 94. Poutet, 'Docteurs', 302, no 562. Bossuet, *Correspondance*, viii, 76, n 8. Landrin, *Un prélat gallican. Pierre de Langle évêque de Boulogne. Répertoire des visites pastorales*, i, 299–303.

Languet de Gergy, Jean-Joseph. Soissons 1715–31, Sens 1731–48 (resign).   Family of Burgundian origins, originally from village of Vitteaux, or possibly Chalon-sur-Saône. Allegedly, Hubert Languet, the Huguenot writer, was one of them, while another source claims that the great-grandfather of bp, Jean Claude Languet, held major position in household of Catherine de' Médici, after which he retired to Burgundy and married Marguerite Pivert. What seems clear is that earliest known generations were lawyers, and that bp's grandfather, Guillaume, thanks to 1622 marriage which brought him into Bouthillier family circle, became SR and actively particpated in financial dealings (esp army supplying and tax-farming) from 1630s to 1650s, which he combined with role as a Condé family business manager (one of many) in Burgundy. The *chambre de justice* of 1661 bankrupted him. His wife, Elisabeth de Bretagne, was closely related by marriage to Bossuet family, also natives of Dijon – thus making the 'eagle of Meaux' and the bp's father 2nd cousins. The latter, after initial service as *cons* in Rouen parlt (1646–53), became *proc-gén* in Dijon parlt in 1654, marrying daughter of a second *prés* in same parlt in 1661. Over several generations Languet family members were heavily involved in religious activities in Dijon and beyond, with strong ties to Carmel (Dijon, Beaune) and Oratory, and to wider *dévot* movement. Bp and his brothers made substantial careers in very different spheres. The most prominent, Jacques-Vincent, was a long-serving career diplomat (for whom Gergy itself, near Chalon-sur-Saône, was elevated to *comté* in 1706); Pierre a general in Wurttemberg army; Jean-Baptiste, a model curé of St-Sulpice in Paris, who studied simultaneously with bp in Paris theol fac; Lazare, abbot of Morimond O Cist, who died as *proc-gén* of Cisterican order in Rome. They also kept some ties to the past, as evidenced by bp's sister marriage to Claude Rigoley, secretary of Burgundian estates and later *pr prés* of *chambre des comptes* of Dijon.

Born Dijon, 25-8-1677, 6th and youngest son of Denis Languet and Marie Robelin. Studies in Jesuit coll des Godrans at Dijon until 1690, when moved to Univ of Paris, MA in Aug 1697, theol bacc exam in Jan 1698, followed by 4th place in 1702 theol lic (his brother was 9th). Doct of theol, Paris (coll of Navarre) 26-4-1702. Entered St-Sulpice seminary in Nov 1691 with elder brother, the future curé, and remained there until March 1702. Priest since 1702. He taught and had some cure of souls in St-Sulpice community and seminary during these years. Bossuet, his relative and mentor, was instrumental in obtaining an almonership to duchess of Burgundy on completion of his theol studies, 1702. Abbot *in comm* of Coetmalouen (Quimper) in 1709, when he was dispensed from court service in order to become vic-gen (and *official*) of the Bourbonnais area of Autun dioc, where he remained for 6 years. St-Simon paints hostile portrait of him as a 'man of the antichamber' who thought *Unigenitus* would be making of him, and which got him see of Soissons and then Sens. His episcopal career was dominated by his anti-Jansenist crusade, and his voluminous works in defence of *Unigenitus* were published in 2 substantial vols in 1752, but it was widely rumoured that he allowed Honoré Tournély, the Paris theol professor, to publish works under his name! Elected to Académie Française in 1723. On resigning Sens in 1748, he retired to abbey of ND de la Couture at Bernay, where he died.

Nom 12-1-1715. Provs 29-5-1715. Consec 23-6-1715. Nom to Sens 20-12-1730. Provs 9-4-1731. Died 11-5-1753.

Sources: ASV, PC 104, fos 481–93. BN, Doss bleus 202, no 4521. Denis Languet, *Lettres*, ed Henri Chevreul (Paris 1880). Frondeville, *Conseillers du parlement de Normandie de 1641 à 1715*, 182–3. Fénelon, *Correspondance*, xvii, 308, n 4. Bossuet, *Correspondance*, viii, 112, n 5. Renty, *Correspondance*, 188ff, 916–17. St-Simon, xviii, 117; xxxvii, 65–70, 392–3. Dessert, *Argent, pouvoir, société*, 620–1; Béguin, *Princes de Condé*, 425. N-M Dawson, 'Mgr Jean Joseph Languet de Gergy, une famille, un réseau', *Etudes Villeneuviennes* (2000) 63–83.

Lanta. *See* **Barthélemy.**

La Parisière. *See* **Rousseau.**

La Poype de Vertrieu, Jean-Claude. Poitiers 1702–32.   The Poype family originated in the Dauphiné and Bresse area, where the name was to be found in 12th c. Bp was born into a junior line, Vertrieu, which had developed in 16th c, and which was widely connected among nobility of the region, enjoying easy access to elite chapters such as St-Jean of Lyon for its clerical offspring. One contemporary claimed that bp's family and that of the king's confessor, La Chaize, were virtual neighbours.

Born in family château de Cornod in Bresse, and baptised 9-2-1655. 2nd son of Edme-François, sgr de Vertrieu, and Claude Louise Marie de Seyturier, married in 1651. No information on early studies, but possibly in SJ coll at Vienne. Further studies in Paris, taking MA before 1672, and theol bacc in July 1675, but he may have taken doct in theol at Bourges at some later date. Tonsured cleric in Paris 7-9-1669, subdeacon in 1674, deacon in March 1682 and priest in April 1683. While studying in Paris, he spent some time in St-Sulpice seminary, which he entered in Nov 1671. Elected canon-count of St-Jean of Lyon 4-5-1678, he later served Abps Villeroy and St-Georges as one of their Gr-vics, with responsbility for the Bresse area, and was vic-gen to St-Georges from 31-10-1697 onwards, having also governed Lyon *sede vacante* after Villeroy's death in 1693. Nom bp of Beziers, which he declined, on 14-4-1702 and then, on the refusal of La Chetardie, the curé of St-Sulpice, to Poitiers, the following day! With a sister at St-Cyr, he took full advantage of his close relations to Mme de Maintenon, Desmarets and others at court to obtain royal support for his policies in Poitiers. An able admin, many of whose vic-gens went on to become bps. He was succeeded by his cousin 'à la mode de Bretagne', i.e., Foudras, son of his aunt, not of his sister.

Nom 15-4-1702. Provs 7-10-1702. Consec 12-11-1702. Died 3-2-1732.

Sources: ASV, PC 95, fos 340–52. AN, G7 542b (corr with Desmarets). BN, MS Fr 32,703, p 70 (*preuves*, St-Pierre of Mâcon chapter). BM Versailles, MS G331 (corr with Maintenon). Fénelon, *Correspondance*, xvii, 117, n 10. Levesque, 'Liste des élèves', no 1097. Beyssac, *Chanoines de Lyon*, 201, 214, 217; Beyssac, *Les Grands Prêtres de Lyon*, 20–1. Paulze-Yvon le Poype, *Un Évêque de Poitiers au xviii siècle* (Poitiers 1899).

La Roche-Aymon, Claude. Le Puy 1704–20.   A Limousin-Marchois family that claimed to trace its lineage back to 12th c, having added the distinguishing 'Aymon' suffix at some intervening date. Connected to similarly old and entrenched families, present episodically at court since at least time of Francis I, they remained somewhat in background, even though 17th c marriages brought connections to Brichantau, La Rochefoucauld, Charpin de Génétines and other families with, *inter alia*, important ecclesiastical connections. Bp's father's marriage extended this particular network: his wife was daughter of Pierre de Lezay, *dit* de Lusignem, a officer in king's *garde du corps*, and Louise Grangier de Liverdis, which made bp of Le Puy a maternal nephew of Bp Lezay of Rodez (1693–1716) and a relative of Bp Grangier of Tréguier (1646–79), not to mention also of the bp of Limoges, Antoine Charpin. Rocheaymon ecclesiastical fortunes rose much higher when bp's nephew, Charles-Antoine (b 1687) became abp of Reims, cardinal and grand almoner of France under Louis XV, spending much of his career improving his family's status and fortunes.

Son of Antoine (d 1697), comte de la Roche-Aymon, and Marie de Lezay de Luzignem, married in Feb 1652. Born in parish of Mainsat, dioc of Limoges, November 1658. Univ studies Paris, MA in Aug 1677, followed by theol bacc, June 1683 and lic in 1686. Tonsured in 1672, he was ordained priest in December 1688, residing in St-Sulpice seminary from March 1685 to Sept 1690. Prior of Ste-Catherine-de-Darnet (Limoges) in 1682. Canon and archdeacon as well as vic-gen of Mende – helped no doubt by eldest brother's marriage in 1680 to niece of Bp Baudry of Mende.

Nom 24-12-1703. Provs 28-4-1703. Consec 22-6-1704. Died 4-6-1720.

Sources: ASV, PC 97, fos 71–84. Levesque, 'Liste des élèves', 102. St-Simon, xiv, 346. Anselme, *Histoire*, ix, 68–75. Nadaud, *Nobiliaire de Limoges*, iv, 32–8. Remacle, *Dictionnaires des familles d'Auvergne*, ii, 331–6. Trépardoux, 'Le Cardinal de la Roche-Aymon et sa famille', 77–91.

La Roque-Priélé, Gaspard. Bayonne 1681–8.   One of the most obscure members of episcopate under Louis XIV. From Tarbes dioc, born Madiran, ca 1623, son of Pierre and Catherine de Gorgue, both dead before his promotion in 1681. Further studies at Toulouse where he was bachelor in canon law, 5-9-1654. Ordained subdeacon in 1651, priest soon afterwards. Abbot *in comm* of La Réole until death, and holder of other benefices, inc priory of Tarast (Tarbes) which he resigned in early 1682. May also have been curé of a parish in Auch, but he was certainly canon of its cath and archpriest of Sangriede.

Nom 30-5-1681. Provs 22-9-1681. Consec 1681. Died 19-6-1688.

Sources: ASV, PC 80, fos 43–74. BIUT, MS 30, fo 254r. BN, MS Fr 20969, fo 86r.

Lascaris d'Urfé, Louis. Limoges 1676–95.   Originating among the Provençal family of Vintimille, a Byzantine imperial marriage in 13th c led them to adopt Lascaris name. It was as comtes de Tende, who in turn intermarried with the Savoyard ducal family and other aristocratic houses, that they subsequently flourished, notably with René, gov of Provence (d 1566), whose grandson, bp's father, would found the Lascaris d'Urfé line. On mother's side, bp's ancestry and connections were no less powerful and longstanding, esp in Auvergne-Forez.

Born 1636 at Alègre in Le Puy dioc. Eldest son of Emmanuel, marquis d'Urfé, and Marguerite d'Alègre, he was baptised 30-3-1647 with young Louis XIV as his godfather. Brought up at court from 1647 onwards in company of king, when known as comte de Sommerive. Made lieut, then capt of light horse of the *maison du roi* a few years later, he quit the court in 1660, and entered St-Sulpice (1-6-1660) under Tronson's direction, while still a layman without even clerical tonsure. 3 of his brothers followed him into the church. After ordination in 1675, he was *prêtre libre* of St-Sulpice parish, so involved in pastoral and charitable work. Long-standing friend of Rancé and Le Camus of Grenoble, who may have had some part in his promotion to Limoges, which he only accepted on condition that Tronson would continue to be his director. Nature of his studies remains obscure, but he hastened to take bacc, lic and doct in canon law in Paris, in March 1676, only a few weeks after nom to Limoges. Initially designted coadj of Limoges, his predecessor died almost immediately, and Lascaris made attempts to resign his title outright, but was dissuaded by Tronson. He brought Sulpician traditions with him to Limoges, where he preferred to live in *séminaire des ordinands* than in episcopal palace, and was surrounded by small group of close collaborators who inc 2 future bps of La Rochelle and Amiens respectively, Étienne de Champflour and Pierre Sabatier. He continued reforming efforts of long-serving predecessor La Fayette, though in different vein. Attempted to retire to La Trappe, but was dissuaded by Tronson and Rancé.

Nom 22-2-1676. Provs. 16-11-1676. Consec 10-1-1677. Died 30-6-1695.

Sources: ASV, PC 75, fos 290–302. AN, MM 1118, fos 37r–8r (degrees, 5–3, 12–3 and 26-3-1676). ASS, Bertrand *fiches*. Levesque, 'Liste des élèves', no 610. Nadaud, *Nobiliaire de Limoges*, iii, 465–8. Rancé, *Correspondance*, ii, no 781105a. Tronson, *Correspondance*, ii, 389–470 (45 letters from Tronson). Aulagne, *La Réforme catholique du xviie siècle dans le diocèse de Limoges*, 355–47. Limouzin-Lamothe, *Le Diocese de Limoges*, 33–4. DBF, xix, 1134, 1141.

La Tour du Pin-Montauban, Louis-Pierre. Toulon 1712–37.   Natives of Dauphiné and Valentinois, this bp's family claimed descent from medieval *dauphins* of the Viennois, based on early 14th c evidence, when they were simply called 'La Tour'. Though related to established Dauphiné families like the Alleman, they did not become prominent until 16th c, when they also began developing numerous collateral branches, of which the La Chau de Montauban (in Rhone valley, not in Guyenne!) was merely one, which explains their complicated name patterns. Bp's grandfather, René (1543–1619), embraced Calvinist cause in the 1560s or 1570s, and played a major part under Lesdiguières in the Wars of Religion in Dauphiné-Provence area, acquiring lands, governorships and offices from Henri IV in particular, and retaining them under Louis XIII. Without attaining equal prominence, his sons and grandsons sustained the military traditions into early 18th c, and included *maréchaux de camp*, brigadiers and lts-gen, serving in all of major theatres of war from Catalonia to the Empire to Hungary (in 1660s), with the bp's uncle, René, becoming lt-gen and *commandant* in Franche-Comté. Their abandonment of Calvinism was relatively slow, and in part post-1685: bp's father converted before 1676, but his mother was a convinced Calvinist who, after her husband's early death, brought up her children as Huguenots. Escaping to Geneva after 1685, she saw her children brought back to France and sequestrated by Louvois, with some of them, like bp, being brought up as Catholics, but with others, like his eldest brother, escaping to serve in Prussia, England and Venice before abjuring and returning to France years later.

3rd son of Alexandre (1625–76), marquis de la Chau and Allex, *maréchal des armées et des camps*, and Lucrèce du Puy-Montbrun, married in 1663, the bp was born at Allex, near Valence, 1676, but he was baptised (or rebaptised?) and subsequently tonsured in Paris, around 1690. On orders of Louvois, he was placed in Jesuit coll of Louis le Grand, Paris, where he studied hum and phil. Also studied theol in Paris, residing in St-Sulpice between April 1700 and Aug 1701, but appears to have taken doct at Univ of Aix. Canon of St-Jean of Lyon in May 1696, resigned in Aug 1699, he became abbot *in comm* of St-Guilhem-du-Desert OSB (Lodève) in Aug 1698. 10 years later, in 1708 he was made vic-gen of the small Provençal see of Apt. As a Jesuit protégé, he was militantly anti-Jansenist before and after *Unigenitus*, but also active and charitable, winning respect for his efforts during the 1720 plague in Toulon.

Nom to Toulon, 15-8-1712. Provs 26-9-1712. Consec 6-11-1712. Died 12-9-1737.

Sources: ASV, PC 93, fos 297–309 (St-Guilhem, 1698). *Gallia Chr Nov,* Toulon, cols 697–82 (and *instrumenta,* col 456). Pinard, *Chronologie,* iv, 277–8; vii, 65–6. Levesque, 'Liste des élèves', no 2113. Haag, *France protestante,* vi, 406–10. Anselme, *Histoire,* ix, pt ii, 54–66. Martin, *Histoire et généalogie de la maison de la Tour du Pin.* DBF, xix, 1254–9.

Laurens. *See* du Laurens.

Laval de Montmorency de Montigny, Charles Guy François. Ypres 1713.   According to Fénelon, the bishop's distant relative by marriage, he was from a family with a great name that had fallen on hard times. Ultimately descended from 13th c Constable Mathieu de Montmorency and his wife Emme de Laval, the Montigny branch was one of several to separate from the main line in 15th c, and were settled at Montigny-sur-Avre, west of Dreux in Chartres dioc. For all their lack of means, they did enjoy extensive connections and their marriages played a part in shaping their fortunes. Bp's grandfather's marriage to Michelle Péricard, sister of François, bp of Evreux (1613–46), meant that they were related to Norman robe and *dévot* groups in which Rouen-based Péricard family was so prominent. Long career of bp of Ypres's uncle, François (1623–1708), successively vicar-apostolic and bp of Quebec, epitomises this. Other members of that generation fought under Condé and Turenne, while one of them became *grand bailli* of the Order of Malta.

Born in 1668. One of 8 children (6 of them sons) of Jean-Louis, sgr de Montigny, and Françoise Chevestre. Early studies unknown and he may not have been initially earmarked for a church career. Only took MA in Paris in Oct 1695, followed by bacc in theol, May 1696 and 2nd place in 1698 lic, with doct on 24-3-1700. Elected *socius* of Sorbonne, May 1700. He was made *official* and canon of Tournai in 1702, it seems, but resigned within 2 years, when Fénelon made him a canon of Cambrai (June 1704) and had him join his household. He became his vic-gen by Oct 1707, and was made archdeacon and *official* in 1709. Though disclaiming any wish to promote him to episcopate, Fénelon drew him to attention of Mme Guyon, the duc de Chevreuse and Tellier, the confessor, in 1710–12. By early 1713 Louis XIV, persuaded of Laval's virtues, nom him to Ypres on understanding that Fénelon would act as his episcopal mentor. His nom was regarded as a coup for the confessor, and a reminder of Fénelon's continuing influence. It was also kept secret until his provs were granted by Rome, but his career, the shortest of any of Louis XIV's bps, put paid to Louis XIV's plans for a French bishop in a soon-to-be foreign dioc!

Nom to Ypres, n.d. (but ca 20-1-1713). Provs 13-2-1713. Consec 6-5-1713. Died 26-8-1713.

Sources: ASV, no PC file; Nunz Fr 226, fos 72, 192. Fénelon, *Correspondance*, i, 81–6, 166; xiv, nos, 1255, 1373, 1626a. Dangeau, xiv, 368. St-Simon, xxiii, 357–8. Bergin, *Making*, 681–2 (Péricard). *Dictionary of Canadian Biography*, i, 358–72.

La Vallière. *See* **La Baume**.

Lavardin. *See* **Beaumanoir**.

Lavergne de Montenard de Tressan, Louis. Vabres 1670–2, Le Mans 1672–1712.   The Lavergne were an old Languedoc noble family resident near Béziers who prided themselves on producing a bp of Lodève as long ago as 1398, but also cardinals, knights of Malta, canons of the St-Jean chapter of Lyon, etc. Some of them converted to Protestantism in 16th c, and actively participated in the religious wars, developing strong ties, based on military service, with the Coligny-Montmorency families, in Languedoc and beyond, at this time; others remained within the old church and in following century seem to have been active in securing re-conversion of their Protestant relatives, who included the generations of bp's parents and grandparents. Their military vocation continued to flourish under Louis XIII and XIV, and one of bp's sisters married marshal Houdancourt, whose family had significant church connections since Richelieu's ministry. Abbé Pierre de la Vergne, an uncle (or older cousin, it seems) of bp of Le Mans, was highly active in attempts to reform the religious orders and convert Protestants, esp in southern France, and become a key figure with very wide contacts within Jansenist circles – 'le saint courrier de l'église', according to prince of Conti, to whose wife he was director of conscience. His moral rigorism made him enemies, but also opened many doors within French ecclesiastical and *dévot* circles for younger family members.

Born 13-9-1630 in château of Tressan in Béziers dioc. 2nd son of François, sgr de Tressan-Lestang, a lt-col of regiment of Mme Royale de Savoie, and Louise de Montenard de la Tour, his 2nd wife, married in 1627. Lic and doct in canon law, Paris, May 1669, *after* nom to Vabres, but little is known about his education. Priest since about 1658, having entered St-Sulpice seminary in Nov 1649 and joined its presbytery in 1651. Vic-gen of Narbonne for 8 years under François Fouquet, his first patron, for whom he deputised at meetings of clergy of Narbonne province after his disgrace in 1661. Probably thanks to Fouquet influence, he became *maître* of chapel and oratory of Gaston d'Orléans, and later (1668) purchased from disgraced Daniel Cosnac, bp of Valence, post of *premier aumônier* to Philippe d'Orléans, which he kept until 1688. Abbot of ND de Quarante in Jan 1667, the king added the rich priory of Cassan (Béziers) in Nov 1673, and Orléans, his main protector and patron, the abbey of Bonneval en Beauce OSB (Chartres) in 1681. His tenure of Vabres was short, and he quickly resigned it to take up Le Mans in 1671. His nephew, also Louis (1669–1733), was successively *aumônier* of duc d'Orléans, member of *conseil de conscience* after Louis XIV's death, and abp of Rouen – 'une belle continuité' in service of the Orléans family.

Nom to Vabres, 15-4-1669. Provs 2-6-1670. Consec 19-10-1670. Nom to Le Mans 17-8-1671. Provs 21-3-1672. Died 26-1-1712.

Sources: ASV, PC 68, fos 680–92 (Vabres); PC 71, fos 218–41 (Le Mans). AN, L 737, pièce 1, no 6; MM 1115, fo 82rv (law degrees 20 and 23-5-1669). BN, MS Fr 7652, no 50. Levesque, 'Liste des élèves', no 138. ASS, *fiches* Bertrand. Cosnac, *Mémoires*, i, 377. St-Simon, xii, 424–5; xxii, 249, 418–19. Blanquie, 'L'Abbé de la Vergne', 373–92. Piolin, *Histoire de l'eglise du Mans*, v, 333–424.

Le Camus, Étienne. Grenoble 1671–1707.   The Le Camus family may have originated in and around Reims in Champagne, but had become prosperous bourgeois of Paris by late 16th c, with bp's grandfather, Nicolas 'le Riche', being ennobled by letters-patent for his entre-preneurial activities in 1603, having married Marie Colbert, from same family as future min-ister, in 1597. In subsequent years he became a major financier and tax-farmer, esp of *gabelles*, opening up attractive career and matrimonial possibilities for his large progeny – from finance to sovereign courts and intendancies, not forgetting church. Close ties to Colbert and Le Tellier ministerial dynasties were invaluable under Louis XIV. Nicolas II, bp's father, moved into parlt office, becoming an intendant in 1635, but died young. One of bp's brothers was a prov inten-dant and *lieutenant-civil* of Paris, a highly influential position, from 1671 to 1710, while a nephew, Étienne, was prov intendant in Béarn.

Born in parish of St-Nicolas-des-Champs, Paris, 24-11-1632. Son of Nicolas II, *proc-gén* of *cour des aides* (d 1637), and Marie de La Barre. Studies at Univ of Paris, where MA in July 1649, 1st place in 1658 theol lic, and doct 4-4-1658. Ordained priest by Bp Neufville of Chartres, 17-2-1658, *sub titulo patrimoniali*. He played active role within theol fac for several years. Royal almoner 'par quartier' in 1653. Failed to become dep to 1660 AC despite Mazarin's early support. He nearly became tutor to Dauphin in 1664, but reputation as a *mondain* worked against him. He changed radically in mid-1660s, lived in Paris Oratory and was tempted by life of retreat there, but friends dissuaded him, and he accepted see of Grenoble, having turned down Bazas in 1666 and been initially tipped to get Condom over Bossuet in 1669, but a dispute between him and Michel Le Tellier scuppered it. He took Antoine Arnauld into his confidence from outset of his episcopate, consulting him on problems in Grenoble. His inde-pendence of judgement, clashes with Jesuits and regulars at Grenoble, his closeness to Inno-cent XI, who gave him the red hat *motu proprio*, made him numerous enemies at court, beginning with the confessor. Epitome of the rigorist bishop, he left a vast fortune at his death in 1707 which embarrassed his defenders.

Nom 5-1-1671. Provs 1-7-1671. Consec 24-8-1671. Cardinal 2-9-1686. Died 12-9-1707.

Sources: ASV, PC 70, fos 393–415. BN, MS Fr 7651, fo 170 (*bienfaits du roi*). *Lettres du car-dinal Le Camus*, ed Ingold; *Lettres*, ed Claude Frère. Bluche, '*Origine*', 248. Smedley-Weill, *Inten-dants de Louis XIV*, 52–3. *Lettres de Séguier*, ii, 1208–9. Blanc, 'Origines', 147–8. Féret, *Docteurs*, iv, 153–60. Esmonin, *Études sur la France des xviie et xviiie siècles*, 383–96. Lesaulnier, *Port-Royal insolite*, 213, 579–80, 605.

Le Comte, Antoine. Grasse 1682–3.   This bp's personal and family obscurity was pre-served by very brevity of his tenure of Grasse, but he was from a Parisan officeholding family, whose career was determined initially by an uncle who was bp of Glandèves (1626–51).

Born in Paris, 29-12-1629. Son of François, *trésorier de l'extraordinaire des guerres*, and Marie Le Clerc, sister of René Le Clerc, bp of Glandèves. Studied Paris, took bacc in canon law there ca 1659, but may also have taken bacc in theol. By the time he was elected to represent 2nd order clergy of Aix province at 1650 AC, in replacement for relative, Thomas Le Clerc, he was already provost of cath of Glandèves, thanks no doubt to his uncle there, even though he was still a student in Paris. Subsequent career is obscure but despite uncle's death in 1651, it prob-ably unfolded in and around Glandèves, which his ordination as priest by Bp Poncet of Sisteron on 30-3-1668 suggests. Narrowly failed to secure election as *ag-gén* by Embrun province in 1675. Resigned provostship of Glandèves in 1679 in return for a priory in Anjou, but exchange seems to have fallen through. One of Louis XIV's shortest-lived bps.

Nom 2-7-1681. Provs 13-7-1682. Consec 16-8-1682. Died 6-9-1683.

Sources: ASV, PC 81, fos 290–300. BN, Doss bleus 207, nos 5246, 5249. AN, G⁸, vol 88 (1650 AC); MC, LXXXVII, 263, 18-10-1683 (IAD of Bp Le Comte). Bergin, *Making*, 653–4.

Le Filleul de la Chapelle, Charles-Alexandre. Vabres 1710–64.   A number of families of this name existed in 17ᵗʰ c Normandy, as well as one in Paris, but bp was descended from a long-standing if not particularly distinguished family, with historic roots in Rouen itself. By 17ᵗʰ c they resided at Château-Gautier, having been ennobled by royal letters in 1522 for Guillaume Le Filleul. Several branches developed thereafter, that of La Chapelle only began with bp's own father.

Born in château of La Chapelle-Gautier near Evreux on 8-7-1676. Son of Louis, sgr of La Chapelle, and Hélene de Guerpel. Studied at Univ of Paris, MA in Aug 1695, 84ᵗʰ place in 1704 theol lic, and doct 31-5-1704. Ordained priest just before then, 22-3-1704. By 1705 he was canon, precentor and later archdeacon in Mende cath, and also vic-gen of elderly bp of Mende, Baudry de Piencourt, who was a fellow Norman, a post he retained under his successor. Elected by Albi province as dep to AC of 1710. The neighbouring dioc of Vabres was regarded as a modest reward.

Nom 12-7-1710. Provs 10-11-1710. Consec 4-1-1711. Died 4-2-1764.

Sources: ASV, no PC file; PC 101a, fo 100v. BN, PO 1155, nos 26, 263–5; Doss bleus 140, nos 3601–3; 270, no 6997; Nouv d'Hozier 134, no 2930. AN, G⁸, vol 89 (1705, 1707, 1710 *liasses*). AD Lozere, G 2129. *Hierarchia Catholica*, v, 'Vabren', 401–2, n 5. *Gallia*, i, col 284. Chaix d'Est-Ange, *Dictionnaire des familles*, xviii, 138.

Le Goux de la Berchère, Charles. Lavaur 1677–93, Albi 1693–1703, Narbonne 1703–19
The Le Goux were a Burgundian robe family, originally from Nuits, but well established in Dijon parlt by later 16ᵗʰ c. In 1627 abp's grandfather became *pr prés* in succession to his father-in-law, Denis Brûlart, and was duly succeeded by Pierre, bp's father, while still only 27. He was moved to same office in Grenoble parlt from 1644 until his death in 1653. Bp's own generation was more diverse in its activities and its matrimonial politics, if not in its *éclat* – 2 MRs, one of whose sons would marry the daughter of Chancellor Voysin in due course, and 2 daughters married to military officers.

Younger son of Pierre, *pr prés*, and Louise Jolly, daughter of a chief *greffier* of parlt and Estates of Burgundy, from a prominent robe family of Dijon. Born Vif in Grenoble dioc, 23-10-1647, *ondoyé* next day, and baptised in Grenoble 24-12-1649. Resident in St-Sulpice seminary from Oct 1672 to March 1673, while studying theol, but after that in a private house in parish. Univ studies in Paris, where he was MA in June 1664, took *tentativa* exam for bacc in theol under presidency of fellow Burgundian Bossuet in early 1668, followed by 9ᵗʰ place 1672 lic, and doct on 27-2-1674. Ordained priest 23-9-1673. Prior *in comm* of St-Maurice-de-Senlis OSA in 1664 episcopate, abbot of St-Gilles (Nîmes) in 1707. Some activity as preacher in Parisian churches, he became royal almoner 4-1-1672. La Chaize, his patron, obtained promotion from Lavaur to Aix in 1685, but after 2 unsuccessful years there, he was transferred to Albi in Jan 1687, which he admin as vic-cap until 1693. St-Simon regarded him as an excellent bp, capable and well respected, close to La Chaize and duc de Beauvillier.

Nom 18-6-1677. Provs 11-10-1677. Consec 12-4-1678. Nom to Albi, 31-1-1687. Provs 12-10-1693. Nom to Narbonne, 15-8-1703. Provs 12-11-1703. Died 2-6-1719.

Sources: ASV, PC 76, fos 1033–51. BN, MS Lat 15440, p 242; MS Lat 15673, p 20; MS Fr 7655, fo 92; MS Fr 32138, p 745. AC Grenoble, GG 49 (baptism). Lacger, *Etats administratifs*, 314. St-Simon, xxxvi, 237–9. Levesque, 'Liste des élèves', no 1133.

Le Jay, Henri-Guillaume. Cahors 1681–93.   During 15ᵗʰ c the Le Jay family were active as cloth merchants settled in Paris. A century later, they moved into the legal profession and municipal politics/office, which began a gradual transition towards royal offices, notably those of SR, the source of their nobility (1543), and the *chambre des comptes*. Nicolas, from the senior branch was a Condé and Richelieu client who rose to become *pr prés* of Paris parlt in 1636, but he had no children. Bp of Cahors, his grandnephew, was from a junior branch of family.

Born in parish of St-Paul, Paris, 1646, son of Charles (nephew of *pr prés* above), MR, and Gabrielle de Lesrat, married in 1640. Studied phil and theol there, taking MA in Feb 1665, and becoming lic in 1670, doct of theol 31-12-1672. Ordained priest 17-9-1672. Royal almoner, later *maître de chapelle* to Philippe d'Orléans. Dep to 1675 AC as delegate for Paris. Nom to Cahors on transfer of future Cardinal Noailles to Châlons-sur-Marne. Energetic bp, he also used his resources to build 2 palaces, at Mercuès and Cahors, but died before finishing the 2nd of them. A gambler, apparently, before the episcopate, but gave it up subsequently.

Nom 6-9-1680. Provs 28-4-1681. Consec 1-6-1681. Died 22-4-1693.

Sources: ASV, PC 80, fos 204–16. BN, MS Fr 10839, fos 2–23 (SR); MS Lat 15673, p 19. AN, Y 180, 251 (c.m. of parents, 20-2-1640). Fénelon, *Correspondance*, iii, 281, n. 4. St-Simon, iv, 193; xi, 471. Bluche, *L'Origine*, 263. Poutet, 'Docteurs', 309, no 648. Fortin de la Hoguette, *Lettres*, ii, 870–1.

Le Neboux de la Brousse, Pierre. St-Pol-de-Léon 1672–1701.   This bp's origins were not merely provincial, but highly obscure. Some sources claim he was son of a surgeon from Angoulême, others that he was related to the Bouthillier family, some of whose members still resided there, and that their Parisian connections provided him with first bridge to a wider world. The latter part of this conjecture is certainly true: it was his first patron, Bp La Barde of St-Brieuc, a Bouthillier by his mother, who shaped his career, and possibly that of a brother or nephew in due course.

Born in parish of St-Amand, Périgueux dioc, 1633, names and status of parents unknown. Education no less obscure, but he took doct in canon law, Paris, date unknown. Entered service of Denis de La Barde, bp of St-Brieuc, a cousin of Bouthillier family, and he was responsible for his rise through the local and provincial ecclesiastical ranks: initially a canon of *collégiale* of St-Guillaume in St-Brieuc, later a canon in cath and archdeacon of Golouix in same dioc. While in household of La Barde, he took orders, becoming a priest in 1658. Finally he served as vic-gen and *official* under La Barde, visiting dioc, holding synods, preaching a good deal. His political skills, acquired in attending Breton Estates along with La Barde, impressed duc de Chaulnes, gov of Brittany, who seems to have made case at court for his episcopal promotion as a valuable royal servant in province. Given St-Pol after Jean de Montigny, who had obtained provs, died before he could take possession of see. As bp, seems to have been an unofficial inspector of naval establishment at Brest, for which he was pensioned by crown. Pressed several times by Louis XIV in 1680 to succeed Caulet in troubled Pyrenean dioc of Pamiers, but he refused such a poisoned chalice; at the time, commentators regarded his admin and rhetorical skills highly. Was given abbey of Landevenec OSB (Quimper) on 24-12-1695.

Nom 24-12-1671. Provs 12-9-1672. Consec Nov 1672. Died 16-9-1701.

Sources: ASV, PC 71, fos 501–13. BN, MS Fr 20969, fo 105v. AN, G^8 88 (Tours, 1675); L 744, dossier 1, no 24, St-Pol-de-Léon. Rancé, *Correspondance*, ii, pp 471–2, no 801218. Bergin, *Making*, 583–4, 644.

Le Normand, Jean. Evreux 1710–33.   By later 17th and 18th c this family was best known for producing financiers, inc a *fermier-général* in latter years of Louis XIV, but it may well be that bp of Evreux was unrelated to him. They did share a common geographical origin, being descended from a group of families of that name in Orléans, where they belonged to merchant bourgeoisie and town hall notables from at least mid-16th c, though they were already establishing connections in Paris which would lead to office in *gr conseil* by late 1570s and marriage ties to families with a foothold in that court. Several family members seem to have fallen foul of the Catholic League in Orléans in the early 1590s and went into exile for a time, returning with Henri IV's support later. Thereafter, their history becomes more obscure and ordinary, as exemplified by the status of bp's father, who apparently only abandoned his activities as a shop-keeper and merchant in 1650s.

Born 1655 Orléans, names and status of parents unknown. Univ studies, beginning with phil in Paris, then 44th place in 1682 theol lic, followed by doct on 5-5-1683. Had previously been received as *socius* of Sorbonne. Ordained priest in 1682. Canon of St-Honoré in Paris since 1685, a post probably held by an uncle and grand-uncle before him. Cardinal Noailles entrusted him with many functions within dioc of Paris, not least that of *official* in 1700, and later syndic of Parisian clergy (1705). He no doubt secured his election as dep for Paris to AC of 1710, during which Louis XIV nom him to Evreux, to which he added the great abbey of St-Taurin of Evreux 4 years later. St-Simon, who regarded him as a tool of Jesuits and undeserving of high office, could not understand why Noailles employed such a man for so long, alleging that he had had to sack him for serious misconduct. But he was still *official* and syndic of Paris when nom to Evreux, for which he was not 1st choice: vacant since 1709, the king's original choice, Gaston Sublet de Heudicourt, nom in Nov 1709, died before obtaining his provs.

Nom 12-7-1710. Provs 10-11-1710. Consec 21-12-1710. Died 7-5-1733.

Sources: AN, MC, LXXXII, 118, 7-8-1710 (Evreux). ASV, PC 104, fos 198-208 (St-Taurin of Evreux). BN, PO 2124, no 48,259, esp fos 122–4; MS Fr 7026–7, Le Normand's papers (mostly concern Jansenist question, *Unigenitus*). St-Simon, xx, 81–2. Trani, 'Conseillers du grand conseil', 173. *Gallia*, xi, col 620.

Le Peletier, Michel. Angers 1692–1706.   The Le Peletier family originated in bourgeoisie of Le Mans, where Pierre was municipal syndic in 1508. His son, Julien (1526–62) moved to Paris and to law practice in parlt which, along with marriage to Germaine le Danois, laid foundation of family future – which was further enhanced by that of son Jean, also a barrister, to Madeleine Chauvelin; their daughters married in identical milieu, that of Paris barristers. Already ecclesiastics figured prominently in the ranks – as they would continue to do – and they boasted canons of Le Mans, docts of theol, and coll heads in Univ of Paris. Early notoriety came via Julien, celebrated ligueur curé of St-Jacques-de-la-Boucherie in Paris, but several other family members fought for cause, too. That did them no lasting damage, and key figure in their subsequent recovery was Louis (1584–1651), son of Jean above, who rose quickly in royal service thanks to early service as *commis* of Villeroy under Henri IV, ending as *prés* of *bureau des finances* of Dauphiné, having briefly been principal secretary to Anne of Austria in mid-1620s. Ennobled via office of SR 1637. In turn it was his sons – Claude, *contr-gén des finances* 1683–9 after Colbert, Michel, sgr de Souzy (who effectively co-managed the finance ministry in collaboration with Claude 1684–9), and Jérôme (priest, *cons*, parlt of Paris, *cons d'état* in 1685) – who were to hold high office under Louis XIV, thanks mainly to patronage of their Le Tellier relatives, but also of the Condé and Orléans families whom they had served for several decades. St-Simon claims his departure from office in 1689 did not reduce king's esteem for Claude Le Peletier (an honest man) who was thus in a position to 'placer les siens', no fewer than 6 of whom, male and female, entered church, during his retirement. Louis, bp's brother, became *pr prés* of Paris parlt 1707–12, while his daughter married marquis de Fénelon. Charles-Maurice Le Peletier, abbot of St-Aubin, was sup-gen of St-Sulpice from 1725 onwards, another influential position within ecclesiastical circles, and did much to extend the Sulpician presence throughout France. The Le Peletier were already related by marriage to Tronson and Leschassier, 2 previous sups-gen.

Born 4-8-1660, Michel was eldest son of Claude, finance minister, and Marguerite Fleuriau. Studied in Paris, where took MA in Aug 1680, brilliantly defended theses at Sorbonne under Bossuet's presidency, with *tentativa* attended by 40 bishops, and obtained 1st place in lic of 1688, doct taken 27-3-1688. Also attended St-Sulpice during these years, and prepared himself for episcopate by accompanying bps of Sens, Châlons and Meaux on their visitations. Abbot *in comm* of Jouy (Sens) 1678, but later swopped it for St-Aubin in Angers with brother Charles-Maurice when he was nom bp of Angers in 1692. Transfer to Orléans March 1706, gets

St-Jean-d'Amiens OSA in April, but dies before *prise de possession* of Orléans. An effective and demanding, if also authoritarian, bp of Angers. Both he and his father strongly opposed his transfer from Angers to Orléans, but king insisted, partly to combat Jansenist influences in Orléans.

Nom to Angers 15-8-1692. Provs 15-10-1692. Consec 16-11-1692. Died 9-8-1706.

Sources: ASV, no PC file. BN, MS Fr 23510, fo 286; MS Fr 20969, fo 24r, 22-11-1678. St-Simon, iv, 272–3, 370–1; xiii, 256–7. Bossuet, *Correspondance*, iv, 139–41; xiv, 299. Fénelon, *Correspondance*, iii, 388, no 241, n 1; xi, 98, n 3. Bluche, *L'Origine*, 271–2. Fortin de la Hoguette, *Lettres*, ii, 872–6. Barnavi, *Le Parti de Dieu*, 32–3, 250. Bayard, *Dictionnaire des surintendants*, 95–8, 135–7. Antoine, *Coeur de l'état*, 332–42.

Le Pileur Henri-Augustin. Saintes 1711–15 (resign). Established among the Parisian bourgeoisie since later 15th c at least, the Le Pileur family seems not to have had the ability over several generations to rise notably in social or officeholding hierarchy. A succession of lawyers and *contrôleurs des guerres* or of *traites foraines* during 16th c led slowly by mid-17th (the generation of bp's own father) to relatively modest offices of *correcteurs* or *auditeurs* in Paris *chambre des comptes*. Father's marriage to daughter of a *trés-gén* of Estates of Normandy in 1647 did not, it seems, transform their fortunes, though it did direct some of their members towards careers in Normandy; on the other hand, financial affinities did not disappear, and an uncle of bp, Du Buisson, was an *intendant des finances* under Louis XIV. Bp's siblings description of themselves as 'écuyers' did not prevent those describing his family in 1711 as composed of 'parents honnêtes', usually a tell-tale sign of commoner status. The 1st parltementaire, a nephew of the bp, did not take office until 1740s. On the other hand, they were heavily involved in religious and charitable projects in Paris which would have brought them into touch with influential *dévot* networks.

Born Paris 16-11-1650, son of Jean, *correcteur aux Comptes* and treasurer in royal household, and Catherine Heudebert, daughter of Constantin, treasurer of Norman Estates. Tonsured 3-7-1669, he was ordained priest 9-5-1683. Meanwhile he had finished his studies in Paris, where he was MA in Oct 1672, and took bacc in theol in July 1673, followed by lic *in utr*, possibly from Orléans rather than Paris. He seems to have specialised in the superiorship of convents of female religious orders, esp the *Filles de la Providence* sponsored by Anne of Austria and others, and he was apostolic visitor of the order of Discalced Carmelites in France by the time of his episcopal nom. Obtained the abbey of St-Martin-d'Epernay OSA (Reims), as well as Bonnevaux O Cist (Vienne) in 1694, which helped to secure election to 1702 AC by province of Vienne.

Nom to Saintes 4-4-1711. Provs 19-10-1711. Consec 21-12-1711. Resign 19-12-1715. Died 25-4-1726.

Sources: AN, MC, LXXXI, 110, 23-5-1711. BN, PO 2277, nos 51,514–16; Doss bleus 524, nos 13720–1; MS Fr 32139, 433–5. *Hierarchia Catholica*, v, 343, n 5. Bluche, *L'Origine*, 274–5. Dangeau, v, 126. Sourches, xi, 311.

Le Sauvage, René. Lavaur 1673–7. From a family resident in and around Granville, north of Avranches in lower Normandy, bp's ancestors included a notary and other minor officials, seigneurial and royal, of no particular distinction. Bp's father's admiralty office under Richelieu was no doubt an advance on their previous attainments but did not transform their status, while his early death threatened what they had achieved. The presence of an uncle, Pierre, among clergy of St-Severin parish in Paris, enabled René to complete studies in Paris and put his talents to use in service of *les grands*, in this case that of Turenne.

Born mid-1630 near Granville. Son of Jean, sr de Vaufevrier, lieut of *amirauté de France* at Granville, and Guyonne de la Rue, both of whom died during 1630s, so he was brought up by elder brother, Nicolas, who held same admiralty office as his father. Early studies locally, but then sent to Paris, where studied at Univ, taking MA in Aug 1650, followed by theol at Sorbonne. Entered St-Sulpice seminary in Jan 1652, but no information on length of stay there.

Bacc of theol in 1654, he briefly taught phil at coll de Presles in 1655. Took 13th place in 1658 lic, and doct in same year. Ordained priest, possibly in 1654. Non-resident curé of Bacilly (Avranches) for several years. Admitted to Compagnie du St-Sacrement, Paris, 1657, by which time he had contacts with Carmelites and Oratory. Preceptor after 1659 of future cardinal de Bouillon, grand almoner of France in 1671, who resigned his abbey of St-Pierre-de-Beaulieu in Limousin to him for his services in Sept 1664, and whose patronage was key to his episcopal elevation. Very active bishop during few years – a synod, ecclesiastical conferences, founds congregation of Filles de la Croix – but plagued by ill-health which curtailed his career.

Nom 28-4-1673. Provs 18-12-1673. Consec 4-2-1674. Died 17-5-1677.

Sources: ASV, no PC file. Lacger, *Etats administratifs*, 349. Coudrey, 'René Le Sauvage, 1–36. Daniel Rivals, 'Un prélat modèle du xviie siècle', 41–81. Poutet, 'Docteurs', 268, no 262. Levesque, 'Liste des élèves', no 194. *Hierarchia Catholica*, v, 406.

Le Sénéchal de Carcado, Eustache. Tréguier 1692–4.   An old Breton family, Le Sénéchal claimed to trace its history back to 11th c, and to their status as hereditary *grand sénéchaux* of *vicomté* de Rohan. By 17th c there were 2 main branches, Molac and Cercado, which were related to well-known families such as the Rosmadec, Rieux d'Asserac, Avaugour, some of which had themselves produced bps and other ecclesiastics. Bp's grandfather rallied to Henri IV against the League's gov, Mercoeur, after 1589, and was rewarded for his fidelity in later years. Like many other Breton nobles, they also moved into royal office: bp's father was a *cons* in Rennes parlt, and his wife was daughter of one. Military careers were not ignored, esp by Molac branch, which produced a brigadier under Louis XIV and a lt-gen under Louis XV, with other members serving in Italy under Louis XIV. Bp's own brother was gov of Dinan.

One of 3 sons of François (d 1639), marquis de Cercado, and Catherine de Lys, married in 1620, he was born ca 1628. Nothing known about his studies, but he apparently held doct of theol, though the univ remains unknown. Secured post of almoner to Anne of Austria in 1653, but quit in 1658 and retired from court. Abbot *in comm* of Geneston OSA (Nantes) in April 1685 on resign of his nephew, Sebastien-Hyacinthe, to become army officer. Louis XIV apparently insisted on appointing him as successor at Tréguier to Baglion du Saillant, transferred to Poitiers, since he was a Breton-speaker and may have been recommended by Baglion. The suspension of provs until 1692 made for a short reign there.

Nom 1-6-1686. Provs 7-7-1692. Consec 7-9-1692. Died 15-5-1694.

Sources: ASV, PC 86, fos 475–97. BN, Doss bleus 610, no 16070; Cab d'Hozier 310, no 8528; MS Fr 7657 (*bienfaits du roi*); MS Fr 23498, fo 95. Pinard, *Chronologie*, iv, 630–2. St-Simon, xiv, 36. Carné, *Chevaliers bretons de St-Michel*, 392–5. Moréri, *Grand Dictionnaire*, vi, 18–23. Griselle, *État de la maison du roi*, 97, no 3607.

Lescure de Valderiès, Jean-François. Luçon. 1699–1723.   The Lescure name and lands passed through more than one set of family hands between their 1st documentary mention in 1012 as a fief dependent on papacy in area near Albi and the mid-15th c when the Salgues family inherited them. They remained relatively obscure until 16th c: their marriages were to regional noble families like Lautrec, Châteauneuf, Vanelle. A separate branch later developed in Bordeaux thanks to a Lescure who was *cons* in the parlt. From 1560s onwards, successive generations participated in the religious wars down to the Huguenot revolts of 1620s in which bp's own father played a major part in Albigeois. His marriage to a Caylus extended his family connections considerably, into court circles around Louis XIV and esp Mme de Maintenon, to whom the Caylus family would become related by marriage in 1680s. His episcopate induced his family to settle in Poitou, which explains why its *chef de famille* died leading the Vendéens against the ungodly republic in 1793!

Born in château Lescure, dioc of Albi, 5-1-1644. Son of François and Anne de Thubières, which makes him 2nd cousin of bp Caylus of Auxerre. Early studies with SJ at Albi, then in Toulouse where he was MA in 1660, and subsequently in Paris where he took 53rd place in lic of 1674, doct 17-5-1674. His long association with St-Sulpice began in Albi, while still a young cleric, and he entered the Paris seminary on 15-12-1660. Subsequently joined community of priests there in 1678, before becoming superior of community at Mont-Valérien which he already belonged to by April 1677. Dep to 1682 AC. Chosen by Harlay of Paris to engage in Cévennes missions to Huguenots with Chevalier de Saulx bp of Alais. Successively canon, *théologal*, penitentiary as well as gr-vic of his native Albi, whose abp, Le Goux de la Berchère, was a protegé (*mignon*) of royal confessor, La Chaize. At request of maternal uncle, comte de Caylus, who had married a niece 'à la mode de Bretagne' of Mme de Maintenon, he was nom to Luçon. She already knew him from his days at Mont Valérien. Pro-Jesuit, known for his anti-Jansenist sentiments before the episcopate, he banned the rigorist pro-Port-Royal catechism of 'three Henries' in Luçon, gave the seminary to SJ to manage. His *instruction pastorale* of 1710 versus Quesnel's *Réflexions morales* was a notorious incident in history of the 'second' Jansenism, and embroiled him in long and bitter conflict with Cardinal Noailles.

Nom 6-6-1699. Provs 5-10-1699. Consec 8-11-1699. Died 23-5-1723.

Sources: ASV, PC 93, fos 310–21. BN, PO 1693, no 39420; Doss bleus 391, no 10550; Morel de Thoisy 267, fos 250–1. AN, L 735, pièce 1, Luçon. BIUT, MS 9, fo 173r (MA). Bossuet, *Correspondance*, xiii, 38. St-Simon, xx, 339–49; xxii, 145–8. Levesque, 'Liste des élèves', no 636. *Les Tarnais, dictionnaire biographique* (Albi 1996), 202–3.

Le Tellier, Charles-Maurice. Reims coadj 1668/71–1710.   Family originated in Champagne, but Paris-based since early 16th c, acquired nobility via *charges* in *chambre des comptes* in 1574. Abp is from main branch (Louvois), which reached pinnacle of political power under Louis XIV, when bp's father and brother held senior ministerial office.

Son of Michel, chancellor, and Elisabeth Turpin. Born Turin 18-7-1642, while father was still intendant of army of Piedmont. Studies in Paris, where he was MA in July 1659. Ranked 1st in theol lic of 1666, he obtained doct on 27-2-1666. Ordained priest *extra tempora* 1666. His father's position opened doors very quickly for him. *Maître de la chapelle-musique* of Louis XIV, Oct 1665, *élu* of the clergy of Burgundy Estates for 1665–8, nom coadj of Langres 30-5-1668, but 10 days later opted instead for that of Reims, where abp, Cardinal Antonio Barberini, was absentee. *Cons d'état ordinaire* in 1679, chevalier of royal orders 1688, proviseur of Sorbonne 1695, also obtained major abbeys *in comm* – Doualas (1651), St-Benigne-de-Dijon (1668), St-Etienne-de-Caen (1667–8), ND de Breteuil (Beauvais), St-Thierry-de-Reims, St-Pierre-de-Lagny (1695). He played an important role in church politics for nearly 40 years, often as counterpart to abps of Paris, esp Harlay, and was also strong adversary of Jesuits. His abilities and achievements were much debated, but he was an able admin at Reims who surrounded himself with well-chosen assistants. Hugely wealthy, he was a collector and patron of letters. Reputation was tarnished by stories of liaisons, and not helped by sharing some of his brother Louvois's legendary rudeness.

Nom 12-6-1668. Provs 8-7-1668. Consec 11-11-1668. Died 22-2-1710.

Sources: ASV, PC 67, fos 579–613. St-Simon, xix, 42–8. Poutet, 'Docteurs', 290, no 447. Gillet, *Mgr Le Tellier archevêque duc de Reims. Lettres de Séguier*, ii, 1213–14. Corvisier, *Louvois*.

Le Tellier, François. Digne 1678–1708.   Little is known about this bp, but he had no blood relation to ministerial family above. Father's origins are unclear, but he was a royal physician who seems to have entered Louis XIII's service in mid-1610s, was still there in 1638, by which time he had obtained reversion to his post for his son, Louis, who worked with him. The connections of bp's maternal family seem to have been far better.

Born Paris, in St-André-des-Arts parish, where baptised 4-11-1630, son of François, *médecin ordinaire* of Louis XIII, and Françoise Bonigalle; godson of François Hennequin, SR, and Françoise le Tellier, wife of Jacques de Miromesnil. Studied phil and theol, took doct of theol of Bourges in 1663. Ordained priest in June 1657. An almoner to Queen Marie-Thérèse about

1660, he also became curé-archiprêtre of St-Severin in March 1663, but was not an especially edifying one. Offered Digne after refusal of Claude Bourlon, brother of bp of Soissons, in July 1677, but apparently engineered by Mlle de Montpensier in order to remove him from St-Séverin rather than as reward for services rendered by him. Dep to ACs of 1702 and 1707, he was not an especially resident or diligent bp of Digne.

Nom 12-10-1677. Provs 28-2-1678. Consec 15-5-1678. Died 11-2-1708.

Sources: ASV, PC 77, fos 244–61. Fisquet, *France pontificale*, Digne et Rieux, 119–20. Ste-Beuve, *Port-Royal*, ii, 1042–3.

Le Tonnelier de Breteuil, Claude. Boulogne 1681–98.   Family's origins lay in Orléans, but after mid-16th c, they took the road to Paris, with *gr conseil* as their 1st route to advancement. Étienne, who lost his office in Orléans for embracing the Catholic League, successively married an Amelot (fellow Orléanais), a Mangot and a Briçonnet! By mid-17th c, they were a highly connected, wealthy and solidly established Parisian robe family, enduringly involved in royal financial admin but also holding parlt office and prov intendancies into 18th c, when ministerial office also materialised. The bp and his brother François (1638–1705) were sons of Louis, who was an MR, intendant, and Colbert's predecessor as *contr-gén* of finances 1657–65 (though without Colbert's powers, which still belonged to Fouquet as *surintendant*). François (above) was also *intendant des finances* 1684–1701.

Born in Paris, son of Louis, MR, and Christine Le Court, 17-11-1644. Studied phil and theol in Paris, MA in April 1669, 85th place in 1674 theol lic, and doct 23-12-1681 – i.e. *after* nom to Boulogne. Ordained priest by bp of Saintes on 18-12-1677.

Nom 2-5-1681. Provs 1-12-1681. Consec 1-2-1682. Died 8-1-1698.

Sources: ASV, PC 80, fos 94–110. *Lettres de Séguier*, ii, 1214–5. St-Simon, vi, 38–9. Antoine, *Gouvernement*, 170–1. Antoine, *Coeur de l'état*, 278, 330. Smedley-Weill, *Intendants de Louis XIV*, 55. Trani, 'Conseillers du grand conseil', 176–7. Pinard, *Chronologie*, vi, 565–6.

Lézay de Lusignan, Paul-Philippe. Rodez 1693–1716.   The Lézay claim to descend from ancient royal and crusading house of Lusignan, most of whose branches had long since died out. It was a myth invented in the 17th c, to scorn of likes of St-Simon, and bp himself was known as Lezay de la Coste in his younger days. The Lézay were nevertheless one of the oldest noble houses from Poitou, where several branches formed and died out over the centuries. Bp belonged to the main Lézay branch which were related to numerous families like them in Poitou and beyond, though their *états de service* in 16th or 17th c do not quite match the mythical origins they were beginning to claim for themselves, nor were they wealthy enough to advance significantly up the noble hierarchy. Bp's father and elder brother both served in guards from 1620s onwards, while latter was sent to Vienna as extraordinary envoy in 1687, and later to Saxe-Luneberg. Bp's mother was sister of Balthasar Grangier de Liverdis, bp of Tréguier in 1646, from of an influential Parisian robe family, and he played a significant role in his nephew's early career. Moreover, in 1652, Bp Lezay's sister, Marie married Antoine, comte de la Rocheaymon, father of Claude, bp of neighbouring see of Le Puy, in 1704.

Born Paris 1639. 2nd son of Pierre and Louise Grangier de Liverdis, married in 1626. Studied litt hum, phil and theol in Paris, where he matriculated and obtained MA in 1655, and 71st place in 1666 theol lic. Tonsured in April 1646, he took minor orders at St-Brieuc in 1660. Subdeacon in 1664 and deacon soon afterwards, he waited until 1680 before becoming a priest. Abbot *in comm* of St-Barthélemy-de-Noyon OSA, in Feb 1668, in succession to uncle, bp Grangier of Tréguier, who also made him canon of Tréguier in 1664, but it is not clear whether he resided there in subsequent years. Dep to 1682 AC. As bp of Rodez he was a 'fort persecuteur d'heretiques' (St-Simon).

Nom 31-5-1684. Provs 12-10-1693. Consec 15-11-1693. Died 25-2-1716.

Sources: ASV, PC 87, fos 635–51. BN, Doss bleus 394, no 10,637; MS Fr 7651, fo 191v; MS Fr 7657, no 57 (*bienfaits du roi*). AUP reg 97, fo 33v. AD Aveyron, G 61 (personal dossier) and

G 256. St-Simon, xiv, 344–7, 476–7. Beauchet-Filleau, *Dictionnaire des familles du Poitou*, vi, 99–116. Boisnard, *Touraine*, no 1381

Lobière du Bouchet, Olivier-Gabriel. Comminges 1711–39 (resign).   A rather obscure Auvergne family, whose name is sometimes given as Lubière, their early history was probably that of minor local notables in area between Randan and Vichy. The du Bouchet title, itself of modest seigneurial rank, was acquired via marriage of bp's grandmother. Ennobled in 1654, they had virtually disappeared a century later. Family connections were similarly unspectacular, and bp's father's position as an *écuyer* in *petite écurie* of Louis XIV was a sinecure which did not open the gates of Versailles to them. It was probably bp's own close connections to Jesuits and 20 years of experience as a canon and gr-vic of Rodez which brought him the mitre.

Born on 8-5-1663 and baptised on 24-9-1663. 3ʳᵈ son of Olivier, sgr du Bouchet, and Marie-Henriette Giraud, also from a local family in St-Pourçain. Early education with SJ, to whom he remained firmly attached thereafter. Univ studies in Paris, where took MA in Mar 1691. Doct of theol 15 years before episcopate, of univ unknown. Priest since about 1690. Also canon and *préchantre* of Rodez cath for 20 years, he was made vic-gen in Nov 1693 and served for at least 8 years. Strongly anti-Jansenist from outset, he appears to have been an efficient bishop and a well-organised admin, but encountered serious opposition among clergy of Val d'Aran, under Spanish jurisdiction, and recalcitrant to efforts at reform since Bp Choiseul's time. He obtained nom of coadj, Antoine de Lastic, nephew of Bp of Tarbes, in 1739, and died only weeks after his provs had been granted.

Nom 11-7-1710. Provs 26-1-1711. Consec 29-3-1711. Resign 1739. Died 9-9-1740.

Sources: ASV, PC 101a, fos 99–107. Remacle, *Dictionnaire des familles de l'Auvergne*, ii, 487–8. Tixier, *Les Anciennes familles bourgeoises dans les institutions judiciaires de Riom 1621–1649*, 201. Tixier, *Les Anciennes familles, 1650–1703*, 203. AD Aveyron, G 253 (vic-gen, 20-11-1693). Fénelon, *Correspondance*, xvii, 118, n 18. Contrasty, *Histoire des évêques de Comminges*, 389–406.

Loménie de Brienne, Charles-François. Coutances 1667–1720.   This bp's family, natives of Limousin, had included a bp of Marseille under Louis XIII. Their hold on ministerial office was much more tenuous by 1660s, but they were well-connected enough to secure ecclesiastical preferment.

Born in St-Germain-des-Prés, Paris 1637. 2ⁿᵈ son of Henri-Auguste de Loménie, comte de Brienne and sec of state to Louis XIV, and late Louise de Béon-Massès, descended from an old noble family from Béarn. Choice of ecclesiastical career may have been his own, having been a page of Louis XIV. Studied at Univ of Paris, MA in July 1656, 77ᵗʰ place in 1664 theol lic, and doct 28-3-1665. Ordained priest in same year. Seems to have engaged in some activity in St-Sulpice parish – confessions, retreats etc. Abbot *in comm* of St-Eloi-Fontaine (Noyon), he added St-Germain of Auxerre in 1661. He was not first choice for Coutances in 1666, Claude Auvry of Avranches having turned it down for some reason. As bp, he looked to Tronson of St-Sulpice as his inspiration and mentor, also in contact with bp with Bossuet via marshal Bellefonds.

Nom 5-12-1666. Provs 12-12-1667. Consec 19-2-1668. Died 7-4-1720.

Sources: ASV, PC 65 fos 284–306. BN, MS Fr 7657, fo 39 (*bienfaits du roi*). St-Simon, v, 420–1. Poutet, 'Docteurs', 289, no 425. Fénelon, *Correspondance*, v, no 406, p 201, n 8. Toustain de Billy, *Histoire ecclésiastique du diocèse de Coutances*, iii, ch vii. Bergin, *Making*, 660–1.

Lusignan/Lusignem. *See* **Lezay.**

Maboul, Jacques. Alet 1710–23.   The Maboul family originated in Niort, in Poitou, where members were *échevins* in every generation for at least a century after 1529, when François Maboul was 1ˢᵗ elected to office there. But the nobility acquired by muncipal office did not transform them into gentry, urban or landed, and they included receivers of taxes in early 17th c, while their marriages were within same social milieu (an *élu*, an apothecary). In fact the Niort branches died out by mid-century, leaving only that of Paris, which dates from bp's father and which survived into 18th c, when it followed suit. Louis, father of bp, began his career in Paris as a modest *procureur* and barrister, before buying office of SR in 1639, and which he held for 20 years before becoming *proc-gén* of *requêtes de l'Hôtel* – both of these offices were later held by bp's elder brother, Louis, marquis de Fors, before going on to become an MR in 1695 – as did his son after him.

Born ca 1650 in Paris, son of Louis and Louise Commeau, daughter of a *procureur* in the Paris parlt, married in 1639. Studied at Univ of Paris, where he took his MA in July 1672, began theol studies but did not, it seems, progress beyond the bacc, though he also took a lic in canon law. Ordained priest about 1696. Vic-gen of Poitiers for several years before nom to Alet, and apparently active in conversion of Huguenots in region traditionally well populated by Protestants. His talent as a preacher was well known, and he gave well received *oraisons funèbres* for Chancellor Le Tellier, Dauphin, Duke and Duchess of Burgundy in 1712, and for Louis XIV himself at ND in 1715. His collected sermons were published in 1749. The Regent had him compose pieces on need to terminate *Unigenitus* affair.

Nom 1-11-1708. Provs 19-2-1710. Consec 13-7-1710. Died 21-5-1723.

Sources: AN, MC, LXXXII, 101, 30-1-1709. BN, PO 1784, no 41,219; Doss bleus 413, no 11,019. St-Simon, vi, 232; xxiii, 50; xxix, 302. Antoine, *Gouvernement*, 173. Beauchet-Filleau, *Dictionnaire des familles du Poitou*, vi, 304–8. DLF, 786–7.

Madot, François. Belley 1705–12, Chalon-sur-Saône 1712–53.   *De père en fils*, the Madot family held office of lt-gen at Guéret *présidial* into early 18th c, but they were not altogether confined by their ancestral ties. One of bp's own brothers Pierre, was a doctor of theol who accompanied his brother to Belley, where he became *théologal*. Another, known as M de St-Vincent, was cavalry officer in regiment of duc de la Feuillade, whose involvement in a duel in 1694 led to exile in Rome and a death sentence in France. His time in Rome brought him into contact with Bossuet's nephew. The future bp was known to Mme de Maintenon by late 1690s, and in return for his services in keeping tabs on her wayward brother, the comte d'Aubigné, she obtained for him the see of Belley, and also probably Chalon.

Born Guéret, Limoges dioc, 13-7-1671, probably son of Sylvain, lt-gen of Guéret *présidial*, and Anne Reydier. Educated by SJ Limoges, then studied either in Paris or Bourges, where he obtained doct in theol, 1696. Ordained priest on 17-3-1696. Resided for many years in St-Sulpice community, and exercised cure of souls in St-Sulpice parish under direction of its curé, where his preaching impressed Bossuet's brother, Antoine, in Dec 1698, which in turn led to interest in him on part of Bossuet, Godet of Chartres, and especially Mme de Mainteon, who formed high regard for him, used him in various capacities, including preaching at St-Cyr and, later, keeping an eye on her wayward brother. Another source also asserts he was confessor to bp of Noyon, Claude Maur d'Aubigné, Maintenon's cousin, who could also have recommended him to royal circle. Before Belley there were signs of royal favour: canon of *collégiale royale* of St-Quentin-de-Noyon (May 1701) and abbot *in comm* of Leroy O Cist (Bourges, April 1702), followed by abbeys Beaulieu (Boulogne, 1706) and Absie under Louis XV. St-Simon was predictably negative about him, given his Sulpician ways and background, but Luynes' *Mémoires* acknowledge him as virtuous and zealous, leaving large amount of money for foundation of pious establishments in dioc.

Nom 11-4-1705. Provs 7-9-1705. Consec 18-10-1705. Nom to Chalon 24-12-1711. Provs 16-3-1712. Died 7-10-1753.

Sources: ASV, PC 98, fos 108–22. BN, PO 1790, dossier 41,381; Doss bleus, 414, no 11,045; MS Fr 20969, fo 164. AN, L 728, pièce 1, nos 66–7; O^1 45,fo 243, 22-5-1701. AD Creuse, E 558–9 (Madot papers). Fénelon, *Correspondance*, vii, 142, n 8. Bossuet, *Correspondance*, x, 328–9. St-Simon, xi, 114.

Mailly, Victor-Augustin. Lavaur 1692–1712.   The Mailly were a long-standing noble family from Picardy, settled at Mailly near Amiens, and admitted to Estates of Burgundy as long ago as 1460. They had seen continuous military service during the Italian wars and later. They were no less well-connected to noble families over several generations, inc that of St-Simon, who was one of friends of François (below) and who expressed surprise that Louis XIV gave him Arles without any prior episcopal experience. The bp of Lavaur's earlier promotion was less unusual, and it was probably facilitated by the marriage of his brother, the comte de Mailly, to a relative of Mme de Maintenon no more than a month before his nom.

Born Paris, 1644 son of Louis, marquis de Mailly, and Jeanne de Monchy, marquise de Nesle-Paris and heiress of Mouchy-Moncarvel line. Both he and brother François were 'élevés' at abbey of St-Victor in Paris, where Victor became canon regular and later grand prior. It was on special request of Chancellor Boucherat that he was admitted to lic in canon law in Paris, Oct 1687, having been nom to Lavaur a few months earlier. Admin Lavaur as vic-gen of the chapter *sede vacante* 1687–92. He reorganised charitable assistance in dioc in 1689, founded a *bureau de charité* at Lavaur, and made the hospital of Lavaur his *héritier universel* in his will. Completed La Berchère's objective of founding a seminary there in 1703, run by Doctrinaires, who already ran the local coll.

Nom to Lavaur 14-8-1687. Provs 15-10-1692. Consec 16-11-1692. Died 23-12-1712.

Sources: ASV, no PC file. AN, MM 1120, p 284. St-Simon, iv, 350. Lacger, *Etats administratifs*, 350–1.

Mailly, François. Arles 1698–1710, Reims 1710–21.   Younger brother of Victor above. Born 4-3-1658. Resident at St-Victor, Paris, he studied in Paris, where he took MA in Aug 1678, 103rd place in 1684 lic in theol. He became royal almoner in 1694, having obtained abbey of Flavigny OSB (Autun) in 1693, Massay in 1695, and St-Etienne-de-Caen in 1720. Dep to 1695 AC for Toulouse province, when he was provost of Lavaur cath, thanks to his brother. Made cardinal by the pope independently in 1719, but dispute over it with crown was soon healed.

Nom to Arles 24-12-1697. Provs 7-4-1698. Consec 11-5-1698. Nom to Reims 12-7-1710. Provs 1-12-1710. Cardinal 29-11-1719. Died 13-9-1721.

Sources: ASV, PC 101a, fos 216–223 (Reims). BN, MS Fr 20969, fo 88–9. Boisnard, *Touraine*, no 1447. Pinard, *Chronologie*, vi, 496–7. Vindry, *État major, gendarmerie*, 313–14. St-Simon, iv, 516–19.

Malezieu, Nicolas. Lavaur 1713–48.   Family of Champagne origins, some of whom may have been involved in silk and cotton trade of Lyon in mid-16th c, although heirs of Raphael Malezieu, Mathieu and Jean, went bankrupt in 1570s. Their subsequent fortunes are much less clear, at least before Louis XIV's reign, and bp of Lavaur was probably descended from a branch that was based in Paris, also from mid-16th c, where successive generations included a *chirurgien du roi* and a *huissier* in parlt. It was bp's own father, Nicolas (1650–1727), son of a 'bourgeois de Paris', who transformed their fortunes. A barrister, he was chosen by the duc de Montausier and Bossuet to teach maths to duc du Maine, an illegitimate son of Louis XIV and Mme de Montespan. He later became favourite of Maine, who successively made him a gentleman of his household, *secrétaire des commandements* for Languedoc, of which Maine was govr, and chancellor of his principality of Dombes. He also tutored Louis XIV's grandson, the duc de Bourgogne, in phil and maths, possibly because of relations with Fénelon. His son followed in his pedagogical footsteps.

Born 1674, probably eldest son of Nicholas, and Françoise Faudel, herself a governess of duc du Maine. He was one of 5 children, one of whom, Elisabeth, was briefly a *vêtue* of St-Cyr. Studies at Univ of Paris, where he took MA in July 1692, defended his theol bacc (*tentativa*) with Bossuet presiding, Nov 1695, 31st place in 1700 theol lic, followed by doct in theol 3-7-1703. Vic-gen of Soissons, nom abbot of Moureilles O Cist (Maillezais), 5-4-1692, which he later exchanged for La Chalade (Verdun), also prior *in comm* in dioc of Sens. Chosen to educate Maine's son, prince of Dombes, in early 1708, and given Lavaur in 1713 on understanding he would complete education of Dombes. An active bp he published new synodal ordinances and partially rebuilt the *hôpital-général* of Lavaur. Showed himself very pro-Roman, pro-*Unigenitus* at outset of his episcopate.

Nom 22-4-1713. Provs 18-9-1713. Consec 22-10-1713. Died 14-3-1748.

Sources: AN, MC, LXXXII, 122, 5-5-1713 (Lavaur). BN, PO 1815, no 41,933; Doss bleus 420, no 11,219; Cab d'Hozier 223, no 5796; MS Fr 20969, fo 130. St-Simon, iv, 82. Bossuet, *Correspondance*, viii, 31, n 6. Fénelon, *Correspondance*, xvii, 134, nn 1–2. Chamillart, *Correspondance*, ii, 226–7. Lacger, *Etats adminsitratifs*, 351. Bluche, *L'Origine*, 294. R Gascon, *Grand commerce et vie urbaine au xvi*ᵉ *siècle* (Paris 1971), 602.

Malier du Houssay, Marc. Tarbes 1668–75.   Nephew of François, bp of Troyes (1641–78) and son of Claude II, his predecessor as bp of Tarbes (1649–68), and Marie le Bailleul, herself the daughter of a Malier. Born in Venice in 1638 while father was ambassador there. Univ studies in Paris, where he took bacc in theol 22-8-1661, 4ᵗʰ place in 1664 lic, and doct in 1666. *Socius* of coll of Navarre, 1666, when also ordained priest. *Premier aumônier* to duchess d'Orléans, like his uncle and his father, who resigned Tarbes in order to make way for him.

Nom 13-4-1668. Provs 3-9-1668. Consec 25-11-1668. Died 3-5-1675.

Sources: ASV, PC 67, fos 721–54. BN, MS Fr 22384, 118v; MS Lat 15440, p 222. *Lettres de Séguier*, ii, 1218. Poutet, 'Docteurs', 293, no 464. Soulet, *Traditions et réformes religieuses*, 92 ff. Bayard, *Dictionnaire des surintendants*, 68–9. Bergin, *Making*, 662–3.

Margarit, Vicenç. Perpignan 1668–72.   Spanish see of Elne fell vacant during French occupation of Roussillon and Catalonia after 1640, and remained vacant, because disputed between the 2 crowns, for several decades until Louis XIV was finally granted an indult to nom to Elne, translated to Perpignan, in late 1660s. A decade earlier, in 1658, Vicent Margarit had already been chosen by Louis XIV to be its next bp – as a reward for his and his family's pro-French stance during Catalan revolt. The Margarit family, from Castell d'Empordà near Gerona, belonged to the 'cavallers' or lower nobility of Catalonia, and were represented among nobility in Catalan Cortès since Charles V's time. His elder brother, Josep (1602–85), perhaps frustrated by his lack of prospects of service/advancement under Olivares, became leading pro-French noble in Catalonia, for which he lost all his lands and titles and was only rebel to be excluded from pardon by the Spaniards after 1651. In partial indemnity, he was made baron de Brens and marquis d'Aguilar by Louis XIV. *His* son, Josep, was abbot of St-Martin-du-Canigou 1692–8, and held ecclesiastical office in Narbonne until death in 1701.

Son of Felip de Margarit i Sunyer and Beatriz de Biure, daughter of a baronial family based near Tarragona, bp was born in Castro, dioc of Gerona, ca 1603. He joined Dominicans young, studied theol at Univ of Gerona, where took his doct, and taught theol and published a work called *Quaestiones de Sancto Thomas*. Subsequently held offices within Dominican order. Priest since about 1638. Nom by French monarchs to sees of Lleida (1642), Solsona (1646), Barcelona (1651) (which he briefly administered without papal provs until revolt there collapsed), but not approved by Rome, which refused to take sides in conflict for control of Catalonia. Nom by Mazarin to Perpignan in 1658, but not approved until 1669. He was also *cons honoraire* in Sovereign Council of Roussillon. His episcopate, long in coming, was short in duration.

Nom initially 1658, renewed 4-5-1668. Provs 12-11-1668. Consec 30-6-1669 at Auch. Died 21-12-1672.

Sources: ASV, PC 66, fos 135–46. Capeille, *Dicionnairet des biographies roussillonnaises*, 354–5. Pinard, *Chronologie*, iv, 101–4. Elliott, *Revolt of the Catalans*. Sala, *Dieu, le roi, les hommes*, 331, 336.

Marion, Pierre. Gap 1662–75.   Figuring among the more obscure of Louis XIV's bps, despite alleged descent from same family, originally from Nevers, as Simon Marion, *avocat-*

général of the Pari parlt under Henri IV. That connection is unproven, and suggestions that he was son (or grandson) of a *procureur* at Paris Châtelet rather than of *avocat-général* do not suffice to clarify it.

Son of Pierre Marion, *commissaire des guerres* in Paris, sgr de Bois-Herpin, and Jeanne Joubert, date of birth unknown, but ca 1611. Early career is obscure, with one source claiming that after an initial spell as a *procureur* at Châtelet in Paris, he was active mostly in Alsace and Champagne as a *commissaire des guerres*. He abandoned it to enter order of Cluny, date unknown but after the Fronde, it seems. He became prior of Lyons near Abbeville, where he encountered difficulties and opposition, and then abbot of St-Paul of Sens. Allegedly spent some time study-ing law and taking a degree in it at Angers after becoming a Benedictine, but there is no real evidence of this. As successor at Gap of Artus de Lionne, father of Louis XIV's 1st foreign min-ister, Hugues, he was handpicked by latter who spent considerable time and effort seeking a candidate who would not be able to resist his (mainly financial) demands in relation to Gap. Lionne's comment might have been made with him in mind – 'it is hard to secure a bishopric for an unknown figure, and it may involve questions of conscience' ('il est pourtant malaisé de faire tomber un évêché a un homme qui n'est pas connu, et peut-etre la conscience y est interessé'). However, Marion's record as bp of Gap shows that Lionne found someone who was capable and energetic, a good admin who raised its revenues, which enabled him, aided by pious legacies, to found and build seminary run by Doctrinaires.

Nom 14-12-1661. Provs 26-6-1662. Consec 8-10-1662. Died 25-8-1675.

Sources: ASV, no PC file. *Hierarchia Catholica*, v, 404. BN, PO 1857, no 42,808; Doss bleus 429, no 11,480. AD Hautes-Alpes, G 1533 (fragments of Vallor-Corse's history of bps of Gap, 18th c). *Archives des Hautes-Aples, Inventaire-sommaire, série G*, iii, pp. xviii–xix. *Gall Chr Nov*, Gap, cols 523–3. Fisquet, *France pontificale*, Gap, 127–9.

Mascaron, Jules. Tulle 1672–9, Agen 1679–1703.   Son of a long established family of urban notables in Marseille, which in the generation of bp's grandfather adhered to Catholic League and its devotional spin-offs. Born Marseille, 14-3-1634. Only son of Pierre, well known *avocat* at Aix parlt (d 1647) and a scholar known for his works on Seneca, and Catherine de Pancis, who died shortly after her husband. His early years were thus difficult. Initial studies in an Oratorian coll, followed by entry to Oratory itself. He studied theol at Saumur coll, and was ordained priest by Lavardin of Le Mans on 15-6-1658, while teaching Rhetoric at Oratorian coll there. He also taught in Marseille coll of Oratory. Began to preach while involved in controversies with Saumur Protestants. Moved to Paris in 1660s, where preached several Lents and Advents before court 1666 and 1679. Involved in preparing Turenne's conversion. *Prédicateur du roi* in 1672, renewed in 1679 when he left Tulle for Agen. Active preacher as bp in south-west, where his *manière douce* in dealings with Huguenots set him apart. Admired by some of greatest literary figures of his time (Sévigné, Rabutin, Fénelon, Scudéry).

Nom 5-1-1671. Provs 21-3-1672. Consec 8-5-1672. Nom to Agen 25-2-1679. Provs 8-1-1680. Died 16-11-1703.

Sources: ASV, PC 71, fos 814–32. AN, L 727, Agen. Abbé Oroux, *Histoire ecclésiastique de la cour*, ii, 510. W Kaiser, *Marseille im Bürgerkrieg* (Göttingen 1991).

Matha. *See* **La Mer**.

Matignon, Jacques de Goyon de. Condom 1672–93 (resign).   2 Matignon brothers suc-ceeded their uncle, Léonor I, bp of Coutances and Lisieux (1632–74) into the episcopate under Louis XIV, when Matignon family power and connections remained undiminished, esp in Nor-mandy, and were comparable to those of Beaumanoir, La Baume de Suze, Noailles and other aristocratic families. One of several reasons for success was intermarriage and close ties to min-isterial (Louvois, Seignelay, Chamillart) families under Louis XIV. Bps' mother was heavily involved with the *dévot* networks in Normandy, patronising Jean Eudes among others.

Jacques was one of 12 children of François, comte de Matignon and Thorigny, lt-gen of lower Normandy, and Anne Malon de Bercy, married in 1631. Born 17-3-1643. Studies in Paris, where he took MA in July 1667, then theol at Sorbonne, possibly leading to bacc, but he took licentiate in canon law before that, in June 1665. Ordained priest 5-4-1670. Dean of Lisieux cath. Prior *in comm* of Le Plessis-Grimault (1652), abbot of Foigny (1693) – the latter exchanged for St-Victor of Marseille (1703).

Nom 25-11-1671. Provs 22-2-1672. Consec 16-4-1673. Resign 1693. Died 15-3-1727.

Sources: ASV, PC 71, fos 271–91. AN, MM 252, fos 107r, 111v (theol fac, Aug and Nov 1667); MM 1115, fo 24v (law degree 3-6 and 5-6-1665). St-Simon, xi, 280–6. Béguin, *Princes de Condé*, 421–2. Berthelot du Chesnay, *Les Missions de Saint Jean Eudes*, 353–4.

Matignon, Léonor II de Goyon de. Lisieux 1675–1714. Elder brother of Jacques. Born at Thorigny, 5-9-1637. Tonsured Paris 24-3-1651. Studied hum and phil at coll of Lisieux, Univ of Paris, where he took MA in Oct 1656. Bachelor in theol at Sorbonne, where he was student in 1659–60, as well as licentiate in canon law from Paris, June 1654, a combination followed by younger brother above. Priest for about 4 years before nom to Lisieux, where he was also dean of cath chapter. Dep to 1660 AC, he also obtained a royal almonership in March 1669 (as successor to Le Camus of Grenoble). Nom to ND de Thorigny O Cist, on uncle's resignation, 27-1-1676, abbot *in comm* of Lessay OSB (Coutances), also on uncle's resignation in Sept 1668.

Nom 20-12-1674. Provs 27-5-1675. Consec 14-3-1677. Died 14-7-1714.

Sources: ASV, PC 74, fos 302–22; Misc Arm XII, 151, fo 14r. AN, MM 1114, fo 20v. BN, MS Fr 7651, fo 220 (*bienfaits du roi*); MS Clairambault 814, fo 359r. *L'Intendance de Caen*, p 222, n 607.

Maupeou, Augustin de. Castres 1693–1705, Auch 1705–12. Bp was from same branch, the Bruyères, of this celebrated but recently ennobled lineage as Jean, bp of Chalon-sur-Saône (1659–77), his uncle. By early 1680s, when Augustin was nom to Castres, their connections within the highest circles of the Parisian robe had strengthened further, enabling them, through patronage of Pontchartrain and other powerful relatives, to envisage high-ranking careers in the next century.

Born in Paris, ca 1649. Son of René II, *prés* in *Enquetes*, Paris parlt, and Marie Doujat, daughter of a *cons* in parlt. Studies in Paris – MA June 1667, 6th place in 1676 theol lic, doct 20-6-1676. Ordained priest at same time. Succeeded uncle, bp of Chalon, as *doyen* of St-Quentin-en-Vermandois (Noyon) on his death in May 1677, a post he retained until 1694. He turned suddenly to a legal career in late 1679 in order to retain post of *avocat-général* in *gr conseil* held by his elder brother, Pierre, who died prematurely in 1679. 3 years later, and just as suddenly, he turned towards episcopate, in order to retain the nom to Castres which another brother had obtained but died before obtaining provs! His nom to Castres came too late in 1682 for speedy confirmation by Rome, and he was compromised by having participated as a dep for Paris to 1682 AC.

Nom 3-7-1682. Provs 7-12-1693. Consec 10-1-1694. Nom to Auch 11-4-1705. Provs 16-11-1705. Died 12-6-1712.

Sources: ASV, PC 87, fos 181–90. BN, Cab d'Hozier, 231, no 6084; MS Fr 32139, pp 181–6. AN, O¹, vol 21, fo 110 (St-Quentin). Lacger, *Etats administratifs*, 333–4. J de Maupeou, *Histoire des Maupeou* (Fontenay-le-Comte 1959). Bergin, *Making*, 669.

Maurel du Chaffaut, Joseph. St-Paul-Trois-Châteaux 1714–17. A classic case of rapid social and political advance in mid-17th c. Until later 16th c they were relatively obscure merchants at La Ciotat near Marseille, and were still cloth merchants at Aix until 1630s, when brothers Antoine and Pierre invested heavily in prov financial offices – posts of controller of postal services, *trés-gén* – as well as in fiefs such as Chaffaut itself, subsequently marrying their children advantageously. Antoine's son, André, bp's father, became *cons* in Aix parlt in 1651 as a result. André's brother, Pierre, was even more successful as a financier, serving several terms as *trés-gén* of Estates after the Fronde, and may have been wealthiest individual in Provence when he died in 1672, only months after royal letters 'rehabilitated' him and his family – i.e. actually ennobling them under guise of restoring an 'authentic' lost nobility. His vast wealth enabled him to advance his children – nearly 20 of them in all – from 3 marriages, with the result that the Maurel were quickly connected to many of the best (even most ancient, like Pontevès, Thomassin, Villeneuve) Provençal families! By 1650s, Pierre had 2 sons and a nephew (brother of future bp of St-Paul) in Aix parlt. A relative/brother of bp, Louis, was provost of Riez cath in 1699.

Born in Aix, 17-10-1658. Son of André Maurel (1630–1717), sgr du Chaffaut et Valbonette, *cons* in Aix parlt, and Marguerite de Villeneuve de Mons, from an old Provençal noble family with a strong ecclesiastical as well as parlt background. Tonsured 11-9-1667, he seems to have attended school and univ in Aix exclusively, where he took bacc in theol, 28-6-1683. Despite being a deacon for many years, he only became priest in 1698, when he also took bacc and lic *in utr* in quick succession, for which he needed (and obtained) a royal dispensation, in order to become a *cons-clerc* in Aix parlt. He was initially a canon and archdeacon of Toulon, but swapped it for that of canon in native Aix cath in July 1686 – again with royal intervention, since Aix, then vacant, was *en régale*. He was among longest-serving Aix canons when he was chosen by chapter as vic-gen *sede vacante* after the death of Abp Cosnac in 1708, a position in which the new abp, Vintimille du Luc, confirmed him (Jan 1709) and which he held, along with that of *official*, until nom to St-Paul. Episcopate was cut short by illness contracted while conducting large-scale preaching missions in his dioc among its ex-Protestant population.

Nom 31-3-1714. Provs 9-7-1714. Consec 26-8-1714. Died 10-3-1717.

Sources: ASV, PC 103, fos 752–60. AAE, MD France 972, fo 50. AD Bouches-du-Rhône, 1G 1320, 11-9-1667; 1G 1273, fos 399–401v, 27-7-1686; 1G 1279, fos 256–7, fo 316v; 1G 1276, fo 268, 10-3-1699; 2 D, 2, fo 632v; 2 D 4, fos 71v–72r. Clapiers-Collongues, *Chronologie*, 96–7, 102, 105, 109, 119. Kettering, *Judicial Politics*, esp 244–6. Pillorget, *Mouvements insurrectionnels*, 92–3. Kettering, *Patrons, Brokers*, 88, 101, 106. Blanc, 'Origines', 370. Dessert, *Argent, pouvoir et société*, no 369, p 644. Bergin, *Making*, 717–18.

Méliand, Victor-Augustin. Gap 1680–4, Alet 1692–8 (resign).　　Natives of Berry, where they produced several *trés de France* at Bourges, although generation of bp's father branched out markedly, both geographically and professionally. Bp's grandfather, Blaise I, sgr d'Egligny, was *trés de France* at Bourges, and SR (source of their noble status) in 1585, while father's career shows a rapid change of fortune. Initially a *cons* in the Paris parlt (1609), then a *prés*, followed by a spell as ambassador to the Swiss cantons and Venice, he was Fouquet's immediate predecessor as *proc-gén* of Paris parlt, a post he had to resign in 1650 to Fouquet because of his inability to keep the court loyal to Mazarin government. By this point, there were 3 Méliand family members in parlt, while their matrimonial strategies in bp's and next generation brought them into relations, however indirect in some cases, with the Colbert, Bossuet, Lamoignon, Creil and Petau families. Bp's own brother, Nicolas, married Marguerite Bossuet, daughter of financier, François, in 1653, cousin of the bp of Meaux.

7th child of Blaise and 1st wife, Geneviève Hurault de Boistaillé, daughter of another distinguished robe family, he was born 9-7-1626, baptised on 10-7 in St-Jean-de-Grève parish church, Paris. Studied phil and theol, but took doct in canon law, spending period March-Oct 1653 in St-Sulpice seminary. Ordained priest by Cardinal Grimaldi in 1657. By then he was associated with the Missions Etrangères de Paris, and was one of the priests sent to Rome to petition pope to appoint 3 bishops for Chinese missions, a project supported by Anne of Austria, to whom Méliand was already attached as an almoner (1661). He remained almoner to Louis XIV after her death. Took active part in preaching missions in various diocs of France, and was superior of ND de la Madelaine de Tresnel near Paris at time of nom. By 1681, he was abbot of St-Etienne-de-Bassac (Saintes), and prior *in comm* of ND de Montluçon, to which he added prévôté of Chardavon by 1686, which he resigned in 1707. His resign of Alet so soon after receiving papal provs is hard to explain, given the length of time he lived thereafter. He retired to Bons-Enfants seminary in Paris where he died.

Nom 21-7-1679. Provs 27-5-1680. Consec 8-1680. Nom to Alet 31-5-1684. Provs 7-7-1692. Resign 29-10-1698. Died 23-9-1713.

Sources: ASV, PC 79, fos 696–706. BN, MS Fr 32139, pp 199–202. AN, L 727, Alet, no 36. Levesque, 'Liste des élèves', no 233. Adrien Launay, *Documents historiques relatifs à la Société des Missions Etrangères*, vol i (Paris 1904), 520–1. *Inventaire-sommaire de la série G des Hautes-Alpes*, iii, pp xix–xx. *Gallia Chr Nov*, Gap, col 524. Bossuet, *Correspondance*, v, 378–9.

Mérinville, Charles-François des Monstiers de. Chartres 1710–46. This family may have migrated from Savoy to Languedoc, and later to Basse-Marche and Poitou, where they were sgrs of Mérinville by 15th c. Their presence among nobility of Languedoc only dates from 1640 when they acquired barony of Rieux (renamed Mérinville) through marriage of bp's grandparents, and which guaranteed a seat in the Estates of Languedoc. Bp's grandfather, who saw extended military service in Roussillon and Catalonia from 1630s to 1650s, was 'lieut du roi' in Provence 1659–69, playing an important role in pacifying that turbulent province after the Fronde, before being replaced in 1669 by comte de Grignan, after which he, and later his son, were govs of Narbonne. More immediately pertinent to bp's career was fact that he was also nephew of Godet des Marais, director of conscience of Mme de Maintenon and his predecessor as bp of Chartres. Later generations furnished another bp of Chartres and of Dijon.

Born 2-2-1682. Son of Charles des Monstiers, comte de Mérinville, and Marguerite Gravé. Originally destined for a military career as a Knight of Malta, but changed his mind, entered St-Sulpice seminary in July 1699, where he resided and studied alongside the duc de Beauvillier's half-brother. He broke off studies once he had completed the bachelor's cycle in Dec 1704, in order to become vic-gen of his uncle at Chartres, where he was already a cath canon and archdeacon of Pinserais. Prospect of episcopal promotion took him back to Sorbonne to join 1709–10 theol lic cycle, which he completed quickly by special dispensation and was even allowed to take doct on 17-10-1709 before lic cycle was finished. Ordained priest about 1706 and was subsequently active in missions. Abbot of St-Calais (Le Mans), which he exchanged for Igny, previously held by his uncle, Bp Godet, soon after nom to Chartres. His uncle also obtained, via Mme de Maintenon, his nom as coadj to him at Chartres in April 1709, but died before coadj could take effect, hence full succession ensued immediately. Close to Maintenon, like his uncle, but too young and inexperienced to take his place as her principal confidant.

Godet's procuration for coadj, 4-4-1709. Nom as coadj 26-4-1709. Provs 10-3-1710. Consec 18-5-1710. Died 10-5-1746.

Sources: AN, MC, LXXXII, 102, 4-4 and 23-4-1709. AN, MM 255, p 251 (doct). BN, MS Fr 7657, no 125. St-Simon, ii, 149; xiii, 434; xviii, 229–40. Anselme, *Histoire*, ix, pt i, 253–4. Pinard, *Chronologie*, iv, 73–4; vii, 38–9. Boisnard, *Touraine*, no 1573. *L'Intendance de Languedoc à la fin du xviie siècle*, 154, n 316. Pillorget, *Mouvements insurrectionnels*, 852–6. Aston, *End of an Elite*, 257, 274.

Meschatin de la Faye, Guillaume. Gap 1677–9. The Meschatin were an established noble family from the Bourbonnais, but there are signs that they were less than dynamic or prosperous in 17th c, despite earlier alliances with La Trémouille, Marconnay and other prominent families. Bp's own father was described as being of limited means from Bourges. Consequently bp's mother's family seems to have been crucial to his career, at least at Lyon, where they were well entrenched in chapter of St-Jean. Perhaps they were also lucky in that another

Lyonnais, the Jesuit La Chaize, had become royal confessor in 1675, and Meschatin was the 1st of many with Lyon connections or origins to attract his attention.

Born in Theneuille in Bourbonnais, Sept 1637, baptised on 7-9-1638. Son of Thomas, sgr de la Faye, and Marie d'Albon, daughter of an old noble family from Lyonnais. Resident in Paris as student in mid-1650s, he took bacc in theol 3-2-1665, 78ᵗʰ place in 1670 lic, doct the same year. Tonsured in April 1650, he spent a month in St-Sulpice seminary at Christmas 1660, and was ordained priest in 1670. Prince of Condé interceded with Lyon primatial chapter to elect him as canon while a student in mid-1651, but he was not successful until Aug 1655. He had some experience as preacher and confessor. Erudite and anti-Jansenist, but in close touch with Port-Royal milieu around 1670. He was in poor health from outset of his brief career at Gap.

Nom 17-9-1675. Provs 24-5-1677. Consec 8-1677. Died 21-2-1679.

Sources: ASV, PC 76, fos 1012–32. BN, PO 1938, no 44,593; Doss bleus 444, no 11,947; Carrés d'Hozier 431, Meschatin. *Inventaire-sommmaire des archives des Hautes-Alpes, série G*, iii, pp xix–xx. AD Hautes-Alpes, G 1533. *Gall Chr Nov*, Gap, 523. Beyssac, *Chanoines de Lyon*, 194, 199, 201, 209, 214. Fisquet, *France pontificale*, Gap, 129. Lesaulnier, *Port-Royal insolite*, 310.

Mesgrigny, Joseph-Ignace, OFM Cap. Grasse 1711–26.　　This Champenois family, originally from Chaumont-en-Bassigny, settled later in Troyes where entered bourgeoisie and held municipal office by mid-15ᵗʰ c. From there they moved in various directions, including Paris, Touraine and, briefly, Provence. The elder branch settled in Paris, where it held offices in *gr conseil* and *chambre des comptes*, where bp's grandfather, Jean, was a *maître* in 1621. Bp's father (d 1678) was successively *cons* in *gr conseil* in 1627, MR in 1634, intendant in Auvergne and Bourbonnais 1636–7, Champagne, 1638, and then on recommendation of the comte d'Alais, gov of Provence, *pr prés* of Aix parlt (1644–8), leaving in April 1648 before Fronde really began there. He increasingly sided with local and parlt interests vs patrons and crown, but formally kept his office despite long absence 1648–55, until sold to Oppède in 1655. Bp's mother had Dinteville and Saulx-Tavannes ancestors, both significant noble families in Champagne, as were their Vignier relatives, who were also present in church and intendancy. 2 of bp's uncles were well-established clerics – Mathieu, doct of theol and abbot of Pontigny (d 1650), and Nicolas, prior of Souvigny, canon of ND de Paris (d 1658).

Son of Jean marquis de Mesgrigny, and Huberte Renée de Bussy-Dinteville. Born Aix, 9-4-1653. Initially embarked on military career, but it seems unlikely he served long enough to become a *mestre de camp*, as one source suggests, since he abandoned the sword to enter the Capuchin order, in which he was professed on 24-3-1672, taking name of Athanasius in religion. Ordained priest 20-9-1681. Had already taken lic in canon law in Paris, 6-8-1672, only months after entry to Capuchins. He preached several missions and held numerous posts of responsibility within Capuchin order (superior of individual houses, master of novices, visitor, provincial) over 30-year period before relatively late call to episcopate in one of France's most remote diocs, where he displayed considerable energy as well as charity.

Nom to Grasse on 5-4-1711. Provs 19-10-1711. Consec 20-12-1711. Died 2-3-1726.

Sources: ASV, PC 101a, fos 121–131. AN, Y 175, fo 217 (c.m. of parents 29-1-1635); MM 1116, fos 33r, 34r (law degrees, 4-8, 6-8-1672). BM Aix, MS 257, p 261. Fénelon, *Correspondance*, xvii, 118, n 19. Frondeville, *Presidents du parlement de Normandie*, pp 374–8. *Lettres de Séguier*, ii, 1221–2. Pillorget, *Mouvements insurrectionnels*, 127, 576–7. Kettering, *Judicial Politics*.

Milon, Louis. Condom 1693–1743.　　'From a family of magistrates of Bourges', is the label usually attached to this bp, but before Bourges, the Milon were resident in Anjou, and especially Tours, where they belonged to ruling municipal oligarchy since 16ᵗʰ c, with several members also becoming canons of St-Martin. Bp's grandfather was a *maître* in *chambre de comptes*, Paris, in 1574 and later a *trés de France* in Tours (1590–1610), a milieu in which bp's own father, based in Bourges, was to distinguish himself over several decades – beginning as simple *commis* he became *trés de France* and finally, under Colbert in 1660s, he was *fermier-général* of both *gabelles* and *cinq grosses fermes*. In this he was following example of his high-flying Tours relatives, since the Milon were connected on both sides of family to major financiers, tax-farmers and officeholders, particularly the Bonneau and Pallu families. Bp's elder brother, Alexandre, became closely associated with prince of Condé and his interests, once he had abandoned church career for which he was originally intended. MR and *cons* in *gr conseil*, he became *intendant de maison* to prince of Conti. He was also a *fermier-général*, in late 17th c. Bp's mother's family, the Pallu, were a similarly well-connected family of notables, with financial and municipal offices, from Tours. Etienne Pallu, *trés de France* at Tours 1642–69 and *maire* of Tours (like his father before him), was brother of François, founder of *Missions Etrangères de Paris* seminary in the capital and one of 1st French missionaries to Far East. Bp's career depended as much on Pallu and Bonneau connections as Milon's. Their milieu was highly *dévot* on every side, Bonneau as much as Pallu – as witness the career of Mme de Miramion, *née* Bonneau, but also the Gault brothers, bps of Marseille under Louis XIII. Also strong Jesuit presence in family.

Bp was younger son of Alexandre (d 1687), sgr d'Amenon, financier and *prés* of *trés de France* at Bourges, and Françoise Pallu, daughter of Etienne Pallu. Born 1655 Bourges. Completed his phil in Univ of Paris, where he took MA in July 1679, followed by bacc in theol, early 1681, 101st place in 1684 lic, completed by doct on 4-7-1685. Succeeded abbé Lionne as an *aumônier du roi* 'en quartier' in early 1682, and was canon of St-Martin of Tours, possibly in succession to a Pallu cousin. He had succeeded his elder brother Alexandre as prior *in comm* of St-Marcel of Bourges in 1674 (which he resigned on accession to episcopate), in gift of prince of Condé. Ordained priest in 1683, by which time, doubtless through influence of uncle, François Pallu, he was closely associated with Missions Etrangères seminary in Paris, of which he was elected a director in March 1688. He formed close ties with Fénelon in 1680s when both men were involved with missions and conversion of Huguenots, esp in western France. Fénelon ensured Milon succeeded him as superior of community of Nouvelles Catholiques and indirectly (through Mme de Maintenon) was instrumental in obtaining episcopal office for him.

Nom 1-11-1693. Provs 22-12-1693. Consec 14-2-1694. Died 24-1-1734.

Sources: ASV, PC, 88, fos 98–106. AN, L 730, pièce 1, nos 7–8; MC, XCII, 285, 8-2-1694. Fénelon, *Correspondance*, iii, 87–8, n 1. Frondeville, *Conseillers du parlement de Normandie, 1641–1715*, 56. Béguin, *Princes de Condé*, 191. Charmeil, *Trésoriers*, 477. Boisnard, *Touraine*, no 1562. Dessert, *Argent, pouvoir et société*, 649.

Monchy d'Hocquincourt, Armand. Verdun 1668–79.   The Monchy were a long-established noble family with roots in Picardy and Artois, and with a number of titles like Hocquincourt and Montcarvel to their name; they were also related to powerful and no less old lineages like the Mailly, who provided 2 bps under Louis XIV. Bp's own mother's family was similarly well-connected, which meant that he was related to the Brûlart and other min-isterial families. His father obtained very substantial rewards from Mazarin for his loyalty during and after the Fronde, but war eventually took its toll on them, and by 1698, the Hoc-quincourt line was reduced to one female, Mme de Feuquières, and an abbé, presumably a nephew of bp, since 2 other sons perished in 1690s. An uncle of bp, the Oratorian Pierre de Monchy (ca 1610–86), was a highly respected figure in Paris, both as preacher and director of conscience, close to leading figures in the French church (Bossuet, Le Tellier of Reims, Rancé, Le Camus of Grenoble, Vialart of Châlons) and served as spiritual mentor to a younger generation which included Fénelon.

One of Louis XIV's youngest bps, he was born at Hocquincourt, Noyon dioc, 1639. 2nd son of Charles, marshal Hocquincourt (1599–1658), and Eleonore d'Étampes de Valançay, he studied at Univ of Paris, where he was MA in July 1656, taking 78th and last place in 1664 theol lic, and doct, also in 1664, becoming *socius* of coll of Navarre. Ordained priest only 5 months before nom to Verdun (ca March 1665). Dep to 1665 AC. Abbé *in comm* of ND de Bohours O Cist (Laon). His confirmation as bp was delayed by Rome for over 2 years because of his strong gallican views in Paris theol fac conflicts of the early 1660s. Close to Port-Royal and *dévot* milieux from his early years, thanks in part to his father and Oratorian uncle, during his relatively brief episcopate he attempted to devise and impose rigorist reforms within his war-torn dioc.

Nom 24-7-1665. Provs 27-2-1668. Consec 6-5-1668. Died 29-10-1679.

Sources: ASV, PC 67, fos 771–85. St-Simon, vi, 161. Fénelon, *Correspondance*, i, 79–80, n 91. Pinard, *Chronologie*, vi, 122–3. Vindry, *État major, gendarmerie*, 314. Poutet, 'Docteurs', 289, no 426. Taveneaux, *Jansenisme en Lorraine*, 170–7. Krailsheimer, *Rancé*, 249–50.

Montgaillard. *See* **Percin.**

Montmorin, Armand de. Die 1692–4, Vienne 1694–1713.   The Montmorin family was among the oldest noble lineages of Auvergne, in the neighbourhood of Billom. Like some of families they were related to – the Alègre, Guiche, Joyeuse, Urfé, Noailles – they spawned numerous branches and spread out across Auvergne and contiguous provinces. The St-Hérem branch went back to mid-15th c. Over centuries they held numerous offices in royal service, and were particularly active as prov govs and as a leading Catholic force in the Auvergne during Wars of Religion; their sons, often as Knights of Malta, served in several of Louis XIV's wars. The marquis de St-Hérem was *grand louvetier* at Louis XIV's court and subsequently capt and gov of Fontainebleau. Their record in ecclesiastical office was perhaps less prominent before end of Louis XIV's reign, but their ancestry guaranteed them a continuous presence in noble-dominated chapters like St-Julien-de-Brioude or St-Jean-de-Lyon.

Born 1645, he was (only surviving) son of Gilbert, gov of Verdun-sur-Saône, killed at Nordlingen in 1645, and Anne Loisilier, married in 1637. He seems to have become a pro-fessed *Feuillant* for a few years in youth but to have quit, possibly due to family pressure for a lay career. But still refusing to marry, he returned to clerical milieu and was ordained priest in 1669. Virtually nothing known about his studies, except that they led to doct in theol, univ unknown (possibly Valence). Spent much time working on missions to Protestants of Nîmes area before episcopate. 1st bp of Die in several centuries, doubtless because experiences at Nîmes equipped him to deal with Protestant problem there. Active and resident there as vic-gen of predecessor, Cosnac, since late 1687, his record, esp during disaster years 1693–4 at Die, impressed court enough to give him Vienne. Also obtained abbey of St-André-de-Vienne in 1709.

Nom to Die 17-1-1687. Provs 7-7-1692. Consec 7-9-1692. Nom to Vienne 10-4-1694. Provs 19-7-1694. Died 6-10-1713.

Sources: ASV, PC 86, fos 500–22. AN, L 746, pièce 1, no 22. St-Simon, vii, 3. Bossuet, *Correspondance*, xii, 302, n 52. Pinard, *Chronologie*, vi, 334. Vindry, *État major, gendarmerie*, 345, 363. Remacle, *Dictionnaire des familles d'Auvergne*, ii, 602–3. Chevalier, *Essai historique sur l'église et la ville de Die*, iii, 525–40.

Montmorin de St-Hérem, Joseph-Gaspard. Aire 1710–23.   This bp was from a cadet branch of the comtes de St-Hérem line, the La Chassaigne, which died out with the bp's own son, Francois-Gaspard, bp of Aire (1723–34) and Langres (1734–70).

Born 24-6-1659, only son of Edouard, sgr de la Chassaigne, and Marie de Champfeu, married in 1655. He became a cavalry officer in a royal regiment and, in Feb 1684, married Louise de Bigny, by whom he had 9 children. When his wife died in Nov 1700, he entered St-Magloire seminary, Paris, studied theol (probably in Paris), but took his doct at Valence in 1703. Ordained subdeacon at Clermont seminary on 22-12-1703. Subsequently acted as vic-gen to his cousin, abp of Vienne, whose patronage obtained election as dep to ACs of 1707 and 1710, when nom to Aire. St-Simon described him as man of 'beaucoup d'esprit'. His son, the abbé de St-Hérem, succeeded him at Aire and later became bp of Langres.

Nom to Aire 12-7-1710. Provs 10-11-1710. Consec 4-1-1711. Died 7-11-1723.

Sources: AN, MC, LXXXII, 118, 9-8-1710. AD Puy-de-Dôme, 6 F 78. St-Simon, ix, 374–8 (appendix 8 on the St-Hérem); xl, 242. Remacle, *Dictionnaire des familles d'Auvergne*, ii, 594–603 (esp 597).

Montmort. *See* **Habert.**

Montpezat de Carbon, Joseph. St-Papoul 1665–75, Toulouse 1675–87.   Younger brother of Jean, bp of St-Papoul etc (1658–85).

Born ca 1620 at Conilh in dioc of Comminges. Son of Jean-Antoine (d 1621) and Louise de St-Paul. Studies culminated in doct in law at Toulouse, but also studied theol up to bacc, which he took in Toulouse on 4-10-1646. Priest since 1654. Held a parish in St-Papoul dioc, but also served as vic-gen of St-Papoul under brother for a few years. Abbot of Homblières until nom to St-Papoul, when it passed to his elder brother, abp of Bourges. Dep to 1660 AC, a useful stepping stone, though not immediately. Given St-Papoul on brother's promotion to Bourges, and then got Toulouse when brother moved to Sens in 1675. Incurred wrath of Innocent XI's for his interventions in Pamiers affair in 1680s.

Nom 20-12-1664. Provs 28-9-1665. Consec 27-12-1665. Nom to Toulouse 21-11-1674. Provs 6-5-1675. Died 17-6-1687.

Sources: ASV, PC 63, fos 399–413. BIUT, MS 28, fo 113r. BN, MS Fr 7657, nos 157–8. Bergin, *Making*, 673.

Moreau, Étienne. Arras 1668–70.   Natives of the area around Louviers in Normandy, from where bp's grandfather seems to have moved by mid-16th c to Paris, where their ensuing presence proved not to be a particularly lengthy. Bp's father's career is obscure, though by time he married he was a *cons* in the *cour des monnaies*, later becoming *proc-gén* in *chambre des comptes*. Of his 2 sons, the elder, Michel (d 1637), became *lt-civil* at the Châtelet and later *prévôt des marchands*, dedicating himself by late 1620s to service of Richelieu, which may have helped his younger brother's early career. His marriage to a Luillier could have opened up greater prospects, but their only son died relatively young in 1655, leaving bp of Arras as only surviving male. His widow, Elisabeth Luillier, remarried Etienne Aligre, a future chancellor of France, whose value to his wife's wider family may not have been insignificant.

Born in Paris and baptised in St-Nicolas-du-Chardonnet 28-10-1594. Son of Jean and Catherine de Thélis, married in 1586. Doct of theol from Univ of Bourges. Ordained priest in 1622. Abbot of St-Josse OSB (Amiens) from early to mid-1620s. Elected *ag-gén* in 1630 by Rouen province (under pressure from Richelieu?), served as secretary of AC of 1635, of which he left a substantial diary. He was initially nom to Arras in 1652 after death of J-P Camus, Mazarin's initial nominee (1650). Moreau took profession of faith as royal nominee before the papal nuncio in 1652, but papacy refused to confirm him until indult granted to Louis XIV in 1669.

Nom 1652, renewed 28-4-1656 and 24-4-1668. Provs 3-9-1668. Consec 21-10-1668. Died 8-1-1670.

Sources: ASV, PC 66, fos 1–34. BN, Doss bleus 471, no 12,434. AN, Y 179, fo 214. Tallemant, *Historiettes*, ii, 443.

Moret de Bourchenu, Flodoard-Ennemond. Vence 1714–27 (resign).   This bp was born into a family practically unknown before his grandfather, but they seem to have been among the *taille*-paying inhabitants of Réaumont in Dauphiné. Ennemond, the grandfather, graduated in law from Valence in 1584 and after 20 years as a barrister, he became a *cons* in Grenoble parlt (1604), and died *doyen* of parlt in 1631. Ennobled by Henri IV in 1606, he was made a city councillor 'de robe longue' in 1610. His elder son, bp's father, held same office until 1680s. Both father and grandfather benefited substantially from their marriages which brought *seigneuries* like Bourchenu (grandfather) and very extensive kin relations (esp his father) in Grenoble elite involving families like Servien, Lionne, St-Germain and others. Bp's elder brother, 'le président de Valbonnais' consolidated these gains, becoming *pr prés* of *chambre des comptes* of Grenoble and enjoying a reputation as a scholar and man of letters in a province well-provided with them. Bp's own early career owed much to his father's only brother, Flodoard, also highly cultivated and independently wealthy, owing partly to his collection of church benefices. Provost of St-André collegiate chapter of Grenoble 1653–87, he opened many doors for future bp.

Born Grenoble 3-7-1663 and baptised in parish of St-Hugues and St-Jean 2 days later. Son of Pierre, *cons* in Grenoble parlt from 1632 to 1677, and Philippe Béatrix-Robert de St-Germain, daughter of a fellow *cons*. Not much known about his studies, but he may have begun in Oratorian coll of ND des Graces in Forez (like his elder brother). He resided for a time in St-Magloire seminary while studying in Paris but, following family custom, took doct of theol at Valence, ca 1690, where he probably also took a doct *in utr*. Succeeded his uncle as *prévôt* of chapter of St-André of Grenoble in 1689, when still mere cleric and bachelor of theol, but was probably ordained priest in 1691. Cardinal Le Camus's successor, the Dauphinois Alleman, made him his *official* in May 1707 and vic-gen in Sept 1709. His brother Valbonnais lobbied hard and effectively for his election as dep to 1700 AC, and possibly also for the much delayed but modest episcopal promotion of 1714. Hopes for promotion to a better see were dashed on several occasions after 1717, until Fleury persuaded him to resign outright in 1727 in return for an abbey (Reigny).

Nom 19-5-1714. Provs 19-11-1714. Consec 6-1-1715. Resign 1727. Died 11-1-1744.

Sources: ASV, PC 103, fos 788–800. BN MS, PO 2049, nos 46,717–18; Doss bleus 472, no 42,472; MS Lat 9156, fo 85v. AC Grenoble, GG 61, p 134 (baptism of future bp). AD Isère, 15 G 454 (St-André chapter deliberations, 27-1-1690, 1-12-1690, 4-6-1691); 4 G 324, fo 5r (*official*), fo 153 (vic-gen). Virieu, 'Parlement de Grenoble', 229. Riollet, 'Valbonnais, sa vie, son oeuvre (1651–1730)' 125–291. H-J Martin, *Les Registres du libraire Nicolas*, i, 222–3.

Nesmond, Henri. Montauban 1692–1703, Albi 1703–22, Toulouse 1722–7. 1st cousin of François, bp of Bayeux (1661–1715), younger brother of André, naval commander under Louis XIV.

Born Bordeaux 27-1-1652, 3rd son and 6th child of Henri Nesmond, *prés* in Bordeaux parlt, and Marie de Tarneau. Univ studies in Paris, where MA in Aug 1676. Took 7th place in theol lic of 1682, and became doct 13-7-1682. Priest since same year. Well-regarded preacher, whose reputation was already made before nom to Montauban, having preached Lenten and Advent stations at court. Elected as Fléchier's successor to Académie Française in 1711. Abbé of St-Pierre-de-Chésy OSB (Soissons) in 1682, on resignation in his favour by bp of Bayeux, followed by that of Mas Granier in 1712. St-Simon, who admired his courage in rebuking Louis XIV for damage done by his wars, claims that he proposed him for post of preceptor to Louis XV. Nom abp of Toulouse in 1719 (bulls delayed until 1722) when Beauvau of Toulouse moved to Narbonne.

Nom 15-8-1687. Provs 15-10-1692. Consec 24-5-1693. Nom to Albi 15-8-1703. Provs 12-11-1703. Nom to Toulouse 16-11-1719. Provs 14-1-1722. Died 27-5-1727.

Sources: ASV, PC 86, fos 678–90. Bossuet, *Correspondance*, iii, 1; xii, 440–62. St-Simon, xxi, 339–40; xxvii, 554–5. Béguin, *Princes de Condé*, 431–2. Bergin, *Making*, 675. Villette Mursay, *Mes campagnes*, 376–7; Vergé-Franceschi, *Officiers généraux*, ii, 1249–63.

Nettancourt de Vaubécourt d'Haussonville, François. Montauban 1704–29 (resign).
This bp's family name was Nettancourt. Comtes de Vaubécourt after 1633, they were one of Champagne's oldest noble families. Known primarily for their military activities, members fought in Hungary, Italy and Empire from Henri IV to Louis XIV. Bp's grandfather, Jean (1575–1642) was made a baron of the Empire for his military service against Turks around 1600, and on returning to France became a *maréchal de camp* and, later, gov of Châlons-sur-Marne. Commanding in Champagne in late 1630 when marshal Marillac was arrested in Italy, he prevented Verdun from being used as a base for possible rebellion against Richelieu. The eldest son, bp's father, inherited Haussonville title and name from his great-uncle, and succeeded his father in 1632 as gov of Châlons, later becoming *lt du roi* in the governorships of Metz and Verdun. These *charges* remained in family hands until end of century, when bp's brother rose to rank of lt-gen in royal army.

Born in Châlons-sur-Marne, 24-4-1659, where baptised 20-10-1659. 3rd son of Nicolas (1603–78), comte de Vaubécourt, and Claire-Guillaume de St-Eulieu, his 2nd wife, daughter of *vidame* of Châlons. Studies in Paris, where he took MA in July 1677, 6th place in 1686 theol lic, culminating in doct of theol, Paris, in March 1688. Tonsured in Dec 1678, he was ordained priest in early 1688, when also made royal almoner (successor to Feydeau of Amiens). Also abbot *in comm* of Chassaigne O Cist (Lyon) in 1691 and Ainay OSB (Lyon) in 1693, retaining the latter until death. Dep to 1702 for Albi province.

Nom 15-8-1703. Provs 11-2-1704. Consec 30-3-1704. Resign 14-11-1729. Died in Paris 17-4-1736.

Sources: ASV, PC 97, fos 326–40. BN, MS Fr 20969, fo 84. St-Simon, i, 264, n 5. Grillon, *Papiers de Richelieu*, v, no 627. *L'Intendance de Champagne à la fin du xvii siècle*, 175, 275. Pinard, *Chronologie*, iv, 100–01, 413–15; vi, 51–3. C Daux, *Histoire de l'église de Montauban*, 2 vols (Paris 1882), ii, 4 période, 1–31.

Neufville de Villeroy, François-Paul. Lyon 1714–31. Nephew of Camille, abp of Lyon (1653–93).
Son of François, maréchal-duc de Villeroy, and Marguerite de Cossé. Born 14-11-1677. Studies in Paris, where he took MA in Aug 1694 in full pomp at Harcourt coll. Obtained 1st place in theol lic of 1702, but left doct until 30-10-1714, *after* his nom to Lyon. Priest 2-6-1703. Vic-gen of Poitiers for about 3 years, from Dec 1702. Abbot *in comm* of Fécamp OSB Rouen since 1698. He got Lyon in 1714 just as father became head of the *conseil des finances*, also in 1714 – undeserving according to St-Simon who thought his morals and ignorance were widely known. Father also got post of 'commandant pour le roi of Lyonnais' for him, which his great uncle Camille had held. But he lacked ability of great uncle, and died relatively young, 'sans réputation et ruiné' (St-Simon).

Nom 15-8-1714. Provs 1-10-1714. Consec 30-11-1714. Died 6-2-1731.

Sources: ASV, PC 103, fos 439–51. BN, MS Fr 20969, fo 141. St-Simon, vi, 596–9; vii, 42–3; xxv, 80–1, 358. Bergin, *Making*, 676–7.

Noailles, Louis-Antoine. Cahors 1679–81, Châlons-sur-Marne 1681–95, Paris 1695–1729. Grandnephew of Charles de Noailles, bp of St-Flour and Rodez (1609–48). Born St-Flour 27-5-1651, but baptised at St-Germain-l'Auxerrois, Paris. Early studies possibly in Jesuit coll at Aurillac, but completed them in Paris, first in coll du Plessis, where he was MA in May 1668, then in Sorbonne, taking 1st place in 1676 theol lic, leading to doct on 14-3-1676. Ordained priest 6-6-1675. He became 1st superior of the Nouvelles Catholiques, a position he held until 1679. He may have refused see of Mende in June 1677. At Châlons, he followed in footsteps of Félix Vialart, a reforming and rigorist bp, and his tenure there enhanced his reputation as a model *dévot* bp, without which he would not have been a candidate for Paris in 1695. His long reign there was dominated by his Jansenist and gallican affiliations, and his lack of political skills made him ill-suited for the conflicts which ensued.

Nom 23-2-1679. Provs 8-5-1679. Consec 18-6-1679. Nom to Châlons-sur-Marne 21-6-1680. Provs 17-3-1681. Nom to Paris 19-8-1695. Provs 19-9-1695. Died 4-5-1729.

Sources: ASV, PC 78, fos 129–42. Sévigné, *Correspondance*, v, 185. Levantal, *Ducs et pairs*, 815–23, 904. Bergin, *Making*, 678.

Noailles, Gaston. Châlons-sur-Marne 1696–1720. Younger brother of Louis-Antoine above, born 8-7-1669. Educated mostly in Paris, where he was tutored in theol by Jean-Jacques Boileau (or Beaulaigue), a correspondent of Fénelon and habitué of Noailles-Luynes circle. MA of Paris in July 1685, followed by theol, leading to 1st place in 1694 theol lic, with doct on 31-3-1694. Attended seminary of St-Sulpice for about 7 years during studies, and gained some pastoral experience there. Ordained priest 6-3-1694. Dep to 1693 AC. Abbot *in comm* of Hautefontaine in 1684 (resigned in 1692), and then got Montierender in March 1693. Added *domnerie* of Aubrac along with Châlons, resigned it in 1706 in order to get Hautvilliers instead. St-Simon thought well of him, while recognising his limited 'lumières et savoir', heavily dependent on his brother for advice and guidance. Even more severe than his brother against Fénelon and quietism, he was also firmly anti-*Unigenitus*, not fearing to defend his position.

Nom 24-12-1695. Prvos 2-4-1696. Consec 20-5-1696. Died 17-9-1720.

Sources: ASV, PC 90 fos 178–86. BN, MS Fr 20969, fo 86r; MS Fr 23214–15, 23206–9 (parts of his correspondence). Fénelon, *Correspondance* v, 17–18, n 1. St-Simon, ii, 361; xxxviii, 11. Levesque, 'Liste des élèves', no 1685.

Novion. *See* **Potier.**

Oppède. *See* **Forbin-Maynier.**

Pajot du Plouy, Séraphim. Die 1694–1701. The various Pajot families resident in Paris in mid-17th c did not all have a common origin. The most prominent under Louis XIV were natives of Pont-sur-Seine, who owed their fortune to patronage of Léon Bouthillier de Chavigny, sgr of Pont. But bp's family originated among the bourgeoisie of Beauvais, where its earliest known members were resident during 16th c, and included receivers of town's finances and *élus* in royal tax admin. By 1600 and later, however, several members were to be found in Paris, *officiers* in parlt, *grand conseil, cour des aides* and *cour des monnaies*. André, sgr du Plouy, father of bp, began as a *correcteur* in *chambre des comptes*, becoming *pr prés* of *cour des monnaies* in Feb 1641, where a relative had already been a *prés*. Intermarriage with Parisian robe families like Rebours, Luillier and Chasteau helped to accelerate the process of integration. In bp's generation, parlt office and military service to crown were combined, though at a relatively modest level. But most decisive factor in bp's own career was probably marriage of his aunt, Françoise Marchant, to Louis Boucherat, successor to Michel Le Tellier as chancellor of France.

Born in Paris, 1644. Son of André, *pr prés* in *cour des monnaies*, and Jeanne Marchand. Univ studies in Paris, where he took MA in Sept 1661, but did not begin formal *primum cursus* in theol until 1673, taking bacc in Feb 1674, 31st place in 1678 lic, and doct on 8-5-1682. Priest since 1683. Frequented a Parisian seminary for some time along with La Broue bp of Mirepoix, according to latter. A resident, active bp in a dioc with large Huguenot population, two-thirds allegedly, but tenure too brief to evaluate his record there.

Nom 10-4-1694. Provs 13-9-1694. Consec 14-11-1694. Died 14-11-1701.

Sources: ASV, PC 88, fos 131–9. BN, PO 2184, no 49,345; Doss bleus 507, no 13,147; MS Fr 32991, fo 121v. Boisnard, *Les Phélypeaux*, 177. Trani, 'Conseillers du grand conseil', 196. Chevalier, *Essai historique sur l'église et la ville de Die*, iii, 541–64.

Pas de Feuquières. Philibert-Charles. Agde 1702–26. Natives of county of St-Pol in Artois, the Pas were already substantial military nobles in royal service during 16th c, both as govs in Artois-Picardy region, and as military commanders with close connections to Guise and Humières families. After 1560, the eldest branch, from which bp was descended, broke with Guise and embraced Huguenot cause. Bp's great-grandfather was *premier chambellan* to Henri IV, while the timely conversion to Catholicism in 1610s of his grandfather Manassès (1590–1640), architect of family's fortunes under Louis XIV, enabled him to move up military hierarchy. A relative of Père Joseph, and enjoying Richelieu's support, he commanded French armies after 1635, and also served as ambassador in Empire and Sweden. But his wife, Anne Arnauld, daughter of Isaac Arnauld, an *intendant des finances* and aunt of Antoine and Henri Arnauld, remained firmly Protestant until her death. Isaac, bp's father and eldest of 8 children, initially followed his mother's example: he converted to Catholicism under paternal pressure, and was variously gov of Verdun, lt-gen of Toul, ambassador to Sweden, Germany and Spain, where he died in 1688. His marriage in 1659 to Anne-Louise de Grammont, daughter of Antoine de Grammont-Guiche and Claude de Montmorency-Bouteville, brought family into even higher aristocratic circles. Several of his brothers served with distinction in both army and navy of Louis XIV, while a foothold in the church was established by yet another of them, François, abbé de Feuquières, who was dean of Verdun (d 1691). Bp's father was made a *conseiller d'etat d'épée* while still ambassador in Stockholm.

6th son of Isaac, marquis de Feuquières, and Anne-Louise de Gramont, baptised at St-Eustache, Paris, 24-6-1657. Univ studies in Paris, where MA in Aug 1674, 98th place in the 1682 theol lic. Doctor of theol 31-5-1686, the year he was ordained priest in Paris. Abbot *in comm* of St-Pierre OSB (Chalon-sur-Saône), which he exchanged in 1691 for Cormeilles OSB (Lisieux). Vic-gen of Sens along with Taffoureau, bp of Alet (1699–1708), with whom he had also studied theol. Represented province of Sens, where he enoyed favour of Abp Fortin de la Hoguette, at 1690 and 1701 ACs. Passed over for Angers succession in 1692 and for Alet in 1692, it seems that it was his uncle, comte de Grammont, who persuaded Louis XIV to give him Agde.

Nom 15-4-1702. Provs 31-7-1702. Consec 10-9-1702. Died 25-7-1726.

Sources: ASV, PC 95, fos 9–23. BN, Doss bleus 512. AN, L 727, pièce 1, no 6. *Lettres aux Feuquières*, 5 vols. St-Simon, xx, 248–9. Pinard, *Chronologie*, i, 480–2; iv, 186–7, 381–4; vi, 95, 251–2, 396. Villette-Mursay, *Mes campagnes*, 324. Fortin de la Hoguette, *Lettres*, ii, 829–30. Sedgwick, *Travails of Conscience*, 15–17 (Arnauld connection).

Paulmy. *See* **Voyer**.

Percin de Montgaillard, Pierre-Jean-François St-Pons 1665–1713. One may doubt the legend of an original Norman family, that of Percy, later dukes of Northumberland, settling in England, only to return later to France and settle in Gascony! A less elevated pedigree seems more likely, as the Percin can only be traced back to Bertrand, a native of Lectoure, who became a *notaire et secrétaire du roi* in 1556, an ennobling office which he appears to have used mainly to slip into the local Gascon nobility, a move which following generations consolidated by military careers. Individual members, of whom the famous *ligueur* preacher, the *feuillant* Bernard de Montgaillard, was the first, achieved fame/notoriety over next century or so. Bp's father was a successful soldier, attaining rank of *mestre de camp*, until he was summarily executed for surrendering fortress of Brema in the Milanais, of which he was gov, in 1630s. His posthumous rehabilitation benefited his sons, one of whom became a officer in Mazarin's *mousquetaires*, and the other bp of St-Pons, where his long career and anti-regular, pro-Jansenist *prises de position* made him one of best-known French bps of his day. They were also related to Fénelon and Murviel families, the 2nd of which played the more prominent part in bp's career, before and during the episcopate.

2nd son of Pierre-Paul, and Françoise de Murviel, niece of Anne, bp of Montauban (1600–52), married in 1623. Born at Montgaillard in Lectoure dioc 23-3-1633. Early studies probably in Montauban and Toulouse, but phil and theol at Univ of Paris, where he matriculated in Mar 1654 and was MA in July 1655, taking 59th place in 1660 theol lic, and the doct 12-9-1661. Made a *socius* of Sorbonne ca 1660, he spent 3 years at St-Sulpice seminary, June 1650 to Nov 1653, and took some minor orders while there. Priest since 1660. Abbot of St-Marcel-de-

Réalville O Cist (Cahors), which he resigned in 1678. Dep to AC of 1660 where he took anti-Jansenist position. As a bp, he was widely suspected of Jansenism given his correspondence with Angélique de St-Jean, Arnauld and Quesnel. He defended *Rituel* of Alet 1678, made liturgical innovations, 1691, and was exceptionally irenical in his *Instruction contre le schisme des Calvinistes* (1685). Interminable troubles with Récollets within his dioc on subject of their exemption and moral-sacramental discipline. Intransigent and polemical, he had numerous disputes with fellow bps over many years, and Rome placed some of his books on Index. His final dispute with Fénelon nearly led to him rather than Quesnel being target of papal condemnation in early 1710s. St-Simon regarded him as a saint, whose 'vertus épiscopales, son grand savoir, une constante résidence depuis 40 années, une vie toute apostolique, une patience humble, courageuse, prudente, invincible, avoient singulièrement illustré sous la persécution des jesuites, qui y engagèrent le roy pendant presque tout son épiscopat'.

Nom 30-6-1664. Provs 17-1-1665. Consec 12-7-1665. Died 13-3-1713.

Sources: ASV, PC 62, fos 284–96. AUP, reg 97, fo 26. BN, MS Fr 7652, fo 57. St-Simon, xxiii, 359. Poutet, 'Docteurs', no 332. E Barnavi, *Parti de Dieu*, 87. J. Sahuc, *Un Ami de Port Royal* (Paris 1909). Levesque, 'Liste des élèves', no 147. Bergin, *Making*, 674–5.

Phélypeaux de la Vrillière, Michel. Uzès 1676–9, Bourges 1679–94.   The most consistent and durable ministerial dynasty of the entire *ancien régime* began as bourgeois of Blois in 14th c, when known by their patronymic of Le Picart. Officeholding in *comté* of Blois followed, where marriages with Morvilliers and Hurault families were a distinct advantage to their later rise. Nobility was secured at end of 16th c, by which time they were beginning to make a major breakthrough (initially via the entourage of ministers like Revol and Villeroy) into direct royal service as secs of state, leading to high ministerial office – the finances, chancellorship – under Louis XIV, and sustaining that presence in following century. Along the way, kinship and marriage with large number of ministerial and robe families of Paris (Talon, Beauharnois, Maupeou), also leading to numerous careers in military and naval spheres, as well as development of several branches which did not always work well together (La Vrillière, Pontchartrain, Herbault). The future *contr-gén* and chancellor owed some of his advancement to Le Pelletier, his predecessor as *contr-gén* during the 1680s. Their legendary durability was demonstrated also by their attention to the church – with 3 bps under Louis XIV, though none was from senior Pontchartrain branch, since Chancellor had only one son. This was their first 'foray' into church, at least at episcopal level.

Born Paris, baptised in St-Eustache church 1642. 3rd and youngest son of Louis (1598–1681), sgr de la Vrillière, sec of state, and Marie Particelli, daugher of Mazarin's pre-Fronde finance minister; brother of Châteauneuf, sec of state. Doctor in canon law, probably Paris. Ordained priest 25-3-1675. Known as abbé La Vrillière, he was successively *cons* at Châtelet (1667), then in parlt of Paris (1671). Abbot *in comm* of St-Lo OSA (Coutances), Nieul OSA and Absie-en-Gâtine OSB (both La Rochelle). Able admin of Bourges, but died heavily indebted on account of vast building projects there.

Nom 31-3-1675. Provs 23-3-1676. Consec 7-6-1676. Nom to Bourges 18-6-1677. Provs 10-4-1679. Died 28-4-1694.

Sources: ASV, PC 75, fos 793- 809. St-Simon, vi, 412, n 2. Boisnard, *Les Phélypeaux*, 105. Frostin, 'La Famillle ministérielle des Phélypeaux', 117-39.

Phélypeaux, Jacques-Antoine. Lodève 1692–1732.   The 2nd of 2 sons of Antoine (d 1665), sgr du Verger, a relatively undistinguished *cons* in parlt and prov intendant of Bourbonnais, and Marie de Villebois, born in 1654. Studied phil and theol in Paris, where he took MA in Sept 1681 and bacc in theol in Feb 1682. He only took doct in theol at Montpellier in Feb 1691, when already present in Lodève dioc as vic-gen. Ordained priest Jan 1685. Probably owed much of his early career to his uncle, Abp Phélypeaux of Bourges, who secured his election to 1680 AC and, in 1685, his election as *ag-gén* by Bourges province. Already well endowed with benefices, he became abbot *in comm* of Bourgmoien OSA (Chartres) 1688 on death of 1st cousin Balthazar, resigned it in 1693 (so that it could be part of endowment for new see of Blois), but got St-Pierre-de-Nants OSB (Vabres) and priory of St-Nicolas in Bar-sur-Seine (Troyes), both in 1694, followed by St-Sauveur-de-Lodève OSB (1697), and St-Gilles-de-Nîmes (1721). Ministerial-family connections and Basville's support enabled him to play an important role in Estates of Languedoc. St-Simon's description of him as an epicurian and a skeptic who lived scandalously, fathering numerous bastards, seems borne out by other sources. Rich but indolent, he apparently died without sacraments despite a lengthy illness. His elder brother had no descendants, so this branch disappeared with bp in 1732.

Nom 1-11-1690. Provs 7-7-1692. Consec 24-8-1692. Died 15-4-1732.

Sources: ASV, PC 86, fos 569–92. BN, MS Fr 20969, fo 65r, 95v. AD Hérault, G 1273, 10-2-1691 (doct). St-Simon, vi, 268ff; xii, 130–1. Boisnard, *Les Phélypeaux*, 77–80. Appolis, *Le Jansénisme dans le diocèse de Lodève*, chs 2–3.

Phélypeaux d'Herbaut, Louis-Balthazar. Riez 1713–51.   2nd son of François, sgr d'Herbault, *cons* in Paris parlt, and Anne Loisel, daughter of a *cons* in Paris parlt. Born Aug 1665. Studies in Paris, where MA in Aug 1685, followed by 103rd (and 2nd last) place in 1694 lic and doct in theol, June 1694. Ordained priest 5-6-1694. By 24-12-1697, when nom abbot *in comm* of St-Laurent-de-Thoronet O Cist (Frejus), he was a canon of ND de Paris (1694), and prior *in comm* of St-Georges OSB (Luçon). He was also a *cons-clerc* in Paris parlt. Dep to 1695 AC, he was elected *ag-gén* in 1702, like his cousin of Lodève before him, whose behaviour he did *not* otherwise imitate. His was a relatively long wait for mitre, which only materialised in a little sought after dioc. Able, active, resident bishop, who built big hospital for poor, and also a seminary.

Nom to Riez 15-8-1713. Provs 27-11-1713. Consec 14-12-1713. Died 31-8-1751.

Sources: AN, MC, LXXXII, 123, 27-8-1713 (Riez); ASV, PC 92, fos 298–308 (St-Laurent-de-Thoronet). BN, MS Fr 20969, fo 139. *Gallia Chr Nov*, iv, cols 643–4. Fisquet, *France pontificale*, Digne et Riez, 439–45.

Ploeuc de Timeur, François-Hyacinthe. Quimper 1707–39.   This family's lands were located around Ploeuc-sur-Lié in Quimper, one of few diocs of France where a linguistic issue could complicate, or even determine choice of candidates for the mitre. Traceable to 15th c if not earlier, they were old enough to be connected to other families of substantial noble status, some of which, such as the Coëtlogon, Kerhoent, Le Prestre, Visdelou and du Louet, themselves produced bps under Louis XIII and Louis XIV: in fact, René du Louet, bp of Quimper, was one of the principal signatories of the marriage contract on Ploeuc side when bp's parents married in 1648. Their military traditions, evident during Wars of Religion, were sustained by 2 of bp's brothers who became Knights of Malta and St-Louis, but his father and elder brother seemed content with role of stay-at-home local nobility. It is not implausible that ecclesiastical preferment for bp was obtained, at least indirectly, by an extremely well-placed *alliée*, Louise de Kergolay, duchess of Portsmouth, mistress of Charles II.

Born in château de Landudec, Quimper dioc, 16-4-1661, Hyacinthe was 2nd of 4 sons and 6 daughters of René (1619–85) and Marie Gourcun, married in 1648. Took bacc in canon law, Paris, in March 1695, followed by lic, probably in 1696, after which he returned to Quimper, where he appears not to have obtained any ecclesiastical benefice. Ordained priest 1699. Vic-gen of bp of Tréguier since 1704. As bp, he participated in politics of Breton Estates, and in 1712 was chosen to present its cahier to Louis XIV. His generosity, esp as expressed in his will, caused serious problems for heirs, and the litigation over his estate endured for decades after his death.

Nom 24-12-1706. Provs 11-4-1707. Consec 19-6-1707. Died 18-1-1739.

Sources: ASV, PC 100, fos 187–99. BN, PO 2305, no 52,078; Doss bleus 528, no 13,871. AN, MM 1099, p 17 (bacc in canon law); 272 AP, vols 5–7 (Ploeuc papers). Vindry, *État major, gendarmerie*, 106. Carné, *Chevaliers bretons de St-Michel*, 304–6. Denis de Thézan, *Histoire généalogique de la maison de Ploeuc* (Beauvais 1873).

Polastron, François-Louis. Lectoure 1692–1717. The Polastron were a long-standing noble family from small dioc of Lombez, west of Toulouse, originating possibly in Guyenne, and with several branches, some of them active politically and militarily under Mazarin and Louis XIV, though their military record was much older than that. Bp's own father, having initially served under marshal Brézé and at Brouage under marshal La Ferté, married daughter of a gov of Bastille in 1653 and ended his career as captain of duc de Mazarin's guards. Further military commands followed during Louis XIV's wars, with 3 successive generations boasting general officers in army, and with bp's own half-brother, an army brigadier, distinguishing himself in arms before being killed at Almanza, 1707. They also included Knights of Malta, with one member becoming *grand prieur* of Toulouse, 1653–62. Bp's mother's family, also from Gascony, was of similar stripe, but they seem to have been better established within church, and it was probably their intervention which secured François-Louis a position of canon of Auch *en régale* in 1675.

Born in 1653 Marennes, where father was posted, but lived at Polastron, south-west of Toulouse, in Lombez dioc. Son of Jacques, sgr de Polastron, and 1st wife, Diane Paule de Montlezun. He studied in SJ coll at Auch up to completion of phil, after which he went on to study at Toulouse, Paris and Bourges. Took bacc in theol at Toulouse in May 1675, and doct at Bourges. Canon and archdeacon for many years in Auch cath, where a maternal uncle Jean-Charles de Montlezun had preceded him, and was vic-gen since 1684 of his native Lombez, next door to his future dioc of Lectoure. He obtained abbey of St-Sauveur-de-Blaye OSB (Bordeaux) in Aug 1687, when he was already a priest.

Nom 5-4-1692. Provs 6-10-1692. Consec 9-11-1692. Died 13-10-1717.

Sources: ASV, PC 86, fos 615–22, 640–56. BN, Doss bleus 530, no 13,937; Chérin 159, no 3226; MS Fr 20969, fo 57rv; MS Lat 17026,fo 49. AN, O^1 19, fo 252v (Auch 1675). St-Simon, xiii, 307. Pinard, *Chronologie*, iv, 407–8; v, 203–5; vi, 449–50; viii, 145. Vindry, *État major, gendarmerie*, 277, 421. Rowlands, *Dynastic State and Army*, 320. Bordes, 'Le Jansénisme dans le diocèse de Lectoure', 107–35, esp 112–14.

Poncet de la Rivière, Michel. Sisteron 1667–75, Bourges 1675–7. The Poncet family belonged to Parisian bourgeoisie by late 15th c, beginning a slow upward movement into robe during 16th and early 17th c, via Châtelet and financial courts (*aides, comptes*), emerging from shadows with Pierre (1590–81), a dependent of Chancellor Séguier who became an MR (1642) and *cons d'état*, father of bp of Uzès and uncle of bp of Sisteron/Bourges. The latter bp's father's office brought them noble status in 1596.

Born Paris, 1609, baptised in St-Gervais parish. Son of Mathieu, sgr de Gournay and Brétigny, *auditeur aux Comptes*, Paris, and Antoinette Pollaër, daughter of a fellow *auditeur aux Comptes*. Studied at Univ of Paris, where MA in Nov 1626 and bachelor of theol in Mar 1631, taking 1st place in 1634 theol lic, when he also became doct and *socius* of Sorbonne. Ordained priest ca 1634. Abbot *in comm* of St-Pierre-d'Airvaux OSA (La Rochelle). Also canon of ND de Chartres and provost of Ingre in Chartres, July 1652. He had become dean of Poitiers before attending 1655 AC, of which he was made *promoteur*. Also involved with superiorship of female convents in Paris. King nom him to succeed Ondedei at Fréjus in 1674, but within a few months he was given Bourges instead.

Nom 12-5-1667. Provs 3-8-1667. Consec 27-11-1667. Nom to Bourges 22-11-1674. Provs 17-6-1675. Died 21-2-1677

Sources: ASV, PC 65, fos 601–31. AN, MM 251, fo 170v. BN, MS Fr 7658, fos 31–4. BSG, MS 941, fo 57v. Bluche, *L'Origine*, 354. Poutet, 'Docteurs', no 25. *Gall Chr Nov*, Sisteron, cols

773–4. Merlet, ed, *Dignitaires de l'eglise ND de Chartres*, 243. Espitalier, 'Eveques de Fréjus', 82–7.

Poncet de la Rivière, Michel. Uzès. 1678–1728.   Born Paris, 1638, baptised in SS Gervais et Prothais parish church. Son of Pierre (1590–1681), marquis d'Ably, MR and later dean of *cons d'état*, and Catherine de Lattaignan. Studies at Univ of Paris, where he took MA in July 1660, 78th place in 1670 theol lic, and doct several years later, 21-1-1676, by which time he was also a *socius* of Sorbonne. Ordained priest 30-12-1675 by Péricard of Angoulême, having done his spiritual exercises before ordination in seminary of Missions Etrangères, where he lived for a time. Some experience as preacher before episcopate. Obtained abbey of St-Eloi-Fontaine OSA (Noyon) in 1669.

Nom 18-6-1677. Provs 14-3-1678. Consec 8-5-1678. Died 18-11-1728.

Sources: ASV, PC 77, fos 641–59. BN, MS Fr 7651, fo 224.

Poncet de la Rivière, Michel. Angers 1706–30.   Nephew of bp of Uzès. Son of Mathieu, MR and prov intendant, and Marie Bétault, daughter of a *prés* in *chambre des comptes*. Born 11-7-1671 Paris. Doctor of theol, Bourges, 1695. Priest since 1696. Abbot *in comm* of St-Pierre-de-Vierzon (1689), and simultaneously obtained a canon's stall in Sarlat via *régale*. Thanks to uncle's patronage he became dean of Navacelles (Uzès) and vic-gen of Uzès in 1695, where he worked strongly in effort to convert Protestants. Elected to Académie Française in 1706, the year he became bp of Angers. He was on shortlist of 3 clerics for post of preceptor to Louis XV in 1714. A talented orator, he preached on several major occasions, e.g. the funeral oration for Louis XIV's grandson, Monseigneur, in 1711, and for the Regent in 1723, but St-Simon regarded his oratorical skills as inadequate for occasions in question. Firm and orthodox like his predecessor Le Peletier on doctrinal issues in a dioc for long governed by Henri Arnauld.

Nom 3-4-1706. Provs 7-6-1706. Consec 1-8-1706. Died 2-8-1730.

Sources: ASV, PC 99, fos 11–25. BN, MS Fr 20969, fo 76r. St-Simon, xxi, 344; xli, 316. Lehoreau, *Cérémonial de l'église d'Angers 1692–1721*, esp 52–60.

Potier de Novion, Jacques. Sisteron 1677–82, Evreux 1682–1709.   From the same Parisian parlt family which produced bps of Beauvais under Henri IV and Louis XIII, and which continued to prosper under Louis XIV, when 2 of its branches obtained peerages, with that of Novion rising to highest echelons of Paris parlt with bp of Sisteron's father.

Born Paris, 1642. Son of Nicolas, *pr prés* in Paris parlt and Catherine Gallard, daughter of the notary of Paris parlt. Studied at Univ of Paris, where took MA in Aug 1665, 98th and last place in 1672 theol lic, but waiting until after his nom to Sisteron before taking doct on 2-7-1676. Priest since November 1675, ordained by Bp Vintimille du Luc of Digne. Gets abbey of L'Aumone O Cist (Chartres) in Jan 1668. He was initially given *brevet* to Fréjus in Jan 1680, but was quickly nom to Evreux before he got bulls for Fréjus. An authoritarian, litigious bp at Evreux.

Nom 21-11-1675. Provs 8-2-1677. Consec 28-10-1677. Nom to Evreux 2-5-1681. Provs 16-2-1682. Died 14-10-1709.

Sources: ASV, PC 76, fos 877- 89. BN, MS Fr 7651, fo 189 (*bienfaits du roi*). St-Simon, vi, 599–605. *Gall Chri Nov*, Sisteron, col 774, Fréjus, col 411. Bluche, *L'Origine* 358. Bergin, *Making*, 686–7.

Potier de Gesvres, Léon. Bourges 1694–1729 (resign).   Son of Léon Potier, duc de Gevres and Marie-Françoise du Val de Fontenay. Born 15-8-1656. Studied in Paris, where he was MA in June 1673, and obtained 88th (and last) place in 1680 theol lic, but only took doct 30-9-1694, a few months *after* nom to Bourges (he was not doctor *of* Bourges, as some sources claim!) Priest for about 6 years by 1694, nom abbot *in comm* of Bernay and St-Geraudd'Aurillac in 1688. A protonotary apostolic while very young, he served Innocent XI in Rome during 1680s as a chamberlain, but the affair of diplomatic franchises in Rome dashed his chances of success there and led him to return to France. Nom to Bourges in 1694 surprised some observers, given Louis XIV's habit of only giving archiepiscopal sees to reigning bps. Cardinal in 1719 at request of King of Poland, *commandeur des ordres* in 1724, resigned see in 1729 when he obtained abbey of St-Remy-de-Reims *in comm* as 'compensation'.

Nom 29-5-1694. Provs 30-8-1694. Consec 23-1-1695. Cardinal 29-11-1719. Resigned see, Jan 1729. Died 12-11-1744.

Sources: ASV, PC 88, fos 57–65. St-Simon, ii, 347; vi, 411–12. Bossuet, *Correspondance*, xi, 165. Levantal, *Ducs et pairs*, 609–14, 934–7.

Poudenx, François. Tarbes 1692–1716.   This family was among the most prominent in the Béarn/Landes area where they were based. Related by marriage to similar families – like Abbadie, Gassion, Albret, who included bps under Henri IV, Louis XIII and XIV – the Poudenx presence over several generations in the church across Béarn and neighbouring areas, was impressive and sustained. Bp of Marseille was, it seems, only one to spread his wings to any real extent, and only fleetingly, and this may have something to do with a namesake and nephew of bp of Tarbes who became an influential Sulpician in the last decades of Louis XIV's reign.

Born in Lescar dioc, 1642. 3rd son of Étienne, baron de Poudenx, syndic of nobility of Bearn and *maréchal des camps*, and Gabrielle de Monluc de Castillon. Studied in Paris, under Guillaume de la Brunetière, later bp of Saintes, and Jacques Gaudin, taking 76th place in 1670 theol lic. Ordained priest 28-3-1671. By time of election as dep to 1675 AC for Auch province, where he was elected *promoteur*, he was canon and archpriest of Maslacq in Lescar cath. His predecessor at Tarbes, La Baume de Suze, was consecrated bishop in Oct 1677, but 2 weeks later Louis XIV transferred him to St-Omer, which he had just conquered. Pope refused to accept king's right to nom to St-Omer until 1686, but by then the *regale*-gallican crisis had erupted, so that bulls not delivered until 1692! It seems that La Baume had remained at Tarbes, perhaps even after Louis XIV had nom him to Auch in 1684, but Poudenx was already active there by then.

Nom to Tarbes on 17-1-1678. Provs 24-3-1692. Consec 24-8-1692. Died 24-6-1716.

Sources: ASV, PC86, fos 332–49. BN, PO 2357, no 52,593. Fénelon, *Correspondance*, ix, 30. A de Cauna, *Armorial des Landes*, 4 vols (Bordeaux 1862-9), i, 339–95. Bertrand, 'Hommes d'église de la famille de Poudenx'. Soulet, *Traditions et réformes religieuses*, 306–8.

Poudenx de Castillon, Bernard-François. Marseille 1708–9.   Born in Lescar dioc in ca 1664, 4th son of Bernard, vicomte de Poudenx, and Jeanne de Baffoigne de Castillon, married in 1645. Little information on his studies, but seems to have taken his theol lic in Bordeaux. Ordained priest ca 1692. Canon and archdeacon, then vic-gen of Tarbes for 12 years under his uncle, playing important role in governing dioc. Dep to 1695 AC, elected as *ag-gén* by province of Auch for 1705 AC, he was secretary of 1707 AC. Obtained abbey of Bonnefonds O Cist (Comminges) in April 1707. Cardinal Noailles was probably instrumental in getting Marseille for him, when Vintimille was promoted to Aix. Arriving there on 22-12-1708, he died within a month, a victim of the terrible winter of 1709 – dying of cholera, and not after long illness as *Gallia* asserts.

Nom 10-2-1708. Provs 30-4-1708. Consec 26-8-1708. Died 19-1-1709.

Sources: ASV, PC 101, fos 167–81 (Marseille); PC 100, fos 166-74 (Bonnefonds). St-Simon, xvii, 227. Soulet, *Traditions et réformes religieuses*, 102. Albanès, *Armorial et sigillographie des évêques de Marseille*, 172–3. Bertrand, 'Les hommes d'Eglise de la famille de Poudenx'.

Pradel, Charles. Montpellier 1676–1706.   Bp was not connected to the Pradel family best known under Louis XIII and Louis XIV via François who rose to become a military commander in 1650s and 1660s, but was from the bourgeoisie of Narbonne – like his uncle, patron and predecessor at Montpellier, François Bosquet. Municipal office was a constant feature of their history from 1580s onwards, enhanced by post of *trés de France* at Montpellier and canon of Narbonne in generation of bp's father, who himself became *greffier* of Narbonne *présidial*. Also his involvement with Estates of Languedoc and wider provincial politics beyond Narbonne was probably due to Bosquet's role as a native prov intendant, one of the few, in Languedoc.

Baptised in parish of St-Paul in Narbonne, 1645. Son of Guillaume and Anne Bosquet, sister of bp of Montpellier. Univ studies in Paris, from mid-1660s, briefly resident at St-Sulpice in Feb–May 1664. Took Paris MA Nov 1669, followed by bacc in theol there in 1673, and was apparently about to take lic at moment of his nom to Montpellier, where he was already vic-gen to his ailing uncle, who had made him canon of Montpellier at early age. Eventually took 93rd and last place in 1676 lic, leading immediately to doct on 19-6-1676. Ordained priest in Beziers, 18-3-1673, by Bp Rotundy. Dep to 1670 AC. His coadjutorship was virtual, since his uncle died 4 days before his consec!

Nom 17-9-1675. Provs 27-4-1676. Consec 28-6-1676. Died 17-9-1696.

Sources: ASV, PC 75, fos 442–60; Acta CC 1676, fos 34–6, 9-1-1676. BN, PO 2368, no 53,192; Doss bleus 542, no 14,178. Bossuet, *Correspondance*, ii, 395. Levesque, 'Liste des élèves', no 809. Bergin, *Making*, 580 (Bosquet).

Puget, Henri de. Digne 1708–28.   From the same Toulouse family which produced a bp of Marseille (1644–68). Under Richelieu and Mazarin the Parisian branch, dominated by celebrated financier, Puget de Montauron, outclassed their Toulousain cousins, but latter continued to prosper in Toulouse, where its various branches, as exemplified by bp's own line, held numerous civil and ecclesiastical offices, and also included Knights of Malta.

Born Toulouse, 1655. Son of François, sgr de St-André, a *prés* in Toulouse parlt, and Françoise de Plas. After early studies in Toulouse, where he took MA in March 1673, he continued in Paris (MA in June 1678), where he obtained 73rd place in 1684 theol lic, but did not take doct. Began career as canon of Lombez, also obtaining priory of St-Loup (Viviers) and, in April 1694, the abbey of Simorre OSB (Auch). For about 8 years in all, he was a busy vic-gen to Bp La Garde de Chambonas of Viviers, who was often absent and relied heavily on his vic-gens to admin his dioc. In 1708 he moved into service of abp of Auch, also as vic-gen. Successor at Digne to Parisian Le Tellier, but far more resident and active in dioc.

Nom 7-4-1708. Provs 3-10-1708. Consec 9-3-1710. Died 22-1-1728.

Sources: ASV, PC 101, fos 110–22. BN, Cab d'Hozier 280, no 7603; Nouv d'Hozier 270, no 6183; MS Fr 20969, fo 90r. BIUT, MS 10, fo 261r. Navelle, *Familles toulousaines*, viii, 297–304. Fisquet, *France pontificale*, Digne et Riez, 120–1. Joret, 'Basville et l'épiscopat', 461.

Quiqueran de Beaujeu, Honoré. Castres 1705–36.   One of the most prominent of Provençal noble families thanks to its extensive alliances and occupations – sword, robe, church, Knights of Malta. They obtained seigneurie of Beaujeu (and with it noble status) in 1439. Their base was Arles, whose nobility was old and uninvolved in commerce, and where family members were often *premiers consuls*. Also allied to certain Aix robe families, the Quiqueran developed several branches, and were to be found among the different Provence political factions under Richelieu and Mazarin, while the Grillé family held municipal offices in Arles since 15th c.

Born Arles 23-6-1655, son of Honoré, baron of Beaujeu, and Hélène de Grillé d'Estoublon. Studied at Oratorian coll, Arles and entered the Oratory in 1672, but seems to have left it 15 years later. Doctor of theol, Bourges, in 1684. Prof of theol at Oratorian colls of Arles, where Massillon was a pupil, and then at Saumur. A noted preacher who performed at court, he was sent on crown-sponsored missions to Huguenots of Poitou and Aunis in mid-1685, subsequently attracting interest of Fléchier who made him canon of Nîmes from outset of his episcopate there, and later his vic-gen. His missionary experience was put to test in his dealing with Huguenots and converts in Nîmes dioc during Camisards uprising in 1703–4, where his stance impressed circles round king, and possibly Louis XIV himself, who placed him on *feuille des bénéfices*. Dep to ACs of 1693 and 1700. He may initially have been nom to Oloron, only for Castres to fall vacant before provs could be sought for Oloron. Founded Castres seminary in 1710, he preached funeral sermon for Louis XIV at St-Denis. Pro-Jansenist and gallican, he was prominent in opposing introduction into French liturgy of the office of Pope Gregory VII. Forbin-Janson, abp of Arles, refused him last sacraments, but he received them from member of his entourage.

Nom 11-4-1705. Provs 7-9-1705. Consec 25-10-1705. Died 26-6-1736.

Sources: ASV, PC 98, fos 197–211. BN, PO 2418, no 54,256; Doss bleus 52, no 14,506. AN, L 729, pièce 1, Castres, no 70. Vindry, *État major, gendarmerie*, 390. Sauzet, *Contre-Réforme*, 435. Lacger, *Etats administratifs*, 334. Blanc, 'Origines', 459–62. Moréri, *Grand Dictionnaire*, viii, 702–3. *Encyclopédie des Bouches du Rhône*, iv, pt ii, 396–9. Renacle, *Ultramontains et gallicans au xviii² siecle: Quiqueran et Forbin*.

Ratabon, Martin de. Ypres 1693-1713, Viviers 1713–23 (resign). The history of this family remains obscure before the career of bp's father, although his grandparents were still residents in 1640s of Severac 30 km north of Millau. Their son Antoine, bp's father, moved initially to Montpellier, where he was *trés-gén de France* (1641–72), and then to Paris, where he was simultaneously *intendant* of both *gabelles* of Languedoc and of *batiments, tapisseries et manu-factures de France*. Key to his Parisian prominence was, it seems, patronage of Sublet des Noyers, Louis XIII's secr of state for war and *surintendant des bâtiments*, who used him as his principal *commis*. After Sublet's disgrace in 1643, Ratabon succeeded in retaining his post, and even taking over as *surintendant des bâtiments* for duration of Mazarin government, being bought out by Louis XIV who wished to give post to Colbert in 1664. The fact that Anne of Austria, Mazarin and senior court figures signed his marriage contract shows he had secured powerful protectors. But throughout these years, his main activities seem to have been financial, as his involvement with *gabelles* shows. During Fronde, he even represented the *bureau des finances* of Montpellier in assemblies of *trés de France* in Paris. Apart from the bp, his offspring included an elder son, Louis, godson of Louis XIV and Anne of Austria, who served as French repre-sentative at Geneva and Liège in 1667, and a daughter, who married Louis de Verjus, comte de Crécy, another career diplomat and brother of bp of Grasse François Verjus (1692–1710).

Born Paris 1654. Son of Antoine and Marie Sanguin, from one of best connected of all Parisian families and which included 2 bps of Senlis (1622–1701). All of his studies were in Paris: MA in Aug 1671, leading to theol at coll of Navarre where took 5th place in 1678 theol lic, but delayed doct until 4-5-1684. Deacon before 1677, he was ordained priest by bp of Tulle at Easter 1682, when he also attended the famous assembly of that year. Abbot *in comm* of Barbeau O Cist (Sens), April 1688. His first clerical patron may have been Abp Michel Phe-lypeaux of Bourges, son of former sec of state. Dep to 1685 AC. Of decisive importance was his nom as vic-gen to francophile Cardinal Fürstenberg, bp of Strasbourg, in 1684, which was probably engineered by Louvois. Episcopal office beckoned but Jesuits failed to obtain Toul for him in 1689, and after his experiences at Strasbourg, he was doubtless judged suitable to take on Ypres after French conquest. Despite hostile portrait in St-Simon (whose views were prob-ably shared by Fénelon), he appears to have been an accomplished admin and a charitable bp in hard times, both in Ypres and Viviers. Resign Ypres in early 1713, knowing it would no longer remain French, and received Viviers instead. When he resigned Viviers in 1723, he obtained abbeys of Mortemer and St-Barthelemy of Noyon as compensation.

Nom 28-5-1689. Provs 12-10-1693. Consec 6-12-1693. Nom to Viviers 22-4-1713. Provs 18-9-1713. Resign 20-2-1723. Died 8-6-1728.

Sources: ASV, PC 87, fos 367–81. BN, PO 2437, no 54,790; Doss bleus 557, no 14,670; Cab d'Hoz 285, no 7753; MS Fr 20969, fos 21r, 54r, 66v; MS Fr 23498, fo 189r (*Nouvelles*

Ecclésiastiques). St-Simon, xxiii, 356–7. Poutet, 'Docteurs', 324. Châtellier, *Tradition chretienne*, 218ff. Charmeil, 136, 249. *Mémoriaux du conseil de 1661*, i, 50–1. *Biographie Nationale Belge*, xvii, cols 763–70. *Recueil des instructions aux ambassadeurs et ministres de France*, xviii (Liège), 143–56. Gatz, *Bischöfe*, 361–1.

Revol, Joseph. Oloron 1705–35 (resign). From the same family as Louis, Henri IV's sec of state, and Antoine, bp of Dol (1603–29). Despite the early, if brief, taste of ministerial office, the family remained provincial rather than Parisian, though activities of successive generations are hard to trace during 17th c. Bp's father's career was typical of such a pattern, and bp himself seemed set to follow it after completing his studies in Paris. Some family members served in parlt of Metz and moved into that of Paris in 18th c, but not clear how they were related to Dauphiné branch to which bp belonged.

Born in dioc of Belley, ca 1663. Son of Pierre, vicomte de Revol, *procureur du roi* in the *cour des aides* of Dauphiné, and Françoise Charlotte de St-Chamand. By his own account, he spent 3 years at St-Magloire seminary, during which he studied at Univ of Paris, where he was an MA in Aug 1686, taking bacc of theol there, but doct at Bourges. He was later made an *agregatus* of the Sapienza in Rome, apparently soon after finishing studies in France. Ordained priest in 1688. *Official* and vic-gen in Belley, and then at Poitiers under Bp La Poype de Vertrieu, with responsibility for ca 150 parishes situated in Angoulême side of dioc, and for all female convents under direct episcopal jurisdiction, reporting directly to bp himself. He also acquired facility and experience as preacher in Poitiers. Efforts were made to obtain Belley, his native dioc, for him in 1705, but his experience of dealing with a large Protestant population may have decided Louis XIV to give him Oloron in Béarn instead, which fell unexpectedly vacant with death of Antoine de Magny, who died only 3 months after receiving papal bulls but before taking possession of the see. A highly able and active, resident bp at Oloron, Revol resigned in 1735 when he was succeeded by his maternal nephew, Chastellane de Montillet (1735–41) who, on becoming abp of Auch in 1741, was succeeded by François de Revol (1741–83) – an impressive record of episcopal nepotism over nearly 80 years!

Nom 11-4-1705. Provs 7-9-1705. Consec 8-11-1705. Resign 26-6-1735. Died 21-3-1739.

Sources: ASV, PC 98, fos 494–506. BN, PO 2468, no 55,528; Doss bleus 562, no 14,874. AN, L 740, pièce 1, Oloron, no 1. Dubarat, *Notices historiques sur les évêques de l'ancien diocèse d'Oloron 506-1792*, 46–51. Michel, *Biographie du parlement de Metz*, 450. Bergin, *Making*, 690.

Rezay. *See* **Bénard.**

Rochebonne. *See* **Châteauneuf.**

Roger, Cosme. Feuillant. Lombez 1672–1710. Identifying the origins, status and connections of this family is difficult, as they seem unrelated to the well-known Roger family of jewellers (and financiers) in service of Marie de' Medici during 1620s. They may have been natives of Limoges, but possibly of Vendômois. It was probably bp's grandfather who moved to Paris, where one son became a sec in employ of Catherine de' Medici. Bp's father was for several decades an *avocat* in parlt, but also involved in running affairs of de Thou family before moving into service of Gaston d'Orléans as his *proc-gén* by late 1620s – not a comfortable position, as he was to discover, when his master was in exile or attacking the Richelieu ministry after 1630! He retired, it seems, by the late 1630s, and may have left Paris altogether, where his 2nd son remained as a modest *commissaire des guerres* by 1641.

Elder son of Michel and Isabelle Trouvé, daughter of a Parisian family, he was baptised at St-Eustache, date unknown, but around 1615. Entered reformed Cistercian congregation of the Feuillants in Paris, 1632, he became a professed monk, under name of Cosme de St-Michel, at St-Bernard-de-Blérancourt (Soissons), and was also ordained priest at Soissons, 20-2-1641. Took no univ degrees because of Feuillants' renunciation of degrees. Later elected assistant and then sup-gen of the Feuillants, he preached in Paris in 1659 and 1660 with considerable success, and then before king and court, beginning in 1662 and at various times during next decade, with funeral sermons for Henri de Condé, Anne of Austria and Turenne among others along the way. He was confessor to Mme de Mongtlas for a time in mid-1660s, and a friend and correspondent of exiled Bussy-Rabutin. His oratorical talents ensured that he was considered as a candidate for translation from Lombez to diocs with Huguenot populations in the 1680s – but he refused the Pamiers succession 3 times in 1680–1, and that of Montauban in 1687! He remained within his dioc, not even attending provincial assemblies of Auch province for elections to ACs from the 1680s onwards.

Nom 5-1-1671. Provs 14-12-1671. Consec 31-1-1672. Died 20-12-1710.

Sources: ASV, PC 70, fos 537–63. BN, PO 2526, Roger dossiers; Doss bleus 576, no 15,170. AN, MC, XXXIV, 16, 18-2-1608; XXXIV, 21, 23-9-1613; Y 181, fo 191, 26-3-1641 (family docs). Grillon, *Papiers de Richelieu*, vi, nos 184, 207. Bussy-Rabutin, *Correspondance*, i, 3–4, 76–8, 79–80, 237–40, 245–8, 358. Rancé, *Correspondance*, i, 359.

Rogier du Crévy, Pierre. Le Mans 1712–23.   Unrelated to similarly named families from Poitou, Provence or Paris, this Breton family, like many others of the province, could trace their roots and their nobility to a more distant non-officeholding past, having participated in the *montres* and *réformations* of nobility of diocs of St-Malo and Rennes during 15th and early 16th c. Parlt office came much later, during the Wars of Religion, when a father (who had previously been *sénéchal* of Ploermel) and son held the post of *proc-gén* of Rennes parlt between 1581 and 1603, at which point the son, François, (great-grandfather of bp?) became a *prés à mortier*, an office he duly passed to *his* son in 1620s. 3 further members of the family, which had by then developed 3 branches, became *cons* in parlt during 1st half of 17th c, and intermarried with similar families, one such marriage making bp of Le Mans a grandnephew of Descartes! The last of them looked set for even higher office when he married only daughter of René de Bourgneuf, *pr prés* of parlt, but he turned his back on opportunities this prestigious alliance offered to become provost and master of ceremonies of royal Order of St-Esprit in 1657, dying in 1678 with massive debts and no male heir. By then the earlier promise of the Rogier family had faded significantly. The senior Villeneuve branch died out in later 17th c, while junior branch of Crévy, to which bp belonged, followed suit in 18th c.

Born ca 1660 Rennes, 2nd son of François, sgr de Crévy, *cons* in Rennes parlt, and Renée Foucault, daughter of a *maître* in *chambre des comptes* at Nantes, married in 1650. Seems to have entered Lazarists while young, but to have left under family pressure. Further studies at Univ of Paris, where MA in August 1673, but did not formally begin theol studies until 1679, taking bacc in March 1680 and 12th place in 1684 theol lic, followed by doct on 3-9-1685, the year in which he was probably ordained priest. Already canon of Rennes, he became grand archdeacon there in Jan 1692, resigning it in 1704 in order to become *chefcier* of Nantes cath, where he was later made vic-gen. At Rennes he had also been superior of the seminary run by St-Sulpice. Dep to 1710 AC for Tours province. Not 1st choice for Le Mans, which he got when abbé de Vassé, aged nearly 80 years, turned down king's nom. His episcopate was dominated by Jansenist question, with local disputes arising from his own indecisiveness.

Nom 8-4-1712. Provs 11-7-1712. Consec 21-8-1712. Died 2-8-1723.

Sources: AN, MC, LXXXII, 118, 13-8-1710. BN, PO 2528, no 56591; Doss bleus 576, no 15186. Anselme, *Histoire*, ix pt i, 654–6. Saulnier, *Parlement de Bretagne*, ii, 767–70 (and 'Additions', 24–6). Sourches, xiii, 353. Piolin, *L'Église du Mans*, vi, 425–54.

Roquette, Gabriel. Autun 1666–1702 (resign).   Bp's family was *not* related to well-known Languedoc military and legal family of same name based in Toulouse since mid-15th. Bp's grandfather appears to have been a modest *procureur du roi* at Villeneuve in Rouergue, but his father, also a lawyer by training, moved to Toulouse where he was a *capitoul* (guaranteeing ennoblement) in 1620. His marriage a few years previously brought him into a much better placed milieu, highly *dévot*, whose best-known member was his own sister-in-law, Marguerite de Sénaux, a Dominican nun in Paris and a well-respected friend of Anne of Austria. These connections probably helped bp's father's own career locally, since by 1640s he was involved in royal finances in Languedoc – but, above all, his son when he moved to Paris in same decade.

Son of François and Anne-Marie de Sénaux, married in 1614, born in Toulouse ca 1624. Doct of theol of Bourges, ca 1661. Priest since 1662. Well before then, probably through his aunt, Marguerite de Sénaux, he had been introduced to Anne of Austria and begun to move in high court circles. Attached initially to Brienne family, then to Condé interests by 1650 when he helped to organise support for rebellion against Mazarin over the imprisonment of princes. Was subsequently employed by prince of Conti as vic-gen for Cluny and St-Denis, as well as Languedoc benefices, presiding his council on these matters. Conti-Condé patronage generally was vital to his career, and was instrumental in obtaining abbey of Grand-Selve in 1661 O Cist (Toulouse) (Mazarin was previous abbot), but also priories of Charlieu O Cluny (Mâcon) and St-Denis-des-Vaux (Chalon-sur-Saône), and reinforced by fact that see of Autun gave him major role in Estates of Burgundy, where Condés were govs! He also won recognition as a preacher from mid-1640s onwards, and continued preaching as a bp – e.g. funeral sermon for princesse de Conti in 1672. His consec attracted a large attendance by the great princely-aristocratic families of France. *Remuant* and ostentatious in search for patrons (e.g. Maintenon, St-Sulpice, Jesuits), often regarded as a buffoon and a prototype of Tartuffe, he was an able and effective reforming bp of Autun (witness the impressive series of pastoral visitations), where he built a magnificent seminary, with royal assistance, and managed by St-Sulpice after 1680. Also had a wide circle of friends and admirers, inc Cardinal Le Camus, Mme de Sévigné, Bussy-Rabutin and others. He wanted the succession to Lyon on Villeroy's death in 1693, and Cardinal Le Camus supported him, but St-Georges, previously nom to Tours, was better placed, even though still unconfirmed by Rome for Tours. He resigned in 1702 in order to ensure succession at Autun of nephew and vic-gen Bertrand de Sénaux, whom Louis XIV had just nom to Saintes, while another ambitious nephew and vic-gen, Henri Emmanuel de Roquette, had to be satisfied with a place in Académie Française.

Nom 1-5-1666. Provs 11-10-1666. Consec 10-4-1667. Resign 22-7-1702. Died 22-2-1707.

Sources: ASV, PC 64, 212–28 (Autun); PC 63, fos 495–509 (Grand-Selve). BN, Chérin 178, no 3556; MS Lat 17022 (Autun). St-Simon, vi, 131–4; xiv, 293–5, 473. Bossuet, *Correspondance*, i, 268, n 3. Fénelon, *Correspondance*, ii, 291. Béguin, *Princes de Condé*, 436. Villain, *La France Moderne*, Haute-Garonne et Ariège, 459–73. *Lettres du cardinal Le Camus* (ed Ingold), 566. Schmitt, *Organisation ecclésiastique*, 8.

Rotundis de Biscarras, Jean-Armand. Lodève 1669–72, Béziers 1672–1702.   Because bp was last suriving member of his generation, relatively little is known about his family's history. The name suggests Italian origins, and they claimed such antecedents, but there is no clear evidence either way. Their 17th c roots lay in Guyenne, where they owned relatively minor seigneuries like Biscarras and Cahusac. Military activities seem beyond dispute, since bp's uncle and father both served as relatively senior officers in royal army by 1620s. His father was dep-gov of Verdun under ill-fated marshal Louis de Marillac, to whom he was closely attached. On and after the Day of the Dupes (1630), he seems to have ignored injunctions from Louis XIII and even Marillac himself to allow loyal army units to enter Verdun; he joined Marie de' Medici in exile in 1631 and participated in 1632 revolt in Languedoc! Possibly because his brother was a Richelieu loyalist, he escaped punishment, and when war began in 1635 he was allowed to return to service, replacing his brother, killed that year, in Richelieu's own regiment. He served with distinction until killed in action, in 1641, becoming successively a *maréchal de camp*, gov of Charleville and Mont-Olimpe. His rehabilitation was epitomised by Richelieu becoming godfather to future bp (as his Christian names demonstrate), while his other son's names, Louis-Jules, suggest that a Mazarin connection also developed. When latter killed in Flanders in 1667, the bp, a priest for 3 years, was only survivor.

Son of Jacques, sgr de Biscarras, and Nicole Françoise Gleisenove (d before 1648). Born in 1636, his univ studies were in Paris, where he was MA in June 1658, and took bacc in theol in May 1659, 76th place in 1664 lic, followed by doct on 31-8-1665. Priest since 27-1-1664, when ordained by Abp of Paris in St-Honoré church. Dep to 1665 AC, when he was also abbot *in comm* of ND de Cendras OSB (Nîmes). Initially nom to Digne in April 1668 on transfer of future Cardinal Janson to Marseille, but before taking possession, he received nom to Lodève. The move to Béziers was due to his friendship with new royal confessor, Ferrier. A talented preacher, he was a champion of Vincent de Paul's Lazarists and Sisters of Mercy in his diocs.

Nom to Lodève 15-4-1669. Provs 5-8-1669. Consec 20-10-1669. Nom to Beziers 5-1-1671. Provs 22-2-1672. Died 15-2-1702.

Sources: ASV, PC 68, fos 419–49 (Lodève); PC 71, fos 136–58 (Béziers). BN, PO 2553, no 57,065; MS Fr 22384, fo 107v; MS Lat 15440, p 221; MS Lat 16573, p 12. Pinard, *Chronologie*, vi, 126–7. Poutet, 'Docteurs', 289, no 432. Grillon, *Papiers de Richelieu*, v, no 632. Fisquet, *France pontificale*, Digne et Riez, 113–16.

Rousseau de la Parisière, Jean-César. Nîmes 1710–36.   Natives of Poitiers, the Rousseau family acquired minor local seigneuries during 16th c, and were exempted from *taille* in 1584, but it was tenure of mayoralty of Poitiers (an ennobling office) in 1595 which best indicates their real status at this point. They retained their urban ties in subsequent generations, and successive members were *prés* and *trés de France* at the Poitiers *bureau des finances* from the 1580s, if not earlier, until at least the Fronde, while others served in royal armies; bp's grandfather became captain of duc de Roannez's guards in 1653. Mingling with turbulent Poitevin nobility, they were notorious for their violent behaviour, not least towards each other. They also got a foothold in local church, with successive members becoming 'regular' abbots of Montierneuf OSB in Poitiers under Henri IV and Louis XIII. One possible reason why they were able to secure a bishopric 2 generations later was their relationship to another Poitevin family, the d'Aubigné, which in turn was connected to Mme de Maintenon, while bp himself may have been assisted by Père Brillac, a Jesuit from Poitou (who may also have been a relative), who presented him to père Tellier, Louis XIV's last confessor.

Born Poitiers 3-5-1667, son of César, sgr de la Parisière, and Marie Reveau de Brétigny, from a well-known Poitiers family, married in 1666. After hum and phil at SJ coll in Poitiers, he studied theol in Paris, during which he spent some time at St-Sulpice. Bachelor of theol in Paris, he took doct at Bourges, after which he returned to Paris, residing at St-Magloire seminary (where Revol of Oloron was a contemporary) and engaging in some preaching activity. Ordained priest 22-9-1703. He obtained priory of Ste Catherine of Bressuire, served as dep of Bordeaux province at 1705 AC. He preached before king, at Whit 1706, and was also vic-gen to fellow Poitevin, bp Aubigné of Laon. He was a well-recommended, orthodox candidate for a mitre just as Jansenist crisis was looming. St-Simon portrayed him as the polar opposite of his predecessor Fléchier ('un homme de la condition la plus obscure'), litigious and an intriguer, manipulated by the royal confessor, Tellier. But the historian of Nîmes, Ménard, who knew him personally, portrayed him otherwise, as a resident and vigilant bp of irreproachable behaviour.

Nom 11-7-1710. Provs 1-12-1710. Consec 8-2-1711. Died 15-11-1736.

Sources: AN, MC, LXXXII 107, 29-9-1710. BN, Doss bleus 586, no 15,401; Cab d'Hozier 300, no 8209. St-Simon, xx, 80–1; xxvi, 90, 383; xxxii, 220–1. Fénelon, *Correspondance*, xv, 91–2, n 1. Ménard, *Histoire civile, ecclésiastique et littéraire de Nimes*, vi, 397–8. 'Maintenues de noblesse . . . de la généralité de Poitiers 1714–1718', *Archives Historiques du Poitou*, 15 (1885), 168; 23 (1893), 219–21. Mesnard, *Pascal et les Roannez*, i, 344–52; ii, 1003.

Rousset. *See* **Des Alries.**

Ruthie. *See* **Charitte.**

Sabatier, Pierre. Amiens 1707–33.   The Sabatier family originated in Istres, settled in Arles in late 15th c, where they were active in commerce, notarial practice, etc until entering municipal office there in 1570s. Ennobled by letters in 1571, their nobility was upheld in 1667 _recherches de noblesse_ and later – facilitated no doubt by their continuing presence in Arles _consulat_. The bp, however, was descended from an offshoot of the family settled at Valréas, in the Comtat Venaissin, who seem to have remained involved in pursuits well short of anything 'ennobling'. His mother's family, Guyon, was a full-blown dynasty of Avignon jurists, magistrates and univ teachers, with a large number of law graduates in each generation which made them a prominent force in Avignon law fac, while one or 2 members had managed to become canons of Avignon cath. Louis-Henri Guyon, bp's maternal uncle, was dean of the Auditors of the Avignon Rota by 1680s. It was probably thanks to the Guyon family's extensive local connections that Sabatier was able to envisage better things beyond Avignon.

Born 14-11-1654 in Valréas (Vaison dioc). Son of Pierre Sabatier and Jeanne Guyon. His initial education was in SJ coll at Avignon, but he moved to Paris in 1673, where he completed his studies, beginning with MA in May 1678, taking 23rd place in 1684 theol lic, and finishing with doct on 27-9-1685. His difficulties in defending the Four Articles of 1682, given his birthplace was Papal territory, caused him some anxiety and even the papal nuncio corresponded with Rome about them! A subdeacon by 1678, he was ordained a priest in 1684. He attended seminary of St-Sulpice from Nov 1673 onwards, joining the Compagnie of St-Sulpice, where he was well regarded by Tronson and Leschassier. He was successively superior of Sulpician seminaries in Limoges (to 1695, where simultaneously vic-gen of dioc for 10 years), after 1695 in Autun (where also vic-gen) and finally at Viviers. Fénelon wanted him in similar role at Cambrai in 1695, but failed to persuade him to leave Autun, though his nom as bp of Amiens may have been some compensation. His close ties with Bp Noailles of Châlons-sur-Marne, brother of Abp of Paris, may also have helped secure the mitre for him. St-Simon regarded him as a 'barbe sale' of St-Sulpice but especially as a _créature_ of P Tellier, even before latter became the king's confessor, and an inadequate successor at Amiens of Feydeau de Brou. Pro-_Unigenitus_, it was he who received Tellier at Amiens after his disgrace following Louis XIV's death.

Nom 15-8-1706. Provs 11-4-1707. Consec 15-5-1707. Died 20-1-1733.

Sources: ASV, PC 100, fos 26–38. BN, MS Lat 17021, fo 162. AN, L 727, Amiens, nos 38-9. Fénelon, _Correspondance_, v, 35, n 2. St-Simon, xiii, 419; xxix, 299, n 4. Blanc, 'Origines', 511–12. Ceyssens, _Autour de la bulle_, 395–6.

Sabran, César de. Glandèves 1702–20.   Sabran was one of oldest and most distinguished of Provençal noble families, tracing its origins to at least 13th c, when they were already powerful in Forcalquier area. Several branches developed, ramified, intermarried with other families (Aube, Arbaud and others) thereafter. But it appears that they declined in significance during 17th c, as is evident from rather limited _états de service_ and marriages – which might also help explain their limited success when it came to episcopal office.

César was 2nd son of Charles, sgr d'Aiguines, and Marguerite de Monier-Cheateaudeuil, born in Romolis, Riez dioc, 1642. Nothing known about his studies, except that he took 2 docts, _in utr_ and theol. Priest for many years before episcopate. Canon of Riez from relatively early age, precentor from June 1662 onwards. Louis XIV used _régale_ to reward him with a _chapellenie_ in St-Mane of Aix in 1693, though he remained essentially at Riez, where he served as vic-gen under 2 successive bps. A very 'local' career in every way.

Nom 3-6-1702. Provs 25-9-1702. Consec 30-11-1702. Died 19-6-1720.

Sources: ASV, PC 95, fos 183–95. BN, PO 2601, no 57,870. AN, L 730, pièce 1, no 31. BM Aix, MS 257, p 255. AD Bouches-du-Rhône, 1 G 1271, fos 252–3v, 26-6-1662; 1 G 1275, fo 221r–v, 29-4-1696. _Encyclopédie des Bouches du Rhône_, iv, pt ii, 436–7.

St-Aulaire. _See_ **Beaupoil.**

St-Esteven (Estève, Esteben), Gabriel. Couserans 1680–1707. With claims to be descended from Spanish family of Pacheco, sgrs of St-Esteben in 14th c, unravelling the history of this family is problematic, as Hozier and others admitted under Louis XIV and Louis XV. Their presence is well attested among minor nobility of Béarn-Navarre from 16th c, while bp's own father was politically active in Estates of Béarn in 1640s and 1650s. From an ecclesiastical perspective, kinship ties with 2 successive bps of Bayonne were equally important: Bertrand Deschaux, bp of Bayonne under Henri IV and abp of Tours under Louis XIII, was son of Catherine de St-Esteven, while marriage in 1646 of an elder brother of the future bp to Marie d'Olce, sister of Jean, bp of Bayonne from 1643 to 1681 (and a nephew of Bp Deschaux!), was probably a key moment: although brief, the marriage strengthened existing ties with the d'Olce and Deschaux families, and provided the future bp with his earliest ecclesiastical preferment. These connections may also have helped bp's generation more widely, with one of his brothers becoming a well-regarded army brigadier who served in king's guards regiment in 1680s and was made gov of Brouage in 1687; the same military activities were repeated in next generation.

Born in Bayonne dioc, 1645. Youngest son of Jean, sgr de St-Esteven, and Marie (or Aymée) Darmandaris. After early studies in SJ coll at Pau and which included some theol, he completed his phil in Paris with MA in Dec 1668, and took bachelor's degree in theol there in May–June 1669, but did not proceed any further. He was already a priest on entry to St-Sulpice seminary on 15-11-1666, which he left in July 1667. Nominally curé of St-Etienne-en-Auberoue (Bayonne) in 1665, he was later abbot of Plaimpied OSA (Bourges) and Combelongue O Prem (Couserans). Attended 1682 AC, where he signed the Four Articles, but he seems to have played no further part in ecclesiastical politics.

Nom 24-2-1680. Provs 15-7-1680. Consec 10-8-1680. Died 24-12-1707.

Sources: ASV, PC 79, fos 141–52. PO 2749, dossier 61,441; Doss bleus 256, no 6562; Chérin 183, no 3650; MS Fr 20969, fo 33r. AN, O¹ 19, fo 97; 21, fo 22v; 23, fo 240; 27, fo 201; 45, fo 78v. Dufau de Maluquer, *Armorial de Béarn*, i, 155. Bergin, *Making*, 606, 678–9 (Deschaux, d'Olce).

St-Georges, Claude de. Lyon 1693–1714. The St-Georges family history straddled a number of *pays* and provinces, though as a relatively common name, it is not easy to decide whether it proliferated widely or whether the different families are simply unrelated to each other. Abp of Lyon was son of a family with branches based in Mâconnais ('l'une des meilleures de la province') and neighbouring Bourbonnais, which may be their place of origin. They 'entered' Estates of Burgundy in 1653, but their nobility was much older than that, as the *preuves de noblesse* required for entry to St-Jean chapter in Lyon, where several generations were represented, make clear, and as intermarriage with prominent families like Aubusson, Rochechouart and Mortemer, confirms.

Born St-Romain d'Urfé 15-4-1632, son of Claude and Marie de Crémeaux, daughter of a family also well established in St-Jean, Lyon. MA in Paris in July 1655, and immediately began theol studies there, taking 62nd (and last) place in 1660 lic, but was only 'admitted' as new doctor of theol 29-8-1673. Tonsured at Mâcon in 1648, he succeeded at second attempt in obtaining canonicate in St-Jean, Lyon, in 1650. Ordained subdeacon in May 1651, priest on 28-3-1671. He was *official primatial* in Lyon, Nov 1670, having been rector of *aumône générale* in 1656 and 1658. Dep to 1682 assembly, where he was prominent member of the *régale* commission. Initial nom to Mâcon in 1682 fell through when Bp Cassagnet of Mâcon decided to remain there, enabling Louis XIV to nom St-Georges to Clermont in his place, in July 1682, followed by nom to Tours in 1687. By time granting of provs resumed in 1692–3, he was on verge of his 3rd episcopal nom, to Lyon. An 'ami intime' of La Chaize, he was strongly and consistently gallican, disapproving of the later Louis XIV's recourse to Rome to deal with religious problems in France.

Nom to Clermont 1-11-1682. Nom to Tours, 12-2-1688. Nom to Lyon, 8-9-1693. Provs 26-10-1693. Consec 22-11-1693. Died 8-6-1714.

Sources: ASV, PC 87, fos 414–24. BN, Chérin 183, no 3665; MS Fr 32703, p 162 (*preuves*, St-Jean). AN, L 736, pièce 1, Lyon. Beyssac, *Chanoines de Lyon*, 208. *Intendance de Bourgogne*, 434.

St-Mauris, Alexandre Chevriers de. Saintes 1702–10.   Not to be confused with the La Croix de Chevrières family of parlt from Dauphiné which produced bps of Grenoble in early 17ᵗʰ c, the Chevriers originated in Dole and Bugey, but moved into Mâconnais in later Middle Ages where they acquired title of St-Mauris; other family members settled in Lyon where they remained bourgeois. During 16ᵗʰ c some of them also served Habsburgs as diplomats, and with distinction. They obtained entry to Burgundian Estates in 1570, by which time 2 branches of family were taking shape. Bp's father, as vicomte du Thil, was head of elder branch, and no doubt consolidated their position by marrying his cousin, but his line died out with bp's elder brother Claude-Joseph, who was *élu* of nobility in Burgundy Estates in 1682. Clearly well anchored among local nobility, their younger sons regularly entered socially exclusive chapter of St-Pierre in Mâcon – as did bp and his brother in their generation.

Born in Mâcon dioc, baptised 29-12-1653. One of 4 sons of Honoré, sgr de St-Mauris and vicomte de Thil, and Claudine Dumas, married in 1640. Further studies in Paris, where MA in July 1677, later took 11ᵗʰ place in 1692 theol lic. Doctor of theol, Paris, on 22-3-1692. Priest for many years before nom to Saintes. Dep to 1695 AC. Canon, then treasurer of St-Pierre cath chapter in Mâcon at time of nom, having received the provostship of St-Pierre from Louis XIV at Christmas 1701. He was nom to Saintes when Bertrand Sénaux withdrew and opted for Autun instead in late July 1702.

Nom to Saintes 15-8-1702. Provs 20-11-1702. Consec 25-3-1703. Died 25-12-1710.

Sources: ASV, PC 95, fos 472–84. BN, Doss bleus 184, no 4790; Cab d'Hozier 93, no 2469; MS Fr 32422, pp 62–3 (*preuves* for St-Pierre-de-Mâcon). Valous, *Patriciat lyonnais aux xiiiᵉ et xivᵉ siecles*, 247–59. Pinard, *Chronologie*, iv, 476–8. *L'Intendance de Bourgogne à la fin du xviiᵉ siècle*, 433–4.

Salette, Charles-François. Oloron 1682–1704.   Grand-nephew and nephew Jean and Jean-Henri, successive bps of Lescar (1609–25, 1629–58). The Salette family consolidated their provincial position in 17ᵗʰ c by military service, entry to Estates of Béarn etc.

Born in Pau, 1640, but not formally baptised until April 1646. One of 11 children of Charles, sgr de Montardon, and Madeleine de Poudenx, married in 1627. Nothing known about his studies, but it seems he took doct in theol, possibly at Bordeaux. He was a priest for over 10 years before nom to Oloron. Thanks to his relative, bp of Lescar, he became canon there, and subsequently, around 1662, *official* in same dioc. Obtained personal *entrée* to Estates of Béarn in 1666. Given abbey of Caignotte OSB (Dax) in Dec 1685.

Nom 16-1-1682. Provs 20-4-1682. Consec n.d. (1682). Died 22-7-1704.

Sources: ASV, PC 81, fos 446–60; fondo Santini 210. Dufau de Maluquer, *Armorial de Béarn*, i, 124; ii, 116–40.

Salignac. *See* **Fénelon.**

Sanzay. *See* **Turpin.**

Saulx. *See* **Chevalier.**

Savary, Mathurin. Sées 1692–8.   The bp's antecedents are difficult to disentangle, as more than one merchant family of this name existed in early 17ᵗʰ c Paris. He was probably related to Jacques Savary, author of the *Parfait Négociant*, but precisely how is unclear – and is even disputed. On both sides of family, bp was from textile-merchant stock. His father's success as a silk merchant enabled his sons to seek more socially attractive careers – as well as bp, they included a *cons* in parlt of Metz (who was also canon of cath there), an *avocat*, an embassy sec. The latter, Jean-Baptiste, served in French embassy in London, and was found murdered in Paris in 1699, with a whiff of high-society scandal as he kept an 'epicurean' house in Montmartre.

Born ca 1642 in St-Eustache parish, Paris, Mathurin was 2nd of 4 sons of Guillaume, bourgeois de Paris, and Marie Baudeau. Studied hum, phil, law, probably in Paris, but took his lic *in utr* at Reims. Apparently took over family business for a time after father's early death. Ordained priest ca 1673 by Louis de Bernage, bp of Grasse. Abbot *in comm* of Isle-en-Barrois O Cist (Toul) and Chehery O Cist (Reims), he was made almoner 'par quartier' of the queen, Marie-Thérèse, and then, in 1678, royal almoner 'ordinaire'. He was, apparently, the only one of her household clerics for whom she requested an episcopal nom. Her death did not close down opportunities for him: in 1689, still awaiting his bulls for Sées, where his activities as a vic-gen *sede vacante* were less than popular with the chapter, he was nom to *primatiale* of Nancy (which he had previously held before nom to Sées, but which was incompatible with episcopal office), he was given a year to decide which of 2 he wished to keep: he opted for the episcopate. Nom to Sées only months too late for papal provs to be granted, he endured a 10-year wait which drastically shortened the episcopate that followed.

Nom 22-5-1682. Provs 24-3-1692. Consec 24-8-1692. Died 16-8-1698

Sources: ASV, PC 86, fos 350–63. BN, PO 2649, no 58905; Doss bleus 602, no 15891; MS Fr 20969, fo 74v, 1-7-1689; MS Fr 32510, fos 30, 34v. AN, L 744, pièce 1, no 40. St-Simon, vi, 200–3. Fisquet, *France pontificale*, Sées, 71–3.

Séguier de la Verrière, Jacques. Lombez 1662-71, Nîmes 1671–87 (resign).   The bp belonged to a collateral branch of this prolific and high-ranking robe family, which was related to most of distinguished robe families of Paris, from the Dupuy to the Bérulle and beyond, and by Louis XIV's time, the court aristocracy (via marriage of chancellor's granddaughters). Bp's grandfather and that of Chancellor Séguier were 1st cousins, but his own father was a modest *maître* in *eaux et forêts* admin, and was probably only made *cons d'état* in 1636 through patronage of chancellor. Later generations seemed to have moved into military careers, but without great distinction.

Born ca 1606 Paris. Eldest son of Jacques, sgr de la Verrière, and Marguerite Tardieu, daughter of an SR. Studies in Paris, where an MA in Jan 1637, took bacc in theol in June 1637, 9th place in 1644 lic, completed by doct 4-7-1644. He seems to have been principal of coll of Fortet (Paris) during these years. Still a cleric, he was canon of ND of Chartres, early 1635, but later moved to similar position in ND de Paris, where he was also made *théologal*, as well as royal almoner. His was not Mazarin's or Louis XIV's 1st choice for Lombez, vacant since 1657, and was only nom after 2 previous nominees had died before entering episcopate. Active and committed bp in both Lombez and Nîmes, conducting visitations, emphasising importance of clerical reform and good behaviour etc, but his (northern?) severity (despite strong pro-Jesuit family sentiments) and authoritarian streak did not endear him to all, esp in Nîmes chapter. His resign has variously been interepreted as a result of his condemning Four Articles of 1682 or his inability, owing to his advanced age, to tackle local Huguenot problem after Revocation of 1685. He was paid off for resigning Nîmes in 1687 with abbeys of Lyre OSB (Evreux) and Livry OSA (Paris), in Aug 1689, with pensions for various family members.

Nom to Lombez, 1-12-1661. Provs 27-2-1662. Consec 6-8-1662. Nom to Nîmes 5-1-1671. Provs 24-8-1671. Resign 1687. Died 8-11-1689.

Sources: ASV, PC 70, fos 764–86 (Nîmes). BN, MS Lat 9153, fo 68v; MS Fr 20969, fo 118r; MS Fr 23498, fo 58. Anselme, *Histoire*, ix, 464–5. Sauzet, *Contre-Réforme*, 405–11. Ménard, *Histoire civile, ecclésiastique et littéraire de Nîmes*, vi, 196.

Sénaux, Bertrand. Autun 1703–9.   A maternal nephew of his direct predecessor at Autun, Roquette, the bp was scion of an established officeholding family of Toulouse, whose presence in parlt is attested from 1570 onwards, their earlier activities and status being difficult to specify. However, evidence also exists for military careers under Charles IX and Henri III, though this option may not have been sustained in subsequent generations.

Born Toulouse, 21-9-1647. 2nd son of Bertrand, *cons* in parlt, and Marie d'Assezat, married in 1638. Further studies in Paris, where he took his MA in Aug 1670, followed by 19th place in 1676 theol lic. Ordained priest in 1677. He owed his career virtually exclusively to his uncle, Roquette, bp of Autun. Cantor of Autun cath, vic-gen of Autun since 1679. Dep to 1682 AC. Nom to abbey *in comm* of ND du Val-St-Benoist O Cist (Autun) in April 1692, which he later exchanged with uncle for priory of St-Fortuné-de-Cherlieu OSB (Mâcon), in 1697. King nom him to Saintes in June 1702, only for Roquette to resign Autun in haste on July 17, opening the way for him to succeed at Autun instead – with Roquette now acting as *his* vic-gen.

Nom 4-8-1702. Provs 12-11-1703. Consec 6-4-1704. Died 30-4-1709.

Sources: ASV, PC 96, fos 202–36. BN, PO 2684, no 59,555; MS Fr 20969, fos 111r, 113v. St-Simon, xiv, 297. Navelle, *Familles toulousaines*, x, 37–8.

Sève de Rochechouart, Guy de. Arras 1670–1724.   A provincial family, possibly originating in Piedmont, but settled in Lyon by early 16th c where Jean de Sève was an *échevin* in 1510, after which they became prominent municipal officeholders. 2 generations later, a Parisian branch was added through Guillaume, sgr de Saint Julien, who held important financial offices (*trés-gén* of *gabelles* of Orléanais, *rec-gén* and *payeur* of *rentes sur le clergé*) under Henri IV and Louis XIII. By now, both Parisian and Lyon branches of family were proliferating and held wide variety of offices, muncipal (esp in Lyon) and royal, notably parlt of Dombes. Bp was born into Parisian branch, but most of the others remained in and around Lyon. In generation of bp's father, Alexandre (d 1674), financial but increasingly non-financial offices loomed large: he married into Rochechouart family, inheriting their name and titles, and became a long-serving prov intendant in Dauphiné, Auvergne and Provence. Marriage over several generations ensured they were related to some of France's best-connected robe families – among them the Camus, Villars, Bernage, Le Clerc de Lesseville, and not least the Colbert, all of whom numbered bps in their ranks before or during Louis XIV's reign.

Born 15-6-1640 in St-Sulpice parish, where baptised 21-6-1640. Son of Alexandre, MR, and Marguerite de Rochechouart. 1st cousin to Louis Tronson, the celebrated sup-gen of St-Sulpice, who formed him there. Studied phil and theol, along with Brienne of Coutances, in Univ of Paris, where took MA in July 1656, 75th place in 1664 theol lic, and doct on 30-3-1666. Ordained priest in church of Visitation convent Paris (with papal dispensation *extra tempora*), 20-3-1666. Abbot *in comm* of St-Michel-en-Thierarche OSB (Laon), 1663. Insufficiently 'cooperative' at the 1681 AC, he was subsequently confined to his dioc and banned from presiding over Estates of Artois. Portrayed as a Jansenist, when, according to some, he was merely a rigorist like Tronson, Fénelon and others, he attracted the animosity of Louvois. Admired in many circles, including Rome under Innocent XI, for his determintion to restore a more rigorist church discipline in his dioc, which brought him into frequent conflict with Jesuits. His collected censures, instructions and *mandements* etc were published and widely diffused inside and outside of France. He remained faithful to Fénelon in *Maximes* affair, one of the few among the episcopate to do so. He attempted to secure a nephew as coadj in 1721, but it fell through, and he died in office 1724.

Nom 17-1-1670. Provs 28-7-1670. Consec 30-11-1670. Died 27-12-1724.

Sources: ASV, PC 69, fos 46–68. BN, MS Fr 32139, p 637. Fénelon, *Correspondance*, i, 163; v, 143. Tronson, *Correspondance*, iii, 58–61. St-Simon, vi, 159. Poutet, 'Docteurs', no 449. Bluche, *L'Origine*, 388–9. *Lettres de Séguier*, i, 121–8. Smedley-Weill, *Intendants des Louis XIV*, 59–60. François Hébert, *Mémoires*, 146–58. Legay, *Les États provinciaux dans la construction de l'état moderne*, 90.

Sillery. *See* **Brûlart**.

Simiane de Gordes, Louis-Marie-Armand. Langres 1671–95.   Simiane was one of oldest of Provence's sword noble families, claiming descent from Charlemagne, boasting several branches (Gordes, la Coste) by 17th c! Like similar families there, their alliances with major noble families were numerous. They played significant roles in military and political history of Provence and Dauphiné during 16–17th centuries, and provided 2 bps of Apt in 16th c. Bp's eldest brother, François, preceded him as canon-count in Lyon, but resign his position to him in 1643: having succeeded his uncle Jean de Pontevès as comte de Carcès, he later became *grand sénéchal* and *lt du roi* in Provence, and was a major political figure in Provence from 1656 to 1659, when he was arrested, disgraced and replaced by Desmontiers de Mérinville for having opposed Mazarin's client-ally, Oppède, in 1658–9. Yet his post of *chevalier d'honneur* at court to Queen Marie-Thérèse, to whom future bp was also *premier aumônier*, showed that disgrace was relative and short-lived.

Born Paris, 1627, 4th son of Guillaume, marquis de Gordes, 1st captain of king's Scots guards, gov of Pont-St-Esprit, and Gabrielle de Pontevès, heiress of comte de Carcès, from another ancient Provençal dynasty, he was baptised at St-Germain-l'Auxerrois. Took doct in canon law 28-1-1671, i.e. 2 weeks *after* nom to Langres. Ordained priest by Ch-M Le Tellier in chapel of Minims, Paris, 28-4-1669. Succeeded in becoming canon of St-Jean, Lyon, at second attempt in 1643, when elder brother vacated seat on his behalf. *Premier aumônier* to Queen Marie-Thérèse, ca 1661. Also held abbeys of La Roe OSA (Angers) and St-Vincent-de-Senlis OSA (1668–81), as well as several priories, one of which he exchanged for abbey of St-Seine OSB (Langres) in 1675. Dep to 1655 AC. 'Le bon Langres' (St-Simon) shared his time between court and dioc, where he held synods and published his own *Rituel* (allegedly inspired by Port Royal), but Louis XIV concluded, after his death, that he had neglected his dioc and was too prone to gambling.

Nom 16-1-1671. Provs 28-9-1671. Consec 30-11-1671. Died 21-11-1695.

Sources: ASV, PC 70, fos 591–617; Misc Arm XII, 151, fo 14. BN, MS Fr 7651, fo 189 (*bienfaits du roi*); MS Fr 20969, fo 15v. BM Aix, MS 257, p 238. Fénelon, *Correspondance*, v, 56, n 9. Vindry, *État major, gendarmerie*, 344, 491. Abbé Roussel, *Le Diocèse de Langres*, i, 121–2. Pillorget, *Mouvements insurrectionnels*, 121, 622. Beyssac, *Chanoines de Lyon*, 201, 202.

Soanen, Jean. Senez 1696–1727.   From a relatively modest family of bourgeois of Riom in Auvergne, the bp probably owed more to his maternal than his paternal relatives. The Sirmond family included Jean, the famous Jesuit scholar and confessor to Louis XIII, but other members also achieved distinction elsewhere. But instead of the Jesuits, he joined the Oratory, where he emerged as an important figure, esp in 1680s and early 1690s, when he was one of Abp Harlay's principal agents within congregation, reporting to him and king on its internal affairs. This 'political' phase, which ensured the support of both Harlay and Jesuit confessor, earned him the mitre, but it contrasts sharply with his later career, when he emerged as a Jansenist martyr, the only bp to be formally deposed between the 1630s and the Revolution.

Born Riom 6-1-1647. Son of Mathieu, *procureur* at *présidial* court of Riom, and Gilberte Sirmond, married in 1638. Early studies in Oratory coll at Riom, and joined Oratory in Paris 15-11-1661, where his director was Pasquier Quesnel! He studied philosopy and theol there, taking *magister's* degree in theol (univ unknown), having already taught in various Oratorian colls at Troyes, Beaune, Dieppe, Riom (where he was resident in 1670). Ordained priest in Caen in 1671. A talented preacher (one of the 'quatre évangélistes' from the Oratory), who performed several times at court, and in many provincial towns, after 1678. Deputy 'pour le roi' at general assembly of Oratory in 1690, where he opposed his sup-gen, Denis de St-Marthe, suspected of Jansenism! In early 1690s both Bossuet and Quesnel had a low opinion of him ('un petit politique . . . il se croit bien fin'). His nom to Senez led to break with fellow Oratorian, Quesnel, but Soanen turned into a resolute Jansenist who opposed the bull *Unigenitus* until he was deprived of his jurisdiction (but not actually deposed) by a specially convened provincial council at Embrun in 1727, after which he was exiled to abbey of Chaise-Dieu where he died.

Nom 8-9-1695. Provs 21-5-1696. Consec 1-7-1696. Deprived Sept 1727. Died 25-12-1740.

Sources: ASV, PC 90, fos 428–36. AN, L 744, pièce 1, no 46. AD Puy-de-Dôme, *Insinuations* B, vol 188, fo 148 (*titre clérical*, 3-12-1670). St-Simon, xxxi, 146–7. Fénelon, *Correspondance*, xvii, 241. Bossuet, *Correspondance*, iv, 66. Quesnel, *Correspondance*, i, 390. Tardieu, *Dictionnaire des anciennes familles de l'Auvergne*, col 370.

Sourches, Jean-Louis du Bouchet de. Dol 1716–48.   St-Simon denigrated the ancestry of this court-based family – 'gentilshommes de bon lieu, mais fort ordinaires, du pays du Mans. Il n'y en a rien à remarquer.' Resident around Sablé since at least mid-15ᵗʰ c, they were militarily and politically active during Wars of Religion. Their presence at court only began with bp's grandfather, who fell foul of Richelieu, but recovered to become *grand prévôt de France* in 1643, a major court post which his son and grandson also held without interruption. He was made marquis de Sourches in 1652, *chevalier* of St-Esprit in 1661. Bp's father also became gov and lt-gen of Maine and Perche in 1670, acquiring Monsoreau lands by marriage. Well placed, as their marriages to Hurault de Cheverny, Vassé, Plessis-Liancourt, Cheverny and Colbert (bp's sister) suggest, rather than wealthy.

Son of Louis François du Bouchet, marquis de Sourches, godson of Louis XIV, gov of Le Mans, Laval, *grand prévôt de l'hôtel et de France*, and Marie-Geneviève de Chambert, daughter and heiress of comte de Montsoreau. Born July 1669, baptised 17-2-1675. Early studies in SJ coll of Clermont, Paris, then at Univ where he took MA July 1686 at coll of Harcourt, followed by 5ᵗʰ place in 1694 theol lic. Priest since 5-6-1694, doctor in theol 26-6-1694. Abbot *in comm* of St-Martin-de-Troarn OSB (Bayeux), in succession to greatuncle, followed by priory of St-Symphorien OSB (Le Mans) in 1678. *Aumônier du roi* in May 1699. St-Simon's portrait of him as a bore who frequented the antechambers of Versailles in search of advancement, was probably coloured by his dislike of St-Sulpice, where Sourches had been briefly resident in late 1687 and early 1688. He missed out on better diocs in Jan 1714 when nom to Dol.

Nom 20-4-1715. Provs 30-3-1716. Consec 12-7-1716. Died 30-6-1748.

Sources: ASV, PC 105, fos 249-60. St-Simon, iv, 150; xiii, 548-9; xxvi, 98; xxxiii, 102. Levesque, 'Liste des élèves', no 1701-2. Pinard, *Chronologie*, iv, 653–6; vi, 325. Vindry, *État major, gendarmerie*, 62. Chaix d'Est-Ange, *Dictionnaire des familles*, vi, 218-24. Raison, 'Un prélat d'ancien régime'.

Taffoureau de Fontaine, Charles-Nicolas. Alet 1699–1708.   The origins of this successor but 2 of the celebrated Pavillon at Alet were relatively modest, as his family were merchants in Sens in late 16ᵗʰ c. Bp's father may have started as a tax receiver there, but later obtained an office of *cons* in Sens *présidial*, which was still in family hands in the 1710s, and therefore suggesting limited means or ambitions. Other family members in mid-17ᵗʰ c were *avocats* and minor landed proprietors, though bp's own entry into cath chapter of Sens and his progress towards episcopate also gives impression of local notables beginning to spread their wings.

Born Sens, 23-8-1655, son of 'noble homme' Jean, sgr de Fontaine, *cons* at *présidial* of Sens, and Louise Moncourt. Higher univ studies in Paris where MA in July 1673, followed by theol (along with Pas de Feuquières and Bazin de Bezons), leading successively to bacc in March 1677, 3ʳᵈ place in 1682 lic (when he was prior of Sorbonne), and finally doct in May 1682. Also ordained priest in 1682. Rancé rebuffed his attempt to become a monk at La Trappe in 1673. His clerical career had begun with post of chaplain of *chapelle* of St-Eutrope in Sens cath, in 1666, but was elected canon there in 1678, later archdeacon of the Gâtinais, and finally dean of chapter in 1694. Meanwhile he had acquired priory of Auxon, and served as a gov and *cellerier* of hôtel-dieu of Sens. Abp Fortin, his patron, played a key role by making him first his *official*, then his gr-vic. As archdeacon, he was spiritual director to Benedictine nuns of Montargis where Colbert's highly *dévot* son-in-law, the duc de Beauvillier, placed most of his daughters in 1690s, which led to life-long ties and correspondence between the 2 men. Indirectly at least, Beauvillier's favourable reports on Taffoureau ensured he was known to king and his advisers – as did those of Abp Fortin, even though in 1698 he solicited Alet for one of Taffoureau's contemporaries from his student days, Pas de Feuquières! Judging by his surviving papers, he was an active, experienced spiritual director to various convents and individuals within Sens, a task he continued by letter after elevation to episcopate.

Nom 1-11-1698. Provs 5-1-1699. Consec 25-3-1699. Died 8-10-1708.

Sources: ASV, PC 93, fos 176–93. BN, PO 2785, no 61934; MS Lat 17021, fo 128. AN, L 727, Alet, no 36. BM Sens, MSS 140–161, 245, 284–5 (Taffoureau papers). 'Lettres du duc de Beauvillier à l'évêque d'Alet'. Rancé, *Correspondance*, iv, 450–2.

Tassi/Tassy. *See* **Félix.**

Tessé. *See* **Froulay.**

Thomassin, Louis. Vence coadj 1671/2–82, Sisteron 1682–1718.   Originating in Pignerol, but settled in Aix since the later 15th c, the Thomassin were ennobled by King René of Anjou in 1479. Having subdivided into numerous branches known individually by their seigneurial titles, they subsequently provided an impressive number of magistrates to parlt and *cour des comptes* of Provence, as well as other *grands magistrats* – there were allegedly 16 family members in Aix parlt in 1647! Bp's father was a *cons* there, and involved in Fronde in 1648 as anti-Mazarin rebel. Family also included clerics and men of learning, inc the well-known Oratorian scholar, Louis. Their St-Paul seigneurie was elevated to rank of marquisat in 1690.

Louis was 3rd son of François, sgr de St-Paul, *cons* in Aix parlt, and Anne (or Jeanne) Duchesne. Born 16-8-1637, baptised in Aix cath. Little is known about his studies, apart from outcome, which was a brace of docts, one in theol at Avignon on 15-11-1660, the other in law, univ unknown. By 1660, he was canon-sacristan of Riez and prior of Montmeyan OSB (Aix) to which he added 2 other priories, Les Arcs OSB and, in 1664, Grambois OSB (both Fréjus). He was ordained priest on 1-6-1670, by which time his preaching talents had blossomed. His coadjutorship to Antoine Godeau was very brief, since Godeau died in 1672, and Louis XIV later transferred him to Sisteron, where he completed the seminary of Manosque founded by his cousin, Claude. Founded *petit séminaire* at Lurs for poor clerics and to encourage vocations. Was killed by wall of episcopal chateau of Lurs falling upon him.

Nom coadj Vence 22-4-1671. Provs 17-4-1672. Consec 21-2-1672. Resign Vence 2-2-1680. Nom to Sisteron 19-5-1681. Died 16-7-1718.

Sources: ASV, PC 70, fos 1243–67 (coadj Vence); PC 81, fos 565–79 (Sisteron). BM Aix, MS 257, p 239. AD Bouches-du-Rhône, 1 G 1271, fos 405–09, May 1664 (Grambois provs, 1664). AD Vaucluse, D 136, fo 108 (Avignon doct). *Gall Chr Nov*, Sisteron, cols 775–6. Fénelon, *Correspondance*, xvii, 313, n 18. Blanc, 'Origines', 553–5. Clapiers-Collongues, *Chronologie*, 79, 88, 162. Kettering, *Judicial Politics*, 182. Pillorget, *Mouvements insurrectionnels*, 228, 876, n 36. Pierre Clair, 'La Famille du père Louis Thomassin', *Oratoriana*, 11 (1965), 122–39.

Thyard de Bissy, Henri-Pons. Toul 1692–1705, Meaux 1705–37.   Between them the Thyard and their Neufchèze relatives held the see of Chalon-sur-Saône without interruption from Charles IX to Mazarin (1571–1658), benefiting from strong royalist stance during Wars of Religion.

Baptised 25-5-1657 in parish of St-Marcel-de-Lierre (?) in Besançon dioc. Eldest son of Claude, former gov of *trois-évêchés*, and Eléonore Angélique de Neufchèze, sister of Jacques, bp of Chalon-sur-Saône. Early studies in Jesuit coll des Godrans in Dijon, then moved to Paris, where took MA in June 1675, 8th place in 1684 lic in theol, finishing with doct, 25-1-1685. Tonsured in 1666, he was subdeacon in Sept 1682, deacon in April 1683 and priest on 23-12-1684. Undertook several missions to Huguenots in dioc of Metz. His preaching at Metz and controversies with RPR attracted attention of court to him. Initially, he was regarded as pro-Jansenist and pro-Port Royal, but he was a weather-cock and intriguer whom St-Simon and La Palatine both despised. Abbot *in comm* of Noaillé OSB (Poitiers) in 1680 on resign of his brother, and Troisfontaines O Cist (Châlons-sur-Marne) in 1698. His nom to Toul in 1687 was a reward as much for father's services as for his own. Refused to leave Toul for Bordeaux in late 1697, but a year later got abbey of Trois-Fontaines. He was one of judges of Fénelon's *Maximes des Saints* in 1697. Succeeded Bossuet at Meaux in 1704, and after death of Godet of Chartres (whom he regarded as his patron) in 1709 he was director of conscience of Maintenon, which helped to get nom for red hat in June 1713, abbey of St-Germain-des-Prés in Dec 1714, and red hat in May 1715, though his anti-Jansenist zeal during these crucial years was not irrelevant either. Retained some ecclesiastical influence after Louis XIV's death, despite Regent's unwillingness to use the services of such a partisan figure. *Commandeur* of St-Esprit in 1724, apparently managed to place several clients in episcopate post-1715.

Nom 29-3-1687. Provs 10-3-1692. Consec 24-8-1692. Nom to Meaux 10-5-1704. Provs 9-2-1705. Cardinal 29-5-1715. Died 26-7-1737.

Sources: ASV, PC 86, fos 290–308. BN, MS Fr 20969, fo 144. Bossuet, *Correspondance*, viii, 304. Fénelon, *Correspondance*, iii, no 253, p 422, n 2. Taveneaux, *Jansénisme en Lorraine*, 200ff. St-Simon, iv, 92; v 36–7. Dangeau, xvi, 78–9. Ceyssens, *Le Sort de l'Unigenitus*, ch 7, 'Le cardinal de Bissy'. Bergin, *Making*, 676, 708.

Tilladet. *See* Cassagnet.

Timeur. *See* Ploeuc.

Tressan. *See* Lavergne.

Trudaine, François-Firmin. Senlis 1714–54.   The Trudaine were by origin merchants in Amiens, where the trout, la *truie*, was their *enseigne* in 16th c. They also used their social capital as rising urban notables to move into royal financial magistracies in Amiens, where several generations of members were *trés de France* and *prés* in *bureau des finances*. They seem to have hesitated about switching to Paris, where the offices they held were for sometime less important than those at Amiens. But it seems equally clear that bp's elevation might not have occurred *without* such a move, in which 2 of his 1st cousins played their part – Charles, MR, prov intendant, and *prévot des marchands* in 1716, and his sister Charlotte, wife of Daniel Voysin, whose elevation to chancellorship of France occurred in same year as bp's own nom to Senlis.

Born Amiens 13-1-1679. Son of François and Marie-Anne Canteraine. Theol studies in Paris, where he was member of coll of Cardinal Lemoine and took 7th place in 1712 lic, followed by doct on 19-4-1712. Ordained priest ca 1706. Canon, chancellor of Amiens cath, vic-gen of Amiens since 1711, when he was elected dep to AC by province of Narbonne where he held priory of St-Martin-de-Gibeleaux.

Nom 19-5-1714. Provs 20-8-1714. Consec 25-11-1714. Died 4-1-1754.

Sources: ASV, PC 103, fos 721–33. BN, MS Fr 32139, pp 761–4. AN, G[8], 89 (1711 AC). St-Simon, xvii, 453–61. Bluche, *L'Origine*, 402–3.

Turgot de St-Clair, Dominique-Barnabé. Sées 1710–27.   The frustrated aspirations of the enlightened reforming minister of young Louis XVI's reign can easily obscure not merely his own previous activities, but those of several generations of ancestors who served as MRs and prov intendants with unparalleled regularity from Louis XIII to Louis XIV! But they also provided a *prévôt des marchands* in Paris under Louis XIV, as well as army officers. Natives of Normandy, where they acquired nobility under Louis XI (1472), they had served as *officiers* in Caen area in 16th c and, by early 17th c, also in Rouen, where they were both *avocats* and *cons* in parlt. Bp's grandfather, having begun his career in Rouen, moved to Paris and was the 1st MR and intendant (from 1630 onwards) of his lineage, possibly because of marriage to Anne Favier, daughter of a family with similar trajectory under Louis XIII. By Louis XIV's reign, 2 branches existed, *both* producing MRs and intendants in each generation! Bp belonged to senior one, St-Clair; Louis XVI's minister to that of Brucourt.

2nd son of Antoine (1625–1713), MR and intendant at Limoges, and Jeanne Marie du Tillet de la Bussière, he was born and baptised in St-Jean-le-Rond parish, Paris, on 26-10-1667, godson of Dominique Turgot de Sousmons, MR, and Marguerite du Tillet, daughter of the *greffier-en-chef* of Paris parlt. Studies in Paris where he became MA in Aug 1684, and undertook theol studies which led to bacc in 1688 and then as far as lic exams in 1692 (though he seems not to have actually taken theol lic), preferring instead to take bacc and lic *in utr* in Paris, 1696. Priest since 1694. Royal almoner in July 1694 (successor of Louis Milon). Canon of Appoigny chapter (Auxerre), he was dep for Sens province to 1707 AC. Elected *ag-gén* in 1708 by province of Auch, his accession to the episcopate seems to have been virtually automatic. Made *premier aumônier* of duc de Berry in 1710. Strongly pro-Jesuit successor at Sées to Louis d'Aquin, suspected of Jansenist leanings.

Nom 12-7-1710. Provs 10-11-1710. Consec 14-12-1710. Died 18-12-1727.

Sources: AN, MC, LXXXII 118, 10-8-1710; MM 254, pp 98, 108, 124, 132, 292 (theol); MM 1099, pp 51, 65 (law). St-Simon, xx, 82, 219; xviii, 114ff. Fénelon, *Correspondance*, xv, 76, n 14. Bluche, *L'Origine*, 404–5. Bluche, *Magistrats du grand conseil*, 141. Fisquet, *France pontificale*, Sées, 76–7. Foncin, 'Remarques sur la généalogie des Turgot', 64–84.

Turpin de Crissé de Sanzay, Christophe-Louis. Rennes 1712–24, Nantes 1724–46. This family's origins go back to 13th c and to the Anjou-Touraine area, spreading out later to Brittany and Berry. They held significant court positions in Loire valley monarchy of late Middle Ages/Renaissance (chamberlains, later *gentilshommes de la chambre*, etc), also served in royal army, and counted 3 bps before 1500. The Sanzay belonged to senior branch of family, and became a distinct line in early 17th c, dying out a century later. Their family alliances were not especially distinguished, with bp's grandfather's marriage to Suzanne Chenu, comtesse de Sanzay, probably most notable among them. Via his mother, they were related to numerous *grande robe* families in Paris, particularly as the Coulange-Turpin relationship seems to have been close. Their traditions of service, apart from court, were military, and these were sustained through 17th c, with bp's elder brother finishing a 30-year military career of some distinction in 1716 with rank of brigadier.

Born in Paris, parish of St-Gervais, 19-9-1670. Son of Louis, comte de Sanzay, and Anne-Marie de Coulange, daughter of Philippe, *maître aux comptes*, Paris, married in 1661. Studies in Paris, where he was MA in Aug 1688. Took theol bacc exam in Paris, Jan 1696, 95th place in 1700 lic, rounded off by doct on 30-4-1701. Priest from same time. Dean of St-Martin of Tours, where his family had founded a *chapelle* in 15th c, and abbot *in comm* of ND de Moreilles O Cist (Poitiers). Also abbot of Quimperlay OSB (Quimper) in 1717 and la Chaume OSB (Nantes) in 1725.

Nom to Rennes 15-8-1711. Provs 1-6-1712. Consec 7-8-1712. Nom to Nantes 17-10-1723. Provs 27-9-1724. Died 29-3-1746.

Sources: AN, MC, LXXXII, 111, 16-9-1711. BN, Doss bleus 650, no 17,257; MS Lat 5496, p 59. Pinard, *Chronologie*, viii, 139. St-Simon, viii, 237; xx, 257ff. Boisnard, *Touraine*, no 2247. Vindry, *État major, gendarmerie*, 64, 173, 409.

Valbelle de Montfuron, Louis-Alphonse. Alet 1678–93, St-Omer 1693–1708.   With 4 major branches (Valbelle, Rians, Montfuron, Tourves), the Valbelle were one of Provence's best-known houses, wielding extensive influence in Marseille itself, their main power base. Despite claims to ancient lineage, they were actually descended from an apothecary who became a 2nd *consul* of Marseille in 1528, when clear filiation begins. Thereafter, they were centrally involved in Marseille factional politics from Wars of Religion until aftermath of Fronde, during which bp's father played major role against crown. But it was in naval service, as Knights of Malta or French officers, that they distinguished themselves under Louis XIII and XIV. The Monfuron branch were also related to Grignan family, which was equally prominent in Provence under Louis XIV, while Tourves was elevated to status of marquisat in 1690.

Born 12-4-1641, 4th son of Antoine, sgr de Montfuron, lieut of admiralty of Marseille, and Françoise Felix, dame de Valserres, from another well connected Marseille family heavily involved in city politics. His godfather was Alphonse de Richelieu, Cardinal of Lyon, his godmother the comtesse d'Alais. Further studies in Paris, initially at coll of Harcourt, then at Sorbonne, where took 76th in 1666 theol lic, followed by doct 10-4-1668. Priest since 1668. Provost of Sisteron cath, he also became royal almoner in 1669, dep to 1665 and 1670 AC, elected *ag-gén* in 1675, usually a stepping stone to episcopate. Chosen in 1677 to succeed Pavillon at Alet, whose pro-Jansenist policies he systematically reversed, and was allowed to serve out his term as *ag-gén*. Purchased office of *maître* of king's chapel in 1682 from disgraced Louis Fouquet bp of Agde, he was the very opposite in behaviour to Pavillon according to Mme de Sévigné. Having presented the *cahiers* of the Languedoc estates to Louis XIV in 1684, he was transferred to St-Omer, but like many others had to wait until 1693 for bulls. He had played active role in ACs of 1680 and 1682, where he showed strong gallican sentiments. Nicknamed 'le Freluquet', he was judged severely by contemporaries for his attacks on his metropolitan Fénelon of Cambrai over his book *Maximes des Saints*. He built the *hôpital-général* of St-Omer.

Nom to Alet 24-12-1677. Provs 14-3-1678. Consec 1-9-1680. Nom to St-Omer 31-5-1684. Provs 9-11-1693. Died 29-10-1708.

Sources: ASV, PC 77, fos 280–96 (Alet); PC 87, fos 134–42 (St-Omer). BN, MS Fr 7651, fo 229 (*bienfaits du roi*); MS Lat 17021, fo 61. BM Aix, MS 257, p 244. Fénelon, *Correspondance*, iv, 21–2; v, 31–2, n 1; ix, 291–2; Bossuet, *Correspondance*, xi, 371. Sévigné, *Correspondance*, iii, 183, 380. St-Simon, vi, 147–60. Clapiers-Collongues, *Chronologie*, 24, 84, 89, 100, 107. Villette-Mursay, *Mes campagnes*, 448–50. Pillorget, *Mouvements insurrectionnels*, 364, 543, 552. Boisnard, *Touraine*, no 2257. Kettering, *Patrons, Brokers and Clients* (passim). Laplane, *Messieurs de Valbelle, évêques de St-Omer*.

Valbelle de Tourves, François. St-Omer 1710–27.   Tourves was a junior branch of the Valbelle family, which included 2 *prés* in Aix parlt 1686 and 1718. Born Aix 25-2-1664, bp was 7th son (and 11th child) of Jean-Baptiste, later marquis de Tourves, *cons* in Aix parlt, and Anne-Marguerite de Vintimille, dame de Tourves, from another local 'episcopal' family. MA in Paris in Aug 1683, he took 9th place in 1692 theol lic, but waited until 21-2-1696 before taking doct there. Priest since 1695. He owed virtually everything to uncle and predecessor at St-Omer, thanks to whom he was successively canon, archdeacon, dean of St-Omer chapter. Also served him as vic-gen from 1696. Obtained royal almonership in 1699 (as successor of Fleury), and succeeded uncle as *maître* of royal chapel in 1703. Dep to 1702 and 1705 ACs. Prior *in comm* of St-Sauveur-de-Tourves, and abbot of ND de Pontron O Cist (Angers) in 1705. Nom to Alet, which his uncle had held in 1670s, in 1708, but as his uncle died shortly afterwards and Estates of Artois and chapter at St-Omer petitioned for him as successor, he was given St-Omer instead. Not many episcopal careers were so 'pre-ordained' as this one.

Nom to St-Omer 1-11-1708. Provs 19-2-1710. Consec 6-4-1710. Died 17-11-1727.

Sources: AN, MC, LXXXXII, 100, 7-12-1708. BM Aix, MS 257, pp 259–60. Boisnard, *Touraine*, no 2257. Laplane, *Messieurs de Valbelle*.

Valderiès. *See* **Lescure.**

Valençay. *See* **Estampes.**

Vallot, Edouard. Nevers 1667–1705 (resign).   The Vallot were a Dijon bourgeois family, who intermarried with families of like background, such as the Bossuet, and whose members still held office in local *chambre des comptes* into 18th c. Antoine (1597–1671), bp's father, a medical doctor trained in Montpellier, was the 2nd of Louis XIV's 'premier' physicians, succeeding the celebrated Vautier in 1652, and retaining the position until his death, surviving even the fall of Fouquet, to whom he was close. Thanks to this, the family fortunes, financially and socially, changed considerably in space of a generation. None of his 4 sons practised medicine – 2 became ecclesiastics, one a military officer, another a parlt. Even so, they fared less well than did the family of his immediate successor, Aquin, whose importunity was legendary.

Born 1638 Paris, where he was baptised in St-Paul parish church. Son of Antoine Vallot, king's *premier médecin*, and Catherine Gayant, daughter of a well-known Parisian family, married in 1634. Studies in Univ of Paris, where matriculated in 1650 and took MA in Aug 1658. Ranked 72nd in 1666 theol lic, followed up with doct 6-9-1666. Elected *socius* of Sorbonne. Priest since Feb 1666. Abbot *in comm* of ND de Nogent OSB (Chartres) and St-Aubin-des-Bois O Cist (St-Brieuc) by 1653 (which enabled him to attend as dep to Estates of Brittany in 1661), and St-Maurin OSB (Agen) in 1658. Royal almoner 'sans quartier' from 1662. Exchanged one of his benefices with Bp Chery of Nevers when latter resigned Nevers in his favour in Sept 1666. He himself resigned Nevers to Bargedé his vic-gen in early 1705, but died before it could take effect, hence Bargedé was promptly renom by king as his full successor.

Nom 26-9-1666 Provs 7-3-1667. Consec 28-8-1667. Died 3-9-1705.

Sources: ASV, PC 65, fos 485–505. BN, PO 2922, no 64,941; Doss bleus 656, no 17398; MS Fr 19212, fo 159r (resign); MS Clairambault 814, fo 357v. AUP, reg 97, fo 5. *Journal de la santé du Louis XIV*, xvi–xx. Poutet, 'Docteurs', p 295, no 491. Fisquet, *France pontificale*, Nevers, 91–2.

Vaubécourt d'Haussonville. *See* **Nettancourt.**

Vény d'Arbouze, Gilbert. Clermont 1664–82.   A 'belle famille seigneuriale' from Auvergne with claims to older origins in Italy and migration to France in 14th c. But this seems pure legend, as one Guillaume Vény was bourgeois and *échevin* of Montferrand in 1491, whose brother acquired title and name of Arbouze by marriage in 1475. They prospered in following century or more, developing several branches and contracted alliances with some of most prominent families of province (Bayard, Marillac, Charpin, Chauvigny de Blot, St-Quentin) and beyond (Epinac, Albon), and holding an array of offices, military and civilian, esp in Auvergne itself. Opportunities in church were not neglected: as well as a strong presence in religious orders like Benedictines and noble chapters like Brioude, bp boasted a great-uncle as abbot-general of Cluny before Richelieu, and a saintly aunt, Marguerite, abbess of Val de Grace (Paris) and a confidante of Anne of Austria.

Born in chateau of Villemont (Clermont) 15-1-1608, 4th son of Gilbert, sgr de Villemont and *bailli* of duchy of Montpensier, and Madeleine de Bayard. He took the Benedictine habit in 1617, followed by vows in abbey of Sauxillanges ca 1623, but left in protest next year. He was subsequently moved from OSB coll at Dole to SJ colls in Lyon and Billom, finishing his hum and phil at La Flèche. Did not attend univ at this point, since his doct in canon law, Paris, was only taken in weeks immediately *following* his nom to Clermont, in April 1664. In fact, his early life was a turbulent one, as exemplified by rejection of monastic life and even the church career outlined for him by his family. He lived as layman for many years after mid-1620s, but had a change of direction ca 1648. Still averse to monastic life, he was only formally relieved of monastic vows in 1657, when he was confirmed as abbot *in comm* of Manglieu, an abbey he had obtained many years previously. Ordained priest, also ca 1648, he spent some time in St-Sulpice parish then or subsequently. Anne of Austria 'presented' him to Louis XIV for nom to Clermont, in accordance with her status as *apanagiste* of 'county' of Clermont. His episcopal career proved to be relatively uneventful, but he seems to have governed his dioc with a firm hand.

Nom 12-4-1664. Provs 11-8-1664. Consec 21-9-1664 (Val de Grace). Died 19-4-1682.

Sources: ASV, PC 61, fos 240–57v. AN, MM 1115, fo 14v (doct, 14-4-1664). AD Puy-de-Dôme, 6 F 185. Remacle, *Dictionnaire des familles de l'Auvergne*, iii, 496–8. Welter, *Réforme ecclésiastique*, 191–237.

Verjus, François. Grasse 1692–1710.   Relatively little is known of earlier history of bp's family, except that from 15th to mid-17th c, they were resident in Joigny in the Brie, where Antoine, possibly bp's grandfather, was a tax official (*élu*) in 1620s and 1630s. It seems highly probable that the bp and his brothers, in different degrees, 'made' each others' careers, because of their highly complementary trajectories. But initial push may have come from Gondi de Retz family, who were counts of Joigny, since bp's eldest brother, Louis, later comte de Crécy (1629–1709), began his long career as sec to last Cardinal de Retz, before becoming a *secrétaire de cabinet* to Louis XIV, who sent him, along with Jesuit brother, to Portugal as *secrétaire des commandements* to its French queen, Isabelle de Savoie-Nemours, in 1666. On return in 1669, several diplomatic missions, esp in Empire, followed in 1670s, he was made French plenipotentiary at Ryswick and accompanied Cardinal Furstenberg to the 1689 conclave in Rome. He married Marie-Marguerite Ratabon, sister of Martin, bp of Ypres and Viviers, whose brother Louis was another 2nd-rank career diplomat. Another brother Jean (1630–63) was doct of theol of Paris, a royal almoner and a respected preacher, whose *Panégyriques* were published after his early death in 1664. Yet another, Antoine, was a Jesuit, who served as sec and confidant of royal confessor Père La Chaize, which cannot have hindered future bp's prospects in 1680s.

Born Joigny, 1633, son of Antoine, *bailli* of Joigny, and Barbe de Champrenaut. His studies, probably in Paris, included 3 years of theol, but he took lic in canon law there instead – he is frequently confused with his brother, a doct of theol, Paris, and well-known preacher. He entered Oratory and was received in the Paris 'Institution' 3-8-1656. After ordination as a priest, he resided in the various Oratorian houses in Paris – at St-Magloire in 1662, then following mentor Sénault to St-Honoré house in 1663 on latter's election as sup-gen of Oratory. When France's German ally, the prince of Neubourg, was given abbey of Fécamp he appointed Verjus, possibly through the good offices of his diplomat-brother, as his 'spiritual' admin there, a post which seems to have caused some tensions with regard to his position within Oratory, leading to suggestions that he had effectively quit by late 1670s. Spent 4 years in Germany after 1680, probably with his diplomat-brother, and on returning he was nom to Grasse, having already been given the abbey of Barbey O Cist (Bayeux) in 1677. Nom to Glandèves before bulls for Grasse arrive, but king again changed mind and renom him to Grasse, the only see he would effectively hold.

Nom 31-5-1684. Provs 24-3-1692. Consec 7-12-1692. Died 17-12-1710.

Sources: ASV, PC 86, fos 309–23. BN, PO 2969, no 65938; Doss bleus 673, no 17,646. Bossuet, *Correspondance*, i, 290; ix, 190. St-Simon, ii, 242–3; iv, 139–42; xviii, 241–2. *Recueil des instructions aux ambassadeurs*, xviii (Diet of Empire), 40. Batterel, *Mémoires domestiques*, iv, 223–6. Pinard, *Chronologie*, vii, 68. Sonnino, *Louis XIV and the Origins of the Dutch War*, esp 135–7.

Verthamon de Villemenon, Jean-Baptiste. Pamiers 1693–1735.   The origins of this family lay in the Limousin, where their filiation was clearly established from 1528. Some members settled in Saintonge, but esp in Paris where they included prominent officeholders and MRs under Louis XIII and Louis XIV, well connected in robe and financial circles, close to Jesuits and *dévot* networks. Precise connections between various branches are not always sufficiently clear, but bp of Pamiers belonged to the Villemenon one, resident in Paris, while the bp of Couserans belonged to Chalucet one, based in Limoges, where it produced a succesion of *trés de France*, followed in 18th c by a *prés* in Bordeaux parlt. By 17th c, family members also figured among canons and dignitaries of Limoges cath, with some also entering ND de Paris. Bp of Pamiers was 1st of them to hold episcopal office, while 2 nephews of bp of Couserans became bps in 18th c – Michel bp of Montauban 1730–62, and Guillaume-Samuel, bp of Luçon 1737–58.

Born Paris 1646, 2nd of 5 sons of François, comte de Villemon, *cons* in Paris parlt, MR in 1653, and Renée Quatresous, daughter of an *auditeur* in *chambre des comptes*, Paris. Studies in Paris, placed 84th in 1674 theol lic. Doctor of theol there 6-9-1678. Priest for same period of time. He was *promoteur* of Ste-Chapelle (Paris) before becoming vic-gen of Pontoise (Rouen dioc) for 6 years before nom to Pamiers. During 1686-93 Pamiers was admin by François de Camps as vic-cap, having been nom to Pamiers on 12-11-1685. But de Camps was such a strong regalist that Rome absolutely refused him bulls for Pamiers, so Louis XIV withdrew his nom and replaced him with Verthamon who, despite Jesuit connections and contrary to expectations, took firmly anti-*Unigenitus* line during 1710s, joining appeal of 1717.

Nom 8-9-1693. Provs 9-11-1693. Consec 3-1-1694. Died 20-3-1735.

Sources: ASV, PC 87, fos 71–80. BN, MS Fr 20969, fo 136, 24-12-1692. St-Simon, xxxviii, 255. Boisnard, *Touraine*, no 2305. Vidal, *Histoire des évêques de Pamiers, viii. Jean-Baptiste de Verthamon (1693–1735)*.

Verthamon, Jean-Jacques. Couserans 1708–25. Born in château of Chalucet, Limoges dioc, 1670. 2nd son of Guillaume II (d 1686), sgr de Malagnac, later baron of Chalucet, successively receiver of *tailles* at Saintes and *trés de France* at Limoges, and Catherine de Romanet. Entering the Oratory very young, he pursued his studies there, before taking doct of theol at Cahors. Ordained priest in 1696. In 1692, he obtained priory of St-Gerald OSA (Limoges) from his cousin, bp of Pamiers, whom he joined to serve as vic-gen by 1702 at latest, having left Oratory with that in mind. Dep to 1705 AC. With Couserans contiguous to Pamiers, his was a very local, family-driven career, but he did try to obtain nom to Embrun in 1719 via Noailles, to whom he spelled out his intellectual gifts, esp his knowledge of Greek and Hebrew.

Nom 14-1-1708. Provs 14-1-1708. Consec 24-6-1708. Died Oct 1725.

Sources: ASV, PC 101, fos 91–99. Fénelon, *Correspondance*, xvii, 118, n 20. AD Ariege, G 1 (letter to Noailles, 15-9-1719). O'Gilvy, *Nobiliaire de Guienne et de Gascogne*, ii, 231–48. Charmeil, *Trésoriers*, 465–6.

Villeneuve de Vence, Charles. Glandèves 1694–1702. From same extended family as Modeste, bp of Apt (1629-70) and Scipion, bp of Grasse (1632–6). Born in town of Groulières in Vence dioc, ca 1645, bp was son, probably, of Jean-Baptiste, sgr de Thorenc, gov of St-Paul-de-Vence (1663), and his cousin Anne-Marie de Villeneuve de Vence, married in 1640, both dead by 1686. Univ studies in Paris, where MA in Aug 1662. Studied theol at coll of Navarre, and took 79th place in 1670 theol lic, completing doct 28-2-1671. Priest since 1670, ordained in Paris. Provost of Grasse cath for ca 10 years before nom as bp. Present at 1682 Assembly, so his gallican sentiments may have secured him nom to Glandèves in 1686.

Nom 26-4-1686. Provs 4-6-1694. Consec 18-4-1694. Died 12-4-1702.

Sources: ASV, PC 88, fos 202–14. Poutet, 'Docteurs', no 599. Blanc, 'Origines', 581–91. AN, O[1] 34, fo 365v. Bergin, *Making*, 717–18.

Villeroy. *See* **Neufville.**

Villeserin. *See* **Aubert.**

Vintimille du Luc, Jean. Digne 1670–6, Toulon 1676–82.   The Vintimille 'of the counts of Marseille' were an old feudal dynasty from Provence (declared noble to 22th degree in 1667) with numerous branches, of which du Luc were 3rd to form during 16th c, and impressively extensive kinship relations with old familes like themselves. Family members were often 1st consuls in Aix in period 1600–60, but they were 'older' in social terms than the equally pro- lific Forbin, to whom they were related by marriage again in 1630s. Le Luc itself became a *marquisat* in 1688. Traditional political and military careers were pursued under Louis XIV, as exemplified by career of brother of bp of Marseille, Charles-François, marquis des Arcs, *dit* le comte du Luc, who served in both army and galleys in 1690s and 1700s, before turning to diplomacy as ambassador to the Swiss 1709–14, Vienna, and the congress of Baden 1714–17. Clerics were present too, with the provostship of Riez cath, among many others, being held by family members for a century or more after 1545.

Born in family château of Le Luc (between Brignoles and Fréjus), in 1615, Jean was 4th son of Madelon, comte du Luc, and Marguerite de Vins, daughter of famous Hubert, baron de Vins, married in 1604. Studied at coll in Aix en Provence and later in Riez. Took doct in canon law during 1630s, univ unknown. Ordained priest in 1638. Initially provost of Riez cath (1633), he failed to secure the provostship of Toulon in 1640 but became dean of Tarascon instead, and later again was made an archdeacon of Avignon. At Digne, he succeeded his relative, the future Cardinal Forbin-Janson, when the latter moved to Marseille, probably through influence of Maynier d'Oppède-Forbin, *pr prés* of Aix parlt and intendant of Provence, who was related to both of them, while his immediate predecessor at Toulon in 1676 was Louis Forbin d'Oppède! As bp, he became embroiled in a bitter, prolonged dispute with Bp Percin de Montgaillard of St-Pons on moral and doctrinal issues.

Nom to Digne 13-9-1669. Provs 2-6-1670. Consec 21-9-1670. Nom to Toulon 17-9-1675. Provs 27-4-1676. Died 15-11-1682.

Sources: ASV, PC 68, fos 227–49. BM Aix, MS 257, p 233. *Gallia Chr Nov*, i, cols 650–1; v, 673. St-Simon, xii, 196; xv, 349. Blanc, 'Origines', 595–9. Pillorget, *Mouvements insurrec- tionnels*, 84, 87, 869, n 14. Kettering, *Patrons, Brokers and Clients*, 101. Pinard, *Chronologie*, vi, 268.

Vintimille du Luc, Charles-Gaspard-Guillaume. Marseille 1692–1708, Aix 1708–29, Paris 1729–46.   Nephew of Jean above. Born 15-11-1655 Fréjus, but lived in Paris since ca 1666. Son of François, comte du Luc (d 1666), and Anne de Forbin-la-Martre, married in 1639. Studies in Paris, where took MA in Sept 1675 and 95th place in 1682 theol. Priest since 1681. Successively canon, and archdeacon of Toulon (via *régale*, 1675), as well as vic-gen of Toulon, thanks to uncle. Dep to 1680 AC. Prior *in comm* of Le Luc OSB (Fréjus). Governed Marseille from Dec 1684 to early 1692 as vic-cap. Moved to Aix in 1708, *commandeur* of Order of St-Esprit in 1724, succeeds Noailles as abp of Paris, 1729. He was strongly anti-Jansenist, hostile to teaching in Aix seminary run by Andre Leget, whose works he condemned. Well endowed with benefices while still at Aix, e.g. abbot of St-Denis-de-Reims and Belleperche, dom of Aubrac. Owed Paris succession in 1729 to Fleury, his former suffragan at Fréjus, but also to his orthodox, anti-Jansenist record. Considering problems of Paris under Noailles, his tenure there was relatively peaceful.

Nom 31-1-1684. Provs 21-1-1692. Consec 25-3-1692. Nom to Aix 10-2-1708. Provs 14- 5-1708. Nom to Paris 10-5-1729. Provs 17-8-1729. Died 15-3-1746.

Sources: ASV, PC 86, fos 90–109. BN, MS 20969, fo 15r. Fénelon, *Correspondance*, xvii, 117, n. 5. *Gallia Chr Nov* (Marseille) 643–7; (Aix) 147–9. Albanès, *Armorial et sigillographie des eveques de Marseille*, 169–71.

Voyer de Paulmy, Gabriel. Rodez 1667–82.   Originally from Touraine, the Voyer, sgrs/vicomtes de Paulmy, had received letters of ennoblement as far back as 1375. Until early 17th c, they were overwhelmingly involved in military activities and royal/aristocratic household service, a tradition sustained, albeit without especial distinction, by the senior Paulmy line into 18th c. The Argenson branch, to which bp of Dol belonged and which emerged in mid-16th c, moved into robe officeholding (parlt of Paris) in 1619 with René I who, after holding several prov intendancies and taking priestly orders in widowhood, died as ambassador to Venice in 1651. His son, René II, father of bp of Dol, failed miserably as his successor in Venice, and his subsequent disgrace (1655) seemed to ruin Voyer d'Argenson's prospects for good. They were rescued from provincial obscurity at Angoulême by bp of Dol's elder brother, Marc-René, lt-gen at Angoulême, though it was initially thanks to his marriage in 1693 to a Lefebvre de Caumartin. This unexpected renaissance was underlined by his appointment as Paris police chief (1697–1718), and minister of state (1718–21), and it was impressively sustained by high ministerial, ambassadorial and other offices during 18th c. Voyer d'Argenson links with the *dévots* of 17th c are well documented: the indispensable chronicle of their *faits et gestes*, the *Annales de la Compagnie du Saint-Sacrement*, was written by René II, who commissioned son François-Elie, to personally present it to Cardinal Noailles of Paris in 1696 in the hope of reviving the Compagnie.

Bp of Rodez, of the Paulmy branch, born in Tours dioc, 1611, 3rd son of Louis (1581–1651), capt of 50 *hommes d'armes*, and Françoise de Larsay, married in 1605. Took MA at coll of Harcourt, Paris, July 1624, but only took bacc in theol, Paris, much later, after 4 years of study there. Priest for only 2 years before nom to Rodez. Also *aumônier du roi* by 1666. Prior *in comm* in 1641 of St-Jacques-de-la-Lande and St-Pierre-de-Vou (both OSB, Tours), St-Martin-de-Julles (1650) and St-Sauveur-de-Loulaye (both OSB, Saintes), Ste-Magdeleine-de-Bernay OSB (Poitiers). Not particularly young on nom to Rodez, yet his studies and orders had only been completed a few years previously, possibly only when/because the prospect of preferment came into view. Successor to Louis Abelly whose brief reign at Rodez was dogged by poor health, and who resigned in Paulmy's favour, this appointment may well have been engineered with assistance of Voyer's relative, Abp Péréfixe of Paris.

Nom 23-4-1666. Provs 7-2-1667. Consec 8-5-1667. Died 11-10-1682.

Sources: ASV, PC 65, fos 569–88. BSG, MS 941, fo 30. Frondeville, *Conseillers du parlement de Normandie de 1641 à 1715*, 101–4. *Lettres de Séguier*, i, 83–112. *Lettres de Fortin de la Hoguette*, ii, 784–5. Combeau, *Le Comte d'Argenson*, ch 1.

Voyer d'Argenson, François-Elie. Dol 1702–15, Embrun 1715–20, Bordeaux 1720–8. Younger brother of Louis XV's minister, bp was 2nd son of René II, sgr d'Argenson, and Marguerite Houllier de la Pyade, daughter of lt-gen at Angoulême. Born Paris 22-9-1656 and baptised in St-Gervais-et-Prothais parish church on 23-9-1656, shortly after his father's recall from Venice. Studied theol in Paris, taking 96th place in 1682 lic, completing it with doct on 9-2-1686. Ordained priest in 1686. Canon and dean of St-Germain-l'Auxerrois, Jan 1694, also prior of St-Nicolas of Poitiers. Presented *cahiers* of Breton Estates to king in Jan 1705, he obtained abbey of St-Pierre-de-Preuilly O Cist (Sens) in Nov 1706, ND de Relecq O Cist (St-Pol-de-Léon) when transferred from Embrun to Bordeaux in 1720. One of 3 *cons d'état d'église* in 1719, a side-effect of his brother's influence as a major political and ministerial figure.

Nom 15-4-1702. Provs 11-12-1702. Consec 18-3-1703. Nom to Embrun 12-1-1715. Provs 16-12-1715. Nom to Bordeaux 23-4-1719. Provs 6-5-1720. Died 25-10-1728.

Sources: ASV, PC 95, fos 146–58 (Dol); PC 104, fos 187–96 (Embrun). AN, Y 167, fo 117 (c.m. of bp's grandparents 18-7-1622). St-Simon, xxvi, 97–8. Fénelon, *Correspondance*, xvii, n 7. Frondeville, *Conseillers du parlement de Normandie de 1641 à 1715*, 104–8. Bayard, *Dictionnaire des surintendants*, 118–21. Antoine, *Gouvernement*, 247–50.

BIBLIOGRAPHY

Manuscript sources

Paris

Archives des Affaires Étrangères (AAE).

Mémoires et documents (MD)
Rome, 8, 91; France, 972, 307, 1234.

Archives Nationales (AN)

AD/XVII, vol 17ᵃ. G⁷ 542A–542B. G⁸ 88–9. L 727–46 (Père Léonard papers). MM 251–55 (Paris theology faculty, 1608–1717). MM 607, 824. MM 1059, 1099, 1110, 1114, 1119–20 (Paris law faculty). O¹ 24, 26, 46. V² 33–4. V⁷ 88.
109 AP vol 14; 257 AP vol 3; 272AP vols 4–6.
Minutier Central (MC), LXXXII, 105, 110–121. XCI, 659. XCII, 229. XCVIII, 364. CXI, 35. CXIII, 217.

Bibliothèque Nationale (BN)

Baluze 112, 121.
Cabinet des titres (subseries):
a) Pièces originales (PO), 2, 39, 41, 44, 117, 120, 164, 196, 222, 249, 296, 373, 395, 413, 416, 529, 542, 564, 570, 609, 618, 679, 687, 714, 1025, 1028, 1033, 1153, 1155, 1248–9, 1254, 1424, 1466, 1518, 1578, 1607, 1616, 1640, 1687, 1683, 1687, 1693, 1701, 1768, 1784, 1790, 1815, 1857, 1887, 1926, 1938, 1950, 1967, 2049, 2124, 2184, 2277, 2305, 2318, 2357, 2368, 2386, 2437, 2468, 2487, 2523, 2526, 2528, 2553–4, 2598, 2601, 2649–50, 2684, 2749, 2785, 2922, 2969.
b) Cabinet d'Hozier (Cab d'Hoz), 1, 17, 23, 27, 30, 36, 68, 80, 86, 92–3, 140, 144, 211, 218, 223, 231, 235, 248, 269, 280, 285, 298–300, 308, 310.
c) Carrés d'Hozier (Carrés Hoz), 69, 106, 179, 265, 431, 453, 652.
d) Chérin, 39, 53, 81, 125, 132, 134, 142, 158–9, 178–9, 183, 188, 202.
e) Dossiers Bleus (Doss bleus), 1, 12–14, 17, 35–6, 49, 55, 57, 64, 77, 80, 103, 108, 139–40, 142, 147–8, 156, 158, 169–70, 178, 183, 190, 202, 207, 241, 256, 270, 275, 293, 295, 336, 344, 355, 369, 373, 381, 387, 391–2, 394, 408, 413–14, 420, 429, 434, 443–4, 471–2, 507, 524, 528, 530, 545, 557, 562, 576, 583, 586, 602, 610, 623, 650, 656, 673.
f) Nouveau d'Hozier (Nouv d'Hoz), 29, 134, 138, 145, 202, 208, 247, 270, 302.
Clairambault, 814.

Français (MS Fr), 6919 (Noailles corr), 7493, 7651–9 (*Dictionnaire des bienfaits du roi*), 7854 (maison du roi), 19211–12 (P Léonard notes), 20052 (abbé Louvois corr), 23206–8 (Noailles corr), 23498–23510 (*Nouvelles Ecclésiastiques* 1675–95), 20969 (extracts from *feuille des bénéfices*), 22404 (Cardinal Fleury papers), 22832–4 (Paris theology faculty), 23206, 23483 (Noailles corr), 32138–9, 32422, 32703, 32757, 32811–12, 32991.

Latin (MS Lat), 5496, 9153–56, 15440, 16573, 17021–30, 17039, 17042, 18389.

Mélanges Colbert, 7, 139, 147, 148, 148b, 156, 156b, 157b, 176b.

Morel de Thoisy, 2, 4, 267.

Nouvelles acquisitions françaises (Naf), 2092–3, 5132, 9651, 13634.

Other Paris Archives and Libraries

Archives de Saint-Sulpice (ASS), Correspondance des supérieurs-généraux, 3 vols; *fiches* Louis Bertrand.

Bibliothèque Sainte-Geneviève (BSG), MSS 941–2.

Bibliothèque de la Sorbonne, Archives de l'ancienne université de Paris (AUP), Reg 97 (rector's book 1650–79).

Missions Étrangères de Paris, MSS 2, 8, 9, 32–3, 94, 1537.

Archives Départementales

Alpes Maritimes, G 136, 1356, 1369, 1385. 1G 448.

Aveyron, G 61, 72, 79–80, 390, 1023.

Bouches-du-Rhône (dépôt Aix), 2D vol 2 11; 4D 4 (University); 1G 1271, 1273, 1275–6, 1275–6, 1279, 1281–2, 1319–21 (*insinuations ecclésiastiques*).

Cher, D 9, 17–18, 409 (Bourges law and theology faculty).

Creuse, E 392–491 (La Roche-Aymon papers); 3E 558–9 (Madot papers). G 687.

Doubs, G 949.

Drôme, B 1331.

Eure, E 2485–8 (Langle papers).

Eure-er-Loir, G 2.

Gers, I 2283.

Hautes-Alpes, G 223–6, 796, 1159, 1162–3, 1185, 1349–50, 1355–6, 1389, 1504, 1533.

Isère, B4212. 1G 276. 4G 86, 87, 161, 163, 165, 179, 181–2, 187, 195, 199, 324; 15G 454.

Lot-et-Garonne, B 35, 73, 90; 3E 120, vol 27. G/D 23; G/E 69, 70 (Hébert dossier).

Lozère, F 396. G 45, 61, 652, 655–6, 2129, 3028, 3095, 3119, 3124.

Puy-de-Dôme, 1G 1780. 2E 408 and 9F 61 (Champflour papers).

Saône-et-Loire, F 604, J 681.

Vaucluse, B 682, 1275. D 36, 136–8, 140.

Vendée, 1G 4–5.

Yonne, G 2–3, 109, 177, 453, 1621.

Provincial Libraries

Aix-en-Provence, Bibliothèque Méjanes. MS 256–7, P Bicaïs, Oratorian, Provençaux devenus évêques; MS 377, Vie de Mme de Venel (Gaillard); MSS 624–5, Papers of Cardinal Janson, from Rome embassy 1690–4; MS 1186 (abrégé de la vie de Jean de Gaillard . . . prince et évêque d'Apt).

Avignon, BM, MS 2648.

Clermont-Ferrand, BM, MS 550, 552–3, 559–61.

Grenoble, AC, CC 424, 725; GG 61; FF100. BM, MS R 7426, *dénombrement des familles annoblies 1587–1634*.

St Malo, AC, GG 25, *La Tour de Babel, ou la division des Evesques de France qui ont eu part a la constitution Unigenitus, depuis l'année 1714*.

Sens, BM, MSS 77, 143, 149–50, 156, 196–7, 245, 284.
Toulouse, Bibliothèque inter-universitaire (BIUT), MSS 8–10, 24, 28, 30.
Versailles, BM, MSS G 329–31, P 52, 66–7.

Rome

Vatican Archives (ASV)

Acta congregationis consistorialis 1668–93 (unnumbered volumes, papers grouped by years).
Miscell Armadio, I, 36, 40.
Fondo Carpegna, 86.
Fondo Santini, 210.
Lettere di Vescovi, 52, 53, 55, 56, 57, 61, 62, 63, 64, 65, 66, 67, 90.
Miscell Arm, XII, 151.
Nunz Fr, 134–5, 141, 144–5, 153–61, 163, 165–7, 180–7, 195, 219, 221, 222, 225, 226,
    332.
Processus consistoriales, 61–105.
Processus Datariae, 55, 90.

Others

Manchester, John Rylands University Library (JRULM), MSS French 89–96, Letters of Mme
    d'Huxelles to marquis de la Garde.

Printed primary sources

Bosuet, Jacques-Bénigne, *Correspondance*, ed Charles Urbain and Eugène Levesque, 15 vols, Paris
    1909–25.
Bussy-Rabutin, Roger de, *Correspondance avec le père René Rapin*, ed C Rouben, Paris 1983.
———, *Correspondance de Bussy-Rabutin*, ed Ludovic Lalanne, 6 vols, Paris 1858–9.
Chamillart, Michel, *Correspondance et papiers inédits*, ed G Esnault, 2 vols, Le Mans 1884.
Choisy, François-Timoléon, abbé de, *Mémoires*, ed Georges Mongrédien, Paris 1966.
*Collection des procès-verbaux des assemblées générales du clergé de France depuis l'année 1560 jusqu'à
    présent*, ed Antoine Duranthon, 9 vols, Paris 1767–78.
Correspondance de M Louis Tronson. Lettres choisies 1676–1700, ed Louis Bertrand, 3 vols, Paris
    1904.
Correspondance des contrôleurs-généraux des finances avec les intendants de province, ed A-M de Bois-
    lisle, 3 vols, Paris 1874–97.
Correspondance des intendants avec le contrôleur-général des finances 1676–1689, ed Annette Smedley-
    Weill, 3 vols, Paris 1989–91.
Correspondance du nonce en France Angelo Ranuzzi, ed Bruno Neveu, 2 vols, Rome 1973.
Correspondance du nonce en France Fabrizio Spada (1674–5), ed Ségolène de Dainville-Barbiche,
    Rome 1982.
Cosnac, Daniel de, *Mémoires*, ed Gabriel-Jules de Cosnac, 2 vols, Paris 1852.
Coulanges, Philippe de, *Mémoires*, ed Louis de Monmerqué, Paris 1820.
Dangeau, Philippe de Courcillon, marquis de, *Journal*, ed E Soulié, L Dussieux and P de
    Chennevières, 19 vols, Paris 1854–60.
Documents historiques relatifs à la Société des Missions Etrangères, ed Adrien Launay, i, Paris 1904.
Documents pour l'histoire de Luçon 1317–1801, ed Louis Delhommeau, Luçon 1971.
*État de la maison du roi Louis XIII, des celles de sa mère, Marie de Médicis, de sa soeur Chrétienne, etc,
    comprenant les années 1601 à 1665*, ed Eugène Griselle, Paris 1912.
Fénelon, François de la Mothe-Salignac de, *Oeuvres*, ed J Gosselin, 10 vols, Paris 1851–2.
———, *Oeuvres* (ed *La Pléiade*), ed J Le Brun, 2 vols, Paris 1983–92.

————, *Correspondance*, ed Jean Orcibal, Jacques Le Brun and Irénée Noye, 17 vols, Paris 1972–99.

Fléchier, Esprit, *Lettres sur divers sujets*, Paris 1711.

Fortin de la Hoguette, Philippe, *Lettres aux frères Dupuy et à leur entourage*, ed Giuliano Ferretti, 2 vols, Florence 1997.

Foucault, Nicolas-Joseph, *Mémoires*, ed F Baudry, Paris 1862.

Hébert, François, *Mémoires*, ed G Girard, Paris 1927.

————, *Testament de feu messire François Hébert évêque et comte d'Agen*, Agen 1728.

Huet, Daniel, *Lettres inedites de P-D Huet évêque d'Avranches à son neveu, M de Charsigné*, ed Armand Gasté, Caen 1901.

Inventaire-sommaire des archives départementales des Hautes-Alpes, série G, ed Paul Guillaume, 3 vols, Gap 1891–1913.

Jarrot, Louis, 'Le Testament de Jean-Joseph Languet de Gergy, archevêque de Sens, membre de l'Académie française', *Bulletin d'Histoire et d'Archéologie Religieuse du Diocèse de Dijon*, 18 (1900), 217–22, 257–8, 278–82.

Journal de la santé du Louis XIV, ed J A Le Roy, Paris 1862.

Journal inédit de Jean-Baptiste Colbert marquis de Torcy, ministre et secrétaire d'état aux affaires étrangères pendant les années 1709, 1710 et 1711, ed Fréderic Masson, Paris 1884.

*L'Intendance de Berry à la fin du xvii*ᵉ *siècle*, ed Claude Michaud, Paris 2000.

L'Intendance de Caen en 1700, ed P Gouhier, Paris 1998.

*L'Intendance de Champagne à la fin du xvii*ᵉ *siècle*, ed J-P Brancourt, Paris 1983.

*L'Intendance de Languedoc à la fin du xvii*ᵉ *siècle*, ed Françoise Moreil, Paris 1985.

L'Intendance de Bourgogne, ed Daniel Ligou, Paris 1988.

L'Intendance du Lyonnais, Beaujolais et Forez en 1698 et 1762, ed J-P Gutton, Paris 1992.

La Bretagne en 1665 d'après le rapport de Colbert de Croissy, ed Jean Kerhervé, François Roudaut and Jean Tanguy, Brest 1978.

Le Gendre, Louis, *Mémoires*, ed M Roux, Paris 1863.

Le Peletier, Claude, *Deux mémoires historiques de Claude le Peletier*, ed Louis André (*thèse complémentaire*) Paris 1905.

Ledieu, François, *Mémoires et Journal sur la vie et les ouvrages de Bossuet*, ed abbé René-François-Wladimir Guettée, 4 vols, Paris 1856–7.

Lehoreau, René, *Cérémonial de l'église d'Angers 1692–1721*, ed François Lebrun, Paris 1967.

Lesaulnier, Jean, ed, *Port-Royal insolite: Receueil critique des choses diverses*, Paris 1992.

L'Estat de la France, nouvellement corrigé et mis en meilleur ordre, où l'on voit de suite tous les officiers de la couronne, avec leurs armoiries . . . avec plusieurs traittez particuliers . . . par N. Besongne, Paris 1661 (and regularly thereafter).

Lettres aux Feuquières, 5 vols, ed Etienne Gallois, Paris 1845.

Lettres de Germain Vuillart ami de Port-Royal à M Louis de Préfontaine (1694–1700), ed Ruth Clark, Geneva-Lille 1951.

Lettres de Jean Chapelain, ed Philippe Tamizey de Larroque, 2 vols, Paris 1880–3.

Lettres de Turenne, ed Suzanne d'Huart, Paris 1971.

Lettres du cardinal Le Camus, évêque et prince de Grenoble (1632–1707), ed A P M Ingold, Paris 1892.

Lettres du cardinal Le Camus, évêque et prince de Grenoble (1632–1707), ed Claude Faure, Grenoble 1933.

'Lettres du duc de Beauvillier à l'évêque d'Alet', ed Léon Lecestre, *Annuaire-Bulletin de la Société d'Histoire de France*, 59 (1922), 186–209.

Lettres et mémoires adressés au chancelier Séguier, ed R Mousnier, 2 vols, Paris 1964.

Louis XIV, *Mémoires for the instruction of the Dauphin*, ed Paul Sonnino, New York 1970.

————, *Mémoires pour l'instruction du dauphin*, ed Pierre Goubert, Paris 1992.

Maintenon, Françoise d'Aubigné, marquise de, *Correspondance générale*, ed Théophile Lavalée, 4 vols, Paris 1864–6 (vol v printed, but not published).

——, *Correspondance de Madame de Maintenon et de la princesse des Ursins: 1709, une année tragique*, ed Marcel Loyau, Paris 2002.

——, *Lettres de Mme de Maintenon*, 8 vols, Amsterdam 1766.

——, *Lettres*, ed Marcel Langlois, 4 vols, Paris 1934–9 (vol 1 never published).

——, 'Lettres inédites de Mme de Maintenon', ed Henri Courteault, *Revue des Etudes Historiques* (1900), 401–13.

——, 'Quarante-six lettres inédites de Madame de Maintenon', ed Théophile Foisset, *Le Correspondant*, 1 (1859), 641–92 (BN tirage à part).

——, 'Quelques lettres de la vieillesse de Mme de Maintenon 1708–16' *Revue de l'Histoire de Versailles et de Seine-et-Oise*, 27 (1925).

——, *Lettres inédites de Mme de Maintenon et de Mme la princesse des Ursins*, ed Bossange frères, 4 vols, Paris 1826.

Mémoriaux du conseil de 1661, ed J de Boislisle, 3 vols, Paris 1905.

Mention, Léon, *Documents rélatifs aux rapports du clergé avec la royauté de 1682 à 1705*, Paris 1893, reprint Geneva 1976.

Ormesson, Olivier Lefèvre d', *Journal et extraits des mémoires d'André Lefèvre d'Ormesson*, ed A Chéruel, 2 vols, Paris 1860–1.

Quesnel, Pasquier, *Correspondance*, ed Mme Albert Le Roy, 2 vols, Paris 1900.

Rancé, Armand-Jean Bouthillier de, *Correspondance*, ed A J Krailsheimer, 4 vols, Paris 1993.

Receueil des mandemens et instructions pastorales de Messeigneurs les Archevêques et Évêques de France pour l'acceptation de la Constitution de N S Père le Pape Clement XI du 8 septembre 1713 contre le livre intitulé: Le Nouveau Testament, en François, avec des Réflexions Morales sur chaque verset. Paris 1715.

Recueil des instructions données aux ambassadeurs et ministres de France depuis les traités de Westphalie jusqu'à la Révolution française, (Rome), ed G Hanotaux and J Hanoteau, 2 vols, Paris 1884–1911.

Renty, Gaston de, *Correspondance*, ed Raymond Triboulet, Paris 1978.

Répertoire des visites pastorales de la France. Première série: anciens diocèses (jusqu'en 1790), 4 vols, Paris 1977–85.

Retz, Cardinal de, *Oeuvres*, ed A Feillet *et al*, 10 vols, Paris 1870–1920.

Richelieu, Armand-Jean du Plessis de, *Les Papiers de Richelieu, politique intérieure*, ed Pierre Grillon, 6 vols, Paris 1975 – in progress.

Saint-Simon, Louis de Rouvroy, duc de *Mémoires*, ed A M de Boislisle, L Lecestre, J de Boislisle, 43 vols, Paris 1879–1930.

——, *Écrits inédits*, ed A P Faugère, 8 vols, Paris 1880–1895.

Sévigné, Marie de Rabutin-Chantal, marquise de, *Lettres*, ed Louis Monmerqué and Paul Mesnard, 14 vols, Paris 1862–6.

Sourches, Louis-François du Bouchet, marquis de, *Mémoires*, ed Gabriel de Cosnac, Arthur Bertrand and E Pontal, 13 vols, Paris 1882–93.

Tallemant des Réaux, Gédéon, *Historiettes*, ed Antoine Adam, 2 vols, Paris 1962.

Villette-Mursay, Philippe de, *Mes Campagnes de mer sous Louis XIV*, ed Michel Vergé-Franceschi, Paris 1991.

Reference Works, Dictionaries, etc

Albanès, J-H, *Armorial et sigillographie des évêques de Marseille*, Marseille 1884.

Andrieu, Jules, *Bibliographie de l'Agenais*, 3 vols, Paris-Agen 1886–91.

Anselme de Sainte-Marie, le Père (Pierre de Gibours), *Histoire généalogique et chronologique de la maison royale de France et des grands officiers de la Couronne*, 9 vols, Paris 1726–30.

Antoine, Michel, *Gouvernement et administration de Louis XV. Dictionnaire biographique*, Paris 1978.

Arundel de Condé, G, *Dictionnaire des anoblis normands 1600–1789*, np 1975.

Bayard, Françoise, *et al*, *Dictionnaire des surintendants et contrôleurs-généraux des finances*, Paris 2000.

Beauchet-Filleau, Henri, and Chergé, Charles de, *Dictionnaire historique et généalogique des familles du Poitou*, 2nd ed, 3 vols, Poitiers 1891–1915.

Bechameil de Nointel, *La Bretagne à la fin du xviie siècle d'après le rapport de Béchameil de Nointel*, ed Jean Meyer and Jean Bérenger, Paris 1976.

Biographie Nationale Belge, 44 vols, Brussels 1866–1986.

Blanc, François-Paul, 'Les Origines des familles provençales maintenues dans le second ordre sous le règne de Louis XIV. Dictionnaire généalogique', unpublished doctoral thesis, Aix-en-Provence 1971.

Boisnard, Luc, *Dictionnaire des anciennes familles de Touraine*, Mayenne 1992.

Borricand, René de, *Nobiliaire de Provence*, 3 vols, Aix-en-Provence 1974–9.

Capeille, Joseph, *Dictionnaire des biographies roussillonnaises*. Paris 1914.

Carné, Gaston de, *Les Chevaliers bretons de Saint-Michel*, Nantes 1884.

Cauna, A de, *Armorial des Landes*, 4 vols, Bordeaux 1862–9.

Cerchiari, Emmanuele, *Capellani Papae et Apostolicae Sedes auditorum causarum sacri palatii apostolici seu Sacra Romana Rota ab origine ad diem usque 2 sept 1870*, 4 vols, Rome 1921.

Chaix d'Est-Ange, Gustave, *Dictionnaire des familles françaises anciennes ou notables à la fin du xixe siècle*, 20 vols, Evreux 1903–29.

Champeval, J-B, *Dictionnaire des familles nobles et notables de la Corrèze*, 2 vols, Tulle 1911–13.

Clapiers-Coulonges, Balthazar, *Chronologie des officiers de cours souveraines*, ed marquis de Boisgelin, Aix 1909–12.

Clergeac, Adrien, *Chronologie des archevêques, évêques et abbés de l'ancienne province ecclésiastique d'Auch et des diocèses de Condom et de Lombez*, Paris 1912.

Dainville, François de, *Cartes anciennes de l'église de France*, Paris 1956.

Dictionary of Canadian Biography, George W Brown *et al*, eds, 12 vols, Toronto 1966–91.

Dictionnaire de Biographie Française, ed Roman d'Amat *et al*, Paris 1934–, in progress.

Dictionnaire de droit canonique, ed R Naz, 7 vols, Paris 1936–65.

Dictionnaire de la noblesse, ed F Aubert de La Chesnaye-Desbois and Badier, 3rd ed, 19 vols, Paris 1866–76.

Dictionnaire d'Histoire et de Géographie Ecclésiastiques, ed A de Meyer et al, Paris 1912–, in progress.

Dictionnaire du grand siècle, ed François Bluche, Paris 1992.

Dictionnaire historique, géographique, et biographique du Maine-et-Loire, ed Célestin Port, 3 vols, Paris and Angers 1874–8.

Dictionnaire historique, topographique et biographique de la Mayenne, ed A Angot and F Gaugain, 4 vols, Laval 1900–10.

Dizionario biografico degli Italiani, Rome 1960–, in progress.

Dufau de Maluquer, Armand, *Armorial de Béarn*, 2 vols, Paris 1889–93.

Durand de Maillane, Pierre-Toussaint, *Dictionnaire de droit canonique et de pratique bénéficiale*, Lyon 1770.

Encylopédie départementale des Bouches-du-Rhône, vol iv, pt ii: *Dictionnaire biographique*, ed Raoul Busquet, Paris-Marseille 1931.

Etchéchoury, Maïté, *Les Maîtres des requêtes de l'hôtel sous les derniers Valois*, Geneva 1991.

Favre-Lejeune, Christine, *Les Secrétaires du Roi de la grande chancellerie de France. Dictionnaire biographique et généalogique, 1672–1789*, Paris 1986.

Foix, V, *Lalanne. Essai généalogique sur les familles nobles ou titres de ce nom*, Dax, n.d.

Frondeville, Henri de, *Les Présidents du parlement de Normandie 1494–1790*, Rouen 1953.

———, *Les Conseillers du parlement de Normandie au xvie siècle 1499–1594*, Rouen and Paris 1960.

———, *Les Conseillers du parlement de Normandie sous Henri IV et Louis XIII*, Rouen and Paris 1964.

————, *Les Conseillers du parlement de Normandie de 1641 à 1715*, Rouen and Paris 1970.

Gallia Christiana, ed Denis de Sainte-Marthe *et al*, 16 vols, Paris 1715–1865.

Gallia Christiana Novissima, ed Joseph Albanès, 7 vols, Valence 1899–1920.

Gatz, Erwin, ed, *Die Bischöfe des Heiligen Römischen Reiches 1648 bis 1803. Ein biographisches Lexikon*, Berlin 1990.

Godet de Soudé, François de, *Dictionnaire des anoblissements. Extrait des registres de la Chambre des Comptes depuis 1345 jusqu'en 1660*, ed E de Barthélemy, Paris 1875.

Guéneau, Victor, *Dictionnaire biographique du Nivernais*, Nevers 1899.

Haag, Eugène and Emile, *La France protestante*, 10 vols, Paris 1846–59.

Hierarchia Catholica medii et recentioris aevi, ed Conrad Eubel *et al*, vols iii–v, Munich 1923–52.

Hommages rendus à la chambre de France. Chambre des comptes de Paris. Série P (xive–xvie siècles), ed L Mirot and J-P Babelon, 3 vols, 1932–85.

Inventaire des arrêts du conseil d'état (règne de Henri IV), ed Noël Valois, 2 vols, Paris 1886–93.

Jean, Armand, *Les Évêques et les archevêques de France depuis 1682 jusqu'à 1801*, Paris 1891.

Lacger, L de, *Etats administratifs des anciens diocèses d'Albi, de Castres et de Lavaur*, Albi-Paris 1921.

Lamant, Hubert, *Armorial français*, np 1975–, in progress.

————, *Armorial de Bayonne, pays Basque et sud-Gascogne*, 2 vols, Bayonne 1981–4.

Lapeyre, André, and Scheurer, Rémy, *Les Notaires et secrétaires du roi sous les règnes de Louis XI, Charles VIII et Louis XII (1461–1515)*, Paris 1978.

Levantal, Christophe, *Ducs et pairs et duchés-pairies laïques à l'époque moderne 1519–1790: dictionnaire prosographique, généalogique, chronologique, topographique et heuristique*, Paris 1996.

Lurion, Roger de, *Nobiliaire de Franche-Comté*, Besançon 1890.

'Maintenues de noblesse prononcées par MM Quentin de Richebourg et Desgalois de Latour, intendants de la généralité de Poitiers 1714–1718', ed A de la Bouraliere. *Archives Historiques du Poitou*, vols 22–23, Poitiers 1892–3.

Merlet, Louis and Robert, eds, *Dignitaires de l'église Notre-Dame de Chartres (Archives du diocese de Chartres, v)*, Paris 1900.

Mesmay, J-T, *Dictionnaire historique, biographique et généalogique des anciennes familles de Franche-Comté*, 5 vols 1958–63.

Moreri, Louis, *Le Grand Dictionnaire historique* (1759 ed), 10 vols, Paris 1759.

Nadaud, Joseph, *Nobiliaire du diocèse et de la généralité de Limoges*, 4 vols, Limoges 1856–80.

Navelle, André, *Familles nobles et notables du midi toulousain au xve et au xvie siècles*, 11 vols, Fenouillet 1991–5.

O'Gilvy, Gabriel, and Bourousse de Laffore, Jules, *Nobiliaire de Guyenne et de Gascogne*, 4 vols, Bordeaux-Paris 1856–83.

Pidoux de la Maduère, Sylvain, *Les Officiers du Parlement de Dôle et leurs familles*, Paris 1961.

Pinard, *Chronologie historique militaire, contenant l'histoire de la création de toutes les charges militaires supérieures, etc*, 8 vols, Paris 1760–78.

Popoff, Michel, *Prosopographie des gens du parlement de Paris (1266–1753)*, Saint-Nazaire-le-Désert 1996.

Recherche générale de la noblesse d'Auvergne de 1656 à 1724, ed L de Ribier, Paris 1907.

Remacle, Albert de, *Dictionnaire généalogique des familles d'Auvergne*, 3 vols, Clermont, 1995.

Rivoire de la Batie, G de, *Armorial de Dauphiné*, Lyon 1867.

Saulnier, Frédéric, *Le Parlement de Bretagne 1551–1790. Répertoire alphabétique et biographique de tous les membres de la cour*, 2 vols, Rennes 1909.

Surgères de Granges, marquis de, *Répertoire biographique et historique de la Gazette*, 4 vols Paris 1902–6.

Tardieu, Ambroise, *Dictionnaire des anciennes familles de l'Auvergne*, Moulins 1884.

Les Tarnais, dictionnaire biographique, ed Jean-Louis Biget, Albi 1996.

Tessereau, Abraham, *Histoire chronologique de la grande chancellerie de France*, 2 vols, Paris 1710.

Thiébaud, J M, *Officiers seigneuriaux et anciennes familles de Franche-Comté*, Lons-le-Saunier 1984.

————, *Les Co-gouvernants de la cité impériale de Besançon, Dictionnaire biographique, historique et généalogique*, Besançon 1996.

Trani, Camille, 'Les Conseillers du grand conseil au xvie siècle (1547–1610)', *Paris et l'Ile-de-France: Mémoires*, 42 (1991), 61–218.

Vergé-Franceschi, Michel, *Les Officiers généraux de la marine royale (1715–1774)*, 7 vols, Paris 1990.

Vidal, Jean-Marie, *Catalogues épiscopaux et listes de bénéfices des anciens diocèses ariégois*, Foix, 1933.

Villain, Jean, *La France moderne*, 3 vols, St-Etienne-Montpellier 1906–13.

Villenaut, A de, *Nobiliaire de Nivernois*, 2 vols, Nevers 1900.

Vindry, Fleury, *Dictionnaire de l'état-major français au xvie siècle. Vol i: la gendarmerie*, Paris 1901.

————, *Les Ambassadeurs permanents français au xvie siècle*, Paris 1903.

————, *Les Parlementaires français au xvie siècle*, 2 vols, Paris 1909–12.

Secondary works

Allier, Raoul, *Une Société secrète au xviie siècle. La Compagnie du très saint-sacrement de l'autel à Marseille*, Paris 1909.

Antoine, Michel, *Le Conseil du roi sous Louis XV*, Geneva-Paris 1970.

————, *Le Coeur de l'état. Surintendance, contrôle général et intendances des finances 1552–1791*, Paris 2003.

Appolis, E, 'Un prélat philojanséniste sous la Régence', in *La Régence* (Paris 1970), 238–45.

————, *Le Jansénisme dans le diocèse de Lodève au xviiie siècle*, Albi 1952.

————, *Entre jansénistes et 'zelanti', le tiers parti catholique au xviiie siècle*, Paris 1960.

Archon, abbé (Jean-Louis), *Histoire ecclésiastique de la chapelle des rois de France*, 2 vols, Paris 1704–11.

Ardoin, Paul, *La Bulle Unigenitus dans les diocèses d'Aix Arles, Marseille, Fréjus, Toulon (1713–1789)*, Marseille 1936.

Armogathe J-R and Joutard, P, 'Baville et la consultation des évêques en 1698' *Revue d'Histoire et de Philosophie Religieuse (1972)*, 157–84.

Arnaud, Etienne, *Les Milon, une famille de Touraine et d'Anjou (xiiie–xixe siècle)*, np, 1988.

Aston, Nigel, *End of an Elite. The French Bishops and the Coming of the Revolution 1786–1790*, Oxford 1992.

Aulagne, J, *La Réforme catholique du xviie siècle dans le diocèse de Limoges*, Paris 1905.

Azéma, Xavier, *Un prélat janséniste. Louis Foucquet évêque et comte d'Agde (1656–1702)*, Paris 1963.

Barnavi, Elie, *Le Parti de Dieu. Étude sociale et politique des chefs de la Ligue parisienne 1585–1594*, Louvain 1980.

Barrio Gozalo, Maximiliano, *Les Obispos de Castilla y León durante en antiguo régimen (1556–1834). Estudio socioeconómico*, Madrid 2000.

Batterel, Louis, *Mémoires domestiques pour servir à l'histoire de l'Oratoire*, ed A M P Ingold, 5 vols, Paris 1902–11.

Baumgartner, Frederic J, *Change and Continuity in the French Episcopate: The Bishops and the Wars of Religion 1547–1610*, Durham, North Carolina 1986.

Bayard, Françoise, *Le Monde des financiers au xviie siècle*, Paris 1988.

————, 'Jean Bochart de Champigny (1561–1630)', *Revue d'Histoire Moderne et Contemporaine*, 46 (1999), 39–52.

Bazin, Jean-Louis, *Histoire des évêques de Chalon-sur-Saône*, vol ii (*Mémoires de la Société d'Histoire et d'Archéologie de Chalon-sur-Saône*, 2nd series, vol xv). Chalon-sur-Saône 1918.

Béguin, Katia, *Les Princes de Condé au xviie siècle. Rebelles, courtesans et mécènes dans la France du grand siècle*, Seyssel 1999.

Beik, William, *Absolutism and Society in Seventeenth-Century France*, Cambridge 1984.

Bély Lucien, *Espions et ambassadeurs au temps de Louis XIV*, Paris 1990.

——, ed, *Dictionnaire de l'ancien régime*, Paris 1996.

Bérengier, Théophile, *Vie de Mgr Henry de Belsunce évêque de Marseille 1670–1755*, 2 vols, Lyon-Paris 1886.

Bergin, Joseph, 'Richelieu and his bishops?', in Joseph Bergin and Laurence Brockliss, eds, *Richelieu and his* Age, Oxford 1992, 175–202.

——, *The Making of the French Episcopate 1589–1661*, New Haven-London 1996.

Berthelot du Chesnay, Charles, *Les Missions de Saint-Jean Eudes*, Paris 1967.

Bertrand, Antoine-Louis, *Histoire des séminaires de Bordeaux et de Bazas*, 3 vols, Bordeaux 1894.

——, *Bibliothèque Sulpicienne*, 3 vols, Paris 1900.

——, *La Vie de Messire Henri de Béthune archevêque de Bordeaux 1604–1680*, 2 vols, Bordeaux 1902.

——, 'Hommes d'église de la famille de Poudenx', Pau 1902 (in *Etudes historiques et religieuses du diocèse de Bayonne*) (BN offprint).

Beyssac, Jean, *Notes pour servir à l'histoire de l'église de Lyon. Les Grands prêtres de Lyon*, Lyon 1903.

——, *Les Chanoines de l'église de Lyon*, Lyon 1914.

Bien, David, 'Offices, Corps and a System of State Credit: the Uses of Privilege under the ancien régime', in Keith M Baker, ed, *The French Revolution and the Creation of Modern Political Culture*, Oxford 1987, 89–114.

Bizocchi, Roberto, *Genealogie incredibili: Scritti di storia nell'Europa moderna*, Bologna 1995.

Black, Jeremy, *From Louis XIV to Napoleon: The Fate of a Great Power*, London 1999.

Blanquie, Christophe, 'L'Abbé de la Vergne', *Chroniques de Port-Royal: Port-Royal et les Protestants*, Paris 1999, 373–92.

Blet, Pierre, *Le Clergé de France et la monarchie*, 2 vols, Rome-Paris 1959.

——, *Les Assemblées du clergé et Louis XIV de 1670 à 1693*, Rome 1972.

——, *Le Clergé de France, Louis XIV et le Saint-Siège de 1695 à 1715*, Vatican City 1989.

——, *Les Nonces du pape à la cour de Louis XIV*, Paris 2002.

——, 'Le Concordat de Bologne et la réforme tridentine', *Gregorianum*, 45 (1964), 241–79.

——, 'Le Camus et le conflit de la régale', in Jean Godel, ed, *Le Cardinal des montagnes. Etienne Le Camus évêque de Grenoble (1671–1707)*, Grenoble 1974, 65–86.

——, 'La nonciature de France et la crise gallicane', in *Kurie und Politik*, ed Alexander Koller, Tübingen 1998, 98–115.

——, 'Louis XIV et les papes aux prises avec le jansénisme', *Archivum Historiae Pontificiae*, 31 (1992), 109–92; 32 (1993), 65–148.

Bliard, P, *Les Mémoires de Saint-Simon et le Père Le Tellier confesseur de Louis XIV*, Paris 1891.

Bluche, François, *L'Origine des magistrats du parlement de Paris au xviiie siècle. Dictionnaire généalogique*, Paris 1956.

——, *Les Magistrats du grand conseil au xviie siècle (1690–1791)*, Paris 1966.

——, 'Social Origins of the Secretaries of State under Louis XIV, 1661–1715', in Ranghild M Hatton, ed, *Louis XIV and Absolutism*, London 1976, 85–97.

——, and Durye, Pierre, *L'Anoblissement par charges avant 1789*, 2 vols (*Les Cahiers nobles*), np 1962.

Boisnard, Luc, *Les Phélypeaux, une famille de ministres sous l'ancien régime*, Paris 1986.

Bonney, Richard, *Political Change in France under Richelieu and Mazarin 1624–1661*, Oxford 1978.

Bordes, Maurice, 'Le Jansénisme dans le diocèse de Lectoure', *Actes du 96e Congrès National des Sociétés Savantes* 2 vols, Toulouse 1971, ii, 107–35.

Bourgeon, Jean-Louis, *Les Colbert avant Colbert*, Paris 1973.

Bourquin, Laurent *La Noblesse dans la France moderne*, Paris 2002.

Bouyssou, Marc, *Réforme catholique et déchristianisation dans le sud du diocèse de Chartres. Les testaments ruraux du Blésois et du Vendômois, xvie–xviiie siècles*, 2 vols, Chartres 1998.

Briggs, Robin, *Communities of Belief. Cultural and Social Tensions in Early Modern France*, Oxford 1989.

Brockliss, L W B, *French Higher Education in the Seventeenth and Eighteenth Centuries*, Oxford 1987.

——, and Jones, Colin, *The Medical World of Early Modern France*, Oxford 1997.

Brunet, Serge, *Les Pêtres des montagnes. La Vie, la mort, la foi dans les Pyrénées centrales sous l'ancien régime*, Aspet 2001.

Bungener, Eric, *Les Descendants d'Agrippa d'Aubigné*, 2 vols, Paris 1998–9.

Busquets, Joan, 'Bisbes espanyols i francesos a Catalunya durant la guerra dels segadors', in Albert Rossich and August Rafanell, eds, *El barroc català*, Barcelona 1989, 61–87.

Campbell, Peter R, *Power and Politics in Old Régime France*, London 1996.

Camps, François de, *Éloge de Messire Hyacinthe Serroni, suivi de son testament*, np, nd.

Cans, Albert, *L'Organisation financière du clergé de France au temps de Louis XIV*, Paris 1910.

Ceyssens, Lucien , 'Les Papiers de Quesnel saisis à Bruxelles et transportés à Paris en 1703 et 1704', *Revue d'Histoire Ecclésiastique*, 44 (1949), 508–51.

——, 'Autour de la bulle Unigenitus. Jean-François de Lescure évêque de Luçon et Etienne de Champflour, évêque de La Rochelle', *Augustiniana*, 38 (1988), 149–204.

——, 'Vineam Domini et le jansénisme français', in *Antonianum*, 64 (1988), 388–430.

——, *Le Sort de la bulle Unigenitus*, Louvain 1992.

——, 'Innocent XII et le jansenisme français', in *Riforme, religione e politica durante il pontificato di Innocenzo XII*, ed Bruno Pellegrino, Lecce 1994, 307–34 (also in *Antonianum*, 67 (1992), 39–66).

——, and Tans, J G A, *Autour de la bulle Unigenitus*, Louvain 1988.

Chantelauze, Régis de, *Le Père de la Chaize confesseur de Louis XIV*, Lyon 1859.

Charmeil, Jean-Paul, *Les Trésoriers de France à l'époque de la Fronde*, Paris 1964.

Charpentier, Léon, *Un évêque d'ancien regime, Louis-Joseph de Grignan (1650–1722)*, Arras 1899.

Châtellier, Louis, *Tradition chrétienne et renouveau catholique dans le cadre de l'ancien diocèse de Strasbourg 1650–1770*, Paris 1981.

——, 'Le Vicaire-général François Blouet de Camilly (1694–1705) et la reconstruction du diocèse de Strasbourg', *Archives de l'Eglise d'Alsace*, 50 (1990–1), 75–92.

Chaunu, Pierre, *La Mort à Paris, xvi*, *xvii*, *xviii* siècles*, Paris 1978.

——, *et al*, *Le Basculement religieux de Paris au xviii* siècle*, Paris 1998.

Chevaillier, R, 'Les Revenus des bénéfices ecclésiastiques au xviii* siècle', *La Revolution Française*, 74 (1921), 113–49.

Chevalier, Jules, *Essai historique sur l'église et la ville de Die*, 3 vols, Montelimar-Valence, 1888–1909.

Church, William F, *Richelieu and Reason of State*, Princeton, NJ, 1972.

Clair, Pierre, 'La Famille du père Louis Thomassin', *Oratoriana* 11 (1965), 122–39.

Collins, James B, *Classes, Estates and Order in Early Modern Brittany*, Cambridge 1994.

——, 'Geographic and Social Mobility in Early Modern France', *Journal of Social History*, 24 (1991), 563–77.

Combarieu, L, 'Testaments de trois évêques de Cahors', *Bulletin de la Société d'Étude du Lot*, 6 (1880), 26–42.

Combeau, Yves, *Le Comte d'Argenson, ministre de Louis XIV*, Paris 1999.

Compère, Marie-Madeleine and Julia, Dominique, *Les Collèges français, 16ᵉ–18ᵉ siècles*, 2 vols, Paris 1984–8.

Contrasty, Jean, *Histoire de la cité de Rieux-Volvestre et de ses évéques*, Toulouse 1936.

——, *Histoire des évêques de Comminges*, Toulouse 1940.

Cornette, Joël, 'L'Histoire au travail. Le nouveau 'Siècle de Louis XIV': un bilan historiographique depuis vingt ans (1977–2000)', *Histoire, Économie et Société*, 19 (2000), 561–620.

Corvisier, André, *Louvois*, Paris 1983.

Couarraze, G, *Au Pays de Savès. Lombez évêché rural*, Lombez 1973.

Coudray, René du, 'René Le Sauvage, évêque de Lavaur 1630–1677', *Le Pays de Grandville*, 5 (1909), 1–36.

Couet, Marie-Emmanuelle, 'Mgr Desmaretz, seigneur-évêque de Saint-Malo', *Histoire, Economie, Société*, 18 (1999), 467–87.

Croix, Alain, *L'Âge d'or de la Bretagne 1532–1675*, Rennes 1993.

Daranatz, J-B, 'Dominique Turgot de Saint-Clair, évêque de Sées en 1710', *Bulletin de la Société des Sciences, Lettres, Arts et Études Régionales de Bayonne*, n s, 1 (1928), 171–5.

Darricau, Raymond, 'Louis XIV et le Saint-Siège. Les Indults de nomination aux bénéfices consistoriaux (1643–1670)', *Bulletin de Littérature Ecclésiastique*, 66 (1965), 16–34.

———, *La Formation des professeurs de séminaire au début du xviiᵉ siècle d'après le directoire de M Jean Bonnet (1664–1735) supérieur général de la congrégation de la Mission*, Piacenza 1966.

———, 'Une heure mémorable dans les rapports entre la France et le Saint-Siège: le pontificat de Clément IX (1667–1669)', *Bolletino Storico Pistoiese*, 61 (1969), 78–98.

———, 'L'arrêt d'Agen', *Revue de l'Agenais*, 103 (1976), 345–55.

———, 'La Correspondance de Louis Lascaris d'Urfé (évêque de Limoges 1676–1696) et de M de Tronson, supérieur général de Saint-Sulpice', in *Le Limousin au xviiᵉ siècle*, Limoges 1979, 205–19.

Dawson, Nelson-Martin, ed, *Crise d'autorité et clientélisme: Mgr Jean Joseph Languet de Gergy et la bulle Unigenitus*, Sherbrooke 1997.

———, ed, *Clientélisme ecclésiastique et antijansénisme*, Sherbrooke 1998.

———, ed, *Fidélités ecclésiastiques et crise janséniste*, Sherbrooke 2001.

———, 'Les Pari de Languet et le Paris antijanséniste', *Revue d'Histoire Ecclésiastique*, 94 (1999), 871–96.

Debal, J, ed, *Histoire d'Orléans et de son terroir*, 2 vols, Roanne 1982–3.

Dedieu, Jean, 'Le Désarroi du jansénisme pendant la période du quesnellisme', in Victor Carrière, ed, *Introduction aux études d'histoire ecclésiastique locale*, 3 vols (Paris 1933–6), iii, 541–89.

Degert, Antoine, *Histoire des évêques d'Aire*, Paris 1908.

———, *Histoire des séminaires français jusqu'à la Révolution*, 2 vols, Paris 1912.

Dejean, Étienne, *Un prélat indépendent au xviiᵉ siècle. Nicolas Pavillon évêque d'Alet (1637–1677)*, Paris 1909.

Delattre, P, *Établissements des Jésuites. Répértoire topo-bibliographique publié à l'occasion du quatrième centenaire de la fondation de la Compagnie de Jésus, 1540–1940*, 4 vols, Enghien 1949–57.

Deregnaucourt, Gilles, 'Fénelon à Cambrai: remarques sur un épiscopat et perspectives de recherches', *XVII Siècle*, 52 (2000), 97–110.

———, and Philippe Guignet, eds, *Fénelon évêque et pasteur en son temps*, Lille 1996.

Desmons, F, *Études historiques, économiques et religieuses sur Tournai durant le règne de Louis XIV. L'épiscopat de Gilbert de Choiseul 1671–1689*, Tournai 1907.

Descimon, Robert, 'Élites parisiennes du xvᵉ au xviiᵉ siècle. Du bon usage du cabinet des titres', *Bibliothèque de l'École des Chartes*, 155 (1997), 607–44.

Dessert, Daniel, *Argent pouvoir et société au grand siècle*, Paris 1984.

———, *La Royale. Vaisseaux et marins du roi-soleil*, Paris 1996.

———, *Tourville*, Paris 2002.

Dinet, Dominique, *Vocation et fidélité. Le recrutement des réguliers dans les diocèses d'Auxerre, Langres et Dijon (xviiᵉ–xviiiᵉ siècles)*, Paris 1988.

———, *Religion et société: les réguliers et la vie régionale dans les diocèses d'Auxerre, Langres et Dijon (fin xviᵉ–fin xviiiᵉ siècles)*, Paris 1999.

———, 'Les Appelants contre la bulle *Unigenitus* d'après Gabriel-Nicolas Nivelle', in *Histoire, Economie Société*, 9 (1990), 365–89.

Doyle, William, *Venality. The Sale of Office in Eighteenth-Century France*, Oxford 1996.

———, *La Vénalité*, Paris 2000.

———, ed, *Old Regime France 1648–1789*, Oxford 2001.

Dubarat, V, *Notices historiques sur les évêques de l'ancien diocèse d'Oloron 1506–1792*, Pau 1888.

———, and Daranatz, J-B, *Recherches sur la ville et l'église de Bayonne*, 3 vols, Bayonne, 1910–30.

Dubé, Jean-Claude, *Les Intendants de la Nouvelle France*, Montreal 1984.

Duffo, François, *Le Cardinal de Forbin-Janson, ses négociations diplomatiques à Rome au sujet de l'Assemblée du clergé de France en 1682 (annees 1691, 92, 93)*, Paris 1932.

Dujarric-Descombes, A, *Essai historique sur Mr Daniel de Francheville, d'après des documents inédits*, Périgueux 1874.

———, *Journal de Mgr de Beauvau, évêque de Sarlat (1688–1701)*, Périgueux 1876.

Dumaine, L-V, *Mgr Louis d'Aquin évêque de Sées 1667–1710*, Paris 1902.

Durand, Valentin, *Le Jansénisme au xviii* siècle et Joachim Colbert évêque de Montpellier (1696–1738)*, Toulouse 1907.

Elliott, J H, *The Revolt of the Catalans*, Cambridge 1963.

Enciclopedia dei Papi, ed Istituto della Enciclopedia Italiana, 3 vols, Rome 2000.

Entraygues, L, *Mgr Daniel de Francheville évêque de Périgueux*, Périgueux 1923.

Esmonin, Edmond, *Études sur la France des xvii* et xviii* siècles*, Paris 1964.

Espitalier, H, *Les Évêques de Fréjus du VI* au XVIII* siècle*, Draguignan 1894.

Everat, E, *La Sénéchaussée d'Auvergne et siège présidial de Riom au xviii* siècle*, Paris 1886.

Féret, Pierre, *La Faculté de théologie et ses docteurs les plus célèbres. Époque moderne*, vol iv, Paris 1906.

Ferté, Jeanne, *La Vie religieuse dans les campagnes parisiennes (1622–1695)*, Paris 1962.

Filsjean, Paul, *Antoine-Pierre I de Grammont archevêque de Besançon*, Besançon 1898.

Firino, Roger, 'Sillery, évêque de Soissons', *Bulletin de la Société Archéologique Historique et Scientifique de Soissons*, 4th series, 2 (1922–6), 105–249.

Fisquet, Honoré, *La France pontificale*, 21 vols, Paris 1865–70.

Flament, Pierre, 'Les Moeurs des laïques au diocèse de Sées sous l'épiscopat de Monseigneur d'Aquin (1699–1710)', *Revue d'Histoire de l'Église de France*, 41 (1955), 235–81.

Fleur, Elie, *Essai sur la vie et les oeuvres de Henry Charles du Cambout duc de Coislin, évêque de Metz*, 2 vols, Nancy 1935–6.

Foncin, Pierre 'Remarques sur la généalogie des Turgot', *Revue Historique*, 115 (1914), 64–84.

Ford, Franklin F, *Strasbourg in Transition*, Cambridge, Mass 1958.

Forrestal, Alison, ' "Fathers, Leaders, Kings": Episcopacy and Episcopal Reform in Seventeenth-Century France', *The Seventeenth Century*, 17 (2002), 24–47.

Fossoyeux, Marcel, 'Le Cardinal de Noailles et l'administration du diocèse de Paris', *Revue Historique*, 114 (1913), 261–84; 115 (1914), 34–54.

Froeschlé-Chopard, Marie-Hélène and Michel, *Atlas de la réforme pastorale en France de 1550 à 1790*, Paris 1986.

Frostin, C, 'La Famillle ministérielle des Phélypeaux: esquisse d'un profil Pontchartrain', *Annales de Bretagne et des Pays de l'Ouest*, 86 (1979), 117–39.

Gallerand, J, 'L'Érection de l'évêché de Blois', *Revue d'Histoire de l'Eglise de France*, 42 (1956), 175–228.

Gaquère, F, *Pierre de Marca (1594–1662), sa vie, ses oeuvres, son gallicanisme*, Paris 1932.

Gascon, Richard, *Grand commerce et vie urbaine au xvi* siècle. Lyon et ses marchands*, 2 vols, Paris 1971.

Gélin, H, *Une famille poitevine d'écrivains célèbres*, Niort 1905.

Gillant, abbé, ' Messire Claude Joly, évêque et comte d'Agen', *Semaine religieuse de Verdun* (1930), 157–60, 166–8, 175, 182–4.

Gillet, Joseph, *Mgr Le Tellier archevêque duc de Reims*, Paris 1881.

Godefroy, Jean, *Bibliothèque des bénédictins de la congrégation de St Vanne et de St Hydulphe*, Paris 1925.

Golden, Richard M, *The Godly Rebellion. Parisian curés and the Religious Fronde 1652–62*, Chapel Hill 1981.

Goldman, Lucien, *The Hidden God. A Study of the Tragic Vision in the Pensées of Pascal and the Tragedies of Racine*, London 1964 (original French edn, Paris 1955).

Goujard, Philippe, *Un Catholicisme bien tempéré. La Vie religieuse dans les paroisses rurales de Normandie 1680–1789*, Paris 1996.

Grès-Gayer, Jacques M, *Théologie et pouvoir en Sorbonne. La Faculté de théologie de Paris et la bulle Unigenitus 1714–1721*, Paris 1991.

———, *Le Jansénisme en Sorbonne 1643–1656*, Paris 1996.

———, *Le Gallicanisme de Sorbonne*, Paris 2002.

———, 'Gallicans et romains en Sorbonne d'après le nonce Bargellini (1670)', *Revue d'Histoire Ecclésiastique*, 87 (1992), 682–744.

———, 'The Magisterium of the Faculty of Theology of Paris in the Seventeenth Century', *Theological Studies* 53 (1992), 424–50.

———, 'Tradition et modernité: la réforme des études en Sorbonne (1673–1715)', *Revue d'Histoire de l'Église de France*, 88 (2002), 341–89.

Gresset, Maurice, 'Un fidèle de Louis XIV en Franche-Comté: Claude Boisot', in Yves Durand, ed, *Hommage à Roland Mousnier. Clientèles et fidélités en Europe à l'époque moderne*, Paris 1981, 169–82.

Grosperrin, B, *L'Influence française et le sentiment national français en Franche-Comté de la conquête à la Révolution (1674–1789)*, Paris 1967.

Guignet, Philippe, 'Évangélisation et apaisement d'un conflit séculaire avec l'archevêché de Reims: les engagements contrastés mais cohérents d'un jeune archevêque de Cambrai (1695)', in Gilles Deregnaucourt and Philippe Guignet, *Fénelon, évêque et pasteur en son temps (1695–1715)*, Lille 1996, 43–61.

Guitton, Georges, *Le Père de la Chaize, confesseur de Louis XIV*, 2 vols, Paris 1959.

Hatton, Ranghild, ed, *Louis XIV and Europe*, London 1976.

Hayden, J Michael and Greenshields, Malcolm, 'Les Réformations catholiques en France. Le témoignage des statuts synodaux', *Revue d'Histoire Moderne et Contemporaine*, 48 (2001), 5–29.

Hermann, Christian, *L'Église d'Espagne sous le patronage royal (1476–1834)*, Madrid 1988.

Hillenaar, Henk, *Fénelon et les Jésuites*, The Hague 1967.

Histoire des diocèses de France, ed J R Palanque et al Paris 1967 – in progress.

Histoire du christianisme, ed Jean-Marie Mayeur et al, 14 vols, Paris 1990–2000.

Hoffman, Philip T, *Church and Community in the Diocese of Lyon 1500–1789*, New Haven-London 1984.

Hufton, Olwen, *The Poor of Eighteenth-Century France 1750–1789*, Oxford 1974.

Hurel, Augustin-Jean, *Les Orateurs sacrés à la cour de Louis XIV*, 2 vols, Paris 1872.

Hurt, John J, *Louis XIV and the Parlements. The Assertion of Royal Power*, Manchester 2002.

Joret, Charles, 'Basville et l'épiscopat de Languedoc', *Annales du Midi*, 6 (1894), 420–64; 7 (1895), 5–51.

Julia, Dominique , 'La Constitution du réseau des collèges en France du xvie au xviiie siècle, in *Objet et Méthodes de l'histoire de la culture*, Budapest-Paris 1982, 73–94.

———, 'L'Éducation des ecclésiastiques en France aux xviie et xviiie siècles', in *Problèmes d'Histoire de l'Éducation* (Collection de l'École Française de Rome, 104), Rome 1988, 141–205.

———, and Revel, Jacques, 'Les Étudiants et leurs études dans la France moderne', in Julia-Revel, eds, *Les Universités européennes du xvie au xviiie siècle*, 2 vols, Paris 1984–8, ii, 25–486.

Keohane, Nannerl O, *Philosophy and the State in France. The Renaissance to the Enlightenment*, Princeton 1980.

Kerviler, René, *La Bretagne à l'Académie française au xviie siècle. Etudes sur les académiciens bretons ou d'origine bretonne*, 2ⁿᵈ ed, Paris 1879.

———, *Le Chancelier Pierre Séguier*, Paris 1874.

Kettering, Sharon, *Judicial Politics and Urban Revolt in Seventeenth-Century France*, Princeton NJ, 1978.

———, *Patrons, Brokers and Clients in Seventeenth-Century France*, Oxford 1986.

———, 'The Household Service of Early Modern French Noblewomen', *French Historical Studies*, 20 (1997), 55–85.

Krailsheimer, Alban J, *Armand-Jean de Rancé, Abbot of La Trappe*, Oxford 1974.

Kwass, Michael, *Privilege and the Politics of Taxation in Eighteenth-Century France*, Cambridge 2000.

La Poype, Paulze-d'Ivoy de, *Un Évêque de Poitiers au xviiⁱ siècle. Mgr Jean-Claude de la Poype de Vertrieu*, Poitiers 1889.

Labande, L-H, *Avignon au xvⁱ siècle*, Paris 1920.

Labatut, Jean-Pierre, *Les Ducs et pairs de France au xviiⁱ siècle*, Paris 1972.

Labau, Denis, *Lescar, histoire d'une cite épiscopale*, 2 vols, Pau 1975.

Labourdette, Jean-Françios, 'Les Aumôniers du roi au xviiiᵉ siècle', in *La Noblesse de la fin du xviⁱ au début du xxⁱ siècle*, ed J Pontet, M Figeac and M Boisson, 2 vols, Anglet 2002, i, 17–42.

Lachiver, Marcel, *Les Années de Misère*, Paris 1991.

Lahargou, Paul, *Messire Jean-Louis de Fromentières évêque d'Aire*, Paris 1892.

Landrin, C, *Un prélat gallican. Pierre de Langle évêque de Boulogne (1644–1725)*, Calais 1905.

Languet de Gergy, Joseph, *La Famille d'Aubigné et l'enfance de Mme de Maintenon, par Théophile Lavallée. Suivi des mémoires inédits de Languet de Gergy, archevêque de Sens, sur Mme de Maintenon et la cour de Louis XIV*, Paris 1863.

Lantenay, A de (Louis Bertrand), *Mélanges de biographie et d'histoire*, Bordeaux 1885.

Laplane, H, *Messieurs de Valbelle évêques de Saint-Omer de 1684 à 1754*.

Latreille, André, 'Les Nonces apostoliques en France et l'église gallicane sous Innocent XI', *Revue d'Histoire de Eglise de France*, 41 (1955), 211–34.

———, 'Innocent XI, pape "janséniste", directeur de conscience de Louis XIV' *Cahiers d'Histoire*, 1 (1956), 9–39.

Le Brun, Jacques, 'Paul Godet des Marais, évêque de Chartres (1648–1709)', *Bulletin de la Société Archéologique d'Eure-et-Loire*, 108ᵗʰ year, *Mémoires*, 23 (1964), 47–78.

Le Roy Ladurie, Emmauel with Fitou, Jean-François, *Saint-Simon ou le système de la cour*, Paris 1997.

Legay, Marie-Laure, *Les États provinciaux dans la construction de l'état moderne*, Geneva 2001.

Lehoreau, René, *Cérémonial de l'église d'Angers 1692–1721*, ed François Lebrun, Paris 1967.

Lemaitre, Nicole, ed, *Histoire des curés*, Paris 2002.

Lemarchand, Guy, 'L'Église, appareil idéologique de l'ancien régime', *Annales Historiques de la Révolution Française*, 51 (1979), 250–79.

Le Roux, Nicolas, *La Faveur du roi. Mignons et courtisans au temps des derniers Valois (vers 1547–vers 1589)*, Seyssel 2000.

Le Person, Xavier, *'Practiques' et 'practiqueurs'. La Vie politique à la fin du règne de Henri III (1584–1589)*, Geneva 2002.

Levesque, Eugène, 'Liste des élèves de l'ancien séminaire de Saint-Sulpice', *Bulletin trimestriel des anciens élèves de Saint-Sulpice* (1905–7).

Limouzin-Lamothe, R, *Le Diocèse de Limoges du xviⁱ siècle à nos jours*, Paris-Strasbourg 1953.

Lossky, Andrew, *Louis XIV and the French Monarchy*, New Brunswick 1994.

Loupès, Philipp, *Chapitres et chanoines de Guyenne aux xviiⁱ et xviiiⁱ siècles*, Paris 1985.

Lynn, John A, *Giant of the Grand Siècle, The French Army 1610–1715*, Cambridge 1996.

———, *The Wars of Louis XIV*, London 1999.

Mahieu, L, 'L'Orientation doctrinale des évêques de Saint-Omer 1667–1769', *Bulletin Historique de la Société des Antiquaires de la Morinie*, 16 (1944), 481–515.

'Maintenues de noblesse prononcées par MM Quentin de Richebourg et Desgalois de Latour, intendants de la généralité de Poitiers 1714–1718', ed A de la Bouralière, in *Archives Historiques du Poitou*, vols xxii–xxiii, Poitiers 1892–3.

Maire, Catherine, *De la cause de Dieu à la cause de la nation. Le Jansénisme au xviiiⁱ siècle*, Paris 1998.

Maral, Alexandre, *La Chapelle royale de Versailles sous Louis XIV, céremonial, liturgie et musique*, Paris 2002.

———, 'Portrait religieux de Louis XIV', *XVII Siècle*, 54 (2002), 697–723.

Martimort, Aimé-Georges, *Le Gallicanisme de Bossuet*, Paris 1953.

Martin, Catherine, *Les Compagnies de la propagation de la foi (1632–1685)*, Geneva 2000.

Martin, Georges, *Histoire et généalogie de la maison de la Tour du Pin*, Ricamarie 1985.

Martin, Henri-Jean, *Les Registres du libraire Nicolas (1645–1668)*, Geneva 1977.

McManners, John, *Church and Society in Eighteenth-Century France*, 2 vols, Oxford 1998.

Ménard, Léon, *Histoire civile, ecclésiastique et littéraire de la ville de Nimes*, vi, Nîmes 1875.

Merlet, Louis and Robert, ed, *Dignitaires de l'eglise Notre-Dame de Chartres* (*Archives du diocèse de Chartres*, vol v), Paris 1900.

Mesnard, Jean, *Pascal et les Roannez*, 2 vols, Paris 1965.

Mettam, Roger, *Power and Faction in Louis XIV's France*, Oxford 1988.

Metz, René, *La Monarchie française et la provision des bénéfices ecclésiastiques en Alsace de la paix de Westphalie à la fin de l'ancien Régime 1648–1789*, Strasbourg-Paris 1947.

Meuvret, Jean, 'Les aspects politiques de la liquidation du conflit gallican (juillet 1691– septembre 1693)', *Revue d'Histoire de l'Église de France*, 33 (1947), 257–70.

Meyer, Jean, *La Noblesse bretonne au xviiiᵉ siècle*, 2 vols, Paris 1966.

Meyer, Véronique 'Les Thèses, leur soutenance et leurs illustrations dans les universités françaises de l'ancien régime', *Mélanges de la Bibliothèque de la Sorbonne* 12 (1993), 87–109.

Michaud, Claude, *L'Église et l'argent sous l'ancien régime: les receveurs-généraux du clergé de France aux xviᵉ–xviiᵉ siècles*, Paris 1991.

Michel, Emmanuel, *Biographie du parlement de Metz*, Metz 1853.

Michel, Marie-José, *Jansénisme et Paris*, Paris 2000.

Minois, Georges, *La Bretagne des prêtres*, np 1987.

———, *Le Confesseur du roi*, Paris 1988.

Moote, A Lloyd, *The Revolt of the Judges. The Parlement of Paris and the Fronde 1643–1652*, Princeton 1971.

Moreau, Bernard, 'Jean-Joseph Languet de Gergy et la lettre des dix-huit évêques au Régent (fin 1715–début 1716)', *Bulletin de la Société des Sciences Historiques et Naturelles de l'Yonne*, 131 (1999), 99–114.

———, 'La Famille et la jeunesse de Jean-Joseph Languet de Gergy, de 1677 à 1715', *Bulletin de la Société des Sciences Historiques et Naturelles et l'Yonne*, 132 (2000), 37–58.

Mousnier, Roland, *La Vénalité des offices sous Henri IV et Louis XIII*, Rouen 1945: 2ⁿᵈ edn, Paris 1971.

Neveu, Bruno *Sébastien Joseph du Cambout de Pontchâteau (1634–1690) et ses missions à Rome, d'après sa correspondance et des documents inédits*, Paris 1969.

———, 'Culture religieuse et aspirations réformistes à la cour d'Innocent XI', in his *Érudition et religion aux xviiᵉ et xviiiᵉ siècles*, Paris 1994.

———, *Érudition et religion aux xviiᵉ et xviiiᵉ siècles* (selected essays), Paris 1994.

———, 'L'Autorité doctrinale de l'église à l'épreuve du jansénisme', *Revue d'Histoire Ecclésiastique*, 95 (2000) 196–210.

Newton, William R, *L'Espace du roi. La cour de France au château de Versailles 1682–1789*, Paris 2000.

Orcibal, Jean, *Louis XIV contre Innocent XI. Les appels au future concile de 1688 et l'opinion française*, Paris 1949.

———, *Louis XIV et les Protestants*, Paris 1951.

———, *Études d'histoire et de littérature religieuses*, Paris 1997.

Oroux, abbé, *Histoire ecclésiastique de la Cour de France, où l'on trouve tout ce qui concerne l'histoire de la chapelle et des principaux officiers ecclésiastiques de nos rois*, 2 vols, Paris 1776.

Parrott, David, *Richelieu's Army*, Cambridge 2001.

Pellot, Charles, *Notes du premier président Pellot sur la Normandie: clergé, gentilshommes et terres principales, officiers de justice (1670–1683)*, ed G-A Prevost, Rouen 1915.

Péronnet, Michel, *Les Évêques de l'ancienne France*, 2 vols, Lille 1978.

Pérouas, Louis, *Le Diocèse de la Rochelle de 1648 à 1724, sociologie et pastorale*, Paris 1964.

Peyrous, Bernard, *La Réforme catholique à Bordeaux (1700–1719)*, 2 vols, Bordeaux 1995.

Pillorget, R, *Les Mouvements insurrectionnels en Provence entre 1596 et 17015*, Paris 1975.

————, and Pillorget, S, *France baroque, France classique*, 2 vols, Paris 1995.

Piolin, Paul, *Histoire de l'église du Mans*, 5 vols, Le Mans-Paris 1851–63.

Playoust-Chaussis, A, *La Vie religieuse dans le diocèse de Boulogne*, Arras 1976.

Poncet, Olivier, 'La Papauté et la provision des abbayes et des évêchés français de 1595 à 1667', unpublished doctoral thesis, Université de Paris IV-Sorbonne, 1998.

————, 'Un aspect de la conquête française de l'Artois: les nominations aux bénéfices majeurs de 1640 à 1668', *Revue d'Histoire de l'Eglise de France*, 82 (1996), 263–99.

————, 'Les Contradictions d'une diplomatie. Le Saint-Siège face aux demandes indultaires des souverains catholiques (Espagne, France, Portugal) de 1640 à 1668', in Lucien Bély, ed, *L'Europe des traités de Westphalie. Esprit de la diplomatie et diplomatie de l'esprit*, Paris 2000, 254–65.

————, 'La Cour de Rome et les créations de diocèses au xviie siècle: L'exemple du diocèse de Blois (1693–1697)', in Gerald Chaix, ed, *Le Diocèse: espaces, représentations, pouvoirs. France xve–xxe siècles*, Paris 2002, 47–66.

Poutet, Yves, *Le XVIIe siècle et origines lasalliennes. Recherches sur la genèse de l'oeuvre scolaire et religieuse de Jean-Baptiste de La Salle (1651–1719)*, 2 vols, Rennes 1970.

————, 'Les Docteurs de Sorbonne et leurs options théologiques au xviie siècle', *Divus Thomas*, 81 (1978), 213–348.

Pouzet, Régine, *Chronique des Pascal*, Paris 2000.

Prevost, Arthur-Émile, *Le Diocèse de Troyes, histoire et documents*, 3 vols, Dijon 1923–6.

Prince-Falmagne, Marie-Thérèse, *Un marquis du grand siècle. Jacques René de Brisay de Denonville, gouverneur de la Nouvelle-France 1637–1710*, Montreal 1965.

Quantin, Jean-Louis, *Le Catholicisme classique et les pères de l'église. Un retour aux sources (1669–1713)*, Paris 1999.

————, *Le Rigorisme chrétien*, Paris 2001.

Raison, abbé, 'Un Prélat d'ancien régime. Mgr Jean-Louis du Bouchet de Sources, évêque de Dol 1716–1738, d'après sa correspondance', *Bulletin et Mémoires de la Société Archéologique du département d'Ile-et-Vilaine*, 57 (1931), 43–96, 58 (1932), 41–91, 59 (1933), 75–167.

Rapin, René, *Mémoires sur l'église et la société, la cour, la ville et le jansénisme*, ed Léon Aubineau, 3 vols, Paris 1865.

Ravitch, Norman, *Sword and Mitre. Government and Episcopate in France and England in the Age of Aristocracy*, The Hague 1966.

Rebelliau, Alfred, *La Compagnie du Très Saint-Sacrement à Marseille*, Paris 1909.

Remacle, Louis, *Ultramontains et gallicans au xviiie siècle: Quiqueran et Forbin*, Marseille 1872.

Richet, Denis, *De la Réforme à la Révolution*, Paris 1991.

Riollet, Marius, 'Valbonnais, sa vie, son oeuvre (1651–1730)', in *Bulletin de l'Académie Delphinale*, 8 (1937), 125–291.

Rivals, Daniel, 'Un prélat modèle du xviie siècle: René Le Sauvage, évêque de Lavaur', *Revue du Tarn*, 117 (1985), 41–81.

Ronseray, Comte de, 'Une grande famille de médecins sous Louis XIII et Louis XIV', *Revue d'Histoire de Versailles et de Seine-et-Oise* (1932), 237–242.

Roussel, abbé, *Le Diocèse de Langres, histoire et statistique*, i, Langres 1873.

Rowen, Herbert H, *The King's State. Proprietary Dynasticism in Early Modern France*, New Brunswick 1980.

Rowlands, Guy, *The Dyanstic State and the Army under Louis XIV. Royal Service and Private Interest 1661–1701*, Cambridge 2002.

Sabatier, Gérard, *Versailles, ou la figure du roi*, Paris 1999.

Sahuc, Joseph, *Un Ami de Port Royal. Messire Pierre-Jean-François de Percin de Montgaillard, évêque de Saint-Pons (1633–1665–1713)*, Paris 1909.

Sainte-Beuve, C A, *Port-Royal*, ed Maxime Le Roy (*Pléiade* edn), 3 vols, Paris 1953–5.

Sala, Raymond, *Dieu, le roi et les hommes. Perpignan et le Roussillon (1580–1830)*, Perpignan 1996.

Sars, Max de, *Le Laonnais féodal*, 5 vols, Paris 1924–34.

Sauzet, Robert, *Contre-Réforme et réforme catholique en Bas-Languedoc. Le Diocèse de Nîmes au xviie siècle*, Paris-Louvain 1979.

———, *Le Notaire et son roi. Étienne Borelly (1633–1718). Un Nîmois sous Louis XIV*, Paris 1998.

———, 'La Création du diocèse d'Alès (1694), prototype de l'érection de celui de Blois', in Gerald Chaix, ed, *Le Diocèse: espaces, représentations, pouvoirs. France xve–xxe siècles*, Paris 2002, 33–46.

Schmitt, Thérèse-Jean, *L'Organisation ecclésiastique et la pratique religieuse dans l'archidiaconé d'Autun de 1650 à 1750*, Autun 1957.

Schoenher, P, *Histoire du séminaire de Saint-Nicolas-du-Chardonnet*, 2 vols, Paris 1909.

Sedgwick, Alexander, *The Travails of Conscience. The Arnauld family and the Ancien Régime*, Cambridge, Mass 1998.

Servières, L, *Histoire de l'église du Rouergue*, Rodez 1874.

Sicard, Augustin, *L'Ancien clergé de France. Les Évêques avant la Révolution*, Paris 1893, 5th edn, 1912.

Smedley-Weill, Anette, *Les Intendants de Louis XIV*, Paris 1995.

Sonnino, Paul, *Louis XIV's View of the Papacy*, Berkeley-Los Angleles 1966.

———, *Louis XIV and the Origins of the Dutch War*, Cambridge 1988.

Soulet, Jean-François, *Traditions et réformes religieuses dans les Pyrénées centrales au xviie siècle*, Pau 1974.

Spedicato, Mario, *Il Mercato della mitra. Episcopato regio e privilegio dell'alternativa nel regno di Napoli in età spagnola (1529–1714)*, Bari 1996.

Staes, Jacques, 'Deux testaments de Monseigneur Joseph de Revol, évêque d'Oloron (1732 et 1735)', *Documents pour servir à l'histoire du département des Pyrénées-Atlantiques* 7 (1986), 141–5.

Stewart, David, *Assimilation and Acculturation in Seventeenth-Century Europe. Roussillon and France (1659–1715)*, Westport, Conn, 1997.

Sturdy, David , *The d'Aligres de la Rivière. Servants of the Bourbon State in the Seventeenth Century*, Woodbridge 1986.

Tackett, Timothy, *Religion, Revolution and Regional Culture in Eighteenth-Century France. The Ecclesiastical Oath of 1791*, Princeton 1986.

———, 'L'Histoire sociale du clergé diocésain dans la France du xviiie siècle', *Revue d'Histoire Moderne et Contemporaine*, 26 (1979), 198–234.

———, and Langlois, Claude 'Ecclesiastical Structures and Clerical Geography on the Eve of the French Revolution', *French Historical Studies*, 11 (1980), 715–45.

Tallon, Alain, *La Compagnie du Saint-Sacrement (1629–1667). Spiritualité et société*, Paris 1990.

Taveneaux, René, *Le Jansénisme en Lorraine 1640–1789*, Paris 1960.

———, *Le Catholicisme dans la France classique*, 2 vols, 2nd edn, Paris 1994.

———, 'L'Évêque selon Port Royal', *Chroniques de Port Royal*, 32 (1983), 21–38 (reprinted in Taveneaux, *Jansénisme et Réforme catholique* (Nancy 1992), 75–87).

Teulé, Alexandre-E, *Chronologie des docteurs en droit civil de l'université d'Avignon*, Paris 1887.

Théry, G, *Catherine de Francheville, fondatrice à Vannes de la première maison de retraite des femmes 1620–89*, 2 vols, Tours 1956.

Thomas, Jules, *Les Bossuet en Bourgogne* (Dijon 1903).

Thouard, Auguste, 'Mgr Charles Brulard de Genlis, archevêque et prince d'Embrun', *Bulletin de la Société d'Études des Hautes Alpes*, 32 (1913) 1–15.

Tixier, Eric, *Les Anciennes Familles bourgeoises dans les institutions judiciaires de Riom 1650–1703*, Clermont 1996.

———, *Les Anciennes Familles bourgeoises dans les institutions judiciaires de Riom 1621–1649*, Clermont 2000.

Torreilles, Philippe, 'L'Annexion du Roussillon à la France. La Vacance du siege d'Elne (1643–1669)', in *Société agricole, scientifique et littéraire des Pyrénées Orientales*, 41 (1900), 165–220.

Toustain de Billy, René, *Histoire ecclésiastique du diocèse de Coutances*, ed A Héron, 3 vols, Rouen 1874–86.

Trépardoux, Francis, 'Le Cardinal de la Rocheaymon et sa famille', *Mémoires de la Société des Sciences Naturelles et Archéologique de la Creuse*, 45 (1993), 77–91.

Valous, Guy de, *Patriciat lyonnais aux xiii* et xiv* siècles*, Paris 1973.

Vidal, Jean-Marie, *Histoire des évêques de Pamiers*, vi, *Jean Cerle et le schisme de la régale au diocèse de Pamiers, 1680–1691*, Toulouse 1939; vii, *Jean-Baptiste de Verthamon (1693–1735)*, Toulouse 1945.

Virieux, Maurice de 'Le Parlement de Grenoble au xviie siècle, étude sociale' unpublished doctoral thesis, University of Paris-IV-Sorbonne, 1986.

Vovelle, Michel, *Piété baroque et déchristianisation en Provence au xviii* siècle. Les attitudes devant la mort d'après les clauses des testaments*, Paris 1973.

Welter, Louise, *La Réforme ecclésiastique du diocèse de Clermont au xvii* siècle*, Clermont-Ferrand 1956.

Woolf, John B, *Louis XIV*, New York 1968.

INDEX

Note. The entries in this index exclude material contained in the two Appendices, which are in part an index. Entries for potentially lengthy items such 'bishops', 'crown', 'Louis XIV' are largely brought together under headings which relate to the principal themes of the book.